Role of Human Resources for Inclusive Leadership, Workplace Diversity, and Equity in Organizations

Caglar Dogru
Ufuk University, Turkey

A volume in the Advances in Human Resources Management and Organizational Development (AHRMOD) Book Series

IGI Global
PUBLISHER of TIMELY KNOWLEDGE

Published in the United States of America by
IGI Global
Business Science Reference (an imprint of IGI Global)
701 E. Chocolate Avenue
Hershey PA, USA 17033
Tel: 717-533-8845
Fax: 717-533-8661
E-mail: cust@igi-global.com
Web site: http://www.igi-global.com

Library of Congress Cataloging-in-Publication Data

Names: Dogru, Caglar, 1983- editor.
Title: Role of human resources for inclusive leadership, workplace diversity, and equity in organizations / edited by Caglar Dogru.
Description: Hershey, PA : Business Science Reference, [2023] | Includes bibliographical references and index. | Summary: "Role of Human Resources for Inclusive Leadership, Workplace Diversity, and Equity in Organizations aims to bring together the emerging topics of inclusive leadership, diversity, equity, and inclusion in organizations in the digital transformation context. The book also offers theoretical infrastructure and the latest empirical research findings on inclusive leadership, diversity, equity, and digital transformation. Covering key topics such as social entrepreneurship, employee motivation, and diverse organizations, this premier reference work is ideal for managers, entrepreneurs, business owners, policymakers, researchers, scholars, academicians, practitioners, instructors, and students"-- Provided by publisher.
Identifiers: LCCN 2022058512 (print) | LCCN 2022058513 (ebook) | ISBN 9781668466025 (hardcover) | ISBN 9781668466032 (paperback) | ISBN 9781668466049 (ebook)
Subjects: LCSH: Leadership. | Personnel management. | Employee motivation. | Diversity in the workplace. | Industrial management--Technological innovations.
Classification: LCC HD57.7 .R65 2023 (print) | LCC HD57.7 (ebook) | DDC 658.4/092--dc23/eng/20221208
LC record available at https://lccn.loc.gov/2022058512
LC ebook record available at https://lccn.loc.gov/2022058513

This book is published in the IGI Global book series Advances in Human Resources Management and Organizational Development (AHRMOD) (ISSN: 2327-3372; eISSN: 2327-3380)

British Cataloguing in Publication Data
A Cataloguing in Publication record for this book is available from the British Library.

Advances in Human Resources Management and Organizational Development (AHRMOD) Book Series

ISSN:2327-3372
EISSN:2327-3380

Editor-in-Chief: Patricia Ordóñez de Pablos, Universidad de Oviedo, Spain

MISSION

A solid foundation is essential to the development and success of any organization and can be accomplished through the effective and careful management of an organization's human capital. Research in human resources management and organizational development is necessary in providing business leaders with the tools and methodologies which will assist in the development and maintenance of their organizational structure.

The **Advances in Human Resources Management and Organizational Development (AHRMOD) Book Series** aims to publish the latest research on all aspects of human resources as well as the latest methodologies, tools, and theories regarding organizational development and sustainability. The **AHRMOD Book Series** intends to provide business professionals, managers, researchers, and students with the necessary resources to effectively develop and implement organizational strategies.

COVERAGE

- Upward Feedback
- Diversity in the Workplace
- Employee Relations
- Change Management
- Talent Identification and Management
- Collaborative Method
- Process Improvement
- Corporate Governance
- Organizational Learning
- Compliance

IGI Global is currently accepting manuscripts for publication within this series. To submit a proposal for a volume in this series, please contact our Acquisition Editors at Acquisitions@igi-global.com or visit: http://www.igi-global.com/publish/.

The Advances in Human Resources Management and Organizational Development (AHRMOD) Book Series (ISSN 2327-3372) is published by IGI Global, 701 E. Chocolate Avenue, Hershey, PA 17033-1240, USA, www.igi-global.com. This series is composed of titles available for purchase individually; each title is edited to be contextually exclusive from any other title within the series. For pricing and ordering information please visit http://www.igi-global.com/book-series/advances-human-resources-management-organizational/73670. Postmaster: Send all address changes to above address.

Titles in this Series

For a list of additional titles in this series, please visit:
http://www.igi-global.com/book-series/advances-human-resources-management-organizational/73670

HR Analytics in an Era of Rapid Automation
Radha Yadav (Christ University, India) Mudita Sinha (CHRIST University (Deemed), India) and Joseph Varghese Kureethara (Christ University, India)
Business Science Reference • copyright 2023 • 350pp • H/C (ISBN: 9781668489420) • US $225.00 (our price)

Socio-Economic Disparities, Vulnerable Communities, and the Future of Work and Entrepreneurship
JoAnn Denise Rolle (Medgar Evers College, City University of New York, USA) and Micah Crump (Medgar Evers College, City University of New York, USA)
Business Science Reference • copyright 2023 • 299pp • H/C (ISBN: 9781668469903) • US $240.00 (our price)

Examining Applied Multicultural Industrial and Organizational Psychology
Bryan Christiansen (Southern New Hampshire University, USA) and Angela M. Even (Purdue University, USA)
Business Science Reference • copyright 2023 • 349pp • H/C (ISBN: 9781668472125) • US $250.00 (our price)

Diversity, Equity, and Inclusion Efforts of Businesses in Rural Areas
Shashi Bala (V.V. Giri National Labour Institute, India) and Puja Singhal (National Centre for School Leadership (NIEPA), India)
Business Science Reference • copyright 2023 • 258pp • H/C (ISBN: 9781668468784) • US $225.00 (our price)

For an entire list of titles in this series, please visit:
http://www.igi-global.com/book-series/advances-human-resources-management-organizational/73670

IGI Global
PUBLISHER of TIMELY KNOWLEDGE

701 East Chocolate Avenue, Hershey, PA 17033, USA
Tel: 717-533-8845 x100 • Fax: 717-533-8661
E-Mail: cust@igi-global.com • www.igi-global.com

Editorial Advisory Board

Table of Contents

Detailed Table of Contents

investments united with the alteration in social attitudes in the employees, there are rare causes why organizations currently are embracing diversity and inclusion as need of an hour to achieve improved organizational fallouts. Corporates have realized that diverse employees can contribute towards commercial developments at different organizational levels. In many ways, the function of diversity and inclusion are like two sides of the same coin. While a diverse workforce has gained popularity in organizations, most of the time its twin-component inclusion is lost. Be it in research or practice, OI remains a concept under development. Diversity awards have also become an upcoming business trend. In recent years, diversity management (DM) has shifted its focus to that of an inclusive environment.

Our world is rich in ethnicity, belief, social and economic differences, social and physical disability, and equality. Inclusion is the understanding of the ability and developmental diversity of human communities to coexist with sociocultural and racial differences as well as different socio-cultural or racial factors, and the understanding of being able to coexist with people with physical, intellectual, and developmental differences while respecting their cultural contexts. The main driving motivation of the inclusive leadership approach is the cooperation of the employees in the organization, the empowerment of the employees by constantly supporting them, the courage to change against the status quo, and the curiosity to learn about cultural diversity and differences. Inclusive culture, on the other hand, increases organizational resilience. In this section, the possible connections between inclusive leadership, organizational resiliency, inclusion, and culture will be revealed through the lens of inclusive organizational culture, interdisciplinary and intercultural.

This chapter discovers how employee resource groups play an important role in fostering organizational diversity within information technology organizations. It examines the activities and practices to improve employee behaviour and also focuses on challenges faced by employees in spite of stress and mental health related issues during the COVID-19 pandemic. The data has been collected from secondary sources. The authors have used desk research and gray literature. The findings showcase increased employee engagement, improvements in diversity and inclusion, and an overall improvement in the inventive and creative skills of employees. It also helps the organization to brand itself better along with better recruitment strategies and practices. The key emphasis of the paper looks at the employees working within information technology organizations and how employee resource groups function to balance, motivate, and empower employees during COVID-19 Pandemic.

Cognitive diversity means having an amalgam of people with different ways of thinking, different skill sets, diverse perspectives, and different viewpoints in the organization. Organizations have realized the importance of diversity in age, gender, qualification, and started taking cognizance of the same. All these are visible forms of diversity. However not much attention is paid to 'cognitive diversity' because it is not visible and is deep level diversity. Organizations need to have cognitive diversity as a part of their diversity and inclusion (D&I) agenda. Cognitive diversity is indeed the way forward. This study is an effort to understand and explore 'cognitive diversity' which is invisible in nature, yet of great importance and relevance for the organizations.

Employees nowadays are more diverse than ever before, and that diversity is manifested in differences in generational cohorts. It has been observed that an organization is composed of distinct age groups, which represent employees of distinct generational cohorts. The key goal of this study is to render an observation and insight into differentiation and comparison in work values, communication style, and leadership style of distinct age group employees at workplace likely boomer, Gen X, Gen Y, and Gen Z. The finding of the study depicted the variations among generations (Boomer, Gen X, Gen Y, and Gen Z) as well as the variation in their styles of leadership, communication, and values of work. The current study has explored only three characteristics. In the organizations, not only is the investigation of distinct generation necessary, but the similarities among them need to be acknowledged. Another limitation is that there is a very less empirical investigation conducted on generational differences.

The central focus of leadership theories in social psychology and organizational studies is on inclusive leadership. Persistent, naturally inclusive leaders seek diverse viewpoints and evaluate their journey. They build strategic intent and cooperate more successfully with others. Inclusive leaders have original social and ethical values, innate personal systems, and moral responsibility. They shape followers' behaviors through consciousness, open-mindedness, fearlessness, humility, and tolerance, fostering an environment where employees from diverse backgrounds feel respected and valued.

The impact of workplace incivility cannot be exaggerated, nor it can be ignored. Academic researchers have demonstrated in their study that 71% of the employees had faced incivility in past five years wherein the fellow court personnel were the instigators and workplace incivility is a source of job stress. Studies have reported that 78% of respondents had experienced supervisor incivility and 8% had gone through co-worker incivility. The stress released from incivility is not only within the workplace, but it is also taken home by the employees to their family domain which causes family antipathy. Haun suggested that incivility has negative impact over work and family domains as well. Employees who experience incivility hide their knowledge, and also retaliate the treatment they are given in workplace. On the days when employees are treated with uncivil behaviour, they tend to have a higher level of stress.

The metaverse is a 3D (three-dimensional) virtual world synchronized with the real world, where users interact with a digital avatar using augmented reality technologies. The transformative impact of this virtual world is making itself felt in many areas, as are the opportunities and challenges it creates. Entrepreneurs' capacity to foresee these risks and assess opportunities may be crucial to the survival of their businesses in the future. This study aims to examine potential business opportunities, obstacles,

Preface

As editor of this reference book, it is with great pleasure that I present to you a comprehensive collection of research and insights on the role of Human Resources for inclusive leadership, workplace diversity, and equity in organizations. In recent years, there has been a remarkable paradigm shift in diversifying the workforce at both national and international levels, driven by the globalization trend that emerged in the twentieth century. The boundaries of many states have opened to foreign workers, and public and private enterprises have been actively contributing to the employment of individuals from diverse ethnicities, races, and genders.

While promising developments have been made in improving workplace diversity and equity, there remains a need for further progress. Although recruiting and placing diversified human resources have received significant attention, this issue cannot be addressed solely by focusing on discrimination and inequalities at the hiring stage. Inclusive leadership and its practices and strategies emerge as a crucial aspect in this regard, offering a paradigm shift from traditional leadership styles to a more groundbreaking approach.

Inclusive leadership, which has gained prominence in today's business context, emphasizes the importance of inclusion in achieving organizational goals by bringing together individuals from diverse backgrounds. It requires leadership approaches that not only acknowledge and respect the differences among members but also motivate them toward common goals. Inclusive leadership fosters a culture of tolerance, respect, and courtesy, making managers and leaders agents of change in creating an organizational environment that embraces diversity and inclusivity. This contemporary leadership style aligns with participative and empowering leadership, enhancing the potential of our diverse human resources.

Furthermore, digital transformation has significantly influenced the dynamics of work life. New forms of work have facilitated human resources diversity within organizations, making diversity and inclusive leadership crucial for the future. Thus, analyzing and evaluating these concepts is essential to generate valuable insights for scholars, practitioners, and students.

This reference book aims to address the emerging topics of inclusive leadership, diversity, equity, and inclusion in organizations within the context of digital transformation. It offers a theoretical foundation and presents the latest empirical research findings on inclusive leadership, diversity, equity, and digital transformation. By combining the most up-to-date research findings with a comprehensive theoretical framework, this book will contribute significantly to contemporary research on these subjects. The chapters cover a range of contemporary topics, mostly based on technological advances, providing readers with the latest management skills and techniques. By examining leadership, diverse organizations, and inclusive strategies, this book fills a critical gap in the management field.

In Chapter 1, the focus is on the implementation of preventative HR practices to foster equity and inclusion in entrepreneurial organizations as they grow. The chapter highlights the potential unintended discrimination perpetuated by common diversity practices when implemented poorly. The authors explore the use of inclusive leadership and an organizational inclusiveness framework to investigate how HR policies can enable the full participation of diverse groups and leverage their diversity for innovative solutions. The chapter emphasizes the importance of establishing a culture that supports diversity and inclusion and discusses the need for resource redistribution and collaboration for true equity. Suggestions for future research in diverse and equitable inclusion are also presented.

Chapter 2 delves into the effects of inclusive leadership on employees' sense of psychological safety and innovative work behaviors. The research examines the potential mediating role of coworker envy and organizational cynicism in the relationship between inclusive leadership and psychological safety, as well as innovative work behavior. The findings, based on data gathered from the hotel industry and analyzed using PLS-SEM, demonstrate a significant positive relationship between inclusive leadership, psychological safety, and innovative work behavior. The chapter also highlights the partial intervening effect of coworker envy and organizational cynicism in this relationship.

Chapter 3 focuses on defining and analyzing performance evaluation methods used by organizations and their limitations. The authors adopt a qualitative approach, using interview surveys as a research tool. The results presented highlight the presence of motivation and performance in the organizations studied, while also noting variations in evaluation methods, implications, and limitations across different organizations. The chapter sheds light on the importance of understanding and addressing the diverse approaches to performance evaluation in organizations.

In Chapter 4, the authors address the need for novel approaches to crisis management in organizations facing limited resources and crisis situations such as the Covid-19 pandemic. The chapter explores the shift from traditional leadership theories to team leadership approaches, emphasizing the importance of team proactivity, self-efficacy, and shared leadership. A conceptual theoretical framework is developed to outline the relationships between team proactivity, self-efficacy, and shared leadership. The chapter also highlights the limited research on team proactivity compared to individual proactivity and proposes avenues for further exploration.

Chapter 5 examines the impact of globalization on the workforce, leading to increased workforce diversity. The authors highlight the importance of inclusive leadership as a strategic mechanism to manage the diverse workforce in 21st-century organizations. Inclusive leadership, characterized by openness, accessibility, self-awareness, and cultural intelligence, is presented as a means to promote employee engagement. The chapter advocates for inclusive leadership as the preferred style to manage a diverse workforce and ends with suggestions for future research.

In Chapter 6, the authors discuss the growing importance of diversity and inclusion in organizations due to globalization and changing social attitudes. The chapter emphasizes the need for organizations to embrace both diversity and inclusion, as they are interconnected and crucial for improved organizational outcomes. The authors highlight the role of diversity and inclusion in contributing to commercial developments and call for further research and practice in this area. The chapter also mentions the emergence of diversity awards as a business trend and the shift of diversity management towards creating an inclusive environment.

Chapter 7 explores the relationship between inclusive leadership, organizational resiliency, inclusion, and culture. The authors highlight the driving motivation behind the inclusive leadership approach, which includes employee cooperation, empowerment, change readiness, and curiosity about cultural diversity. The chapter discusses the potential connections between inclusive leadership, organizational resiliency, and an inclusive organizational culture, taking an interdisciplinary and intercultural perspective. The chapter aims to reveal these connections and their implications.

Chapter 8 focuses on the role of Employee Resource Groups (ERGs) in fostering organizational diversity within Information Technology (IT) organizations. The chapter examines the activities and practices undertaken by ERGs to improve employee behavior and addresses the challenges faced by employees, including stress and mental health issues during the COVID-19 pandemic. The findings highlight increased employee engagement, improvements in diversity and inclusion, and enhanced inventive and creative skills. The chapter emphasizes the importance of ERGs in branding, recruitment, and overall organizational development.

Chapter 9 explores the concept of cognitive diversity, which refers to differences in thinking, skill sets, perspectives, and viewpoints within organizations. The authors argue for the inclusion of cognitive diversity as part of the Diversity and Inclusion (D&I) agenda in organizations. The chapter emphasizes the importance and relevance of cognitive diversity, despite its invisible nature, and discusses its significance for organizational success. The authors highlight the need for further research and understanding of cognitive diversity in organizations.

Chapter 10 examines the differentiation and comparison of work values, communication styles, and leadership styles among different generational cohorts, including boomers, Gen X, Gen Y, and Gen Z. The study explores the variations in these characteristics and highlights the importance of acknowledging both the differences and similarities among generations in organizations. The chapter suggests that further empirical research is needed to deepen the understanding of generational differences and their impact on the workplace.

In Chapter 11, the focus is on leadership from a lay perspective and its consistency of behaviors, morals, and responsibility. The chapter aims to provide insights into the journey of leadership, its theory, and its significance in social psychology. The authors discuss the inclusive leadership philosophy and the importance of persistent leaders who are aware of their biases. The chapter emphasizes the significance of maintaining moral and ethical standards throughout the leadership journey.

Chapter 12 highlights the significant impact of workplace incivility and its implications for organizations. The authors present findings from academic research, indicating the prevalence of incivility and its sources, such as fellow court personnel and supervisors. The chapter emphasizes the negative impact of incivility on job stress and its spillover effects into the family domain. The authors also discuss the tendency of employees to hide knowledge and retaliate against uncivil treatment. The chapter underscores the importance of addressing workplace incivility for overall well-being.

Chapter 13 focuses on the metaverse, a 3D virtual world synchronized with the real world, and explores the potential business opportunities, obstacles, and risks it presents for entrepreneurs. The chapter examines existing literature on the metaverse and identifies various business opportunities in different fields. The authors emphasize the importance for entrepreneurs to invest in the metaverse and capitalize on these opportunities. The chapter sheds light on the transformative impact of the metaverse and its implications for future business endeavors.

The intended audience for this book includes scholars from universities worldwide, as well as undergraduate and graduate students studying leadership, gender studies, migrants and refugees, organizational behavior, human resources management, and management information systems. Moreover, professionals such as managers, specialists, consultants, educators, and employees of social organizations globally will find this reference book valuable in their respective fields.

The topics covered in this reference book span a wide range of areas, including Human Resources Management, Inclusive Leadership, Leadership Styles for Inclusion, Leadership Styles for Diversity and Equity, Leadership Approaches, Diverse Organizations, Organizational Strategies for Diversity, Equity and Inclusion,

Managing Diversity in Organizations, Gender Equality in Organizations, Women's Empowerment, Inclusion of Migrants and Refugees, Elimination of Discrimination in Organizations, Workplace Equity, Human Resources Practices for Inclusion, Human Resources Management for Gender Equality, Organizational Behavior, Employee Motivation, Diverse Workforce Motivation and Organizational Commitment, Digital Transformation, Diversity and Inclusion in Technology, Data-Driven Approach in Diversity and Inclusion, Data Analytics, Women Entrepreneurship, Innovation Capabilities and Entrepreneurship, Inclusive Leadership and Digitalization, Technological Capabilities and Organizations, Technology and Organizations, Organizational Strategy, Corporate Social Responsibility, Social Entrepreneurship, and Strategic Leadership.

My hope is that this reference book will serve as a valuable resource, offering insights and guidance for understanding today's business organizations operating in a global, dynamic, and complex environment. May the knowledge shared within these pages contribute to fostering inclusive leadership, workplace diversity, and equity, leading us toward a more inclusive and equitable future.

Çağlar Doğru
Ufuk University, Turkey

Chapter 1
Advancing Meaningful Inclusion in the Workplace:
A Model for Avoiding Tokenism and Marginalization

Ryan Payne
https://orcid.org/0000-0002-1165-8655
Queensland University of Technology, Australia

Michelle Keeffe
Queensland University of Technology, Australia

ABSTRACT

This chapter examines how implementing preventative HR practices can promote equity and inclusion in entrepreneurial organizations as they grow. Common diversity practices, like HR policies and affirmative action initiatives, can unintentionally perpetuate discrimination when implemented poorly. To foster an inclusive environment, the authors use inclusive leadership and a framework for organizational inclusiveness to investigate how HR policies can enable diverse groups to participate fully. This approach not only allows for the full participation of diverse groups but also enables individuals to leverage their diversity for innovative solutions. Organizational leaders can create an inclusive climate by establishing a culture that supports diversity and inclusion. Achieving true equity requires redistributing resources and ensuring an inclusive culture throughout the organization, facilitated by collaboration and diverse voices in decision-making. This chapter explores challenges faced by emerging businesses and proposes suggestions for future research in diverse and equitable inclusion.

DOI: 10.4018/978-1-6684-6602-5.ch001

INTRODUCTION

Workplace Diversity is well recognized for having many benefits, not only for the organization, but also for the stakeholders within the organization as well. Likewise, entrepreneurship, especially intrapreneurship is well recognized as having a wide range of benefits for different stakeholders too including employment generation, social and economic benefits (Luke et al., 2007; Steyaert & Katz, 2004; Valliere & Peterson, 2009). However, in the workplace, there continues to be a struggle for workplace diversity, and the underrepresentation of different groups of people in entrepreneurship is still prevalent. These groups include migrants, individuals belonging to ethnic minorities, individuals who identify as living with disabilities or impairments, individuals from low educational attainment or socio-economic status (Blackburn & Smallbone, 2015; Wishart, 2018), and those who feel stigmatized for an aspect of their daily living and being (Veldman et al., 2021).

Including a more diverse group of people can reduce gender inequalities and poverty (Gu & Nie, 2021), increase economic freedom (Kimhi, 2010) and promote economic and social development (Ge et al., 2022; Sajjad et al., 2020). It can also lead to higher levels of innovation (PriceWaterhouseCoopers International, 2019), better idea generation (Burgess & Tharenou, 2002) and improved decision-making and problem-solving (Trehan, 2018). These traits are also linked with successful entrepreneurship, therefore it is important to understand how emerging entrepreneurs can benefit from such insights. Further, while the management literature is captivated with promoting diverse sets of leaders (Bassett-Jones, 2005), entrepreneurs are different from managers and therefore have different principles and practices which guide their operations, and how such diversity may be included in their business. For example, most emerging entrepreneurs have limited resources and unestablished HR policies, therefore often they rely on proximity and their personal leadership to guide human resource based developments, such as the office culture, within their organization. While both management and entrepreneurship literature work to enhance diversity in the workplace, it has generally concentrated on building and maintaining stakeholder and social capital (Wishart, 2018) with a lack of tackling the structural obstacles and organizational practices that hinder different groups of individual's involvement.

This chapter outlines how preventative HR practices at the inception of an organization can avoid the need for large shifts and adjustments later in a corporation's development to promote equity and equality amongst diverse workplace populations as a business grows and develops. Through the notion of inclusive leadership (Boekhorst, 2015), and previous work on avoiding tokenism of entrepreneurs (Payne et al., 2023) a conceptualized framework for organizational inclusiveness framework is utilized to explore how HR practices shape the ability for diverse groups of people to freely and equally participate in an inclusive environment. It further highlights how such HR policies invite, foster and support the full participation of diverse groups of people in entrepreneurial ventures, and allows for each person to use their diversity for creative innovations. The chapter concludes by offering suggestions for future research in the area of diverse and equitable inclusion and potential application outside the entrepreneurial field.

BACKGROUND

Fillion (2021) redefines the traditional understanding of an entrepreneur from simply a business owner and leader, to include the following qualities: "an individual who detects opportunities for innovation, makes moderately risky decisions, and efficiently uses resources to create added value" (Fillion, 2021, p.78). In this regard, to effectively use resources includes the usage of each person, and their diverse backgrounds and skill sets, within an organization for the business's success.

This is important to entrepreneurship literature as often within emerging entrepreneurial ventures, rather than comparing them as equal because of gender and just focusing on entrepreneurial or personality traits, gendered or cultural traits are still used to define the reasons for success or failure (Snellman & Solal, 2022). This is important, as men still typically have higher levels of expert and legitimate power in workplaces, which results in greater levels of influence (Carli, 1999), it also means a greater issue on how structural systems and leadership styles create patterns of access and work that disadvantage diverse populations are overlooked or not addressed. For example, it is common as an entrepreneurial recruitment process to rely on drawing from social networks (Acker, 2006). This preference for hiring from one's own social networks can result in a lack of diversity in other areas, as it is shown people prefer to hire those similar to themselves (whether in education level or by other demographic traits). For example, Acker (2006) suggests that recruitment often favors those similar in characteristics, such that white men typically hire from within their network of white men. For those who have managed to break into such organizations, there can be detrimental career effects if they seek to disrupt this status quo (Smith-Tran, 2020), even though this status quo can be detrimental to the creativity, innovation and ultimately success of the organization (Cunningham et al., 2017). This creates a paradigm to consider on how to balance between the convenience and ease of social networks when emerging, and ensuring a business is representative in its workforce that all employees feel valued/included.

Leadership and HR Policy Development

To address this topic we look to use an adapted version of Boekhort's Inclusive Leadership model. Boekhorst's (2015) model of inclusive leadership has been widely used in the literature for addressing workplace hiring and diversity, but it lacks certain elements that Bourke and associates (2019, 2020) have identified as crucial for establishing and maintaining an inclusive culture. Specifically, the Boekhorst model does not include sustainable metrics at an organizational level or address the attributes that make an inclusive leader effective in fostering inclusion within their organization. Therefore, we utilize the adapted *Organizational Inclusiveness Framework* (Payne et al., 2023) (See figure 1 below). This model's subparts have previously been fully outlined (Payne et al., 2023); this article looks to highlight within the organizational factors, the workplace or work group diversity, and how human resources can create policies which facilitate a sustainable climate for inclusion.

Workplace diversity is associated with the composition of people who make up an organization (Triandis et al., 1994) and the variety within an organization. Workgroup diversity is crucial for creating an inclusive climate and avoiding perceptions of tokenism. A diverse organizational membership can also prevent groupthink and challenge established norms and practices that may marginalize certain members (Tarmo & Issa, 2022). In order to achieve workgroup diversity, recruitment and selection practices must be examined, but it also requires a commitment to creating organizational policies and practices that support and retain diverse staff members.

A Social Justice Approach to Workgroup Diversity

In opposition to this repetitive social network hiring cycle, is the addressing of diversity and equality through the principles of equity, equality, and need, as informed by social justice (Folger et al., 1995; Wagstaff, 1994). These concepts acknowledge that while equality aims to treat all individuals the same, equity focuses on providing individuals with what they need to succeed, taking into account individual differences and needs (Espinoza, 2007). This approach recognizes that equal treatment may not always result in fair outcomes for all individuals.

The image of two people trying to pick apples from a tree, as shown in Figure 2, illustrates the concept that providing equal resources and support does not necessarily result in equal access for all. In the image labeled "inequality," both individuals are standing on the ground, however the abundance of apples and lean of the tree to the left indicates that one individual has greater access to opportunities than the other. The second box labeled "equality?" shows both individuals standing on ladders, both of the same height, suggesting an equal access to resources and assistance. However, the ladder only aids the first person to collect more apples, while the

Figure 1. Organizational inclusiveness framework
Source: Payne, R., Kruwinnus, J. & Grant-Smith, D., (2022).In Perez-Uribe, R. I., Ocampo-Guzman, D. & Moreno-Monsalve, N. (eds.) Handbook of Research on Promoting an Inclusive Organizational Culture for Entrepreneurial Sustainability. . IGI Global, p. 86-109.

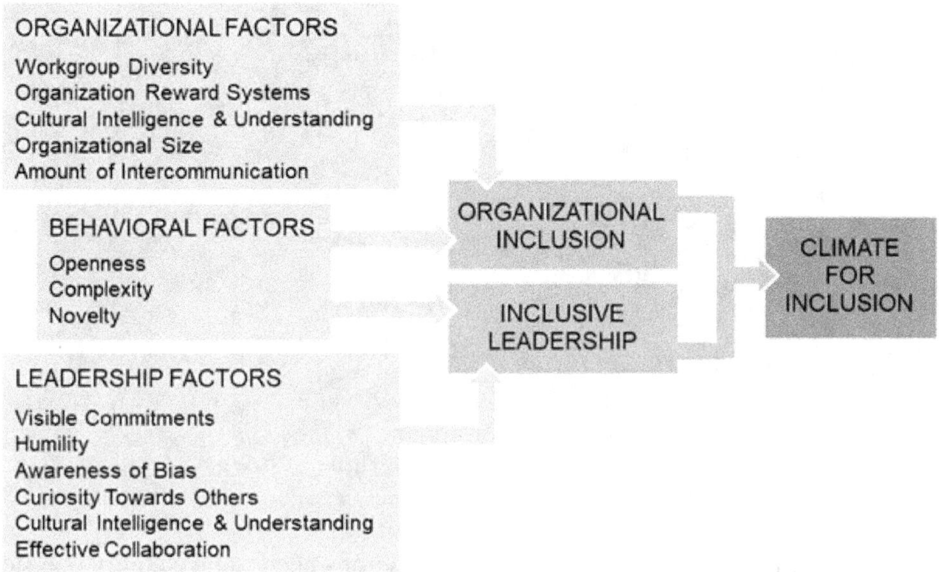

second person's ability to pick apples remains hindered, showing that individuals have different needs that must be considered.

The third image, titled "equity," focuses on distributing resources and support fairly, taking into account individual differences. It shows both individuals on ladders, with the access to resources and assistance represented by the height of ladders adjusted so that both individuals can pick apples from the tree. The individual on the left still has their ladder and can pick apples, while the person on the right now has a longer ladder and can also pick apples. This highlights the fact that an equitable distribution of resources and assistance can provide access to all without taking away access from anyone.

The final image, where the apple tree has been reinforced with supports and ropes to grow 'evenly', eliminates the need for ladders with different heights. This version is titled "justice", as the barrier to participation and access has been removed for all, resulting in long-term, sustainable, and equitable access. Justice, as defined by Rawls (1971), is achieved when all individuals have equal basic rights and a fair distribution of opportunities, which may require providing additional support to disadvantaged people.

Figure 2. Equality, equity, and social justice illustration
Image Credit: Tony Ruth in 2019 Design in Tech Report | Addressing Imbalance (Maeda, 2019)

To achieve justice in the workplace, organizations need to take equity one step further by removing the systemic barriers that are currently producing and reinforcing inequality. For example, instead of asking managers to nominate employees for an internal mentoring program, they could develop an open application process that considers the needs of the individual rather than the 'merits' already achieved by the employee. This approach enables those employees who feel they would benefit from mentoring to apply rather for a program while reducing the potential for managers to favor employees with similar characteristics to themselves. Additionally, this approach opens opportunities to those m who may already have the capability, access to resources or networks to assist them developing their professional careers.

Entrepreneurial HR Practices

As emerging entrepreneurs are known for limited resources and bootstrapping when beginning (Grichnik et al., 2014), the ability to define strong equitable and justice based HR policies is often limited. Rather entrepreneurial HR policies are shown to emerge from experiences as the business grows and develops (Barringer et al., 2005). Therefore, while its thought no entrepreneur seeks to create biased or inequitable organizations, with limitations on time and resources, often HR policies for diversity take a backseat to revenue generated tasks; and further, convenience and the previously noted social network bias naturally emerge within an organization.

These unintentional behaviors foster the grounds for a lack of diversity and inclusion. Therefore, while entrepreneurs recognize their need for HR practices, they often focus on the perceived support immediately needed. These include giving subordinates the information, knowledge, and ability they need to make decisions, and also to have a system that rewards good performance (Lawler, 1994). However, it is also important to have a supportive work environment that allows for empowerment (Kaminski et al., 2000). These empowering activities include giving out authority, sharing information, giving rewards, building trust, having a positive company culture, having knowledge, and having good leadership (Srivastava et al., 2006; Spreitzer, 1995; Conger and Kanungo, 1988; Lawler, 1994; Wang et al., 2019).

Such empowerment systems and policies emerge from the leadership, human resources and human capital division of a business. Therefore, an effective human resource (HR) system is a fundamental component that can aid an organization in attaining operational efficiency and a competitive advantage as it develops (Becker & Huselid, 1998). The distinctiveness and internal consistency of HR values play a crucial role in strengthening the HR system and fostering shared, collective perceptions, attitudes, and behaviors among employees especially as the business is growing and developing (Bowen & Ostroff, 2004). Given the positive impact of a well-defined organizational blueprint on new ventures (Leung et al., 2013), it is imperative to comprehend the factors that contribute to the distinctiveness and consistency of HR values and specifically examine how entrepreneurs can develop strong HR systems which foster representation, avoid producing false supports/ fairness and circumvent unintended bias in recruitment practices.

Established Firms

Contrary to popular belief, gender stereotypes in organizations are not only perpetrated by those in the normative group (Brady, Kaiser, Major, & Kirby, 2015). Common practice diversity practices, such as HR policies, diversity and inclusion training, and affirmative action initiatives, which are designed to legally protect minority groups within organizations have been shown to unintentionally perpetuate discrimination when implemented ineffectively (Brady et al., 2015; Faniko, Ellemers, Derks, & Lorenzi-Cioldi, 2017). These practices can produce "illusions of fairness" amongst employees (Brady et al., 2015, p. 100), resulting in instances of discrimination being overlooked as the practice is perceived to be fair to all employees. Unfortunately, this 'illusion' is not isolated to those employees that fit the organizational norm. Numerous studies (e.g., Brady et al., 2015; Faniko et al., 2017) have revealed that formal diversity policies and practices can be enough to give diversity groups, including women, the impression they are being treated fairly in the organization. The implications of these false impressions are two-fold. First, an organization might observe lower support from their employees for diversity initiatives and affirmative action to address discrimination; and second, individuals may minimize their experiences of discrimination within the organization (Brady et al., 2015; Faniko et al., 2017; Miner et al., 2018).

It is typical for organizations (and society) to acknowledge the disadvantage and inequality faced by minority groups, while failing to recognise the privileged position of one's own group. This lack of acknowledgement, or "half-blindedness of privilege", unintentionally promotes the dominance of certain groups over others, further exacerbating the power imbalances within an organization (Pratto & Stewart, 2012). While this presents challenges for HR and leaders wanting to address issues of gender inequality, there are actions they can take to reduce the power imbalances in their organizations. Haslam (2004) suggests that HR teams and leaders can combat the automatic preference for the dominant group by advocating for and valuing women and minority groups. Additionally, a leader can leverage their status to positively influence the perception of the minority groups' social status (Haslam, 2004).

To effect change, HR and leaders need to be champions for women and other minority groups, supporting them to achieve their goals and making their contributions visible (Metcalfe, 2011). Championing not only reinforces the value of the minority group but serves to reduce perceived differences between dominant and minority groups, helping to foster organizational inclusion (Haslam, 2004; Schwarzwald et al., 2005; Cadinu & Galdi, 2012; Derks, Van Laar, & Ellemers, 2016). HR, supported by an organization's leadership, plays a crucial role in this process as they produce and enact diversity policies and practices that promote inclusive organizational cultures. This includes raising awareness of implicit biases and harmful stereotypes, effective communication of policies and inclusive practices, and fostering collaboration between different groups. Effective communication can also help address concerns about perceived threats to the organization's culture and reinforce the benefits of a diverse, and inclusive, workplace for individuals, teams and organizations. Leaders can also work to strengthen the inclusive culture of the organization by emphasizing common goals and the contributions of both dominant and minority groups to the success of the organization. Additionally, when leaders foster collaboration between these groups, they are assisting HR and the organization to challenge the status quo and combat individual biases that contribute to gender inequality (Haslam, 2004; Kelly & Breinlinger, 1995; Derks et al., 2016; Iyer & Ryan, 2009; Subašić et al., 2018).

While HR can develop policy and leaders can implement changes within their teams, addressing systemic organizational change is crucial for the long-term sustainability of an inclusive culture within the organization. Collaboratively, HR and leaders can reduce inequality by increasing awareness of implicit bias and gender inequality, promoting gender equality as a common cause between men and women, and leveraging their status within the organization to advocate for others. Research demonstrates that diversity practices and initiatives that empower people from a wide variety of backgrounds are more effective in promoting sustainable change than initiatives that focus only on empowering females or a select group of individuals. (Brady et al., 2015; Subašić et al., 2018; Haslam, 2004; Simpson & Macy, 2004)

Such shifts within an organization may not be enough to foster a culture of inclusion and allow diverse groups of people to participate equally and freely within the organization. Rather, often HR policies in addition to leadership support are required to "course correct" an organization back towards inclusion.

These policies can vary greatly, however, traditionally have focused on hiring practices, and specifically having spaces for different groups of people to seed the company with more diversity (missing the errors of such practices). This practice is commonly referred to as quota spaces. Quotas for increasing diversity in the workplace can have negative consequences, such as increasing discrimination (Rudman & Fairchild, 2004; Pande & Ford, 2012) and creating a patronizing environment where women are perceived as not being chosen based on their talent but rather on their gender. This can lead to lack of support for career advancement, being viewed as tokens rather than having earned their position through merit (Koopman et al. 2016) and being offered "few valued resources but a great deal of seemingly disingenuous praise" (Vescio et al., 2005, p. 659).This can impede the advancement of diverse groups of people to top leadership positions and undermine the goal of true equality in the workplace. Further, is in direct opposition to treating a diverse workforce as a human capital collection of resources (Baron & Armstrong, 2007), which should be prioritized for having a difference of opinions and ideations.

While the actions outlined above can be effective in reducing gender inequality it is important to note that some individuals may perceive a reduction in their group's dominance as a threat to their status, which can lead to negative responses such as further distancing from the minority group or lack of participation in diversity initiatives. Leaders should be aware of this potential barrier and use effective communication to address these concerns and emphasize the benefits of diversity and inclusion to the work team and the organization.

Recommendations

Therefore, to foster a collaborative environment as an entrepreneur we look to highlight the need for early advancement of inclusion within the workplace. While recognizing the bias towards similar people and their ease of connection and proximity, we advocate for education for entrepreneurs on the inclusion organizational framework, which highlights the needs for an equitable, diverse and inclusive workplace. Through the emergence of these startup and early adoption behaviours naturally an organization will grow into having a wider range of workplace employees, as different groups of people from the beginning, while they might have higher similar traits in others, will have a wider inclusion of these smaller tribes which ultimately leads to a more inclusive environment.

Second, while an education based approach might reach emerging entrepreneurs in formalized education settings, we recognize that new practices to promote equality and equity are required to stem the structural inequality which is perpetuated in common workplaces (Metcalfe, 2011). Therefore, HR practices to educate on the value of equity, diversity and inclusion are required to promote the value of having a diverse workplace. Such policies would highlight the potential benefits that organizations can realize through the promotion of inclusivity. These benefits can be driven by both ethical and economic considerations (Isidro & Sobral, 2015). For example, research has shown that diversity and inclusion can lead to improved decision-making, increased talent attraction, and increased revenue (Fine et al., 2020). In addition, feelings of inclusion have been linked to individual performance (Fine et al., 2020). Such promotions would subtly contribute or potentially stop the bias towards hiring like minded individuals and perpetuating the social injustice a lack of diversity within a workplace creates.

Finally, effecting significant changes within an organization necessitates the leadership of an entrepreneurial figure who adheres to a principled approach (Payne et al., 2023). It is widely acknowledged that individuals do not purposefully create adverse circumstances, such as instances of hiring-related inequality or discrimination. Nonetheless, actions undertaken with the best of intentions may not necessarily benefit the organization as a whole. Thus, corporate social responsibility initiatives geared towards both employees and the employer (entrepreneur), are indispensable for promoting a workplace environment that is open and inclusive (Boekhorst et al., 2015). Such initiatives are vital in ensuring that employees feel engaged and included, as well as empowered to fully utilize their capabilities.

Future Research Directions

Further investigation is necessary to determine the effectiveness of the framework proposed in this chapter in facilitating the advancement of a diverse and equitable workplace for entrepreneurs within organizations. This can be achieved by monitoring their career development and evaluating their perceptions of the organizational climate, with a specific focus on the role of inclusive and authentic leadership in providing support.

There is also a need for future research to examine the potential positive impact of the framework utilized in this paper (Payne et al., 2023) on the participation and advancement outcomes of other equity groups, such as Indigenous people and individuals with diverse sexual orientation, gender identity and expression, and sexual characteristics. It would be beneficial to investigate the unique challenges and opportunities faced by these groups and how their experiences differ from those of female entrepreneurs. Additionally, research could explore the effectiveness of various theories and public policies in promoting gender equality and increasing the representation of women in key positions in entrepreneurial organisations. While these questions are beyond the scope of our research, they are crucial in advancing the goal of achieving equality for all members of society and are essential to realizing our shared ideals.

CONCLUSION

Organizational leaders have the power to establish an inclusive climate through the organizational culture they create, even as they strive to achieve their vision. This is especially true for leaders starting new organizations. Entrepreneurs, in particular, have the opportunity to develop a new workplace culture that promotes inclusion. However, achieving equality within an organization requires introspection by those involved or those who influence the demonstrated behaviors. Diversity is the starting point for creating an inclusive culture, and paradoxically, it is also the outcome. However, to achieve true equity, leaders must be willing to redistribute resources and ensure that their vision for an inclusive culture permeates throughout the entire organization to maintain an inclusive climate. This requires a commitment to humility and an openness to collaboration by providing an environment that supports a diverse range of voices at all levels of the organization in decision-making.

Although inclusive leaders may have good intentions, their actions and the perceptions they create may blind them, and their intentions may not trickle down to middle and lower management positions, where segregation and other social injustices are most common. To make significant changes within an organization, principled entrepreneurial leadership is essential, along with corporate social responsibility initiatives geared towards employees and the employer. Such actions create the ability within an organization for a more open and inclusive workplace environment that is vital to ensure employees feel engaged, included, and empowered to fully utilize their capabilities.

Our writing presents the Organizational Inclusiveness Framework as an ideation to compare and measure progress in achieving equity and ultimately equality. Through structuring policies around human resources to ensure a wider and more encompassing/diverse set of individuals we believe can help to achieve a more inclusive workplace culture for emerging entrepreneurs, and those who chose to follow these pioneers. We hope that with time, equity is fully achieved, and the tokenistic actions often displayed in corporations no longer exist.

ACKNOWLEDGMENT

The first author, as always, would like to thank God, his family and friends, as well as the second author, who has been a pleasure to work with on this book chapter. The second author is forever thankful for her family and friends, and the opportunity to work on this book chapter with the first author.

REFERENCES

Acker, J. (2006). Inequality regimes: Gender, class, and race in organizations. *Gender & Society*, *20*(4), 441–464. doi:10.1177/0891243206289499

Baron, A., & Armstrong, M. (2007). *Human capital management: achieving added value through people*. Kogan Page. https://www.123library.org/book_details/?id=98763

Barringer, B. R., Jones, F. F., & Neubaum, D. O. (2005). A quantitative content analysis of the characteristics of rapid-growth firms and their founders. *Journal of Business Venturing*, *20*(5), 663–687. doi:10.1016/j.jbusvent.2004.03.004

Bassett-Jones, N. (2005). The paradox of diversity management, creativity and innovation. *Creativity and Innovation Management*, *14*(2), 169–175. doi:10.1111/j.1467-8691.00337.x

Becker, B. E., & Huselid, M. A. (1998). Human resources strategies, complementarities, and firm performance. *SUNY Buffalo: Unpublished manuscript*.

Blackburn, D., & Smallbone, D. (2015). *Sustaining self-employment for disadvantaged entrepreneurs: A background paper for the OECD Centre for Entrepreneurship, SMEs and Local Development*. OECD and LEED.

Boekhorst, J. A. (2015). The role of authentic leadership in fostering workplace inclusion: A social information processing perspective. *Human Resource Management*, *54*(2), 241–264. doi:10.1002/hrm.21669

Bourke, J., & Espedido, A. (2019). Why inclusive leaders are good for organizations, and how to become one. *Harvard Business Review*, *96*, 3–8.

Bourke, J., & Titus, A. (2020). The key to inclusive leadership. *Harvard Business Review, 97*, 2–5.

Bowen, D. E., & Ostroff, C. (2004). Understanding HRM–firm performance linkages: The role of the "strength" of the HRM system. *Academy of Management Review, 29*(2), 203–221.

Brady, L. M., Kaiser, C. R., Major, B., & Kirby, T. A. (2015). It's fair for us: Diversity structures cause women to legitimize discrimination. *Journal of Experimental Social Psychology, 57*, 100–110. doi:10.1016/j.jesp.2014.11.010

Burgess, Z., & Tharenou, P. (2002). Women board directors: Characteristics of the few. *Journal of Business Ethics, 37*(1), 39–49. doi:10.1023/A:1014726001155

Cadinu, M., & Galdi, S. (2012). Gender differences in implicit gender self-categorization lead to stronger gender self-stereotyping by women than by men [Article]. *European Journal of Social Psychology, 42*(5), 546–551. doi:10.1002/ejsp.1881

Carli, L. L. (1999). Gender, interpersonal power, and social influence. *The Journal of Social Issues, 55*(1), 81–99. doi:10.1111/0022-4537.00106

Conger, J. A., & Kanungo, R. N. (1988). The empowerment process: Integrating theory and practice. *Academy of Management Review, 13*(3), 471–482. doi:10.2307/258093

Cunningham, J., O'Reilly, P., Dolan, B., O'Kane, C., & Mangematin, V. (2017). Gender differences and academic entrepreneurship: A study of scientists in the principal investigator role. In A. Link (Ed.), *Gender and entrepreneurial activity* (pp. 221–251). Edward Elgar. doi:10.4337/9781785364747.00013

Derks, B., Van Laar, C., & Ellemers, N. (2016). The queen bee phenomenon: Why women leaders distance themselves from junior women. *The Leadership Quarterly, 27*(3), 456–469. doi:10.1016/j.leaqua.2015.12.007

Espinoza, O. (2007). Solving the equity–equality conceptual dilemma: A new model for analysis of the educational process. *Educational Research, 49*(4), 343–363. doi:10.1080/00131880701717198

Faniko, K., Ellemers, N., Derks, B., & Lorenzi-Cioldi, F. (2017). Nothing Changes, Really: Why Women Who Break Through the Glass Ceiling End Up Reinforcing It. *Personality and Social Psychology Bulletin, 43*(5), 638–651. doi:10.1177/0146167217695551 PMID:28903635

Filion, L. J. (2021). Defining the entrepreneur. In L. P. Dana (Ed.), *World encyclopedia of entrepreneurship* (2nd ed., pp. 72–83). Edward Elgar Publishing. doi:10.4337/9781839104145.00015

Fine, C., Sojo, V., & Lawford-Smith, H. (2020). Why does workplace gender diversity matter? Justice, organizational benefits, and policy. *Social Issues and Policy Review, 14*(1), 36–72. doi:10.1111ipr.12064

Folger, R., Sheppard, B. H., & Buttram, R. T. (1995). Equity, equality, and need: Three faces of social justice. In B. B. Bunker & J. Z. Rubin (Eds.), *Conflict, cooperation, and justice: Essays inspired by the work of Morton Deutsch* (pp. 261–289). Jossey-Bass/Wiley.

Ge, T., Abbas, J., Ullah, R., Abbas, A., Sadiq, I., & Zhang, R. (2022). Women's entrepreneurial contribution to family income: Innovative technologies promote females' entrepreneurship amid COVID-19 crisis. *Frontiers in Psychology, 13*, 1–10. doi:10.3389/fpsyg.2022.828040 PMID:35422737

Grichnik, D., Brinckmann, J., Singh, L., & Manigart, S. (2014). Beyond environmental scarcity: Human and social capital as driving forces of bootstrapping activities. *Journal of Business Venturing, 29*(2), 310–326. doi:10.1016/j.jbusvent.2013.02.006

Gu, R., & Nie, F. Y. (2021). Does empowering women benefit poverty reduction? Evidence from a multi-component program in the Inner Mongolia Autonomous Region of China. *Journal of Integrative Agriculture, 20*(4), 1092–1106. doi:10.1016/S2095-3119(20)63436-0

Haslam, S. A. (2004). *Psychology in Organizations: The Social Identity Approach* (2nd ed.). SAGE Publications.

Isidro, H., & Sobral, M. (2015). The effects of women on corporate boards on firm value, financial performance, and ethical and social compliance. *Journal of Business Ethics, 132*(1), 1–19. doi:10.100710551-014-2302-9

Iyer, A., & Ryan, M. K. (2009). Why Do Men and Women Challenge Gender Discrimination in the Workplace? The Role of Group Status and In-group Identification in Predicting Pathways to Collective Action. *The Journal of Social Issues, 65*(4), 791–814. doi:10.1111/j.1540-4560.2009.01625.x

Kaminski, M., Kaufman, J. S., Graubarth, R., & Robins, T. G. (2000). How do people become empowered? A case study of union activists. *Human Relations, 53*(10), 1357–1383. doi:10.1177/a014108

Kelly, C., & Breinlinger, S. (1995). Identity and injustice: Exploring women's participation in collective action. *Journal of Community & Applied Social Psychology*, *5*(1), 41–57. doi:10.1002/casp.2450050104

Kimhi, A. (2010). Entrepreneurship and income inequality in southern Ethiopia. *Small Business Economics*, *34*(1), 81–91. doi:10.100711187-009-9196-4

Koopman, J., Lanaj, K., & Scott, B. A. (2016). Integrating the bright and dark sides of OCB: A daily investigation of the benefits and costs of helping others. *Academy of Management Journal*, *59*(2), 414–435. doi:10.5465/amj.2014.0262

Lawler, E. E. III. (1994). Performance management: The next generation. *Compensation and Benefits Review*, *26*(3), 16–19. doi:10.1177/088636879402600303

Leung, A., Der Foo, M., & Chaturvedi, S. (2013). Imprinting effects of founding core teams on HR values in new ventures. *Entrepreneurship Theory and Practice*, *37*(1), 87–106. doi:10.1111/j.1540-6520.2012.00532.x

Luke, B., Verreynne, M. L., & Kearins, K. (2007). Measuring the benefits of entrepreneurship at different levels of analysis. *Journal of Management & Organization*, *13*(4), 312–330. doi:10.5172/jmo.2007.13.4.312

Maeda, J. (2019). *Design in Tech Report*. Design InTech. https://designintech.report/wp-content/uploads/2019/03/dit2019_v00.pdf

Metcalfe, B. D. (2011). Women, work organization, and social change: Human resource development in Arab Gulf States. *Human Resource Development International*, *14*(2), 123–129. doi:10.1080/13678868.2011.558309

Pande, R. & Ford, D. (2012). Gender Quotas And Female Leadership: A Review. *Background Paper For The World Development Report On Gender*.

Payne, R., Kruwinnus, J., & Grant-Smith, D. (2023). Handbook of Research on Promoting an Inclusive Organizational Culture for Entrepreneurial Sustainability, p. 86-109. IGI Global.

Pratto, F., & Stewart, A. L. (2012). Group Dominance and the Half-Blindness of Privilege [Article]. *The Journal of Social Issues*, *68*(1), 28–45. doi:10.1111/j.1540-4560.2011.01734.x

PricewaterhouseCoopers International. (2019). *Unraveling the fabric ceiling*. PricewaterhouseCoopers. https://www.pwc.com/us/en/industries/consumer-markets/assets/pwc-unraveling-the-fabric-ceiling.pdf

Rawls, J. (1971). *A theory of justice*. Belknap Press. doi:10.4159/9780674042605

Rudman, L. A., & Fairchild, K. (2004). Reactions to Counterstereotypic Behavior: The Role of Backlash in Cultural Stereotype Maintenance. *Journal of Personality and Social Psychology, 87*(2), 157–176. doi:10.1037/0022-3514.87.2.157 PMID:15301625

Sajjad, M., Kaleem, N., Chani, M. I., & Ahmed, M. (2020). Worldwide role of women entrepreneurs in economic development. *Asia Pacific Journal of Innovation & Entrepreneurship, 14*(2), 151–160. doi:10.1108/APJIE-06-2019-0041

Schwarzwald, J., Koslowsky, M., & Allouf, M. (2005). Group Membership, Status, and Social Power Preference. *Journal of Applied Social Psychology, 35*(3), 644–665. doi:10.1111/j.1559-1816.2005.tb02139.x

Simpson, B., & Macy, M. W. (2004). Power, Identity, and Collective Action in Social Exchange. *Social Forces, 82*(4), 1373–1409. doi:10.1353of.2004.0096

Smith-Tran, A. (2020). Exploring the benefits and drawbacks of age disclosure among women faculty of color. *Teaching Sociology, 48*(1), 3–12. doi:10.1177/0092055X19869983

Snellman, K., & Solal, I. (2022). Does investor gender matter for the success of female entrepreneurs? Gender homophily and the stigma of incompetence in entrepreneurial finance. *Organization Science*.

Spreitzer, G. M. (1995). Psychological empowerment in the workplace: Dimensions, measurement, and validation. *Academy of Management Journal, 38*(5), 1442–1465. doi:10.2307/256865

Srivastava, A., Bartol, K. M., & Locke, E. A. (2006). Empowering leadership in management teams: Effects on knowledge sharing, efficacy, and performance. *Academy of Management Journal, 49*(6), 1239–1251. doi:10.5465/amj.2006.23478718

Steyaert, C., & Katz, J. (2004). Reclaiming the space of entrepreneurship in society: Geographical, discursive and social dimensions. *Entrepreneurship and Regional Development, 16*(3), 179–196. doi:10.1080/0898562042000197135

Subašić, E., Hardacre, S., Elton, B., Branscombe, N. R., Ryan, M. K., & Reynolds, K. J. (2018). "We for She": Mobilizing men and women to act in solidarity for gender equality. *Group Processes & Intergroup Relations, 21*(5), 707–724. doi:10.1177/1368430218763272

Tarmo, C. G., & Issa, F. H. (2022). An analysis of groupthink and decision making in a collectivism culture: The case of a public organization in Tanzania. *International Journal of Public Leadership, 18*(1), 15–29. doi:10.1108/IJPL-08-2020-0072

Trehan, K. (2018, October 18). Why the world needs more women CEOs. *The Conversation.* https://theconversation.com/why-the-world-needs-more-women-ceos-104876

Triandis, H. C., Kurowski, L. L., & Gelfand, M. J. (1994). Workplace diversity. In H. Triandis, M. Dunnette, & L. Hough (Eds.), *Handbook of industrial and organizational psychology* (pp. 769–827). Consulting Psychologists Press.

Valliere, D., & Peterson, R. (2009). Entrepreneurship and economic growth: Evidence from emerging and developed countries. *Entrepreneurship and Regional Development*, *21*(5-6), 459–480. doi:10.1080/08985620802332723

Van Laar, C., Meeussen, L., Veldman, J., Van Grootel, S., Sterk, N., & Jacobs, C. (2019). Coping with stigma in the workplace: Understanding the role of threat regulation, supportive factors, and potential hidden costs. *Frontiers in Psychology*, *10*, 1879. doi:10.3389/fpsyg.2019.01879 PMID:31507478

Veldman, J., Van Laar, C., Meeussen, L., & Lo Bue, S. (2021). Daily coping with social identity threat in outgroup-dominated contexts: Self-group distancing among female soldiers. *Personality and Social Psychology Bulletin*, *47*(1), 118–130. doi:10.1177/0146167220921054 PMID:32431224

Vescio, T., Gervais, S. J., Snyder, M., & Hoover, A. "Power and the Creation of patronizing Environments: The Stereotype-Based Behaviors of the Powerful and Their Effects on Female Performance in Masculine Domains" (2005). Faculty Publications, Department of Psychology. 341.

Wagstaff, G. F. (1994). Equity, equality, and need: Three principles of justice or one? An analysis of 'equity as desert'. *Current Psychological Research & Reviews*, *13*(2), 138–152. doi:10.1007/BF02686797

Wang, Z., Xu, S., Sun, Y., & Liu, Y. (2019). Transformational leadership and employee voice: An affective perspective. *Frontiers of Business Research in China*, *13*(1), 2. doi:10.118611782-019-0049-y

Wishart, M. (2018). *Under represented entrepreneurs: A literature review.* Enterprise Research Centre. https://www.enterpriseresearch.ac.uk/wp-content/uploads/2018/07/Under-represented-entrepreneurs-Revised-10.18.pdf

ADDITIONAL READING

Brief, A. P. (Ed.). (2008). *Diversity at work*. Cambridge University Press. doi:10.1017/CBO9780511753725

Cabrera, E. F. (2009). Fixing the Leaky Pipeline: Five Ways to Retain Female Talent. *People and Strategy*, *32*(1), 40–45.

Ellemers, N. (2014). Women at Work: How Organizational Features Impact Career Development. *Policy Insights from the Behavioral and Brain Sciences*, *1*(1), 46–54. doi:10.1177/2372732214549327

Fine, M. G. (1996). Cultural diversity in the workplace: The state of the field. *The Journal of Business Communication (1973), 33*(4), 485-502.

Green, K. A., López, M., Wysocki, A., & Kepner, K. (2002). Diversity in the Workplace: Benefits, Challenges, and the Required Managerial Tools: HR022/HR022, 7/2002. *Edis, 2002*(2).

Gross-Gołacka, E., Kupczyk, T., & Wiktorowicz, J. (2022). Towards a Better Workplace Environment—Empirical Measurement to Manage Diversity in the Workplace. *International Journal of Environmental Research and Public Health*, *19*(23), 15851. doi:10.3390/ijerph192315851 PMID:36497925

Kilian, M. C., Hukai, D., & McCarty, E. C. (2005). Building diversity in the pipeline to corporate leadership. *Journal of Management Development*, *24*(2), 155–168. doi:10.1108/02621710510579518

Kossek, E. E., & Buzzanell, P. M. (2018). Women's career equality and leadership in organizations: Creating an evidence-based positive change. *Human Resource Management*, *57*(4), 813–822. doi:10.1002/hrm.21936

Martin, G. C. (2014). The effects of cultural diversity in the workplace. *Journal of diversity management (JDM), 9*(2), 89-92.

KEY TERMS AND DEFINITIONS

Entrepreneurship: The process of doing something new and something different for the purpose of creating wealth for the individual and adding value to society. Gender parity: Achieving equal participation of men and women in all aspects of a workplace based on their proportion within the company. Human Resources: the division of a business responsible for finding, screening, recruiting, developing and training job applicants. Inclusive Leadership: a specific form of relational leadership that establishes the workplace (organizational) climate to allow for the access of all members within an organization to feel included and equal members of an organization.

Social Justice: A theoretical practice which concerns itself with society, particularly with social institutions and their allocation of duties and rights. (see Rawls, 1971)

Tokenism: Perfunctory or symbolic efforts recruiting a small number of people from under-represented groups to give the appearance of equality within a workforce the difference of one member of a group from most of the group. Tokenism can occur based on gender, race, or other characteristics. (see Yoder et al. 1996)

Workplace Diversity: A consideration of having different groups of people based on age, gender, religion, political affiliation, psychology or behavioral traits inside and working together inside a communal place of work (physically or digitally).

Chapter 2
Inclusive Leadership and Innovative Work Behaviour:
Empirical Evidence From the Indian Hospitality Industry

Diksha Dhar
Assam University, Silchar, India

Sachitaa Srivastava
Babasaheb Bhimrao Ambedkar University, India

Lata Bajpai Singh
https://orcid.org/0000-0002-5386-3630
Babasaheb Bhimrao Ambedkar University, India

ABSTRACT

This research attempts to inspect the effects of inclusive leadership on employees and their sense of psychological safety and innovative work behaviours. It examines whether coworker envy and organizational cynicism acts as an intervening measure in the link between inclusive leadership and psychological safety. It also endeavours to look into the role of coworker envy and organizational cynicism as a mediating factor in the association between inclusive leadership and innovative work behaviour. For the present research, information was gathered from 279 people employed in the hotel industry. SmartPLS 3 software was used to analyse the data using the PLS-SEM (partial least square-structural equation modelling) method. The findings indicate a significant positive relationship amongst inclusive leadership, psychological safety, and innovative work behaviour. In addition, a partial intervening effect of coworker envy and organizational cynicism was also observed.

DOI: 10.4018/978-1-6684-6602-5.ch002

INTRODUCTION

The hospitality industry is constantly evolving. As the world becomes gradually more interconnected and technologically advanced, hotels are finding it extremely difficult to keep up with the ever-changing demands of their customers and their changing expectations. Offering the same services and products in a similar manner does not please their clients, as what is novel and innovative today will eventually become ordinary (Ko, 2015). Because of this, hotels view innovation as a key strategy for competing with the rising competition and as a weapon of excellence (Al-Ababneh, 2015). In order to boost an organization's innovativeness and ensure long-term progress, especially in the service industry, it is critical to support its employees' innovative behaviour (Li *et al.*, 2016). For a business that relies heavily on human resources, the hospitality industry has the potential to benefit from the innovative behaviour of its employees.

Customers' dynamic desires have created an urgent need for enterprises to explore new approaches to foster innovation (Hu *et al.,* 2017). Evidence from past studies suggests that employees are crucial in driving innovation and ensuring a company's success in the long term (Lee and Wong, 2017). Personnel utilise their skills while simultaneously engaging in discretionary behaviour, which leads to the conception, development, and adoption of novel concepts (Naqshbandi *et a*l., 2019; Theurer *et al.*, 2018). Therefore, these roles have an impact on how innovative workers behave (Javed *et al.,* 2017). Further, leadership is seen as a vital element in reinforcing employees' independent functioning and has been demonstrated to encourage employees' innovative behaviour at work (Khalili, 2016; Mahmood *et al.,* 2019). Since it forms the basis for employees' innovative work behaviours, the inclusive leadership perspective is especially well-suited for creating innovative settings (Choi *et al.,* 2015; Weintraub and McKee 2019). Employees' innovative work behaviour can be explained as the voluntary extra-role effort that personnel make to benefit their employer over time (Eid & Agag, 2020; Zhang *et al.*, 2021). Corporate leaders must promote and support innovative work behaviours among their workforce, though, by utilising inclusive leadership strategies.

Nembhard and Edmondson (2006) explained inclusive leadership as "leaders' positive behaviour that motivates people to contribute to the organization." Personnel are more likely to consider themselves included in their job duties when they feel psychologically safe as a result of mutually advantageous exchange relationships with their supervisors (Javed *et al.,* 2019). Psychological safety is a state in which people are free to express themselves without worrying about the possible repercussions on their self-perception, social standing, or professional prospects (Kahn, 1990). It is possible for employees to believe that they are receiving favourable treatment from the organisation if they are supported and helped by inclusive leaders (Carmeli *et al.,* 2010; Nembhard & Edmonson, 2006). Carmeli *et al.* (2010) examined the effects of inclusive leadership, and the results suggested that inclusive leadership enhanced psychological safety. Employees' views of psychological safety are highly influenced by the associations between superiors and subordinates, particularly those felt by employees. Being able to create a suitable work atmosphere that allows for indirect information sharing can have an effect on employees' psychological safety (van der Berg, 2010).

The study of inclusive leadership's benefits in the hotel industry is still very much in its initial phases, and there is scant empirical proof of its consequences, especially in the context of India (Du *et al.,* 2021; Jolly & Lee, 2021). Studies have been conducted in the past where the effect of inclusive leadership on psychological safety and innovative work behaviour has been established (Mansoor *et al.*, 2021; Siyal *et al.,* 2021; Wang *et al.*, 2021; Wang and Shi, 2021). Also, the significance of psychological safety as an intervening construct between employees' innovative work behavior and their comprehension of the leadership philosophies they believe they experience has been investigated in a very small number of studies. But, a lack of research is there in the hospitality industry on how to encourage employee innovative work behavior and psychological safety, and how these factors relate to inclusive leadership. Also, none of the studies have examined the function of coworker envy and organizational cynicism as a mediating link between inclusive leadership, psychological safety, and innovative work behavior.

This research attempts to analyze and offer a conceptual framework of the aspects that might be important in the relationship between inclusive leadership and employees' innovative work behaviours and their psychological safety in the hotel industry, with the mediating roles of coworker envy and organisational cynicism. As a result, this study first presents a summary of the literature, a proposed conceptual model that identifies the elements that may obstruct innovative work behaviour and psychological safety. It concludes by offering a suggestion for future study. The researchers also propose that the variables under investigation will be replaced by their acronyms: inclusive leadership (IL), co-worker envy (CE), organisational cynicism (OC), psychological safety (PS), and innovative work behaviour (IWB).

LITERATURE REVIEW AND HYPOTHESIS DEVELOPMENT

Inclusive Leadership (IL)

The phrase IL was first used by Nembhard and Edmondson (2006). It refers to a leader's words and actions that show gratitude for the significant contribution of others and an invitation to participate in deliberations in which their views and opinions might otherwise be absent. It is a new paradigm of research which promotes diversity through educating team members and treating everyone impartially in a biased free manner. In the wake of globalisation clubbed with COVID-19, it is imperative for organisations to be inventive to persist in the current market state, accomplish desired goals, and remain ahead of competitors (Siyal *et al.,* 2021). The occurrence of IL within the organizations stimulates innovative thinking among the subordinates and followers to implement modern ideas (Siyal *et al.,* 2021; Mansoor *et al.*, 2021; Aboramadan *et al.,* 2021), creativity i.e., to produce innovative and valuable ideas (Zhu *et al.,* 2020), orienting organisational members towards their work responsibilities (Cenkci *et al.*, 2020) and reducing unfavourable effects such as psychological distress, trauma and other health problems (Zhao *et al.*, 2020).

Coworker's Envy (CE)

Earlier work by Vecchio (1995) can be seen as the foundation for the concept of CE, who defined it as negative feelings and thoughts brought on by the belief that a coworker has accomplished goals or possesses skills that one desperately seeks. Prior research work on CE has predominantly focused on envious employees (Hilal, 2021; Duffy *et al.*, 2012), ignoring the viewpoint of targets who are envied (Vecchio, 2005; Lee *et al.*, 2018). Being the object of envy from less successful colleagues is what is meant by CE (Lee *et al.,* 2018).

In a workplace, an employee becomes a target of CE when they perceive something of better quality or are distributed better resources, such as a salary hike, promotion, recognition, status, and so on, which their counterparts lack but desire (Parrot and Smith, 1993). In such a pursuit, high-performing employees have to face group pressure and the burden of envy from their colleagues (Mao *et al.*, 2020). Consequently, envied employees foster a feeling of negativity because they feel that they are being neglected or disregarded by envious coworkers (Kim and Glomb, 2014).

Organizational Cynicism (OC)

OC is conceptualised as an unfavourable perspective toward their employer (Dean *et al.*, 1998), which is tied to the discernment that the organization lacks trustworthiness and integrity. OC has increased recently as a result of incompetent management and self-centered leadership in the workplace (Arslan and Roudaki, 2019). Cynics believe that the firms do not care about their employees, and thereby they develop a bad attitude towards one employer. As a result, employees develop a negative mood of pessimism, anger, and hopelessness towards their employers and the organization, which creates an imbalance and leads to unfavourable consequences.

Psychological Safety (PS)

The term PS from organizational management literature was first originated from the earlier work by Schein and Bennis (1965) which focused on organizational change and concerning employees feeling safer and confident within work environment backed by supportive behavior of leaders (Ghafoor and Haar, 2020). PS helps in creating an environment that is favourable for rational thinking and allows a forum for open participation by all without the fear of being penalised (Kostopoulos and Bozionelos, 2011). This in turn facilitates exploring new knowledge and exploiting existing resources among employees, leading to higher organizational performance. The inclusion of PS is attributed to collective intelligence (Shankar and Tewari, 2021), career adaptability (Gong *et al.*, 2020), leader inclusiveness (Hirak *et al.*, 2012), worker expertise (Lee *et al.*, 2011), and so forth.

Innovative Work Behavior (IWB)

Scott and Bruce (1994) described IWB as a multifaceted behaviour entailing the development, introduction, or implementation of fresh, relevant notions, procedures, and remedies. A work environment exhibiting IWB fosters new and innovative business opportunities and provides opportunities and solutions for improving organizational performance (Scott and Bruce, 1994). Consequently, this helps in establishing organizational sustainability, which helps in managing complex problems with innovative solutions. Thus, to foster IWB it becomes crucial for managers to plan and execute modern methods of functioning and completing daily tasks and other responsibilities by employees.

Additionally, employees engaging in IWB experience decreased burnout and have lower turnover intentions (Hammond *et al.*, 2019), which helps fulfil their basic needs (Devloo *et al.*, 2016). Furthermore, it helps in increasing individual performance as well as team performance within the organization (Hughes *et al.*, 2018).

IL and PS

Inclusive leaders are in a unique position to define the standards of conduct required to foster an environment of PS in the workplace because of their intimate ties with their followers (Nembhard and Edmondson, 2006). There are ways in which a leader's inclusive actions might impact his or her team's sense of PS. For instance, within the context of social exchange theory, they consistently model behaviours of transparency, accessibility, and availability to aid their followers in achieving their own aims and desires (Carmeli *et al.*, 2010). Employees can feel comfortable to deliberate facts about their work and expressing their genuine thoughts in a supportive work environment (Choi *et al.,* 2015). Because of the assistance they give to their staff, inclusive leaders help to create a work atmosphere where people will feel psychologically safe (Javed *et al.,* 2019). In light of this argument, it is hypothesized:

H1- *IL is positively associated with PS.*

IL and IWB

IL promotes a strong association with workforces and creates an encouraging atmosphere for subordinates by giving them more autonomy and allowing them to adopt unique ideas that aid in creative thinking (Bannay *et al.,* 2020). These qualities of IL empower workforces and encourage them to participate actively in creative operations (Javed *et al.*, 2018). As per the social exchange theory, leaders that model a culture of inclusion and encourage subordinates to take on hard tasks encourage employees to adopt innovative work practises (Siyal *et al.*, 2021). Numerous empirical studies have been found to be crucial in encouraging personnel to participate in innovative work practises and to show a high level of excitement and dedication to their jobs (Javed *et al.,* 2018; Mansoor *et al.,* 2021; Scott and Bruce, 1994). Furthermore, this motivates individuals to meet or even surpass the organization's current demands by utilising their capabilities, resources, and skills to the fullest extent possible. Based on this, it is clear that IL and IWB have a positive association. As a result, it's possible to speculate that:

H2- *IL is positively associated with IWB.*

CE as Mediator

Being envied by coworkers means that you're the target of jealousy from those who aren't as successful (Lee *et al.,* 2018). Unfavorable social comparisons may play a role in this feeling of isolation (Lee *et al.*, 2018; Ye *et al.,* 2021). It is discovered that being envied is a complicated emotion that can result in job and interpersonal stress, as well as intent to leave (Scott *et al.,* 2015; Yu & Duffy, 2016). The researchers are interested in determining if an IL style is linked with CE because the lives of the team members are greatly impacted by the team leaders. Regardless of their position within the organisational hierarchy, Hassan and Jiang (2019) contend that IL guarantees the acceptance of subordinates' ideas. This has been proven to be a good strategy for workplace engagement (Wang *et al.,* 2019), creativity (Mikyoung & Moon, 2019), innovative behaviour (Javed *et al.,* 2017), and the creation of an educational environment (Hassan & Jiang, 2019; Hirak *et al.*, 2012). During stressful occasions, leaders' behaviour can either exacerbate or calm the psychological state of workforces (Hannah *et al.,* 2009). An inclusive leader can help decrease tension by routinely connecting with subordinates and listening to their concerns. Anxiety about one's work can be lessened with the assistance of their leaders. Moreover, when CE reduces due to IL, consequently, it will also lower the adverse impact of OC. For the reason stated above, we propose:

H3: *CE mediates the relationship between IL and OC.*

OC as Mediator

A common and pervasive symptom of widespread employee dissatisfaction with one's boss and the organisation for which they work is known as "OC" (Neves, 2012). In the context of an organization, the meaning of cynicism is "an adverse attitude about one's employer defined by three dimensions: (1) a conviction that there is a lack of integrity in the organisation; (2) an unfavourable outlook toward the organization; and (3) inclinations to degrade and critique the organization in line with these attitudes and beliefs" (Dean et al., 1998). According to several researchers, some workplace attitudes and actions are often linked to OC, along with strong negative feelings like frustration, tension, or anxiety (Abraham, 2000; Dean *et al*., 1998). An employee may react adversely if they believe their coworkers are envious of them (Mao *et al.*, 2020). Possessing a negative outlook on one's workplace increases the likelihood that one may engage in disruptive behaviour on the job (Abubakar & Arasli, 2016). A cynical viewpoint of employees has a negative effect on job satisfaction and organizational commitment (Reichers *et al.,* 1997). Job satisfaction and organizational commitment have been shown to be inversely linked to workplace unsafe behaviour (Morrow and Crum 1998). Furthermore, highly cynical employees may already consider the workplace unsafe as a byproduct of their overall negative opinions regarding the organisation (i.e., low PS) (Jiang *et al.*, 2019). Using this justification as support, we hypothesize:

H4: *OC mediates the relationship between CE and PS.*

Cynicism in organisations manifests itself in three ways, including employees' attitudes, sentiments, and behaviours toward the organisation (Neves, 2012). As an attitude, OC (Dean *et al.,* 1998) is likely to affect workplace behaviours like in-role job performance, organisational citizenship behaviour and IWB. Whereas, IWB is explained as "the deliberate invention, advancement, and execution of novel concepts within a work role, group, or organisation" (Janssen and Van Yperen, 2004). Making a significant investment of intellectual, psychological, and physical resources in IWB (Montani *et al.,* 2015; Scott and Bruce, 1994) is seen as an activity requiring resources (Janssen, 2004). When working in a stressful environment, an employee spends a significant amount of their focus and time dealing with and handling pressure, which further depletes their resources and reduces their likelihood of displaying IWB (Agarwal *et al.,* 2016). Numerous scholars have examined the association between OC, job burnout (Simha *et al.,* 2014), and outcomes (Nafei, 2014). Cynicism can have an impact on employees' performance and the willingness and efficiency of their work (Dean *et al.*, 1998; Harrell-Cook *et al.,* 1999). A cynical view of the workplace, as well as a lack of commitment to the company, might have a damaging impact on efficiency (Dean *et al.*, 1998; Johnson & O'Leary-Kelly, 2003). As a result, the high level of OC may lead to a decrease in creative activity. Thus, on the basis of the above-given arguments, we posit:

H5: OC mediates the relationship between CE and IWB.

METHODOLOGY

Sample and Procedure

This research relied on the cooperation of numerous hotels to collect their employees' data in Guwahati, Assam, and was acquired using standardised closed-ended questionnaires. Despite the fact that the questionnaire was written in English, a number of respondents requested that certain questions be translated into their native Assamese, which was done as requested. The sample size is 279 individuals.

According to the demographic profile of respondents, males made up 58.9 percent of the total and females made up 41.1 percent. Furthermore, 66.3 percent of respondents had less than five years of job experience, 27.6 percent had five to ten years of work experience, and 6.1 percent had more than ten years of work

Figure 1. Conceptual model

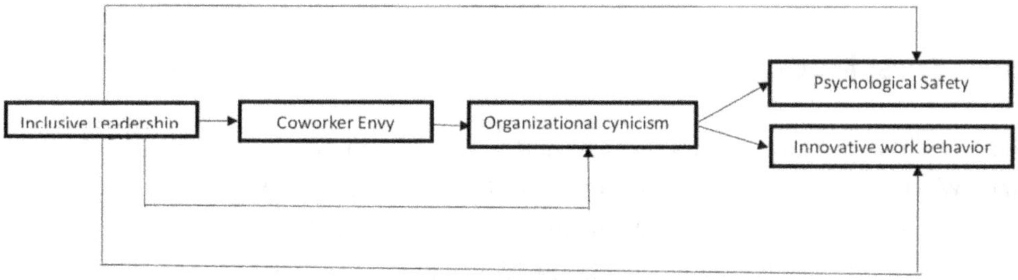

experience. Furthermore, 76.8 percent of respondents had worked in the current organisation for 0–3 years, 20 percent of respondents had worked for 4–7 years, and 3.2 percent of respondents had worked for more than 7 years.

Measures

Five different scales were used for the purpose of this quantitative study. Using a nine-item scale, IL was evaluated (Carmeli *et al.*, 2010). To measure the respondent's perception of CE, a three-item scale (Vecchio, 2005) was used. A five-item scale was used to assess OC (Bang & Reio, 2017), whereas the respondents' PS was measured using a three-item scale proposed by May *et al.* (2004), and a ten-item scale (De Jong & Den Hartog, 2010) was employed to assess IWB.

Measurement Model

All five variables in the measurement model were tested for reliability, convergent validity, and discriminant validity. At a threshold level of 0.70, the variables under examination were reliable according to composite reliability and Cronbach's alpha (Table II) (Nunnally, 1978). The variables demonstrated a high amount of convergent validity, as evidenced by the average variance extracted (AVE) values for the five reflecting constructs being larger than 0.50. (MacKenzie *et al.,* 2011).

A number of methods were employed to assess the discriminant validity of the model, with the factor loading criteria being the first. The requirements stipulate that the average factor loading for each construct must be higher than 0.7 and that the factor loading for each indicator on its linked construct must be higher than 0.05 (Table I). Second, the Fornell-Larcker test was used to see if each construct's AVE square root value exceeded the highest correlation with any other construct (Table 2). To verify discriminant validity, the hetreotrait-monotrait (HTMT) ratio of correlations of the constructs under research was also evaluated. Because the HTMT ratios for all of the constructs investigated were less than the 0.85 threshold limit, this indicated that they had discriminant validity. (Henseler *et al.,* 2015). The chi square test was shown to be significant in determining whether the measurement model was an adequate fit, hence verifying the measurement model's fit.

Structural Model

This study's structural model investigated the direct and indirect impacts of IL on PS and IWB through CE and OC. Table IV contains the findings of the experiment. The collinearity values, significance, and applicability of structural model relationships, the coefficient of determination (R square values), the impact of path coefficients

Table 1. Construct validity and reliability

Construct	Item remained	Loadings	Cronbach's alpha	Composite reliability	AVE
CE	CE 1	0.89	0.893	0.932	0.822
	CE 2	0.943			
	CE 3	0.884			
IL	IL 1	0.806	0.939	0.949	0.7
	IL 2	0.772			
	IL 3	0.817			
	IL 4	0.96			
	IL 5	0.888			
	IL 6	0.73			
	IL 7	0.902			
	IL 8	0.858			
PS	PS 1	0.827	0.733	0.851	0.655
	PS 2	0.811			
	PS 3	0.791			
IWB	IWB 1	0.743	0.909	0.928	0.648
	IWB 2	0.796			
	IWB 3	0.839			
	IWB 4	0.822			
	IWB 5	0.837			
	IWB 6	0.839			
	IWB 7	0.753			
OC	OC 1	0.743	0.828	0.886	0.66
	OC 2	0.817			
	OC 3	0.826			
	OC 4	0.861			

CE: Coworker's envy; IL: Inclusive leadership; PS: Psychological safety; IWB: Innovative work behavior; OC: Organizational cynicism

(f2 values), the predictive applicability (Stone-Geisser Q2) of endogenous variables, and the SRMR values are used to assess the overall structural model fit. There was no evidence of collinearity in the model, which had a variance inflation factor (VIF) of under 5 for all variables.

The model's path coefficient indicates a positive and significant association between IL and PS ($\beta = 0.399$, $t = 8.032$, $p<0.05$), corroborating hypothesis H1. Similarly, the direct association between CE and IWB was shown to be significant (β= 0.541, t = 11.85, p<0.05), corroborating hypothesis H2. Table IV contains further correlations between constructs.

Mediation Analysis

To evaluate the indirect effect of IL on PS and IWB via CE and OC, a bias-corrected bootstrapping approach was applied. CE partially mediated the relationship between IL and OC, which validates H3 (β = -0.09, t = 3.363, p=0). The effect of IL on PS was found to be significant in the presence of CE and OC (β = 0.019, t = 2.598, p=0), implying that CE and OC partially mediate the association between IL and PS, verifying hypothesis H4. Similarly, the indirect effect of IL on IWB was shown to be significant via CE and OC (β = 0.021, t = 2.657, p= 0), validating hypothesis H5. As a result, it is possible to conclude that CE and OC mediate the link between IL and PS, as well as IWB.

The coefficient of determination (R2) values for all endogenous variables, namely PS, were reported to be 0.249, 0.408 for IWB, 0.064 for CE, and 0.186 for OC. The structural model's effect size was also calculated as the value of f2 and compared to the recommended values provided by Cohen (1988) as small (0.02), medium (0.15), and large (0.35). The effect size of IL on PS is medium, and for IWB-large, it is large. Whereas, for CE and OC it is small. The relationship between CE and OC was medium, and that between OC and PS as well as OC and IWB was small.

In addition to R2 and f2, the model's predictive significance was evaluated using "Stone-Q2 Geisser's value" (Woodside, 2013). The blindfolded cross-validation results show that for PS (Q2 = 0.159), IWB (Q2 = 0.260), CE (Q2 = 0.048), and OC (Q2 = 0.119). Because the Q2 values for these variables are greater than 0.0, the model's predictive relevance is determined to be sufficient (Henseler *et al.*, 2015). Finally, the standardised root-mean square residual (SRMR) value is 0.644

Table 2. Discriminant validity

Fornell- Larcker Test						HTMT Ratio					
	CE	IL	PS	IWB	OC		CE	IL	PS	IWB	OC
CE	0.906					CE					
IL	-0.262	0.837				IL	0.265				
PS	-0.251	0.457	0.81			PS	0.318	0.541			
IWB	-0.143	0.594	0.349	0.805		IWB	0.152	0.645	0.421		
OC	0.401	-0.264	-0.318	-0.37	0.813	OC	0.437	0.286	0.407	0.423	

CE: Coworker's envy; IL: Inclusive leadership; PS: Psychological safety; IWB: Innovative work behavior; OC: Organizational cynicism

Table 3. Total effect

Relationship	Path	t value	p value
CE-PS	-0.077	3.812	0
CE-IWB	-0.082	4.301	0
CE-OC	0.358	7.548	0
IL-CE	-0.252	3.842	0
IL-PS	0.454	9.402	0
IL-IWB	0.599	13.71	0
IL-OC	-0.258	5.162	0
OC-PS	-0.214	4.395	0
OC-IWB	-0.228	5.705	0

Table 4. Direct -effect (path coefficient)

Relationship	Path	t value	p value	Hypothesis
CE-OC	0.358	7.548	0	Significance
IL-CE	-0.252	3.842	0	Significance
IL-PS	0.399	8.032	0	Significance
IL-IWB	0.541	11.85	0	Significance
IL-OC	-0.167	3.195	0.001	Significance
OC-PS	-0.214	4.395	0	Significance
OC-IWB	-0.228	5.705	0	Significance

CE: Coworker's envy; IL: Inclusive leadership; PS: Psychological safety; IWB: Innovative work behavior; OC: Organizational cynicism

Table 5. Indirect -effect

Path	Indirect effect	t value	p value	LLCI	ULCI
IL-CE-OC-PS	0.019	2.598	0.01	0.008	0.037
IL-CE-OC	-0.09	3.363	0.001	-0.143	-0.044
IL-CE-OC-IWB	0.021	2.657	0.008	0.008	0.038
IL-OC-PS	0.036	2.458	0.014	0.012	0.0067
CE-OC-IWB	-0.082	4.301	0	-0.126	-0.048
CE-OC-PS	-0.077	3.812	0	-0.118	-0.042
IL-OC-IWB	0.038	3.107	0.002	0.014	0.063

CE: Coworker's envy; IL: Inclusive leadership; S: Psychological safety; IWB: Innovative work behavior;

Table 6. F square

	CE	IL	PS	IWB	OC
CE					0.48
IL	0.068		0.198	0.461	0.032
PS					
IWB					
OC			0.057	0.082	

CE: Coworker's envy; IL: Inclusive leadership; PS: Psychological safety; IWB: Innovative work behavior; OC: Organizational cynicism

Table 7. Explanatory power of structural model

<table>
<tr><th>Predictor</th><th>Outcome Variables</th><th>R^2</th><th>Q^2</th><th>Model fit</th></tr>
<tr><td rowspan="4">IL</td><td>CE</td><td>0.064</td><td>0.048</td><td rowspan="2">0.644</td></tr>
<tr><td>PS</td><td>0.249</td><td>0.159</td></tr>
<tr><td>IWB</td><td>0.408</td><td>0.26</td><td rowspan="2">NFI- 0.816</td></tr>
<tr><td>OC</td><td>0.186</td><td>0.119</td></tr>
</table>

CE: Coworker's envy; PS: Psychological safety; IWB: Innovative work behavior; OC: Organizational cynicism

which is less than the required value of 0.10, and the NFI is 0.816, indicating that the structural model is well-fitting overall (Henseler *et al.*, 2015).

DISCUSSION

Businesses require employees to be creative in order to address the volatility of the external environment and the limited energy and capabilities of the managers. The study's purpose was to understand how to organically encourage people to adopt IWB. The outcomes of this research indicate that IL has a favourable effect on PS and IWB among employees. From a cultural viewpoint, it is possible to gauge the significance of the study's findings because the Indian sample employed in it (unlike the majority of other research utilising Western samples) uses a different reactance method than their Western counterparts when it comes to the leadership conduct.

The study's findings are in accordance with our premise that IL enhances PS for workers. This is as per past studies' findings that showed IL could raise workers' PS-related positive cognition (Zeng *et al.*, 2020; Khan *et al.*, 2020). Employees feel emotionally safe when their boss provides them with PS such as genuine political support, financial recompense, time off, and a safe environment in which to voice their opinions (Nembhard and Edmondson, 2006; Choi *et al.*, 2015).

Next, the study attempts to discover if IL leads to employees' IWB. The outcomes suggest that IL and IWB had a significant relationship, which is validated by earlier studies as well (Bannay *et al.*, 2020; Javed *et al.*, 2019). IL, as a kind of relational leadership, invites workers to participate directly in making decisions and enables them to exhibit participatory behaviour throughout work procedures. Thus, in an inclusive atmosphere where workers consider leaders to be inclusive of their new processes and ideas, their sense of worth is strengthened, which results in more IWB.

Next, the outcomes of the research suggest that CE mediated the relationship between CE and OC. In the presence of inclusive leaders, CE reduces which further diminishes the cynical behaviour of employees. Further, the researchers looked at the indirect influence of CE and OC on the association between IL and PS in this study. This research adds to the existing literature by examining the IL-CE-OC-PS linkage. The study demonstrates that CE and OC weaken the link between IL and PS. Similarly, the intervening effect of CE and OC was also studied between IL and IWB. The outcomes demonstrate that CE and OC partially mediate this relationship, which weakens the link between IL and IWB.

PRACTICAL IMPLICATIONS

The present research has numerous practical applications for business leaders and managers. Management should hire such candidates who have the quality of being inclusive and attitude of working with team. Such candidates can be further considered for succession planning and to fulfil important job roles in the future. Management should be aware of the factors that encourage innovative work behaviour among their staff. In order to create an atmosphere where workers feel at ease voicing their thoughts and opinions, we suggest that managers build an inclusive leadership style by placing an emphasis on openness, availability, and accessibility. Therefore, it is critical for leaders to establish connections with their teams through social events and training initiatives. Training sessions should be arranged for the leaders to better enhance their capabilities, whereas mentoring sessions should be arranged for those employees who have the potential to be inclusive leaders in the future. In addition, to encourage employees to take initiative, organisations should foster an open environment by providing clear direction at work and showing genuine concern for their psychological safety. It is important to provide them with opportunities for training and other resources to help them become more self-sufficient. Moreover, it's important for businesses to foster a culture that promotes respect and esteem for employees. The negative effects of jealousy or envy on both the company and its employees are clear: lower productivity and morale among workers, and less cohesive teams. This disengagement from an organization's environment, which destroys psychological safety, appears to be amplified in poorly led organisations. The organisation should promote equality among their employees; all the employees must get equal opportunities and resources for their growth and success, so that feelings of jealousy and envy among the employees can be reduced to a minimum. An employee's perception of their own worth at work is measured by how competent and appreciated they are by their superiors. If that sense of self-worth is shaken by feelings of envy, it can quickly give way to cynicism. Managers can start a culture of having open conversations with their superiors by starting a dialogue between their subordinates and superiors. They may start a monthly event such as "An evening with the manager," where they promote open dialogue and the negative opinions of the employees about the organisation can be addressed. The key aspects of healthy empathy are trust, open interactions that make employees feel valued, and maintaining positive ties. When there is a lot of trust in an organisation, everyone works together better and the leadership is more efficient. An individual's level of confidence in an organisation is directly related to the degree to which they are treated impartially (regardless of their status), respected, and credibly. So, it is recommended to create a healthy environment among co-workers that may result in better psychological safety and innovative work behaviour.

LIMITATIONS AND FUTURE RESEARCH DIRECTIONS

The study's findings provided us with some crucial knowledge regarding inclusive leadership and its relationship to psychological safety and innovative work practices. Our research does have certain limitations, though. First, information was gathered from employees in the Indian hospitality sector; however, it was unclear if the data came from supervisors or subordinates. To better comprehend how to evaluate their behaviour, future research can focus on one of the two separately. Another disadvantage is the relatively small sample size; future studies should employ larger samples. As a result, it will be relatively easier to generalise the study's findings. Another problem is the geographical position of the respondents. It would be wise to exercise caution when extrapolating any inferences from our findings to other countries with different cultural traditions, as we chose to conduct our inclusive leadership research in India. Researchers wishing to broaden their findings may look into this route in the future.

CONCLUSION

Our results support prior research while also advancing our understanding of the direct and indirect effects that IL has on PS and IWB. A sample of full-time employees in India's hospitality industry served as the basis for our hypothesis testing. Our results indicate how CE and OC hamper the PS and IWB of employees. The data implies that all of the variables studied are linked and that IL has an impact on the PS and IWB of employees, with CE and OC mediating the relationship.

REFERENCES

Aboramadan, M., Dahleez, K. A., & Farao, C. (2022). Inclusive leadership and extra-role behaviors in higher education: Does organizational learning mediate the relationship? *International Journal of Educational Management*, *36*(4), 397–418.

Abraham, R. (2000). Organizational cynicism: Bases and consequences. *Genetic, Social, and General Psychology Monographs*, *126*(3), 269–292. PMID:10950198

Abubakar, A. M., & Arasli, H. (2016). Dear top management please don't make me cynic: Intention to sabotage. *Journal of Management Development*, *35*(10), 1266–1286. doi:10.1108/JMD-11-2015-0164

Agarwal, U. A., Stokes, P., & Smith, S. (2016). Examining perceived organizational politics among Indian managers: Engagement as mediator and locus of control as moderator. *The International Journal of Organizational Analysis*, *24*(3), 415–437. doi:10.1108/IJOA-07-2014-0786

Al-Ababneh, M. M. (2015). Employees' service innovation behavior and new service development in four- and five-star hotels. *International Journal of Tourism & Hospitality Reviews*, *1*(1), 13–22. doi:10.18510/ijthr.2014.113

Arslan, M., & Roudaki, J. (2019). Examining the role of employee engagement in the relationship between organisational cynicism and employee performance. *The International Journal of Sociology and Social Policy*, *39*(1/2), 118–137. doi:10.1108/IJSSP-06-2018-0087

Bang, H., & Reio, T. G. Jr. (2017). Examining the role of cynicism in the relationships between burnout and employee behavior. *Journal of Work and Organizational Psychology*, *33*(3), 217–227. doi:10.1016/j.rpto.2017.07.002

Bannay, D. F., Hadi, M. J., & Amanah, A. A. (2020). The impact of inclusive leadership behaviors on innovative workplace behavior with an emphasis on the mediating role of work engagement. *Problems and Perspectives in Management, 18*(3), 479.5e5

Carmeli, A., Reiter-Palmon, R., & Ziv, E. (2010). Inclusive leadership and employee involvement in creative tasks in the workplace: The mediating role of psychological safety. *Creativity Research Journal, 22*(3), 250–260. doi:10.1080/10400419.2010.504654

Cenkci, A. T., Bircan, T., & Zimmerman, J. (2020). Inclusive leadership and work engagement: The mediating role of procedural justice. *Management Research Review, 44*(1), 158–180. doi:10.1108/MRR-03-2020-0146

Choi, S. B., Tran, T. B. H., & Park, B. I. (2015). Inclusive leadership and work engagement: Mediating roles of affective organizational commitment and creativity. *Social Behavior and Personality, 43*(6), 931–943. doi:10.2224bp.2015.43.6.931

Cohen, J. (1988). *Statistical power analysis for the behavioural sciences*. Lawrence Erlbaum Associates.

De Jong, J., & Den Hartog, D. (2010). Measuring innovative work behaviour. *Creativity and Innovation Management, 19*(1), 23–36. doi:10.1111/j.1467-8691.2010.00547.x

Dean, J. W. Jr, Brandes, P., & Dharwadkar, R. (1998). Organizational cynicism. *Academy of Management Review, 23*(2), 341–352. doi:10.2307/259378

Devloo, T., Anseel, F., De Beuckelaer, A., & Feys, M. (2016). When the fire dies: Perceived success and support for innovation shape the motivating potential of innovative work behaviour. *European Journal of Work and Organizational Psychology, 25*(4), 512–524. doi:10.1080/1359432X.2016.1182157

Du, J., Ma, E., & Lin, X. (2021). Can proactivity translate to creativity? Examinations at individual and team levels. *International Journal of Hospitality Management, 98*, 103034. doi:10.1016/j.ijhm.2021.103034

Duffy, M. K., Scott, K. L., Shaw, J. D., Tepper, B. J., & Aquino, K. (2012). A social context model of envy and social undermining. *Academy of Management Journal, 55*(3), 643–666. doi:10.5465/amj.2009.0804

Eaton, J. A. (2000). *A social motivation approach to organizational cynicism*. York University.

Edmondson, A. C., Kramer, R. M., & Cook, K. S. (2004). Psychological safety, trust, and learning in organizations: A group-level lens. *Trust and distrust in organizations: Dilemmas and approaches, 12*, 239-272.

Eid, R., & Agag, G. (2020). Determinants of innovative behaviour in the hotel industry: A cross-cultural study. *International Journal of Hospitality Management, 91*, 102642. doi:10.1016/j.ijhm.2020.102642

Ghafoor, A., & Haar, J. (2020). A climate and personality approach towards creativity behaviours: A moderated mediation study. *International Journal of Innovation Management, 24*(06), 2050080. doi:10.1142/S1363919620500802

Gong, Z., Yang, J., Gilal, F. G., Van Swol, L. M., & Yin, K. (2020). Repairing police psychological safety: The role of career adaptability, feedback environment, and goal-self concordance based on the conservation of resources theory. *SAGE Open, 10*(2), 2158244020919510. doi:10.1177/2158244020919510

Hammond, M., Cross, C., Farrell, C., & Eubanks, D. (2019). Burnout and innovative work behaviours for survivors of downsizing: An investigation of boundary conditions. *Creativity and Innovation Management, 28*(3), 306–317. doi:10.1111/caim.12327

Harrell-Cook, G., Ferris, G. R., & Dulebohn, J. H. (1999). Political behaviors as moderators of the perceptions of organizational politics—Work outcomes relationships. *Journal of Organizational Behavior, 20*(7), 1093–1105. doi:10.1002/(SICI)1099-1379(199912)20:7<1093::AID-JOB945>3.0.CO;2-#

Hassan, S., & Jiang, Z. (2021). Facilitating learning to improve performance of law enforcement workgroups: The role of inclusive leadership behavior. *International Public Management Journal, 24*(1), 106–130. doi:10.1080/10967494.2019.1680465

Henseler, J., Ringle, C. M., & Sarstedt, M. (2015). A new criterion for assessing discriminant validity in variance-based structural equation modeling. *Journal of the Academy of Marketing Science, 43*(1), 115–135. doi:10.100711747-014-0403-8

Hilal, O. A. (2021). The moderating role of self-efficacy in the relationship between workplace envy and social undermining. *Global Business and Organizational Excellence, 40*(6), 28–40. doi:10.1002/joe.22091

Hirak, R., Peng, A. C., Carmeli, A., & Schaubroeck, J. M. (2012). Linking leader inclusiveness to work unit performance: The importance of psychological safety and learning from failures. *The Leadership Quarterly, 23*(1), 107–117. doi:10.1016/j.leaqua.2011.11.009

Hu, N., Wu, J., & Gu, J. (2019). Cultural intelligence and employees' creative performance: The moderating role of team conflict in interorganizational teams. *Journal of Management & Organization*, *25*(1), 96–116. doi:10.1017/jmo.2016.64

Hughes, M., Rigtering, J. C., Covin, J. G., Bouncken, R. B., & Kraus, S. (2018). Innovative behaviour, trust and perceived workplace performance. *British Journal of Management*, *29*(4), 750–768. doi:10.1111/1467-8551.12305

Janssen, O. (2004). How fairness perceptions make innovative behavior more or less stressful. *Journal of Organizational Behavior*, *25*(2), 201–215. doi:10.1002/job.238

Janssen, O., & Van Yperen, N. W. (2004). Employees' goal orientations, the quality of leader-member exchange, and the outcomes of job performance and job satisfaction. *Academy of Management Journal*, *47*(3), 368–384. doi:10.2307/20159587

Javed, B., Khan, A. K., & Quratulain, S. (2018). Inclusive leadership and innovative work behavior: Examination of LMX perspective in small capitalized textile firms. *The Journal of Psychology*, *152*(8), 594–612. doi:10.1080/00223980.2018.1489767 PMID:30260768

Javed, B., Naqvi, S. M. M. R., Khan, A. K., Arjoon, S., & Tayyeb, H. H. (2017). Impact of inclusive leadership on innovative work behavior: The role of psychological safety. *Journal of Management & Organization*, *25*(1), 117–136. doi:10.1017/jmo.2017.3

Javed, B., Naqvi, S. M. M. R., Khan, A. K., Arjoon, S., & Tayyeb, H. H. (2019). Impact of inclusive leadership on innovative work behavior: The role of psychological safety. *Journal of Management & Organization*, *25*(1), 117–136. doi:10.1017/jmo.2017.3

Jiang, Z., Hu, X., Wang, Z., & Jiang, X. (2019). Knowledge hiding as a barrier to thriving: The mediating role of psychological safety and moderating role of organizational cynicism. *Journal of Organizational Behavior*, *40*(7), 800–818. doi:10.1002/job.2358

Johnson, J. L., & O'Leary-Kelly, A. M. (2003). The effects of psychological contract breach and organizational cynicism: Not all social exchange violations are created equal. *Journal of Organizational Behavior: The International Journal of Industrial. Journal of Organizational Behavior*, *24*(5), 627–647. doi:10.1002/job.207

Jolly, P. M., & Lee, L. (2021). Silence is not golden: Motivating employee voice through inclusive leadership. *Journal of Hospitality & Tourism Research (Washington, D.C.)*, *45*(6), 1092–1113. doi:10.1177/1096348020963699

Kahn, W. A. (1990). Psychological conditions of personal engagement and disengagement at work. *Academy of Management Journal, 33*(4), 692–724. doi:10.2307/256287

Khalili, A. (2016). Linking transformational leadership, creativity, innovation, and innovation-supportive climate. *Management Decision, 54*(9), 2277–2293. doi:10.1108/MD-03-2016-0196

Khan, J., Jaafar, M., Javed, B., Mubarak, N., & Saudagar, T. (2020). Does inclusive leadership affect project success? The mediating role of perceived psychological empowerment and psychological safety. *International Journal of Managing Projects in Business, 13*(5), 1077–1096. doi:10.1108/IJMPB-10-2019-0267

Kim, E., & Glomb, T. M. (2014). Victimization of high performers: The roles of envy and work group identification. *The Journal of Applied Psychology, 99*(4), 619–634. doi:10.1037/a0035789 PMID:24490964

Ko, C. H. (2015). Exploring the Motivators Stimulating Hotel Employees' Innovation. *Journal of Human Resource and Sustainability Studies, 3*(03), 156–161. doi:10.4236/jhrss.2015.33021

Kostopoulos, K. C., & Bozionelos, N. (2011). Team exploratory and exploitative learning: Psychological safety, task conflict, and team performance. *Group & Organization Management, 36*(3), 385–415. doi:10.1177/1059601111405985

Lee, C., & Wong, C. S. (2019). The effect of team emotional intelligence on team process and effectiveness. *Journal of Management & Organization, 25*(6), 844–859. doi:10.1017/jmo.2017.43

Lee, J. Y., Swink, M., & Pandejpong, T. (2011). The roles of worker expertise, information sharing quality, and psychological safety in manufacturing process innovation: An intellectual capital perspective. *Production and Operations Management, 20*(4), 556–570. doi:10.1111/j.1937-5956.2010.01172.x

Lee, K., Duffy, M. K., Scott, K. L., & Schippers, M. C. (2018). The experience of being envied at work: How being envied shapes employee feelings and motivation. *Personnel Psychology, 71*(2), 181–200. doi:10.1111/peps.12251

Li, M., & Hsu, C. H. (2016). Linking customer-employee exchange and employee innovative behavior. *International Journal of Hospitality Management, 56*, 87–97. doi:10.1016/j.ijhm.2016.04.015

MacKenzie, S. B., Podsakoff, P. M., & Podsakoff, N. P. (2011). Construct measurement and validation procedures in MIS and behavioral research: Integrating new and existing techniques. *Management Information Systems Quarterly*, *35*(2), 293–334. doi:10.2307/23044045

Mahmood, M., Uddin, M. A., & Fan, L. (2018). The influence of transformational leadership on employees' creative process engagement: A multi-level analysis. *Management Decision*, *57*(3), 741–764. doi:10.1108/MD-07-2017-0707

Mansoor, A., Farrukh, M., Wu, Y., & Abdul Wahab, S. (2021). Does inclusive leadership incite innovative work behavior? *Human Systems Management*, *40*(1), 93–102. doi:10.3233/HSM-200972

Mansoor, A., Wahab, S. A., & Jahan, S. (2021). Stimulation of innovative behavior through the inclusive leaders and engaged workers. *Business: Theory and Practice*, *22*(2), 249–255. doi:10.3846/btp.2021.13363

Mao, Y., He, J., & Yang, D. (2021). The dark sides of engaging in creative processes: Coworker envy, workplace ostracism, and incivility. *Asia Pacific Journal of Management*, *38*(4), 1261–1281. doi:10.100710490-020-09707-z

May, D. R., Gilson, R. L., & Harter, L. M. (2004). The psychological conditions of meaningfulness, safety and availability and the engagement of the human spirit at work. *Journal of Occupational and Organizational Psychology*, *77*(1), 11–37. doi:10.1348/096317904322915892

Mikyoung, K., & Moon, J. (2019). Inclusive leadership and creative performance: The role of psychological safety, feedback-seeking behavior and power-distance. *Korean Journal of Human Resources Development*, *22*(4), 181–205. doi:10.24991/KJHRD.2019.12.22.4.181

Montani, F., Odoardi, C., & Battistelli, A. (2015). Envisioning, planning and innovating: A closer investigation of proactive goal generation, innovative work behaviour and boundary conditions. *Journal of Business and Psychology*, *30*(3), 415–433. doi:10.100710869-014-9371-8

Morrow, P. C., & Crum, M. R. (1998). The effects of perceived and objective safety risk on employee outcomes. *Journal of Vocational Behavior*, *53*(2), 300–313. doi:10.1006/jvbe.1997.1620

Nafei, W. (2015). The effects of job embeddedness on organizational cynicism and employee performance: A study on Sadat City University. *International Journal of Business Administration*, *6*(1), 8.

Naqshbandi, M. M., Tabche, I., & Choudhary, N. (2018). Managing open innovation: The roles of empowering leadership and employee involvement climate. *Management Decision*, *57*(3), 703–723. doi:10.1108/MD-07-2017-0660

Nembhard, I. M., & Edmondson, A. C. (2006). Making it safe: The effects of leader inclusiveness and professional status on psychological safety and improvement efforts in health care teams. *Journal of Organizational Behavior*, *27*(7), 941–966. doi:10.1002/job.413

Neves, P. (2012). Organizational cynicism: Spillover effects on supervisor–subordinate relationships and performance. *The Leadership Quarterly*, *23*(5), 965–976. doi:10.1016/j.leaqua.2012.06.006

Nunnally, J. C. (1978). *Psychometric Theory* (2nd ed.). McGraw-Hill.

Parrott, W. G., & Smith, R. H. (1993). Distinguishing the experiences of envy and jealousy. *Journal of Personality and Social Psychology*, *64*(6), 906–920. doi:10.1037/0022-3514.64.6.906 PMID:8326472

Podsakoff, N. P., LePine, J. A., & LePine, M. A. (2007). Differential challenge stressor-hindrance stressor relationships with job attitudes, turnover intentions, turnover, and withdrawal behavior: A meta-analysis. *The Journal of Applied Psychology*, *92*(2), 438–454. doi:10.1037/0021-9010.92.2.438 PMID:17371090

Prajogo, W., Kusumawati, H., & Wijaya, N. H. S. (2020). Organizational culture as determinant of employee-based antecedents to organizational cynicism. *Humanities & Social Sciences Reviews*, *8*(1), 881–886. doi:10.18510/hssr.2020.81105

Rayisi, A., & Nastiezaie, N. (2019). The Relationship between organizational cynicism and organizational anti-citizenship behavior with the mediating role of organizational envy. *Career and Organizational Counseling*, *11*(38), 117–136. doi:10.29252/jcoc.11.1.117

Reichers, A. E., Wanous, J. P., & Austin, J. T. (1997). Understanding and managing cynicism about organizational change. *The Academy of Management Perspectives*, *11*(1), 48–59. doi:10.5465/ame.1997.9707100659

Schein, E. H., & Bennis, W. G. (1965). *Personal and organizational change through group methods: The laboratory approach*. Wiley.

Scott, K. L., Tams, S., Schippers, M. C., & Lee, K. (2015). Opening the black box: Why and when workplace exclusion affects social reconnection behaviour, health, and attitudes. *European Journal of Work and Organizational Psychology*, *24*(2), 239–255. doi:10.1080/1359432X.2014.894978

Scott, S. G., & Bruce, R. A. (1994). Determinants of innovative behavior: A path model of individual innovation in the workplace. *Academy of Management Journal*, *37*(3), 580–607. doi:10.2307/256701

Shakil, R. M., Memon, M. A., & Ting, H. (2021). Inclusive leadership and innovative work behaviour: The mediating role of job autonomy. *Quality & Quantity*, 1–15. doi:10.100711135-021-01102-0

Shankar, S., & Tewari, V. (2021). Impact of Collective Intelligence and Collective Emotional Intelligence on the Psychological Safety of the Organizations. *Vision (Basel)*, 9722629211012256.

Simha, A., Elloy, D. F., & Huang, H. C. (2014). The moderated relationship between job burnout and organizational cynicism. *Management Decision*, *52*(3), 482–504. doi:10.1108/MD-08-2013-0422

Siyal, S., Xin, C., Umrani, W. A., Fatima, S., & Pal, D. (2021). How do leaders influence innovation and creativity in employees? The mediating role of intrinsic motivation. *Administration & Society*, *53*(9), 1337–1361. doi:10.1177/0095399721997427

Tabatabaei, S. A. N., & Bigdelli, E. (2015). The mediating role of employee cynicism in the relationship between perceived organizational justice and employee silence. *Journal UMP Social Sciences and Technology Management*, *3*(3), 121–127.

Theurer, C. P., Tumasjan, A., & Welpe, I. M. (2018). Contextual work design and employee innovative work behavior: When does autonomy matter? *PLoS One*, *13*(10), e0204089. doi:10.1371/journal.pone.0204089 PMID:30286104

van der Berg, P. (2010). Stimulating Knowledge Sharing by Error Management and Leader-Member Exchange: Psychological Safety as a Mediator. *Psihologia Resurselor Umane*, *8*(2), 42–52. doi:10.24837/pru.v8i2.417

Vecchio, R. (2005). Explorations in employee envy: Feeling envious and feeling envied. *Cognition and Emotion*, *19*(1), 69–81. doi:10.1080/02699930441000148

Vecchio, R. P. (1995). It's not easy being green: Jealousy and envy in the workplace. In G. R. Ferris (Ed.), *Research in personnel and human resources management* (Vol. 13, pp. 201–244). JAI Press.

Wang, F., & Shi, W. (2021). Inclusive leadership and pro-social rule breaking: The role of psychological safety, leadership identification and leader-member exchange. *Psychological Reports*, *124*(5), 2155–2179. doi:10.1177/0033294120953558 PMID:32878545

Wang, H., Chen, M., & Li, X. (2021). Moderating multiple mediation model of the impact of inclusive leadership on employee innovative behavior. *Frontiers in Psychology*, *12*, 666477. doi:10.3389/fpsyg.2021.666477 PMID:34456787

Wang, Y. X., Yang, Y. J., Wang, Y., Su, D., Li, S. W., Zhang, T., & Li, H. P. (2019). The mediating role of inclusive leadership: Work engagement and innovative behaviour among Chinese head nurses. *Journal of Nursing Management*, *27*(4), 688–696. doi:10.1111/jonm.12754 PMID:30702790

Weintraub, P., & McKee, M. (2019). Leadership for innovation in healthcare: An exploration. *International Journal of Health Policy and Management*, *8*(3), 138–144. doi:10.15171/ijhpm.2018.122 PMID:30980629

Woodside, A. G. (2013). Moving beyond multiple regression analysis to algorithms: Calling for adoption of a paradigm shift from symmetric to asymmetric thinking in data analysis and crafting theory. *Journal of Business Research*, *66*(4), 463–472. doi:10.1016/j.jbusres.2012.12.021

Ye, Y., Lyu, Y., Kwan, H. K., Chen, X., & Cheng, X. M. (2021). The antecedents and consequences of being envied by coworkers: An investigation from the victim perspective. *International Journal of Hospitality Management*, *94*, 102751. doi:10.1016/j.ijhm.2020.102751

Yu, L., & Duffy, M. K. (2016). A moral licensing perspective of abusive supervision and career consequences. In Academy of Management Proceedings (pp. 15269). Academy of Management. doi:10.5465/ambpp.2016.15269abstract

Zeng, H., Zhao, L., & Zhao, Y. (2020). Inclusive leadership and taking-charge behavior: Roles of psychological safety and thriving at work. *Frontiers in Psychology*, *11*, 62. doi:10.3389/fpsyg.2020.00062 PMID:32153448

Zhao, F., Ahmed, F., & Faraz, N. A. (2020). Caring for the caregiver during COVID-19 outbreak: Does inclusive leadership improve psychological safety and curb psychological distress? A cross-sectional study. *International Journal of Nursing Studies*, *110*, 103725. doi:10.1016/j.ijnurstu.2020.103725 PMID:32810720

Zhu, J., Xu, S., & Zhang, B. (2020). The paradoxical effect of inclusive leadership on subordinates' creativity. *Frontiers in Psychology*, *10*, 2960. doi:10.3389/fpsyg.2019.02960 PMID:32038369

ADDITIONAL READING

Bourke, J., & Espedido, A. (2019). Why inclusive leaders are good for organizations, and how to become one. *Harvard Business Review*, *29*(03).

Kuknor, S., & Bhattacharya, S. (2021). Exploring organizational inclusion and inclusive leadership in Indian companies. *European Business Review*, *33*(3), 450-464.

Kuknor, S. C., & Bhattacharya, S. (2022). Inclusive leadership: new age leadership to foster organizational inclusion. *European Journal of Training and Development*, *46*(9), 771-797.

Srivastava, S., & Singh, L.B. (2022). Inclusive Leadership and innovative work behavior: mediating role of thriving at work. *Corporate Governance Insight*, *4*(2).

KEY TERMS AND DEFINITIONS

Coworker Envy: Coworker's envy from the perspective of a targeted victim is the feeling of being resented or judged negatively by a colleague because of qualities or achievements that evoke jealousy or inadequacy.

Inclusive Leadership: Inclusive leadership refers to the practice of cultivating an environment of respect, belonging, and fairness for all individuals in a given organization, regardless of their personal differences or backgrounds.

Innovative Work Behavior: Innovative work behavior is the process of developing and implementing new and creative ideas and solutions in the workplace. It involves taking risks, challenging the status quo, and thinking outside the box to develop novel approaches to problem-solving.

Organizational Cynicism: Organizational cynicism refers to a negative work attitude characterized by distrust, skepticism, and disillusionment toward an organization and its members.

Psychological Safety: It is the degree to which individuals in a group or team feel that they can speak up, share their thoughts, express their ideas, and challenge the status quo without feeling embarrassed, judged or punished.

Chapter 3
The Influence of Human Resources in the Motivation and Performance of Employees:
Performance Evaluation/Appraisal

Inês Maximino
ISAG-European Business School, Portugal & Research Center in Business Sciences and Tourism (CICET-FCVC), Portugal

Ana Pinto Borges
https://orcid.org/0000-0002-4942-079X
ISAG-European Business School, Portugal & Research Center in Business Sciences and Tourism (CICET-FCVC), Portugal & Research Centre in Organizations, Markets and Industrial Management (COMEGI), Portugal

Bruno Miguel Vieira
ISAG-European Business School, Portugal & Research Center in Business Sciences and Tourism (CICET-FCVC), Portugal

Elvira Vieira
https://orcid.org/0000-0002-9296-3896
ISAG-European Business School, Portugal & Research Center in Business Sciences and Tourism (CICET-FCVC), Portugal & Polytechnic Institute of Viana do Castelo (IPVC), Portugal & Applied Management Research Unit (UNIAG), Portugal

Henrique Pires
ISAG-European Business School, Portugal & Research Center in Business Sciences and Tourism (CICET-FCVC), Portugal

DOI: 10.4018/978-1-6684-6602-5.ch003

ABSTRACT

This chapter seeks to define and analyse performance evaluation, which are the methods used by organizations to evaluate the performance of employees and their limitations. Based on a qualitative methodological approach, the interview survey was used as a research tool. The results presented demonstrate that motivation and performance are very present in the organizations addressed, although the stipulated evaluation methods differ from organization to organization, as well as the implications and limitations that may arise from performance evaluation.

INTRODUCTION

Currently, Human Resource Management is considered one of the most important areas for an organisation because its main objective is to ensure the sustainability of the organisation, especially in the development of People Management or in the search for a balanced organisational climate that enables teamwork, facilitating communication and integration among all stakeholders and, on the other hand, it seeks to ensure that all elements of the organisation are able to perform their functions effectively and demonstrate motivation and work performance (Beck et al., 2014; Dias & Paraíso, 2011). Human Resource Management is more focused on the employee because it aims to identify the employee's professional skills, the goals to be achieved, as well as the objectives set out. In this sense, we can say that the Human Resources area aims to guide all tasks and policies involving professional skills and the engagement of each element of the organisation to achieve the expected results.

One of the areas analysed by the Human Resources Management is the employee's performance and how it is ensuring the business success, for example through recommendations for behavioural improvement, as well as suggestions for organisational improvement (Pfeffer, 2007; Topcic, Baum, & Kabst, 2016; Dias & Paraíso, 2011).

Reward management system is a core role of human resource management. Besides, it has an important function on job outcome. Remuneration reward system have most important impact on organizations capability to hiring, retain and motivate high potential employees and as a result getting the high levels of performance (Agustiningsih et al. 2016; DeNisi & Murphy, 2017). Remuneration reward system is usually applied to motivate employees so that they perform better, are more productive, don't leave the organisation, establish a service oriented behaviour, and avoid corruption. Remuneration can be in the way of salary, fixed allowances, variable allowances, incentives and other facilities. Remuneration is the total compensation received by the employees in return for the services that they have done (Sun, Aryee, & Law, 2007; Wright, Gardner, & Moynihan, 2003; Agustiningsih et al. 2016).

It is pertinent to evaluate, and consequently reward employees through the merit of results achieved and this will only be possible through Performance Evaluation. Thus, this study aims to explore the Human Resources practices and its importance for the organisation, and on the other hand, to analyse and interpret how the performance and motivation of employees in an organisation are evaluated, to define some of the existing evaluation methods, and finally, to verify the possible implications or gaps that may arise in the performance evaluation for employees and for the organisation itself, aiming to minimise its effects (Beck et al., 2014; DeNisi & Murphy, 2017).

THEORETICAL BACKGROUND

The Evolution of Human Resources and Their Importance to the Organisation

In the context of Human Resources Management it is essential to demonstrate its changes over the last decades, particularly in People Management. In the past, the Human Resources area was limited to addressing specific problems that emerged in the organisation, without establishing any strategic concern; its function was merely to comply with the organisation's rules and norms. However, as of the 1960s, Human Resource Management leaned towards the development of procedures and practices directed towards the employee, i.e. towards people management, namely: the responsibility for selection methods, the development of training to ensure that all employees had the necessary procedures to perform tasks, benefit and reward policies, needs planning, and, finally, performance evaluation (DeNisi & Murphy, 2017). The tension between the traditional and newer approaches stems from a long-running dispute.

From this perspective, the scientific area of Human Resources Management, directed towards the development of people management, encompasses various aspects, namely the way in which the individual's behaviour is structured and guided within an organisation. Thus, the role of Human Resource managers is to seek to humanise organisations, i.e., in addition to the results obtained and goals achieved by the organisation, they should consider the personal and professional characteristics of each employee, what needs to be improved by each element of the organisation, trying to minimise their gaps (Aguinis, 2013; Pulakos & O'Leary, 2011; Beck et al., 2014).

Therefore, it is the responsibility of the Human Resources Management department to analyse and evaluate the individual and organisational skills of employees, to verify whether they have the necessary conditions to perform a particular function, whether they have the intellectual and professional conditions and whether they have the essential resources and means to obtain a favourable and motivating performance focused on the intended objectives (Boxall & Macky, 2009; Gardner et al., 2011; Corrêa, 2015; Agustiningsih et al. 2016). Also, it is within the scope of the Human Resources department to attract, to motivate and to retain employees to perform their functions. Attracting and motivating the right employees for the right functions and seeking to retain them in their jobs is essential and vital for the organisation (Pfeffer, 2007; Topcic, Baum, & Kabst, 2016), since any organisation is made of people, who manifest themselves, who produce, who achieve results and who give recognition to the organisation. However, with new technologies, new market trends have emerged and that, in turn the business environment has become increasingly competitive, making it necessary for companies to adapt to these divergences and seek to attract, motivate, and retain the best people so that the organization ensures a sustainable competitive advantage over its competitors. (Wright et al., 2001; Chiavenato, 2014).

So, organisations must be prepared to develop a strategy to attract, motivate and retain employees. In order to attract the right employees with the required competences, the organisation has to ensure a true, real and appropriate image and reputation, to make the employee feel engage, safe and integrated (Boxall & Macky, 2009; Gardner et al., 2011). It should be noted that an employee is not attracted by an organisation that loses its employees, that does not try to develop them, that does not guarantee career succession. The organisation has to be able to guarantee the employee's development and progression. However, in this sense, it is only possible to retain employees when they achieve the expected results, when they show progression in their work because much of the success of employees in an organisation depends on the efficient and effective way in which they are attracted (Gardner et al., 2007; Joaquim Vicente Rodrigues, 2013).

In addition, motivation is an indispensable tool to ensure a quality and efficient work, it is defined as a driver that moves towards its goals, so motivation and organizational goals should be aligned in order to guide the future strategies of the organization (Aguinis, 2013; Pulakos & O'Leary, 2011). On the other hand, when people are motivated in the job they are doing, they become more productive, act with greater satisfaction, show greater performance and tend to achieve the expected results, and may even exceed them, and thus show greater commitment to the organization where they work (Meyer et al., 2004; Boxall & Macky, 2009; Gardner et al., 2011; José Osmir Fiorelli, 2018). Thus, we can conclude that the organisation should develop and implement strategies that enable a greater motivation and satisfaction of the employee (Gardner et al., 2007).

Therefore, Human Resources Management involves the development and implementation of a set of policies and practices in the organisation that allow the set objectives to be achieved. It also develops a set of Human Resources Management activities that have a significant impact on employee performance, motivation and satisfaction, increasing the organisation's productivity (Pfeffer, 2007; Topcic, Baum, & Kabst, 2016). One of the main activities carried out by Human Resources is training, which assumes a primordial role in the employees (Aguinis, 2013; Beck et al., 2014). Training and development are a strategic Human Resources practices and should be considered as an investment due to the fact that it allows for an increase in employee productivity and profitability (Rego et al., 2015). On the other hand, training is considered an essential tool for improving knowledge and reviewing the organisation's processes, with the purpose of preparing employees for market demands and performing their functions efficiently and effectively.

Performance Evaluation

Returning to the progress of Human Resource Management already mentioned, we can see that one of the most valued characteristics of this area is the analysis, observation and evaluation of each employee, safeguarding that each person has a certain adaptability and flexibility in the organisation (DeNisi & Murphy, 2017). Each person is unique and complex, with different characteristics, for this reason an individual performance evaluation is necessary. Centred on the individual, it is possible to evaluate all their potentialities, their professional and personal competencies, as well as their weaknesses and limitations, seeking through the performance evaluation to improve their weaknesses and highlight their strengths, demonstrating how their contribution is indispensable for the organisation (Aguinis, 2013; Pulakos & O'Leary, 2011; Beck et al., 2014).

Before addressing the performance evaluation, it is necessary to define *performance*, since we will not be able to assess something without first defining its specificity. Performance refers to a particular action, the result of this action, and the analysis of this result, based on a comparison with a certain standard (Mills et al., 2016). From the author's perspective, we may define performance as an observable behaviour against an expectation or a standard of desirable behaviour of a given organisation.

Nevertheless, the Performance Evaluation is essential to identify possible future inconsistencies, as well as allows us to properly integrate the employees by checking whether they are fit for the function they are performing, and from there identify their potentials, as well as their weaknesses, seeking to adopt measures to improve their performance in the organisation (DeNisi & Murphy, 2017; Gomes & Cesário, 2014; Agustiningsih et al. 2016). Performance evaluation does not have a specific concept, as it is defined in different ways by different authors (DeNisi & Murphy, 2017). Performance evaluation is a systematic process intended at assessing the individual results of employees against the timely defined objectives, allowing for the analysis of deviations that require greater attention and preparation (Silva, 2019). In this way, it is pertinent to reinforce that performance evaluation is a systematic and continuous process that allows for the assessment of the work developed by employees in a certain established period, i.e. performance evaluations can be guided by organisations on a weekly, monthly, quarterly, half-yearly or annual basis, depending on what the organisation seeks and what is most advantageous and efficient (DeNisi & Murphy, 2017; Almeida, 2019).

In this context, it is fundamental that employees are aware of their contribution to the organisation, realise their importance and recognise their professional and personal skills. The fact that employees are aware of what they are within the organisation and of their importance to it, allows all the feedback transmitted by the performance evaluation to be seen as a support, a tool to help them improve their gaps and to enable their development within the organisation. It is this awareness that differentiates the impact on employee motivation, because when the performance evaluation is prepared and carried out in an ideal way, it contributes to an improvement in the work processes, in the goals that each employee intends to achieve from an individual point of view and in the favouring of his own motivation and development (Gardner et al., 2007).

As already mentioned, the Performance Management and Performance Evaluation purpose is to analyse and assess the practices, procedures, policies of salaries, career promotions, training and development, and the attribution of benefits and merit-based compensation to employees who demonstrate good performance and who achieve the proposed goals (DeNisi & Murphy, 2017; Murphy, Cleveland, & Hanscom, 2018).

Limitations and Implications of Performance Evaluation

Performance evaluation could be a personal, complex and ambiguous process, which is why anomalies may occur by the appraiser or even on the part of the organisation, which makes its effectiveness questionable. Among the limitations and implications, we can highlight some, such as: a certain mistrust in the process, the appraiser may not feel secure in the methods or processes previously established by the organisation, not having the assurance that it will work properly, which may lead to a drop in motivation (Aguinis, 2013; Pulakos & O'Leary, 2011). Additionally, the complexity by which should be assessed the individual performance is so demanding that it may not occur effectively, such as the difficulty in evaluating group activities, knowing who effectively participated and which members cooperated more for the development of the process (Lazear & Gibbs, 2011). The achievement of these group objectives often depends on the contribution of several employees, so their observation is not always clear. The disadvantages of these objectives are mainly the difficulty of measurement and the possibility of evaluators making biased assessments (DeNisi & Murphy, 2017). Therefore, it is necessary to seek to eliminate these gaps and implications that may emerge within an organisation.

Performance Evaluation Methods

Performance evaluation has usually been considered an critical facet of performance management and human resources practices, however it would seem that the best possibility of establishing a link between organization performance development and individual performance development would be to consider this activity as only one of a boarder set of the human resources practices that involve aligning staffing, incentives, feedback, and supervision with the strategic objectives of organizations (DeNisi & Murphy, 2017). For this a set of performance methods are used by organizations at the time and that the appraiser is making decisions (DeNisi & Murphy, 2017). It should be noted that the Performance Evaluation of an organization may be translated into a single method or into several, according to the existing reality in each organization and the previously established goals (Silva, 2019). Among the most varied existing assessment methods, we can highlight: those oriented to behaviour, i.e., to commitment, and those oriented to results.

Regarding the methods oriented to the employee's behaviour, we may highlight the method by Graphic Rating Scale or Attributes Scale, considered a method that classifies the performance of each element of the organisation, through a set of parameters to be evaluated that includes a numeric scale that may go from insufficient to excellent, in order to evaluate the individual's behaviour within the organisation. This method brings several advantages, such as: being a method which translates into reduced costs, easy to use and the scope it has in the most varied areas and different functions. However, it also brings disadvantages, such as: fallacious or poorly defined criteria, due to the different areas and functions and, on the other hand, the defined parameters may be interpreted differently by each evaluator (Rego et al., 2015).

Another method, oriented towards the employee's behaviour, is the Narrative Appraisals or Essay Appraisals, in which the appraiser describes and analyses in writing the employee's strengths, i.e. the most evident professional and personal skills, potentials, contribution to the organisation, whether the employee is following the organisation's processes and objectives, and analyses and describes the weaknesses and offers recommendations for improvement in order to overcome them. When it is well developed and planned, this method promotes a favourable reaction from all stakeholders because it is considered a development-oriented method (Murphy, Cleveland, & Hanscom, 2018).

Subsequently, there are result-oriented methods which we can point out: the Management by Objectives method in which these are outlined in a strategic manner for each of the areas within the organisation according to the function performed. The assessment is measured through the contribution that the assessed employee makes to the organisation, i.e. what is his effort, motivation and performance, since the main objective should be to achieve the strategic success of the organisation (Murphy, Cleveland, & Hanscom, 2018; Pereira, 2013).

Therefore, we highlight the Balanced Scorecard method in which its elaboration and application guarantees that performance is evaluated from a set of previously established criteria. This method translates an organisation's strategy into performance objectives, measures, targets, and initiatives.

METHOD

The present study requires a research process based on an adequate methodology, in order to facilitate the research, and the analysis of results. The research process is considered a crucial tool for any study, which should be developed in a demanding and rigorous approach so that, according to the answers acquired, it is possible to establish a relationship with the literature review. The qualitative methodology was used, and was based on a detailed description of phenomena, information and methods and techniques involving it (Rebelo, 2013). It is defined as a fundamental resource that aims to facilitate research with the purpose of finding the most appropriate answers to the object under study (Chizzotti, 2003). Therefore, the qualitative methodology differs from the quantitative method by the fact that it is not only based on statistical data, but also by data analysis and interpretation of its results, i.e. the main objective of the qualitative methodology is to analyse and interpret the data transmitted by the intervenient, which may be from subjective answers and it is necessary to decode them (Bardin, 1977; Braun & Clarke, 2006; Marconi & Lakatos, 2017).

The objective of this qualitative study is to analyse and interpret from the interviewee's answers, the way motivation, performance and performance evaluation of employees is approached and applied in a particular organisation and to compare its applicability with the other organisations.

Participants

For this study, twenty-five companies were invited to participate, but only six accepted to take part. Of the six interviews scheduled, only five were carried out, due to the non-attendance without justification of a participant representing the organisation. A semi-structured interview was conducted with Human Resources managers from five organisations who previously agreed to participate. The participants belonged to companies in the field of temporary work, industry, education, and consulting. Four of the participants were male and one was female, and their ages ranged from 25 to 55 years.

Interview Procedure

For the preparation of the interview questions, some categories already described in the literature review, and which are fundamental to the Human Resources Management of an organisation were chosen. In a first part, we sought to know the functioning of the organisation portrayed, more specifically in Human Resources and its main current and future strategies for the organisation. Therefore, in a second phase of the interview, the questions were directed towards Human Resources practices, namely the importance of motivation and performance of employees in the organisation, how human resources can act to ensure a better performance of its employees, and how it is possible to attract, motivate and retain employees. Finally, in the last part, the topic of performance evaluation was focused, i.e. how is performance evaluation carried out in the organisation and what methods are used. The implications or limitations of performance evaluation were also explored.

Thus, the interviews were conducted via digital platform (Zoom), lasting approximately forty minutes each. The interviews were conducted within a two-

Table 1. Participant's characteristics

Interviewee 1 (I1)	Human Resource Manager of an organization that specializes in human resources and is responsible for managing the assiduity and accounting of employees, evaluating their metrics and providing support on the operations side. The organization has the responsibility to recruit and select an employee, based on appropriate specifics, to perform functions in a particular organization. He has been working in the company for 6 years.
Interviewee 2 (I2)	Corporate Director of Human Resources of an organization, in which supervises the human resources of all countries in which the group is present. It is an organization that has its main focus on the customer and aims for an integrated and global logistics solution that makes it possible to integrate the products on the market in a fast, safe and effective way, in order to satisfy its customers. He has been working in the company for 24 years.
Interviewee 3 (I3)	Human Resources consultant in a Spanish organization, based in Portugal, which operates transversally in the area of Human Resources in 3 main pillars: specialized recruitment; recruitment and selection and temporary work. He has been working in the company for 2 years.
Interviewee 4 (I4)	Human Resources Manager in a public school, with public purposes and aims to prepare students for the future. In which he performs functions of people management, economist, and advisor. She has been working in the company for 2 years.
Interviewee 5 (I5)	Human Resources Manager in an organization specialized in Human Resources specializing in the processes of recruitment and management of employees. Has worked in the organisation for 2 years.

week time frame, where the dates were set by the interviewees according to their availability and workload.

In conclusion, in all interviews conducted, the participants provided all the information requested, were available for any additional question and, if necessary, scheduled a new face-to-face interview, in order to clarify any possible doubts that might arise when processing the data.

Analytic Approach

The interviews were fully transcribed, having been read for an initial familiarisation with the data that had been collected. After this phase, the interviews were analysed using the content analysis method. A categorical analysis was performed, in which the verbal data was, in a first phase, individually dissected so that a detailed access to what was said was possible and, subsequently, this same information was regrouped and organised into broader categories, where the categorisation criteria were respected.

In the categorical content analysis, a thematic analysis was performed where there was a concern to list all themes emerging during the interviews, trying to understand if they were groupable and comparable, thus trying to create cohesive category patterns. It was possible to give a categorisation within the listed themes to each unit of meaning of the interviews (Bardin, 1977; Braun & Clarke, 2006).

Sample Characterization

Regarding the first question, the participants were asked to give a brief description of the organisation where they work. We wanted to know what position they occupy in the organisation and how long they have been working in this organisation. This question is pertinent in a first stage because it allows to know the organisation from the point of view of the members of the Human Resources team, i.e. whether they are satisfied with the work they are doing, whether they have had a progression in the organisation or whether their professional experience in the organisation was only restricted by the Human Resources department, or whether they had other functions in the organisation. The objective of this first question was to get to know the more individual side of the participants on a professional level, to try to understand if they were satisfied with their work, if it was meeting their expectations, why they work in this organisation, what are the functions they carry out. This type of question makes it possible to establish a link and greater security between interviewee and interviewer for the following questions.

Alignment Between Human Resources Practices and the Organisation's Strategy

The second question was prepared based on the main current and future strategies in terms of Human Resources Management of the organisation, with the aim of getting to know the Human Resources department of each of the five organisations from a strategic point of view, in order to explain their goals, their main concerns and how they intend to address them. On the other hand, it was also intended to verify if their current and future strategies were aligned with the development of people management.

Motivation Management

The third question concerns the topic of motivation management, trying to understand to what extent the Human Resources department could motivate the performance of the employees. It is the responsibility of Human Resources to guarantee the motivation and performance of employees. This is only possible through the adoption of a set of strategies, such as: performance recognition, professional and personal skills, career progression, or even an investment in training.

Attract, Motivate, and Retain Employees

The fourth question is related to how the Human Resources department should act to attract, motivate, and retain employees in the organization. The aim of this question is to try to understand which of the three variables are the most important for the participant, although both are mutually related. Attract talent is key factor for any organisation, however retaining it can be even more important. And sometimes, when employees are willing to leave, it's up to the Human Resources department to motivate and retain them by, for example: checking their dissatisfactions regarding the work they are performing, their future goals, how they can be rewarded through a career progression. However, not all employees achieve the expected results or perform well and, therefore, it is often only possible to retain an employee who effectively demonstrates that deserves a career progression for achieve the expected goals (Joaquim Vicente Rodrigues, 2013).

Nevertheless, more than attracting and retaining, it is essential that the employee is motivated at work, because motivation could be one of the key instruments to achieve a good performance and achieve the expected results. This question sought to understand how organizations contribute to the enhancement of their employees (José Osmir Fiorelli, 2018).

Human Resources Practices to Improve Motivation and Performance

The aim of question five was to analyse how the existing activities in the organisation encourage more motivation or performance from the employees, such as: the making of training courses adjusted and aligned to the needs assessment analysis to perform the functions, to improve their development or to establish a good organisational climate. For instance, the elaboration of questionnaires, with the purpose of understanding if the employees are satisfied and motivated, what suggestions for improvement they want to transmit to the organisation to solve a certain problem, can be a useful tool.

Performance Evaluation

In questions six, seven and eight, we aimed to frame the theme of performance evaluation, namely, to understand how it is analysed and interpreted, and also what its evolution and contribution to the organisation is. Firstly, the system should be easy to understand, the employee should easily realize how their performance could be linked to the benefits. Secondly, that the employees' performance should be under their control, if for example performance is assessed by targets that are out of the employee's scope, then the system will have no motivating effect. It is also important that the benefits are linked to all facets of the job done by the employee. If they are only linked to one part of the job, it is likely that the employee will work harder on the part that gives them access to the benefits and neglect the rest. Finally, it is necessary that the employee has the skills and capabilities to achieve high performance and that he/she has access to training to fill some of the gaps. It should be noted that each organisation establishes the methods of Performance Evaluation according to its interests and objectives. Performance Evaluation is essential to any organization because it allows analyse the failures and gaps existing at both, the organizational process level, and the individual level of the organization's employees. It also allows reporting the feedback on the assessment results so that employees have the possibility to improve their performance and, therefore, generate better results for the organization (Mulvaney et al., 2012). The specific nature of the objectives to be achieved is particularly delicate, ideally, they should be quantifiable and easily observable.

Question seven aimed to examine the methods adopted by each organisation in the Performance Evaluation, since there is a set of methods that organisations can use. For example: the Management by Objectives Method, which is designed based on a set of objectives to assess the contribution that the employee makes to the organisation (Pereira, 2013). On the other hand, the assessment by Graphic Rating Scale Method, each employee is assessed based on a set of parameters where a numerical scale ranging from insufficient to excellent is evidenced (Rego et al., 2015). Finally, we can highlight the Balanced Scorecard Method, which assesses employees based on a set of previously established criteria. (Pereira, 2013). These methods were defined in more detail in the literature review, however it is important to highlight that in addition to the methods evidenced, there are still more that we can point out and analyse according to the answers given by the participants.

RESULTS AND DISCUSSION

In this study we intend to analyse how organisations act to develop the motivation and performance of their employees and how Performance Evaluation is fundamental for the development of the employee and the organisation itself.

In question one it was intended to understand the function of the interviewees (see Table 1). The results show that the organisations were heterogeneous, namely interviewee one and interviewee five work in an organisation specialised in Human Resources, while, for example, interviewee four works as a member of Human Resources in a private institution. However, despite being organisations of different natures, the role of the interviewee is generally similar in all the organisations interviewed. It was aimed to interview exclusively members of Human Resources in order to make the present study more robust and precise.

Alignment Between Human Resources Practices and the Organisation's Strategy

Therefore, in question two when the interviewees are asked for the current and future strategies in terms of Human Resource Management of the organisation. As mentioned in the literature review, the main concerns of the interviewees as Human Resource managers are people, and all policies and practices adopted in terms of Human Resource Management are employee-oriented.

Interviewee two, interviewee four and interviewee five described the organisation's strategies, based on valuing and welcoming people and on digitalisation to ensure that employees have the necessary tools to carry out their tasks efficiently.

'Adjusting the work according to the current pandemic situation, adapting to teleworking and trying to adjust tools and processes according to the current state we live in. On the other hand, establishing greater control over the work of employees and it was necessary to reinvent new policies and practices' I1

'The current and future strategy of the organisation is digitalisation, there is a huge effort in giving the necessary tools to employees to be digital. Another one of the key strategies is on-the-job training, training that people have to be able to do what they are hired to do. But in fact the focus of the organisation is to develop people, prepare them for the future because having people prepared for the future, the company doesn't have to be afraid.' I2

'The current and future strategy of the company aims to achieve a higher revenue volume than 2020 and, in terms of Human Resources management, to work in a logic of constant training both by training to act and learn in a work context, as well as systematically seeking to provide online training in the most diverse themes that each consultant needs to exercise their function.' I3

'The current strategy goes through a on-boarding process in the first moments that the person is integrated into the institution, o ue, an office training is carried out, in order to present all the departments and the people who constitute it in order to facilitate integration into the group.' I4

'The main strategy is recognition. Nowadays, and for the younger generation, what keeps employees motivated is not only the rewards attributed, but the working conditions, the valorisation of the employee, because if an employee feels recognised, it is essential to remain in the organisation.' I5

Motivation Management

Question three refers to the motivation and performance of employees, assuming that motivation is a crucial instrument for any organisation because when employees demonstrate commitment and motivation to perform their function they become more productive, demonstrate greater performance in order to achieve the desired results.

Interviewee two, interviewee three and interviewee five present the development of appropriate training to create mechanisms to meet the needs of employees, or even, as mentioned by interviewee five the best way to ensure the motivation and performance of employees is through meetings to check how the work is going, if it meets their expectations, what suggestions for improvement they give to the organisation. In this way, employees also feel that their contribution is essential for the success of the organisation, thus increasing their motivation (DeNisi & Murphy, 2017). Contrary to what was mentioned above by the other interviewees, it can be seen that interviewee one considers that the solution to ensure the motivation and performance of employees is through the allocation of performance bonuses, i.e. the higher the productivity, the greater the benefit granted. also through the preparation of satisfaction questionnaires to understand how they feel motivated and how to encourage higher motivation or performance. Similarly, interviewee four indicates that it is possible to ensure a higher motivation of employees by offering days before holidays, to ensure that employees who need to be absent due to family situations will not be affected, thus assuming a great flexibility of schedules to meet everyone's needs, and this ensures a higher performance of employees.

'By giving performance rewards or by developing satisfaction questionnaires, individual meetings with employees to have feedback on their performance and seek to motivate them to improve their performance.' I1

'From the previously defined strategies. It is possible to motivate the performance of employees from adequate training, one of them strategic in organisational terms and another one strategic for people and create these mechanisms of response to the need. In order to analyse the motivation and performance of employees, it is necessary to carry out a competence assessment where we will check if people are prepared for the future and if people are satisfied with the work to be developed.' I2

'The Human Resources department gives the necessary tools for employees to progress, to improve their performance and to achieve better results. When the employee feels motivated in a company the performance is automatically positive and of course this is dependent on a daily performance of the Human Resources department.' I3

'By offering a large part of the days before public holidays, if the person is on sick leave for example and is able to telework a shorter schedule, they are paid the same, and on the other hand there is also a great importance for the family. There is great flexibility in terms of working hours, holidays, breaks and public holidays, which motivates the employee's performance.'I4

'The secret is to establish direct contact with all employees, through meetings, to know if the work is meeting expectations, what are the suggestions for improvement, and these meetings are fundamental to motivate the performance of employees. It can also be analysed through the monthly performance evaluation. When a meeting is held, the key is to end on a positive note in order to motivate the employee.' I5

Attract, Motivate, and Retain Employees

Question four addressed the issue of the extent to which companies favour certain characteristics over others. To attract the right people, it is up to the organisation to ensure a true, real and appropriate image. Therefore, as mentioned by interviewee two, interviewee four and interviewee five, to attract is very much related to the first contact, the way the organisation is presented to employees and how it works, as well as ensuring a favourable organisational climate that provides a favourable group dynamic. Both interviewees gave special emphasis to the topic of attracting workers. Consequently, retention arises when employees are not satisfied in the organisations or have other future plans. As already mentioned in the literature review, it is only possible to retain an employee when they possess the required competencies, which may eventually allow career progression. The answers of interviewees one and five refer exactly to this perspective, employee retention depends on their performance and professionalism. Whereas interviewees two and four state that it is difficult to retain any employee, because before they indicate a desire to leave, the organisation has already noticed their dissatisfaction, future goals, underlying concerns in their work and that limit their motivation.

'To attract and to motivate is the most important for the organization because if the employees are motivated and satisfied with their work they will remain loyal to the organization. Regarding retaining employees, progression may not always occur because this does not depend only on Human Resources but also on other departments, and sometimes it is not possible to retain the employee by increasing his/her salary or changing his/her hierarchical position in the organisation.' I1

'The attraction is very much related to the way in which the recruitment and selection of employees is carried out. It is possible to motivate the performance of employees through appropriate training and create mechanisms to meet their needs. Regarding retaining, it is visible the offers that the organisation has for career progression, motivation and guaranteeing the performance of the employees, so it is hardly necessary to retain an employee.' I2

'New generations care more about career progression, rather than the salary component. To attract them, the company must develop its Employer branding to the maximum. To motivate and retain them, the company has a well-supported remuneration plan that promotes promotion and employee development.' I3

'Mainly the functioning of the organisation, that is, if the person is in an institution that is well run, that has integrated them properly, that they feel their work is rewarded and recognised, all these components lead to motivation. Retaining is not very visible in the institution.' I4

'To attract the employee, the first contact that the employee has with the human resources member is fundamental in order to get to know the company, its dynamics and processes. To motivate, we give employees small gifts so that they remain satisfied. To retain employees, it is necessary to take into account the reasons for leaving and the organisation only tries to retain them when it sees that there will be the possibility of career progression.' I5

Human Resources Practices to Improve Motivation and Performance

Regarding question five on the theme of practices to attract, motivate and retain, there is some discrepancy in the participants' answers. While interviewees two, four and three attempt to develop a set of fundamental activities both for the employee and for the organisation, namely the creation of training courses to ensure higher employee productivity, a work method review, and consolidation of knowledge involved within the organisation. Interviewees one and five consider that the most predominant activities of the organisation that guarantee the motivation and satisfaction of its employees are the elaboration of satisfaction questionnaires or meetings on a periodic basis to develop group integration.

'At the moment, only the elaboration of satisfaction questionnaires. I consider that no activities have taken place in order to maintain an organisational climate, group integration, but that I consider wrong because all colleagues in the team should know each other'. I1

'We have various activities and events to try to develop people, in some aspects, not always related to work, but with the use of the necessary tools to have the will to self-training, a company is fine when employees want to train themselves, this is a sign that employees want to learn. On the other hand, the company intends to create some mechanisms and rituals, seeking to innovate in communication both in the social networks and in internal communication.'I2

'Yes. Human resources systematically tries to promote activities that help the team relationship and that promote the well-being of all within the organisation in order to promote a favourable organisational climate. On the other hand, trainings are also held periodically with the aim of reviewing processes, giving group feedback, getting to know new work tools.'I3

'Periodic training, favourable organisational climate, all the members of the company know each other and therefore it facilitates the integration of a new element in the

team, which in turn promotes greater motivation and performance on the part of all.' I4

'Yes! Through satisfaction questionnaires, trainings that are requested by the client who hires the organisation when there is a line transition or when a new process occurs. Rarely are trainings done by Human Resources members, but by the quality department. Human Resources conducts group meetings in order to promote group integration.' I5

Performance Evaluation

Regarding question six, again we found different characteristics defined by the interviewee in relation to how the Performance Evaluation is assessed. While interviewees one and five stated that they only assess employee performance in terms of commitment and absenteeism on a monthly basis as a way of checking whether they are satisfied with their work, analysing their contribution and their shortcomings regarding scheduling flexibility and adaptability and seeking what key strategies should be adopted to improve their contribution (Mulvaney et al., 2012). Interviewees three and four highlight that the performance evaluation is performed annually in order to analyse their performance throughout the year and assess the future expectations of employees. It should be emphasised that although performance evaluation is a systematic and continuous process, it may be analysed weekly, monthly, or annually, depending on what is most favourable for the organisation, always with the purpose of achieving the objectives established (Almeida, 2019). In addition, interviewee two refers that the Performance Evaluation is performed through five mandatory objectives which are designed based on the company, based on the team and the last three objectives based on the employee. The relevance of the employee's assessment aims to evaluate their results in individual terms, making it possible to analyse their gaps that need greater dedication and attention (Silva, 2019).

'As Human Resources what we assess most is commitment and absenteeism, in relation to performance metrics, motivation who carries out this assessment is the quality department of the organisation, which in turn gives feedback on the assessment to the members of Human Resources.'I1

'Performance evaluation is conducted each month and all human resources members have a panel of 5 objectives that are mandatory and are created according to the company, team and another 3 according to the individual. All people have performance evaluation, and all people have competencies evaluation.'I2

'In terms of performance methods, each employee is assessed annually. This assessment is divided between the human resources department and the direct manager of each employee and also between the leader responsible for the organisation at a regional level, where a final report is drawn up on the development that took place during the year, and on the other hand a briefing is made on what the employee is expected to achieve next year, what expectations they have of the employee and what results are expected.'I3

'It is done annually by a jury that evaluates the performance of employees and over the years we will see if the person has improved, if they have kept the same posture, and the jury is composed of 4 completely different people, in which 2 work directly with employees and the rest is an external jury, we can evaluate their performance and also the employees themselves make a self-evaluation of their performance and from there we can see the evolution of each one.'I4

'As a member of Human Resources, there are 3 methods that we have total control over: the behavioural part of the agents; the agents' absenteeism; and the agents' rescissions. The evaluation is done through observation, through contribution and commitment. The participant reinforces that at the quality level (of process management) they don't have access to our results, only if perhaps, the client shares with the Human Resources department.'I5

In relation to question seven, it was found that among the methods presented in the literature review, the vast majority of interviewees use Management by Objectives as a method of performance evaluation, namely interviewee two, interviewee three and interviewee five mention that in the performance evaluation goals are set for each of the existing areas in the organization according to the function performed (Pereira, 2013).

'Balanced scorecard, performance is evaluated according to customer-oriented criteria, competencies, processes, learning, assuity. However, all evaluation metrics related to productivity and quality are handled by the quality department of the organisation, but all employees are subject to this method.'I1

'The organisation's performance evaluation methods differ from department to department. Performance appraisal is defined through management by objectives or performance by objectives because both are similar. It is evident that in the Human Resources department the objectives portrayed are different than the warehouse objectives, they are unequally characterised.'I2

'The method used is management by objectives, in which the assessment is made through each employee's contribution to achieving the strategic success of the organisation and through the objectives initially proposed it will be verified if the employee has fulfilled them and how they have achieved them.'I3

'Performance evaluation is carried out through specific parameters on a graphic scale, where the parameters of assiduity, accomplishment of tasks; team spirit.'I4

'Evaluation methods are based on management by objectives in terms of commitment, absenteeism and terminations and are assessed in percentiles.'I5

Finally, question eight was examined what the implications and limitations based on the Performance Evaluation. Through the interviewees' responses we could highlight the contradiction between interviewee two and the other interviewees. While interviewee two states that in his organisation there is no implication or limitation in the Performance Evaluation because the method plan design is properly agreed. The remaining interviewees consider that there are poorly structured Performance Evaluations, due to the fact that the complexity by which the performance is assessed. Sometimes is so demanding that it may not run effectively (Mulvaney et al., 2012). On the other hand, interviewee four refers to the personal relationships between appraisers and appraisees that can influence the Performance Evaluation.

When properly executed it is a good mechanism for determining appropriate corrective measures and actions to improve future performance. It is important that the organisation clarifies the evaluation criteria in advance and communicates them to the employee. The employees should also know the level of performance that is expected of them. The participation of the employee in the process may encourage them to identify more strongly with the objectives established (DeNisi & Murphy, 2017).

'Initially employees when given feedback indicate that they will try to improve their processes and overcome their faults and mistakes, but in practice this often does not happen. When this happens, the employee is warned again about his constant behaviour, and if this continues, it is necessary to take measures.'I1

'No, because the method plan is agreed. And the more technical tables are validated by the Human Resources area, through a member who is dedicated solely and exclusively to that area of choosing methods. When you set up assessment methods you can run the risk of going wrong but the only solution is to correct them quickly, you need people focused on that.'I2

'The performance evaluation has to be elaborated through a well structured and organised plan that enhances the mutual growth of the employees and the organisation. There are inadequately structured performance evaluations that do nothing to promote organisational development and individual development, so the human resources department should pay special attention when elaborating the parameters that will be present in the performance evaluation.'I3

'Yes, the jury is composed of 4 people who remain from year to year, that is, they have been evaluating the same employees for many years, because it is only in the last year that they have begun to recruit new people, and in this sense I feel that the jury makes the mistake of evaluating the employee according to their personal relationship, and ends up influencing the performance evaluation of the person evaluated.'I4

'Yes, the parameters are defined according to the project, so it is normal that there are changes in the parameters and sometimes they may not be the most efficient. The evaluation parameters are drawn up according to the client's requirements, there are clients who value quality more, others who value productivity more, so these parameters have to be adjusted.'I5

CONCLUSION

This study contributed to understand the importance of Human Resources practices on organization performance, its contribution on employee's performance and verify their role in people management. It is pertinent to make a brief reflection on the proposed objectives. Human Resources Management seeks to design scenarios and practices that are aligned with the objectives of the organisation and, in turn, of the employees. Human Resources practices are usually known to positively impact employee and organization performance across numerous dimensions (Bloom, Sadun, & Van Reenen, 2012). In particular, some researches have demonstrated how Human Resources practices are able to motivate and encourage desired employee behaviours and attitudes focusing on performance evaluation, reward systems, and job design (Pfeffer, 2007; Topcic, Baum, & Kabst, 2016). Performance management include a set of practices that enhance employees' skills, motivation, and participation, inducing engagement in efforts that result in better performance (DeNisi & Murphy, 2017).

The preparation of the interviews was planned from the literature review, from the subtopics present in the review such as: the role of Human Resources, the Performance Management, the Performance Evaluation Methods and the limitations and implications based on the Performance Evaluation. A set of questions were outlined to cover all organisations. The results presented by the intervening parties met all expectations, all sought to demonstrate the functioning of the organisation in the most diverse aspects and contributed efficiently and pragmatically in answering of objective of this study.

The purpose for many of this Performance Management practices is to improve motivation, morale, reduce turnover, increase productivity, and boost guest satisfaction. However, there is no consensus on literature about which specific Human Resources practices have an impact on performance, some of the most frequently cited practices include selective hiring, widespread development and training, performance feedback, performance-linked compensation, and employees' participatory instruments (Sun, Aryee, & Law, 2007; Wright, Gardner, & Moynihan, 2003). For example, some Human Resources practices improve employees' motivation; others have an effect on their knowledge, competencies and skills or empower and encourage employee's participative behaviours. Which Human Resources practices promote each of these potential impacts remains an open debate in the literature (Boxall & Macky, 2009; Gardner et al., 2011).

Results suggest that managers should pursue Human Resources practices that increase employees' motivation and performance. According to these findings, some practices will help enhance both performance and motivation, while other practices, such as compensation and incentives, have an impact more primarily through motivation. Managers should make their final decisions about which Human Resources practices to invest in after considering the types of outcomes expected from those practices, such as skill enhancement, motivation, or empowerment (Meyer et al., 2004; Pfeffer, 2007; Topcic, Baum, & Kabst, 2016).

Therefore, Performance Management is a configuration of Human Resources management practices that encompasses aspects such as goal setting, performance evaluation and compensation. Thus, (1) performance objectives are defined; (2) the employees are evaluated on how they have achieved these objectives; (3) according to this evaluation, they are compensated; (4) they are subject to training and development actions so that the objectives are achieved, and their performance improves (Boxall & Macky, 2009; Gardner et al., 2007).

Successful performance management implies that there is an appropriate definition of objectives, both from an individual and organisational point of view. It is essential that individuals are assessed according to the degree to which they have achieved those objectives. To do so, it is necessary that they are well acquainted with, for example, the criteria against which they are assessed. It is fundamental that the achievement of objectives and high performance is correctly compensated both in terms of remuneration and career pay. Training and development actions are especially important for individuals to be able to achieve the desired objectives. They are also relevant for employees with poor performance evaluation to address gaps, take corrective action and improve future performance (Sun, Aryee, & Law, 2007; Wright, Gardner, & Moynihan, 2003; Agustiningsih et al. 2016).

Additionally, the effectiveness of the Performance Evaluation comes to a considerable extent from the possibility to encourage performance. An important condition for this is the perceived fairness of the process. Several elements can contribute to this, such as participating in the process, having the possibility to appeal the rating, perceiving that the appraisal is based on accurate and precise information. It is important that the employee has access to training and development programmes that allow him to meet the performance objectives set and to correct deficiencies detected in the performance appraisal. It is also essential that the employee knows in advance if and how his performance will be related to compensation. The performance evaluation should contribute to career development (Aguinis, 2013; Pulakos & O'Leary, 2011; Beck et al., 2014) .

An additional difficulty in the goal setting on the Performance Evaluation is related to team versus individual goals. Individual objectives induce more commitment because they allow access to individual rewards. However, this type of rewards does not promote cooperation among the team. Team goals have the advantage of fostering cooperation among team members. But it may lead some team members to attenuate their effort because they are aware that no matter how hard they work and how well they perform, they will receive the same reward as the other members. On the other hand, hard-working members of staff may be less committed because they feel that less committed staff members will receive the same reward. Feelings of unfairness may also emerge, with consequences for trust, cooperation and commitment (Wright et al., 2001; Sun, Aryee, & Law, 2007; Wright et al., 2003).

Organizations in general, and Human Resources managers in particular, should pay attention to the way Human Resources practices are being understood by employees. Understanding about how employees give meaning these practices can help managers and organisations get involved and ensure that the availability of these practices, as well as their appropriate purpose and functioning are understood by all group members. The results of this study are also relevant for government policymakers. Organizations' investments in HR practices can be encouraged through national policies, such as tax benefits that induce organizations to invest in practices aimed to help employees improve their performances (Pfeffer, 2007; Topcic, Baum, & Kabst, 2016).

Finally, this study contribute for insights into Performance Evaluation helps develop more reflections about Human Resources practices, but it has some limitations. Namely, we took an interpretative approach to our study question and our analysis was based on qualitative data from a small number of interviews in a very specific context of Human Resources Management. We do not see this as a limitation as we did not set out to generalize from our study but to pursue more nuanced insight into the topics we describe. Further research can circumvent these limitations.

Future Research Directions

Future research might explore the possibility of formalising Performance Management practises and policies, and it is advised to do a longitudinal study to track changes over time and identify any potential organisational cultures. Relevant would also be a comparison of the various economic activity sectors.

REFERENCES

Aguinis, H. (2013). *Performance management* (3rd ed.). Pearson/Prentice-Hall.

Agustiningsih, H. N., Armanu, T., Djumilah, H., & Noermijati, N. (2016). The effect of remuneration, job satisfaction and OCB on the employee performance. *Science Journal of Business and Management, 4*(6), 212–222. doi:10.11648/j.sjbm.20160406.16

Bardin, L. (1977). *Análise de conteúdo*. Edições 70.

Beck, J. W., Beatty, A. S., & Sackett, P. R. (2014). On the distribution of job performance: The role of measurement characteristics in observed departures from normality. *Personnel Psychology, 67*, 531–566.

Bloom, N., Sadun, R., & Van Reenen, J. (2012). Does management really work? *Harvard Business Review, 90*(11), 76–82. PMID:23155999

Boxall, P., & Macky, K. (2009). Research and theory on high-performance work systems: Progressing the high-involvement stream. *Human Resource Management Journal, 19*(1), 3–23. doi:10.1111/j.1748-8583.2008.00082.x

Braun, V., & Clarke, V. (2006). Using thematic analysis in psychology. *Qualitative Research in Psychology, 3*(2), 77–101. doi:10.1191/1478088706qp063oa

DeNisi, A., Wilson, M., & Biteman, J. (2014). Research and practice in hrm: A historical perspective. *Human Resource Management Review, 14*(3), 219–231. doi:10.1016/j.hrmr.2014.03.004

DeNisi, A. S., & Murphy, K. R. (2017). Performance appraisal and performance management: 100 years of progress? *The Journal of Applied Psychology, 102*(3), 421–433. doi:10.1037/apl0000085 PMID:28125265

Dias, J. H., & Paraíso, I. (2011). O sistema de gestão e avaliação do desempenho na Administração Pública Portuguesa: Efeitos da sua prática no contrato psicológico dos colaboradores. *Interações*, *20*, 101–132. https://www.interacoes-ismt.com/index.php/revista/article/viewFile/276/282

Gardner, P., Moynihan, T., & Wright, L. (2007). The influence of human resource practices on the performance of business units. *Human Resource Management Journal*, *13*, 21–36.

Gardner, T. M., Wright, P. M., & Moynihan, L. M. (2011). The impact of motivation, empowerment, and skill-enhancing practices on aggregate voluntary turnover: The mediating effect of collective affective commitment. *Personnel Psychology*, *64*(2), 315–350. doi:10.1111/j.1744-6570.2011.01212.x

Gerhart, B., & Fang, M. (2015). Pay, intrinsic motivation, extrinsic motivation, performance, and creativity in the workplace: Revisiting long-held beliefs. *Annual Review of Organizational Psychology and Organizational Behavior*, *2*(1), 489–521. doi:10.1146/annurev-orgpsych-032414-111418

Lazear, E. P., & Gibbs, M. (2014). *Personnel economics in practice*. John Wiley & Sons.

Meyer, J. P., Becker, T. E., & Vandenberghe, C. (2004). Employee commitment and motivation: A conceptual analysis and integrative model. *The Journal of Applied Psychology*, *89*(6), 991–1007. doi:10.1037/0021-9010.89.6.991 PMID:15584837

Mulvaney, M. A., McKinney, W. R., & Grodsky, R. (2012). The development of a pay-for-performance appraisal system for municipal agencies: A case study. *Public Personnel Management*, *41*(3), 505–533. doi:10.1177/009102601204100307

Murphy, K. R., Cleveland, J. N., & Hanscom, M. (2018). Performance appraisal and management: Why does it fail and how can it be fixed? *Sage (Atlanta, Ga.)*.

Nae, E. Y., Moon, H. K., & Choi, B. K. (2015). Seeking feedback but unable to improve work performance? Qualified feedback from trusted supervisors matters. *Career Development International*, *20*(1), 81–100. doi:10.1108/CDI-08-2014-0107

Pfeffer, J. (2007). Human resources from an organizational behavior perspective: Some paradoxes explained. *The Journal of Economic Perspectives*, *21*(4), 115–134. doi:10.1257/jep.21.4.115

Pulakos, E. D., & O'Leary, R. S. (2011). Why is performance management so broken? *Industrial and Organizational Psychology: Perspectives on Science and Practice*, *4*(2), 146–164. doi:10.1111/j.1754-9434.2011.01315.x

Sun, L. Y., Aryee, S., & Law, K. S. (2007). High performance human resources practices, citizenship behavior, and organizational performance: A relational perspective. *Academy of Management Journal, 50*(3), 558–577. doi:10.5465/amj.2007.25525821

Topcic, M., Baum, M., & Kabst, R. (2016). Are high-performance work practices related to individually perceived stress? A job demands-resources perspective. *International Journal of Human Resource Management, 27*(1), 45–66. doi:10.1080/09585192.2015.1043136

Wright, M. P., Gardner, M. T., & Moynihan, M. L. (2003). The impact of HR practices on the performance of business units. *Human Resource Management Journal, 13*(3), 21–36. doi:10.1111/j.1748-8583.2003.tb00096.x

Wright, P. M., Dunford, B. B., & Snell, S. A. (2001). Human resources and the resource based view of the firm. *Journal of Management, 27*(6), 701–721. doi:10.1177/014920630102700607

Zaitouni, M., Harraf, A., & Kisswani, A. M. (2020). Resources for development: The relationship of HRM practices and continuous learning culture with training success. *International Journal of Human Resources Development and Management, 20*(1), 75–92. doi:10.1504/IJHRDM.2020.105099

ADDITIONAL READING

P., A., Dey, C., Santhanam, N., & Bin Ahmad, K.Z. (2023). Strategic HRM practices, learning orientation and learning competence: study from retail industry. *The Learning Organization, 30*(4), 406-425. doi:10.1108/TLO-05-2022-0066

Potnuru, R. K. G., Sahoo, C. K., & Parle, K. C. (2021). HRD practices, employee competencies and organizational effectiveness: Role of organizational learning culture. *Journal of Asia Business Studies, 15*(3), 401–419. doi:10.1108/JABS-06-2020-0237

Tripathi, A. & Dhir, S. (2022). HRD interventions, learning agility and organizational innovation: a PLS-SEM modelling approach. *International Journal of Organizational Analysis*. doi:10.1108/IJOA-12-2021-3064

KEY TERMS AND DEFINITIONS

Assessment methods in Human Resources: They are used to gauge the performance, potential, and potential of employees and job prospects. Performance reviews, psychometric testing, skills evaluations, behavioural observation, interviews, assessment centres, portfolio or work sample reviews, and peer evaluations are a few examples of these techniques. These evaluation techniques are used to acquire trustworthy and valid data that can be used to influence decisions about employee development, hiring and placement, performance management, and other Human Resources -related procedures.

Human Resources Management: It includes the strategic method and practice of properly managing the people in an organization. To accomplish the goals and objectives of the organization, it entails the planning, recruitment, selection, development, and retention of people. Job analysis, performance management, training and development, pay and benefits, employee relations, and Human Resources rules and procedures are just a few of the many responsibilities covered by Human Resource Management. To create a productive and motivated workforce that contributes to the organization's overall performance, Human Resources Management's main goal is to make sure that the right people with the correct skills and talents are in the right roles.

Human Resources Performance: It describes the measurement and assessment of the efficacy and efficiency of the Human Resources function within a company. It entails evaluating the degree to which Human Resources initiatives and tactics support the overarching organizational goals and objectives. Employee satisfaction, retention rates, the success of recruitment, the results of training and development, and the effectiveness of Human Resources operations are common criteria used to assess the performance of Human Resources. To improve organizational performance, employee engagement, and overall success, Human Resources practices are to be optimized.

Performance Evaluation: It is also referred to as performance appraisal or performance review, is a methodical procedure for gauging a person's effectiveness on the job and contribution to the organization. The appraisal of a worker's abilities, successes, and behaviours in light of established performance standards and objectives is a part of this process. A formal evaluation report or rating is frequently produced as a result of performance evaluations, which are frequently carried out using a combination of feedback, assessment, and documentation. Performance evaluation serves a variety of purposes, including giving feedback, highlighting successes, pointing out areas for development, assisting in making educated judgements about awards and promotions, and coordinating individual performance with organizational goals.

Chapter 4
Shared Leadership, Self-Efficacy, and Team Proactive Effectiveness in a Theoretical Conceptual Framework:
Management in Crisis

Chérine Jneid
Azm University, Lebanon

Sam El Nemar
Azm University, Lebanon

ABSTRACT

As organizations become more crisis-ridden, they are struggling with limited resources for business survival and continuity in crisis management. Lately, Covid-19 imposed social distancing which reflects on alternative ways of performing jobs through virtual teams and online jobs. Traditional leadership theories seem inadequate in these new job contexts, proactive crisis theories are still minor, and new leadership theories consistently proved the need to switch to team leadership approaches as shared leadership. The authors aim through this chapter to address the need for novel approaches to crisis management through team proactivity, self-efficacy, and shared leadership. The authors develop a conceptual theoretical framework that outlines the relationships between the concepts of team proactivity, self-efficacy, and shared leadership. This study extends the literature review through exploring team proactivity which is marginally studied in comparison to individual proactivity.

DOI: 10.4018/978-1-6684-6602-5.ch004

INTRODUCTION

Research on organizational crisis effectiveness has been prominent over the decades because of the occurrence of a variety of types of crisis in past decades and its repercussions on organization survival (Faulkner, 2001). However, in recent times, business environment leaders are challenged with unexpected new natures of crisis which are unprecedented, large scale and unbounded. OECD (2011) stated that unbounded crisis, such as spread of viruses and terrorists, may develop to become a costly "global shock" threatening a combination of different global systems as health, social, financial and/or climate systems. Traditional organizational structures and processes become insufficient while unforeseen events like 11 September 2001, Hurricane Katrina in 2005 and the latest Covid-19 pandemic in 2020 occur. Recently, the new demands of shifting to online work and virtual teamwork in organizations create new leadership challenges.

Scholars from different disciplines as psychology, public administration, business and others offered interesting links between crisis theory and its practices (Fowler et al., 2007). Team leadership has become a prominent approach of crisis-ridden organizations. Houghton et al. (2003) demonstrated the urgency to expand the traditional leadership research which relies on formal leaders to study new team leadership approaches, as shared leadership concept, in the increased investment of organizations in its skilled professionals. However, Burke et al. (2003) revealed that the effectiveness is not guaranteed in all team leadership approaches because of the lack of coordination between team members.

Cloudman and Hallahan (2006) recommended considering the team proactivity approach in crisis management to reduce the crisis' negative influences by consistently acquiring the needed strategic competencies for prevention and preparedness for potential crisis (Jaques, 2007). For that reason, we may argue that team proactivity is a predictor to a successful crisis management process. However, we found out that exploring the team proactivity concept, its antecedents, its mediating and moderating effects and its consequences are slightly studied in organizational research comparing to the individual proactivity.

In addition, this study also considers the shared leadership concept, this approach is gaining increased interest in the studies of team leadership. Pearce and Conger (2003) defined shared leadership as "a dynamic, interactive influence process among individuals in groups for which the objective is to lead one another to the achievement of group or organizational goals or both". The "dynamic interactive influence process among individuals" in shared leadership teams makes the difference with the traditional teams where the social interactions are limited to downward and upward influence processes (Xu and Zhao, 2022). In specific crisis situations and its repercussions on job performance, traditional leadership loses on its power on maintaining the traditional role of leaders in communication, control and performance assessment. So that, team leadership approaches may be more suitable in crisis management. In 1982, Johnson & Johnson adopted the shared leadership approach to face the Tylenol crisis. Same in 2018, Southwest Airlines relied on their shared leadership to become proactive on safety issues. However, little is known about antecedents and consequences of shared leadership in theory (Petrie et al., 2021). More specifically, theoretical studies lack of understanding how the human-level constructs may impact the development constructs of team leadership. In this paper, it is assumed that it is worthy to explore how individual self-efficacy beliefs may have a significant relationship with the shared leadership concept.

Our proposed conceptual theoretical framework also includes the self-efficacy concept. Self-efficacy is defined as one's belief about their ability to produce designated levels of performance to influence the external events that affect his or her life (Esmaeilikia and Groth, 2022; Schwarz et al., 2016; Bandura 1977, 1997). Self-efficacy is also considered a specific domain (Bandura 1977, 1997). It was found that cognitive and task oriented domains of self-efficacy in workplace gained important attention from researchers and practitioners (Judge and Bono, 2001; Stajkovic and Luthans, 1998). However, there has been relatively little attention devoted to understanding how self-efficacy might be theoretically and empirically linked to shared leadership (Schwarz et al., 2016). Pearce and Manz (2005) assumed that there is a need for organizations to shift from a formal leader engaged in a unidirectional influence process of traditional teams to multiple leaders engaged in dynamic interactive influence processes of shared leadership (Bligh et al., 2006). We argue, that high levels of self-efficacy beliefs within team members in shared leadership might be a moderator for more team proactive effectiveness which leads to a better crisis management. As both concepts of self-efficacy and shared leadership rely on the capabilities of the team members, we believe that studying the relationships between these theories may provide interesting outcomes, specifically related to crisis management (Han and Hazard, 2022). Seers el al. (2003) argued that minor theoretical research studied the role of influence processes within organizations. Accordingly, we tried to explain through theoretical reasons the influence processes role of shared leadership in the relationship between the information sources of self-efficacy improvements and the team proactive effectiveness in crisis management (Mohammed and Hadi, 2022). Our proposed conceptual theoretical framework provides a multi-level approach where individual-level beliefs may be upgraded to team level through reciprocated social interactions.

In the next section, we review the literature on teams in the crisis management literature with a particular focus on the shared leadership potential outcomes on team proactivity behaviors and the capacity of the influence processes between its team members to facilitate the upgrade of self-efficacy sources effectiveness from an individual level to team level. We consequently propose a conceptual theoretical framework that outlines the relationship between shared leadership and team proactive effectiveness in crisis management focusing on intermediary concepts related to self-efficacy beliefs and its improvement sources (Figure 1). We conclude with some theoretical and practical implications of this framework.

BACKGROUND OF THE STUDY

From Traditional Teams to Shared Leadership Teams

Crisis management research studied the need of effective communication and coordination between specialized teams emerging in time of crisis (Nembhard and Edmondson, 2006) to cope with changing conditions (Burke el al. 2006). Researchers revealed how the different crisis teams as crisis management team, emergency teams, specialist teams and incident management teams become interdependent in the chaotic time (Nembhard and Edmondson, 2006). These emerging crisis teams are cross-functional in general and are related to reactive organizational behavior (King, 2002).

Organizational researchers assumed that organizations do not adapt the same behavior when facing a crisis. Iyer and Miller (2008) and Shimizu (2007) considered that some organizations embrace rigidity and/or deviant behaviors (Kuusela et al., 2017), while Miller and Chen (2004) argued that other organizations adapt to change and innovate in the crisis context. In crisis situations, organizations face adversity, limited resources, uncertainty and negative stakeholders' perceptions of trust and

Figure 1. Moderating effect of self-efficacy between shared leadership and team proactive effectiveness in crisis management; a conceptual theoretical framework

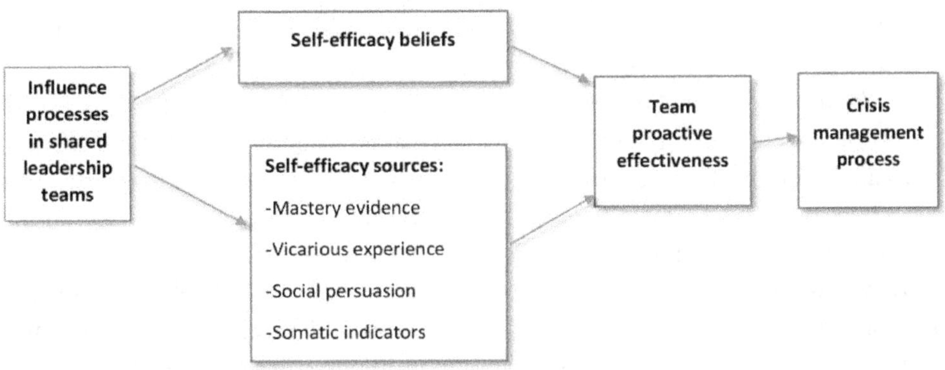

legitimacy. Managers and employees are consequently operating in a high level of occupational stress leading to emotions of fear, anxiety, anger and sadness (Lazarus, 1991). Studies assumed that the appropriate coping strategies increase the survival and continuity prospects of the organizations (Champion, 1999). Moreover, Danneels (2002) urged the firms to recognize the need of innovation in the journey of crisis management whether it is in technology (Bushee, 1998) or marketing (Naidoo, 2010) innovations. However, the role of teams in transforming the crisis from loss to opportunity is understudied in organizational behavior research despite the fact that many studies revealed interesting findings in crisis and crisis management. Ucal et al. (2010) and Coombs and Holladay (2002) studied the antecedents and causes of crisis, while Rogov (2006) investigated the characteristics of crisis situation; Murphy (2006), Bundy and Pfarrer (2015), Kahn et al. (2013) studied how organizations behave to overcome the burden of the crisis. Other scholars focused on crisis communication (Gillespie and Dietz, 2009; Pfarrer et al., 2008) and the organizational learning behavior (Bundy et al., 2017; Lampel et al., Shapira, 2009). Mitroff and Alpaslan (2003) and Paraskevas (2006) examined the proactive crisis management where teams in organizations can detect the early signs of a potential crisis and be proactive on adopting the best practices to deal effectively with potential business losses. Sapriel (2003) assumed that majority of organizations failed to respond successfully to crisis events in contrary to others which invested in advance on necessary resources to prepare suitable responses to crisis when occurring.

Traditional Teams in Research

Traditionally, the need for teamwork in organizations is critical because of the advanced need of innovation and creativity and the immense dependency on the organizational knowledge to keep competitive advantage in an increased global competition (Sundstrom et al., 1990). Kozlowski and Klein (2000) assumed that team effectiveness is a process which needs the engagement of team members in both task work and teamwork. King (2002) realized that both individual and team characteristics influence the crisis teams' effectiveness. The researcher showed that previous interactions between crisis team members may be an antecedent for a better business performance during the crisis journey (King, 2002). King (2002) also advised to compose heterogeneous crisis teams, where members have different values and opinions, for a successful crisis management in organizations. However, researchers demonstrated that social loafing (Hüffmeier et al., 2012; Karau and Williams, 1993), can create motivation losses in task-performing groups (Kerr, 1983) which can lead to a blocking effect on productivity (Diehl and Stroebe, 1991), and affect all teamwork process losses (Kerr and Tindale, 2004). Moreover, Wise (2006) identified team communication problem as a serious barrier of team effectiveness during crisis. Few studies revealed the role of leaders on coaching the team members to ensure an efficient information flow management in crisis process (Hackman and Wagemen, 2005).

Virtual Teams in Research

Recently, the breadth of Covid-19 and its repercussions of global lockdown and economic threat unexpectedly urged majority of traditional teams to turn to virtual teams. Prior to the event of Covid-19, research focused moderately on understanding the management of virtual teams and their structures because of the growing global organizations and the advances in information and communication technology (Hertel et al., 2005). Virtual teams were mostly employed at large organizations (Hertel et al. 2005). They are created and disbanded according to need. Nowadays, business performance, including SMEs performance, depend on the effectiveness of virtual teams for an extended period of time. Leenders et al. (2003) considered that virtual teams have the same constructs as traditional teams with the fact that team members are geographically dispersed within or outside their organization. Cascio and Shurygailo (2003) showed how problematic it is to define virtual teams across multiple institutional contexts. Anderson et al. (2007) highlighted the agility of virtual teams as an important advantage for organizations in a dynamic environment while other researchers demonstrated some pitfalls of virtual teams (Ramarajan and Reid, 2013). Employees in virtual teams not only share the same problems of individuals in traditional teams, they are also overwhelmed by too much information and communication technologies to perform their tasks (Avolio and Kahai, 2003; Belanger and Watson-Manheim, 2006). In addition, Jarvenpaa and Tanriverdi (2002) assumed that virtual teams' structures are strong on dealing with complexity of the tasks and information while they fail to support adequately the interpersonal relationships. Ryssen and Godar (2000) proposed that specific training modules and motivational practices are necessary for virtual team effectiveness. Studies are not mature enough on what leadership strategies (Mukherjee et al., 2012) and policies are most suitable for virtual teams and building trust between its members (Jarvenpaa et al., 2004). Hertel et al. (2005) and Walvoord et al., (2008) acknowledged that the team leadership approach that relies on empowerment of employees is the most suitable for the virtual teams' effectiveness. Lin et al. (2008) and King (2002) assumed that the quality of the social interactions between virtual team members also have consequences on its effectiveness.

Shared Leadership and Team Proactive Effectiveness

Coombs (2007) stated that crisis management is a process which includes three sequential phases of actions: pre crisis, evolution of crisis and post crisis which can be translated to preparation and/ or prevention phase, containing and damage control phase and business recovery and learning phase (Schwarz et al., 2017). Studies showed that, in the sudden occurrence of crisis, organizations rely mostly on specific teams and leaders to manage the situation with minimum business losses (Nembhard and Edmondson, 2006; Burke et al., 2006; King, 2002). However, researchers argued that crisis management will have better outcomes when organizations follow a proactive approach (Cloudman and Hallahan, 2006; Jaques, 2007). This paper will contribute to the research by studying the antecedents of the team proactive effectiveness on crisis management despite the adversity of the crisis characteristics related to its types, scales, repercussions and geographical expansion (Xu et al., 2019).

Numerous studies focused on the understanding of the determinants of individual level proactivity and demonstrating its influence on the organizational performance (Bindl and Parker, 2011; Williams et al., 2010; Frese et al., 1997; Bateman and Crant, 1993; Frese and Fay, 2001; Parker et al., 2006). Crant and Bateman (2000) defined individual proactivity as the personal disposition to take initiative on identifying opportunities and persevere on adopting adequate actions and behaviors till reaching a significant change.

Team level proactivity is still understudied in organizational behavior research (Williams et al., 2010). Team proactivity is a collective level concept which is functionally similar to individual level proactivity (Morgeson and Hofmann, 1999). Many researchers pinpointed that individual proactivity elements can identify team proactivity as well (Grant and Ashford, 2008; Grant et al., 2011; Kirkman and Rosen, 1999). Strauss et al. (2009) hypothesized that team proactivity does not match with the total proactivity performances of its members. Effective proactive behaviors of different members within the team, as suggesting some process improvements, do not guarantee a team proactive effectiveness if the team interactions are not well managed (Marks et al., 2001). Williams et al. (2010) and Parker et al. (2006) identified team proactivity as the collective tendency to adopt self-management approach, future oriented actions to change the undesired external context and self-improvements activities. The few existing studies related to team proactivity effectiveness were restricted to certain domains as maintenance work groups (Hyatt and Ruddy, 1997), customer service teams (Kirkman and Rosen, 1999), road crews (Tesluk and Mathieu, 1999) and short-term students' projects (Williams et al., 2010). Researchers found that proactive teams have shorter response time to problems, higher productivity and better learning in challenging events (Erkutlu and Chafra, 2012; Hyatt and Ruddy, 1997; Kirkman and Rosen, 1999; Tesluk and Mathieu, 1999; Williams et al., 2010).

It is worthy to explore the potential of these positive organizational outcomes to be translated to organizations in crisis management. Therefore this study suggests:

P1: Higher team proactive effectiveness in organizations predicts more effectiveness in understanding the warning signs and taking the adequate measures in the pre-crisis phase.
P2: Higher team proactive effectiveness in organizations predicts more effectiveness in business performance during the crisis evolution phase.
P3: Higher team proactive effectiveness in organizations predicts more effectiveness in learning and business survival in the after-crisis phase.

Scholars assumed that both individual beliefs as role self-efficacy (Strauss et al., 2009) and contextual characteristics as organizational culture and leadership approaches (Erkutlu, 2012) influence the team proactivity level and its outcomes. Team leadership theories evolved rapidly in the latest years to identify and understand a more collective form of leadership such the shared leadership concept that allows the involvement of all skilled employees in the organizations (Arnold et al., 2000; Pearce, 2007). Translated to crisis context, it may be worthy for the contemporary business environment to consider the shared leadership which is a follower-centered leadership approach (Costello et al., 2002). However, previous studies focused on the leader's role and the importance of coordination between team members to guarantee the shared leadership effectiveness in organizations (Burke et al., 2006). Research demonstrated also the positive relationship between the shared leadership construct and team performance (Carson et al., 2007; Pearce and Conger, 2003; Hoch, 2013; Wang et al., 2014), proactivity and productivity (Erkutlu, 2012), improvements in performance (Carson et al., 2007; D'Innocenzo et al., 2014) and effectiveness (Berson et al., 2016; Daspit et al., 2013; Wang et al., 2014). So that, we propose:

P4: Higher levels of shared-leadership within team members will be significantly and positively related to higher levels of team proactive effectiveness related to crisis management.

Self-Efficacy Theory in Shared Leadership Teams

Bandura (1977, 1997) expanded the Social Cognitive Theory SCT to develop the Self-Efficacy Theory SET. Bandura (1997) defined self-efficacy as the confidence of an individual on their own capacity to attain challenging objectives in specific contexts. Bandura (1977) demonstrated that self-efficacy is domain specific and assumed that social influences shape the individual's assessment of self-efficacy. Bandura (2002) positively associated high levels of self-efficacy in individuals to better performance in coping with change, optimizing in resources and overcoming challenges by engaging in positive productive organizational behaviors as teamwork, empathy and cooperation. Organizational behavior research is increasingly focusing on self-efficacy as a vital construct of productive organizational behavior (Jneid, 2022; Heuven et al., 2006; Judge and Bono, 2001; Luthans et al., 2007). Referring to the dynamic interactive influence processes that are stated in the shared leadership definition, we assume that:

P5: Better influence process in shared leadership teams leads to higher self-efficacy within employees in pre-crisis phase.
P6: Better influence process in shared leadership teams leads to higher self-efficacy within employees during the crisis evolution phase.
P7: Better influence process in shared leadership teams leads to higher self-efficacy within employees in post-crisis phase.

Bandura (1997) considered that information is critical in self-efficacy theory. He suggested four different information resources related to the enhancement of self-efficacy beliefs.

Mastery experience is the first information resource for self-efficacy (Tasa et al., 2007; Bandura, 1997). The researcher considered that the individuals who proved past success stories on changing previous obstacles to opportunities have higher self-efficacy in future challenging events. Translated to a crisis context, employees who enactive mastery experience show more awareness to warning signs in pre-crisis phase, mobilize adequately the necessary resources to cope adequately with the crisis and take responsibility of organization survival in the post crisis phase. We suggest consequently that:

P8: Higher levels of influence processes within shared leadership is significantly and positively related to the capacity of upgrading the mastery experience in crisis management from individual level to team level.
P9: The capacity of shared leadership teams to interpret and understand successfully their organizational mastery crisis experience is significantly and positively moderating the team proactive effectiveness in the crisis management process.

Bandura (1997) demonstrated also the importance of observing others' success stories (vicarious experience) as another resource of information for self-efficacy improvement. The researcher argued that individuals, who lack on mastery experience, observe more sensitively others' actions which can either strengthen their self-efficacy or weaken it. Research demonstrated that vicarious experience effectiveness depends on social influences and becomes higher when individuals show high capacity to perceive similarities between their situations and others' events. Bandura (1986) considered that vicarious experience reflects on applying mastery modeling which leads to the development of a variety of productive organizational competencies. Translated into shared leadership in crisis management, we assume:

P10: Higher levels of influence processes within shared leadership is significantly and positively related to the capacity of upgrading the vicarious experience in crisis management from individual level to team level.
P11: The capacity of shared leadership teams to perceive similarities between their crisis events and others' events is significantly and positively moderating the team proactive effectiveness in crisis management process.

The third information resource for self-efficacy is social persuasion which is close to social influence of others (Bandura, 1997). Previous studies showed that social effectiveness in workplace affects positively the organizational citizenship behaviors and the business performance in challenging situations (Luo et al., 2019; Chiaburu and Harrison, 2008; Cullen et al., 2014; Scott, 2013). Blau (1964) assumed that positive social interactions within team members lead to a positive work environment where empathy, altruism and resilience behaviors are reciprocated. In translation to shared leadership teams, influence processes are also reciprocated and impact, in consequence, its members' behaviors. We suggest that:

P12: Higher levels of influence processes within shared leadership is significantly and positively related to the capacity of upgrading the social persuasion in crisis management from individual level to team level.
P13: The power of social persuasion in shared leadership teams is significantly and positively moderating the team proactive effectiveness in crisis management process.

Bandura (1997) named the somatic indicators as the fourth information resource for self-efficacy improvement through reducing stress levels, controlling negative emotional tendencies and enhancing physical status (Cioffi, 1991). Research demonstrated that occupational stress and anxiety in employees affect negatively their productivity and assessment of their self-efficacy (Bandura, 1997). The crisis process increases the stress and anxiety levels within employees. Dynamic social interactions in shared leadership teams, which encourage well-being and positive emotional states within employees, shape positively their self-efficacy (Bandura 1997) and consequently their capacity to overcome the depression, anxiety and occupational stress (Mikolajczak et al., 2007; Ullrich et al., 2012) that accompany the crisis process. We propose:

P14: Higher levels of influence processes within shared leadership is significantly and positively related to the capacity of influencing emotional states in crisis management from individual level to team level.

P15: The power of influencing the emotional states in shared leadership teams is significantly and positively moderating the team proactive effectiveness in crisis management process.

PRACTICAL IMPLICATIONS

Our paper has also some practical implications. We think that there is an increased need to develop a proactive crisis management process in organizations through motivating team proactivity (Cloudman and Hallahan, 2006). An effective proactive team is more aware to understand pre-crisis signs, more prepared to face the crisis with minimum business losses and take better decisions for business survival and continuity. We propose that shared leadership teams may be a critical antecedent to team proactive effectiveness. So that, investment on facilitating the development of successful shared leadership in organizations is a milestone to a better crisis management.

In organizations, switching from traditional leadership to shared leadership is challenging. Coaching team members on adopting positive reciprocal social interactions is crucial for a successful shared leadership teams. In addition, shared leadership concept must be translated in the compensation and benefits plan in organizations; so that, organizational and team incentives become critical motivators for managers and team members to commit to this new leadership approach.

We suggested the moderating effect of self-efficacy of individuals in our framework. Bandura (1997) assumed that social influences shape the self-efficacy beliefs of individuals. Organizations may rethink the quality of its social interactions and incorporate training plans that encourage constructive feedback, empathy, proactivity and teamwork.

FUTURE RESEARCH DIRECTIONS

Our conceptual theoretical framework focuses on the critical role of the dynamic interactive influence processes in shared leadership to expand the self-efficacy sources outcomes from individual level to a team level in crisis management. We conceptualize shared leadership as a social influence process which refers to team dynamics and social interactions (Bligh et al., 2004; Pearce and Conger, 2003; Shamir and Howell, 1999) which leads to future research area related to the characteristics of individuals and teams, organizational values and national culture that may be less or more supportive to the facilitation of shared leadership between employees.

Sharing leadership within team members can be a critical factor for effectiveness of teams (Houghton et al., 2003). However, organizations which invested for a long period of time on vertical leadership and individual achievements find the shared leadership approach difficult to attain. We assumed that research to understand the moderators of shared leadership for the development of positive organizational outcomes, its antecedents and consequences may be important, particularly as business environments are increasingly in need for more agility to adapt to changes that result from crisis. We introduced a theoretical framework that studies how self-efficacy of individuals may moderate the relationship between shared leadership and team proactivity effectiveness. Other factors related to team, organizational and cultural levels may be worth to explore because of their potential mediating or moderating roles in the relationship between shared leadership and team proactive effectiveness.

One important limitation of our framework is our assumption that individual self-efficacy has no dark side that may inhibits the positive relationship between shared leadership and team proactivity effectiveness. Despite the large number of studies that support the positive effects of self-efficacy, only few studies tackled the negative effects of high levels of self-efficacy as overconfidence (Vancouver and Kendall, 2006) and rigidity on keeping previous successful practices despite changes (Audia et al., 2000). We consider that studying the impact of negative side of self-efficacy on the relationship between shared leadership and team proactivity in crisis management is an important subject for researchers.

Bandura (1997) assumed that self-efficacy is domain specific. We think that there is a benefit to expand the literature of self-efficacy by considering the crisis self-efficacy dimension. Organizational studies have important role on understanding the crisis self-efficacy in organizations.

Another limitation of our framework is our assumption that that the team members are already encouraged by organizational and team incentives to commit to a shared leadership approach. Previous studies demonstrated that positive workplace environment (Carson et al., 2007; Daspit et al., 2013), perception of leadership role (Hackman and Wagemen, 2005), employees' empowerment and trust (Small and Rentsch, 2010) and the perception of the team members of the incentive plans influence the development and maintenance of shared leadership.

We also showed in this paper the importance of proactive crisis management in the recent years and we suggested that team proactive effectiveness may be critical to a better management of the crisis process. Although team leadership theories explicit the need for new leadership approaches for challenging events and self-efficacy theories demonstrate the importance of high levels of self-efficacy to attain objectives in any specific context, little theoretical and empirical attention was given to understand the relationship between these two theories in organizations, specifically in crisis management.

CONCLUSION

In conclusion, we assume that the combination of shared leadership, self-efficacy and team proactiveness are vital for the effective crisis management at organizations.

Team members that trust their own skills and capabilities, as well as their colleagues' competencies, are more likely able to share responsibilities and efforts effectively in times of crises. They, successfully, lead and address the negative impacts of the crises when occurring. This shared leadership fosters a collaborative and dynamic environment that facilitates a proactive crisis management.

Furthermore, team proactiveness and high self-efficacy play vital roles on assessing potential risks, anticipating them, avoiding or facing these risks effectively through preparedness and finally making improvements for better crisis management.

Finally, organizations that invest on shared leadership culture are more capable to benefit from the enhanced problem solving capabilities of their teams as well as their proactive behaviors to effectively overcome complex and unpredictable crises.

REFERENCES

Anderson, AH, McEwan, R, Bal, J & Carletta, J. (2007). Virtual team meetings: An analysis of communication and context. *Computers in Human Behavior*, *23*(5), 2558- 2580.

Arnold, J. A., Arad, S., Rhoades, J. A., & Drasgow, F. (2000). The empowering leadership questionnaire: The construction and validation of a new scale for measuring leader behaviors. *Journal of Organizational Behavior*, *21*(3), 249–269. doi:10.1002/(SICI)1099-1379(200005)21:3<249::AID-JOB10>3.0.CO;2-#

Audia, G., Locke, E. A., & Smith, K. G. (2000). The paradox of success: An archival and laboratory study of strategic persistence following a radical environmental change. *Academy of Management Journal*, *43*(5), 837–853. doi:10.2307/1556413

Avolio, B., & Kahai, S. (2003). Adding the 'E' to E-leadership: How it may impact your leadership. *Organizational Dynamics*, *31*(4), 325–338. doi:10.1016/S0090-2616(02)00133-X

Bandura, A. (1977). Self-efficacy: Toward a unifying theory of behavioral change. *Psychological Review*, *84*(2), 191–215. doi:10.1037/0033-295X.84.2.191 PMID:847061

Bandura, A. (1986). *Social foundation of thought and action: A social cognitive theory*. Prentice-Hall.

Bandura, A. (1997). *Self-efficacy: The exercise of control*. Freeman.

Bandura, A. (2002). Social cognitive theory in cultural context. *Applied Psychology*, *51*(2), 269–290. doi:10.1111/1464-0597.00092

Bateman, T. S., & Crant, J. M. (1993). The proactive component of organizational behavior: Ameasure and correlates. *Journal of Organizational Behavior*, *14*(2), 103–118. doi:10.1002/job.4030140202

Belanger, F., & Watson-Manheim, M. B. (2006). Virtual teams and multiple media: Structuring media use to attain strategic goals. *Group Decision and Negotiation*, *15*(4), 299–321. doi:10.100710726-006-9044-8

Berson, Y., Waldman, D. A., & Pearce, C. L. (2016). Enhancing our understanding of vision in organizations: Toward an integration of leader and follower processes. *Organizational Psychology Review*, *6*(2), 171–191. doi:10.1177/2041386615583736

Bindl, U. K., & Parker, S. K. (2011). Proactive work behavior: Forward-thinking and change-oriented action in organizations. In S. Zedeck (Ed.), APA handbook of industrial and organizational psychology, Vol. 2. Selecting and developing members for the organization (pp. 567–598). American Psychological Association. doi:10.1037/12170-019

Blau, P. M. (1964). *Exchange and power in social life*. Wiley.

Bligh, M. C., Kohles, J. C., & Meindl, J. R. (2004). Charisma under crisis: Presidential leadership, rhetoric, and media responses before and after the September 11th terrorist attacks. *The Leadership Quarterly*, *15*(2), 211–239. doi:10.1016/j.leaqua.2004.02.005

Bligh, M. C., Pearce, C. L., & Kohles, J. C. (2006). The importance of self- and shared leadership in team based knowledge work: A meso-level model of leadership dynamics. *Journal of Managerial Psychology*, *21*(4), 296–318. doi:10.1108/02683940610663105

Bundy, J., & Pfarrer, M. D. (2015). A burden of responsibility: The role of social approval at the onset of a crisis. *Academy of Management Review*, *40*(3), 345–369. doi:10.5465/amr.2013.0027

Bundy, J., Pfarrer, M. D., Short, C. E., & Coombs, W. T. (2017). Crises and crisis management: Integration, interpretation, and research development. *Journal of Management, 43*(6), 1661–1692. doi:10.1177/0149206316680030

Burke, C. S., Fiore, S. M., & Salas, E. (2003). The role of shared cognition in enabling shared leadership and team adaptability. In C. L. Pearce & J. A. Conger (Eds.), *Shared Leadership: Reframing the Hows and Whys of Leadership* (pp. 103–122). Sage Publications. doi:10.4135/9781452229539.n5

Burke, C. S., Stagl, K. C., Salas, E., Pierce, L., & Kendall, D. (2006). Understanding team adoption: A conceptual analysis and model. *The Journal of Applied Psychology, 91*(6), 1189–1207. doi:10.1037/0021-9010.91.6.1189 PMID:17100478

Bushee, B. J. (1998). The influence of institutional investors on myopic R&D investment behavior. *The Accounting Review, 73*, 305–333.

Carson, J. B., Tesluk, P. E., & Marrone, J. A. (2007). Shared leadership in teams: An investigation of antecedent conditions and performance. *Academy of Management Journal, 50*, 1217–1234.

Cascio, W. F., & Shurygailo, S. (2003). E-Leadership and Virtual Teams. *Organizational Dynamics, 31*(4), 362–376. doi:10.1016/S0090-2616(02)00130-4

Champion, D. (1999). The price of under management. *Harvard Business Review, 77*(2), 14–15.

Chiaburu, D. S., & Harrison, D. A. (2008). Do peers make the place? Conceptual synthesis and meta-analysis of coworker effects on perceptions, attitudes, OCBs, and performance. *The Journal of Applied Psychology, 93*(5), 1082–1103. doi:10.1037/0021-9010.93.5.1082 PMID:18808227

Cioffi, D. (1991). Beyond attentional strategies: A cognitive-perceptual model of somatic interpretation. *Psychological Bulletin, 109*(1), 25–41. doi:10.1037/0033-2909.109.1.25 PMID:2006227

Cloudman, R., & Hallahan, K. (2006). Crisis communication preparedness among U.S. organizations: Activities and assessments by public relations practitioners. *Public Relations Review, 32*(4), 367–376. doi:10.1016/j.pubrev.2006.09.005

Coombs, W. (2007). *Ongoing Crisis Communication: Planning, Managing and Responding* (2nd ed.). Sage.

Coombs, W. T., & Holladay, S. J. (2002). Helping crisis managers protect reputational assets. *Management Communication Quarterly, 16*(2), 165–186. doi:10.1177/089331802237233

Costello, M. L., Brunner, P. W., & Hasty, K. (2002). Preparing students for the empowered workplace: The risks and rewards in a management classroom. *Active Learning in Higher Education*, *3*(2), 117–127. doi:10.1177/1469787402003002002

Crant, J. M., & Bateman, T. S. (2000). Charismatic leadership viewed from above: The impact of proactive personality. *Journal of Organizational Behavior*, *21*(1), 63–75. doi:10.1002/(SICI)1099-1379(200002)21:1<63::AID-JOB8>3.0.CO;2-J

Cullen, K. L., Fan, J., & Liu, C. (2014). Employee popularity mediates the relationship between political skill and workplace interpersonal mistreatment. *Journal of Management*, *40*(6), 1760–1778. doi:10.1177/0149206311435104

D'Innocenzo, L., Mathieu, J. E., & Kukenberger, M. R. (2014). A Meta-Analysis of Different Forms of Shared Leadership–Team Performance Relations. *Journal of Management*, *20*(10), 1–28.

Danneels, E. (2002). The dynamics of product innovation and firm competences. *Strategic Management Journal*, *23*(12), 1095–1121. doi:10.1002mj.275

Daspit, J., Tillman, C., Boyd, N., & Mckee, V. (2013). Cross-functional team effectiveness: An examination of internal team environment, shared leadership, and cohesion influences. *Team Performance Management*, *19*(1/2), 19. doi:10.1108/13527591311312088

Diehl, M., & Stroebe, W. (1991). Productivity loss in idea-generating groups: Tracking down the blocking effect. *Journal of Personality and Social Psychology*, *61*(3), 392–403. doi:10.1037/0022-3514.61.3.392

Erkutlu, H. (2012). The impact of organizational culture on the relationship between shared leadership and team proactivity. *Team Performance Management*, *18*(1/2), 102–119. doi:10.1108/13527591211207734

Erkutlu, H., & Chafra, J. (2012). The impact of team empowerment on proactivity: The moderating roles of leader's emotional intelligence and proactive personality. *Journal of Health Organization and Management*, *26*(5), 560–577. doi:10.1108/14777261211256918 PMID:23115905

Esmaeilikia, M., & Groth, M. (2022). A motivational approach to emotional labor: Examining the link between goal orientation and emotional labor strategies. *Journal of Management & Organization*, *28*(6), 1280–1300. doi:10.1017/jmo.2019.63

Faulkner, B. (2001). Towards a framework for tourism disaster management. *Tourism Management*, *22*(2), 135–147. doi:10.1016/S0261-5177(00)00048-0

Fowler, K. L., Kling, N. D., & Larson, M. D. (2007). Organizational preparedness for coping with a major crisis or disaster. *Business & Society*, *46*(1), 88–103. doi:10.1177/0007650306293390

Frese, M., & Fay, D. (2001). Personal initiative: An active performance concept for the 21st century. In B. M. Staw & R. I. Sutton (Eds.), *Research in Organizational Behavior,23, 133–187*. JAI Press. doi:10.1016/S0191-3085(01)23005-6

Frese, M., Fay, D., Hilburger, T., Leng, K., & Tag, A. (1997). The concept of personal initiative: Operationalization, reliability and validity in two German samples. *Journal of Occupational and Organizational Psychology*, *70*(2), 139–161. doi:10.1111/j.2044-8325.1997.tb00639.x

Gillespie, N., & Dietz, C. (2009). Trust Repair after an Organization-Level Failure. *Academy of Management Review*, *34*(1), 127–145. doi:10.5465/amr.2009.35713319

Grant, A. M., & Ashford, S. J. (2008). The dynamics of proactivity at work. *Research in Organizational Behavior*, *28*, 3–34. doi:10.1016/j.riob.2008.04.002

Grant, A. M., Gino, F., & Hofmann, D. A. (2011). Reversing the extraverted leadership advantage: The role of employee proactivity. *Academy of Management Journal*, *54*(3), 528–550. doi:10.5465/amj.2011.61968043

Hackman, J., & Wageman, R. (2005). A Theory of Team Coaching. *Academy of Management Review*, *302*(2), 269–287. doi:10.5465/amr.2005.16387885

Han, S. J., & Hazard, N. (2022). Shared Leadership in Virtual Teams at Work: Practical Strategies and Research Suggestions for Human Resource Development. *Human Resource Development Review*, *21*(3), 300–323. doi:10.1177/15344843221093376

Hertel, G. T., Geister, S., & Konradt, U. (2005). Managing virtual teams: A review of current empirical research. *Human Resource Management Review*, *15*(1), 69–95. doi:10.1016/j.hrmr.2005.01.002

Heuven, E., Bakker, A. B., Schaufeli, W. B., & Huisman, N. (2006). The role of self-efficacy in performing emotion work. *Journal of Vocational Behavior*, *69*(2), 222–235. doi:10.1016/j.jvb.2006.03.002

Hoch, J. E. (2013). Shared leadership and innovation: The role of vertical leadership and employee integrity. *Journal of Business and Psychology*, *28*(2), 159–174. doi:10.100710869-012-9273-6

Houghton, J., Neck, C. P., & Manz, C. C. (2003). Self-leadership and SuperLeadership: the heart and the art of creating shared leadership in teams. In C. L. Pearce & J. A. Conger (Eds.), *Shared Leadership: Reframing the Hows and Whys of Leadership* (pp. 123–140). Sage Publications. doi:10.4135/9781452229539.n6

Hüffmeier, J., Krumm, S., Kanthak, J., & Hertel, G. (2012). "Don't let the group down": Facets of instrumentality moderate the motivating effects of groups in a field experiment. *European Journal of Social Psychology*, *42*(5), 533–538. doi:10.1002/ejsp.1875

Hyatt, D. E., & Ruddy, T. M. (1997). An examination of the relationship between work group characteristics and performance: Once more into the breech. *Personnel Psychology*, *50*(3), 553–585. doi:10.1111/j.1744-6570.1997.tb00703.x

Iyer, D. N., & Miller, K. D. (2008). Performance feedback, slack, and the timing of acquisitions. *Academy of Management Journal*, *51*(4), 808–822.

Jaques, T. (2007). Issue management and crisis management: An integrated, non-linear, relational construct. *Public Relations Review*, *33*(2), 147–157. doi:10.1016/j.pubrev.2007.02.001

Jarvenpaa, S. L., Shaw, T. R., & Staples, D. S. (2004). Toward contextualized theories of trust: The role of trust in global virtual teams. *Information Systems Research*, *15*(3), 250–267. doi:10.1287/isre.1040.0028

Jarvenpaa, S. L., & Tanriverdi, H. (2002). Leading virtual knowledge networks. *Organizational Dynamics*, *31*(4), 403–412. doi:10.1016/S0090-2616(02)00127-4

Jneid, C. (2022). How Social Self-Efficacy and Emotional Self-Efficacy moderate the relationship between Occupational stress and knowledge hiding in Brazilian software industry. Evidence-based HRM: a global forum for empirical scholarship. doi:10.1108/EBHRM-03-2021-0040

Judge, T. A., & Bono, J. E. (2001). Relationship of core self-evaluations trait self-esteem, generalized self-efficacy. Locus of control, and emotional stability – with job satisfaction and job performance: A meta-analysis. *The Journal of Applied Psychology*, *86*(1), 80–92. doi:10.1037/0021-9010.86.1.80 PMID:11302235

Kahn, W. A., Barton, M. A., & Fellows, S. (2013). Organizational crises and the disturbance of relational systems. *Academy of Management Review*, *38*(3), 377–396. doi:10.5465/amr.2011.0363

Karau, S. J., & Williams, K. D. (1993). Social loafing: A meta-analytic review and theoretical integration. *Journal of Personality and Social Psychology*, *65*(4), 681–706. doi:10.1037/0022-3514.65.4.681

Kerr, N. L. (1983). Motivation losses in task-performing groups: A social dilemma analysis. *Journal of Personality and Social Psychology*, *45*(4), 819–828. doi:10.1037/0022-3514.45.4.819

Kerr, N. L., & Tindale, R. S. (2004). Group performance and decision making. *Annual Review of Psychology*, *55*(1), 623–655. doi:10.1146/annurev.psych.55.090902.142009 PMID:14744229

King, G. III. (2002). Crisis management and team effectiveness: A closer examination. *Journal of Business Ethics*, *41*(3), 235–249. doi:10.1023/A:1021200514323

Kirkman, B. L., & Rosen, B. (1999). Beyond self-management: Antecedents and consequences of team empowerment. *Academy of Management Journal*, *42*(1), 58–74. doi:10.2307/256874

Kozlowski, S. W. J., & Klein, K. J. (2000). A Multilevel Approach to Theory and Research in Organizations: Contextual, Temporal, and Emergent Processes. In K. J. Klein & S. W. J. Kozlowski (Eds.), *Multilevel Theory, Research, and Methods in Organizations: Foundations, Extensions, and New Directions* (pp. 3–90). Jossey-Bass.

Kuusela, P., Keil, T., & Maula, M. (2017). Driven by aspirations, but in what direction? Performance shortfalls, slack resources, and resource-consuming vs. resource-freeing organizational change. *Strategic Management Journal*, *38*(5), 1101–1120. doi:10.1002mj.2544

Lampel, J., Shamsie, J., & Shapira, Z. (2009). Experiencing the improbable: Rare events and organizational learning. *Organization Science*, *20*(5), 835–845. doi:10.1287/orsc.1090.0479

Lazarus, R. S. (1991). *Emotion and adaptation*. Oxford university press.

Leenders, R. T. A. J., Engelen, J. M. L. V., & Kratzer, J. (2003). Virtuality, communication, and new product team creativity: A social network perspective. *Journal of Engineering and Technology Management*, *2003*(20), 69–92. doi:10.1016/S0923-4748(03)00005-5

Lin, C., Standing, C., & Liu, Y. C. (2008). A model to develop effective virtual teams. *Decision Support Systems*, *45*(4), 1031–1045. doi:10.1016/j.dss.2008.04.002

Luo, Y., Permzadian, V., Fan, J., & Meng, H. (2019). Employees' social self-efficacy and work outcomes: Testing the mediating role of social status. *Journal of Career Assessment*, *27*(4), 661–674. doi:10.1177/1069072718795401

Luthans, F., Avolio, B. J., Avey, J. B., & Norman, S. M. (2007). Positive psychological capital: Measurement and relationship with performance and satisfaction. *Personnel Psychology*, *60*(3), 541–572. doi:10.1111/j.1744-6570.2007.00083.x

Marks, M. A., Mathieu, J. E., & Zaccaro, S. J. (2001). A temporally based framework and taxonomy of team processes. *Academy of Management Review*, *26*(3), 356–376. doi:10.2307/259182

Mikolajczak, M., Menil, C., & Luminet, O. (2007). Explaining the protective effect of trait emotional intelligence regarding occupational stress: Exploration of emotional labor processes. *Journal of Research in Personality*, *41*(5), 1107–1117. doi:10.1016/j.jrp.2007.01.003

Miller, K. D., & Chen, W. R. (2004). Variable organizational risk preferences: Tests of the march-Shapira model. *Academy of Management Journal*, *47*(1), 105–115. doi:10.2307/20159563

Mitroff, I. I., & Alpaslan, M. C. (2003). Preparing for Evil. *Harvard Business Review*, *81*(4), 109–115. PMID:12687925

Mohammed, A. A., & Hadi, A. A. (2022). The impact of empowering and transformational leadership on organizational performance and innovation: the mediating role of shared leadership and moderating role of organizational culture in the Iraqi healthcare sector. *International Journal of Organizational Analysis*.

Morgeson, F. P., & Hofmann, D. A. (1999). The structure and function of collective constructs: Implications for multilevel research and theory development. *Academy of Management Review*, *24*(2), 249–265. doi:10.2307/259081

Mukherjee, D., Lahiri, S., & Billing, T. K. (2012). Leading virtual teams: How do social, cognitive, and behavioral capabilities matter? *Management Decision*, *50*(2), 273–290. doi:10.1108/00251741211203560

Murphy, P. (2006). Chaos Theory As A Model For Managing Issues And Crises. *Public Relations Review*, *22*(2), 95–113. doi:10.1016/S0363-8111(96)90001-6

Naidoo, V. (2010). Firm survival through a crisis: The influence of market orientation, marketing innovation and business strategy. *Industrial Marketing Management*, *39*(8), 1311–1320. doi:10.1016/j.indmarman.2010.02.005

Nembhard, I., & Edmondson, A. (2006). Making It Safe: The Effects of Leader Inclusiveness and Professional Status on Psychological Safety and Improvement Efforts in Health Care Teams. *Journal of Organizational Behavior*, *27*(7), 941–966. doi:10.1002/job.413

OECD. (2011). *OECD Reviews of Risk Management Policies, Future Global Shocks, Improving Risk Governance*. OECD Publishing.

Paraskevas, A. (2006). Crisis Management or Crisis Response System? A Complexity Science Approach to Organizational Crises. *Management Decision*, *44*(7), 892–907. doi:10.1108/00251740610680587

Parker, S. K., Williams, H., & Turner, N. (2006). Modeling the antecedents of proactive behavior at work. *The Journal of Applied Psychology*, *91*(3), 636–652. doi:10.1037/0021-9010.91.3.636 PMID:16737360

Pearce, C. L. (2007). The future of leadership development: The importance of identity, multilevel approaches, self-leadership, physical fitness, shared leadership, networking, creativity, emotions, spirituality and on-boarding processes. *Human Resource Management Review*, *17*(4), 355–359. doi:10.1016/j.hrmr.2007.08.006

Pearce, C. L., & Conger, J. A. (2003). *Shared leadership: Reframing the hows and whys of leadership*. Sage. doi:10.4135/9781452229539

Pearce, C. L., & Manz, C. C. (2005). The new silver bullets of leadership: The importance of self and shared leadership in knowledge work. *Organizational Dynamics*, *34*(2), 130–140. doi:10.1016/j.orgdyn.2005.03.003

Petrie, E. J., Nieto, A. G., & Andrews, K. (2021). Racial Differences in Perceptions of Shared Leadership Among IT Managers. In *Effective Strategies for Communicating Insights in Business* (pp. 101–128). IGI Global. doi:10.4018/978-1-7998-3964-4.ch007

Pfarrer, M. D., DeCelles, K. A., Smith, K. G., & Taylor, M. S. (2008). After the fall: Reintegrating the corrupt organization. *Academy of Management Review*, *33*(3), 730–749. doi:10.5465/amr.2008.32465757

Ramarajan, L., & Reid, E. (2013). Shattering the myth of separate worlds: Negotiating non work identities at work. *Academy of Management Review*, *38*(4), 621–644. doi:10.5465/amr.2011.0314

Rese, M., & Fay, D. (2001). *Personal initiative: An active performance concept forthe 21st century.*

Rogov, M. A. (2006). Global Risk Factors. *Journal of Business Economics and Management*, *7*(1), 25–28. doi:10.3846/16111699.2006.9636119

Ryssen, S. V., & Godar, S. H. (2000). Going international without going international: Multinational virtual teams. *Journal of International Management*, *6*(1), 49–60. doi:10.1016/S1075-4253(00)00019-3

Sapriel, C. (2003). Effective crisis management: Tools and best practice for the new millennium. *Journal of Communication Management (London)*, *7*(4), 348–355. doi:10.1108/13632540310807485

Schwarz, A., Seeger, M. W., & Auer, C. (Eds.). (2016). *The handbook of international crisis communication research*. John Wiley & Sons. doi:10.1002/9781118516812

Scott, B. A. (2013). A conceptual framework for the study of popularity in the workplace. *Organizational Psychology Review*, *3*(2), 161–186. doi:10.1177/2041386612464092

Seers, A., Keller, T., & Wilkerson, J. M. (2003). Can team members share leadership? Foundations in research and theory. In C. L. Pearce & J. A. Conger (Eds.), *Shared Leadership: Reframing the Hows and Whys of Leadership* (pp. 77–102). Sage Publications. doi:10.4135/9781452229539.n4

Shamir, B., & Howell, J. M. (1999). Organizational and contextual influences on the emergence and effectiveness of charismatic leadership. *The Leadership Quarterly*, *10*(2), 257–283. doi:10.1016/S1048-9843(99)00014-4

Shimizu, K. (2007). Prospect theory, behavioral theory, and the threat-rigidity thesis: Combinative effects on organizational decisions to divest formerly acquired units. *Academy of Management Journal, 50*(6), 1495-1514.

Small, E. E., & Rentsch, J. R. (2010). Shared leadership in teams: A matter of distribution. *Journal of Personnel Psychology*, *9*(4), 203–211. doi:10.1027/1866-5888/a000017

Stajkovic, A. D., & Luthans, F. (1998). Self-efficacy and work-related per-formance: A meta-analysis. *Psychological Bulletin*, *124*(2), 240–261. doi:10.1037/0033-2909.124.2.240

Staw, I. B. M., & Sutton, R. I. (Eds.), *Research in Organizational Behavior* (Vol. 23, pp. 133–187). JAIPress.

Strauss, K., Griffin, M. A., & Rafferty, A. E. (2009). Proactivity directed toward the team and organization: The role of leadership, commitment and role-breadth self-efficacy. *British Journal of Management*, *20*(3), 279–291. doi:10.1111/j.1467-8551.2008.00590.x

Sundstrom, E., De Meuse, K. P., & Futrell, D. (1990). Work Teams: Applications and Effectiveness. *The American Psychologist*, *45*(2), 120–133. doi:10.1037/0003-066X.45.2.120

Tasa, K., Taggar, S., & Seijts, G. H. (2007). The development of collective efficacy in teams: A multilevel and longitudinal perspective. *The Journal of Applied Psychology*, *92*(1), 17–27. doi:10.1037/0021-9010.92.1.17 PMID:17227148

Tesluk, P. E., & Mathieu, J. E. (1999). Overcoming roadblocks to effectiveness: Incorporating management of performance barriers into models of work group effectiveness. *The Journal of Applied Psychology*, *84*(2), 200–217. doi:10.1037/0021-9010.84.2.200

Ucal, M., Ozcan, K. M., Bilgin, M. H., & Mungo, J. (2010). Relationship Between Financial Crisis And Foreign Direct Investment in Developing Countries Using Semiparametric Regression Approach. *Journal of Business Economics and Management*, *11*(1), 20–33. doi:10.3846/jbem.2010.02

Ullrich, A., Lambert, R. G., & McCarthy, C. J. (2012). Relationship of German elementary teachers' occupational experience, stress, and coping resources to burnout symptoms. *International Journal of Stress Management*, *19*(4), 333–342. doi:10.1037/a0030121

Vancouver, J. B., & Kendall, L. N. (2006). When self-efficacy negatively relates to motivation and performance in a learning context. *The Journal of Applied Psychology*, *91*(5), 1146–1153. doi:10.1037/0021-9010.91.5.1146 PMID:16953775

Walvoord, A. A. G., Redden, E. R., Elliot, L. R., & Coovert, M. D. (2008). Empowering followers in virtual teams: Guiding principles from theory and practice. *Computers in Human Behavior*, *24*(5), 1884–1906. doi:10.1016/j.chb.2008.02.006

Wang, D., Waldman, D. A., & Zhang, Z. (2014). A meta-analysis of shared leadership and team effectiveness. *The Journal of Applied Psychology*, *99*(2), 181–198. doi:10.1037/a0034531 PMID:24188392

Williams, H. M., Parker, S. K., & Turner, N. (2010). Proactively performing teams: The role of work design, transformational leadership, and team composition. *Journal of Occupational and Organizational Psychology*, *83*(2), 301–324. doi:10.1348/096317910X502494

Wise, C. R. (2006). Organizing for homeland security after Katrina: Is adaptive management what's missing? *Public Administration Review*, *66*(3), 302–318. doi:10.1111/j.1540-6210.2006.00587.x

Xu, C., & Zhao, L. (2022). Collective achievement, cohesive support, complementary expertise: 3Cs emergent model for shared leadership. *Human Resource Development International*, 1–26.

Xu, X., Jiang, L., & Wang, H. J. (2019). How to build your team for innovation? A cross-level mediation model of team personality, team climate for innovation, creativity, and job crafting. *Journal of Occupational and Organizational Psychology*, *92*(4), 848–872. doi:10.1111/joop.12277

ADDITIONAL READINGS

Boin, A., & Lagadec, P. (2000). Preparing for the future: Critical challenges in crisis management. *Journal of Contingencies and Crisis Management*, *8*(4), 185–191. doi:10.1111/1468-5973.00138

KEY TERMS AND DEFINITIONS

Shared leadership: This refers to collective leadership, where everyone is accountable to contribute to the achievement of the organizational goals.

Self-efficacy: This refers to the individual or team's belief in their skills and capacity to overcome many challenges. Teams with high self-efficacy are resilient and motivated to achieve successful goals.

Team proactive effectiveness: This refers to the ability of the teams to expect crises, increase preparedness and overcome the crises with the minimum negative impacts possible.

Crisis management: This refers to the systematic process of identifying risks and crises, planning for preparedness, responding, or avoiding risks and crises, recovering and learning lessons.

Chapter 5
Diversity and Employee Engagement in the 21st Century Organisation:
A Focus on Inclusive Leadership

Theresa Obuobisa-Darko
Ghana Communication Technology University, Ghana

Evans Sokro
Central University, Ghana

Richard Afedzie
Pentecost University, Ghana

ABSTRACT

Globalisation has affected the work environment, leading to an increase in the workforce. Workforce diversity describes ways employees differ by way of values, beliefs, experiences, backgrounds, preferences, and behaviours. While organisational success depends on effective management of its workforce by leaders, the adoption of appropriate leadership style, like inclusive leadership, has become one of the strategic mechanisms to manage the diverse workforce in the 21st century organisation. Inclusive leadership, a relational leadership style, tends to be open, accessible, available, self-aware, committed, collaborative and culturally intelligent. Premised on social exchange theory, these unique characteristics make the diverse subordinates of inclusive leaders feel valued and reciprocate by being dedicated, absorbed, and working with vigour. The chapter advocates for inclusive leadership style as the preferred leadership style to manage diverse workforce to promote employee engagement in the 21st century organisation. The chapter ends with suggestions for future research.

DOI: 10.4018/978-1-6684-6602-5.ch005

INTRODUCTION

Globalisation has affected the work environment leading to an increase in the diversity of workforce in organisations (Ehsan, 2021; Ongori & Agolla, 2007; Choy, 2007). Diversity denotes the differences that exist between persons based on their personal characteristics and this influence how individuals perceive one another (Ragins & Gonzalez, 2003). Workforce diversity can therefore be based on ethnic origin, gender, age, religious beliefs, political beliefs, and all other ways in which people differ. These differences are meaningful and relevant tools for the promotion of innovative ways of accomplishing individual and organisational goals efficiently (Ehsan, 2021; Roberge & Van Dick, 2010). Workforce diversity has therefore become an antecedent to organisational success. It is therefore imperative that the appropriate leadership style is used to manage the diverse workforce to benefit for organisational success.

The 21st century organisation is characterised by increase knowledge sharing, increase focus and demand on employee competencies, cultural transformation, and workforce diversity (Krebs, 2007; Ployhart, 2006). It has been established that organisations can survive only where these diverse employees, are well managed through improved connectivity (Meraku, 2017; Krebs, 2007). Consequently, the effective management of workforce diversity has become a core strategic value that managers perceive they have a duty to understand (Ragins & Gonzalez, 2003; Ongori & Agolla, 2007), uphold and follow for employees to feel connected, inclusive and perform in the organisation (Roberge & Van Dick, 2010; Saxena, 2014; Ashikali & Groeneveld, 2015). This is because Inclusiveness, in the long run matters most to ensure organisational growth (Riffkin & Harter, 2016). Further, "diverse workforce provides better quality and innovative superior solutions to organizational problems than the homogenous groups; which can ultimately lead to organizational efficiency, effectiveness, and profitability" (Ehsan, 2021, p. 2). The question then is what leadership style should be adopted to ensure diverse employees in organisation feel inclusive?

This chapter seeks to advocate for inclusive leadership in the 21st century organisation to effectively manage the diverse workforce to feel inclusive. Inclusive leadership is a specific relational leadership style where such leaders tend to be open, accessible and available (Carmeli et al., 2010; Nembhard & Edmondson, 2006). The argument then is, inclusive leader with its unique characteristics is preferred as compared with other leadership styles to manage diverse workforce for them to feel inclusive.

Research on inclusive leadership has attracted attention of both practitioners and scholars', hence over the last one and half decades after Nembhard and Edmondson (2006) introduced the concept of inclusive leadership in the field of management, numerous researchers have shown much interest in its studies (Nishii et al. 2009; Choi et al., 2017; Fang et al., 2021). This interest is due to the significant positive effects inclusive leadership (IL) has on employee work behaviors and attitudes because of the cordial relationship such leaders foster (Ospina, 2011). Regardless of the interest, there remains paucity of critical academic literature on IL, and relatively little is known about how it influences employee behaviour in general and specifically, employee engagement (Vakira et al., 2022; Choi et al., 2015).

Engaged employees play a significant role in organisations because they have a positive fulfilling work-related state of mind which is characterized by vigour, dedication, and absorption (Schaufeli, et al., 2002, p. 74). Hence, engaged employees employ their cognitive, emotional and physical energies in performing their roles, making them assets to every organisation due to their immense contribution. Engaged employees therefore seem to be the 'magic wand' for organisational success in this century, where due to globalisation there is high workforce diversity and innovation among employees.

Several studies suggest a relationship between leadership in the organisation and employee behaviour and attitude (Tran & Choi 2019; Walumbwa et al., 2008) such as their level of engagement (Obuobisa-Darko & Ameyaw-Domfeh, 2019; Busse & Regenberg, 2019; Vakira et al., 2022). Leadership is a process not a person with the leader who is an individual being at the centre of the process and making employees feel valued and inclusive. One such leadership style that makes employees feel inclusive is the inclusive leadership style. The adoption of the inclusive leadership styles makes the leader supportive, interested in their team members' contributions, engage in open communication, and available to their subordinates (Choi et al., 2017). These unique characteristics of the inclusive leaders make them not to discriminate but value the diversity among the employees, open to their diverse views and opinion, and this make their subordinates feel valued (Carmeli et al., 2010; Choi et al., 2017; Hollander, 2009). There is, however, a dearth of theoretical and empirical research regarding how the inclusive leader can manage diverse workforce in organisations feel inclusive and valued. Anchored on the Social Exchange theory (SET), one of the most influential theories for understanding workplace behaviours, proposes that, all social relationships are rooted within an exchange framework. This chapter contributes to existing knowledge in the field of leadership by extending the SET-inclusive leadership, workforce diversity management and employee engagement literature. It adopts a literature review approach through which information is gathered from textbooks, journal articles and other relevant sources to explain the relationship between workplace employee diversity, employee engagement and inclusive leadership in the 21st century.

This chapter is organised as follows. Following this introduction is a discussion of the social exchange theory, leadership, inclusive leadership and characteristics of inclusive leaders. The next is a review on employee diversity, and Employee

Engagement. Following this is examination of the nexus between inclusive leaders, diverse workforce and employee engagement and concludes the chapter with future research direction.

Social Exchange Theory

The social exchange theory (SET), a theory considered as one of the most influential conceptual models to help clarify workplace behaviour (Cropanzano & Mitchell, 2005), is based on the works of Homan (1958, 1961, 1974) and Blau (1960, 1964). It emphasises how strong social relationship, seen in the form of professional relationship, organisational groupings, friendship, and diversity management, are imperative towards the creation of positive employee behaviour and attitude (Nishii et al., 2018; Nishii & Mayer, 2009; Aryee et al., 2002; Chiaburu et al., 2011). The theory postulates that social behaviour is the outcome of a social exchange process. This social exchange, a process which has central significance in social life (Cook et al., 2013) refers to the voluntary actions of individuals that are motivated by the returns they are expected to bring and typically do in fact bring from others (Blau, 1964). From a similar perspective Gouldner (1960) had earlier explained social exchange as a "mutually contingent exchange of benefits between two or more units" (p. 164). Thus, the impetus of this dyadic social exchange is to get the maximum benefits out of the relationship and minimise costs. In this chapter the SET therefore serves as a framework for explaining the inclusive leadership, employee engagement, and diversity management relationship.

The social exchange theory is characterised by four (4) features (Cropanzano et al., 2017). Firstly, that social life involves a series of sequential transactions which take place between two or more individuals. The social life exchanges which usually takes place in a sequential manner, leads to either a positive or a negative attitude or behaviour in each one of the parties involved. Since behaviour is a function of payoff (Cook et al., 2013), when the inclusive leader relates well with their subordinates, for them to feel inclusive, there will be a positive payoff which will be seen in their high levels of engagement (Ariani, 2014; Decuypere & Schaufeli, 2020).

The second characteristic indicates that social exchange relationship involves an exchange of resources through a process of reciprocity. Reciprocity is regarded as "the pattern of exchange through which the mutual dependence of people, brought about by the division of labour, is realised (Gouldner, 1960, pp. 170-171). Hence, it is important that leaders as well as individuals appreciate the mutual dependence and the exchange of both material and non-material resources in relationship.

Thirdly, the quality of these exchanges is sometimes influenced by the kind of relationship between the parties involved (Cropanzano et al., 2017). This makes the quality of exchanges between the leader and his subordinates very critical. A good quality relationship between the leader and his subordinates will encourage these subordinates to feel obliged to reciprocate by using their discretion at work, be dedicated and work with vigour (Ariani, 2014; Alam et al., 2022) and vice versa.

Lastly, social exchanges involve trust and flexibility. Trust is an individual's willingness to be vulnerable to the actions of another individual based on the belief that this person will act as expected, even if that individual is unable to monitor their behaviour (Granovetter, 1985). Since trust is an indispensable component for the survival of an organisation (Black et al., 2000; Rezvani et al., 2016), leaders have to ensure positive social exchanges to build the trust. Behavioural flexibility represents employees' ability to adjust and adapt as opposed to routine behaviour and therefore able to adapt to situation-specific demands (Lepine et al., 2000; Bhattacharya et al., 2005). Since flexibility impacts organisational performance positively (Bhattacharya, et al., 2005), it is imperative that leaders ensure high level of flexibility in their social exchanges with their subordinates for organisational success.

LEADERSHIP AND INCLUSIVE LEADERSHIP

Leadership is about "doing things with people, rather than to people", which is the crux of inclusion (Hollander, 2009). Inclusive leadership (IL) is a relatively new construct, and therefore full conceptualization is not at the advanced stages in the management and leadership literature, and this has resulted in varied definitions. First, coined by Nembhard and Edmondson (2006), they described leader inclusiveness, as leaders' whose 'words and deeds indicate an invitation and appreciation for others' contribution" (p. 947). Such leaders encourage and permit their followers to share their views by being open, available and accessible, thus helping to shape their perception about how valuable they are (Bortini et al., 2018; Hollander, 2009). Thus, inclusivity describes the degree to which employees perceive the acceptance of their uniqueness and their opinion by their leaders, and therefore treated fairly within the organisation, which lead to the satisfaction of their need to feel belonging (Shore et al., 2011).

Carmeli et al. (2010) in defining inclusive leadership stated that, it is a kind of leadership that exhibits openness, accessibility, and availability in their interaction with followers" (p. 250). Similarly, Choi, Tran, and Kang (2017) explained inclusive leaders as leaders who are "open, willing to listen to employees and discuss new ways for achieving the work goals and paying attention to new opportunities (p.1880). Such attributes result in the leaders' willingness to explore different perspectives and experiences (Lall-Trail et al., 2021) and create an enabling environment where both the leader and his followers are able to express themselves for mutual gains (Bortini et al., 2018; Kouzes & Posner, 2023). This explains why Korkmaz et al.

(2022) described inclusive leadership as the leadership style that goes beyond just fostering uniqueness but also strengthening belongingness in the organisation.

More recently, IL has been described as those leaders who permit their followers to share their views and inputs by being open, available, and accessible, which help shape employees' perception that their voices are genuinely heard (Fang et al., 2021). Inclusive leadership is therefore that kind of leadership that values openness and therefore creates an atmosphere where employees perceive them as accessible, available, and willing to accept different perspectives from diverse individuals without any discrimination.

These characteristics of the IL make it unique and different from other well-known leadership constructs such as transformational, responsible and servant leaderships, even though there are some commonalities. Whiles the Inclusive leaders focus on being available, accessible, and open which helps build quality relationship between themselves and their followers, other leadership styles do not exhibit all of them. The transformational leader is oriented towards motivating their followers towards believing in the vision of the organisation and following them (Daft, 2001) and not paying much attention to creating an environment with a high level of inclusivity, unlike the IL whose main characteristic is inclusiveness and identity (Hollander, 2009, Randel et al., 2018). Responsible leaders are known to pay attention to issues of responsibility, including accountability, appropriate moral decision-making, and trust (Pless & Maak, 2011), while the IL aims at encouraging others to contribute, take active part, and appreciate their followers for their inputs (Randel et al., 2018). Servant leadership on the other hand, focuses on the level of success of employees but does not address the importance of employee belongingness, an essential human need (Filstad et al., 2019), unlike the IL who embraces followers for who they are and ensures their need for belongingness is met (Jolly & Lee, 2021). Overall, the inclusive leader tends to be open, accessible, available, culturally intelligent, committed, self-aware and promote collaboration. It therefore stands to argue that inclusive leadership is a unique leadership style different from other existing leadership styles.

Inclusive leadership is perceived to be a specific relational leadership (Carmeli et al., 2010; Jolly & Lee, 2021). A relational leadership is a "social influence process through which emergent coordination (i.e., evolving social order) and change (i.e., new values, attitudes, approaches, behaviour, ideologies, etc.) are constructed and produced" (Uhl-Bien, 2006, p. 668). This implies, inclusive leadership is not just a process that is interested in the quality of relationship between the leader and follower, as purported by SET, but also the dynamics within the society upon which the relationship is formed.

CHARACTERISTICS OF INCLUSIVE LEADERSHIP

Inclusive leadership, being one of the relational leadership styles has some characteristics similar to other relational leadership styles such as transformational, transactional, responsible and participative leadership styles. Different authors have outlined different characteristics of the IL. One of such classification is that from Carmeli et al. (2010) and Nembhard and Edmondson (2006) who indicated that the IL is characterised as being open, available, and accessible.

Openness is one's willingness to explore different perspectives and experiences. It refers to a leader's ability to motivate their subordinates to think creatively, come up with innovative ideas, listen to their opinions actively, and involve them in decision-making (Khattak et al., 2022). The openness attribute of the inclusive leader result in they are sharing their vision and guide his followers to share in it, give them the confidence to offer feedback about the vision, which improves the quality of the relationship (Bailey, et al., 2017). The improvement in the quality of relationship goes a long way to positively impact on employees' behaviour and attitude (Shu & Lazatkhan, 2017; Li et al., 2014).

Being accessible, is more about what you do by being fair, than just what you say (Shore, & Chung, 2022). Fairness is an outcome of integrity, where leaders' decisions are unbiased and honest (Colquitt & Rodell, 2011) and this leader behaviour helps to build greater trust among their subordinates (Guinaliu & Jordan, 2016). Thus, when leaders are accessible and therefore fair (Shore & Chung, 2022), they keep personal connections and develop a strong relationship with their followers by providing them with the needed attention, fair treatment, develop an others-first attitude and invest in and connect with them (Rayner, 2009).

The third characteristics describe the concerted effort made by the IL to be available to their followers. Availability describes the leader's ability to offer timely assistance to their followers when they encounter difficulties in performing their work (Khattak et al., 2022). Being available therefore is a function of time management. Leaders who are available consider team members a priority and make time for scheduled and unscheduled conversations. The leaders' availability therefore tends to have a positive impact on the employees' behaviour and attitude (Perry et al., 2020; Vakira et al., 2022).

While Prime and Salib (2014) view the characteristics of the inclusive leader as empowering followers, humility, courage and accountability, Dillon, and Bourke (2016) on the other hand, espouses six characteristics of an IL which are re-enforcing and interrelated and include: curiosity, cultural intelligence, collaboration, commitment, courage and cognizance of bias.

The demonstration of inclusivity requires the leader to be curious (Dillon & Bourke, 2016). Curiosity is theorised as a motivational state and a personality trait of individuals (Grossnickle, 2016). A curious individual demonstrates an open mind set, listens without judgment, and seeks with empathy to understand those around them (Bourke & Espedido, 2020). As a result, leaders who are curious are exposed to different ideas and experiences that allows for growth (Dillon & Bourke, 2016; Mohanty et al., 2015) and leader effectiveness (Khan, 2022).

With the open-minded characteristic of the IL, they lean towards being ready to listen, support and show interest in the contributions of their team members (Choi et al., 2017; Hollander, 2009; Roberson & Perry, 2022). In so doing, they tend not to be judgemental, but attempt to understand, those around them and this makes these followers feel valued (Obuobisa-Darko & Ameyaw-Domfeh, 2019; MacLeod, & Clarke, 2011).

Cultural intelligence, another characteristic of the IL, is the ability that individuals have to interact effectively across cultural contexts and with culturally different individuals" (Thomas et al., 2015, p. 2). Such persons are attentive to others' culture, and therefore able adapt when confronted with problems arising in interactions with people or artefacts of diverse cultures when required (Sternberg et al., 2021; Bourke & Espedido, 2020). Cultural intelligence includes three interactional elements: cognitive, behavioural, and motivational (Thomas et al., 2015; Earley & Mosakowski, 2004). The cognitive facet of cultural intelligence reflects the cognitive processes that individuals use to gain knowledge about the norms, practices, and conventions in different cultures (Harrison & Brower, 2011; Liao & Thomas, 2020). Persons with high levels of the cognitive facet understand the similarities and differences across cultures and the knowledge specific to the context which enables them operate efficiently and effectively within specific domains (Van Dyne et al., 2012). Consequently, the culturally intelligent individual will value and appreciate contributions from different individuals. The motivational dimension of cultural intelligence reflects readiness to learn and adapt to new cultural environment (Earley & Mosakowski, 2004). They added that persons with a high level of motivational cultural intelligence are ready to direct their attention towards learning and performing well in a new cultural surrounding. Behavioural cultural intelligence on the other hand, reveals a person's ability to exhibit appropriate verbal and nonverbal actions and responses when interacting with people from different cultures (Thomas et al., 2015; Earley & Mosakowski, 2004). In essence, the acquisition of knowledge and its understanding increases the leaders' understanding of their own cultures (Sternberg et al., 2022), appreciate what shapes and cause patterns of behaviours and interactions within cultures, and why behaviours and interactions differ across cultures (Ang & Van Dyne, 2008).

The IL is known to be a good collaborator (Dillon & Bourke, 2016). Collaboration is the process where employees work together in a collegiate manner, for a "common purpose" which often involves finding solutions (Goulet et al., 2003). Leaders usually take the initiative, but it requires followers for the implementation of these initiatives and therefore the need for collaboration (Maalouf, 2019; Witte, 2012). Collaboration among members is crucial to ensure efficiency and effectiveness, build consensus of the plan, obtain high quality results and participation, and make improved, objective, and democratic decisions in organisations (Cheng et al., 2022; Fu et al., 2020). Collaboration has become an important act required by leaders because through effective collaboration leaders are able empower others, pay attention to diversity of thinking and psychological safety, and focus on team cohesion (Bourke & Espedido, 2020). This is beneficial to the organisation since the existence of a diverse-thinking team is greater than the sum of its parts (Dillon & Bourke, 2016). Leaders, therefore, have to collaborate and in doing so, maintain a healthy and productive relationships between employees by listening, having an open-minded attitude; and being calm and patient in relating with their employees (Ang'ana & Chiroma, 2021). Hence, there is a call for a shift from the command-and-control leadership style towards embracing a collaborative leadership characteristic seen in the potential inclusive leader, to motivate employees (Mayan et al., 2016), boost the overall collaborative functioning (Shu & Wang, 2021) and facilitate project performance and sustainability (Chak et al., 2022).

Staying the course of any activity an employee embarks on is usually difficult (Dillon & Bourke, 2016) and therefore requires commitment. Commitment, one of the unique characteristics of inclusive leaders (Dillon & Bourke, 2016) describes the extent to which employees' and leaders identify with an organisation and its goals and desires to be part of the organisation (Robbins & Judge, 2017). The IL therefore has a sense of responsibility and feel obliged to ensure the achievement of the targets set, by dedicating much time, energy, and other resources to foster inclusiveness.

Demonstration of inclusivity requires courage by the leader (Dillon & Bourke, 2016). Courage involves putting one's personal interest aside to achieve what needs to be done (Prime & Salib, 2014, p. 7). Individuals who are courageous therefore prefer to pursue moral goals even if there exist a threat but see the goal as important (Woodard & Pury, 2007). Courage is about having that voluntary willingness to act, with or without a level of fear to achieve an important goal (Chen et al., 2019). An inclusive leader will therefore be prepared and not scared to speak his mind, challenge the status quo, and accept his weakness where necessary in a bid to achieve set goals.

The inclusive leader is aware of his biases (Dillon & Bourke, 2016). Cognizance of biases combined with empathy and humility greatly improve the level of employees' perception and feeling of inclusivity (Bourke & Espedido, 2020). Biases reflect an individual's inability to be neutral in situations, hence, the tendency to be inclined towards or away from a particular thing or thought. Being conscious of one's biases reflects self-awareness which is an individual's ability to be mindful of the different facets of the self through reflection and introspection (Van Gulick, 2000). The recognition of the biases empowers an individual to manage these biases to prevent them from influencing his actions and choices negatively.

The characteristics of inclusive leadership are not independent of each other but are interrelated and re-enforce each other. It therefore stands to argue that inclusive leadership is a unique leadership style different from other existing leadership styles.

DIVERSITY AT THE WORKPLACE

Work environment in the 21st century is characterised by increasing employee diversity (Mathis & Jackson, 2010). As a result, both researchers and practitioners have developed interest in diversity at the workplace (Buengeler et al., 2018) and putting in much effort in creating an inclusive work environment (Roberson, 2006) and better understand the attitudes towards diversity and diversity initiatives (Fujimoto & Hartel, 2017). Diversity, a multi-dimensional concept can broadly be defined as "a characteristic of social grouping that reflects the degree to which objective or subjective differences exist between group members" (Van Knippenberg & Schippers, 2007, p. 516). It is the differences between individuals on any attribute that may lead to the perception that another person is different from self" (Van Knippenberg et al.,

Figure 1. Inclusive leadership characteristics

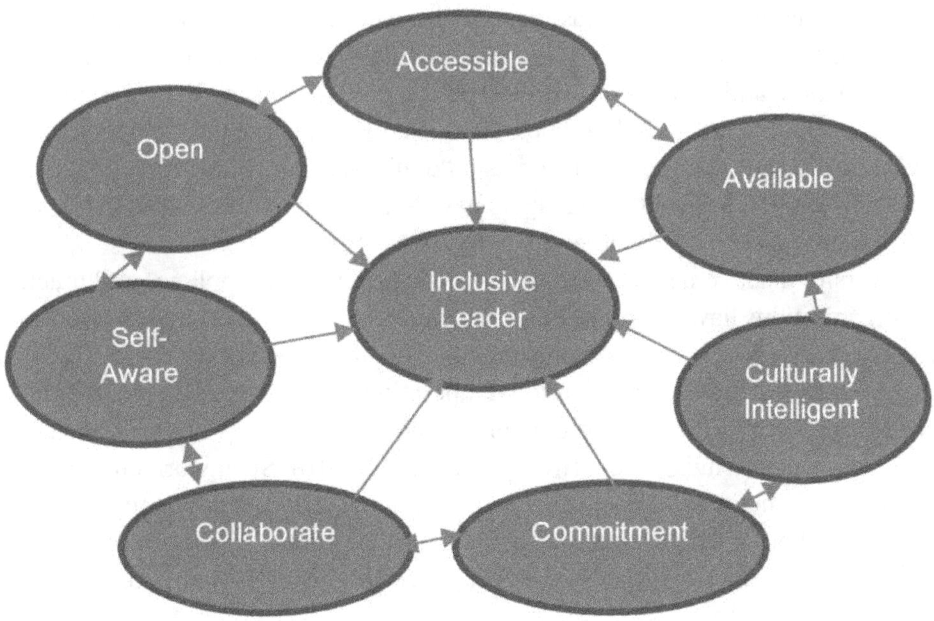

2004 p. 1008). Simply, it is the dissimilarity among group members based on certain traits (Guillaume et al., 2013). These traits may include gender, age, ethnicity, marital status, sexual orientation, parental status, education, income, work experience, job tenure, physical disability, nationality, social status, language, among others (Saxena, 2014; Rijamampianina & Carmichael, 2005; Shen et al., 2009). Diversity, hence, denotes the existence of differences and/or a state of being different.

All these differences are put into varied categories by different authors. For example, Hsiao et al. (2015) put it into two major categorisations: primary and secondary. The primary category of diversity cannot change, and usually influences the personality of the individual and the self-image (Hsiao et al., 2015). On the other hand, the secondary dimension can be modified and adjusted by different factors like education, job level and, geographical location (Hsiao et al., 2015). There are others that does not fit into neither the primary nor secondary dimension and these are what Rijamampianina and Carmichael (2005) describe as the tertiary dimension. These authors categorised diversity into primary, secondary, and tertiary.

There is a plethora of literature that argue that having diversity of employees can be a blessing to managers in different ways such as level of engagement, creativity, improved performance and innovation (Luu et al., 2019; Tuan, 2019; Triguero-Sánchez et al., 2018). This is because diverse workforce brings in more inclusiveness and diversity in representatives, improve the corporate image, better quality, creative and innovative superior solutions, team effectiveness, and employee engagement (Ehsan, 2021; Blouch & Azeem, 2019; Roberge & Van Dick, 2010). On the contrary, others posit that a diverse workforce can create challenges such as increase in conflict and tension among subgroups, decrease group cohesiveness, lower employee satisfaction, reduce well-being, increase high turnover, counterproductive work behaviours like discrimination, and derogation (Guillaume et al., 2013, Ehsan, 2021; Cunningham & Sagas, 2004; Roberge & Van Dick 2010; Van Knippenberg & Schippers 2007). Diversity can therefore be described as a "double-edged sword" since it has both pros and cons. Consequently, managers have to adopt appropriate leadership styles and strategies to ensure effective diversity management.

Diversity management (DM), "the specific programmes, policies and practices that organisations have developed and implemented to manage a diverse workforce effectively and to promote organisational equality" (Dennissen et al., 2020, p. 220), greatly influence organisational operations. These management policies, practices and programs when implemented and enforced, help create and maintain an inclusive work environment (Mor Barak et al., 2016). Such work environments with its fair policies and programs when implemented create a positive employee perception about the organisation (Garcia-Rodriguez et al., 2020) and facilitate the effective management of the diverse workforce (Manoharan et al., 2021; Ashikali & Groeneveld, 2015).

Leaders therefore play a significant role towards diversity management. They ensure the formulation and implementation of these policies, practices and programs to positively impact employees' perception on how the organisation value them and therefore are ready to integrate and support them through reasonable and impartial enforcement of employment policies, practices and procedures (Kundu & Mor, 2017). This explains why managers have great influence on the equality and diversity workplace climate which employees experience on daily basis (Kirton & Greene, 2015).

INCLUSIVE LEADERSHIP AND WORKPLACE DIVERSITY

Diverse workforce has several benefits to the organisation such as improved performance (Blouch & Azeem, 2019), employee work engagement (Goswami & Kishor, 2018; Luu et al., 2019) and job satisfaction (Madera et al., 2013). When the diverse employees do not feel heard, seen, and valued they take their talents away which negatively impacts the organisation. However, if leaders ensure that diverse employees feel their unique characteristics are appreciated, valued and their welfare is of interest to the leader, they tend to stay (Nishii & Mayer, 2009) and give off their best to the organisation. Therefore, managers of organisations must create a safe and inclusive workplace so that employees can reach their full potential. Inclusive leadership, an emerging unique leadership style reflects a leader's capability which help organizations to adapt to diverse customers, markets, ideas and talents (Bourke & Espedido, 2020; Roberson & Perry, 2022). Inclusive leadership, therefore, with its unique characteristics of being open, available and accessible (Carmeli et al., 2010; Nembhard & Edmondson, 2006), curious, cultural intelligence, collaborate, committed, courageous, and cognizance of bias (Dillon & Bourke, 2016), is able create this inclusive workplace where employees can speak up and take part in decision making, feel valued and therefore ready to stay and support the leader to achieve the organisation's goals. In sum, the adoption of inclusive leadership style positively impacts diversity and inclusive initiatives and affect the management of employee diversity in organisations.

EMPLOYEE ENGAGEMENT

Ensuring employee engagement (EE) in recent times has been of interest to practitioner, academics and researchers alike due to their significant contribution towards organisational outcomes (Saks & Gruman, 2014) such as organisation citizenship behaviour (Ariani, 2014), job performance (Rich et al, 2010; Liu et al.,

2022), job satisfaction (Saks, 2006; Vorina et al, 2017), and as a source of competitive advantage (Kular et al., 2008; Kumar & Pansari, 2016). Consequently, a decline in EE has a negative effect on productivity, customer service and performance (Mone et al., 2011; Liu et al., 2022).

Over thirty (30) years after Kahn (1990) introduced EE, the debate on what it entails is still ongoing. There exist four major approaches to the definition of EE (Shuck, 2011). These include Kahn (1990) Need-Satisfying approach, Maslach et al. (2001) burnout-antithesis approach, Harter et al. (2002) Satisfaction-engagement approach and Sak (2006) multidimensional approach.

The first definition of employee engagement (EE) from the management literature by Kahn (1990), from the need-satisfaction approach, explains that EE refers to “the harnessing of organisational members’ selves to their role; in engagement, people employ and express themselves physically, cognitively, and emotionally during role performance” (p. 694). Kahn (1990) indicated that employees perform different roles in organizations, and employ different degrees of themselves, be it emotional, cognitive, and physical in performing these roles to satisfy a need.

Maslach et al. (2001) theorised that employee engagement was the positive antithesis to burnout. They explained employee engagement on the engagement-burnout continuum, with engagement at one end and burnout on the other end. Engagement describes the energy (high levels of mental and physical resources in the task to be performed), involvement (attentive, attached response) and efficacy (ability to do a quality work and a feeling of being competent), while burnout describes a state of exhaustion, cynicism and inefficacy (Maslach et al (2001). Thus, a person who is engaged will have a high level of energy to perform, be highly involved in all activities at the workplace and perform a good quality work.

Schaufeli et al. (2002) on their part explained that EE is “a positive, fulfilling, work-related state of mind that is characterized by vigor, dedication and absorption” (p.74). Vigour describes a person’s possession of high level of energy and mental resilience at work, dedication is an individual’s sense of pride, enthusiasm, and inspiration, while absorption reflects the level at which a person concentrates fully and deeply involved in the job assigned (Schaufeli et al., 2002). Hence, engaged employees are physically devoting to their work, cognitively absorbed and attentive, and emotionally motivated and excited about their work (Shen & Jiang, 2019; Saks, 2006).

From the satisfaction-engagement approach, Harter et al. (2002) the first to consider EE from the business level, posit that EE refers to an “individual’s involvement and satisfaction with as well as enthusiasm for work” (Harter et al., 2002, p. 269). Engaged employees are connected to their work, and this is improved when managers involve them in activities and decisions (Obuobisa-Darko & Ameyaw Domfeh, 2019; Khan & Altaf, 2015) which lead them to work with high levels of enthusiasm.

Similar to the definition by Kahn (1990), Saks (2006) described EE as a distinct and unique construct that consists of cognitive, emotional, and behavioural components, that is associated with individual role performance. An engaged employee is therefore willing and ready to offer discretionary effort and a high level of mental resilience at work to achieve individual and organisational goals (Shen & Jiang, 2019). Engagement therefore reflects a person's emotional, cognitive, mental, and physical commitment towards achieving both his personal goals and that of the organization at large. Such employees understand and accept their leaders and so are motivated to work with high levels of energies, commitment, dedication, and vigour to ensure organisational success (Saks, 2006; Harter et al., 2002; Schaufeli et al., 2002).

INCLUSIVE LEADERSHIP, EMPLOYEE ENGAGEMENT, AND WORKPLACE DIVERSITY NEXUS

Understanding the nexus between IL and EE is considered critical due to globalisation, including the current rapidly changing and competitive nature of the 21st century's organisational environment. There are several antecedents to EE, but leadership stands out (Obuobisa-Darko & Ameyaw Domfeh, 2019; Alam et al., 2022). Leader behaviour significantly influences employee engagement (Bailey et al., 2017; MacLeod & Clarke, 2011; Malik, et al., 2017; Obuobisa-Darko & Ameyaw Domfeh, 2019). Consequently, when leaders exhibit certain characteristics as they relate with their followers, it causes EE. The leader-employee engagement relationship is explained from the Social Exchange Theory (SET) perspective. The SET emphasizes that all social behaviour relationships involve reciprocity which is guided by rules of exchange. When both the leader and the followers' behaviour are guided by these exchange rules, the relationship over time, evolves into a trusting loyal one (Cropanzano & Mitchell, 2005). Hence, if leaders offer subordinates the resources, treat them in a friendly manner, are open and available, committed to their wellbeing, it develops into a trusting loyal relationship, where the subordinates respond in a positive manner. Since inclusive leaders are known to offer subordinates the required resources and support; involve them in all activities, open and accessible (Carmeli et al., 2010; Nembhard & Edmondson, 2006; Choi et al., 2017). Consequently, these employees tend to perceive their leaders to be interested in their wellbeing, open to diverse views, available and therefore offer timely assistance and attention required. They in turn reciprocate by being dedicated, work with vigour, show enthusiasm in performing their jobs (Choi et al., 2015; Malik et al., 2017; Vakira et al., 2022).

Inclusive leaders listen, provide needed attention to their followers (Roberson & Perry, 2022) and this communicates and makes the followers perceive their leader to be available and accessible (Hollander, 2009). This perception provides favourable and conducive work environment which fosters positive employee outcomes such as increased job performance (Randel et al., 2018; Hirak et al., 2012; Obuobisa-Darko & Ameyaw-Domfeh, 2019); psychological safety (Carmeli et al., 2010; Hirak et al., 2012) employee well-being (Choi et al., 2017) commitment, (Prime and Salib, 2014), dedication (Obuobisa-Darko & Ameyaw-Domfeh, 2019), creativity and innovative behavior (Randel et al., 2018; Choi et al., 2017), are all characteristics of engaged employees.

Where the IL collaborate with subordinates, it sends a signal to followers that their views are valued and makes them feel that they are esteemed members of the organisation and this perception helps satisfy their need for belongingness and uniqueness (Shore et al., 2011). The satisfaction of this need increases employees' willingness to contribute intellectually, experience positive emotions, thereby becoming committed to the organisation's goals and values. As such, the IL creates an atmosphere where the subordinates become engaged and therefore reciprocate by applying their discretionary efforts and go beyond what is a typically expected relationship (Malik et al., 2017; Vakira et al., 2022).

Several studies have proven that there is a significant positive relationship between engaged employees and organisational performance and success (Liu et al., 2022; MacLeod & Clarke, 2011). To increase the level of engagement and organisational performance require the management of employees' diversity and ensuring inclusivity, increase engagement and organisational performance (Downey et al., 2015; Goswami & Kishor, 2018; Itam & Bagali, 2019). Additionally, if managers are able to manage the differences among their employees and create a conducive organisational climate it will influence these employees positively to be highly engaged (Jones & Harter, 2005) and ensure a feeling of inclusivity. In contrast, organisations which does not value inclusivity and diversity at the workplace have been cited as having highly disengaged employees (Riffkin & Harter, 2016; Mor Barak et al., 2016).

From the social exchange theory's perspective (Cropanzano et al., 2017; Cropanzano & Mitchell, 2005), employees tend to behave positively and put in extra effort when they perceive the organisation values their diversity, existence and contributions (Cropanzano & Mitchell, 2005). Therefore, if leaders fail to adopt appropriate diversity management practices, it will increase biases and discrimination which significantly and negatively impact employee engagement (James et al., 2013; Shenoy & Kumar, 2021). Consequently, drawing from the SET's perspective and the characteristics of the inclusive leader, the conclusion is, subordinates of the inclusive leader will reciprocate the leader's openness, availability, readiness to accept their diversity by exhibiting the characteristics of an engaged employee which will impact positively on organisational outcomes.

PRACTICAL IMPLICATIONS

This study offers various attributes for inclusive leader behaviour, which can be espoused by organisations that desire to benefit from inclusion at the workplace. As the role of the leader is critical in fostering inclusion, it is necessary for organisations to consciously upskill and promote inclusive behaviours. Accordingly, the study encourages leadership in organisations to adopt a broader view of diversity and inclusion programmes as the effective implementation of such programmes could have significant implications for employee engagement and work performance outcomes. It has been recognised that leaders who use shared vision and participative decision-making to empower their followers can positively influence team performance and effectiveness (Ye et al., 2018).

In addition, the study highlights the need for human resource practitioners to effectively manage workforce diversity and ensure they foster inclusive work environment. Leader behaviour has been acknowledged to impact inclusion at workplace. As such, employees' positive perception of being consulted in decision-making could influence their work engagement and overall performance. For organisations to improve leader behaviour and encourage diversity, top management must develop new policies or modify existing ones to promote inclusion. As suggested by Hollander (2009), leadership in organisations must view inclusion and development as a strategic business imperative, integrate them into employee development policies and ensure accountability at all levels.

Finally, our study underscores the critical role of inclusive leadership in achieving an inclusive work environment using human resource diversity policies and practices. Managers, must therefore, add inclusive leadership as part of management development programmes. This will enable managers appreciate the benefits of inclusion as they manage workforce diversity in contemporary organisations.

CONCLUSION AND FUTURE RESEARCH DIRECTIONS

Ensuring the best is derived from diverse employees can be a daunting task. This is because having a diverse workforce has both benefits and challenges. Consequently, there is the need to address the diversity issues comprehensively and manage the employees by adopting the appropriate leadership style. On account of this, organisations need a leader who is open to new ideas, available and accessible to the diverse workforce, promote collaboration, culturally intelligent and self-aware, and one of such is the inclusive leadership style. Once the inclusive leader exhibits these characteristics as he relates with the diverse workforce, it will create a positive exchange relationship between the inclusive leader and the diverse workforce and affect their engagement levels positively.

Employee engagement is extremely beneficial to any organization and more importantly in this 21st century organisation that has diverse workforce and characterised by demand for employees' competencies. Engaged employees boost organisational productivity, enhances the organisation's image, increase customer satisfaction, remain committed and attached emotionally, cognitively and physically to the organization. Inclusive leadership behaviours communicate openness, accessibility, availability to followers, committed to employee wellbeing, ready to collaborate and culturally intelligent. (Carmeli et al., 2010; Dillion & Bourke, 2016; Nembhard & Edmondson, 2006). These unique characteristics of IL make employees perceive these leaders as caring, valuing their contribution and being interested in their wellbeing, thereby boosting and enhancing their exhibition of an engaged employee characteristics.

The SET explains the inclusive leadership, employee engagement and diversity management nexus. From this theory's perspective, the social exchanges that take place at the workplace, involve series of interactions that engender unspecified obligations (Xanthopoulou et al., 2009). As a result of the exchanges between the leader and his subordinates, such employees feel obliged to reciprocate when the inclusive leader is open, available and provide them with the economic and socio-emotional resources (Cropanzano & Mitchell, 2005). This, they do, by being engaged since "one way for individuals to repay their organisation is through their level of engagement (Saks, 2006, p.603). Thus, employees will choose to engage themselves to varying degrees in response to the resources they receive from their organisation. That is why ''employees who perceive that the organisation cares about their well-being through the provision of adequate resource allocation are more likely to be motivated and engaged (Dollard & Bakker, 2010, p. 583). It can thus, be concluded that, when employees perceive they are autonomous, receive support, have access to the leader, and their unique and diverse needs are addressed, they reciprocate by showing higher levels of engagement.

Even though there is clear evidence that the inclusive leader is able to manage employees' diversity effectively which results in employee engagement, as well as the importance of diversity and inclusion practices in organisation, review of the literature indicates that research on these areas are marginal. Aside the quantum, minimal studies have been carried out in the developing countries context. It is therefore recommended that empirical studies be conducted to ascertain the relationship between these variables in the developing countries. Future research should also identify variables that can serve as mediators and moderators in the workplace diversity, employee engagement and inclusive leadership relationship. Aside the SET, future researchers can explore other theoretical perspectives such as the resource-based view of the firm, the psychological contract theory and the theory of met expectations to explain the relationships among the variables.

Although some organisations realise the importance of introducing and implementing diversity and inclusion practices, the most appropriate leadership to adopt to ensure the effective management of diverse workforce and ensure inclusiveness are not much considered. Therefore, the chapter considered inclusive leadership and how it ensured effective management of diverse employees to enhance inclusiveness and engagement.

REFERENCES

Alam, J., Mendelson, M., Boamah, M. I., & Gauthier, M. (2022). Exploring the antecedents of employee engagement. *International Journal of Organizational Analysis*.

Albrecht, S. L. (2015). Meaningful work: Some key questions for research and practice. In R. J. Burke, K. M. Page, & C. L. Cooper (Eds.), *Flourishing in life, work, and careers: Individual wellbeing and career experiences* (pp. 210–234). Edward Elgar. doi:10.4337/9781783474103.00021

Alfes, K., Truss, C., Soane, E., Rees, C., & Gatenby, M. (2010). *Creating an engaged workforce: findings from the Kingston employee engagement consortium project.* Chartered Institute of Personnel and Development.

Ang, S., & Van Dyne, L. (2008). Conceptualization of cultural intelligence: Definition, distinctiveness, and nomological network. In S. Ang & L. Van Dyne (Eds.), *Handbook of Cultural Intelligence: Theory, Measurement, and Applications* (pp. 3–15). M. E. Sharpe.

Ang'ana, G. A., & Chiroma, J. A. (2021). Collaborative Leadership and its Influence in Building and Sustaining Successful Cross-Functional Relationships in Organizations in Kenya. *Journal of Business and Management*, *23*(8), 18–26.

Ariani, D. W. (2014). Relationship leadership, employee engagement, and organizational citizenship behavior. *International Journal of business and social research, 4*(8), 74-90.

Aryee, S., Budhwar, P. S., & Chen, Z. X. (2002). Trust as a mediator of the relationship between organizational justice and work outcomes: Test of a social exchange model. *Journal of Organizational Behavior*, *23*(3), 267–285. doi:10.1002/job.138

Ashikali, T., & Groeneveld, S. (2015). Diversity management in public organizations and its effect on employees' affective commitment: The role of transformational leadership and the inclusiveness of the organizational culture. *Review of Public Personnel Administration, 35*(2), 146–168. doi:10.1177/0734371X13511088

Bailey, C., Madden, A., Alfes, K., & Fletcher, L. (2017). The meaning, antecedents and outcomes of employee engagement: A narrative synthesis. *International Journal of Management Reviews, 19*(1), 31–53. doi:10.1111/ijmr.12077

Bhattacharya, M., Gibson, D. E., & Doty, D. H. (2005). The effects of flexibility in employee skills, employee behaviors, and human resource practices on firm performance. *Journal of Management, 31*(4), 622–640. doi:10.1177/0149206304272347

Black, C., Akintoye, A., & Fitzgerald, E. (2000). An analysis of success factors and benefits of partnering in construction. *International Journal of Project Management, 18*(6), 423–434. doi:10.1016/S0263-7863(99)00046-0

Blau, P. M. (1964). Justice in social exchange. *Sociological Inquiry, 34*(2), 193–206. doi:10.1111/j.1475-682X.1964.tb00583.x

Blouch, R., & Azeem, M. F. (2019). Effects of perceived diversity on perceived organizational performance: Mediating role of perceived organizational justice. *Employee Relations, 41*(5), 1079–1097. doi:10.1108/ER-05-2018-0150

Bortini, P., Paci, A., Rise, A., & Rojnik, I. (2018). *Inclusive leadership: Theoretical framework*. Inclusive Leadership. http://inclusiveleadership. eu/ il_theoreticalframework_en. pdf.

Bourke, J., Titus, A., & Espedido, A. (2020). The key to inclusive leadership. *Harvard Business Review*, 6.

Brown, J. (2019). *How to be an inclusive leader: Your role in creating cultures of belonging where everyone can thrive*. Berrett-Koehler Publishers.

Buengeler, C., Leroy, H., & De Stobbeleir, K. (2018). How leaders shape the impact of HR's diversity practices on employee inclusion. *Human Resource Management Review, 28*(3), 289–303. doi:10.1016/j.hrmr.2018.02.005

Busse, R., & Regenberg, S. (2019). Revisiting the "authoritarian versus participative" leadership style legacy: A new model of the impact of leadership inclusiveness on employee engagement. *Journal of Leadership & Organizational Studies, 26*(4), 510–525. doi:10.1177/1548051818810135

Carmeli, A., Reiter-Palmon, R., & Ziv, E. (2010). Inclusive leadership and employee involvement in creative tasks in the workplace: The mediating role of psychological safety. *Creativity Research Journal, 22*(3), 250–260. doi:10.1080/10400419.2010.504654

Chak, C. M., Carminati, L., & Wilderom, C. P. (2022). Hope, goal-commitment and-stress mediating between collaborative leadership, financial resources, and performance. *International Journal of Productivity and Performance Management.*

Chen, Y., Wang, L., Liu, X., Chen, H., Hu, Y., & Yang, H. (2019). The trickle-down effect of leaders' pro-social rule breaking: Joint moderating role of empowering leadership and courage. *Frontiers in Psychology, 9*, 2647. doi:10.3389/fpsyg.2018.02647 PMID:30666224

Cheng, X., Liu, W., & Li, Y. (2022). Is online collaboration process suitable for digital youth organization? A design approach. *Journal of Electronic Business & Digital Economics.*

Chiaburu, D. S., Diaz, I., & Pitts, V. E. (2011). Social and economic exchanges with the organization: Do leader behaviors matter? *Leadership and Organization Development Journal, 32*(5), 442–461. doi:10.1108/01437731111146569

Choi, S. B., Tran, T. B. H., & Kang, S. W. (2017). Inclusive leadership and employee well-being: The mediating role of person-job fit. *Journal of Happiness Studies, 18*(6), 1877–1901. doi:10.100710902-016-9801-6

Choi, S. B., Tran, T. B. H., & Park, B. I. (2015). Inclusive leadership and work engagement: Mediating roles of affective organizational commitment and creativity. *Social Behavior and Personality, 43*(6), 931–943. doi:10.2224bp.2015.43.6.931

Choy, W. K. (2007). Globalisation and workforce diversity: HRM implications for multinational corporations in Singapore. *Singapore Management Review, 29*(2), 1–20.

Colquitt, J. A., & Rodell, J. B. (2011). Justice, trust, and trustworthiness: A longitudinal analysis integrating three theoretical perspectives. *Academy of Management Journal, 54*(6), 1183–1206. doi:10.5465/amj.2007.0572

Cook, K. S., Cheshire, C., Rice, E. R., & Nakagawa, S. (2013). Social exchange theory. In *Handbook of social psychology* (pp. 61–88). Springer. doi:10.1007/978-94-007-6772-0_3

Cropanzano, R., Anthony, E. L., Daniels, S. R., & Hall, A. V. (2017). Social exchange theory: A critical review with theoretical remedies. *The Academy of Management Annals, 11*(1), 479–516. doi:10.5465/annals.2015.0099

Cropanzano, R., & Mitchell, M. S. (2005). Social exchange theory: An interdisciplinary review. *Journal of Management, 31*(6), 874–900. doi:10.1177/0149206305279602

Cunningham, G. B., & Sagas, M. (2004). Group diversity, occupational commitment, and occupational turnover intentions among NCAA Division IA football coaching staffs. *Journal of Sport Management, 18*(3), 236–254. doi:10.1123/jsm.18.3.236

Daft, R. L. (2001). *Organization theory and design*. Australia, South-western Thomson learning.

De Jong, J. P., & Den Hartog, D. N. (2007). How leaders influence employees' innovative behaviour. *European Journal of Innovation Management, 10*(1), 41–64. doi:10.1108/14601060710720546

Decuypere, A., & Schaufeli, W. (2020). Leadership and work engagement: Exploring explanatory mechanisms. *German Journal of Human Resource Management, 34*(1), 69–95. doi:10.1177/2397002219892197

Dennissen, M., Benschop, Y., & van den Brink, M. (2020). Rethinking diversity management: An intersectional analysis of diversity networks. *Organization Studies, 41*(2), 219–240. doi:10.1177/0170840618800103

Dillon, B., & Bourke, J. (2016). *The six signature traits of inclusive leadership: Thriving in a diverse new world.* Deloitte University Press. https://www2.deloitte.com/content/dam/Deloitte/au/Documents/human-capital/ deloitte-au-hc-six-signature-traits-inclusive-leadership020516.pdf

Downey, S. N., van der Werff, L., Thomas, K. M., & Plaut, V. C. (2015). The role of diversity practices and inclusion in promoting trust and employee engagement. *Journal of Applied Social Psychology, 45*(1), 35–44. doi:10.1111/jasp.12273

Earley, P. C., & Mosakowski, E. (2004). Cultural intelligence. *Harvard Business Review, 82*(10), 139–146. PMID:15559582

Ehsan, S. M. A. (2021). Managing Workforce Diversity Through Human Resource Management. A. Farazmand (ed.), Global Encyclopedia of Public Administration, Public Policy, and Governance, 1-9. Cornell University.

Fang, Y., Dai, X., & Zhang, X. (2021). An empirical study of the relationship between inclusive leadership and business model innovation. *Leadership and Organization Development Journal, 42*(3), 480–494. doi:10.1108/LODJ-11-2019-0484

Filstad, C., Traavik, L. E., & Gorli, M. (2019). Belonging at work: The experiences, representations, and meanings of belonging. *Journal of Workplace Learning, 31*(2), 116–142. doi:10.1108/JWL-06-2018-0081

Fu, S., Cheng, X., Su, L., Bilgihan, A., & Okumus, F. (2020). Designing collaboration process facilitation in hotel management teams to improve collaboration performance. *International Journal of Hospitality Management, 88*, 102527. doi:10.1016/j.ijhm.2020.102527

Fujimoto, Y., & Härtel, C. E. J. (2017). Organizational diversity learning framework: Going beyond diversity training programs. *Personnel Review, 46*(6), 1120–1141. doi:10.1108/PR-09-2015-0254

Gibbons, J. M. (2006). *Employee engagement: A review of current research and its implications*. Conference Board.

Goswami, S., & Kishor, B. (2018). Exploring the relationship between workforce diversity, inclusion and employee engagement. *Drishtikon: A Management Journal, 9*(1), 65-89.

Gouldner, A. W. (1960). The norm of reciprocity: A preliminary statement. *American Sociological Review, 25*(2), 161–178. doi:10.2307/2092623

Goulet, L., Krentz, C., & Christiansen, H. (2003). Collaboration in education: The phenomenon and process of working together. *The Alberta Journal of Educational Research, 49*(4), 325–340.

Granovetter, M. (1985). Economic action and social structure: The problem of embeddedness. *American Journal of Sociology, 91*(3), 481–510. doi:10.1086/228311

Grossnickle, E. M. (2016). Disentangling curiosity: Dimensionality, definitions, and distinctions from interest in educational contexts. *Educational Psychology Review, 28*(1), 23–60. doi:10.100710648-014-9294-y

Guillaume, Y. R., Dawson, J. F., Woods, S. A., Sacramento, C. A., & West, M. A. (2013). Getting diversity at work to work: What we know and what we still don't know. *Journal of Occupational and Organizational Psychology, 86*(2), 123–141. doi:10.1111/joop.12009

Guinalíu, M., & Jordán, P. (2016). Building trust in the leader of virtual work teams. *Spanish Journal of Marketing-ESIC, 20*(1), 58–70. doi:10.1016/j.reimke.2016.01.003

Harrison, J. K., & Brower, H. H. (2011). The impact of cultural intelligence and psychological hardiness on homesickness among study abroad students. *Frontiers: The Interdisciplinary Journal of Study Abroad, 21*(1), 41–62. doi:10.36366/frontiers.v21i1.303

Harter, J. K., Schmidt, F. L., & Hayes, T. L. (2002). Business-unit-level relationship between employee satisfaction, employee engagement, and business outcomes: A meta-analysis. *The Journal of Applied Psychology*, *87*(2), 268–279. doi:10.1037/0021-9010.87.2.268 PMID:12002955

Hirak, R., Peng, A. C., Carmeli, A., & Schaubroeck, J. M. (2012). Linking leader inclusiveness to work unit performance: The importance of psychological safety and learning from failures. *The Leadership Quarterly*, *23*(1), 107–117. doi:10.1016/j.leaqua.2011.11.009

Hollander, E. P. (2009). *Inclusive leadership: The essential leader-follower relationship*. Routledge.

Hsiao, A., Auld, C., & Ma, E. (2015). Perceived organizational diversity and employee behavior. *International Journal of Hospitality Management*, *48*, 102–112. doi:10.1016/j.ijhm.2015.04.009

IES. (2004). *Employee Studies*. The Institute for Employment Studies. http://www.employmentstudies. co.uk/system/files/resources/files/408.pdf

Itam, U., & Bagali, M. M. (2019). Diversity and inclusion management: a focus on employee engagement. In Gender and Diversity: Concepts, Methodologies, Tools, and Applications (pp. 1771-1788). IGI Global.. doi:10.4018/978-1-5225-6912-1.ch093

James, J. B., McKechnie, S., Swanberg, J., & Besen, E. (2013). Exploring the workplace impact of intentional/unintentional age discrimination. *Journal of Managerial Psychology*, *28*(7/8), 907–927. doi:10.1108/JMP-06-2013-0179

Jolly, P. M., & Lee, L. (2021). Silence is not golden: Motivating employee voice through inclusive leadership. *Journal of Hospitality & Tourism Research (Washington, D.C.)*, *45*(6), 1092–1113. doi:10.1177/1096348020963699

Jones, J. R., & Harter, J. K. (2005). Race effects on the employee engagement turnover intention relationship. *Journal of Leadership & Organizational Studies*, *11*(2), 78–88. doi:10.1177/107179190501100208

Kahn, W. A. (1990). Psychological conditions of personal engagement and disengagement at work. *Academy of Management Journal*, *33*(4), 692–724. doi:10.2307/256287

Khan, M. W., & Altaf, M. (2015). Important dimensions influencing employee engagement in organizations of Pakistan. *Journal of Business and Management Research*, *9*(1), 270–275.

Khattak, S. R., Zada, M., Nouman, M., Rahman, S. U., Fayaz, M., Ullah, R., Salazar-Sepúlveda, G., Vega-Muñoz, A., & Contreras-Barraza, N. (2022). Investigating Inclusive Leadership and Pro-Social Rule Breaking in Hospitality Industry: Important Role of Psychological Safety and Leadership Identification. *International Journal of Environmental Research and Public Health, 19*(14), 8291. doi:10.3390/ijerph19148291 PMID:35886142

Kirton, G., & Greene, A. M. (2015). *The Dynamics of Managing Diversity: A Critical Approach*. Routledge. doi:10.4324/9781315767147

Korkmaz, A. V., van Engen, M. L., Knappert, L., & Schalk, R. (2022). About and beyond leading uniqueness and belongingness: A systematic review of inclusive leadership research. *Human Resource Management Review, 32*(4), 100894. doi:10.1016/j.hrmr.2022.100894

Kouzes, J. M., & Posner, B. Z. (2023). *The leadership challenge: How to make extraordinary things happen in organizations*. John Wiley & Sons.

Krebs, V. (2007). Managing the 21st century organization. *ihrim Journal, 11*(4), 2-8.

Kular, S., Gatenby, M., Rees, C., Soane, E., and Truss, K. (2008). *Employee Engagement: A literature review*. Kingston University.

Kumar, V., & Pansari, A. (2016). Competitive advantage through engagement. *JMR, Journal of Marketing Research, 53*(4), 497–514. doi:10.1509/jmr.15.0044

Kundu, S. C., & Mor, A. (2017). Workforce diversity and organizational performance: A study of IT industry in India. *Employee Relations, 39*(2), 160–183. doi:10.1108/ER-06-2015-0114

Lall-Trail, S. F., Salter, N. P., & Xu, X. (2021). How Personality Relates to Attitudes Toward Diversity and Workplace Diversity Initiatives. *Personality and Social Psychology Bulletin*, 01461672211057755. PMID:34930046

Landells, E. M., & Albrecht, S. L. (2019). Perceived organizational politics, engagement, and stress: The mediating influence of meaningful work. *Frontiers in Psychology, 10*, 1612. doi:10.3389/fpsyg.2019.01612 PMID:31354596

LePine, J. A., Colquitt, J. A., & Erez, A. (2000). Adaptability to changing task contexts: Effects of general cognitive ability, conscientiousness, and openness to experience. *Personnel Psychology, 53*(3), 563–593. doi:10.1111/j.1744-6570.2000.tb00214.x

Li, H., Feng, Z., Liu, C., & Cheng, D. (2014). The impact of relative leader-member exchange on employees' work behaviors as mediated by psychological contract fulfillment. *Social Behavior and Personality, 42*(1), 79–88. doi:10.2224bp.2014.42.1.79

Liao, Y., & Thomas, D. C. (2020). Conceptualizing cultural intelligence. In *Cultural intelligence in the world of work* (pp. 17–30). Springer. doi:10.1007/978-3-030-18171-0_2

Liu, X. R., Yu, J. J., Guo, Q., & Li, J. J. (2022). Employee engagement, its antecedents and effects on business performance in hospitality industry: a multilevel analysis. *International Journal of Contemporary Hospitality Management.*

Luu, T. T., Rowley, C., & Vo, T. T. (2019). Addressing employee diversity to foster their work engagement. *Journal of Business Research*, *95*, 303–315. doi:10.1016/j.jbusres.2018.08.017

Maalouf, G. Y. (2019). Effects of collaborative leadership on organizational performance. *International Journal of Multidisciplinary Research and Development*, *6*(1), 138–144. doi:10.22271/ijmrd.2019.v6.i1.25

MacLeod, D., & Clarke, N. (2011). *Engaging for success: enhancing performance through employee engagement, a report to Government.* IoE.

Madera, J. M., Dawson, M., & Neal, J. A. (2013). Hotel managers' perceived diversity climate and job satisfaction: The mediating effects of role ambiguity and conflict. *International Journal of Hospitality Management*, *35*, 28–34. doi:10.1016/j.ijhm.2013.05.001

Malik, M. S., Suleman, F., Ali, N., & Arshad, F. (2017). An Empirical Analysis of Impact of Inclusive Leadership on Employee Engagement in International Non-Government Organizations (INGO's) of Punjab (Pakistan). *International Journal of Economics and Management Science*, *6*, 2–6.

Manoharan, A., Madera, J. M., & Singal, M. (2021). Walking the talk in diversity management: Exploring links between strategic statements, management practices, and external recognition. *International Journal of Hospitality Management*, *94*, 102864. doi:10.1016/j.ijhm.2021.102864

Maslach, C., Schaufeli, W. B., & Leiter, M. P. (2001). Job burnout. *Annual Review of Psychology*, *52*(1), 397–422. doi:10.1146/annurev.psych.52.1.397 PMID:11148311

Mathis, R. L., & Jackson, J. H. (2010). *Human resource management.* South-Western College.

Mayan, M., Lo, S., Oleschuk, M., Paucholo, A., & Laing, D. (2016). Leadership in community-based participatory research: Individual to collective. *Engaged Scholar Journal: Community-Engaged Research, Teaching, and Learning*, *2*(2), 11–24.

Meraku, A. (2017). Role of leadership in organizational effectiveness. *Journal of Economics. Business and Management*, *5*(11), 336–340.

Mohanty, A., Pradhan, R. K., & Jena, L. K. (2015). Curiosity and Meaning of life leading towards Personal Growth: The role of Emotional Intelligence. *Journal of the Indian Academy of Applied Psychology*, *41*(2), 1–35.

Mone, E., Eisinger, C., Guggenheim, K., Price, B., & Stine, C. (2011). Performance management at the wheel: Driving employee engagement in organizations. *Journal of Business and Psychology*, *26*(2), 205–212. doi:10.100710869-011-9222-9

Mor Barak, M. E., Lizano, E. L., Kim, A., Duan, L., Rhee, M. K., Hsiao, H. Y., & Brimhall, K. C. (2016). The promise of diversity management for climate of inclusion: A state-of-the-art review and meta-analysis. *Human Service Organizations, Management, Leadership & Governance*, *40*(4), 305–333. doi:10.1080/23303131.2016.1138915

Nembhard, I. M., & Edmondson, A. C. (2006). Making it safe: The effects of leader inclusiveness and professional status on psychological safety and improvement efforts in health care teams. Journal of Organizational Behavior: *The International Journal of Industrial. Journal of Organizational Behavior*, *27*(7), 941–966. doi:10.1002/job.413

Nishii, L. H., Khattab, J., Shemla, M., & Paluch, R. M. (2018). A multi-level process model for understanding diversity practice effectiveness. *The Academy of Management Annals*, *12*(1), 37–82. doi:10.5465/annals.2016.0044

Nishii, L. H., & Mayer, D. M. (2009). Do inclusive leaders help to reduce turnover in diverse groups? The moderating role of leader–member exchange in the diversity to turnover relationship. *The Journal of Applied Psychology*, *94*(6), 1412–1426. doi:10.1037/a0017190 PMID:19916652

Obuobisa-Darko, T., & Domfeh, K. A. (2019). Leader behaviour to achieve employee engagement in Ghana: A qualitative study. *International Journal of Public Leadership*, *15*(1), 19–37. doi:10.1108/IJPL-04-2018-0018

Ongori, H., & Agolla, J. E. (2007). Critical review of literature on workforce diversity. *African journal of business management, 1*(4). 072-076

Perrin, T. (2003). Working today: Understanding what drives employee engagement. *The 2003 Towers Perrin talent report.* Perrin Talent. http://www.keepem.com/doc_files/Towers_Perrin_Talent_2003%28TheFinal%29.pdf

Perry, E. L., Block, C. J., & Noumair, D. A. (2020). Leading in: Inclusive leadership, inclusive climates and sexual harassment. *Equality, Diversity and Inclusion*, *40*(4), 430–447. doi:10.1108/EDI-04-2019-0120

Prime, J., & Salib, E. R. (2014). *Inclusive leadership: The view from six countries.* Catalyst. https://www.catalyst.org/research/inclusive-leadership-the-view-from-six-countries/

Ragins, B. R., & Gonzalez, J. A. (2003). Understanding diversity in organizations: getting a grip on a slippery construct. In J. Greenberg (Ed.), *Organizational Behavior: The State of the Science* (2nd ed., pp. 125–163). Lawrence Erlbaum Associates.

Randel, A. E., Galvin, B. M., Shore, L. M., Ehrhart, K. H., Chung, B. G., Dean, M. A., & Kedharnath, U. (2018). Inclusive leadership: Realizing positive outcomes through belongingness and being valued for uniqueness. *Human Resource Management Review*, *28*(2), 190–203. doi:10.1016/j.hrmr.2017.07.002

Rayner, S. (2009). Educational diversity and learning leadership: A proposition, some principles and a model of inclusive leadership? *Educational Review*, *61*(4), 433–447. doi:10.1080/00131910903404004

Rezvani, A., Chang, A., Wiewiora, A., Ashkanasy, N. M., Jordan, P. J., & Zolin, R. (2016). Manager emotional intelligence and project success: The mediating role of job satisfaction and trust. *International Journal of Project Management*, *34*(7), 1112–1122. doi:10.1016/j.ijproman.2016.05.012

Rich, B. L., Lepine, J. A., & Crawford, E. R. (2010). Job engagement: Antecedents and effects on job performance. *Academy of Management Journal*, *53*(3), 617–635. doi:10.5465/amj.2010.51468988

Riffkin, R., & Harter, J. (2016). *Using Employee Engagement to Build a Diverse Workforce*. Gallup Inc.

Rijamampianina, R., & Carmichael, T. (2005). A pragmatic and holistic approach to managing diversity. *Problems and Perspectives in Management*, (1), 109–117.

Robbins, S. P., & Judge, T. (2017). *Organizational behavior*. Pearson Boston.

Roberge, M. É., & Van Dick, R. (2010). Recognizing the benefits of diversity: When and how does diversity increase group performance? *Human Resource Management Review*, *20*(4), 295–308. doi:10.1016/j.hrmr.2009.09.002

Roberson, Q., & Perry, J. L. (2022). Inclusive leadership in thought and action: A thematic analysis. *Group & Organization Management*, *47*(4), 755–778. doi:10.1177/10596011211013161

Roberson, Q. M. (2006). Disentangling the meanings of diversity and inclusion in organizations. *Group & Organization Management, 31*(2), 212–236. doi:10.1177/1059601104273064

Saks, A. M. (2006). Antecedents and consequences of employee engagement. *Journal of Managerial Psychology, 21*(7), 600–619. doi:10.1108/02683940610690169

Saks, A. M., & Gruman, J. A. (2014). What do we really know about employee engagement? *Human Resource Development Quarterly, 25*(2), 155–182. doi:10.1002/hrdq.21187

Saxena, A. (2014). Workforce diversity: A key to improve productivity. *Procedia Economics and Finance, 11*, 76–85. doi:10.1016/S2212-5671(14)00178-6

Schaufeli, W. B., Salanova, M., González-Romá, V., & Bakker, A. B. (2002). The measurement of engagement and burnout: A two sample confirmatory factor analytic approach. *Journal of Happiness Studies, 3*(1), 71–92. doi:10.1023/A:1015630930326

Sharma, N. E., Chaudhary, N. E., & Singh, V. K. E. (2019). *Management techniques for employee engagement in contemporary organizations*. Business Science Reference/IGI Global. doi:10.4018/978-1-5225-7799-7

Shen, H., & Jiang, H. (2019). Engaged at work? An employee engagement model in public relations. *Journal of Public Relations Research, 31*(1-2), 32–49. doi:10.1080/1062726X.2019.1585855

Shen, J., Chanda, A., D'netto, B., & Monga, M. (2009). Managing diversity through human resource management: An international perspective and conceptual framework. *International Journal of Human Resource Management, 20*(2), 235–251. doi:10.1080/09585190802670516

Shenoy, V., & Kumar, M. (2021). Common biases found in the workplace: Visible and invisible inequalities. *Strategic HR Review, 20*(5), 183–185. doi:10.1108/SHR-10-2021-188

Shore, L., Randel, A., Chung, B., Dean, M., Ehrhart, K., & Singh, G. (2011). Inclusion and diversity in work groups: A review and model for future research. *Journal of Management, 37*(4), 1262–1289. doi:10.1177/0149206310385943

Shore, L. M., & Chung, B. G. (2022). Inclusive leadership: How leaders sustain or discourage work group inclusion. *Group & Organization Management, 47*(4), 723–754. doi:10.1177/1059601121999580

Shu, C. Y., & Lazatkhan, J. (2017). Effect of leader-member exchange on employee envy and work behavior moderated by self-esteem and neuroticism. *Journal of Work and Organizational Psychology, 33*(1), 69–81. doi:10.1016/j.rpto.2016.12.002

Shu, Q., & Wang, Y. (2021). Collaborative leadership, collective action, and community governance against public health crises under uncertainty: A case study of the quanjingwan community in China. *International Journal of Environmental Research and Public Health, 18*(2), 598. doi:10.3390/ijerph18020598 PMID:33445697

Shuck, B. (2011). Four Emerging Perspectives of Employee Engagement: An integrative literature review. *Human Resource Development Review, 10*(3), 304–328. doi:10.1177/1534484311410840

Shuck, B., Osam, K., Zigarmi, D., & Nimon, K. (2017). Definitional and conceptual muddling: Identifying the positionality of employee engagement and defining the construct. *Human Resource Development Review, 16*(3), 263–293. doi:10.1177/1534484317720622

Shuck, B., & Wollard, K. (2010). Employee engagement and HRD: A seminal review of the foundations. *Human Resource Development Review, 9*(1), 89–110. doi:10.1177/1534484309353560

Sternberg, R. J., Siriner, I., Oh, J., & Wong, C. H. (2022). Cultural Intelligence: What Is It and How Can It Effectively Be Measured? *Journal of Intelligence, 10*(3), 54. doi:10.3390/jintelligence10030054 PMID:35997410

Sternberg, R. J., Wong, C. H., & Kreisel, A. P. (2021). Understanding and assessing cultural intelligence: Maximum-performance and typical-performance approaches. *Journal of Intelligence, 9*(3), 45. doi:10.3390/jintelligence9030045 PMID:34564293

Thomas, D. C., Liao, Y., Aycan, Z., Cerdin, J. L., Pekerti, A. A., Ravlin, E. C., Stahl, G. K., Lazarova, M. B., Fock, H., Arli, D., Moeller, M., Okimoto, T. G., & Van De Vijver, F. (2015). Cultural intelligence: A theory-based, short form measure. *Journal of International Business Studies, 46*(9), 1099–1118. doi:10.1057/jibs.2014.67

Tran, T. B. H., & Choi, S. B. (2019). Effects of inclusive leadership on organizational citizenship behaviour: The mediating roles of organizational justice and learning culture. *Journal of Pacific Rim Psychology, 13*, 1–11.

Triguero-Sánchez, R., Peña-Vinces, J., & Guillen, J. (2018). How to improve firm performance through employee diversity and organisational culture. *Revista Brasileira de Gestão de Negócios, 20*(3), 378–400. doi:10.7819/rbgn.v20i3.3303

Uhl-Bien, M. (2006). Relational leadership theory: Exploring the social processes of leadership and organizing. *The Leadership Quarterly*, *17*(6), 654–676. doi:10.1016/j.leaqua.2006.10.007

Vakira, E., Shereni, N. C., Ncube, C. M., & Ndlovu, N. (2022). The effect of inclusive leadership on employee engagement, mediated by psychological safety in the hospitality industry. *Journal of Hospitality and Tourism Insights*.

Van Dyne, L., Ang, S., Ng, K. Y., Rockstuhl, T., Tan, M. L., & Koh, C. (2012). Sub-dimensions of the four factor model of cultural intelligence: Expanding the conceptualization and measurement of cultural intelligence. *Social and Personality Psychology Compass*, *6*(4), 295–313. doi:10.1111/j.1751-9004.2012.00429.x

Van Gulick, R. (2000). Inward and upward: Reflection, introspection, and self-awareness. *Philosophical Topics*, *28*(2), 275–305. doi:10.5840/philtopics200028222

Van Knippenberg, D., De Dreu, C. K., & Homan, A. C. (2004). Work group diversity and group performance: An integrative model and research agenda. *The Journal of Applied Psychology*, *89*(6), 1008–1022. doi:10.1037/0021-9010.89.6.1008 PMID:15584838

Van Knippenberg, D., & Schippers, M. C. (2007). Work group diversity. *Annual Review of Psychology*, *58*(1), 515–541. doi:10.1146/annurev.psych.58.110405.085546 PMID:16903805

Vorina, A., Simonič, M., & Vlasova, M. (2017). An analysis of the relationship between job satisfaction and employee engagement. *Economic themes, 55*(2), 243-262

Walumbwa, F. O., Wu, C., & Orwa, B. (2008). Contingent reward transactional leadership, work attitudes, and organizational citizenship behavior: The role of procedural justice climate perceptions and strength. *The Leadership Quarterly*, *19*(3), 251–265. doi:10.1016/j.leaqua.2008.03.004

Witte, L. (2012). Creating and Leading in an Environment of Collaboration. *SPNHA Review*, *8*(1), 7.

Woodard, C. R., & Pury, C. L. (2007). The construct of courage: Categorization and measurement. *Consulting Psychology Journal*, *59*(2), 135–147. doi:10.1037/1065-9293.59.2.135

Xanthopoulou, D., Bakker, A. B., Demerouti, E., & Schaufeli, W. B. (2009). Reciprocal relationships between job resources, personal resources, and work engagement. *Journal of Vocational Behavior*, *74*(3), 235–244. doi:10.1016/j.jvb.2008.11.003

Ye, Q., Wang, D., & Li, X. (2018). Promoting employees' learning from errors by inclusive leadership: Do positive mood and gender matter? *Baltic Journal of Management*, *13*(1), 125–142. doi:10.1108/BJM-05-2017-0160

ADDITIONAL READING

Byrne, Z. S. (2022). *Understanding employee engagement: Theory, research, and practice*. Routledge. doi:10.4324/9781003171133

Ferdman, B. M., & Deane, B. (2014). *Diversity at work: The practice of inclusion*. Jossey-Bass.

Jerónimo, H. M., Henriques, P. L., & Carvalho, S. I. (2022). Being inclusive boosts impact of diversity practices on employee engagement. *Management Research: Journal of the Iberoamerican Academy of Management*, *20*(2), 129–147. doi:10.1108/MRJIAM-05-2021-1175

Kuknor, S. C., & Bhattacharya, S. (2022). Inclusive leadership: New age leadership to foster organizational inclusion. *European Journal of Training and Development*, *46*(9), 771–797. doi:10.1108/EJTD-07-2019-0132

Van Knippenberg, D., & van Ginkel, W. P. (2022). A diversity mindset perspective on inclusive leadership. *Group & Organization Management*, *47*(4), 779–797. doi:10.1177/1059601121997229

Wuffli, P. A. (2016). *Inclusive leadership: A framework for the global era*. Springer. doi:10.1007/978-3-319-23561-5

KEY TERMS AND DEFINITIONS

Diversity: Diversity, a multidimensional concept, refer to the existence of differences and/or a state of being different among persons based on personal characteristics such as gender, age, ethnicity, marital status, sexual orientation, parental status, education, income, work experience, physical disability, nationality, social status, language, among others.

Employee engagement: An employee's emotional, cognitive, mental and physical commitment towards achieving both his personal and organisational goals.

Employee Management: unified set of activities and processes to effectively use available employee resources to achieve set targets at the individual, departmental and organisational levels.

Inclusive Leadership: The kind of leader who commits to diversity, inclusion and equity and therefore seek to be accessible, available and willing to accept different perspectives from varied individuals without any discrimination.

Leaders: They are individuals who influence their followers to achieve set goals.

Leadership: It is a process of influencing persons to accomplish set targets by using leadership skills and competencies.

Chapter 6
The Need of the Hour in the Corporate Sector:
Inclusive Leadership

Ashwini Yogendra Sonawane
Vishwakarma University, Pune, India

ABSTRACT

Speedy progress in globalization has made corporates and societies very heterogeneous. The way trade is directed and the modes individuals live their work lives are being altered. With an upsurge in cross-cultural groups and foreign investments united with the alteration in social attitudes in the employees, there are rare causes why organizations currently are embracing diversity and inclusion as need of an hour to achieve improved organizational fallouts. Corporates have realized that diverse employees can contribute towards commercial developments at different organizational levels. In many ways, the function of diversity and inclusion are like two sides of the same coin. While a diverse workforce has gained popularity in organizations, most of the time its twin-component inclusion is lost. Be it in research or practice, OI remains a concept under development. Diversity awards have also become an upcoming business trend. In recent years, diversity management (DM) has shifted its focus to that of an inclusive environment.

INTRODUCTION

Inclusion" has developed a catchword in current globalized business domain. Specialists and academicians alike have comprised inclusion as main for the unrelenting competitive advantage of establishments as well as the healthiness and

DOI: 10.4018/978-1-6684-6602-5.ch006

well-being of their personnel. Inclusion is planned as an idiosyncratic diversity management approach (Roberson, 2006) that discourses diversity definitely, slightly than as a trouble that wants to be allocated with (Shore et al., 2009; Zanoni & Janssens, 2007). Inclusion can be allowed by concentrating on the concurrent satisfaction of employees' wants for individuality and belongingness (Shore et al., 2011), so that personnel can be their exclusive natures at exertion while also suffering the sensitivity of being "home-based." When efficiently arranged, this perfect authorizations establishments to ultimately go afar the mere getting of diversity to afford a just and impartial work where every person is preserved as an insider (Ainscow & Sandill, 2010; Hope Pelled, Ledford Jr, & Albers Mohrman, 1999). Consequently, employees can unbridle their full possible, answer to contests, collaborate with others crosswise boundaries, and improve their workplace experiences (Ainscow & Sandill, 2010; Holvino, Ferdman, & Merrill-Sands, 2004; Panicker, Agrawal, & Khandelwal, 2018; Pless & Maak, 2004; Randel et al., 2018; Roberson, 2006; Shore et al., 2011).

Leaders have an imperative role in safeguarding the application of inclusion (Brannen & Thomas, 2010; Chrobot-Mason, Ruderman, & Nishii, 2013; Mor Barak, 2011; Nembhard & Edmondson, 2006). Shore et al. (2011) offered inclusive leadership as one of the background issues donating to inclusion, together with inclusive surrounding and inclusive performs. Over the past three eras, a rivulet of research has been devoted to investigating the confident impressions of inclusive leadership on, for instance, psychosomatic protection (Nembhard & Edmondson, 2006), engrossment in artistic waged (Carmeli, Reiter-Palmon, & Ziv, 2010), facility to cram from blunders (Ye, Wang, & Guo, 2019; Ye, Wang, & Li, 2019), and effort engagement (Choi, Tran, & Park, 2015). Yet, notwithstanding the evidentiary base for the position of inclusive leadership and the courtesy leadership has conventional in the writings (Lacerenza, Reyes, Marlow, Joseph, & Salas, 2017; Parris & Peachey, 2013), inclusive leadership is a recent growth, and several important questions about its conceptualization and theorization endure unrequited (Boekhorst, 2015; Shore & Chung, 2021).

Research on inclusive leadership is pigeon-holed by a variability of standpoints and conceptualizations (e.g., Carmeli et al., 2010; Nembhard & Edmondson, 2006) on which there is as yet no shared covenant (Randel, Dean, Ehrhart, Chung, & Shore, 2016). While researchers have enhanced surviving descriptions with their miscellaneous understandings (e.g., Choi et al., 2015) and stimulated the theory advancing with progressive research models (e.g., Hanh Tran & Choi, 2019; Ye, Wang, & Guo, 2019; Ye, Wang, & Li, 2019), the gradation to which specific charities were beached in model has diverse. This unfinished considerate of the concept and its instruments may create misperception about the environment and special effects of inclusive leadership (Van Knippenberg & Sitkin, 2013) and eventually hinder theoretical breakthroughs (Randel et al., 2018). Consequently, we goal here to examine the prose and combine the available knowledge to provide a conceptualization of inclusive leadership, an overview of the research models calculated to date, and an empathetic of where the pitch stances in footings of its sustaining theories. More explicitly, in this systematic literature review, we discourse two questions:

1. How are inclusive leadership behaviors well-defined in the literature, and how can these descriptions escort the arena in emergent an amalgamated conceptualization of inclusive leadership?
2. How is inclusive leadership hypothesized: What are the backgrounds, devices (mediators), results, and possibilities (moderators) of inclusive leadership, and which supporting theories explain the recommended associations?

To speech the first query, we ran a content analysis and then consolidated the available definitions and descriptions of inclusive leadership behaviors to address the dearth of clearness in investigation and rehearsal about what leaders should do to be inclusive (Shore & Chung, 2021). Ranging existing research and reviews on the topic (e.g., Randel et al., 2018; Shore et al., 2011; Shore & Chung, 2021), our study (1) includes studies published up until April 2021 in this quickly developing field; (2) provides a context-spanning conceptualization (as we did not focus on one specific industry); (3) uncovers nuances of leadership related to belongingness and uniqueness that have not previously been presented thoroughly (e.g., the importance of employee learning and development for uniqueness); and (4) proposes that inclusive leadership goes beyond behaviors targeted at the employee and the team to also include, for example, those supporting organizational initiatives. Whereas earlier work mostly presented inclusive leadership at or within the work group level (Mor Barak, Luria, & Brimhall, 2021), our conceptualization accounts for the multi-level nature of leadership and explicitly considers how inclusive leadership plays out at the organizational level (in addition to the employee and team levels).

To answer the second research question, we analyzed quantitative inclusive leadership studies and provide an overview of the antecedents, mechanisms, outcomes, and contingencies of inclusive leadership and the underpinning theories used. The resulting nomological network, and the overview of theories with the examples of relationships they explain, offer a final key aspect of this study that sets the stage for future theoretical advancements on inclusive leadership.

Below mentioned is the diagrammatic representation of Process of reviewing based on PRISMA-2020. It shows identification of studies via data base in detail.

Ayfer Veli Korkmaz, Marloes L. van Engen, Lena Knappert, René Schalk, Human Resource Management Review,Volume 32, Issue 4, 2022, 100894, ISSN 1053-4822, https://doi.org/10.1016/j.hrmr.2022.100894.(https://www.sciencedirect.com/science/article/pii/S105348222200002X)

Figure 1. Process of reviewing based on PRISMA-2020
Source- https://www.sciencedirect.com/science/article/pii/S105348222200002X

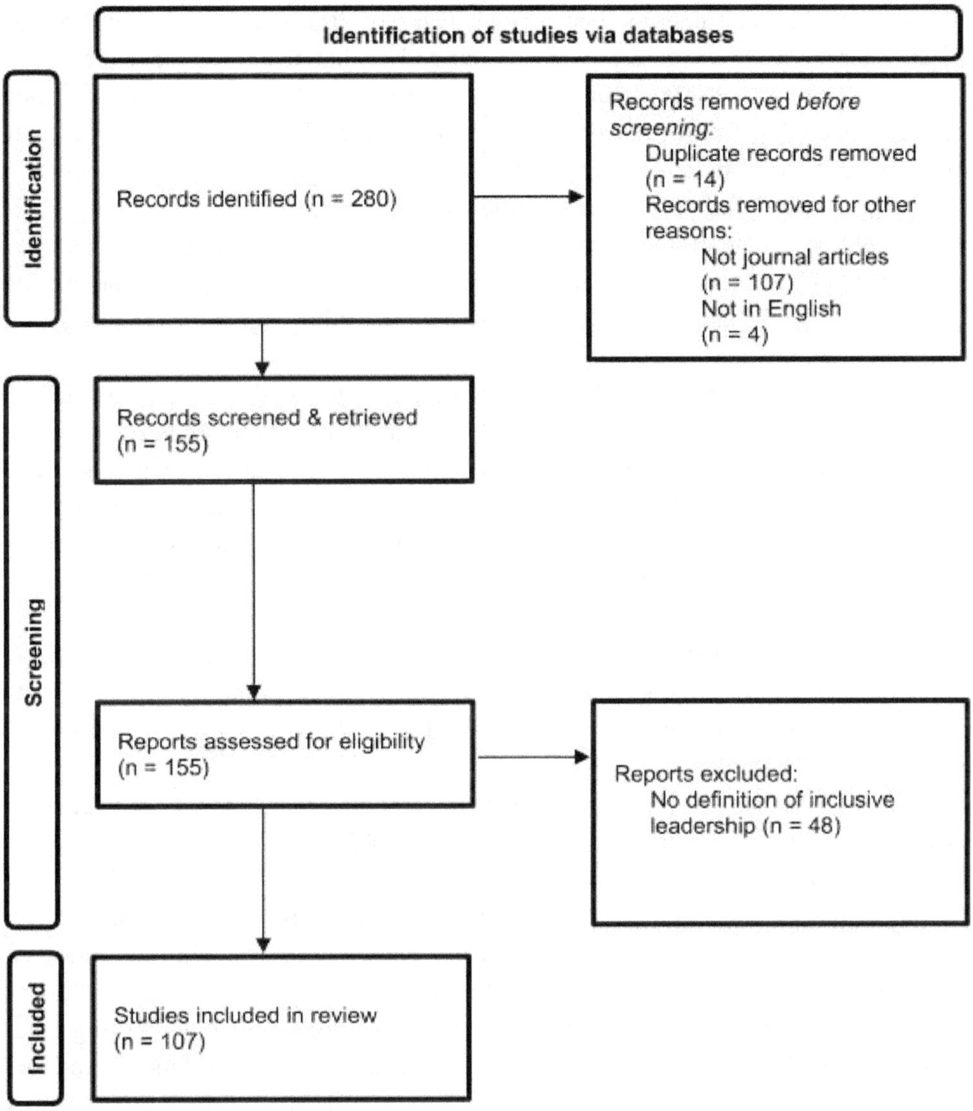

Analysis Approach

We initially assessed and categorised articles based on their study methodology. Our dataset* included 58 quantitative studies (like Javed et al., 2019), 24 conceptual papers (like reviews and discussion papers; Perry, Block, and Noumair, 2020; Shore and Chung, 2021), 18 qualitative studies (like interviews and ethnographic designs;

Sugiyama, Cavanagh, van Esch, Bilimoria, and Brown, 2016), and seven mixed-methods studies (e.g., Weiss, Kolbe, Grote, Spahn, & Grande, 2018). The data was then subjected to a content analysis (Elo & Kyngäs, 2008). The first author began the analysis using the exact terms (first-order codes) that described inclusive leader behaviours from the articles, such as "valuing variety" and "tolerating errors." After that, we reduced the first-order codes into common second-order codes (themes) that still represent different behaviours of inclusive leaders, such as "ensure everyone is fairly represented" and "praise achievements".

We held open discussions among the author team to make sure the themes were categorised into the most pertinent categories. In order to better organise the themes (N = 63), eleven broad categories were created, including "guarantee equity" and "recognise employees' contributions."

Next, it was explained what levels these inclusive leadership behaviours aim to affect (employee, team, or organization). The target level for each theme (of the 63) was separately coded by eight researchers (in leadership, organisational behaviour, and/or human resources [HR]), including the authors, in order to assemble a diverse variety of expert viewpoints on this subject. It was necessary to choose the level (i.e., employee, team, or organisation) that the researchers felt was most relevant to each topic.

The percentage agreement (PA) formula, which calculates interrater agreement as the number of concordant responses divided by the total number of responses by 100%, was used to determine the levels. PA >62.5% was used to define the percentage agreement.

The levels for each subject and consequently category were changed as necessary based on the level that garnered the highest level of agreement. The author team made the final judgement when the level of agreement was low (PA 62.5%) or when researchers added additional remarks regarding the themes. We made the decision to omit certain themes in certain instances because their descriptions (such as "contributes to group processes") lacked clarity, were overly detailed (such as "invite team to social initiatives"), or overlapped with other codes (such as "having open communication") (N = 12). In order to make several topics more understandable for readers, we also chose to reword some of the descriptions (for example, "helps group members fully contribute" was changed to "helps employee to contribute") (N=5). Finally, we ended up with 50 themes mapped against 10 categories.

In the end, we had 50 themes mapped to 10 categories. We discovered four fundamental dimensions by taking both theory and categories into account (Gioia, Corley, & Hamilton, 2013): (1) promoting an employee's individuality, which includes the categories "supporting employees as individuals," "promoting diversity," "empowering employees," and "contributing to employees' L&D"; (2) enhancing team cohesiveness, which includes the categories "ensuring equity," "building relationships," and "sharing decision-making"; (3) expressing gratitude, which includes the category "recognising efforts and contributions"; and (4) providing support. In the findings section, it is further explained what these dimensions and categories represent.

Theorizing about inclusive leadership was the topic of our second research question. We addressed this by limiting our article collection to quantitative research solely and gathering data on the antecedents, mechanisms, outcomes, and contingencies of inclusive leadership that have been experimentally explored, as well as the theories employed to investigate the suggested correlations. Before clustering the variables based on the variables they are linked with, we first grouped the variables based on their types (for example, antecedents). Employee variables are those that are connected to employees. They indicate factors specific to each employee, such as their own actions or experiences (such as good spirits among employees or organisational citizenship activity). Team variables (such as team performance) and organisational factors underwent a similar grouping (e.g., power distance). In addition, we discovered leader-related variables that we added to the overview as a leader variable (such as conflicts between leaders' work and family obligations). After completing this process, we created a nomological network that visualised the list of variables used in earlier empirical study (see Eva, Robin, Sendjaya, van Dierendonck, & Liden, 2019). In order to understand how these theories might aid academics in the area in comprehending the existence and nature of inclusive leadership, we collated the underlying theories describing the links between inclusive leadership and other characteristics.

RESULTS

While conducting this study, we first noted that the field of inclusive leadership is developing and has been the subject of theoretical and empirical papers. From a variety of angles, the conceptual papers and reviews offered insights regarding inclusive leadership. Other conceptual papers and reviews intended to comprehend inclusive leadership in various contexts, such as virtual teams or the health care industry, while others sought to comprehend inclusive leadership in relation to other leadership styles, such as spiritual leadership (Gotsis & Grimani, 2017). (Bradley, 2020).

The relationship between inclusive leadership and organisational factors like the climate for inclusion (Mor Barak et al., 2021), organisational inclusion (Kuknor and Bhattacharya, 2020a, 2020b), or sexual harassment was covered in a few conceptual articles (Perry et al., 2020). The focus on conceptual papers also included studies on the influence of inclusive leaders on underrepresented workers (Shore & Chung,

2021) and the benefits of inclusive leadership in relation to gender stereotyping (Minehart, Foldy, Long & Weller, 2020).

Also, a lot of studies helped to conceptualise inclusive leadership. For instance, leader inclusion is described as one of the organisational inclusion structures in a review on inclusive workplaces (Shore, Cleveland, & Sanchez, 2018). Similar to this, one study (Randel et al., 2018) focuses on inclusive leadership and offers a conceptualization based on optimal uniqueness theory (Brewer, 1991) and the definition of inclusion at work put forth by Shore et al (2011).

We recognise the importance of the contributions made by these conceptual works and reviews. While each publication contributes to our understanding of inclusive leadership, we also note several areas where our systematic literature evaluation might be expanded. It is possible to advance the conceptualization and theorization of inclusive leadership by integrating both the conceptual and empirical works.

A Comprehensive Theory of Inclusive Leadership

Based on the themes (N = 50), categories (N = 10) and dimensions (N = 4) found at the conclusion of our content analysis, which are shown in Table 1, we have created a consolidated conception of inclusive leadership. We have included references to the articles where the topics may be found in the table. Sometimes writers cited definitions from earlier works that weren't included in the sample of papers under examination. In these instances, we provide indirect reference to the concept ("as referenced in").

Fostering Individuality in Employees

This first dimension consists of four categories that we conceptualise on the employee level because they are based on the relationship between the leader and their employees. This first dimension resonates with the need for uniqueness defined in optimal distinctiveness theory (Brewer, 1991; Shore et al., 2011). The first category is "supporting workers as persons," which entails leaders paying attention to the employee (for instance, their sentiments, Ye, Wang, & Li, 2019), providing direction (for instance, Wang et al., 2019), and demonstrating availability (Carmeli et al., 2010). The second category is "promoting diversity," which is based on the notions that inclusive leaders are able to respect an employee's distinctive qualities (e.g., Randel et al., 2018) or actively encourage an employee to contribute (e.g., Bradley, 2020). (e.g., Derven, 2016).

"Empowering employees" is a category that includes allowing The third category is "empowering workers," which involves giving each employee the freedom to decide for themselves what to do (Mansoor, Farrukh, Wu, & Abdul Wahab, 2021).

Table 1. Aspects, divisions, and themes of inclusive leadership

Aspects	Divisions	Themes
Fostering Employee's Uniqueness (E*)	Supporting employees as individuals	Shows concern about employee's feelings (e.g., Ye, Wang, & Li, 2019)
		Shows concern about employee's expectations (e.g., Wang et al., 2019)
		Shows concern about employee's interests (e.g., Hollander, 2009 as cited in Choi et al., 2017)
		Offers guidance to the employee (e.g., Wang et al., 2019)
		Exhibits accessibility to the employee (e.g., Carmeli et al., 2010)
		Exhibits availability to the employee (e.g., Carmeli et al., 2010)
		Shows emotional support to the employee (e.g., Hollander, 2009 as cited in Fang et al., 2021)
	Promoting diversity	Recognizes employee's individual differences (e.g., Bradley, 2020)
		Exhibits openness to the employee (e.g., Carmeli et al., 2010)
		Values employee's uniqueness (e.g., Randel et al., 2018)
		Helps employee to contribute (e.g., Derven, 2016)
		Listens to employee's ideas (e.g., Meeuwissen, Gijselaers, van Oorschot, Wolfhagen, & Oude Egbrink, 2021)
	Empowering employees	Collaborating during decision-making with the employee (e.g., Nembhard & Edmondson, 2006)
		Encourages the employee to become involved in organizational activities (e.g., Randel et al., 2018)
		Promotes opportunity to share the ideas on how to perform work (e.g., Mir et al., 2021)
	Contributing to employees' Learning and Development (L&D)	Is open to the needs of the employee for development and growth (e.g., Rayner, 2009)
		Helps the employee advance their career prospects (e.g., Sabharwal, 2014 as cited in *Gotsis and Grimani, 2016a, *Gotsis and Grimani, 2016b)
		Provides feedback to the employee (e.g., Hollander, 2009 as cited in Chen et al., 2020)
		Cultivates the ability of the employee to learn and work (e.g., Wang et al., 2019)
		Guides the employee when mistakes are made (e.g., Ospina & El Hadidy, 2011 as cited in Qi et al., 2019)
		Focuses on the employee training (e.g., Fang, Chen, Wang, & Chen, 2019)
Strengthening Belongingness within a Team (T*)	Ensuring equity	Shows moral behavior (e.g., Rayner, 2009)
		Shows unbiased judgement (e.g., Kelan, 2020)
		Ensures justice (e.g., Liu et al., as cited in Fang et al., 2019)
		Distributes reward fairly (e.g., Siyal et al., 2021)
		Makes sure everyone is fairly represented (e.g., Saxena et al., 2019)
	Building relationships	Makes team members feel like they belong and matter (e.g., Sugiyama et al., 2016)
		Supports employees as team members (e.g., Randel et al., 2018)
		Enables effective function of diverse work groups (e.g., *Kuknor and Bhattacharya, 2020b)
		Builds closer connections with employees (e.g., Gallegoes, 2014 as cited in Gotsis & Grimani, 2017)
		Fosters relationships (e.g., Xiaotao et al., 2018)
		Enables respectful interactions within the team (e.g., Minehart et al., 2020)
	Sharing decision-making	Provides reasoning for practices (e.g., *Gotsis and Grimani, 2016a, *Gotsis and Grimani, 2016b)
		Takes actions in collaboration with employees rather than to people (e.g., Amin et al., 2018)
		Fosters transparent decision-making (e.g., Ferdman, 2014 as cited in *Gotsis and Grimani, 2016a, *Gotsis and Grimani, 2016b)
		Consults with workers (e.g., (Nembhard & Edmondson, 2006)
		Builds consensus (e.g., Meeuwissen et al., 2021)
		Includes others in decisions (e.g., Ahmed et al., 2020)

continued on following page

Table 1. Continued

Aspects	Divisions	Themes
Showing Appreciation (E*&T*)	Recognizing efforts and contributions	Notices the efforts (e.g., Hollander, 2009 as cited in Javed et al., 2019)
		Affirms contributions (e.g., Ryan, 2006 as cited in Wang & Shi, 2020)
		Praises achievements (e.g., Qi et al., 2019)
Supporting Organizational Efforts (O*)	Being open to organizational change	Promotes change (e.g., Mansoor et al., 2021)
		Pays attention to new opportunities (e.g., Choi et al., 2017)
		Focuses on organizational development (e.g., Caron et al., 2019)
		Understands and engages with resistance (e.g., Ferdman, 2014 as cited in Gotsis & Grimani, 2017)
	Promoting organizational mission on inclusion	Creates an environment where everyone is heard (e.g., Derven, 2016)
		Communicates how inclusion is related to mission and vision (e.g., Ferdman, 2014 as cited in *Gotsis and Grimani, 2016a, *Gotsis and Grimani, 2016b)
		Facilitates a diverse workforce and inclusion (e.g., Norman et al., 2018)
		Explains how organizational practices and inclusion are aligned (e.g., Luu, 2021)
		Promotes participative management mechanisms (e.g., *Gotsis and Grimani, 2016a, *Gotsis and Grimani, 2016b)

E* = Employee level.
T* = Team level.
O* = Organizational level.

By working together with the staff when making decisions (e.g., Nembhard & Edmondson, 2006), or by encouraging chances for staff to express ideas about how they wish to carry out their work, leaders may ensure employee empowerment (e.g., Mir, Rafique, & Mubarak, 2021). The last benefit of inclusive leaders is "employee learning and development (L&D)." Employees have the chance to strengthen their areas of weakness and build their strengths through L&D as a personal journey. The examined publications define inclusive leadership on this dimension as leaders clearly saying that they are receptive to employees' demands for professional development.

Enhancing Sense of Community Within a Team

The optimum uniqueness theory's inclusion of the demand for belongingness is connected to the second aspect of inclusive leadership (Brewer, 1991; Shore et al., 2011). Because it involves the interactions between the leader and the team as well as among team members, we conceptualise it at the level of the team. According to reviewed articles, leaders can increase a sense of belongingness by "ensuring equity" (Mansoor et al., 2021). This can be done, for instance, by acting morally (Rayner, 2009), making fair decisions (Kelan, 2020), distributing rewards fairly (Siyal, Xin, Umrani, Fatima, & Pal, 2021), or ensuring that team members are fairly represented (e.g., Saxena et al., 2021). According to Sugiyama et al. (2016), establishing belongingness requires leaders to focus on "creating connections," which calls for them to focus on their interactions both with the team as a whole and with each other in order to promote good partnerships (e.g., Xiaotao, Yang, Diaz, & Yu, 2018).

Showing Gratitude

This dimension, which contains the area of "recognising efforts and contributions," deals with how leaders respond to accomplishments and efforts. Leaders acknowledge efforts (e.g., Hollander, 2009 as quoted in Javed et al., 2019), confirm contributions (e.g., Ryan, 2006 as cited in Wang & Shi, 2020), and commend accomplishments to accomplish this (Qi et al., 2019). Due to the fact that efforts can be demonstrated by either one employee or by the team as a whole, the dimension of displaying gratitude is defined across two levels. Similarly, the accomplishments might be made by the team or by the people alone. As a result, both individual employee and team accomplishments may be the focus of the response to efforts and successes, which is characterised as acknowledgment in this dimension.

Assisting Organisational Initiatives

As the fourth and final component of inclusive leadership involves leader behaviours connected to organisational strategy and transformation around inclusion, we define this dimension at the organisational level. This dimension focuses on the relationship between leaders and the organisation, how they support organisational issues, and how they advance the organisations' inclusionary stance. More particularly, the papers under consideration stress the need of inclusive leaders "being open to organisational change," as this may offer up possibilities for experimenting with new concepts and methods of goal-achieving (such as inclusion). Leaders are advised to encourage change (Mansoor et al., 2021), be aware of new opportunities (e.g., Choi, Tran, & Kang, 2017), or concentrate on organisational growth (e.g., Caron et al., 2019). Also, executives who "promote the company objective on the actions listed under "conveying inclusion" include building a diverse workforce, describing how organisational policies are in line with inclusion, and communicating how inclusion is connected to the purpose and vision (e.g., Ferdman, 2014 as referenced in Gotsis and Grimani, 2016a, 2016b) (e.g., Luu, 2021).

An Inclusive Leadership Network With Several Levels

Ayfer Veli Korkmaz, Marloes L. van Engen, Lena Knappert, René Schalk, Human Resource Management Review,Volume 32, Issue 4, 2022, 100894, ISSN 1053-4822, https://doi.org/10.1016/j.hrmr.2022.100894.(https://www.sciencedirect.com/science/article/pii/S105348222200002X)

Figure 2. Based on these data, proposes a comprehensive framework of inclusive leadership
Source- https://www.sciencedirect.com/science/article/pii/S105348222200002X

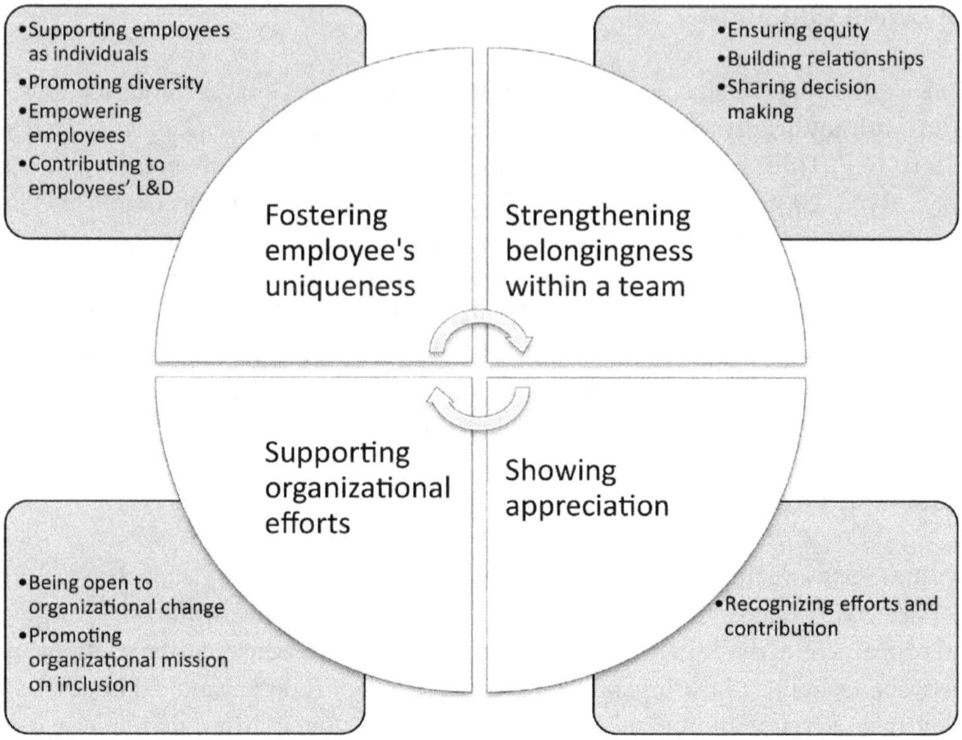

We looked for empirically validated links between inclusive leadership and its antecedents, outcomes, moderators, or mediators and took stock of the underlying theories employed by the researchers in the related studies in order to map the body of literature on inclusive leadership. Our research is shown in Fig. 3 as a nomological network that distinguishes across variables depending on whether a leader's action is directed at the organisational, team, or employee level.

Ayfer Veli Korkmaz, Marloes L. van Engen, Lena Knappert, René Schalk, Human Resource Management Review,Volume 32, Issue 4, 2022, 100894, ISSN 1053-4822,https://doi.org/10.1016/j.hrmr.2022.100894.(https://www.sciencedirect.com/science/article/pii/S105348222200002X)

First, there is a knowledge gap regarding potential strategies to encourage leaders to adopt inclusive leadership behaviours or to choose leaders who already exhibit inclusive leadership behaviours. Antecedents of inclusive leadership have received very little empirical research attention (e.g., Lin, Tsai, & Liu, 2016). In contrast, the effects of inclusive leadership have been extensively researched at

Figure 3. An overview of the variables used in previous empirical studies, shown as a nomological network
Source- https://www.sciencedirect.com/science/article/pii/S105348222200002X

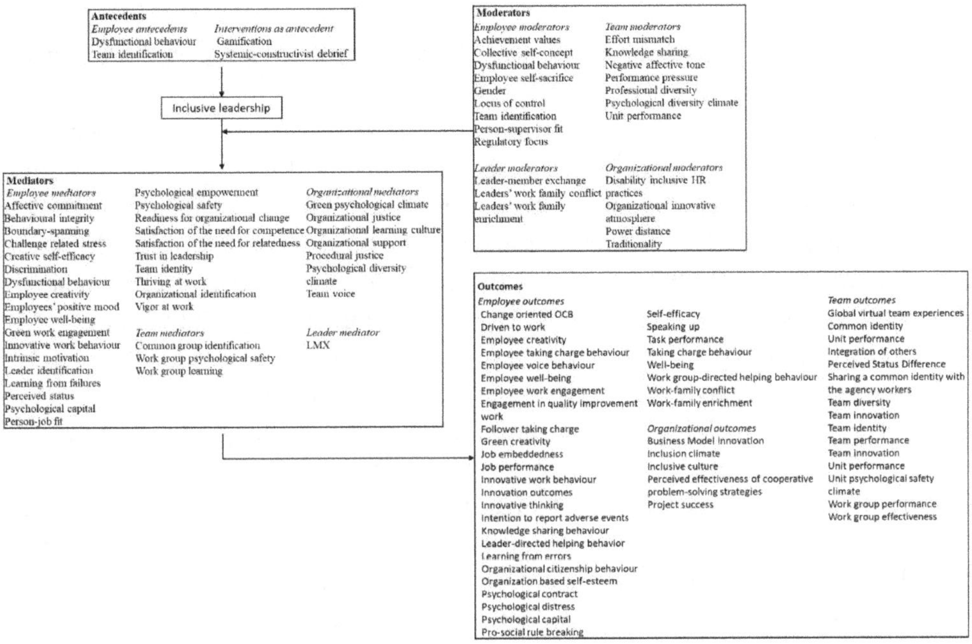

the organisational, team, and employee levels. For instance, Hirak, Peng, Carmeli, and Schaubroeck (2012) looked at unit performance as a team outcome whereas Ye, Wang, and Li (2018) explored employees' learning from mistakes as a result of inclusive leadership. The literature pays very little attention to organisational results. However, there is very little information in the literature about how inclusive leadership affects leaders themselves. A number of processes that operate at different levels have been discovered in relation to mediators. For instance, Fatima, Majeed, and Zulfiqar Ali Shah (2021) discovered that inclusive leadership affects workers' motivation to work through the employee-level theme of employee preparedness for organisational transformation. The connection between inclusive leadership and organisational citizenship behaviour is further mediated by organisational justice, according to Hanh Tran and Choi's (2019) analysis. In contrast, mechanisms aimed at the team level need greater consideration.

The investigation of team-related contingencies, such as the influence of performance pressure on the relationship between inclusive leadership and team voice, has dominated existing research on moderators (Ye, Wang, & Guo, 2019; Ye, Wang, & Li, 2019). However, employee variables have also been taken into account, such as the moderating effect of innovative work behaviour on the relationship between inclusive leadership and challenge-oriented organisational citizenship behaviour (Wang, Wang, Zhou, Li, & Wang, 2020).

The Underlying Concepts of the Researched Research Models

According to the direction of numerous underlying theories, which are mentioned in Table 2 with some instances of the researched relationships organised according to the theories that address them, academics study research models in inclusive leadership research. Our research reveals a wide range of ideas driving the study of inclusive leadership. The dominant theory in the literature is social exchange theory, which is followed by leader-member exchange theory. Both contribute to the understanding of the relationship between inclusive leadership and employee- and organization-related outcomes (e.g., organisational learning culture, Hanh Tran & Choi, 2019; business model innovation, Fang, Dai, & Zhang, 2021). Examples include employee voice, readiness for organisational change, and business model innovation. A crucial theoretical foundation for comprehending the links explored in the literature is also provided by social identity theory. Academics have literature. Social identity theory has mostly been used by academics to describe how inclusive leadership results in employee-related outcomes through encouraging identification with the team or business (e.g., affective commitment, Wang et al., 2020; job embeddedness, Elsaied, 2020).

DISCUSSION

The goal of this systematic literature review is to advance the field of inclusive leadership scholarship by (1) providing a unified conceptualization of inclusive leadership that incorporates earlier definitions and (2) organising the variables under investigation into a nomological network and critically examining theories that have been applied in inclusive leadership research. We shall go into great depth about our results and their theoretical ramifications in the paragraphs that follow.

Integrated Leadership Paradigm That is Inclusive

Our study focuses on the lack of integration between the conceptualizations of inclusive leadership and attempts to address it by building a consolidated conceptualization of inclusive leadership based on the current definitions and descriptions. In order to do this, we consider two factors: what the themes stand for and the level at which a leader is functioning, namely the individual, team, and organisational level. As a consequence, categories and dimensions were established. The first two aspects of inclusive leadership's design, fostering employee individuality and promoting belongingness within a team, were reasonably predictable because each dimension represented one level. Moreover, the notions of uniqueness and belongingness were already the main emphasis of inclusion theory. Expressing thankfulness appears to be a more challenging component due to its dual goals of the individual and the team. Last but not least, supporting organisational activities is a critical component that concentrates on a leader's actions that are focused on organisational factors.

The first two components of our conception basically match a previously proposed paradigm (Randel et al., 2018). Yet, after further refining the element of encouraging employee individuality, our judgement gives this paradigm some new nuance. We believe that "supporting people as individuals" is the first step that leaders should take to promote individuality within their workforce. Inclusive leaders build on the encouragement they currently offer by actively "supporting diversity" and continue with "empowerment of workers." Employee empowerment may provide them a sense of encouragement (Ahearne, Mathieu, & Rapp, 2005; Raub & Robert, 2013).

As L&D enhances employees' distinctive features, it is necessary to "contribute to workers' learning and development (L&D)" in order to realise uniqueness. We view "building connections" as a crucial category that adds to a more comprehensive understanding of the dimension of strengthening belongingness within a team, in addition to "ensuring equality" and "sharing decision-making." Building connections encompasses both the interaction between the team and the leader and the impact leaders have on the relationships within the team itself since leadership is considered as a shared activity between and among individuals (Komives, Lucas, & McMahon, 2013).

According to the desired level, acknowledgment can be given to both specific employees and the entire team. So, we suggest that expressing gratitude may apply to both the specific employee and the team. The notion of appreciation has been studied both independently and as a component of other constructs (such as leadership) in the literature, in addition to its duality in levels (Pfister, Jacobshagen, Kälin, & Semmer, 2020; Siegrist, 2005). Moreover, academics recommended that because of the benefits of appreciation (such as well-being), the idea should be researched in a wider context but as a distinct idea (Baumeister, 2012; Pfister et al., 2020; Sarason, Sarason, Brock, & Pierce, 1996; Stocker et al., 2019). Following the definition of expressing gratitude, the levels it seeks to achieve, and lastly, we propose demonstrating appreciation as a different dimension from the literature's recommendations for studying the subject in isolation.

We have furthermore highlighted encouraging organisational endeavours as a component of inclusive leadership. The literature has acknowledged the value of leadership. As an illustration, companies encourage senior executives to advance justice and decreased prejudice in addition to other activities. According to Dwertmann et al. (2016), leaders are responsible for diversity objectives, and it is critical that leaders and human resource management (HRM) in a company act in a way that promotes inclusion. In other words, the level of support that leaders provide for organisational efforts to promote diversity and inclusion may lessen or change the impact of those efforts (Buengeler, Leroy, & De Stobbeleir, 2018). Hence, encouraging the organization's inclusion mission and being open to organisational change are also necessary for inclusive leadership. As was said throughout the section, we thought about inclusive leadership's multi-level character as we developed a consolidated picture of it.

Future Research Suggestions

In this systematic literature review, we attempted to explain what inclusive leadership means and summarise the present status of research on this issue by reviewing the factors researched together with the theories supporting these variables. We have sought to construct a framework of inclusive leadership that is indicative of the concepts brought forward to date by the numerous scholars working in this topic. The necessity for this endeavour stemmed from the existence of a substantial number of definitions of inclusive leadership and the misalignment between different conceptualizations.

We now provide a conceptualization of inclusive leadership, a framework that provides an overview of the multiple factors associated to inclusive leadership, and the several theories explaining how these variables relate to inclusive leadership. We urge future researchers to expand upon this literature evaluation to clarify a number of aspects.

Secondly, we propose that the four characteristics of inclusive leadership should be explored simultaneously. Understanding if some aspects need to be handled more prominently in particular circumstances is also crucial. For instance, during the COVID-19 epidemic, many workers began working from home, and businesses sought out strategies to foster a sense of community. Future studies should thus look at whether certain variables (such as a crisis or the state of the market) necessitate that inclusive leaders primarily exhibit behaviours connected to particular dimensions. Managers will receive advice on how to adapt their inclusive leadership practises to certain situations thanks to this expertise.

Second, we advise researchers to look into the connections between the various aspects of inclusive leadership to see whether they have an impact on one another. Another topic to be addressed is if putting effort into the different characteristics of inclusive leadership has varied consequences. Would we, for instance, anticipate managers to encourage a sense of individuality as a means of achieving creativity inside the organisation? Similar inquiries might be answered to improve the anticipated benefits of inclusive leadership.

Finally, despite the fact that we included research papers conducted in both Western and Eastern cultures, we see that research from Western nations contributed disproportionately to the notion of inclusive leadership, which in turn inspired research originating from Eastern cultures. This might be a concern since cultural values can affect how inclusive leadership is seen and how people feel about it, just as cultural values can affect how employees feel about their leaders (Kirkman, Chen, Farh, Chen, & Lowe, 2009). For instance, it is well known that hierarchy plays a significant role in Eastern civilizations. As a result, employees in these nations are less likely to disagree with their bosses when making decisions, which is a crucial component of inclusive leadership.

Also, while examining the overall findings, we identify a few key points whose clarification would advance the field's understanding of inclusive leadership. First and foremost, our idea is predicated on previously published scientific publications. Perspectives from additional sources, such as book chapters and conference papers, may be used in future study. We also recommend that future studies gather input from the field, i.e., from leaders and employees, to learn how people see inclusive leadership, as definitions of inclusive leadership are established on the input of scholars. Incorporating this knowledge with recent findings from the literature will lead to a more accurate conceptualization (Shore et al., 2018), which might aid in determining how the employees are concurrently experiencing the many aspects of inclusive leadership.

We also encourage academics to look at inclusive leadership alongside closely linked leadership philosophies. For instance, the traits of servant leadership include encouraging and developing staff (Van Dierendonck, 2011). Understanding the current research on such typical behaviours would help us better grasp inclusive leadership theory since comparable behaviours are exhibited in the inclusive leadership style. For instance, we may draw conclusions about the relationship between inclusive leadership and operational success from research that looked at the connection between servant leadership and operational performance (Overstreet, Hazen, Skipper, & Hanna, 2014). Also, this would help to close certain gaps in the study of inclusive leadership, such how inclusive leadership and different organisational level characteristics relate to one another.

Suggestions

Our recommendations for practise are also based on the findings of this review article. First and foremost, we recommend that HR departments work more closely with managers to help them acquire the abilities and attitudes needed to concurrently achieve each aspect of inclusive leadership. The targeted levels can be used to determine how each dimension should be applied. For instance, managers must comprehend organisational efforts and the motivations behind them in order to support organisational efforts (leadership at the organisational level). Hence, HR personnel should work closely with managers to explain, for instance, why initiatives linked to inclusion are vital, what their aims are, and how leaders may aid in achieving these goals. Managers should then get assistance in implementing the essential conduct to improve their participation in the pertinent HR activities, such as encouraging the employment of a diverse staff (Nishii & Paluch, 2018; Woodrow & Guest, 2014). By giving managers the right tools, mentoring, and training, this may be accomplished.

Second, we advise firms to create a method for managers to provide feedback on their experiences in implementing inclusive leadership. For instance, managers can provide feedback on how each employee is experiencing being shown gratitude and whether there are any differences between each employee's experiences. These findings can help firms design more intricate compensation plans that satisfy the needs of a varied workforce.

Our last proposal is that companies and researchers engage in determining the variables in need of examination in inclusive leadership research (Kalinoski et al., 2013). This is crucial because organisations' experiences and demands will assist researchers better serve real-world needs in their research and direct studies on inclusive leadership and organisational practises towards higher efficacy.

Limitations

There are several restrictions on this study. First, we restricted our attention to the Web of Science database, which may have impacted our findings because other (unpublished) publications might have been accessible that had more details on ideas, connections, and underlying hypotheses. Relatedly, our results imply that most assumptions in the literature are accepted, which leaves it unclear whether recommended components of inclusive leadership may in fact be unsuccessful. This might be due to the bias towards studies with substantial discoveries in publications generally (Dickersin, 1997; Franco, Malhotra, & Simonovits, 2014). It would be extremely desirable for academics to discuss inclusive leadership research's less-than-significant findings openly since they could offer insightful tips for future thinking and investigation.

CONCLUSION

This review demonstrates that there has been considerable progress in inclusive leadership in regard to its conceptualization and research models. Although this provides hope for future research, a more structured approach (e.g., considering the multi-level perspective) will be required for this field to develop further.

We aimed to provide a comprehensive overview of the variables related to inclusive leadership as well as their guiding theories in our review, which was a systematic literature review produced by synthesising the knowledge of research in the field of inclusive leadership (Elsbach & van Knippenberg, 2020; Eva et al., 2019; Randel et al., 2016; Torraco, 2005). We addressed leadership behaviours and looked at the data based on leadership at several levels, especially at the employee, team, and organisational levels, in each of these domains (Dionne et al., 2014; Yammarino & Dansereau, 2008).

REFERENCE

Adams, B. G., Meyers, M. C., & Sekaja, L. (2020). Positive leadership: Relationships with employee inclusion, discrimination, and well-being. *Applied Psychology*, *69*(4), 1145–1173. doi:10.1111/apps.12230

Ahearne, M., Mathieu, J., & Rapp, A. (2005). To empower or not to empower your sales force? An empirical examination of the influence of leadership empowerment behavior on customer satisfaction and performance. *The Journal of Applied Psychology*, *90*(5), 945–955. doi:10.1037/0021-9010.90.5.945 PMID:16162066

Ahmed, F., Zhao, F., & Faraz, N. A. (2020). How and when does inclusive leadership curb psychological distress during a crisis? Evidence from the COVID-19 outbreak. *Frontiers in Psychology*, *11*, 1898. doi:10.3389/fpsyg.2020.01898 PMID:32849111

Ahmed, F., Zhao, F., Faraz, N. A., & Qin, Y. J. (2021). How inclusive leadership paves way for psychological well-being of employees during trauma and crisis: A three-wave longitudinal mediation study. *Journal of Advanced Nursing*, *77*(2), 819–831. doi:10.1111/jan.14637 PMID:33231300

Ainscow, M., & Sandill, A. (2010). Developing inclusive education systems: The role of organisational cultures and leadership. *International Journal of Inclusive Education*, *14*(4), 401–416. doi:10.1080/13603110802504903

Amin, M., Till, A., & McKimm, J. (2018). Inclusive and person-centred leadership: Creating a culture that involves everyone. *British Journal of Hospital Medicine*, *79*(7), 402–407. doi:10.12968/hmed.2018.79.7.402 PMID:29995546

Bass, B. M., & Riggio, R. E. (2006). *Transformational leadership* (2nd ed.). Lawrence Erlbaum Associates. doi:10.4324/9781410617095

Baumeister, R. F. (2012). Need-to-belong theory. In P. A. M. van Lange, A. W. Kruglanski, & E. T. Higgins (Eds.), Handbook of theories of social psychology (pp. 121–140). Thousand Oaks, CA: Sage. doi:10.4135/9781446249222.n32

Blau, P. M. (1964). *Exchange and Power in Social Life*. John Wiley and Sons.

Boekhorst, J. A. (2015). The role of authentic leadership in fostering workplace inclusion: A social information processing perspective. *Human Resource Management*, *54*(2), 241–264. doi:10.1002/hrm.21669

Bradley, E. H. (2020). Diversity, inclusive leadership, and health outcomes. *International Journal of Health Policy and Management*, *9*(7), 266–268. doi:10.15171/ijhpm.2020.12 PMID:32613797

Brannen, M. Y., & Thomas, D. C. (2010). Bicultural individuals in organizations: Implications and opportunity. *International Journal of Cross Cultural Management*, *10*(1), 5–16. doi:10.1177/1470595809359580

Brewer, M. B. (1991). The social self: On being the same and different at the same time. *Personality and Social Psychology Bulletin*, *17*(5), 475–482. doi:10.1177/0146167291175001

Buengeler, C., Leroy, H., & De Stobbeleir, K. (2018). How leaders shape the impact of HR's diversity practices on employee inclusion. *Human Resource Management Review*, *28*(3), 289–303. doi:10.1016/j.hrmr.2018.02.005

Burke, P. J. (1991). Identity processes and social stress. *American Sociological Review*, *56*(6), 836–849. doi:10.2307/2096259

Carmeli, A., Reiter-Palmon, R., & Ziv, E. (2010). Inclusive leadership and employee involvement in creative tasks in the workplace: The mediating role of psychological safety. *Creativity Research Journal*, *22*(3), 250–260. doi:10.1080/10400419.2010.504654

Caron, J., Asselin, H., Beaudoin, J. M., & Muresanu, D. (2019). Promoting perceived insider status of indigenous employees. *Cross Cultural & Strategic Management*, *26*(4), 609–638. doi:10.1108/CCSM-02-2019-0031

Chen, L., Luo, F., Zhu, X., Huang, X., & Liu, Y. (2020). Inclusive leadership promotes challenge-oriented organizational citizenship behavior through the mediation of work engagement and moderation of organizational innovative atmosphere. *Frontiers in Psychology, 11*, 560594. doi:10.3389/fpsyg.2020.560594 PMID:33329187

Choi, S. B., Tran, T. B. H., & Kang, S. W. (2017). Inclusive leadership and employee well-being: The mediating role of person-job fit. *Journal of Happiness Studies, 18*(6), 1877–1901. doi:10.100710902-016-9801-6

Choi, S. B., Tran, T. B. H., & Park, B. I. (2015). Inclusive leadership and work engagement: Mediating roles of affective organizational commitment and creativity. *Social Behavior and Personality, 43*(6), 931–943. doi:10.2224bp.2015.43.6.931

Chrobot-Mason, D., Ruderman, M., & Nishii, L. (2013). Leadership in a diverse workplace. In Q. Roberson (Ed.), *The Oxford handbook of diversity and work* (pp. 315–340). University Press. doi:10.1093/oxfordhb/9780199736355.013.0018

Derven, M. (2016). Four drivers to enhance global virtual teams. *Industrial and Commercial Training, 48*(1), 1–8. doi:10.1108/ICT-08-2015-0056

Dickersin, K. (1997). How important is publication bias? A synthesis of available data. *AIDS Education and Prevention, 9*, 15–21. PMID:9083596

Dionne, S. D., Gupta, A., Sotak, K. L., Shirreffs, K., Serban, A., Hao, C., & Yammarino, F. J. (2014). A 25-year perspective on levels of analysis in leadership research. *The Leadership Quarterly, 25*(1), 6–35. doi:10.1016/j.leaqua.2013.11.002

Dwertmann, D. J., Nishii, L. H., & Van Knippenberg, D. (2016). Disentangling the fairness & discrimination and synergy perspectives on diversity climate: Moving the field forward. *Journal of Management, 42*(5), 1136–1168. doi:10.1177/0149206316630380

Elsaied, M. M. (2020). A moderated mediation model for the relationship between inclusive leadership and job embeddedness. *American Journal of Business, 35*(3/4), 191–210. doi:10.1108/AJB-06-2019-0035

Elsbach, K. D., & van Knippenberg, D. (2020). Creating high-impact literature reviews: An argument for 'integrative reviews'. *Journal of Management Studies, 57*(6), 1277–1289. doi:10.1111/joms.12581

Eva, N., Robin, M., Sendjaya, S., van Dierendonck, D., & Liden, R. C. (2019). Servant leadership: A systematic review and call for future research. *The Leadership Quarterly, 30*(1), 111–132. doi:10.1016/j.leaqua.2018.07.004

Fang, Y., Dai, X., & Zhang, X. (2021). An empirical study of the relationship between inclusive leadership and business model innovation. *Leadership and Organization Development Journal*, *42*(3), 480–494. doi:10.1108/LODJ-11-2019-0484

Fang, Y. C., Chen, J. Y., Wang, M. J., & Chen, C. Y. (2019). The impact of inclusive leadership on employees' innovative behaviors: The mediation of psychological capital. *Frontiers in Psychology*, *10*, 1803. doi:10.3389/fpsyg.2019.01803 PMID:31447740

Fatima, T., Majeed, M., & Zulfiqar Ali Shah, S. (2021). A moderating mediation model of the antecedents of being driven to work: The role of inclusive leaders as change agents. *Canadian Journal of Administrative Sciences/Revue Canadienne des Sciences de l'Administration*, 1–21. doi:10.1002/cjas.1605

Franco, A., Malhotra, N., & Simonovits, G. (2014). Publication bias in the social sciences: Unlocking the file drawer. *Science*, *345*(6203), 1502–1505. doi:10.1126cience.1255484 PMID:25170047

Gioia, D. A., Corley, K. G., & Hamilton, A. L. (2013). Seeking qualitative rigor in inductive research: Notes on the Gioia methodology. *Organizational Research Methods*, *16*(1), 15–31. doi:10.1177/1094428112452151

Godkin, L., Parayitam, S., & Natarajan, L. (2010). An empirical study of attitudes toward recognition among civilian municipal employees in a U.S. City. Journal of Organizational Culture. *Communication and Conflict*, *14*(2), 51–61.

Gotsis, G., & Grimani, K. (2016a). The role of servant leadership in fostering inclusive organizations. *Journal of Management Development*, *35*(8), 985–1010. doi:10.1108/JMD-07-2015-0095

Gotsis, G., & Grimani, K. (2016b). Diversity as an aspect of effective leadership: Integrating and moving forward. *Leadership and Organization Development Journal*, *2*(37), 241–264. doi:10.1108/LODJ-06-2014-0107

Gotsis, G., & Grimani, K. (2017). The role of spiritual leadership in fostering inclusive workplaces. *Personnel Review*, *46*(5), 908–935. doi:10.1108/PR-11-2015-0286

Guo, Y., Zhu, Y., & Zhang, L. (2020). Inclusive leadership, leader identification and employee voice behavior: The moderating role of power distance. *Current Psychology (New Brunswick, N.J.)*, 1–10. doi:10.100712144-020-00647-x

Hanh Tran, T. B., & Choi, S. B. (2019). Effects of inclusive leadership on organizational citizenship behavior: The mediating roles of organizational justice and learning culture. *Journal of Pacific Rim Psychology*, *13*(17), e17. doi:10.1017/prp.2019.10

Hirak, R., Peng, A. C., Carmeli, A., & Schaubroeck, J. M. (2012). Linking leader inclusiveness to work unit performance: The importance of psychological safety and learning from failures. *The Leadership Quarterly*, *23*(1), 107–117. doi:10.1016/j.leaqua.2011.11.009

Holvino, E., Ferdman, B. M., & Merrill-Sands, D. (2004). *Creating and sustaining diversity and inclusion in organizations: Strategies and approaches.*

Hope Pelled, L., Ledford, G. E. Jr, & Albers Mohrman, S. (1999). Demographic dissimilarity and workplace inclusion. *Journal of Management Studies*, *36*(7), 1013–1031. doi:10.1111/1467-6486.00168

Javed, B., Naqvi, S. M. M. R., Khan, A. K., Arjoon, S., & Tayyeb, H. H. (2019). Impact of inclusive leadership on innovative work behavior: The role of psychological safety. *Journal of Management & Organization*, *25*(1), 117–136. doi:10.1017/jmo.2017.3

Kalinoski, Z. T., Steele-Johnson, D., Peyton, E. J., Leas, K. A., Steinke, J., & Bowling, N. A. (2013). A meta-analytic evaluation of diversity training outcomes. *Journal of Organizational Behavior*, *34*(8), 1076–1104. doi:10.1002/job.1839

Kelan, E. K. (2020). The inclusive leader, the smart strategist and the forced altruist: Subject positions for men as gender equality partners. *European Management Review*, *17*(3), 603–613. doi:10.1111/emre.12372

Kirkman, B. L., Chen, G., Farh, J. L., Chen, Z. X., & Lowe, K. B. (2009). Individual power distance orientation and follower reactions to transformational leaders: A cross-level, cross-cultural examination. *Academy of Management Journal*, *52*(4), 744–764. doi:10.5465/amj.2009.43669971

Komives, S. R., Lucas, N., & McMahon, T. R. (2013). *Exploring leadership: For college students who want to make a difference* (3rd ed.). Jossey-Bass.

Korkmaz, A. V., Van Engen, M. L., Knappert, L., & Schalk, R. (2022). About and beyond leading uniqueness and belongingness: A systematic review of inclusive leadership research. *Human Resource Management Review*, *32*(4), 100894. doi:10.1016/j.hrmr.2022.100894

Kuknor, S., & Bhattacharya, S. (2020b). Exploring organizational inclusion and inclusive leadership in Indian companies. *European Business Review*, *33*(3), 450–464. doi:10.1108/EBR-04-2020-0089

Kuknor, S. C., & Bhattacharya, S. (2020a). Inclusive leadership: New age leadership to foster organizational inclusion. *European Journal of Training and Development*. doi:10.1108/EJTD-07-2019-0132

Lacerenza, C. N., Reyes, D. L., Marlow, S. L., Joseph, D. L., & Salas, E. (2017). Leadership training design, delivery, and implementation: A meta-analysis. *The Journal of Applied Psychology*, *102*(12), 1686–1718. doi:10.1037/apl0000241 PMID:28749153

Luu, T. T. (2021). A tale of two countries: How do employees with disabilities respond to disability inclusive HR practices in tourism and hospitality industry? *Journal of Sustainable Tourism*, 1–31. doi:10.1080/09669582.2021.1876073

Mansoor, A., Farrukh, M., Wu, Y., & Abdul Wahab, S. (2021). Does inclusive leadership incite innovative work behavior? *Human Systems Management*, *40*(1), 93–102. doi:10.3233/HSM-200972

Meeuwissen, S. N. E., Gijselaers, W. H., van Oorschot, T. D., Wolfhagen, I. H. A. P., & Oude Egbrink, M. G. A. (2021). Enhancing team learning through leader inclusiveness: A one-year ethnographic case study of an interdisciplinary teacher team. *Teaching and Learning in Medicine*, *33*(5), 498–508. doi:10.1080/10401334.2021.1887738 PMID:33632034

Minehart, R. D., Foldy, E. G., Long, J. A., & Weller, J. M. (2020). Challenging gender stereotypes and advancing inclusive leadership in the operating theatre. *British Journal of Anaesthesia*, *124*(3), e148–e154. doi:10.1016/j.bja.2019.12.015 PMID:32000976

Mir, A., Rafique, M., & Mubarak, N. (2021). Impact of inclusive leadership on project success: Testing of a model in information technology projects. *International Journal of Information Technology Project Management*, *12*(1), 63–79. doi:10.4018/IJITPM.2021010103

Mor Barak, M. E. (2011). *Managing diversity: Toward a globally inclusive workplace*. Sage.

Mor Barak, M. E., Luria, G., & Brimhall, K. C. (2021). What leaders say versus what they do: Inclusive leadership, policy-practice decoupling, and the anomaly of climate for inclusion. *Group & Organization Management*. doi:10.1177/2F10596011211005916

Nembhard, I. M., & Edmondson, A. C. (2006). Making it safe: The effects of leader inclusiveness and professional status on psychological safety and improvement efforts in health care teams. *Journal of Organizational Behavior*, *27*(7), 941–966. doi:10.1002/job.413

Nishii, L. H. (2013). The benefits of climate for inclusion for gender-diverse groups. *Academy of Management Journal*, *56*(6), 1754–1774. doi:10.5465/amj.2009.0823

Nishii, L. H., & Mayer, D. M. (2009). Do inclusive leaders help to reduce turnover in diverse groups? The moderating role of leader–member exchange in the diversity to turnover relationship. *The Journal of Applied Psychology*, *94*(6), 1412–1426. doi:10.1037/a0017190 PMID:19916652

Nishii, L. H., & Ozbilgin, ¨. M. F. (2007). Global diversity management: Towards a conceptual framework. *International Journal of Human Resource Management*, *18*(11), 1883–1894. doi:10.1080/09585190701638077

Nishii, L. H., & Paluch, R. M. (2018). Leaders as HR sensegivers: Four HR implementation behaviors that create strong HR systems. *Human Resource Management Review*, *28*(3), 319–323. doi:10.1016/j.hrmr.2018.02.007

Norman, L., Rankin-Wright, A. J., & Allison, W. (2018). "It'sa concrete ceiling; it's not even glass": Understanding tenets of organizational culture that supports the progression of women as coaches and coach developers. *Journal of Sport and Social Issues*, *42*(5), 393–414. doi:10.1177/0193723518790086

Overstreet, R. E., Hazen, B. T., Skipper, J. B., & Hanna, J. B. (2014). Bridging the gap between strategy and performance: Using leadership style to enable structural elements. *Journal of Business Logistics*, *35*(2), 136–149. doi:10.1111/jbl.12043

Panicker, A., Agrawal, R. K., & Khandelwal, U. (2018). Inclusive workplace and organizational citizenship behavior. *Equality, Diversity and Inclusion*, *37*(6), 530–550. doi:10.1108/EDI-03-2017-0054

Parris, D. L., & Peachey, J. W. (2013). A systematic literature review of servant leadership theory in organizational contexts. *Journal of Business Ethics*, *113*(3), 377–393. doi:10.100710551-012-1322-6

Perry, E. L., Block, C. J., & Noumair, D. A. (2020). Leading in: Inclusive leadership, inclusive climates and sexual harassment. *Equality, Diversity and Inclusion*, *4*(40), 430–477. doi:10.1108/EDI-04-2019-0120

Pfister, I. B., Jacobshagen, N., Kalin, W., & Semmer, N. K. (2020). How does appreciation lead to higher job satisfaction? *Journal of Managerial Psychology*, *35*(6), 465–479. doi:10.1108/JMP-12-2018-0555

Pless, N., & Maak, T. (2004). Building an inclusive diversity culture: Principles, processes and practice. *Journal of Business Ethics*, *54*(2), 129–147. doi:10.100710551-004-9465-8

Qi, L., Liu, B., Wei, X., & Hu, Y. (2019). Impact of inclusive leadership on employee innovative behavior: Perceived organizational support as a mediator. *PLoS One*, *14*(2), e0212091. doi:10.1371/journal.pone.0212091 PMID:30817753

Randel, A. E., Dean, M. A., Ehrhart, K. H., Chung, B., & Shore, L. (2016). Leader inclusiveness, psychological diversity climate, and helping behaviors. *Journal of Managerial Psychology*, *31*(1), 216–234. doi:10.1108/JMP-04-2013-0123

Randel, A. E., Galvin, B. M., Shore, L. M., Ehrhart, K. H., Chung, B. G., Dean, M. A., & Kedharnath, U. (2018). Inclusive leadership: Realizing positive outcomes through belongingness and being valued for uniqueness. *Human Resource Management Review*, *28*(2), 190–203. doi:10.1016/j.hrmr.2017.07.002

Raub, S., & Robert, C. (2013). Empowerment, organizational commitment, and voice behavior in the hospitality industry: Evidence from a multinational sample. *Cornell Hospitality Quarterly*, *54*(2), 136–148. doi:10.1177/1938965512457240

Rayner, S. (2009). Educational diversity and learning leadership: A proposition, some principles and a model of inclusive leadership? *Educational Review*, *61*(4), 433–447. doi:10.1080/00131910903404004

Roberson, Q. M. (2006). Disentangling the meanings of diversity and inclusion in organizations. *Group & Organization Management*, *31*(2), 212–236. doi:10.1177/1059601104273064

Ryan, R. M., & Deci, E. L. (2000). Self-determination theory and the facilitation of intrinsic motivation, social development, and well-being. *The American Psychologist*, *55*(1), 68–78. doi:10.1037/0003-066X.55.1.68 PMID:11392867

Sarason, I. G., Sarason, B. R., Brock, D. M., & Pierce, G. R. (1996). Social support: Current status, current issues. Stress and Emotion. *Anxiety, Anger, and Curiosity*, *16*, 3–27.

Saxena, A., Meschino, D., Hazelton, L., Chan, M., Benrimoh, D., Matlow, A., Dath, D., & Busari, J. (2019). Power and physician leadership. *BMJ Leader*, *3*(3), 92–98. doi:10.1136/leader-2019-000139

Shore, L. M., & Chung, B. G. (2021). Inclusive leadership: How leaders sustain or discourage work group inclusion. *Group & Organization Management*. doi:10.1177/2F1059601121999580

Shore, L. M., Chung-Herrera, B. G., Dean, M. A., Ehrhart, K. H., Jung, D. I., Randel, A. E., & Singh, G. (2009). Diversity in organizations: Where are we now and where are we going? *Human Resource Management Review*, *19*(2), 117–133. doi:10.1016/j.hrmr.2008.10.004

Shore, L. M., Cleveland, J. N., & Sanchez, D. (2018). Inclusive workplaces: A review and model. *Human Resource Management Review*, *28*(2), 176–189. doi:10.1016/j.hrmr.2017.07.003

Shore, L. M., Randel, A. E., Chung, B. G., Dean, M. A., Holcombe Ehrhart, K., & Singh, G. (2011). Inclusion and diversity in work groups: A review and model for future research. *Journal of Management*, *37*(4), 1262–1289. doi:10.1177/0149206310385943

Siegrist, J. (2005). Social reciprocity and health: New scientific evidence and policy implications. *Psychoneuroendocrinology*, *30*(10), 1033–1038. doi:10.1016/j.psyneuen.2005.03.017 PMID:15951124

Siyal, S., Xin, C., Umrani, W. A., Fatima, S., & Pal, D. (2021). How do leaders influence innovation and creativity in employees? The mediating role of intrinsic motivation. *Administration & Society*, *53*(9), 1337–1361. doi:10.1177/0095399721997427

Stocker, D., Keller, A. C., Meier, L. L., Elfering, A., Pfister, I. B., Jacobshagen, N., & Semmer, N. K. (2019). Appreciation by supervisors buffers the impact of work interruptions on well-being longitudinally. *International Journal of Stress Management*, *26*(4), 331–343. doi:10.1037tr0000111

Sugiyama, K., Cavanagh, K. V., van Esch, C., Bilimoria, D., & Brown, C. (2016). Inclusive leadership development: Drawing from pedagogies of women's and general leadership development programs. *Journal of Management Education*, *40*(3), 253–292. doi:10.1177/1052562916632553

Torraco, R. J. (2005). Writing integrative literature reviews: Guidelines and examples. *Human Resource Development Review*, *4*(3), 356–367. doi:10.1177/1534484305278283

Van Dierendonck, D. (2011). Servant leadership: A review and synthesis. *Journal of Management*, *37*(4), 1228–1261. doi:10.1177/0149206310380462

Van Knippenberg, D., & Sitkin, S. B. (2013). A critical assessment of charismatic—transformational leadership research: Back to the drawing board? *The Academy of Management Annals*, *7*(1), 1–60. doi:10.5465/19416520.2013.759433

Wang, F., & Shi, W. (2020). Inclusive leadership and pro-social rule breaking: The role of psychological safety, leadership identification and leader-member exchange. *Psychological Reports*. doi:10.1177/2F0033294120953558 PMID:32878545

Wang, Q., Wang, J., Zhou, X., Li, F., & Wang, M. (2020). How inclusive leadership enhances follower taking charge: The mediating role of affective commitment and the moderating role of traditionality. *Psychology Research and Behavior Management*, *13*, 1103–1114. doi:10.2147/PRBM.S280911 PMID:33299363

Wang, Y. X., Yang, Y. J., Wang, Y., Su, D., Li, S. W., Zhang, T., & Li, H. P. (2019). The mediating role of inclusive leadership: Work engagement and innovative behaviour among Chinese head nurses. *Journal of Nursing Management*, *27*(4), 688–696. doi:10.1111/jonm.12754 PMID:30702790

Weiss, M., Kolbe, M., Grote, G., Spahn, D. R., & Grande, B. (2018). We can do it! Inclusive leader language promotes voice behavior in multi-professional teams. *The Leadership Quarterly*, *29*(3), 389–402. doi:10.1016/j.leaqua.2017.09.002

Woodrow, C., & Guest, D. E. (2014). When good HR gets bad results: Exploring the challenge of HR implementation in the case of workplace bullying. *Human Resource Management Journal*, *24*(1), 38–56. doi:10.1111/1748-8583.12021

Xiaotao, Z., Yang, X., Diaz, I., & Yu, M. (2018). Is too much inclusive leadership a good thing? An examination of curvilinear relationship between inclusive leadership and employees' task performance. *International Journal of Manpower*, *39*(7), 882–895. doi:10.1108/IJM-01-2017-0011

Yammarino, F. J., & Dansereau, F. (2008). Multi-level nature of and multi-level approaches to leadership. *The Leadership Quarterly*, *19*(2), 135–141. doi:10.1016/j.leaqua.2008.01.001

Ye, Q., Wang, D., & Guo, W. (2019). Inclusive leadership and team innovation: The role of team voice and performance pressure. *European Management Journal*, *37*(4), 468–480. doi:10.1016/j.emj.2019.01.006

Ye, Q., Wang, D., & Li, X. (2018). Promoting employees' learning from errors by inclusive leadership. *Baltic Journal of Management*, *13*(1), 125–142. doi:10.1108/BJM-05-2017-0160

Ye, Q., Wang, D., & Li, X. (2019). Inclusive leadership and employees' learning from errors: A moderated mediation model. *Australian Journal of Management*, *44*(3), 462–481. doi:10.1177/0312896218805796

Zanoni, P., & Janssens, M. (2007). Minority employees engaging with (diversity) management: An analysis of control, agency, and micro-emancipation. *Journal of Management Studies*, *44*(8), 1371–1397. doi:10.1111/j.1467-6486.2007.00700.x

ADDITIONAL READING

Adams, B. G., Meyers, M. C., & Sekaja, L. (2020). Positive leadership: Relationships with employee inclusion, discrimination, and well-being. *Applied Psychology*, *69*(4), 1145–1173. doi:10.1111/apps.12230

Allen, K. A., Gray, D. L., Baumeister, R. F., & Leary, M. R. (2022). The need to belong: A deep dive into the origins, implications, and future of a foundational construct. *Educational Psychology Review*, *34*(2), 1133–1156. doi:10.100710648-021-09633-6 PMID:34483627

Amundsen, S., & Martinsen, Ø. L. (2014). Empowering leadership: Construct clarification, conceptualization, and validation of a new scale. *The Leadership Quarterly*, *25*(3), 487–511. doi:10.1016/j.leaqua.2013.11.009

Antonakis, J., Schriesheim, C. A., Donovan, J. A., Gopalakrishna-Pillai, K., Pellegrini, E. K., & Rossomme, J. L. (2004). Methods for studying leadership. *The nature of leadership*, 48-70.

Ashikali, T., Groeneveld, S., & Kuipers, B. (2021). The role of inclusive leadership in supporting an inclusive climate in diverse public sector teams. *Review of Public Personnel Administration*, *41*(3), 497–519. doi:10.1177/0734371X19899722

Avolio, B. J., & Bass, B. M. (Eds.). (2001). *Developing potential across a full range of Leadership Tm: Cases on transactional and transformational leadership*. Psychology Press. doi:10.4324/9781410603975

Avolio, B. J., Sosik, J. J., Jung, D. I., & Berson, Y. (2003). *Leadership models, methods, and applications*. APA.

Bass, B. M., & Riggio, R. E. (2006). *Transformational leadership*. APA.

Bhutto, T. A., Farooq, R., Talwar, S., Awan, U., & Dhir, A. (2021). Green inclusive leadership and green creativity in the tourism and hospitality sector: Serial mediation of green psychological climate and work engagement. *Journal of Sustainable Tourism*, *29*(10), 1716–1737. doi:10.1080/09669582.2020.1867864

Blau, P. (1964). *Power and exchange in social life*. Taylor & Francis.

Booysen, L. (2013). The development of inclusive leadership practice and processes. *Diversity at work: The practice of inclusion*, 296-329.

Burke, P. J. (1991). Identity processes and social stress. *American Sociological Review*, *56*(6), 836–849. doi:10.2307/2096259

Byrne, D. E. (1971). *The attraction paradigm* (Vol. 462). Academic press.

Byron, K., & Peterson, S. (2002). The impact of a large-scale traumatic event on individual and organizational outcomes: Exploring employee and company reactions to September 11, 2001. *Journal of Organizational Behavior*, *23*(8), 895–910. doi:10.1002/job.176

Carson, J. B., Tesluk, P. E., & Marrone, J. A. (2007). Shared leadership in teams: An investigation of antecedent conditions and performance. *Academy of Management Journal*, *50*(5), 1217–1234.

Dansereau, F., Alutto, J. A., & Yammarino, F. J. (1984). *Theory testing in organizational behavior: The varient approach.* Prentice Hall.

Dvir, T., Eden, D., Avolio, B. J., & Shamir, B. (2002). Impact of transformational leadership on follower development and performance: A field experiment. *Academy of Management Journal*, *45*(4), 735–744. doi:10.2307/3069307

Graen, G. B., & Uhl-Bien, M. (1995). Relationship-based approach to leadership: Development of leader-member exchange (LMX) theory of leadership over 25 years: Applying a multi-level multi-domain perspective. *The Leadership Quarterly*, *6*(2), 219–247. doi:10.1016/1048-9843(95)90036-5

Hogg, M. A. (2020). *Learning who we are from our leaders: How leaders shape group and organizational norms and identities*. Quinnipiac University.

Kramer, T. J. (2007). Transformational Leadership. Lawrence Erlbaum Associates.

Meyers, M. C., Adams, B. G., Sekaja, L., Buzea, C., Cazan, A. M., Gotea, M., Stefenel, D., & van Woerkom, M. (2019). Perceived organizational support for the use of employees' strengths and employee well-being: A cross-country comparison. *Journal of Happiness Studies*, *20*(6), 1825–1841. doi:10.100710902-018-0026-8

Ryan, J. (2007). Inclusive leadership: A review. *Journal of Educational Administration and Foundations*, *18*(1-2), 92–125.

Salib, E. R. (2014). *A model of inclusion and inclusive leadership in the US* [Doctoral dissertation, Rutgers University-Graduate School-New Brunswick].

Korkmaz, A. V., Van Engen, M. L., Knappert, L., & Schalk, R. (2022). About and beyond leading uniqueness and belongingness: A systematic review of inclusive leadership research. *Human Resource Management Review*, •••, 100894.

Thompson, H., & Matkin, G. (2020). The Evolution of Inclusive Leadership Studies: A literature review. *Journal of Leadership Education, 19*(3). Advance online publication. doi:10.12806/V19/I3/R2

Zhao, F., Ahmed, F., & Faraz, N. A. (2020). Caring for the caregiver during COVID-19 outbreak: Does inclusive leadership improve psychological safety and curb psychological distress? A cross-sectional study. *International Journal of Nursing Studies, 110*, 103725. doi:10.1016/j.ijnurstu.2020.103725 PMID:32810720

KEY TERMS AND DEFINITIONS

Diversity Management: Diversity management is a structural procedure used to endorse diversity and inclusion in the workroom. This progression includes instigating strategies and tactics in hiring, supervision, training, and more.

Inclusive Leadership: Inclusive leadership is a style of leadership that standards team adherents, calls varied perceptions, and generates an atmosphere where individuals feel their ideas and aids to progress the business's well-being. In workplace culture, inclusive leadership is developing as a prevalent and essential form of business development.

Chapter 7 The Role of Inclusiveness in Organizational Resilience: Overcoming Xenophobia With Inclusiveness

Olcay Okun
Turkish Military Academy, Turkey

ABSTRACT

Our world is rich in ethnicity, belief, social and economic differences, social and physical disability, and equality. Inclusion is the understanding of the ability and developmental diversity of human communities to coexist with sociocultural and racial differences as well as different socio-cultural or racial factors, and the understanding of being able to coexist with people with physical, intellectual, and developmental differences while respecting their cultural contexts. The main driving motivation of the inclusive leadership approach is the cooperation of the employees in the organization, the empowerment of the employees by constantly supporting them, the courage to change against the status quo, and the curiosity to learn about cultural diversity and differences. Inclusive culture, on the other hand, increases organizational resilience. In this section, the possible connections between inclusive leadership, organizational resiliency, inclusion, and culture will be revealed through the lens of inclusive organizational culture, interdisciplinary and intercultural.

INTRODUCTION

People have had to leave their geographies for various reasons in the historical flow. This separation, which is expressed with the concept of migration, has brought along

DOI: 10.4018/978-1-6684-6602-5.ch007

a multifaceted effect on people and geography. Experienced migrations have paved the way for changes and transformations in beliefs, thoughts, rules, and structures about human beings (Ekici & Tuncel, 2015). Due to wars, conflicts, and political and economic instability in today's world, people are forced to leave the countries where they live intensely. These changes have brought about radical changes in the organizations created by people. Multiculturalism of human resources, which includes differences in many contexts such as race, language, religion, culture, and physical ability, leads at the beginning of the changes for organizations.

We live in societies that try to convince us that there is only one way to be "normal" as individuals. We often feel measured by a strict standard: white, strong, young, intelligent, successful, attractive, thin, and preferably male. Normality is defined by society and it is a tight bell curve that allows very little deviation. Even those who feel within the confines of the curve feel pressure to adapt to the normal, while those who fall outside of the normal inclined to see themselves as not only different but also incomplete (Klift & Kunc, 2019). Human societies are based on race, gender, language, color, religion, talent, and sexual orientation and are very diverse. Understanding that diversity, not uniformity, is the real social norm, living with respect for differences, has to be an important feature of productive and peaceful cultures. Diversity, if managed well, can be a source of collective strength for organizations. Different cultures and different orientations can enhance the capacity of organizations to increase their organizational resilience by giving more flexible responses to turbulence.

Inclusiveness can be defined as the practice or policy of providing equal access, opportunities, and participation for all individuals, regardless of their background, identity, or characteristics. It involves creating an environment where everyone feels respected, valued, and included, and where diversity is celebrated. Inclusiveness is about creating a society, organization, or community where everyone is embraced, respected, and provided with equal opportunities to thrive and contribute their full potential (Anand, 2022; Brown, 2019). Leaders have transformative effects on the culture of the organization (House et al., 2004; Madi Odeh et al., 2021). In today's organizations with high human resource diversity, inclusiveness is becoming a fundamental understanding for success. Due to their transformative and decisive role on culture, leaders should be aware of this capacity and evolve the organizational culture with inclusive organizational culture components.

The main aim of inclusive culture should be to eliminate social exclusion, which is the result of responses to diversity in race, language, religion, social class, ethnicity, political affiliation, gender, tribe, disability, and other diversity. The inclusive leadership allows employees in diverse groups, workplaces, and communities to do their best without assuming other cultures and hiding their differences (Woll, 2021). It also creates conditions that encourage employees to behave in this way. Inclusive leaders facilitate participation, voice, and belonging while promoting equality and fairness across multiple identities without requiring assimilation (Ferdman et al., 2020). The most distinctive feature of an inclusive leader is that employees with different backgrounds, cultures, and values are treated fairly, valued for their contributions, and included in the decision-making process (Nishii, 2013). In this context, the performance of inclusive leaders, transformation of this performance into an inclusive organizational culture and related feedback on it, especially in organizations comprised of employees from different cultures, are interesting research topics.

Organizational resilience is expressed as the ability of organizations to cope with negative situations, as well as the ability to adapt to a different and risky environment (Starr et al., 2003). Today, globalization, intense migration flows, natural disasters, recently developing digital currency exchanges, and turmoil, which can be exemplified by sudden economic fluctuations, push organizations to struggle to exist in an unpredictable environment. Organizations have become much more fragile in this new field of struggle, which requires determining the direction of change at the strategic management level. The flexibility of organizations can be expressed with the concept of organizational resilience framework (Coutu, 2002). There are very close links between the resilience capacities of organizations and leadership and organizational culture. Inclusive leadership and inclusive organizational culture (Su et al., 2022) have the potential to contribute significantly to the resilience capacities of organizations, especially where employees from different cultures are concentrated. Management provides all the elements needed to integrate, technology, facilities, processes, and people into an organization's resilience culture, risk management, and enterprise resilience management system. Organizational resilience management culture is built on the core values of the organization. In this framework, the management approach shaped around the inclusive organizational culture will facilitate the integration of people with an integrative understanding and will determine one of the main components of the organizational resilience management culture as the understanding of inclusiveness. In this context, it will be the main purpose of this chapter to examine the relationships between the phenomena that shape the activities of organizations today and to reveal the theoretical foundations in a way that adds value to the organizations.

INCLUSIVE ORGANIZATIONAL CULTURE

If diversity and differences are well managed, they can be a unique resource for organization in today's global, complex, and turbulent work environment in the context of the synergetic results of ideas of different colors. An inclusive culture can be created in which everyone's voice is heard, understood, and integrated for practice, thanks to the effective management provided by the management, and the fact that individuals with differences understand each other and resolve their conflicts in a functional way (Mujtaba, 2013). The main key to this synergy is the umbrella concept of inclusivity that embraces difference and diversity. Management and organizational behavior phenomena that fall under the umbrella of inclusivity will surround all employees. Below, some key elements that define inclusion are listed and explained (Anand, 2022; Brown, 2019; Ferdman et al., 2020; Johnson, 2020).

- Respect and acceptance: Inclusiveness involves treating all individuals with respect, dignity, and acceptance, regardless of their differences in race, ethnicity, gender, sexual orientation, religion, disability, or any other characteristic.
- Equal opportunities: Inclusiveness means ensuring that all individuals have equal opportunities to participate, contribute, and succeed. This includes access to education, employment, healthcare, and other essential resources and services.
- Valuing diversity: Inclusiveness recognizes and values the diversity of backgrounds, perspectives, and experiences that individuals bring. It appreciates the unique contributions and strengths that come from diverse voices and cultures.
- Removing barriers: Inclusiveness involves identifying and removing barriers that hinder individuals from fully participating and accessing opportunities. This includes addressing systemic inequalities, discrimination, prejudice, and bias.
- Creating a safe and inclusive environment: Inclusiveness requires creating an environment where individuals feel safe, supported, and empowered to express themselves authentically. It involves fostering a culture of openness, collaboration, and understanding.
- Collaboration and participation: Inclusiveness encourages active participation, collaboration, and engagement from all individuals. It recognizes that diverse perspectives and contributions enhance decision-making, creativity, and innovation.
- Continuous learning and improvement: Inclusiveness is a dynamic and ongoing process. It requires a commitment to continuous learning, self-reflection, and improvement. It involves staying informed about evolving social issues, challenging one's biases, and actively seeking feedback from diverse voices.

Inclusive leaders are at the forefront of the main actors in creating an inclusive culture for the organization. A stable executive group can contribute to the establishment of an inclusive culture as they know the organization and its culture in detail and know the change requirements and personnel structure. But stability can also bring its reluctance to change. Therefore, transformation into an inclusive culture requires intercultural inclusive leadership that mobilizes and harmonizes the dimensions and diverse resources of organizational culture. This democratic and qualified leadership is what is driving a shift towards management models that match diverse inclusive practices. Leaders must understand diversity, encourage inclusive practices, and continually improve connections among employees (Kuknor & Bhattacharya, 2022; Moliner et al., 2011a). In an inclusive culture, groups can be diverse, and a strong competitive advantage can be created by respecting and accepting these differences and producing teamwork through their unique cultural codes (Mujtaba, 2013). Inclusive leaders constantly strive to maintain an inclusive culture and are aware of its benefits in organizations

Cultural changes in organizations not only happen by targeting and desiring change, but also take place through transformations in the practices, accepted norms, and core values of the organization. Cultural changes do not occur without organizational transformation (Hesselbein, 1999). Transforming the perceptions of the organization is primarily a managerial responsibility. Managers have a responsibility to adapt their organizations to changing and updated ecosystems (Ince, 2022). They should strive for cultural change at the strategic level through practices that encompass all the diversity of the organization, including those who are affected by the decisions and those who implement them. Also they should develop practices that will reinforce every change in perception they achieve. The achievements will pass into the culture over time and become the basic norms of inclusive organizational culture.

One of the areas where the seeds of inclusive culture will be planted is the school. The idea is that each individual is equally important and respected in the social chain and that diversity in societies is a cultural and social wealth that should be instilled in the culture from a young age (Dallalfar, 2011; Valle-Flórez et al., 2022). The most basic pedagogical aspect of developing an inclusive culture may be to accept the universal humanistic values of education, to correct exclusionary definitions and concepts that conflict with these values, and to display a management approach that strengthens friendly, positive and functional communication for the organization (Dubovitskaya et al., 2022). Considering today's ethnic differences and the fact that students from different socio-economic backgrounds are in the same classrooms, it is thought that it will not be difficult for inclusiveness, which accepts the norm to show the respect that each individual deserves, to be embedded in the culture. The university campus can be nurtured toward a sustainable and inclusive society that does not reject faith and spirituality but incorporates diverse worldviews, cultures, and beliefs. Here students should experience interdependence and feel that being together is better and more fun than being alone (Shah, 2022). Inclusive understanding can be made permanent during the university period. It is reflected in all areas of life. Differences and diversity are melted under the umbrella of inclusive culture in organizations in working life. Final stage of globalization necessitates an inclusive organizational culture with a basic requirement for the implementation of policies and practices that promote a sense of belonging, satisfaction and commitment in employees (Findler et al., 2007). Individuals who grow up with an understanding of inclusive culture will adapt to the components of inclusive organizational culture more quickly in working life.

INCLUSIVE LEADERSHIP

Leaders are people who develop a common vision for their followers and the future of the organization and manage relationships with processes to achieve this vision. The hallmark of inclusive leadership is openness. Inclusive leaders acknowledge and respect individual differences among organizational employees. Inclusive leadership directly and consistently helps the innovations produced by the employees in the organization. Therefore, inclusive leadership is a solid and promising leadership model (Carmeli et al., 2010; Lee, 2021). Inclusive leaders satisfy employees' sense of belonging and uniqueness in the organization. Leader behaviors make employees feel included in the organization (Randel et al., 2018). Inclusive leaders seek and appreciate the contributions of those working in the organization through their behavior and communication. They are leaders who are open, accessible, and available in their communication and interaction with staff working in the organization (Nembhard & Edmondson, 2006). Inclusive leadership encourages hierarchically flattened organizations with equal and horizontal relationships, not accepting distinctions related to race, gender, class, and status (Ryan, 2014). Inclusive leaders drive the organization in this direction with their behavior that defies the status quo.

While traditional leadership approaches work around the leader's personality traits, behaviors, and abilities, they push the employees in the organization into the background. Inclusive leadership rises based on establishing cooperation with the employees of the organization, effective communication, and involving them in the processes. Inclusive leadership is successful in bringing the organization to desired results and making strategic decisions by overlapping common goals with differences (Adapa & Sheridan, 2018). The inclusive leader is the assurance and insurance of all diversity working in the organization. Organizational employees know that their inclusive leader will listen to them and value their views. Organization employees who act with this self-confidence will be more committed to the organization, their participation will be higher, and they will be more productive.

Six characteristics of inclusive leaders can be mentioned. *Commitment* is the overlapping of personality traits with belief in differences. *Courage* is challenging the existing structure of the organization and the status quo. *Being aware of bias* is being aware of the areas in the organization that need to be corrected. *Curiosity* is understanding the differences by empathizing with the employees in the organization. *Cultural intelligence* is the capacity to understand the different cultural backgrounds of those working in the organization. *Collaboration* is the ability to run processes together with employees in the organization (Bourke & Dillon, 2018). These capabilities are the main arguments of the inclusive leader in running all the processes of the organization. The embedding of these arguments into the management processes will affect the organizational culture in the direction of these arguments.

The themes used by the inclusive leader can be explained as follows. (Roberson & Perry, 2022).

- Forming teams of organizational employees with differences so that different ideas arise.
- Incorporating and using diversity in the organization's processes.
- Avoiding restrictive ideas by having a broad perspective.
- To know the employees of the organization and to realize their skills by communicating effectively.
- To increase group work and cooperation.
- To create group belonging by bringing together the employees in the organization.
- Demonstrate that as a leader, you want to learn from the people working in the organization.
- Being equal and fair as a leader.
- Creating an inclusive organizational culture as a leader.
- Encouraging employee voice behavior.
- To ensure the participation of the employees of the organization and to make them feel aware of the contribution made.
- To create a sense of trust in all areas of the organization

The inclusive leader should create an inclusive organizational culture shaped by these themes. Inclusive leadership and inclusive organizational culture should instill a sense of trust in each component of the organization (Shore & Chung, 2022). Since the feeling of trust will strengthen the perception that differences will be accepted, the employees of the organization will not have to show toxic behaviors such as hiding themselves and staying silent. The sense of trust that will permeate the walls of the organization will also be a determinant of the continuity of the organization.

Although the leader leads in giving direction, the contributions of the followers are also of unique importance. Leadership is not a one-way relationship, but a two-way interaction in which active followers are involved. The four R's of Inclusive Leadership are *Respect, Recognition, Responsiveness*, and *Responsibility*. The inclusive leader seeks to improve decision-making and achieve desired results, without relying solely on his or her abilities. It creates an atmosphere that promotes and enforces justice for the entire organization. The Inclusive Leader respects competition and collaboration as part of a participatory process (Hollander, 2009). The existence of inclusive leaders means that the feeling of trust permeates every area of the organization.

Inclusiveness, culture, and inclusion leadership is a capacity that can be developed. Schools can offer leadership and management education at a very early age to children who have the potential to raise future leaders in line with the cultures, traditions, social history, and festivals of the countries. There are many social activities performed in schools within the context listed above. Scout groups, sports teams, social activity branches and hobby branches in schools and students at different socio-economic, physical, ethnic and disability levels can be integrated, and inclusive leadership capacity can be developed with group leadership selected for certain periods in the unifying inclusive culture (Shah, 2022). Students with ethnic, socioeconomic, disability, and physical differences will have the ability to show the respect they deserve for differences and manage differences by leading the group for a certain period. They start to value differences from an early age and are more likely to respect them in the future. In this way, human skills are built and valued, and xenophobia is overcome. Inclusion is not a static situation that can be reached in a short time, but a process that needs to be developed and strengthened as much as possible. Moreover, inclusive education is not an end in itself, but a means to the end, namely the realization of an inclusive society (Hassanein, 2015). Understanding the meaning of inclusive education as "seeing human diversity as a fundamental way of seeing and responding to for the benefit of all involved" provides an opportunity to begin imagining a more humane world (Lawrence-Brown et al., 2014). Inclusive leadership is an important construct that works in great perspective. In addition to their leadership, organizations need inclusive leaders and even inclusive governments in their countries. The current conflict in Iraq and the Syrian civil war can be a good example of this situation. The decades-long civil war in Syria has created a major refugee crisis. Millions have fled their homes to neighboring Lebanon, Jordan, Turkey, and Iraq. In addition to the turmoil in neighboring countries, an inclusive government could not be established within the country and conflicts continued. Similarly, the conflict in Iraq, which has been going on since 2003, continues because it cannot be combined around inclusive leadership and policies. While inclusive governments that will be shaped in the context of inclusive culture have the chance to make a recovery, this opportunity is wasted in the clash of differences.

XENOPHOBİA: FEAR OF DIFFERENCE AND INCLUSIVENESS

There is no single agreed definition of xenophobia in human rights discourses and international law. Xenophobia is a set of beliefs and ideas based on the premise that foreigners pose a threat to the nation and the people of that country as an expression of ideology. Xenophobia breeds irrational fear, distance, and further hatred towards foreigners and immigrants, and considers foreigners as the cause of all kinds of bad events. Social scientists and historians say that xenophobia tends to rise and decrease with wars and crises, rapid demographic changes, and economic, political, and social crises (Lee, 2021). The racist foundations of xenophobia stem from the connection between nationality and territory. Waves of immigration and newcomers tend to be seen as the primary source of current social ills and possible sources of potential future harm. Xenophobia towards newcomers can vary and may be continually focused on race, religion, cultural practices, place of origin, language skills, and other factors. In addition, the immigration and citizenship reform packages and the socio-economic support provided by the rulers of the countries may fuel the fears of those who feel threatened by the newcomers (Okun et al., 2021). Differences are a phenomenon that presents strong arguments in every period of history to be afraid and to create fear.

The concept of xenophobia can be thought of as "fear of strangers". Xenophobia is keeping others at a distance because they are perceived differently. Xenophobia is mainly associated with fear of the other (Delanty & O'Mahony, 2002). Xenophobia also operates ideologically to create prejudice based on gender, class, religion, and sexual orientation. It is possible to see the reflections of the tendency to see differences and immigrants as the source of all kinds of problems in social events. The reason for the current Covid-19 pandemic has been seen as immigrants of Asian origin and xenophobic behaviors towards these people have increased (He et al., 2021). The ideas that immigrant women are the cause of extramarital affairs and illegitimate children and that terrorist activities are committed by members of a religious group are based on the Xenophobia ideology, not accepting and excluding differences and diversity, evolves into the behavior of not tolerating and being hostile.

Common to all exclusionary approaches is the strong presence of fundamentalist assumptions about group membership and thus a high degree of exclusion; The identity of the self - "the people" - is the negation of the other. The individual has absolute subordination to the collectivity (group). Belongings are based on authoritarian cultural codes of belonging that include xenophobia. The understanding is built that exclusion is a descriptive justification, not a consequence (Delanty & O'Mahony, 2002). The security discourses spoken by administrators are shaped around a national self confronting one or more threatening others with radically different identities. These discourses are powerful and can build fear in people. To praise one group in rhetoric is to form the "other group" (Cooper-Cunningham, 2020). Xenophobia is a key issue in the narratives of authors who have become immigrants for different reasons. From the author's point of view, xenophobia can be thought of as a global situation affected by factors such as displacement, cultural alienation, religion, and education. This situation in immigrant narratives emphasizes the ubiquity and universality of racism, (negative) stereotyping, and xenophobic attitudes. In general, the new culture, which includes immigrants, works in a way that strongly associates immigrants with feelings of anxiety (Mohr, 2008). Fear has consequences for individuals and communities. From time to time, underlying prejudices and primitive fears against groups defined as distinct by social distinctions such as race, class, sexuality, ethnicity, religion, nationality, or political affiliation can resurface.

Identity is a construct that relates to what we are and how we are recognized, rather than what we choose or consent to. Identity needs difference to exist and tends to transform difference into otherness to secure its certainty (Connolly, 1995). The dichotomies that underlie the discursive structures of human identity are never fixed, they are stable, and unalterable: they can always be questioned, deconstructed, or avoided. Political discourses and identities can be rethought, defined, framed, and have the potential to open up new political spaces (Cooper-Cunningham, 2020). Thinking and questioning the concept of identity generally increase in times of trouble and depression. When political discourse wants to create an "other" for its benefit, it can bend the concept of the "other" in the direction it desires by making use of these basic building blocks of the concept of identity. By framing social diversity such as language, religion, race, gender, color, and preference differences according to political choices, society can be seperated into different others. This situation can be reflected in society in general as intolerance and xenophobia in the simplest terms, leaving common sense aside.

The implicit or overtly critical approaches of policymakers to immigrants, foreigners, or differences can make xenophobia or intolerance of differences culturally acceptable in societies. Therefore, policymakers' implementation of an inclusive language and policy aiming at social integration and cohesion rather than short-term gains will allow an inclusive culture to be established in society in the long run. The far-right and populist approaches made through discrimination will always have the potential to bring social conflicts, as can be seen in the historical flow. Several factors facilitate the development and activation of a subculture that fears differences and is xenophobic. The first factor is the media and politicians. A media that does not want to include differences and spreads fear and anxiety over immigrants will support the formation of a non-inclusive subculture. Policymakers who are fed by the fear of strangers and tolerant or ignoring the fear of differences will allow these negative feelings to form layers in society. The second factor is that the control institutions from the public and non-governmental organizations do not take the initiative to the required extent, ignore them, are insensitive, and do not fulfill their functions in a way that directs the society. In this case, the lack of tolerance and xenophobia and related actions may be triggered more (Kurthen et al., 1997). Discrimination incidents that may be triggered in or around the institution or negative thoughts about differences in society can negatively affect the resilience capacity of institutions and make the institution more vulnerable to possible turmoil. The dampening of toxic effects within the organization such as xenophobia and intolerance to differences, which gnaw the organization's resilience capacity, is an argument that needs to be understood in depth. In this context, the cultures of organizations should evolve towards inclusive understandings.

It is possible to examine the inclusive organizational culture and transformation through the immigrants of Syrian and Afghan origin, who created intense migration movements. The numerical density of citizens of Afghanistan and Syria draw attention in the global migration. Afghanistan and Syria are normative, hierarchical, and collectivistic, with high preferences for avoiding uncertainty in society. In this framework, the general characteristics of people shaped by culture can be defined in the following perspective. People of this culture accept a hierarchical order where everyone has a place and needs no further justification. Hierarchy, and centralization in the organization are popular, subordinates wait to be told what to do, and the ideal boss is a benevolent autocrat. A close, long-term commitment to the family and member "group" is evident. Loyalty is paramount in a collectivist culture and overrides many other societal rules and regulations. Society develops strong relationships where everyone takes responsibility for the other members of their group. Recruitment and promotion decisions in the organization are made by considering the employee's in-group situation. People are highly uncertainty avoidant, maintain strict codes of belief and behavior and are intolerant of unorthodox behavior and ideas are strongly interested in establishing absolute truth; They are normative in their thinking, show great respect for tradition, tend to save relatively little for the future, and focus on achieving quick results (Arun & Kahraman Gedik, 2022; Hofstede, 2023). This projection, made on citizens migrating from Afghanistan and Syria, can be simulated to organizations that have gradually turned into a heterogeneous structure with the globalization trend that started in the 20th century and the opening of borders of many states to foreign workers in the international business environment. How can a leadership and organizational culture be defined as suitable for employees of different ethnicities, cultures, races, and genders working for the same organization? This question is a challenge for today's organizations. We see the answer to this challenge as inclusiveness as it has been covered so far in this chapter. Based on the understanding of inclusiveness, inclusive leadership and inclusive organizational culture are key phenomena that enable organizational differences to be turned into an advantage.

In this context, newcomers to countries with migration waves or globalization, on the one hand, are faced with intolerance to differences, xenophobia, and similar toxic effects, on the one hand, they have to work to continue their lives. The organizational culture, climate, and leadership that immigrants will encounter in the organizations they are involved in are of great importance for both the immigrant employee and the healthy progress of the organization. Inclusivity, a culture of inclusivity, and inclusive leadership are the antidotes to xenophobia and intolerance of differences. The inclusive leader is aware of prejudices against differences, dares to break the sharpened status quo of the organization, understands and empathizes with individuals with differences in cultural intelligence, cooperates with all individuals in the organization, identifies and corrects perceptions and areas that need to be corrected with this mechanism. Inclusive leaders form teams of organizational employees, incorporating differences into the organization's processes and using these capacities. They have a broad perspective and avoid divisive and restrictive ideas, increase group work and cooperation, build a sense of trust in all areas of the organization. (Bourke & Dillon, 2018; Hollander, 2009; House, 2004; Roberson & Perry, 2022). Inclusivity and its manifestation on the leader and organizational culture work as an organizational capacity to heal and cure.

Organizational culture encompasses the shared values and practices of the organization. The norms, values, and beliefs shared among the employees of the organization become the organizational culture. Leaders who shape the organization have a transformative capacity to shape and transform culture. Leaders are one of the main figures in transforming the organizational culture towards an inclusive culture (House et al., 2004). Inclusive organizational culture is the culture of living in diversity. Assuming diversity by accepting individuals as different individuals with their unique characteristics and way of being and living; is to see diversity and differences as an organizational value and as a way of organizational mutual enrichment (Moliner et al., 2011b). Inclusive organizational culture transformation refers to the change of perspectives of organizational personnel within the framework of this paradigm. The organizational culture that will be shaped around this point of view, can create a paradigm for the inclusion of employees in organizations consisting of Afghan and Syrian refugees who are exposed to intense migration movements. Since the employees with differences included in the group will work for the higher goals of the organization, the differences will start to melt in a pot.

Looking at the paradigm we have developed, due to the current turmoil in Afghanistan and Syria from a wider perspective, can produce beneficial results for today's organizations. As a result of globalization and the intense migration wave affecting all countries of the world, people have joined organizations in their countries to survive. Since it can be foreseen that this situation will continue shortly, it is a critical issue for organizations to melt the cultural characteristics listed above into the same pot with the cultural characteristics of the migrated country and to develop a "culture of working together with differences" by accepting the differences as wealth for the organization. In this context, inclusive organizational culture is a culture in which individual contributions in many different lines are recognized, evaluated, and used (Mor-Barak, 2013). Inclusive organizational culture melts different cultures in a single pot and brings the differences arising from cultural backgrounds to the limits that can be considered normal. Employees from different cultures, who will be clamped around the inclusive culture under the same organization, will achieve organizational goals more easily and will stay away from intolerance to differences and toxic effects for organizations such as xenophobia.

ORGANIZATIONAL RESILIENCE AND INCLUSIVENESS

In an age of high uncertainty, all organizations strive to be more resilient, absorb the negative effects of change, adapt, recover, and thrive after disruptions. (Lisdiono et al., 2022). Resilience is a fundamental capacity that can be adapted to individuals, organizations, systems, and groups as the ability to achieve beneficial results from disruptive changes (Home & Orr, 1997). Organizational resilience capacity has a strong theoretical background based on social and basic sciences. Organizational resilience is the ability to absorb tension and recover from undesirable events through continuous restructuring and refers to the capacity to be strong under conditions of stress and change (Coutu, 2002). Organizational resilience is defined as the ability to go forward, adapt, and survive in the face of turmoil, just like human resilience. Resilience is modeled by the integration of resilience capacities of different parts of the organization. Organizational resilience is the resilience of an entire system. The resilience capacities of individuals, which are the most basic building blocks of the organization, also indicate organizational resilience (van Breda, 2016). Inclusivity, which is defined as the use of practices that foster a sense of belonging by encouraging meaningful interactions between individuals and groups representing different characteristics, perceptions, and experiences (Metzger et al., 2020), will make positive contributions to the resilience capacity of the employees in the organization.

Many activities must be defined and managed for the organization to function effectively. Any activity that is managed and uses resources to transform inputs into outputs can be considered as a process. In organizations, the output of one process often forms the input to the next process. The implementation of a system of processes, the identification, and interaction of these processes, and their management within the organization is called the "process approach". The management systems approach encourages organizations to analyze corporate and stakeholder needs and identify processes that contribute to success. A good management system provides a framework of understanding for continuous improvement to increase safety, preparedness, response, continuity, and resilience. A process approach should be adopted to establish, implement, operate, monitor, review, maintain and improve the organization's organizational resilience management system. In general terms, the importance of the following items should be understood in the process approach for organizational resilience management (ASIS, 2009). The understanding of inclusiveness can be digested into the planning of each of the processes listed below. Since this planning process will be handled at the strategic level, inclusive leaders can plan all processes within the framework of the understanding of inclusivism within the existing structure of the organization. The inclusivity that permeates each process will increase the potential for the goals to be accepted more quickly, as a common understanding within the organization has developed around the goals. Consensus in achieving agreed common goals will also have the potential to support organizational resilience (ISO, 2011; Lisdiono et al., 2022).

I) Understand the organization's risk, safety, preparedness, response, continuity, and recovery requirements;
II) Establishing a policy and objectives to manage Observed Risks;
III) Implementing and operating controls to manage risks in the context of the organization's mission;
IV) Monitoring and reviewing the performance and effectiveness of the organizational resilience management system;
V) Continuous improvement based on objective measurement.

Organizational structures, with their conservative aspects, often act as barriers to organizational resilience. This is because most organizational structures were based on people, culture, understanding, and choice when diversity was low, information was scarce, and competition was not as global as it is today (L. Mallak, 1998; L. A. Mallak, 1998). Top management must develop behavioral norms that support organizational resilience by thinking strategically with input and participation from all levels of the organization to design an organizational structure that fits the organization's strategy and operations. Inclusive leadership and inclusive culture provide the organization with a unique resource at this point because organizational resilience can be achieved through the creation and maintenance of cognitive, emotional, relational, or structural abilities that can be sufficiently transformed and shaped to cope with a dynamic environment. Inclusive leaders can transform the growing richness of people, ideas, cultures, and preferences into innovative ideas and the soundness of strategic decisions from an inclusive cultural perspective. For organizational resilience, leaders must develop strategies that incorporate the unique characteristics of the organization. Inclusive leaders know that their strength depends on their strong knowledge of the organization's employees and the inclusive culture created around strong group belonging and communication.

Innovative talent is a driving engine for building organizational resilience. Innovating the organizational culture in the direction of inclusive organizational culture will provide support to increase the organizational resilience capacity as well as the dynamism it will bring to the organization and the ability to keep up with the present. In organizational resilience management, four challenges that are embedded in the organizational structure should be studied (Hamel & Valikangas, 2004). Each challenge should be reviewed from the perspective of inclusiveness, and differences should be provided through each difficulty gate.

Cognitive Difficulty: The organization must be free from being stuck in the past, the perception that everything it does is right, and arrogance. The organization must understand what has changed. Inclusive leaders challenge the status quo (Bourke & Dillon, 2018). Leadership perceptions are about developing and changing the existing order. The organization tries to move forward by organizing its employees as a team. It attempts tries to use the differences as the driving force of this changing and be willing to consider how these changes will be reflected in the present.

Strategic Challenge: Organizational resilience requires an awareness of what has changed, as well as the ability to create multiple new strategic options. Inclusive leaders collaborate with employees of the organization. The polyphonic environment created by this collaborative and inclusive understanding brings with it a wide repertoire of ideas and operations (Adapa & Sheridan, 2018). The inclusive leader develops his ability to create strategic options with the power he gets from the employees in the organization.

Political Challenge: The organization must be able to shift its current resources to future products rather than past products. Creating talent for new productions planned with a realistic vision based on innovation is a critical capacity for organizational resilience. It will be easier for new ideas to germinate in an environment of trust provided by an inclusive leader and an inclusive culture. Inclusive leadership and inclusive culture will create a working environment suitable for innovative developments that will add value to the organization and gain a competitive advantage (Javed et al., 2019; Ye et al., 2019). The behavior of inclusive leaders is perceived by organizational employees as providing assistance rather than command. Any support provided has the potential to increase innovation capacity.

The Ideological Challenge: Rather than an understanding of the temporal renewal of the organization's business models, it is necessary to adopt a belief in opportunity-oriented and continuous falsification (Hamel & Valikangas, 2004). Inclusive leaders can sense opportunities and turn them into advantages, thanks to their strong communication and empathy skills.

Each component of organizational culture can provide information to predict the resilience of many components of the organization.(Borekci et al., 2014). The reason for this is that the unity of norms, behavior, and practices provided by the organizational culture has an impact on the performance and outputs of the components of the organization. Organizational culture makes the organization more resilient to turmoil, changes, and uncertainty by directing the attitudes of organizational employees on information sharing, teamwork, and risk-taking (Mandal, 2017; Madi Odeh et al., 2021). In this context, organizational culture is a predictor of organizational resilience (Morales et al., 2019). Since an inclusive organizational culture will include differences, the synergy that differences will add to the organization will positively improve organizational resilience.

When the transformational leader taps into the morals and values of individuals and incorporates them into a collective vision, a lasting, sustainable transformation characteristic of a resilient organization can be created (Sommer et al., 2016). Because inclusive leaders display transformative leadership behaviors that challenge the status quo, the change they create supports organizational resilience. Inclusive leaders should be aware that components of organizational culture contribute to supporting organizational resilience. Inclusive organizational culture equipped with inclusive practices increases organizational resilience with participation, group belonging, innovation, and many other positive organizational outputs.

FUTURE RESEARCH DIRECTIONS

Future research on inclusion, inclusiveness and inclusive leadership should aim to discover the latest trends, strategies and impacts in these fields. Some research proposals have been made on these topics. First, the role of technology in inclusion can be explored. Research can be conducted to examine the effects of technology on inclusion and diversity. For example, how can online platforms and AI tools be used to create an inclusive environment? What technological solutions can help advance equity and accessibility?

With globalization, cultural diversity has gained importance. In this context, it may be an important topic to explore the effects of different cultures on inclusiveness processes and how cultural differences can be incorporated into inclusion strategies.

Studies can be conducted to investigate the impact of inclusion practices in businesses on business performance, innovation and competitive advantage, examine how inclusiveness and diversity contribute to the sustainability, profitability and employee engagement of businesses.

Research focusing on the impact and importance of inclusive leadership can be conducted. What are inclusive leadership qualities and skills? How can inclusive leadership development programs and training be designed? How to measure the impact and results of inclusive leaders in organizations. How can inclusive leadership be developed in correlation with organizational culture?

Integration of inclusiveness into education systems, accompanied by inclusive public policies, can be another area of research. Research can be conducted on how inclusion and diversity issues can be integrated in educational institutions. Studies can be carried out in areas such as inclusive education models, curriculum design, teacher training and student participation.

CONCLUSION

Inclusive leaders treat and respect employees in the organization with fairness and respect for their diverse talents without stereotyping them. They focus on the values and belonging of employees in the organization and ensure high performance through trust and inspiration. Leaders and those working in the organization are socially together, and employees of the organization contribute to all processes of leadership (Adapa & Sheridan, 2018). Inclusive leadership is about running the processes in the organization together with the employees. It is the inclusion of employee differences in all possible processes of the organization and the development of the organization's vision in this direction.

There is a wide range of positions for leaders and those running the organization to manage the organizational culture and have a strong, systematic, purposeful influence on the values, beliefs, ideas, and meanings of their subordinates. They can influence organizational culture with their behavior and organizational practices through more visible values and norms expressed in various organizational subsystems such as leadership and management, rituals, organizational structure, and control systems (Alvesson & Sveningsson, 2015). Leaders determine what values should be shared, which goals are worth striving for, what beliefs employees should adhere to, and past events and current goals are worth striving for, what beliefs employees should adhere to, and what interpretations should be made in a way that benefits organizations (Fitzgerald, 1988). The leader, who is a kind of compass of the organization, plays a critical role in the formation of the culture of the organization (Okun et al., 2020). In this context, it will be an expected result that the leader, who has a management understanding of the concept of an inclusive leader, will bend the culture of the organization towards the target culture in line with his vision.

Education plays a crucial role in preparing future generations to participate in inclusive communities. It can provide children with a sharing experience from a young age in line with the education systems, cultures, traditions, social history, and festivals of the countries. Inclusive education is not just a specialized program for students with disabilities, but rather a commitment to critical pedagogy and social justice that addresses disability, race, class, gender, sexuality, and ethnicity as intersecting categories that impact student experiences in transformative ways (Lawrence-Brown et al., 2014; Lyons et al., 2016). All children, with their distinctive voices, strengths, abilities, and contributions, are valued members of their country's communities. Inclusive communities embrace and expand children's sociocultural repertoires while also addressing debate and conflict in creative and constructive ways. Policymakers should consider that schools characterized by structures of inclusion rather than exclusion can be life-affirming catalysts for change. Inclusive education practices to be developed by policymakers will contribute greatly to the transformation of society's culture.

Organizations with inclusive leaders emphasize developing workplace culture and exploring new components. The development and exploratory approach of the inclusive culture, which is shaped around the perception of the inclusive leader, is rewarded with the encouragement and appreciation of innovative and creative employees and the return of this creativity as a new product, service, and market (Randel et al., 2018; Ye et al., 2019). Inclusive leaders accept employees in the organization with their unique values and create a working environment where they can be beneficial. It increases the perception that they are a part of the organization by giving employees the chance to belong to the organization and to be themselves. It embraces differences within the organization. Although this situation seems contrary to the concepts of status and belonging created by the similarities often emphasized in social identity theories, the inclusive culture supported by the inclusive leader melts the different identities of the group into one pot and unites the employees of the organization around the group super identity (Jans et al., 2012; Shore & Chung, 2022). Organizational employees, with their differences, come together to form a superior group identity around an inclusive leader and inclusive culture. There are many organizational benefits for the group to come together in a sense of belonging. The richness of diversity is reflected in the decisions the inclusive leader makes about the organization. The decision-making repertoire expands with approaches to combining ideas in group affiliation. Since the decision repertoire that inclusive leaders can use can contribute to the decisions of the employees of the institution they work with, the wider the decision repertoire, the more accurate the decisions will be. The right decisions taken about the organization carry the organization to its goals and success.

Conflicts such as refugee crises, violence, intergroup conflicts, and acts of hatred around the world show how much we need inclusive communities. Our ecosystem is the most inclusive of the communities we share as citizens of the world, and so we must cooperate to care for this common home, even if we do not agree on whether it is an integral part of it for even more. Human beings on earth have to mobilize their intellectual capacities, and multiple cultural and religious traditions to create a common ecological living climate (Rupp, 2015). Beyond the rational or cognitive as a collective experience, knowledge has a crucial dimension that has been overlooked by modern social science – living spirituality, cultural diversity, and the human dimension (Shah, 2022). Phobia, lack of respect, and distrust towards communities with different backgrounds may cause the socio-economic level of these groups to go backward, as well as interrupt beneficial economic contributions to the country's economy. The distrust of diverse communities and their traditions of trust, wisdom, and interdependence can keep us abreast of what is going on and how business and finance work in these communities. Today we live in a time when we have no choice but to accept and work with existing communities, no matter what their ethnic origins, beliefs, and traditions, to pursue development goals. The world is getting flatter and we are becoming a part of the whole. An inclusive society includes people in all their diversity, accepting, respecting, and avoiding prejudices about race, gender, sexual orientation, and religion, as well as disability, diversity, and diverse identities in all contexts related to those situations (Jones & Danforth, 2015). As an umbrella concept, inclusiveness offers countries and organizations unique opportunities to transform differences into strengths and collaborate. Organizations should increase their resilience by protecting themselves from toxic effects such as xenophobia and intolerance of differences, and develop their inclusiveness capacity by spreading it to all areas of the organization.

ACKNOWLEDGMENT

This research received no specific grant from any funding agency in the public, commercial, or not-for-profit sectors.

REFERENCES

Adapa, S., & Sheridan, A. (Eds.). (2018). *Inclusive Leadership*. Springer International Publishing. doi:10.1007/978-3-319-60666-8

Alvesson, M., & Sveningsson, S. (2015). *Changing Organizational Culture: Cultural change work in progress* (2nd ed.). Routledge., doi:10.4324/9781315688404

Anand, R. (2022). *Leading global diversity, equity, and inclusion: A guide for systemic change in multinational organizations* (1st ed.). Berrett-Koehler.

Arun, K., & Kahraman Gedik, N. (2022). Impact of Asian cultural values upon leadership roles and styles. *International Review of Administrative Sciences*, *88*(2), 428–448. doi:10.1177/0020852320935982

ASIS. (2009). *Organizational Resilience: Security, Preparedness, and Continuity Management Systems - Requirements with Guidance for Use ASIS SPC 1-2009*. ASIS.

Borekci, D., Rofcanin, Y., & Sahin, M. (2014). Effects of organizational culture and organizational resilience over subcontractor riskiness: A multi-method study in longitudinal time setting. *European Business Review*, *26*(1), 2–22. doi:10.1108/EBR-07-2013-0099

Bourke, J., & Dillon, B. (2018). The diversity and inclusion revolution: Eight powerful truths. *Deloitte Review*, *22*, 82–95.

Brown, J. (2019). *How to be an inclusive leader: Your role in creating cultures of belonging where everyone can thrive* (1st ed.). Berrett-Koehler Publishers, Inc.

Carmeli, A., Reiter-Palmon, R., & Ziv, E. (2010). Inclusive Leadership and Employee Involvement in Creative Tasks in the Workplace: The Mediating Role of Psychological Safety. *Creativity Research Journal*, *22*(3), 250–260. doi:10.1080/10400419.2010.504654

Connolly, W. E. (1995). *The ethos of pluralization*. University of Minnesota Press.

Cooper-Cunningham, D. (2020). Drawing Fear of Difference: Race, Gender, and National Identity in *Ms. Marvel* Comics. *Millennium*, *48*(2), 165–197. doi:10.1177/0305829819889133

Coutu, D. L. (2002). How resilience works. *Harvard Business Review*, *80*(5), 46–56. PMID:12024758

Dallalfar, A. (2011). *Transforming classroom culture inclusive pedagogical practices*. Palgrave Macmillan. doi:10.1057/9780230370319

Delanty, G., & O'Mahony, P. (2002). Nationalism and social theory: Modernity and the recalcitrance of the nation. *Sage (Atlanta, Ga.)*.

Dubovitskaya, T., Maznichenko, M., Romanova, G., & Yakubova, F. (2022). *The Teacher's Inclusive Culture: Assessing, Adjusting and Nurturing*. 351–369. doi:10.3897/ap.5.e0351

Ekíci, S., & Tuncel, G. (2015). Göç ve İnsan. *Birey ve Toplum Sosyal Bilimler Dergisi*, *5*(1), 9. doi:10.20493/bt.71783

Ferdman, B. M., Prime, J., & Riggio, R. E. (2020). *Inclusive Leadership: Transforming Diverse Lives, Workplaces, and Societies* (B. M. Ferdman, J. Prime, & R. E. Riggio, Eds.; 1st ed.). Routledge. doi:10.4324/9780429449673

Findler, L., Wind, L. H., & Barak, M. E. M. (2007). The Challenge of Workforce Management in a Global Society: Modeling the Relationship Between Diversity, Inclusion, Organizational Culture, and Employee Well-Being, Job Satisfaction and Organizational Commitment. *Administration in Social Work*, *31*(3), 63–94. doi:10.1300/J147v31n03_05

Fitzgerald, T. H. (1988). Can change in organizational culture really be managed? *Organizational Dynamics*, *17*(2), 5–15. doi:10.1016/0090-2616(88)90015-0

Hamel, G., & Valikangas, L. (2004). The quest for resilience. *Icade. Revista de la Facultad de Derecho (Montevideo)*, *62*, 355–358.

Hassanein, E. E. A. (2015). *Inclusion, Disability and Culture*. SensePublishers. doi:10.1007/978-94-6209-923-4

He, L., Zhou, W., He, M., Nie, X., & He, J. (2021). Openness and COVID-19 induced xenophobia: The roles of trade and migration in sustainable development. *PLoS One*, *16*(4), e0249579. doi:10.1371/journal.pone.0249579 PMID:33831012

Hesselbein, F. (1999). The key to cultural transformation: THE KEY TO CULTURAL TRANSFORMATION. *Leader to Leader*, *1999*(12), 1–7. doi:10.1002/ltl.40619991201

Hofstede, G. (2023). Hofstede insights: Country comparison tool. *Hofstede-Insights (E-Article),* Https://Www. Hofstede-Insights. Com/.

Hollander, E. P. (2009). *Inclusive leadership: The essential leader-follower relationship*. Routledge.

Home, J. F. III, & Orr, J. E. (1997). Assessing behaviors that create resilient organizations. *Employment Relations Today*, *24*(4), 29–39. doi:10.1002/ert.3910240405

House, R. J., & Global Leadership and Organizational Behavior Effectiveness Research Program (Eds.). (2004). *Culture, leadership, and organizations: The GLOBE study of 62 societies*. Sage Publications.

Ince, F. (2022). Transformational Leadership in a Diverse and Inclusive Organizational Culture. In R. I. Perez-Uribe, D. Ocampo-Guzman, & N. Moreno-Monsalve (Eds.), (pp. 188–201). Advances in Human Resources Management and Organizational Development. IGI Global., doi:10.4018/978-1-6684-5216-5.ch010

ISO. (2011). *ISO 28002:2011(en), Security management systems for the supply chain—Development of resilience in the supply chain—Requirements with guidance for use*. ISO. https://www.iso.org/obp/ui/fr/#iso:std:iso:28002:ed-1:v1:en

Jans, L., Postmes, T., & Van der Zee, K. I. (2012). Sharing differences: The inductive route to social identity formation. *Journal of Experimental Social Psychology*, *48*(5), 1145–1149. doi:10.1016/j.jesp.2012.04.013

Javed, B., Naqvi, S. M. M. R., Khan, A. K., Arjoon, S., & Tayyeb, H. H. (2019). Impact of inclusive leadership on innovative work behavior: The role of psychological safety. *Journal of Management & Organization*, *25*(1), 117–136. doi:10.1017/jmo.2017.3

Johnson, S. K. (2020). *Inclusify: The power of uniqueness and belonging to build innovative teams*. Harper Business, an imprint of HarperCollins Publishers.

Jones, P., & Danforth, S. (Eds.). (2015). *Foundations of inclusive education research* (1st ed.). Emerald. doi:10.1108/S1479-363620156

Kuknor, S. C., & Bhattacharya, S. (2022). Inclusive leadership: New age leadership to foster organizational inclusion. *European Journal of Training and Development*, *46*(9), 771–797. doi:10.1108/EJTD-07-2019-0132

Kurthen, H., Bergmann, W., & Erb, R. (Eds.). (1997). *Antisemitism and xenophobia in Germany after unification*. Oxford University Press.

Lawrence-Brown, D., Sapon-Shevin, M., & Erevelles, N. (2014). *Condition critical: Key principles for equitable and inclusive education*. Teachers College Press.

Lee, E. (2021). America for Americans: A history of xenophobia in the United States. Basic Books.

Lisdiono, P., Said, J., Yusoff, H., & Hermawan, A., A. (2022). Risk management practice, alliance management capability, and enterprise resilience: Findings from Indonesian state-owned enterprises. *Problems and Perspectives in Management*, *20*(1), 190–202. doi:10.21511/ppm.20(1).2022.17

Lyons, W. E., Thompson, S. A., & Timmons, V. (2016). 'We are inclusive. We are a team. Let's just do it': Commitment, collective efficacy, and agency in four inclusive schools. *International Journal of Inclusive Education*, *20*(8), 889–907. doi:10.1080/13603116.2015.1122841

Madi Odeh, R. B. S., Obeidat, B. Y., Jaradat, M. O., Masa'deh, R., & Alshurideh, M. T. (2021). The transformational leadership role in achieving organizational resilience through adaptive cultures: The case of Dubai service sector. *International Journal of Productivity and Performance Management*. Advance online publication. doi:10.1108/IJPPM-02-2021-0093

Mallak, L. (1998). Putting organizational resilience to work. *Industrial Management-Chicago Then Atlanta*, 8–13.

Mallak, L. A. (1998). Measuring resilience in health care provider organizations. *Health Manpower Management*, *24*(4), 148–152. doi:10.1108/09552069810215755 PMID:10346317

Mandal, S. (2017). The influence of organizational culture on healthcare supply chain resilience: Moderating role of technology orientation. *Journal of Business and Industrial Marketing*, *32*(8), 1021–1037. doi:10.1108/JBIM-08-2016-0187

Metzger, M., Dowling, T., Guinn, J., & Wilson, D. T. (2020). Inclusivity in Baccalaureate Nursing Education: A Scoping Study. *Journal of Professional Nursing*, *36*(1), 5–14. doi:10.1016/j.profnurs.2019.06.002 PMID:32044053

Mohr, D. M. (2008). *Embracing the other: Addressing xenophobia in the new literatures in English*. Rodopi. doi:10.1163/9789401205672

Moliner, O., Sales, A., Ferrández, R., & Traver, J. (2011a). Inclusive cultures, policies and practices in Spanish compulsory secondary education schools: Teachers' perceptions in ordinary and specific teaching contexts. *International Journal of Inclusive Education*, *15*(5), 557–572. doi:10.1080/13603110903165158

Moliner, O., Sales, A., Ferrández, R., & Traver, J. (2011b). Inclusive cultures, policies and practices in Spanish compulsory secondary education schools: Teachers' perceptions in ordinary and specific teaching contexts. *International Journal of Inclusive Education*, *15*(5), 557–572. doi:10.1080/13603110903165158

Mor-Barak, M. E. (2013). *Managing diversity: Toward a globally inclusive workplace* (3rd ed.). SAGE Publications.

Morales, S. N., Martínez, L. R., Gómez, J. A. H., López, R. R., & Torres-Argüelles, V. (2019). Predictors of organizational resilience by factorial analysis. *International Journal of Engineering Business Management*, *11*, 184797901983704. doi:10.1177/1847979019837046

Mujtaba, B. G. (2013). Ethnic diversity, distrust and corruption in Afghanistan: Reflections on the creation of an inclusive culture. *Equality, Diversity and Inclusion*, *32*(3), 245–261. doi:10.1108/EDI-12-2012-0113

Nembhard, I. M., & Edmondson, A. C. (2006). Making it safe: The effects of leader inclusiveness and professional status on psychological safety and improvement efforts in health care teams. *Journal of Organizational Behavior*, *27*(7), 941–966. doi:10.1002/job.413

Nishii, L. H. (2013). The Benefits of Climate for Inclusion for Gender-Diverse Groups. *Academy of Management Journal*, *56*(6), 1754–1774. doi:10.5465/amj.2009.0823

Okun, O., Şen,Cem, & Arun, K. (2020). How Do Paternalistic Leader Behaviors Shape Xenophobia in Business Life? *International Journal of Organizational Leadership*. doi:10.33844/ijol.2020.60487

Okun, O., Arun, K., & Kılınç, S. (2021). Organizational Xenophobia: Effects of Leadership with Moderation of Satisfaction with Life: A field study in the Sample of Dense Migrated Province. *Journal for East European Management Studies*, *26*(4), 665–687. doi:10.5771/0949-6181-2021-4-665

Randel, A. E., Galvin, B. M., Shore, L. M., Ehrhart, K. H., Chung, B. G., Dean, M. A., & Kedharnath, U. (2018). Inclusive leadership: Realizing positive outcomes through belongingness and being valued for uniqueness. *Human Resource Management Review*, *28*(2), 190–203. doi:10.1016/j.hrmr.2017.07.002

Roberson, Q., & Perry, J. L. (2022). Inclusive Leadership in Thought and Action: A Thematic Analysis. *Group & Organization Management*, *47*(4), 755–778. doi:10.1177/10596011211013161

Rupp, G. (2015). *Beyond individualism: The challenge of inclusive communities*. Columbia University Press. doi:10.7312/columbia/9780231174282.001.0001

Ryan, S. M. (2014). An inclusive rural post secondary education program for students with intellectual disabilities. *Rural Special Education Quarterly*, *33*(2), 18–28. doi:10.1177/875687051403300204

Shah, A. K. (2022). *Inclusive and Sustainable Finance: Leadership, Ethics and Culture* (1st ed.). Routledge., doi:10.4324/9781003164746

Shore, L. M., & Chung, B. G. (2022). Inclusive Leadership: How Leaders Sustain or Discourage Work Group Inclusion. *Group & Organization Management, 47*(4), 723–754. doi:10.1177/1059601121999580

Sommer, S. A., Howell, J. M., & Hadley, C. N. (2016). Keeping Positive and Building Strength: The Role of Affect and Team Leadership in Developing Resilience During an Organizational Crisis. *Group & Organization Management, 41*(2), 172–202. doi:10.1177/1059601115578027

Starr, R., Newfrock, J., & Delurey, M. (2003). Enterprise resilience: Managing risk in the networked economy. *Strategy & Business, 30*, 70–79.

Su, S., Baird, K., & Munir, R. (2022). Organisational resilience: The role of organisational culture from an organisational life cycle perspective. *International Journal of Manpower*. doi:10.1108/IJM-11-2021-0631

Valle-Flórez, R.-E., de Caso Fuertes, A. M., Baelo, R., & Marcos-Santiago, R. (2022). Inclusive Culture in Compulsory Education Centers: Values, Participation and Teachers' Perceptions. *Children (Basel, Switzerland), 9*(6), 813. doi:10.3390/children9060813 PMID:35740750

van Breda, A. D. (2016). Building Resilient Human Service Organizations. *Human Service Organizations, Management, Leadership & Governance, 40*(1), 62–73. doi:10.1080/23303131.2015.1093571

van der Klift, E., & Kunc, N. (2019). *Being realistic isn't realistic: Collected essays on disability, identity, inclusion and innovation*. Tellwell Talent.

Woll, E. S. M. (2021). *Inclusive Leadership: 6 Behaviors to Embody*. Betterup. https://www.betterup.com/blog/what-makes-an-inclusive-leader-and-6-ways-to-up-your-game

Ye, Q., Wang, D., & Guo, W. (2019). Inclusive leadership and team innovation: The role of team voice and performance pressure. *European Management Journal, 37*(4), 468–480. doi:10.1016/j.emj.2019.01.006

ADDITIONAL READING

Anand, R. (2022). *Leading global diversity, equity, and inclusion: A guide for systemic change in multinational organizations* (1st ed.). Berrett-Koehler.

Brown, J. (2019). *How to be an inclusive leader: Your role in creating cultures of belonging where everyone can thrive* (1st ed.). Berrett-Koehler Publishers, Inc.

Johnson, S. K. (2020). *Inclusify: The power of uniqueness and belonging to build innovative teams*. Harper Business, an imprint of HarperCollins Publishers.

Shah, A. K. (2022). *Inclusive and Sustainable Finance: Leadership, Ethics and Culture* (1st ed.). Routledge., doi:10.4324/9781003164746

KEY TERMS AND DEFINITIONS

Inclusive Culture: Culture in which everyone's voice is heard, understood, and integrated for practice, thanks to the effective management provided by the management, and the fact that individuals with differences understand each other and resolve their conflicts in a functional way.

Inclusive Leadership: It rises on the basis of accepting and respecting the individual differences among employees, and involving them in the processes by establishing cooperation and effective communication with them. Inclusive leadership is successful in bringing the organization to desired results and making strategic decisions by overlapping common goals with differences. The inclusive leader is the assurance and insurance of all diversity working in the organisation.

Inclusiveness: The practice or policy of providing equal access, opportunities, and participation for all individuals, regardless of their background, identity, or characteristics. It involves creating an environment where everyone feels respected, valued, and included, and where diversity is celebrated.

Leader: Person on charge who has transformative effects on the culture of the organization

Organizational Resilience: Ability of organizations to cope with negative situations, as well as the ability to adapt to a different and risky environment.

Xenophobia: Set of beliefs and ideas based on the assumption that foreigners pose a threat to the nation and people of that country as an expression of ideology. Xenophobia breeds irrational fear, distance and hatred towards differences, foreigners and immigrants, and sees foreigners as the cause of all bad things.

Chapter 8
Role of Employee Resource Groups (ERGs) in Fostering Workforce Diversity in Information Technology (IT) Organizations After COVID-19

P. Ramshankar
CHRIST University (Deemed), India

Mary Rani Thomas
https://orcid.org/0000-0003-1372-3032
CHRIST University (Deemed), India

ABSTRACT

This chapter discovers how employee resource groups play an important role in fostering organizational diversity within information technology organizations. It examines the activities and practices to improve employee behaviour and also focuses on challenges faced by employees in spite of stress and mental health related issues during the COVID-19 pandemic. The data has been collected from secondary sources. The authors have used desk research and gray literature. The findings showcase increased employee engagement, improvements in diversity and inclusion, and an overall improvement in the inventive and creative skills of employees. It also helps the organization to brand itself better along with better recruitment strategies and practices. The key emphasis of the paper looks at the employees working within information technology organizations and how employee resource groups function to balance, motivate, and empower employees during COVID-19 Pandemic.

DOI: 10.4018/978-1-6684-6602-5.ch008

INTRODUCTION

The Information Technology Sector

As leading businesses across industries continue to push for the widespread use of digital technology, The Information Technology Sector has become one of the industries with the highest demand for professionals on the job market today. The information technology sector has undergone significant changes as a result of the introduction of new technologies, shifting client needs, and adjustments to the global economy.

In a number of areas, including the information technology industry, artificial intelligence and machine learning are being employed more regularly. Artificial intelligence and machine learning are used by businesses to automate processes, boost efficiency, and enhance consumer experiences (Varshney, 2020). Additionally, the 29% growth in job listings in this industry predicted for 2020 demonstrates how swiftly the need for specialists in artificial intelligence and machine learning is growing. LinkedIn, 2020.More companies are migrating their operations to the cloud as the information technology industry adopts cloud computing at a faster rate in order to scale operations, reduce expenses, and enhance security (Flexera, 2020). The epidemic has accelerated this trend as remote workforces require increasingly dependable cloud infrastructure to run their businesses.

Cloud computing services are expected to be the primary driver of demand for information technology services. The decision by businesses to store their data on the cloud is driving up demand for IT services. Significant advancements in the information technology sector have been made possible by new technology, changing customer needs, and adjustments to the global economy. Businesses in the information technology industry need to continually adjusting to these trends and developments in order to remain competitive and relevant.

Information Technology as a White-Collar Job

Most occupations in the Information Technology industry are categorized as white-collar. The Bureau of Labor Statistics reports, "White-collar employees handle managerial, professional, or administrative tasks. They often earn salaries and work in an office environment" (BLS, 2021). Software developers, network and computer systems administrators, and computer and information systems managers are examples of these jobs in the Information Technology sector.

The designation of Information Technology positions as white-collar jobs, made after 2018, is supported by research. According to a study done by the job-search website Glassdoor, white-collar positions, including enterprise architect, software development manager, and software engineering manager, had the highest salaries in the technology sector (Glassdoor, 2019). A further finding of the survey was that the median base pay for white-collar occupations in the technology sector was $97,859, while the median base pay for blue-collar professions was $45,377.

According to a 2020 McKinsey & Company report, the Information Technology industry had one of the highest percentages of white-collar positions of any industry, with 88% of Information Technology jobs falling into this category (McKinsey & Company, 2020). The study also discovered that white-collar Information Technology positions had a higher share of remote work potential than blue-collar jobs, making them more adaptable to the shifting workplace caused by the COVID-19 epidemic.

In addition, a 2018 report by the National Skills Coalition discovered that the Information Technology sector has the highest concentration of professional and technical jobs (National Skills Coalition, 2018) reinforcing that white-collar employment in Information Technology Sector constitutes the majority. These professions are primarily compensated office positions that demand employee organizational duties. Also supporting this categorization are the high median earnings, the high proportion of white-collar employment, and the possibility of remote work.

Current Global Scenario of the IT Workforce on a Worldwide Scale

The global market for information technology expanded at a compound annual growth rate (CAGR) of 8.2%, from $8179.48 billion in 2022 to $8852.41 billion in 2023. A temporary COVID-19 pandemic-related global economic recovery was impeded by the conflict between Russia and Ukraine. Economic sanctions on multiple countries, a rise in commodity prices, and disruptions in the supply chain as a result of the conflict between these two countries have increased the cost of goods and services and had an influence on many global markets. The market for information technology is anticipated to grow at a CAGR of 7.9% and reach $11995.97 billion in 2027.

According to pre-corona estimates, there will be 55.3 million full-time Information Technology workers worldwide in 2020, up 3.9 percent from 2019. Geographically, the average compensation for Information Technology workers can range from tens of thousands of dollars to over one hundred thousand. Naturally, executives in the worldwide Information Technology industry earn the highest salaries, followed by workers in the cloud computing industry, which is expanding quickly in the modern information age. Information Technology workers can also earn certifications that raise their worth in the eyes of recruiters and employers. For instance, Google's Professional Cloud Architect is the highest-paying qualification for Information Technology specialists globally in 2020.

The global information technology workforce is experiencing a rapid evolution. The development of new technologies, shifting consumer preferences, and changes in the global economy, has introduced rapid expansion throughout the years. The Information Technology sector has persisted in innovation and adaptation, employing cutting-edge tools like e-commerce, cloud computing, artificial intelligence and machine learning. Companies will need to spend in talent development and retention to stay competitive in the global market as long as there is a strong demand for competent Information Technology experts. The Information Technology workforce plays a crucial role in promoting innovation, economic growth, and digital transformation, and its significance is expected to increase over the following years.

Diversity in the Information Technology Sector

Diversity has gained importance in the information technology (IT) industry over the years after understanding benefits of a diverse workforce. Diverse teams produce more creative solutions and superior business results, according to study. Societal Inequality can be improved by developing a more diverse and inclusive Information Technology workforce, helping to aid in advancing economic development.

There is a growing understanding of the value of diversity in the tech sector. Businesses are trying to increase inclusivity and diversity through recent studies on diversity in the Information Technology industry and initiatives to promote diversity in this response.

Under-Representation of Minorities and Women

Despite initiatives to increase diversity, women and minorities remain disproportionately underrepresented in the Information Technology industry. Women make up only 24% of the computing workforce and only 11% of senior Information Technology leadership jobs, according to research by the National Center for Women & Information Technology (NCWIT) (2019). Similarly, minorities are underrepresented, with Black, Hispanic, and Native American workers making up only 9% of the computing workforce.

Advantages of Diversity in Information Technology

The Information Technology industry needs diversity to foster a more inventive and imaginative staff. A Herring (2019) study found that diverse teams are better equipped to serve a diverse consumer base and are more likely to produce innovative solutions and products. Additionally, a study by Jackson, Ruderman, and DeFillippi (2019) discovered that diverse teams are more imaginative and creative than homogeneous ones.

Initiatives to Expand Diversity in Information Technology

Numerous IT-related businesses are making efforts to broaden their diversity and inclusivity. For instance, Microsoft has pledged to raise the proportion of women and minorities in its workforce and has established goals. Google has also started several programs to promote diversity, such as a program to give underrepresented groups access to coding courses.

Obstacles to Broadening Diversity in Information Technology

Despite these efforts, increasing diversity in the Information Technology industry can take time and effort. The "pipeline problem," which refers to the reality that fewer women and minorities are studying and joining computer science, is one difficulty. Bias in hiring and promotion procedures is another problem that can lead to the exclusion of underrepresented groups.

Diversity in the Information Technology industry is crucial since it might result in a more innovative and creative workforce. Despite obstacles, many businesses are working to solve this problem and foster a more welcoming workplace culture.

Diversity

Differences, acknowledgement, acceptance, and respect are all aspects of diversity. Every individual possesses unique qualities results in a diverse population. In order to have "transcendence," or human attributes that are unique from our own and exist outside of the social groups to which we belong, diversity is necessary. One individual differs from another based on a variety of characteristics. Every country with a sizable immigrant population, whether developed or developing, has been the focus of research and controversy. Race, gender, ethnicity, religion, and geographical areas are the usual categories used to categorise diversity.

The word "diversity" has gained widespread acceptance by the 1990s. Diversity has drawn a lot of attention recently, yet it still poses a serious concern for our society. Diversity is a concept that involves valuing and accepting individual differences. In a study published in the year 2020 and published in the journal Social Psychological and Personality Science, it was found that diverse teams are more innovative than homogeneous teams. According to the researchers, when people from different backgrounds work together, they bring a wider range of information, abilities, and perspectives to the table, which encourages the development of more original ideas and solutions (Wang, Ku, & Galinsky, 2020).

A 2021 study found that higher levels of diversity in healthcare organisations are linked to better patient outcomes. The study was published in the journal Social

Science & Medicine. Researchers discovered that hospitals with more ethnically and racially diverse staffs had lower mortality and readmission rates and higher patient satisfaction scores (Makowsky et al., 2021).

Diversity is a practical method to improve outcomes in various sectors, in addition to being a question of social justice and equity. By embracing variety, we can build a more vibrant and inclusive society that honours and uses each person's talents and experiences.

Workforce Diversity

The term "Workforce Diversity" refers to the variety of differences between employees. A few examples of these discrepancies include those based on age, gender, colour, ethnicity, sexual orientation, religion, education, skills, and cultural background. Diversity fosters exceptional originality, innovation, and adaptation within a company, which is a valuable asset.

Workforce diversity aids in ensuring that there is room for simultaneous, equal, and increased growth for both the individuals and the organisation. The idea of workforce diversity is now more widely accepted across a wide range of businesses. Human resource managers within organisations make it their primary and implied duty to ensure that every employee working within the organisation is taken care of individually with regard and respect to the ethical, religious, and customary beliefs held by different employees working within the organisation.

Before establishing diversity as the research focus, women in management had been a topic of interest for academics since the 1970s. Businesses and Human Resource Management expanded the diversity scale by including new factors like physical ailments, religious beliefs, and educational background.

Organizations have persevered and continued to strive and compete more effectively worldwide as businesses grow gradually or more competitive; however, this can be made possible by creating highly qualified staff. It is challenging for businesses to find skilled staff. Mostly, business organizations are forced to look outside for talent, increasing the workforce's overall diversity. Despite the complexity, due to the tremendous variety of talent within the global world, it is recognized as a vital aspect of human resources and a constant challenge for businesses to manage effectively.

Diversity recruitment is one of the best ways to influence job seekers' perceptions of a firm's attractive workforce, increasing workplace beauty. Programs for diversity training are created to lessen conflicts between organizations, helping to creating an equitable and comfortable atmosphere for the workforce as a whole.

BENEFITS OF WORKFORCE DIVERSITY

Improved innovation, enhanced creativity, and improved problem-solving are also few of the numerous benefits that firms strive to foster in their staff. Including people from various backgrounds, viewpoints, and experiences in the workforce. A diverse workforce can foster fresh ideas and ways of thinking because people from various backgrounds bring their perspectives and insights. Ultimately, worker diversity is a crucial component of contemporary workplaces and can support businesses in thriving and succeeding in a world that is becoming more linked and complex.

Many forms of diversity are widely acknowledged, including:

Demographic Diversity

Individual disparities in age, gender, race, ethnicity, and other demographic factors are called demographic diversity. According to research, demographic diversity can have various sound effects on businesses, such as improved organizational performance and increased creativity and innovation.

The overall connectivity between demographic diversity and creativity in organizations was investigated in a study by Herring et al. (2019). The authors discovered that teams with higher demographic diversity tended to be more creative, but this effect was tempered by team trust and communication. To fully reap the rewards of demographic diversity, the authors recommended that businesses concentrate on creating a culture of openness and trust.

The importance of demographic diversity in fostering innovation and competitive advantage in businesses was covered in an article by Roberson et al. (2019). The writers made the case that businesses should respect diversity and inclusion and seek out people with diverse experiences and viewpoints to foster innovation and success.

The connection between demographic diversity and team effectiveness in the financial services sector was examined in a study by Liu et al. (2020). The researchers discovered that teams with more demographic diversity tended to perform better, but this effect was tempered by effective teamwork and communication. The authors recommended that companies concentrate on creating a culture of cooperation and open communication to fully reap the rewards of demographic diversity. The significance of demographic diversity in fostering organizational resilience in the face of disasters was covered in an essay by Cox and Blake (2021). The authors made the case that various viewpoints are especially beneficial in times of uncertainty and upheaval and offered suggestions on how businesses can easily create and use diverse teams to handle crises.

The relationship between demographic diversity and innovation in the healthcare sector was investigated in a study by Lüscher et al. (2021). According to the authors, firms with greater demographic diversity tended to be more inventive, although this effect was tempered by organizational culture and leadership. According to the authors, organizations should put their efforts into cultivating an inclusive culture and valuing different viewpoints to reap the rewards of demographic diversity fully.

These studies highlight the value of demographic diversity in fostering creative thinking, sound judgment, and organizational effectiveness. In today's multicultural and international business climate, organizations that promote diversity and assemble teams with various experiences and opinions are more likely to be successful.

Cognitive Diversity

Cognitive diversity is the term used to describe variations in how people reason, process information, and approach challenges. The term "cognitive diversity" describes the variations in how people approach problem-solving and decision-making. Decision-making, innovation, and organizational performance have all been demonstrated to benefit from cognitive diversity, according to research. Cognitive diversity can promote creativity, improve the standard of decision-making, and produce fresh ideas and viewpoints by bringing together people with various backgrounds, experiences, and ways of thinking.

A Fernandes et al. (2018) study investigated the association between cognitive diversity and team creativity. The authors discovered that teams with higher cognitive diversity tended to be more creative, albeit this effect was tempered by team size and communication effectiveness. To foster innovation, the authors recommended that corporations concentrate on forming teams with various cognitive viewpoints. The significance of cognitive diversity in fostering creativity and success in businesses was covered in a research article by Miller (2019). According to the author, organizations must value different viewpoints and welcome fresh concepts to remain competitive. The author gave examples of businesses that have effectively used cognitive diversity to promote innovation and growth.

The connectivity between cognitive diversity and team effectiveness in professional service organizations was examined in a study by Jackson et al. (2020). The scientists discovered that teams with more cognitive variety tended to perform better but that this effect was tempered by the degree of team cohesion and coordination.

The significance of cognitive variety in leading teams through crises was covered by Rock and Grant (2020). In addition to suggesting how leaders might use cognitive diversity to manage crises effectively, the authors made the case that varied viewpoints are particularly beneficial in challenging and unpredictable circumstances.

The association between cognitive diversity and company performance was investigated by Di Stefano et al. (2021). The authors discovered that organizations with more cognitive diversity typically outperformed their competitors in terms of financial performance but that this effect was tempered by organizational culture and structure. To fully reap the rewards of cognitive diversity, the authors recommended that firms concentrate on developing an inclusive culture and valuing different viewpoints.

To fully capitalise on cognitive diversity's advantages, it's critical to foster an environment where people feel free to express their individual viewpoints and thoughts. Cognitive diversity can be a potent instrument for fostering innovation and success, but it necessitates conscious effort to manage and harness differences successfully.

Cultural Diversity

Several cultural groups existing inside societal organizations are called cultural diversity. According to research, cultural diversity can improve both individual and organizational outcomes. The relationship between cultural diversity and creative thinking in teams was investigated in a study by Galinsky et al. (2018). The researchers discovered that while teams with greater ethnic variety tended to be more creative, this effect was tempered by team trust and communication. According to the authors, firms should cultivate an inclusive culture and value different viewpoints to reap the rewards of cultural diversity fully.

The value of cultural diversity in fostering innovation and business success was covered in an article by Kanter (2018). The author made the case that firms that value diversity is better equipped to access fresh perspectives and offered instances of businesses that have effectively benefited from cultural variety to gain a competitive advantage. The relationship between cultural diversity and team performance in international organizations was the subject of research by Homan et al. (2019). The authors discovered that teams with more cultural variety typically performed better, albeit the presence of cultural intelligence and a shared sense of identity among team members tempered this effect. To fully reap the rewards of cultural diversity, the authors recommended that businesses concentrate on developing cultural intelligence and fostering a sense of shared identity.

The significance of cultural agility in leading heterogeneous teams was covered in an article by Neeley (2020). The author made the case that leaders must adjust to various cultural norms and communication styles to manage heterogeneous teams effectively. The author offered suggestions for how leaders might achieve cultural adaptability, such as looking for different viewpoints and forging solid connections across cultural barriers. The relationship between cultural diversity and innovation in businesses was investigated in a study by Gallicano et al. (2021). The authors discovered that businesses with greater ethnic variety tended to have more inventive cultures, but elements like organizational structure and leadership tempered this effect. Organizations will only be able to accomplish their objectives by monitoring or controlling the job performance of multicultural staff. A two-way procedure is required to maximize the work output of a team with various cultural backgrounds.

Organizations with diverse workforces should start by switching from domestic human resource management techniques to international human resource management practices that promote multicultural workplaces and foster psychological diversity climates to increase employees' job satisfaction (Cletus et al., 2018). According to Cletus et al. (2018), merely initiating and implementing diversity programs is insufficient for local human resource management slants and approaches to addressing cultural variations across ethnic origins (Aluwi & Saihani, 2013).

Researchers have sought to highlight which aspects of global human resource management are essential to improve multicultural workforce performance and job satisfaction to create a diverse workplace. Though it is based on the cultural revolution, managing diversity is a practical business strategy that emphasizes maximizing the workforce's effectiveness, innovation, and dedication while meeting the needs of various client groups.

Functional Diversity

Functional diversity is the term used to describe the disparities in abilities, wisdom, and experience among group or organization members. According to research, functional diversity has been linked to improved problem-solving, judgment, and organizational performance. The association between functional diversity and team effectiveness in healthcare organizations was investigated in a study by Tzafrir et al. (2018). The authors discovered that teams with more functional diversity tended to perform better, but this effect was tempered by team coordination and communication. To fully reap the rewards of functional diversity, the authors recommended that organizations concentrate on creating a culture of cooperation and open communication.

The value of available variety in fostering creativity and innovation in businesses was covered in a paper by Johnson and Johnson (2019). According to the authors, to foster innovation, businesses should value different points of view and look for people with complementary backgrounds and abilities. The correlation between functional diversity and business success in the technology sector was examined in a study by Kim et al. (2020). The authors discovered that organizations with greater functional diversity tended to do better financially, but this effect was tempered by the degree of team cohesion and communication. To fully capitalize on the advantages of functional diversity, the authors recommended that organizations concentrate on creating a culture of trust and transparency.

The significance of functional variation in managing teams in distant work situations was covered in a Hinds and Mortensen (2021) essay. The authors claimed that functional diversity could be especially beneficial in remote teams, where members may have varying skill sets and specialties. The writers advised managers on creating remote teams with diverse functional expertise.

The association between functional diversity and team creativity in the industrial sector was investigated by Huang et al. in their study from 2021. The authors discovered that teams with greater functional variety tended to be more creative, but this effect was tempered by the team's degree of psychological safety and communication.

These studies highlight the value of functional diversity in fostering creativity, sound judgment, and organizational performance. Organizations will likely thrive in today's fast-paced and dynamic business climate by valuing varied perspectives and creating teams with complementary skills and experiences.

Organizational Diversity

"Organizational Diversity" refers to various distinctions, including age, gender, ethnicity, race, religion, sexual orientation, socioeconomic status, and talents, among employees, management, and leadership. Increasing productivity, lowering attrition rates, and boosting employee morale are all advantages for organizations that support diversity. Diversity in organizational levels, divisions, and functions is also called organizational diversity.

Adina Sterling and Sameer Srivastava's (2018) study examines the relationship between diversity and team innovation. However, the authors find that heterogeneous teams are typically more creative when they have a shared identity or objective that can bring them together to the authors. To fully reap the rewards of diversity, managers should foster a sense of shared identity among team members.

The value of inclusive leadership in fostering diverse and inclusive organizations is covered in a paper by David Thomas and Robin Ely(2019). The authors contend that leaders must go beyond simply encouraging diversity and fostering an inclusive culture where all employees feel valued and supported. The authors offer a paradigm for inclusive leadership that includes aggressively seeking various viewpoints, fostering psychological safety, and developing a sense of common purpose.

The relationship between diversity and team effectiveness in healthcare companies is examined in a study by Samuel Hunter and colleagues (2020). According to the authors, teams with more diversity typically have better patient outcomes, higher efficiency, and reduced costs. According to the authors, healthcare institutions should develop an inclusive culture that celebrates diversity and encourages all staff members to contribute their distinct viewpoints and expertise.

The significance of intersectionality in developing genuinely diverse and inclusive organizations is covered in an article by Stefanie Johnson and David Hekman (2021). The authors contend that to establish genuinely inclusive workplaces, intersectionality—or the ways that various facets of identity (such as race, gender, and sexual orientation) overlap and interact with one another—must be taken into consideration. The authors guide managers and organizations in developing intersectional diversity and inclusion strategies, such as valuing and recognizing all workers' diverse experiences and viewpoints.

The relationship between diversity and team innovation is examined in a meta-analysis by Sylvia van Baalen and others (2021). The authors discover that diverse teams typically exhibit higher levels of creativity. However, the type of diversity present and the environment in which the team operates moderate this effect. According to the authors, managers should develop a culture of psychological safety and receptivity to different viewpoints to fully reap the rewards of diversity.

Workers who experience a sense of value and respect are likely to be engaged and satisfied with their jobs. Employee morale can be raised by providing a varied and inclusive work environment that makes people feel appreciated and respected (Roberson, 2019).

These studies indicate that organizational diversity can have various advantages, from more significant innovation and team performance to increased employee well-being and creativity. In order to create truly diverse and inclusive companies, it is crucial to approach diversity and inclusion strategies cautiously and understand the importance of intersectionality, inclusive leadership, and context. Managing diversity entails fostering an atmosphere where everyone, despite differences, feels appreciated and respected.

IMPORTANCE OF WORKFORCE DIVERSITY

Any organization's personnel is a crucial element, significantly impacting the company's success. Talented and driven personnel can help a business stand out from the competition. A Deloitte analysis claims that companies that invest in the growth and happiness of their workers outperform their competitors more frequently. (Deloitte, 2019). A varied and inclusive workforce can foster creativity and innovation. According to a McKinsey study, businesses with the highest racial and cultural diversity levels are more likely to be profitable than the industry average. (McKinsey, 2020). Also, more customer satisfaction may result from an empowered and engaged workforce due to increased performance. According to a Gallup study, motivated workers are 21% more likely to boost productivity, profitability, and customer satisfaction. (Gallup, 2019)

Organizations can overcome problems and changes in the business environment with an adaptive and resilient staff. According to a PwC analysis, businesses with a strong culture of adaptation are 1.5 times more likely than their peers to record growth. (PwC, 2019).An organization's reputation can be improved by a workforce dedicated to acting morally and responsibly. Consumers feel that a company's reputation for ethical behavior is a deciding factor in their purchasing decisions, according to a survey by Edelman that found 64% of consumers. (Edelman, 2019)

The workforce plays a crucial role in the success of an organization by influencing variables, including innovation, customer happiness, competitiveness, flexibility, and reputation. Companies can improve their performance and set themselves up for long-term success by investing in their workforce's diversity, well-being, and growth. Such organizations are more likely than their counterparts to report growth. (PwC, 2019)

THE IMPACT OF THE COVID-19 PANDEMIC ON THE WORKFORCE

The COVID-19 disease outbreak had a significant negative impact on the information technology market in 2020 as trade restrictions disrupted supply chains and employees had trouble communicating and using infrastructure due to lockdowns imposed by governments around the world, which forced them to work from home.

Early in 2020, after the COVID-19 epidemic broke out, drastic alteration happened in & how people interacted with one another and their communities. As a result of the closure of schools, companies, and community centers to stop the virus' spread, society underwent a great deal of stress and change. One of the areas of life where the virus had the most significant impact was the workplace. Before COVID-19, 23% of employees who could work from home did so; nevertheless, at the height of the epidemic, about 70% of employees were doing so (Parker et al., 2022) for the "essential workers," who were unable to perform their duties remotely, being at work introduced new dangers from disease and infection. Employees were under tremendous pressure from these working conditions since they had to adjust to new health and well-being realities. The workplace is an excellent venue to treat mental health issues (Center for Disease Control and Prevention, 2019). While there is a growing understanding of the necessity of addressing employee mental health, the US remains well behind its peer countries. For instance, since 2013, Canada has had a national Commission on Mental Health emphasizing employees' mental health. This Commission has developed a collection of optional guidelines and tools for companies to meet the mental health needs of their staff members (Mental Health Commission Canada, 2022). With the COVID-19 issue, businesses must have solid mental health assistance plans for their staff. This article examines the most recent developments in workplace mental health.

The Covid-19 pandemic has significantly changed the Information Technology workforce, accelerating current trends and posing new difficulties for both employers and employees. The pandemic's effects on remote work, job security, mental health, and diversity and inclusion in the Information Technology industry are now a subject of an expanding body of research.

One of the pandemic's most immediate effects was the shift to remote work, with many Information Technology professionals doing so for the first time. According to research, this shift affects the Information Technology workforce positively and negatively. Besides, remote work has boosted employee flexibility and work-life balance and reduced enterprise costs. The adverse effects of remote work include an uptick in feelings of loneliness and burnout and a blurring of the lines between work and personal life (Kenski, 2021).

The pandemic's effects on Information Technology workers' job security and financial stability remain another. With rising demand for digital technologies and services, the Information Technology sector has remained resilient throughout the epidemic. However, there have also been job losses and recruiting freezes in several areas. Likewise, employees who cannot work remotely or are responsible for caring for others may experience job loss and economic uncertainty more severely (McKinsey, 2020).

The importance of mental health and wellbeing in the Information Technology sector has also been brought to light by the epidemic. According to research, the pandemic has made Information Technology professionals more stressed, anxious, and depressed. Many also report having a more challenging time juggling their personal and professional lives with their work obligations. Businesses have reacted by providing more mental health resources and assistance to workers, but more must be done to address the pandemic's long-term effects on mental health (American Psychological Association, 2021).Third, the epidemic has bolstered and challenged initiatives to advance inclusion and diversity in the Information Technology sector. Inequities and inequality in access to technology, healthcare, and economic possibilities have been brought to light by the pandemic, especially for underrepresented groups. Contrarily, the pandemic has also raised awareness of and prompted action on issues related to diversity and inclusion, with numerous groups stepping up their dedication to equity and social justice (Hunt & Ajao, 2021).

The Covid-19 epidemic has significantly affected the Information Technology workforce, accelerating current trends and posing new difficulties for both employers and individuals. Employers and employees must adjust to these changes as the pandemic develops and collaborate to foster resilience, wellbeing, diversity, and inclusion in the Information Technology sector.

THE ESSENTIALITY TO KEEP THE WORKFORCE HAPPY AND UPDATED WITHIN ORGANIZATIONS

According to Carnevale and Hatak (2020) and Yldrm and Solmaz (2020), the Coronavirus illness 2019 (COVID-19) has rapidly spread throughout the world, generating an unprecedented worldwide crisis that has notably impacted the operations of numerous service businesses. More than 52,398,474 verified COVID-19 cases had been reported as of November 13th, 2020, affecting 212 countries and territories (World Health Organization, 2020). According to recent studies, COVID-19 can cause a variety of psychological issues, including stress, anxiety, and depression, as well as negatively impact happiness (Arslan et al., 2020; Brooks et al., 2020).

It is evident that stress has a detrimental influence on people's lives, but the severity of that impact differs depending on how well-equipped each person is to deal with situations that cause stress (Babore et al., 2020; Folkman, 2010). The dangerous consequences of stress on general well-being and happiness must be controlled (Rabenu et al., 2017; Xu, 2019).Due to different pressures, COVID-19-related stress harms employees' enjoyment at work and jeopardizes their mental health. According to research, stressors like home confinement (Wang et al., 2020), precautionary measures (Brooks et al., 2020), social exclusion (Tuzovic & Kabadayi, 2020), fear of infection (Labrague & De Los Santos, 2020), uncertainty about pandemics (Zandifar & Badrfam, 2020), and episodes of job loss (Venkatesh, 2020) hurt employee happiness.

Given the apparent link between stress and happiness, COVID-19-related stress management interventions should reduce psychological discomfort and enhance subjective well-being or happiness. At the individual level, developing healthy coping mechanisms and using psychological assets like optimism, self-efficacy, resilience, and hope are two potential strategies for achieving this.

The pandemic has altered the playing field regarding working from home or the workplace. Focusing on stress management is essential since excessive worry and fear have infiltrated the lives of many individuals.

EMPLOYEE RESOURCE GROUPS (ERGS)

Employee resource groups (ERGs) are voluntary, employee-led organizations that aim to support, champion, and celebrate inclusion and diversity. Employee Resource Groups (ERGs) are associations of coworkers who help one another and enhance their careers by coming together around shared interests or identities. Companies use Employee Resource Groups more frequently to encourage workplace diversity, equality, and inclusion (DEI). Employee Resource Groups can be based on a specific aspect of diversity, such as color, gender, or sexual orientation. They can be used for several things, including facilitating networking opportunities, supporting career development and mentoring, and planning social and community outreach activities. Employee Resource Groups(ERGs) have been defined as follows by Catalyst. This non-profit organization has been researching them for over 20 years. “Employee Resource Groups are employee groups created by organizations to serve as resources for both the members and the group as a whole. Employee Resource Groups are voluntary, employee-led organizations with a small or large number of members. Organizations have used employee resource groups (ERGs) for over 40 years. Affinity groups, employee networks, and diversity councils are a few names given to Employee Resource Groups. Although the organization sponsors Employee Resource Groups, volunteers staff them. By joining one or more Employee Resource Groups at their companies, employees with paid employment decide to put in the additional unpaid time to support the organization. They are best categorized as bottom-up phenomena becoming common in many Fortune 500 companies and gaining traction in mid-size companies. Employee Resource Groups, which employee volunteers primarily run, allow people to interact personally and professionally and encourage one another to create a sense of belonging within the company (Cordivano, 2019). Employee resource groups are regularly joined by employees for relationships with others who share their identities, professional development, mentorship support, and networking (Lopez, 2018).

Employees who belong to employee resource groups are more engaged and have higher work satisfaction, per a survey from the Centre for Talent Innovation. By encouraging a sense of belonging, employee research groups can also improve retention. (Centre for Talent Innovation, 2018). A Deloitte analysis claims that employee resource groups can promote brand perception, enhance customer interactions, and aid companies in discovering new business prospects. (Deloitte, 2019)

A Human Rights Campaign Foundation report indicated that Employee Research Groups could offer employees opportunities for leadership development and assist businesses in creating a pipeline of diverse talent for leadership positions. (Human Rights Campaign Foundation, 2019).Employee Resource Groups should have company support and financing, according to a Society for Human Resource Management research. This support and funding should include funding, training, and senior leadership access. (Society for Human Resource Management, 2020)

Employee Resource Groups should endeavor to be inclusive of all employees and recognize and celebrate the intersectionality of employees’ identities, according to the Employee Research Groups’ inclusive and intersectional stance. According to a Catalyst analysis, inclusive Employee Research Groups can promote Diversity, Equity, and Inclusion initiatives and assist businesses in fostering a sense of belonging. (Catalyst, 2018).Employee resource groups (ERGs) provide participants with access to a "community" of people who are similar to them and have similar goals (Green, 2018).

Employee Research Groups act as a path for advocacy (e.g., help promote learning about their causes and positive change, such as working for equality via LGBT organizations), function as a means for information sharing (e.g., programs for black history month, teaching about women leaders), and serve as a source of social and professional support for members.

Despite the expansion and complexity of Employee Resource Groups in big and mid-sized enterprises, more study needs to be done on how they affect people, Employee Resource Groups members, the Employee Resource group itself, or the company. Even though these corporate-sponsored, voluntary groups have been around longer and are still undergoing significant development, much more research is still needed. Most beginning Human Resource Management textbooks, organizational behavior instruction, and undoubtedly academic research on diversity and inclusion have ignored the expansion and comeback of Employee Resource Groups.

IMPORTANCE OF EMPLOYEE RESOURCE GROUPS (ERGS) POST COVID-19

Employee resource groups (ERGs) are crucial tools for promoting inclusion and diversity in the workplace. Within the past five years, crucial emphasis has been given to promoting workplace inclusion and diversity organizations that support inclusion and diversity into significant players in corporate strategy and daily operations. Multicultural competence and awareness are essential for commercial success in today's global economy. Employee resource groups (ERGs) can make use of employee knowledge and expertise for talent management (recruiting/retaining diverse employees), to develop products, marketing, and customer service that are sensitive to cultural differences, as well as supplier diversity, and to create an inclusive and engaged workforce.

In one study, workforce diversity and creativity were compared by Jackson, Ruderman, and DeFillippi (2019). According to the study, diverse teams were more creative than homogeneous teams. According to the authors, this is because diverse teams can draw from a greater variety of viewpoints and experiences, which enables them to produce more original and creative ideas. Hunt, Layton, and Prince (2019) examined the connection between workforce diversity and financial performance in another study. According to the survey, businesses with more diverse executive teams outperformed their less diverse counterparts regarding profitability and financial performance. According to the authors, this is because various teams can better comprehend and cater to a diverse consumer base. Wang, Hu, and He (2020) looked at the connection between employee turnover and workforce diversity in their third study. According to the study, diversified teams saw less turnover than homogeneous teams. According to the authors, this occurs because employees feel more appreciated and included in diverse teams, which increases job satisfaction and decreases turnover.

These studies indicate that workforce diversity can benefit firms in several ways. Employee Resource Groups can promote workplace diversity in several ways, including the following,

Giving Employees a Feeling of Community

Employee Research Groups give employees who might feel alone or underrepresented in the workplace a sense of community. They establish a setting where people can meet others with similar backgrounds, experiences, and interests and form deep connections.

Promoting Professional Growth

Employee Resource Groups can offer beneficial professional growth opportunities, like mentoring, instruction, and skill-building seminars. Employee Resource Groups participants can benefit from networking opportunities, leadership training, and professional advancement through these groups.

Promoting Cultural Change

Within a company, Employee Resource Groups can be used to promote cultural change. They can promote change, advocate for issues related to diversity and inclusion, and offer feedback on procedures and policies that affect workers.

Fostering a Greater Understanding of Cultures

Employee Resource Groups can contribute to the advancement of intercultural understanding by giving members a chance to converse with others about their experiences, viewpoints, and cultural practices. This can promote better empathy and understanding while assisting in dismantling prejudices.

Business Goals Advancement

Employee Resource Groups can assist firms in accomplishing their goals by enhancing employee engagement, retention, and productivity, as well as helping them better understand and serve their diverse client bases.

Overall, by creating a welcoming and inclusive atmosphere for workers to connect, learn, and grow, Employee Resource Groups can be crucial in promoting workplace diversity. Employee Resource Groups can assist businesses in maximizing the advantages of a diverse workforce and developing a more welcoming workplace environment that promotes success for all employees.

FINDINGS AND IMPLICATIONS

Effectiveness of Employee Resource Groups

Employee resource groups may be advantageous to both individuals and organisations, according to a growing body of research. Key conclusions are as follows:

Increased Employee Engagement and Retention

According to research by the Center for Talent Innovation, employees who participate in employee resource groups are more engaged at work and less likely to leave their jobs than those who do not. Employee resource groups can promote a feeling of connection and individual worth among staff members, according to the study.

Improvements in Diversity and Inclusion

Employee resource groups can serve as a forum for promoting change inside an organisation and bringing attention to issues related to diversity and inclusion. Employee resource groups may be essential in furthering programmes for diversity and inclusion, according to a McKinsey & Company study that found that organisations with more diverse leadership teams outperform their peers.

Improved Invention and Creativity

Employee resource groups can provide a space for staff members to discuss ideas, leading to novel discoveries and approaches. According to Deloitte's study, diverse and inclusive teams are more creative and innovative, which suggests that employee resource groups might help businesses become more adaptable and competitive.

Better Branding and Recruitment

Employee Resource Groups can help businesses attract and retain top talent by demonstrating a commitment to inclusion and diversity. More than half of job seekers consider the diversity and inclusion policies of an organisation when making a career decision, according to a Society for Human Resource Management survey.

These are only a few examples of research studies and papers that confirm the effectiveness of employee resource groups. The statistics show that Employee Resource Groups can be a useful instrument for promoting diversity and inclusion within organisations, having a variety of positive benefits on people and organisations alike.

Strategies that Employee Resource Groups (ERGs) Can Employ to Improve Workplace Diversity

Informing Managers of the Advantages of Diversity in the Workplace

Managers and employees need to get along. The main reason why people quit their employment is that they do not like their supervisors. Only a select few managers are knowledgeable in managing a diverse team and are aware of its value. Provide them with the instruction they require to build and manage a diverse team to aid them. A practical first step is scheduling sensitivity training for cultural and other considerations.

Recruiting and Cultivating Diverse and High Potential Candidates

Without tokenism, it is possible to accomplish diversity and performance. This workplace diversity improvement technique requires strategic preparation and execution. Efforts must be taken to find out which of the organization's applicants have a diverse, high potential. Organizations should ensure that leadership is dedicated to giving high-potential employees who lack necessary skills such as mentoring, coaching, and growth opportunities, or consider assigning such people to a stretch role.

Streamlining the Interview Process

Using digital, structured interviewing to create diverse teams is an excellent strategy. The organization may lessen the possibility of hiring discrimination and ensure a fair, consistent interview process by posing the same questions to all job seekers in the same order and format. Using this method, Organizations can hire individuals who are more accurately and objectively representative of the human race. Organizations can speed up the earliest stages of the hiring process while removing the unconscious bias of the recruiters by using Artificial Intelligence powered recruiting tools.

Recognizing and Appreciating Every Diverse Element Within the Organization

Organizations must acknowledge and value each employee's skills, regardless of variances. Regularly expressing appreciation to the staff can be done by conversing and paying attention to what they say. Efforts must be taken to know each of the staff. When workers feel valued and welcomed, they will go above and beyond. Managing diversity is vital to creating an environment where individuals feel their voices are heard and what they say matters. This includes making people feel like they belong and are active in activities. People want to be treated equally and according to their qualities; they do not want to be treated differently.

Establishing Efficient and Effective Policies for Hiring That Promote Diversity and Inclusion

The human resources division must encourage diversity and inclusion in the workforce; recruiters, in particular, must be diversity drivers. This suggests that to develop a diverse and inclusive talent shortlist for the final interview stage, they must build the proper mentality and consider diversity during the selection process.

Usage of Technologically Advanced Recruitment Tools That Reduce Unconscious Bias

Digitizing and streamlining the hiring process becomes essential to driving a contemporary and effective hiring process. The earliest stages of the hiring process are expedited by using Artificial Intelligence driven recruiting software, which also eliminates the unconscious bias of the recruiters. However, after the initial computerized matching of applicants with job requirements, recruiters will be involved in the selection process. As a result, organizations should also spend money on training programs for hiring managers and recruiters to assist them in identifying and managing unconscious prejudice.

Providing Opportunities Meaningful for Employee Engagement

Organizations can consider allowing employees to visit other locations in a different city, state, or nation if the organization's business practices and functions have numerous locations. Organizational efforts must be made to plan internal and external employee engagement activities by surveying the staff to learn where they like to volunteer or spend their free time. Employees could also see how other places handle issues and circumstances of a similar nature. This might inspire the staff to think creatively and contribute such thoughts to their teams.

Creating Diversity and Inclusion Training Initiatives

Top-down training on diversity and inclusion should be given to all employees in the company. The process starts by requesting assistance from the administrative leadership in developing the organization's training program. Training should include raising people's awareness of implicit bias and reducing prejudice that could harm managerial decisions. Organizations should make diversity education a volunteer endeavor. It should ensure it is widely accessible and well-publicized within the organization.

Evaluation of all HR Facets That Have an Impact on Diversity

Organizations should think about systems rather than gestures to avoid the tokenism trap. Efforts must be taken to analyze all facets of human resources that impact diversity, including hiring, salary, career mobility, and benefits for financial wellness. By addressing the whole system, organizations can impact all associated activities, achieve long-term equity, and create a more varied and diverse workplace.

Initiation of Efforts and Measures to Track Organizational Efforts

For an organization to succeed, diversification is crucial. To ensure organizational efforts are impacting, organizations should start measuring the efforts taken for diversification. As the organization begins taking measurements, the management will be able to see how the needle is going. Without metrics to look at and analyze, the organizational management will not know whether employee performance is improving or moving forward.

LIMITATIONS

Employee Resource Groups (ERGs) have been well-liked for encouraging workplace diversity in Information Technology Organizations. ERGs can promote diversity and inclusion in the workplace, but they also have limitations, and more research is required to fully appreciate their potential and difficulties.

Employee Resource Groups can be perceived as exclusive or divisive, which feeds preconceptions and fosters silos within the organization. This can occur when Employee Resource Groups emphasize the requirements of their particular identity group and disregard the general objective of fostering diversity and inclusion for all workers. Researchers discovered that depending on how they were set up and handled, Employee Resource Groups in the technology sector might be empowering and constraining. To foster an inclusive work environment for all employees, they advised that Employee Resource Groups should align with the company's broader diversity and inclusion strategy and participate in cross-functional collaboration (Noland et al., 2019).

Employee Resource Groups may not be accessible to or relevant to all employees. Due to the voluntary nature and self-organization of Employee Resource Groups, some employees may feel uncomfortable participating or need more time or resources. However, certain identity groups might need more support to establish their own Employee Resource Groups because they are underrepresented or marginalized within the organization. Several organizations have begun to use a "network of allies" strategy to overcome these obstacles. Allies support diversity and inclusion programs and are prepared to speak out for underrepresented groups, even if they do not belong to those groups (Witkowski, 2021).

Despite these drawbacks, Employee Resource Groups are a well-liked and valuable tool for fostering workplace diversity inside Information Technology Organizations. Employee resource groups (ERGs) can give disenfranchised or isolated workers a sense of belonging and community and help the organization become more conscious of and comprehend diversity concerns. In order to keep their Employee Resource Group strategies efficient, inclusive, and in line with the organization's overarching goals and values, it will be crucial for businesses to continuously assess and modify them as the diversity and inclusion field develops.

FUTURE RESEARCH DIRECTIONS

Since 2018, the function of Employee Resource Groups (ERGs) in encouraging workplace diversity inside Information Technology Organizations has changed, with new research emphasizing both the potential and difficulties of Employee Resource Groups in doing so.

Promoting intersectionality and allyship is one area where Employee Resource Groups have more room to grow. The term "intersectionality" describes how a person's various identities and experiences interact and influence their lives, such as being a woman of color or a member of the LGBTQ+ community who is differently abled. Research has indicated that Employee Resource Groups can be more effective when they acknowledge and address the intersectional experiences of their members and when they involve allies who might not have the same identity but are dedicated to supporting diversity and inclusion efforts (Catalyst, 2020).

Employee Resource Groups can also play a more prominent role in advancing social justice and equity inside and outside the workplace. Many organizations have widened their diversity and inclusion initiatives in response to social and political movements like #MeToo, and Black Lives Matter to address more extensive problems of structural inequality and discrimination. Employee Resource Groups can contribute by promoting policy modifications, assisting neighborhood projects, and participating in social action in collaboration with other organizations and stakeholders (Carter & Brown, 2020).

The ability of Employee Resource Groups to promote workplace diversity within Information Technology organizations continues to face difficulties and restrictions in addition to these additional areas of focus. Making sure Employee Resource Groups are included in the organization's more considerable diversity and inclusion strategy rather than being viewed as a distinct or ancillary endeavor is one problem. To ensure that Employee Resource Groups are fulfilling their aims and objectives, this calls for ongoing review and feedback, as well as clear communication and alignment between Employee Resource Groups leaders and corporate leadership (Dorsey & Villwock, 2020).

Expanding Employee Resource Groups to promote workplace diversity within Information Technology firms is encouraging but necessitates continued care and effort. Employee Resource Groups can be vital in fostering inclusive and just workplaces that benefit all workers by identifying and addressing intersectionality, fostering equity and social justice, and integrating with the larger organizational plan.

CONCLUSION

Following the COVID-19 epidemic, Employee resource groups (ERGs) have been essential in fostering diversity in the workforce within organisations. Employee resource groups provide a platform for workers from diverse backgrounds to communicate, collaborate, and create a more friendly work environment. Employee resource groups also offer a network of assistance and a stage for underrepresented groups to discuss the concerns that are unique to them.

After the epidemic, businesses are converting to a more diverse and inclusive workforce to remain competitive. This transition would not have been possible without the safe space that Employee Resource Groups offer for employees to share their experiences, ideas, and points of view. Employee resource groups have also helped businesses attract and retain a diverse workforce, stimulate greater innovation, and enhance problem-solving. Additionally, it has been demonstrated that employee resource groups successfully promote cultural awareness and understanding, aiding in reducing prejudice and discrimination inside workplaces. Employee resource groups have helped businesses create positive workplace environments by boosting employee morale and participation. To conclude, in the post-COVID-19 era, Employee Resource Groups are a useful tool for businesses wanting to promote inclusivity and diversity.

REFERENCES

Aluwi, A. R., & Saihani, M. S. (2013). Managing diversity at the workplace: A case study in a Malaysian government agency. *Journal of Management and Sustainability*, *3*(4), 155–167.

American Psychological Association. (2021). *COVID-19 one year later: Workplace mental health matters more than ever*. APA.

Bureau of Labor Statistics. (2021). *White-collar workers: An overview*. Bureau of Labor Statistics.

Carter, R. T., & Brown, S. A. (2020). Racialized trauma and the use of employee resource groups for support and advocacy. *The American Psychologist*, *75*(5), 661–670.

Catalyst. (2018). *The business case for employee resource groups*. Catalyst. https://www.catalyst.org/research/business-case-employee-resource-groups/

Catalyst. (2020). *Intersectionality: A critical lens for gender equality*. Ccatalyst.

Center for Talent Innovation. (2018). *Sponsorship and the high-potential employee: A guide to understanding and overcoming the barriers*. Center for Talent Innovation.

Cletus, U., Isah, M. A., & Kifordu, A. A. (2018). Diversity management and performance of selected Nigerian firms. [CompTIA.]. *African Journal of Economic and Management Studies*, *9*(1), 71–84.

Cox, C. B., & Blake, A. (2021). Diversity and organizational resilience: Insights for leaders navigating COVID-19. *Journal of Leadership Studies*, *15*(1), 81–88. doi:10.1002/jls.21686

Deloitte. (2018). *The Diversity and Inclusion Revolution: Eight Powerful Truths*. Deloitte.

Deloitte. (2019). *Leading the social enterprise: Reinvent with a human focus*. Deloitte.

Di Stefano, G., Gambardella, A., & Verona, G. (2021). Cognitive diversity, team performance, and firm growth: Evidence from a large panel of firms. *Strategic Management Journal, 42*(2), 301–329. doi:10.1002mj.3218

Dorsey, S., & Villwock, J. (2020). Employee resource groups: Best practices for organizational success. *Journal of Business Diversity, 20*(2), 1–16.

Edelman. (2019). 2019 Edelman trust barometer. *The Importance of Employee Engagement in the Modern Workplace*. Entrepreneur.

eMarketer. (2021). *Global e-commerce update 2021: Amid a pandemic shockwave*. eMarketer.

Fernandes, C., de Carvalho, G. B., & de Oliveira Cruz, G. (2018). The relationship between cognitive diversity and team creativity. *Journal of Business Research, 86*, 78–86. doi:10.1016/j.jbusres.2018.01.040

Flexera. (2020). *2020 State of the cloud report*. Flexera.

Forbes. (2019). Why the Human Workforce Is Still the Future of Work. *Forbes*.

Galinsky, A. D., Maddux, W. W., White, J. B., & Dubois, D. (2018). Cultural borders and mental barriers: The relationship between living abroad and creativity. *Journal of Personality and Social Psychology, 114*(2), 168–184. doi:10.1037/pspp0000138

Gallicano, T. D., Martin, L. M., & Wingreen, S. C. (2021). A multilevel examination of cultural diversity, diversity climate, and innovation in US organizations. *Journal of Business Research, 131*, 731–743. doi:10.1016/j.jbusres.2021.03.038

Gallup. (2019). *State of the American workplace*. Gallup.

Harvard Business Review. (2019). The Business Case for Diversity in the Workforce. *Harvard Business Review*.

Harvard Business Review. (2019). The Importance of a Skilled Workforce in the Digital Age. *Harvard Business Review*.

Herring, C. (2019). Does diversity pay? Race, gender, and the business case for diversity. *American Sociological Review, 84*(2), 208–235. doi:10.1177/000312240907400203

Herring, C., Woolley, A. W., & Xin, K. R. (2019). Demographic diversity and creativity in small groups: A review and integration of the literature. *Small Group Research, 50*(6), 715–770. doi:10.1177/1046496419883426

Hinds, P. J., & Mortensen, M. (2021). The key to managing remote work: Functional diversity. *Harvard Business Review, 99*(1), 124–133.

Homan, A. C., Buengeler, C., Eckhoff, R. A., Ginkel, W. P. V., & Voelpel, S. C. (2019). The interplay of diversity training and diversity beliefs on team creativity in nationality diverse teams. *Journal of Organizational Behavior, 40*(7), 812–832. doi:10.1002/job.2381

Huang, X., Wang, J., & Zhang, Y. (2021). Exploring the relationship between functional diversity and team innovation in the manufacturing industry: The role of organizational learning capability. *Sustainability, 13*(3), 1102. doi:10.3390u13031102

Human Rights Campaign Foundation. (2019). *LGBTQ diversity and inclusion in ERGs*. HRCF.

Hunt, V., & Ajao, B. (2021). How to promote diversity and inclusion during a crisis. *Harvard Business Review*.

Hunt, V., Layton, D., & Prince, S. (2019). *Diversity wins: How inclusion matters*. McKinsey & Company.

Hunter, S. T., Ouimet, G., Thompson, L. F., & Lee, M. K. (2020). Diversity, faultlines, and team effectiveness in health care organizations. *Journal of Health Organization and Management, 34*(2), 236–249.

Jackson, S. E., Li, Y., Zhao, Y., & Liu, J. (2020). The effects of cognitive diversity on team effectiveness in professional service organizations. *Journal of Organizational Behavior, 41*(8), 801–818. doi:10.1002/job.2391

Jackson, S. E., Ruderman, M. N., & DeFillippi, R. J. (2019). Diversity, creativity, and innovation: A meta-analytic review of the relationship. *Journal of Business and Psychology, 34*(1), 3–26.

Johnson, R. E., & Johnson, D. W. (2019). Functional diversity and innovation in interdisciplinary teams. *The Journal of Creative Behavior, 53*(4), 501–515. doi:10.1002/jocb.398

Johnson, S. K., & Hekman, D. R. (2021). Intersectionality as a necessary framework for diverse and inclusive organizations. *Academy of Management Review, 46*(2), 221–231. doi:10.5465/amr.2019.0464

Kanter, R. M. (2018). The diversity and inclusion revolution: Eight powerful truths. *Harvard Business Review, 96*(1), 54–61.

Kenski, K. (2021). *The impact of COVID-19 on the IT workforce: A year of disruption*.

Kim, J., Kim, J. N., & Park, H. J. (2020). The relationship between functional diversity and firm performance in the technology industry: The moderating role of environmental dynamism. *Asia Pacific Journal of Management, 37*(1), 81–107. doi:10.100710490-019-09657-9

LinkedIn. (2020). *The most in-demand hard and soft skills of 2020*. LinkedIn.

Liu, Y., Dai, X., & Zhu, W. (2020). The impact of demographic diversity on team performance in the financial services industry. *International Journal of Human Resource Management, 31*(8), 1082–1107. doi:10.1080/09585192.2017.1418659

Lüscher, L. S., Scholz, R. W., Berlowitz, I., & Schwaninger, M. (2021). Diversity, culture and innovation in health care: Insights from a Swiss case study. *European Journal of Innovation Management, 24*(1), 149–172. doi:10.1108/EJIM-03-2019-0080

McKinsey & Company. (2020). *Diversity Wins: How Inclusion Matters*. McKinsey.

McKinsey & Company. (2020). *COVID-19 and jobs: Monitoring the real-time effects on the labor market*. McKinsey.

Miller, C. C. (2019). The power of cognitive diversity. *Harvard Business Review, 97*(3), 96–103.

National Center for Women & Information Technology. (2019). *By the numbers*. NCWIT. https://www.ncwit.org/bythenumbers

Neeley, T. B. (2020). The challenge of leading diverse teams. *Harvard Business Review, 98*(6), 62–71.

Noland, C. M., Steffens, N. K., & Haslam, S. A. (2019). When empowerment limits diversity: A study of employee resource groups in the technology sector. *Frontiers in Psychology, 10*, 2149. 10

PwC. (2019). *Global Culture Survey 2018: Building a culture of innovation and purpose*. PwC.

Reuters. (2021). *Google to train 100,000 African coders in digital skills program*. Reuters.

Roberson, Q. M. (2019). Diversity, equity, and inclusion at work: A review and research agenda. *Journal of Organizational Behavior, 40*(4), 387–400. doi:10.1002/job.2353

Roberson, Q. M., Kulik, C. T., & Pepper, M. B. (2019). The threat of increasing diversity: Why organizations need psychological safety for diversity initiatives. *Organizational Dynamics*, *48*(1), 36–44. doi:10.1016/j.orgdyn.2018.10.004

Rock, D., & Grant, H. (2020). Leading through cognitive diversity. *Harvard Business Review*, *98*(4), 76–84.

Society for Human Resource Management. (2020). *How to support employee resource groups*. SHRM.

Sterling, A., & Srivastava, S. B. (2018). *The inclusion dividend: Why investing in diversity & inclusion pays off*. Center for Talent Innovation.

Thomas, D. A., & Ely, R. J. (2019). Making work more meaningful for everyone. *Harvard Business Review*, *97*(5), 118–127.

Tzafrir, S. S., Dolan, S. L., & Yakhnich, L. (2018). Functional diversity and team performance in health care organizations: The role of transformational leadership. *Journal of Health Organization and Management*, *32*(2), 254–270. doi:10.1108/JHOM-05-2017-0117

van Baalen, S., Alessandri, G., Perugini, M., & Borgogni, L. (2021). The relationship between team diversity and team innovation: A meta-analysis. *European Journal of Work and Organizational Psychology*, *30*(1), 87–111. doi:10.1080/1359432X.2020.1840199

Varshney, R.(2020). AI and machine learning trends in 2020. *Forbes*.

Wang, M., Hu, Q., & He, W. (2020). The relationship between workforce diversity and turnover: A meta-analysis. *Journal of Management*, *46*(7), 1097–1125.

Witkowski, E. (2021). Ally networks: The future of employee resource groups. *Harvard Business Review*.

KEY TERMS & REFERENCES

COVID-19: Pandemic that originated from China and caused widespread havoc to the world.

Diversity: Phenomenon that incorporates the differences across various sections of society.

Employee Resource Groups: Voluntary and collective group of people working inside organizations.

Information Technology: Advanced technological infrastructure utilized for ease of working.

Workforce: Group of people working for profit by achievement of goals set by the organization.

Chapter 9
Cognitive Diversity:
Vital but Invisible

Sukhada Tambe
IES's Management College and Research Centre, Mumbai, India

ABSTRACT

Cognitive diversity means having an amalgam of people with different ways of thinking, different skill sets, diverse perspectives, and different viewpoints in the organization. Organizations have realized the importance of diversity in age, gender, qualification, and started taking cognizance of the same. All these are visible forms of diversity. However not much attention is paid to 'cognitive diversity' because it is not visible and is deep level diversity. Organizations need to have cognitive diversity as a part of their diversity and inclusion (D&I) agenda. Cognitive diversity is indeed the way forward. This study is an effort to understand and explore 'cognitive diversity' which is invisible in nature, yet of great importance and relevance for the organizations.

INTRODUCTION

In recent years, organizations have started paying special attention to diversity. Diversity has now become a business imperative. From the organization's perspective diversity is important for value creation and increasing the bottom line. Many times the terms 'diversity' and 'multiculturalism' are used interchangeably. Diversity refers to the differences that exist among individuals and multiculturalism is the acceptance of these differences by the organizations. Organizations having multiculturalism encourage and promote diversity thus leading to inclusiveness.

Diversity is undeniably very crucial for the organization and has become a buzzword for the organizations in recent years. Ensuring workplace diversity is

DOI: 10.4018/978-1-6684-6602-5.ch009

typically the HR function in most of the organizations and it is ensured by having a workforce comprising of individuals of varying race, religion, differently abled people, age, gender, qualification, region, ethnicity, educational background, cultural background, language, skills, citizenship status, military service and mental and physical conditions. The function of managing diversity is taken care by a senior HR professional in the organization and some organizations have 'Chief Diversity Officer'.

BACKGROUND

Most of the literature available on cognitive diversity is in articles, newspapers and blogs. Moreover, most of the literature on diversity talks about gender diversity. The purpose of this paper is to understand and explore 'cognitive diversity' which is of great importance and relevance for the organizations and to put forth the nature and importance of cognitive diversity, which cannot be seen prima facie, but is very vital for organizational success. Cognitive diversity means having a combination of employees with different ways of thinking, understanding, interpreting, analysing, varied skill sets and diverse viewpoints in the organization. It is observed that organizations have started understanding the importance of diversity as far as qualification, gender, age, experience is concerned. However, despite of all these diversities, the teams may still be homogeneous in their approach if there is no cognitive diversity. Organizations have started taking cognizance of the fact that cognitive diversity encourages and enables creativity, innovation and divergent thinking.

A study conducted by Tata Communications (Goldberg & Kumar, 2018) revealed that 81% of the respondents indicated that demographic diversity in the workplace is important or very important and 90% of the respondents believed that cognitive diversity is essential for management. Further, the respondents also agreed that it is vital to increase cognitive diversity in teams. The study also hinted that in years to come, artificial intelligence could help CEOs gather teams with cognitive diversity. Literature suggests that 'Human Capital' is also an industry (Neal, 1995). If the organizations have to make optimum use of this resource, they must pay special attention to diversity. Diversity is the long term element in the success and sustainability of organizations. It would be highly beneficial for organizations to team people who think differently in order to solve problems with newer approach and innovative ways.

Diversity: A Holistic Perspective

Diversity has become a much discussed topic in the HR domain. In the past few years, organizations have started paying special focus on diversity. The Society for Human Resource Management (SHRM) defines diversity as "the collective mixture of differences and similarities that include, for example, individual and organizational characteristics, values, beliefs, experiences, backgrounds, preferences, and behaviours." Diversity is defined as "the distribution of differences among the members of a unit with respect to a common attribute such as tenure, ethnicity" (Harrison & Klein, 2007). Gardenswartz and Rowe (1994) in their Four Layers of Diversity Model, depicted diversity similar to an onion, which has several layers which once peeled away paves the way for the centre. According to Gardenswartz and Rowe (1994) the four layers of diversity are: organizational factors, internal factors, external factors, and individual identity.

The overall perspective about diversity has changed over the years. While the older generations viewed diversity and inclusion though the lens of fairness, equity and civil rights, the millennials view it from the perspective of teamwork and collaboration. Diversity at the workplace has become a global trend. A diverse workforce gives a competitive advantage to the organization.

Diversity can be divided into two subcategories viz. surface-level diversity and deep-level diversity. Surface-level diversity refers to diversity seen in the visible demographic characteristics among the members of the team; this could be age, gender, race, experience. Deep-level diversity is identified as differences in unique psychological characteristics such as beliefs, values, and attitudes that can only be learned through extended interactions and information gathering (Harrison, Price, & Bell, 1998). It is not so easy to detect deep-level diversity.

Research on diversity mostly focuses on the 'visible diversity' which means the outward signs of difference which are quite obvious and easy to recognize and categorize e.g. age, ethnicity, gender, qualification, experience, etc. However diversity is not only about the visible factors. There are also certain invisible elements that add to diversity. These invisible elements are less outwardly apparent. They include cognitive skills, abilities, values, personality traits, attitudes, etc.

Cognitive Diversity

Diversity is a known topic and a very popular cliché in the HR domain. However cognitive diversity is relatively a very novel term which gives a new and fresh perspective to the term 'Diversity'. According to the Deloitte Review (2018), cognitive diversity is often an overlooked facet of diversity, probably because cognitive diversity is less visible. Deloitte's research reveals that high performing teams are cognitively as well as demographically diverse (Bourke, 2018). Cognitive diversity is based on differences among the group in terms of beliefs, preferences, thinking styles, and assumptions (Liao & Long, 2016; Miller, Burke, & Glick, 1998).

Researchers from psychology and management background have predominantly conducted a lot of research on cognitive diversity. However researchers from other fields including communication, education, criminal justice, military, and health care have also contributed to the literature (Mello & Rentsch, 2015). Knowledge, skills, attitudes, and perceptions may be considered as the acquired cognitive diversity variables. Cognitive diversity research has also been conducted across various countries and cultures (e.g., Sauer, Felsing, & Rüttinger, 2006; Wei & Wu, 2013)

Cognitive diversity is based on the psychological features of the members of the group. It is the intellectual diversity. Cognitive diversity is differences in experiences, knowledge, abilities, and skills of individuals owing to which these individuals differ in their beliefs, attitudes, perspectives and cognitive styles. While defining 'cognitive diversity', some researchers have added the aspect of 'expertise' to the existing definition of cognitive diversity thus referring to expertness diversity (Pandolfo, 2017).

Kress, Steinert, & Price (2012) in their study hypothesized that cognitive diversity is independent of other diversity measures. The results of this study revealed that cognitive diversity as measured by variance is not correlated with the size, age or gender composition of the team. Thus the results supported their hypothesis.

Cognitive diversity is the difference in how people think and process information. It is about nurturing and cultivating a team with differences in perspectives. Cognitively diverse teams perform better when it comes to problem solving, processing information, approaching change and performing in difficult and complex situations.

As stated by Denning (2012), according to Page (2007) cognitive diversity has four dimensions which are as follows: perspectives, interpretations, heuristics and predictive models. The first dimension is 'Diverse Perspective' which means that people have different ways of looking at situations and problems and accordingly their approach for envisioning the set of possibilities confronting them also differ. The second dimension is 'Diverse Interpretations'. According to this perspective, people put things into different categories and classifications. And each of their interpretations would be true. They are diverse and different interpretation of the same phenomenon. The next dimension is 'Diverse Heuristics' Individuals have different ways of generating solutions to problems. Some people like to discuss the problems, some prefer to write down their solutions and then talk. Each has a different approach to arrive at a solution to the problem. The last dimension is 'Diverse predictive models'. Each person may take a different route. Some people want to analyse the situation while others may look for the story, logic and continuity. Each may adopt a different predictive model.

Cognitive diversity is usually studied in relation to the 'outcome' measures like creativity, decision making and there certain moderators like conflict management, psychological safety (Pandolfo, 2017). Researchers have studied cognitive diversity in relation to 'outcome' measures like creativity (Kurtzberg, 2005; Shin, Kim, Lee, & Bian, 2012) and decision-making results (Olson, Bao, & Paravitam, 2007), and with moderators such as conflict management (Mello & Delise, 2015), trust (Olson et al., 2007), and psychological safety (Martins, Schilpzand, Kirkman, Ivanaj, & Ivanaj, 2013).

Cognitive diversity can include culturally-acquired ways of thinking which are acquired as a result of experiences over past several years across diverse cultures. Cultural diversity helps to create a cognitively diverse workforce as people coming from diverse cultures will have varied cultural perspectives and experiences. Cognitive diversity may also be learned, which include various skills and abilities acquired by individuals. Cognitively diverse teams include individuals across various cultures and also across various educational backgrounds.

Cognitive style varies between individuals and can therefore create diversity within a team. Cognitively diverse teams will outperform homogeneous teams as they will have variety in their viewpoints, approach and perspective. Scott E. Page (2017), in his book 'The Diversity Bonus' has underscored the importance of cognitive diversity. Cognitive diversity is the difference in how humans perceive, interpret, reason and solve in human groups. Greater diversity gives more opportunities to discover insights and novel approaches.

In a survey conducted by Quantum Workplace (2020), 55% of the employees opined that there has to be diversity in the way of thinking. Thus rating cognitive diversity as the most important and receiving highest votes.

Cognitive diversity helps to thrive the workplace culture. Cognitive diversity can enhance team innovation up to 20%, and can reduce risks taken by to up 30% (Bourke, 2016).

It gives an advantage to the teams and as a result they are able to solve problems faster when they are cognitively diverse.

Chow (2018) studied the mechanisms through which cognitive diversity affects creativity. His findings indicate that team leaning and inclusion mediate the effect of cognitive diversity on creativity. Cognitive diversity helps to ensure better performance of teams. However, as warned by Jiang and Zhang (2014), the relationship between cognitive diversity and performance outcomes is more complex than expected. Cognitive diversity plays a vital role when a team has to come up with new ideas and entrusted to find solutions to the issues faced by the team or the organization (Yuan & Zhou, 2015).

The benefit of cognitive diversity can be enjoyed in many ways. Cognitive diversity helps to avoid the pitfall of groupthink in decision making (Janis, 1972).

This type of diversity enhances the cognitive resource capacity of the team. Cognitive diversity exposes an individual to novel and diverse ideas and encourages new ways of looking at a problem, situation or issue, thus fostering creative performance of an individual.

A workplace may be diverse demographically, but it may still be cognitively uniform. The organization may have preference for a particular college / institute while hiring candidates. Or unknowingly the management may fill a position by giving preference to same background and experience as the employee who left. Lack of cognitive diversity may limit the organization's capabilities and achievements. According to one study, that cognitive diversity can enhance team innovation up to 20%, and can reduce risks taken by to up 30% (Bourke, 2018).

A cognitively diverse team will solve problems faster. According to Deloitte Review (2018), cognitive diversity also refers to the diversity in the metal framework that individuals use to solve problems. A complex problems requires input from six different perspectives or mental framework or approaches viz. evidence, options, outcomes, people, process and risk. In reality, no one is equally good at all the six and this is where the team members with cognitive diversity can complement each other.

Cognitive Style

Each person has a unique and distinct way in which he obtains, stores, retrieves, processes and transforms the information. This is known as the cognitive style. Cognitive Style undoubtedly plays a crucial role in organisational behaviour and has received the attention of researchers and practising managers alike. Cognitive style is the way in which people process information, in order to make decisions. Cognitive style differs from person to person. It is based on an individual's mental ability, past experiences, way of thinking, learning, and several other factors.

Messick (1984) opined that cognitive styles "appear to serve as high level heuristics that organize lower-level strategies, operations, and propensities – often including abilities – in such complex sequential processes as problem solving and learning."

Cognitive style refers to the way people organize, process, and conceptualize information to solve problems or make decisions. A cognitive style is the knowledge and processes that a person uses to frame problems, organize information, and approach tasks (Kurtzberg, 2005; Mello & Delise, 2015). A cognitive style is a psychological dimension that represents consistencies in how someone acquires and processes information (Ausburn & Ausburn, 1978; Messick, 1984)

Maria Kozhevnikov, a neurologist from Harvard, defined cognitive style as - relatively stable individual differences in preferred ways of organizing and processing information that cut across the personality and cognitive characteristics of an individual (2007).

Cognitive style, is a variable associated with how individual team members assess, process, and organize information (Allinson & Hayes, 1996), Cognitive style has been defined as 'consistent individual differences in preferred ways of organizing and processing information and experience' (Messick, 1976).

In the opinion of Dongrey & Rokade (2020) cognitive styles may lie anywhere in the continuum with 'intuitive' and 'analytical' at the two ends of a continuum. The manager's cognitive style can be developed and moved from one continuum to another through training and also enhancing his knowledge and experience.

Cognitive style is the information processing style of an individual and his approach towards a situation or a problem. Depending on the cognitive style of a person, he may exhibit a step by step approach or may take a holistic approach. Again, to reiterate, cognitive style may be anywhere in the range between analytical and intuitive.

According to Rayner and Riding (1997) cognitive style is a person's typical or habitual mode of problem solving, thinking, perceiving and remembering. The difference in cognitive style has an influence on interpretation, analysis, judgement and decision making process for individuals.

Measuring Cognitive Diversity

Van der Vegt and Janssen (2003) developed a 4-item scale to measure cognitive diversity. This is one of the most popular and commonly used scale to measure cognitive diversity. According to this scale, the statements are measured on a 7-point Likert scale from 1 (to a very small extent) to 7 (to a very large extent). The participants indicate how they personally perceive their team members in their organization. The scoring method is based on the average, with a higher score indicating that respondents perceive their teams are more cognitively diverse. This scale measures the extent to which members of the work group differ in their way of thinking, their knowledge and skills, view of the world and their values and beliefs.

The Kirton Adaption - Innovation Inventory was developed by Kirton and was published in the Journal of Applied Psychology in the year 1976. He intended to explain cognitive tendencies and problem-solving styles. Kirton (1976) stated, "The contention… is that everyone can be located on a continuum ranging from an ability to 'do things better' to an ability to 'do things differently,' and the ends of this continuum are labelled adaptive and innovative, respectively". Adaptors desire to do things better while; Innovators seek to do things differently. He developed a self-reporting inventory consisting of 32 questions / statements. This inventory helped to place the respondent on a continuum between high adaptation and high innovation. The scores could range from 32 to 160. An individual with an adaptive cognitive style will score in the 60 to 90 range. Someone with an innovative style will score between 110 and 140.

Allinson and Hayes (1996) developed the Cognitive Style Index (CSI) which was designed specifically for managerial and professional groups. Approximately 1000 adults participated in the development of this CSI. This study had a dual objective. First objective was to come up with a psychometrically sound instrument suitable for application in large-scale organizational studies and the second objective was to confirm empirically the generic intuition-analysis dimension of cognitive style.

Cognitive Style Indicator (CoSI) was developed by Cools and Van den Broeck (2007). CoSI consists of 18 items spread across three sub-scales and measured on a five-point likert scale. The three subscales are - knowing style, planning style and creating style. CoSI assesses differences in participants' preferences for information processing by distinguishing between three cognitive styles (a) a knowing style that emphasizes logic, objectivity, and precision; (b) a planning style that emphasizes structure, control, and routines, and (c) a creating style that emphasizes subjectivity, impulsivity, and openness to possibilities (Cools and Van den Broeck, 2007).

Sussex Cognitive Styles Questionnaire (SCSQ) was developed in 2016 by Mealor, Simner, Rothen, Carmichael, and Ward. This is relatively a recent instrument to measure cognitive diversity. The purpose was to investigate visual and verbal processing preferences and incorporate global / local processing orientations and systemising into a single, comprehensive measure. SCSO consists of six sub-scales viz. Imagery Ability, Technical / Spatial, Language & Word Forms, Need for Organisation, Global Bias, and Systemising Tendency. There are in all 60 questions in the SCSQ.

Cognitive Diversity: Contrarian View

While we discuss and adulate the benefits of diversity, there could also be a minor flip side to it. Cognitive diversity may introduce conflicts in the organizational system (Türkmen, 2013). People have a tendency to prefer working with those whom they consider similar. It is a popular saying 'great minds think alike'. Hence there is a fear of friction or non-performance when cognitively diverse people come together. Negative effects of diversity are also seen in the form of conflicts, misunderstandings, uncooperative behaviours among team members. It is a popular belief that increasing diversity may lead to conflicts between the group members. Cognitive diversity leads to heterogeneity in the human resource pool, but it may also lead to significant difficulties in communication and coordination (Horwitz & Horwitz, 2007; Jehn, Northcraft, & Neale, 1999). Cognitive diversity may not always be the solution. Nooteboom (2000) opined that for learning to happen, some level of cognitive proximity or complementarity is required. For certain tasks, it is required that workers with similar skills should work to ensure higher productivity (Kremer, 1993). Devine & Philips (2001) conducted an empirical research to study the relationship between cognitive diversity and team performance. Their study found that there is no relationship between diversity in cognitive ability and team performance. The benefits of diversity can be reaped only when the people involved in the task are able to work together.

Certain teams may resort to and perform better with convergent thinking rather than divergent thinking. For such teams cognitive diversity may be an impediment rather than an advantage.

There are some studies, which found conflicting results with regard to the relationship between a team's cognitive diversity and its performance (Mello & Rentsch, 2015). As a result of cognitive bias; which happens subconsciously, people have a tendency to recognize, reinforce and accept ideas which are similar to their own and dismiss conflicting ideas, thoughts and inputs. Potential negative effects of cognitive diversity can be seen due to lack of cohesion based on differences in thought process.

The results of the study conducted by Aggarwal, Woolley, Chabris & Malone (2019) showed that high levels of cognitive style diversity curb team learning indirectly by reducing collective intelligence. Thus lowering the rate at which the team learns.

Cognitive diversity is a double edged sword which needs to be handled carefully. There is also some research giving interesting insight regarding cognitive style diversity, which states that in teams with high cognitive diversity, people may suffer interpersonally, but may still outperform homogeneous teams. A study by Basadur & Head (2001) revealed that there is higher dissatisfaction among the cognitively diverse teams, but these teams do come up with more innovative outputs. Priola, Smith & Armstrong (2004) found in their study found that though, in general, the homogenous cognitive style teams were more satisfied and cohesive than the diverse teams, and the performance of these homogeneous teams was low.

Cronin and Weingart (2007), in their study found that cognitive differences lead to negative outcomes like conflict, tension and misunderstanding. This may harm team performance, hamper innovation and can be a hindrance to individual performance also. Moreover, there is a difficulty faced by the group to come to consensus.

Implications for Organizations

Apple Inc. believes that 'The most innovative company must also be the most diverse' (Deloitte Review, 2018). The organization takes a holistic view of diversity and encourages varied perspective from the employees. Apple Inc. recognises that new ideas come from diverse ways of looking at things.

There is a possibility that a demographically diverse workplace can also be cognitively uniform. This is because, despite of having employees from wide-ranging background, region, religion, age, they stall can be thinking alike and working akin. Boschma (2005), cautioned that too much cognitive proximity might create a lock-in problem that may limit the capability of organizations to adopt new technologies and market potentials. Cognitive Styles influence not only problem solving but also the behaviour, personality and interactions with others. Cognitive styles have a significant influence on individual behaviour which in turn influences the team dynamics and the performance outcome of the team.

Cognitive diversity is indeed the way forward. Cognitive consensus will have its own limitations as the teams will not have a variety in ideas, approaches, to solve a complex problem. However, diversity cannot be at the cost of merit. Cognitive diversity is invisible in nature. Thus it is difficult to see or notice cognitive diversity prima facie. Cognitive diversity in teams is a topic of multidisciplinary and international interest and research has been conducted in number of contents and across nationalities on this topic (Mello & Rentsch, 2015)

Google endeavours to hire people with diverse interests and skills while also ensuring that the incumbents also have the basic skills required to execute their jobs in Google. People must open up and be vocal about cognitive diversity. Cognitively diverse teams are essential to create and nurture a culture of innovation. In order to promote and ensure cognitive diversity, the organizations must pay special attention to 'culture-add' rather than 'culture-fit'.

One of the important reasons that organizations do not pay much attention to cognitive diversity is that it is not a mandatory compliance. Though cognitive diversity is not a mandate, organizations cannot turn a blind eye to it. Infact, at the time of recruitment and selection itself organizations can pay special attention to cognitive diversity. It is critical for hiring. Psychometric tests and assessments can give a fair idea as to how the candidates would most likely respond to certain situations. In addition to the tests and assessments even at the time of interview some consideration can definitely be given to cognitive diversity.

Learning and development is another important initiative for organizations to nurture cognitive diversity. Employees need to be provided with continuous learning opportunities to ensure that they are constantly innovating, problem-solving and developing new ideas. Learning opportunities to be provided to foster diverse thinking among the employees. Cognitive diversity may not always come from within the company. It would be a good idea to invite outside experts to facilitate workshops, training programs and projects to encourage innovative thinking.

Work Environment also plays a very important role to create conducive climate to encourage and foster cognitive diversity. The psychological environment should be such that the employees feel free to express their thoughts and ideas in a group.

Most importantly, psychological safety must be assured. In case the psychological safety is violated due to difference in perceived power status, members with lower status might suppress their opinions in order to protect themselves (Nembhard & Edmondson, 2006). Employees should be encouraged to share ideas, criticisms, and suggestions without any fear. It is the responsibility of organizations to create a safe working environment that allows cognitive diversity to flourish. The best way to achieve cognitive diversity at the workplace is to integrate it into all aspects of company culture. Cognitive diversity also helps to safeguard organizations from 'Groupthink'. Groupthink is fully functional in the absence of cognitive diversity which may have ill-effects on the organization.

Cognitive diversity helps in problem solving. If there are two teams; one with cognitive diversity and the other with individuals who have a similar approach to problem solving, then there is a high probability that the team with cognitive diversity will solve a complex problem faster than the other team. Page (2007) opined that in some situations, a group of ordinary people who exhibit cognitive diversity can defeat a group of like-minded experts. One study from the Harvard Business Review (Reynolds & Lewis, 2017) showed that teams with greater thought diversity were able to solve problems up to three times faster than teams which consisted of like-minded individuals. Similarly, a Deloitte study (2018) found that cognitively diverse teams can boost innovation by about 20 percent.

Creativity and innovation are of great importance in today's dynamic and highly competitive world. Creativity involves cognitive process. Suzue (2020) in his doctoral dissertation explored whether cognitive diversity significantly influences individual creative performance. Several simple and multiple linear regression analyses were conducted to test the model on a sample of 122 employees who were employees of U.S. organizations with headquarters in Japan. The results of the study showed that cognitive diversity significantly predicted individual creative performance.

Organizations talk of innovation and take up many initiatives in that direction. Cognitive diversity is a must to have a culture of innovation and encourage people to think differently. According to Page (2007), cognitive diversity may not contribute much in improving performance when it comes to routine tasks which are mundane in nature. But when we are dealing with complex tasks like engineering problems, or tasks requiring creativity and innovation, or managerial issues, cognitive diversity is a key variable for enhancing the performance. Organizations talk of innovation and take up many initiatives in that direction.

FUTURE RESEARCH DIRECTIONS

Diversity in general and also cognitive diversity in particular is emerging as a topic of interest for academicians and practising professionals worldwide. There are significant studies available on the visible forms of diversity. However there is dearth of research on the invisible forms of diversity. Cognitive diversity is not much researched in India. However, there are Indians but they are not the residents of India who have done research on cognitive diversity. It would also be interesting to explore the intersection between cognitive style diversity and other forms of diversity both visible as well as invisible. Study of cognitive diversity may be extended to design thinking. Design thinking would be a powerful tool to unlock the power of cognitive diversity. There is a scope to explore the relationship between cognitive diversity and gender diversity as it is believed that men and women do not think alike. A study on cognitive diversity of the work group and its effect on quality of innovation will be of immense help to organizations. In addition to cognitive diversity, several other invisible forms of diversity like knowledge diversity, identity diversity, perceived diversity, experiential diversity and expertness diversity may also be probed and explored further.

CONCLUSION

In the given business environment, diversity is a quite complex concept. It is important to understand that organizations must enjoy the benefits of 'working with diversity' rather than struggling with 'managing diversity'. Diversity at work place and making it a success is everybody's responsibility. Diversity may be an HR initiative, but involvement of all the individuals both emotionally and intellectually is required, to make this initiative a success. Cognitive diversity is a topic of interest internationally and is also of importance in interdisciplinary research. Organizations have to make an extra effort to increasing cognitive diversity in its workforce, as it is invisible. Attention must also be paid to surface cognitive diversity which must be hidden amongst the existing workforce.

Diversity in thinking, intellectual capabilities, and perspectives will definitely have an impact on organization's work culture, systems, and work practices; social relations and employee behaviour at work. Teams do need cognitively versatile people. It is much easier for the cognitively diverse teams to catch each other's blind spots, which facilitate performance across domains. Cognitive diversity brings the individuals out of their comfort zones, thus making them feel uncomfortable. This is the platform where innovative and diverge ideas thrive. People come up with different ways of thinking and different ways of doing things.

Organizations must create conducive environment to create, nurture and sustain cognitive diversity. There is a need to cultivate workplace culture, where conflicting ideas, perspectives, viewpoints are listened to and paid attention with respect.

Diversity is not merely the process of acknowledging the differences among employees in the organization. Rather 'Diversity' is an endeavour to create an environment where mutual respect is encouraged and nurtured and inclusion is ensured. Visible forms of diversity viz. demographic diversity, gender diversity, etc. are likely to cause social categorization processes but deep diversity, such as cognitive diversity, is likely to promote creativity among the team members. Diversity certainly helps to improve organizational performance, but cognitive diversity goes a long way in giving a competitive edge to the organization and help to outperform the competitors.

REFERENCES

Aggarwal, I., Woolley, A. W., Chabris, C. F., & Malone, T. W. (2019). The impact of cognitive style diversity on implicit learning in teams. *Frontiers in Psychology*, *10*, 112. doi:10.3389/fpsyg.2019.00112 PMID:30792672

Allinson, C. W., & Hayes, J. (1996). The cognitive style index: A measure of intuition-analysis for organizational research. *Journal of Management Studies*, *33*(1), 119–135. doi:10.1111/j.1467-6486.1996.tb00801.x

Allinson, C. W., & Hayes, J. (1996). The cognitive style index: A measure of intuition-analysis for organizational research. *Journal of Management Studies*, *33*(1), 119–135. doi:10.1111/j.1467-6486.1996.tb00801.x

Ausburn, L. J., & Ausburn, F. B. (1978). Cognitive styles: Some information and implications for instructional design. *Educational Communication and Technology*, *26*(4), 337–354. doi:10.1007/BF02766370

Basadur, M. S., & Head, M. M. (2001). Team performance and satisfaction: A link to cognitive style within a process framework. *The Journal of Creative Behavior*, *35*(3), 1–22. doi:10.1002/j.2162-6057.2001.tb01048.x

Boschma, R. (2005). Proximity and innovation: A critical assessment. *Regional Studies*, *39*(1), 61–74. doi:10.1080/0034340052000320887

Bourke, J. (2016). *Which Two Heads Are Better Than One?: How Diverse Teams Create Breakthrough Ideas and Make Smarter Decisions*. Australian Institute of Company Directors.

Bourke, J. (2018). The diversity and inclusion revolution: Eight powerful truths. *Deloitte Review* (22). https://www2.deloitte.com/us/en/insights/deloitte-review/issue-22/diversity-and-inclusion-at-work-eight-powerful-truths.html.

Chow, I. H. S. (2018). Cognitive diversity and creativity in teams: The mediating roles of team learning and inclusion. *Chinese Management Studies*, *12*(2), 369–383. doi:10.1108/CMS-09-2017-0262

Cools, E., & Van den Broeck, H. (2007). Development and validation of the Cognitive Style Indicator. *The Journal of Psychology*, *141*(4), 359–387. doi:10.3200/JRLP.141.4.359-388 PMID:17725071

Cronin, M. A., & Weingart, L. R. (2007). Representational gaps, information processing, and conflict in functionally diverse teams. *Academy of Management Review*, *32*(3), 761–773. doi:10.5465/amr.2007.25275511

Denning, S. (2012). Why is diversity vital for innovation. *Forbes*. https://www.forbes.com/sites/stevedenning/2012/01/16/why-is-diversity-vital-for-innovation/?sh=6c63f62c13e2. *Retrieved on December*, 20, 2022.

Devine, D. J., & Philips, J. L. (2001). Do smarter teams do better: A meta-analysis of cognitive ability and team performance. *Small Group Research*, *32*(5), 507–532. doi:10.1177/104649640103200501

Dongrey, R., & Rokade, V. (2022). A Framework to Assess the Impact of Employee Perceived Equality on Contextual Performance and Mediating Role of Affective Commitment to Enhance and Sustain Positive Work Behavior. *Discrete Dynamics in Nature and Society*, *2022*, 1–14. doi:10.1155/2022/5407947

Gardenswartz, L., & Rowe, A. (1994). Diversity management: Practical application in a health care organization. *Frontiers of Health Services Management*, *11*(2), 36–40. doi:10.1097/01974520-199410000-00004 PMID:10139136

Goldberg, K., & Kumar, V. (2018). Cognitive Diversity: AI & The Future of Work. Tata Communications. https://www.tatacommunications.com/wp-content/uploads/2018/09/Report_Cognitive-Diversity_AI-and-The-Future-of-Work.pdf

Harrison, D. A., & Klein, K. J. (2007). What's the difference? Diversity constructs as separation, variety, or disparity in organizations. *Academy of Management Review*, *32*(4), 1199–1228. doi:10.5465/amr.2007.26586096

Harrison, D. A., Price, K. H., & Bell, M. P. (1998). Beyond relational demography: Time and the effects of surface- and deep-level diversity on work group cohesion. *Academy of Management Journal, 41*(1), 96–107. doi:10.2307/256901

Horwitz, S. K., & Horwitz, I. B. (2007). The effects of team diversity on team outcomes: A meta-analytic review of team demography. *Journal of Management, 33*(6), 987–1015. doi:10.1177/0149206307308587

Janis, I. L. (1972). *Victims of Groupthink: A Psychological Study of Foreign-Policy Decisions and Fiascoes*. Houghton Mifflin.

Jehn, K. A., Northcraft, G. B., & Neale, M. A. (1999). Why differences make a difference: A field study of diversity, conflict and performance in workgroups. *Administrative Science Quarterly, 44*(4), 741–763. doi:10.2307/2667054

Jiang, H., & Zhang, Q. P. (2014). Development and validation of team creativity measures: A complex systems perspective. *Creativity and Innovation Management, 23*(3), 264–275. doi:10.1111/caim.12078

Kirton, M. (1976). Adaptors and innovators: A description and measure. *The Journal of Applied Psychology, 61*(5), 622–629. doi:10.1037/0021-9010.61.5.622

Kozhevnikov, M. (2007). Cognitive styles in the context of modern psychology: Toward an integrated framework of cognitive style. *Psychological Bulletin, 133*(3), 464–481. doi:10.1037/0033-2909.133.3.464 PMID:17469987

Kremer, M. (1993). The O-ring theory of economic development. *The Quarterly Journal of Economics, 108*(3), 551–575. doi:10.2307/2118400

Kress, G., Steinert, M., & Price, T. (2012). Cognition as a measure of team diversity. In *2012 2nd interdisciplinary engineering design education conference (IEDEC)* (pp. 67-72). 10.1109/IEDEC.2012.6186925

Kurtzberg, T. R. (2005). Feeling creative, being creative: An empirical study of diversity and creativity in teams. *Creativity Research Journal, 17*(1), 51–65. doi:10.120715326934crj1701_5

Liao, Z., & Long, S. (2016). Cognitive diversity, alertness, and team performance. *Social Behavior and Personality, 44*(2), 209–220. doi:10.2224bp.2016.44.2.209

Martins, L. L., Schilpzand, M. C., Kirkman, B. L., Ivanaj, S., & Ivanaj, V. (2013). A contingency view of the effects of cognitive diversity on team performance: The moderating roles of team psychological safety and relationship conflict. *Small Group Research, 44*(2), 96–126. doi:10.1177/1046496412466921

Mealor, A. D., Simner, J., Rothen, N., Carmichael, D. A., & Ward, J. (2016). Different dimensions of cognitive style in typical and atypical cognition: New evidence and a new measurement tool. *PLoS One*, *11*(5), e0155483. doi:10.1371/journal.pone.0155483 PMID:27191169

Mello, A., & Rentsch, J. (2014). Cognitive style diversity in decision making teams: A conceptual framework. *International Journal of Business and Social Research*, *4*(4), 123–135.

Mello, A. L., & Delise, L. A. (2015). Cognitive diversity to team outcomes: The roles of cohesion and conflict management. *Small Group Research*, *46*(2), 204–226. doi:10.1177/1046496415570916

Mello, A. L., & Rentsch, J. R. (2015). Cognitive diversity in teams: A multidisciplinary review. *Small Group Research*, *46*(6), 623–658. doi:10.1177/1046496415602558

Messick, S. (1976). Personality consistencies in cognition and creativity. In S. Messick & ... (Eds.), *Individuality in Learning* (pp. 4–22). Jossey-Bass.

Messick, S. (1984). The nature of cognitive styles: Problems and promise in educational practice. *Educational Psychologist*, *19*(2), 59–74. doi:10.1080/00461528409529283

Messick, S. (1984). The nature of cognitive styles: Problems and promise in educational practice. *Educational Psychologist*, *19*(2), 59–74. doi:10.1080/00461528409529283

Miller, C. C., Burke, L. M., & Glick, W. H. (1998). Cognitive diversity among upper-echelon executives: Implications for strategic decision processes. *Strategic Management Journal*, *19*(1), 39–58. doi:10.1002/(SICI)1097-0266(199801)19:1<39::AID-SMJ932>3.0.CO;2-A

Neal, D. (1995). Industry-specific human capital: Evidence from displaced workers. *Journal of Labor Economics*, *13*(4), 653–677. doi:10.1086/298388

Nembhard, I. M., & Edmondson, A. C. (2006). Making it safe: The effects of leader inclusiveness and professional status on psychological safety and improvement efforts in health care teams. *Journal of Organizational Behavior*, *27*(7), 941–966. doi:10.1002/job.413

Nooteboom, B. (2000). *Learning and innovation in organizations and economies*. OUP Oxford.

Olson, B. J., Parayitam, S., & Bao, Y. (2007). Strategic decision making: The effects of cognitive diversity, conflict, and trust on decision outcomes. *Journal of Management*, *33*(2), 196–222. doi:10.1177/0149206306298657

Page, S. (2017). The diversity bonus. In *The Diversity Bonus*. Princeton University Press. doi:10.2307/j.ctvc77c0h

Page, S. E. (2007). Making the difference: Applying a logic of diversity. *The Academy of Management Perspectives*, *21*(4), 6–20. doi:10.5465/amp.2007.27895335

Pandolfo, A. M. (2017). What is the "cognitive" in cognitive diversity? *Investigating the convergent validity of cognitive diversity measures.* UWO. https://ir.lib.uwo.ca/cgi/viewcontent.cgi?article=1034&context=psychd_uht.

Priola, V., Smith, J. L., & Armstrong, S. J. (2004). Group work and cognitive style: A discursive investigation. *Small Group Research*, *35*(5), 565–595. doi:10.1177/1046496404265143

Rayner, S., & Riding, R. (1997). Towards a categorisation of cognitive styles and learning styles. *Educational Psychology*, *17*(1-2), 5–27. doi:10.1080/0144341970170101

Reynolds, A., & Lewis, D. (2017). Teams solve problems faster when they're more cognitively diverse. *Harvard Business Review*, *30*, 1–8.

Sauer, J., Felsing, T., Franke, H., & Rüttinger, B. (2006). Cognitive diversity and team performance in a complex multiple task environment. *Ergonomics*, *49*(10), 934–954. doi:10.1080/00140130600577502 PMID:16803725

Shin, S. J., Kim, T. Y., Lee, J. Y., & Bian, L. (2012). Cognitive team diversity and individual team member creativity: A cross-level interaction. *Academy of Management Journal*, *55*(1), 197–212. doi:10.5465/amj.2010.0270

Suzue, K. (2020). *The Cognitive Diversity-creative Performance Relationship and the Mediating Effect of Power-distance Orientation: A Study of Japan-based Organizations in the US* [Doctoral dissertation, The Chicago School of Professional Psychology].

Turkmen, A. A. (2013). *Cognitive diversity and innovation: Does cognitive diversity in multinational corporations influence workgroup innovation?* [Doctoral dissertation, Fielding Graduate University].

Van der Vegt, G. S., & Janssen, O. (2003). Joint impact of interdependence and group diversity on innovation. *Journal of Management*, *29*(5), 729–751. doi:10.1016/S0149-2063_03_00033-3

Wei, L. Q., & Wu, L. (2013). What a diverse top management team means: Testing an integrated model. *Journal of Management Studies*, *50*(3), 389–412. doi:10.1111/joms.12013

Quantum Workplace. (2020). Future of work: 17 performance review templates to motivate employees. *Quantum Workplace.* https://www.quantumworkplace.com/future-of-work/17-performance-review-templates-to-motivate-employees.

Yuan, F., & Zhou, J. (2015). Effects of cultural power distance on group creativity and individual group member creativity. *Journal of Organizational Behavior, 36*(7), 990–1007. doi:10.1002/job.2022

ADDITIONAL READING

Basnight-Brown, D., Janssen, S. M. J., & Thomas, A. K. (2023). Exploration of human cognitive universals and human cognitive diversity. *Memory & Cognition, 51*(3), 505–508. doi:10.375813421-023-01410-w PMID:36859524

Blom, T., du Plessis, Y., & Kazeroony, H. H. (2021). Enabling Sustainable Organizational Change: A Case of Cognitive Diversity in the Automotive Industry. *International Journal of Applied Management & Technology, 20*(1), 143–166. doi:10.5590/IJAMT.2021.20.1.08

Chen, X., Liu, J., Zhang, H., & Kwan, H. K. (2019). Cognitive diversity and innovative work behaviour: The mediating roles of task reflexivity and relationship conflict and the moderating role of perceived support. *Journal of Occupational and Organizational Psychology, 92*(3), 671–694. doi:10.1111/joop.12259

Egler, M. (2021). Who's afraid of cognitive diversity? *Inquiry (Oslo, Norway),* 1–27. doi:10.1080/0020174X.2021.1942977

Kang, J.-K., Kim, S., & Oh, S. (2022). Does Board Demographic Diversity Enhance Cognitive Diversity and Monitoring? *The Accounting Review, 97*(6), 385–415. doi:10.2308/TAR-2020-0702

Qi, M., Armstrong, S. J., Yang, Z., & Li, X. (2022). Cognitive diversity and team creativity: Effects of demographic faultlines, subgroup imbalance and information elaboration. *Journal of Business Research, 139*, 819–830. doi:10.1016/j.jbusres.2021.10.027

Schumpe, B. M., Bélanger, J. J., Nisa, C. F., & Pierro, A. (2023). When diversity leads to closed-mindedness: Cognitive factors explain the effects of perceived diversity. *Current Psychology (New Brunswick, N.J.), 42*(11), 9324–9338. doi:10.100712144-021-02184-7

Smith, A., & Angood, P. B. (2020). Diversity & Inclusion: Tough Decisions, Rich Rewards: Hiring based on gender and diversity does not mean settling for less-qualified candidates. It means hiring those who are most qualified AND increasing your organization's competitive edge through cognitive diversity. Is that even possible? Yes —if you make it a priority. *Physician Leadership Journal*, *7*(4), 20–25.

KEY TERMS AND DEFINITIONS

Cognitive Diversity: Diversity exhibited by individuals in terms of thinking and perceiving, processing and analysing and coming up with diverse ideas.

Cognitive Style: The unique way in which an individual acquires, accumulates, retrieves, processes and transforms the information.

Creativity: Refers to the mental ability of imagining, originality in thinking and coming up with new ideas.

Diversity: Differences among individuals working in the organization on account of region, religion, skills, language, qualifications and many such differences.

Groupthink: A psychological phenomenon wherein the group members conform to the majority opinion with an intention to maintain group harmony, rather than asserting their own opinions.

Innovation: Implementing ideas generated as an outcome of creativity to create value and translate them into reality.

Invisible Diversity: Refers to those aspects of diversity that cannot be easily seen or recognized and are less outwardly apparent e.g., values, cognitive skills, abilities, beliefs, attitudes, personality traits, etc.

Problem Solving: The mental process of analysing a complex problem and coming up with solutions.

Teamwork: Group of people coming together to achieve a common goal.

Visible Diversity: Refers to those aspects of diversity that can be easily seen or recognized e.g., age, qualification, race, experience, language, etc.

Chapter 10
Differences in Work Value, Communication Style, and Leadership Style Among Generational Cohorts at the Workplace:
An Overview

Soni Rathi
https://orcid.org/0000-0002-2997-8622
Chandigarh University, India

Praveen Kumar
Chandigarh University, India

ABSTRACT

Employees nowadays are more diverse than ever before, and that diversity is manifested in differences in generational cohorts. It has been observed that an organization is composed of distinct age groups, which represent employees of distinct generational cohorts. The key goal of this study is to render an observation and insight into differentiation and comparison in work values, communication style, and leadership style of distinct age group employees at workplace likely boomer, Gen X, Gen Y, and Gen Z. The finding of the study depicted the variations among generations (Boomer, Gen X, Gen Y, and Gen Z) as well as the variation in their styles of leadership, communication, and values of work. The current study has explored only three characteristics. In the organizations, not only is the investigation of distinct generation necessary, but the similarities among them need to be acknowledged. Another limitation is that there is a very less empirical investigation conducted on generational differences.

DOI: 10.4018/978-1-6684-6602-5.ch010

1. INTRODUCTION

Nowadays, in the organization, one of the most significant issues is Generational diversity. The experienced workforce is delaying retirement while the younger Generation workforce continues to participate in the organizations. Each Generation is bringing its demands and needs to the workplace. The records of the current group of workers from distinct Generations are working beside each other and closely with those people who are as younger as their youngsters and as old as their parents (Zemke et al., 2000). There are various unique characteristics of each Generation such as views on authority, attitude towards work, and communication style (Coulter and Faulkner, 2014). Macky et al., (2008) found variations in personality profiles across Generations and variations in attitudes toward jobs. The term Generation (also "cohort", or "Generational cohort") is described as "a group of people born within similar historical and sociocultural environments, who experience the same formative experiences and make unifying similarities as a repercussion" (Lyons and Kuron, 2014). It may be seen as a form of diversity that influences the place of business which needs to be taken into consideration together with different dimensions of diversity to better understand personnel (Lancaster and Stillman, 2002). The Generational cohort has unique values, characteristics, and skills based on their experiences of life-defining events. The commonality of reports makes Generational identities, which can be the point of view that every cohort has on life, love, work, family, politics, and society (Kovary, 2012). There are four Generations in the organization which are confronted with four distinct, and rarely conflicting techniques to work. When the Generations reach work conflict, the effects are escalated turnover. In the current business organization, there are five generational cohorts noted such as boomers (born 1943–1960), Generation X (born 1961–1981), Generation Y or millennials (born after 1982) (Strauss and Howe, 1991), and Generation Z or post-Millennials or centennials (born 1997-2012) (Dimock, 2019) (see Table 1 & 2).

1.1 Definitions

"Generations is defined as an identifiable group that shares birth years, age, location, and significant life events at critical development stages (times)" (Salahuddin, 2014). *Generational difference is coined as differences in the values, beliefs, and opinions among different Generations of people"* (McNamara). Distinct age groups are classified as boomer, Gen X, Gen Y or millennials, and Gen Z or iGen or centennial.

Table 1. Classification of generations

S no:	Name of the Generation	Birth period
1.	Boomer	1946 - 1960
2.	Gen X	1960 - 1980
3.	Gen Y or Millennials	1980 - 1995
4.	Gen Z or iGen or Centennial	1995 - 2010

Source: (Zemke et al., 2000)

Table 2. Classification of generations

S no:	Name of the Generation	Birth period
1.	Baby boomer	1946 - 1964
2.	Gen X	1965 - 1980
3.	Gen Y / Millennials	1981 - 1996
4.	Gen Z / iGen	1997 - 2012

Source: (Dimock, 2019)

2. RESEARCH QUESTION

What are the differences or comparisons among four distinct age groups of employees (boomer, Gen X, Gen Y or millennials, and Gen Z or iGen or centennial) in work values, communication style, and leadership style?

3. BACKGROUND OF THE STUDY

3.1 Generational Difference

Lately, there has been one concept i.e. generational differences at work studied by researchers widely. The personality of discrete generations ascertains what are the requirements of employees at work. and what type of organizational atmosphere they demand. and what are their notions to achieve them? Because of Generational distinctiveness, these demands or requirements tend to differ from Generation to Generation. Thus, employees of discrete Generations can confront problems in comprehending others' perspectives of the work, which can be disturbing, difficult, twisting, and irritating in a stressful & challenging place of work. (Rotting, 2007). Among distinct generations, a lot of variations in personality profiles can be seen as well as in perspective towards jobs or duties. Conversely, effect sizes are not big enough & prominent stereotypes regarding differences among various Generations with some findings are conflicting in nature. Further, variations in work values and motivations have very little aid (Macky et al., 2008).

Parker (2007), presented significant differences in engagement in person initiative behavior, perceptions of stake, and usage of programs that have been found among baby boomers and millennials. While significant differences in program usage were found amid baby boomers and Generation X. Moreover, there have been no significant outcomes for gender variations in perceived work-life balance throughout the Generations. Beutell and Berman (2008), revealed that matures were significantly more content than baby boomers and Generation X. Boomer and Generation X are not unequal in their perceived ability to experience a work-life balance while Generation Y experiences more work-life balance as compared to Generation X. Fenzel (2013), depicted that this research would not identify statistically significant distinctiveness among boomers, generation X, and generation Y in work-role centrality and self- obsession. Whereas, it would determine significant differences of opinion in employee engagement among the baby boomer and Generation Y. Ozkan and Solmaz (2015), represented that Generation Z is more helpful than Generation Y. Moreover, this gen is also represented as respectful, interested in learning about work life, and open to every kind of idea.

Aydemir et al., (2016), found that Generational differences partly exist and have a considerable amount of effect on the employees' work-life balances and work values. Moreover, the attitude toward work-life balance does not differ much from Generation to Generation. Pasko et al., (2020), demonstrated employees of distinct generations have distinct opinions on four work-related variables likely job safety, promotion, work-life balance, and organizational leadership. Ahmed (2016), mentioned that the boomers have a rich experience and a robust drive to deliver in the organization. Generation X is self-supporting or independent, self-confident & balance oriented while Generation Y aims at nurturing itself and also looks at the bigger picture. Because of changes in demography, distinctive age groups have to agree with one all in an identical workplace environment. Echo boomers, also known as Gen Y or digital natives are self-reliant, outcomes-oriented, and seek extension in expectations (Arora and Dhole, 2019). Gen Y and iGen or centennial have distinct subjective values as compared to previous cohorts.

3.2 Characteristics of Generations at the Workplace

3.2.1 Work Value

A Value is ascertained as 'what is to be reckoned by the people Generally accurate or inaccurate' (Wey and Sutton, 2002). Chu (2007) depicted that heeding employees' value is essential to the point where employees render importance to the workplace and influence their behavior toward work. In the organization work values reforms the workers' opinions of likes, having a direct influence over employee attitudes, perception, and behaviors (Dose, 1997). D'Amato and Herzfeldt (2008) presented that distinct age groups have identical opinions, beliefs, and life experiences that vary from other cohorts to create work-related values. Crowder (2017), revealed a positive association between the Generational cohort and the preferred work-related values of the different generations. It was also depicted that several work-related values were different among discrete generations tied up all day, altruistic, supervising employees what to do and keeping skilled & loyal colleagues. Kicheva (2017) showed values of difference live among employees and the outcome of their likes is an organizational success.

Twenge et al., (2010) found in organizations, among the current generation of employees, there is a significant work-value difference exists. Baby boomers are depicted as cutthroat and reliable, busy bees, career-oriented who give importance to liberty and determination (Gibson et al., 2009) known for their work, having power, knowledge & liberty, and experiencing poor work-life balance (Coulter and Faulkner, 2014). According to Gursoy et al., (2013), there were several factors of work values identified for instance, job equilibrium, refusal to comply with rules or regulations, technological difficulty, work & family harmony, supervision, authority, and acknowledgment. Generation X had the same viewpoints either with baby boomers or Generation Y on residue factors. These outcomes confirm that to close the gap between boomers and Gen Y, Gen X had to consider these factors to maintain a good relationship with them. On the contrary, Generation X employees are more fun-loving, cynical, informal, and independent and look for more of a balance amid work and family (Gibson et al., 2009). According to Coulter and Faulkner (2014), Generation X is capable of using technology, gives importance to work-life balance, and does not have faith in authority.

Hurrelmann and Albrecht (2014), stated that Generation Y (born between 1985 and 2000) has a significant impact on the new values in today's rapidly evolving organizational environment and many other areas. Confidence, trust or belief, tech-savvy, and work for wealth are the characteristics of millennials (Coulter and Faulkner 2014). Gibson et al., (2009), depicted that in workplace the generation Y employees are also featured as optimistic, socially sensitive, technologically adept, ambitious, curious, and easily get tedious (see Figure 1 & Table 3). Generation X employees and baby boomer employees have a difference in work values when it is related to the public and career objectives. Sirias et al., (2007) presented work-value variances among baby boomers and Generation X employees which will lead to conflict. Generation X preferred job liberty and give value to wealth & position. Whereas, Generation Y opted the job adaptability compared to job liberty and give importance to wealth and position (Beutell and Berman, 2008). Gursoy et al., (2008), investigated whether baby boomers are honest, give respect to hierarchy & authority, live to work, and awaiting for rewards and promotions at the workplace. On the contrary, Generation X rebels against authority, work to live as well as expects quick recognition via pay, praise, promotion, and title. Furthermore, there is another generation that is known as millennials (Generation Y) which believes in teamwork with an optimistic attitude and faith in focused authorization. They also present a robust determination or self-discipline to achieve goals with good intent.

Nowadays in the current atmosphere, the new Generation is better addressed as Generation Z (born after the year 1995) with their new values. Alexander (2018), mentioned that Generation Z is characterized as optimistic, a workaholic, (Dolot, 2018) multitasking, and efficient in utilizing new technology as compared to other generations. According to Rohei (2019), Generation Z is self-directed and prefers an independent approach to learning. This Generation also gives value to work-life balance and does not want to think about work after working hours. Berkup (2014), indicated that in organizations centennials have various traits like multitasking, do not work as a team, innovation, efficiency in technology utilization, international perception, and prefer unusual & personalized activities.

3.2.2 Communication Style

Russette et al., (2008), depicted that communication is a coherent and persuasive imagination that is needed to match distinct Generations to the organizational objectives. Various modifications have been done in the organization, one of those modifications is how is the interaction among the Generational cohorts and with managers (Miller, 2012). Berger and Iyengar (2013), represented that to communicate with each other in the organization superiors and supervisors choose a verbal or written method of communication. Oral communication involves one on one communication and telephonic conversation, however, written communication involves texting, tweeting, and virtual interactions. To illustrate, the workforce of the veteran's cohorts opt one for one interaction or via telephone instead of mailing via electronic mail. To be able to reform the flow of records researchers explicitly the value of communication among Generations in the organization. Hartman and McCambridge (2011) mentioned in their study that effective generation is based on verbal communication skills such as teamwork, solving problems and ability are the essential aspect of organizational achievement. Salahuddin (2010) mentioned that firms are facing problems with efficient interaction (verbal) skills among discrete age groups. Supervisors may additionally require to have expertise and understanding in communication (verbal) skills and predictions & perceptions of each of the generational cohorts (Gursoy et al., 2013).

Goudreau (2013), reported that with these different techniques of communication, disappointment or frustration may appear and might make a contribution to negative perceptions among the different Generational cohorts. Salahuddin (2014), presented that expertise in communication can clear variations that take one generation to another generation as missing the sense of appreciation, faith, and openness. People with an affirmative age stereotype towards the other generations found a higher degree of inter-generational communication satisfaction and a lower degree of inter-generational communication discontentment than those who had got negative or natural stereotypes. According to Milligan (2016), employees perceived that business leaders, managers, and supervisors did have not sufficient information to communicate with their employees successfully from different generations of the organizations as well as they perceived that failures of communication and lack of interaction among the diverse generations generated conflict. Lester et al., (2012), depicted that along with discrete age groups of the workforce at the workplace, some examples are presented when employees from various generational backgrounds are called upon to work side-by-side or function as contributing members of a group. It is also identified that baby boomers give importance to one on one interaction for admiration compared to current generations.

French and Shim (2016) reported that generation x and millennials choose electronic-mail communication instead of one on one interaction (see Figure 1 & Table 3). Millennials (Generation Y) prefer broad-minded and steady interaction with their leaders, and the atmosphere at the workplace where the targets, perceptions, operations, issues, and conflicts of the companies are dispensed along every employee (Reed, 2014). Furthermore, generation Y workers need more information in managerial matters and want to escalate responses and interaction via organization compared with other generations (Gallicano et al., 2012). The current generation relies on technology and tends to speak eloquently and can interact more efficiently through cell phones and social websites. According to Rohei (2019), Generation Z is steady or regular, prompt, fast, and believes in one on one communication than boomers, Gen Xers, and Gen Y. According to the study by Schawbel (2014), Generation Z wants that supervisors listen to their point of views and give importance to them. It also depicts that the organization has to be less concerned about age and more concerned about opinion and efforts. Furthermore, open-minded & honest leaders are needed by centennials who do not conceal info on account of their young age or job designations (see Figure 1 & Table 3). Valickas and Jakstaite (2017) presented that different generations of employees themselves find it critical to interact with each other & organizations' managers struggle to discover a way that ascertains smooth communication between employees as well to make a productive and amicable working environment.

3.2.3 Leadership Style

In organizational studies, leaders have been playing a pivotal role and yet they are the essential elements for organizational or managerial efficiency at the individual level, group level, and organizational level (Burke et al., 2007). It has been probed that there is an existence of differences in the leadership styles amid distinct age groups of the workforce. In the current organizations, if generations such as Gen X and baby boomers were completely productive then there will be distinct leadership styles (Price, 2000). According to the theory of Leader-Member, leadership is coined as a practice of a common association and communication among superiors and subordinates (Northhouse, 2004). A leadership model which highlights the convolution, maintaining equity throughout the critical situations and actions of leaders. Innovative leadership needs a plethora of qualities likely professional qualities, experience, and intellect. There is an approach through which a leader can guide others toward attaining a goal i.e. leadership style (Eagly and Johnson, 1990). The leader's styles are based on the work quality, personnel, and individuality of the leader.

The old or common leadership style tends to discourage all multi-Generational employees. However, the current generation's leadership needs innovative qualities, circumstances, education, and similarity or empathy along with innovative tech (Rodriguez et al., 2003). Leadership style like participative takes to qualitative judgment, consent & affirmation, comprehending the judgments, reform decision-making skills, encouragements, work contentment, team building, and conflict resolution. Baby boomers follow it and they face issues in implementing it in the organizations. This also needs a sense of comprehension, compassion, listening, interacting, motivating, and delegating. Contrarily, boomer leadership or supervision influenced Generation Xer's leadership. They even challenge the belief & notions of other employees and the decision-making procedure. Further, they lack interpersonal skills, and sometimes their frank and blunt behavior influences the retentivity of the workforce. Next or new Generations in the organizations may have a chance to work as a leader (Salahuddin, 2010). Yu and Miller (2005) predicted that boomers and Generation X have distinct forms of being leaders. Generation X employees have selected the 'participative decision-making' style where they can include people and desired freedom & liberty, this is called the 'relationship-oriented leadership style'. While, boomers needed direction from their supervisors, which is called the 'task-oriented leadership style'. In the organizations, the leadership style preferences of generations are different like baby boomers such as cordial and compassionate, believe in equality, mission-defined, democratic approach. Generation Xers are direct, cordial, adjustable, competent, concrete results & real, and backing up learning opportunities. Generation Y is inspirational, cooperative, affirmative, educational, able to coach, organized, and achievement-oriented (Lockwood, 2OO9).

According to Lockwood (2004), boomers preferred leadership styles are cooperative and harmonious, display admiration for enthusiasm and hard work, approach other employees for their accomplishments, take part in the organizational itinerary and implement modifications, render challenging tasks to resolve the organizational issues, work as leaders and render support to work/life balance. Generation X's preferred leadership styles are giving esteem or appreciation to the experiences that have given shape to the perceptions, telling the truth, honoring the sense of work-life balance and arranging training programs, interacting clearly and scrutinizing quality, clearly ascertaining boundaries, and providing learning opportunities. Preferred millennials' leadership styles are time-consuming according to organizational culture, give robust leadership, comprehensible expectations, and long-term objectives, and render training programs. Al-Asfour and Lettau (2014),

Figure 1. Generational cohorts and their characteristics
Source: *Author(s) own*

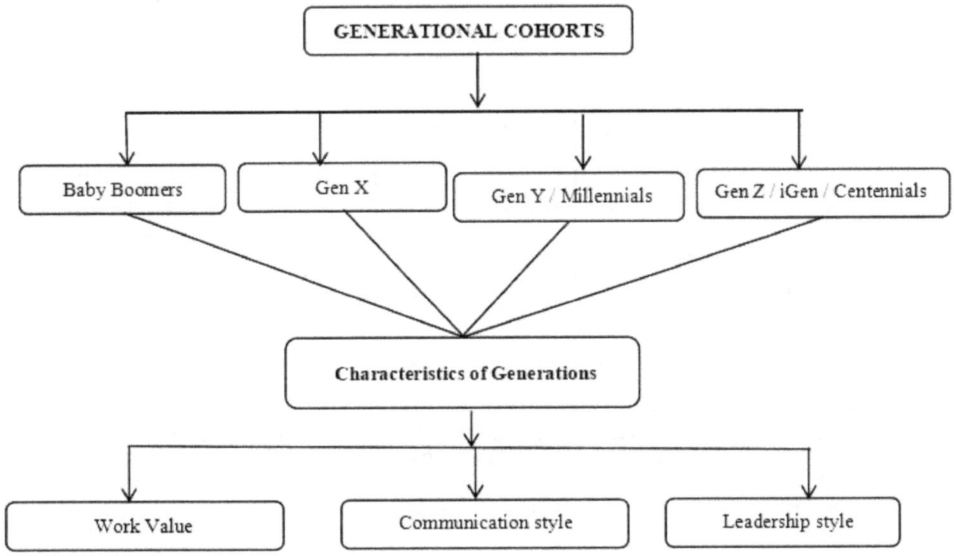

Table 3. Comparison of work values, communication style, and leadership style amid distinct age groups of personnels at the Workplace

Characteristics	Boomers	Gen X	Gen Y / Millennials	Generation Z / iGen/ Centennials
Work value	Competitive, reliable workaholics, honest, give respect to hierarchy & authority, live to work, and awaiting rewards and promotions, Patience, Hardworking, Soft skills, Respect for traditions, commitment; self-motivated	Fun-loving, cynical, informal, independent, prefer work-life balance, job liberty, give importance to work-life balance, prefer diversity, Hardworking, Openness, Curiosity, Practicality, Adaptive, loyal, success-oriented	Confident, assertive, optimistic, socially sensitive, technologically adept, ambitious, curious and easily get tedious, job adaptability, goal-oriented, long-term relationship with supervisors, Flexibility, Mobility, Success-oriented, Creativity, Mobility, brave, creativity	Optimistic, workaholic, tech-savvy, practical, value work-life balance, multi-taskers, Living in the present, Brave, Speedy reactions and access to info, Respect for diversity, energetic, curiosity
Leadership style	Task-oriented, warm, and caring, belief in equality, mission-defined, democratic approach, cooperative and harmonious, deserving praise and respect for their enthusiasm and hard work, target employees on account of their skills or accomplishments, target other employees who participate in the organizational guidance and execution of modified initiatives, challenge employees to participate in resolving the managerial disputes, render opportunities to work as a leader and render help to work-life balance.	Relationship-oriented, participative decision making, direct, cordial, adjustable, competent, concrete results, real, backing up learning opportunities, admire or value the experiences that have given shape to their perceptions, honest, value work-life balance and provide training programs, give repetitive tasks clearly and provide a qualitative job, clearly ascertain boundaries.	Inspirational, cooperative, optimistic, intellectual, able to coach, structured or reformed, action-oriented, time-consuming decisions according to organizational lifestyle or customs, provide knowledge and robust leadership, comprehensible expectations and long-term objectives, and render training or scrutinizing programs, courteous association with superiors, team building, and managerial style.	Flourish in the distinct workforce, multi-taskers, work independently, interact, do not accept traditional office hierarchy, seek their resources to get info and boost up the morale of employees, instead of waiting for a meeting or conference call on other days.
Communication Style	Focus only on face-to-face communication	Face-to-face, email, or call communication	Collaborative (Emails/text/ phones/ computers)	Steady or regular, prompt, fast, and believe in face-to-face & smooth communication via technology, online communication more than in person, amiable communicator, Texts/ tweets with emoji for a shortcut.

Sources: Table 3 was designed by the researchers and compiled from the literature (Lockwood, 2OO9; Gibson et al., 2009; Perilus, 2020; McCrindle 2020; Blazek, 2016).

presented the leadership style of millennials (Generation Y) and they represent a 'well-mannered association with sovereignty'.

Teamwork and managerial style are the forte of this Gen who could bind people and like collective actions. Sessa et al., (2007), depicted that current Generation leaders prefer to use a more individualistic leadership style, however, boomers prefer to choose harmonious and team-oriented leadership styles. McCrindle (2020), found that for Generation Z employees, leadership shifting has taken place when these centennials have changed from older and experienced experts to leaders who encourage and connect with others within the workplace. An efficient superior is a person who could connect via relations, communicate rationally, manage practically, and lead with direction and strategy. Blazek, (2016), showed that Generation Z may prefer a culture that allows modification and the requirement to lead toward a technology-driven environment, automatic processes, and interactive usage of technology in all views of the business to modify outcomes. They also may take the side to work freely and solitarily, not dependent on outdated organizational hierarchy. Furthermore, to find out the information quickly they prefer to search for their informants and boost the morale of employees, instead of waiting for a meeting or conference call on another day. Managers realize it even critical to guarantee the effective achievement of organizational objectives and well-ordered leadership at the workplace (Valickas and Jakstaite, 2017).

Table 3 illustrates the comparison of distinct age groups (Generational cohorts) of employees at the workplace likely Boomer, Gen X, Gen Y (millennials), and Gen Z (iGen or centennial) in work values, communication style, and leadership style at the workplace.

4. RESEARCH GAPS

Many studies have been conducted to comprehend the Generations and their connections with work value, communication style, and leadership style, however, it is considered that the previous research has not focused on the newest generation i.e Generation Z. Most of them were stopped at Millennials, which is safe to verify that millennials (generation Y employees) and other generations were with more studies performed so far. Four-generation orientations of personnel or employees are not universally acknowledged. The categories of distinct age groups (Generation cohort) of employees presented here were determined via academic studies and practitioners' articles. So, to continue the studies of the relationship of work value, communication style, and leadership style with Generations, and to try to fill gaps from previous studies, this paper is endeavoring to identify the differentiation and comparison in work values, communication style, and leadership style of distinct age group employees at workplace likely boomer, Gen X, Gen Y (millennials) and Gen Z (iGen or centennial).

5. LIMITATION

In the current investigation, only three characteristics likely work value, communication style, and leadership style have been studied meticulously among boomers, Gen X, Gen Y or millennials, and Gen Z or iGen or centennial at the workplace. There are other characteristics that need to be explored. In organizations, not only investigation of distinct Generations is necessary, but, similarities among them need to be acknowledged. Another limitation is that less empirical and theoretical investigation has been done on Generational differences, especially on the current Generations likely Gen Y or Millennials and Gen Z or iGen or centennial. Future research should include qualitative research on the cohort theory that shared historical experiences to shape distinct generations. There is also clearly a need for comparative studies to test the notion that generational cohorts are shaped by the significant political, economic, cultural, and other events of their times.

6. DISCUSSION

The current research has unearthed cohort disparities and comparisons in work value, leadership style, and communication which are essential to the workplace. These disparities are genuine and intriguing, but in comparative terms, they are not big enough. Comprehending the disparities or comparisons amid cohorts at work helps meet various workforce essentials. It is essential to proceed with the probation of discrete generations in the firms or companies, however, it is also essential to accredit the differences or comparisons and commonalities among the workforce of distinct age groups and experiences (Cennamo and Gardner, 2008). As discussed theoretically in the paper a fact is not supposed to be shunned and that is organizations include distinct age groups workforce, which are distinct in the job context. Moreover, classifying and generalizing the work values, leadership styles, and communication styles of the boomer, gen X, gen Y (millennials), and gen Z (iGen or centennial) workforce are shown to be critical as each of them has its important characteristics. There is concrete evidence of disparities like boomers workforce live to do a job, value management & respect the organizations, the Gen X workforce support harmonious relation amid work life and family life and Gen Y employees do a job to survive, (Zemke et al., 2000), want management to consider that they are trustworthy & consistently confront authorities (Gursoy et al., 2008).

Generation Y has a significant impact on their new values, in a rapidly evolving business environment and many other areas (Hurrelmann and Albrecht, 2014). Confidence, trust or belief, tech usage, and work for wealth are the characteristics of millennials (Coulter and Faulkner 2014). On the contrary, the generation Z workforce is characterized as optimistic, a workaholic, (Dolot, 2018) multitasking, efficient in utilizing new technology, (Rohei, 2019) self-directed, and prefers an independent approach to learning. This generation also gives value to work-life balance and does not want to think about work after working hours. Boomers believe in maintaining a harmonious association and render importance to consistent one on one interactions and perceptions based on morals & values.

For Gen Y communication either through one on one or social networking sites is essential to create trust. Further, Gen X favors one on one meetings or social sites for communication. Millennials opt for open and free flow of virtual communication using technology (Shrivastava, 2019). The Gen Z workforce wants to listen to the point of view of supervisors and give importance to them. Open-minded & honest leaders are needed by centennials who do not conceal info from them because of their young age or title (Schawbel, 2014). This generation is also steady or regular, prompt, fast, and believes in one on one communication more than boomers, Gen Xers, and Gen Y (Rohei, 2019). The leaders' styles are based on the work quality, personnel, and individuality of the leader. The old or common leadership style tends to discourage all multi-generational employees. However, in the current generation, leadership needs innovative qualities, circumstances, education, and similarity or empathy along with innovative tech (Rodriguez et al., 2003). Distinct Generations perceive the leadership style distinctly. Significant disparities amid boomers and Xers in preferred leadership style in the Taiwan manufacturing industry is unearthed. However, in the educator sector in Taiwan, the investigation could find out no disparities in leadership style amid distinct age groups (Yu, and Miller, 2005). Boomer leadership styles are cooperative, display admiration for enthusiasm and hard work, target insightful and skilled workforce, participate in organizational itinerary and implement modifications, render challenging tasks to resolve the organizational issues, do the job as leaders, and support work/life balance. Generation X workforce gives esteem or appreciation to the experiences that have given shape to the perceptions, is reliable, honors the sense of work-life balance and arranges training programs, interacting clearly and scrutinizing quality, and ascertains boundaries. Millennials are time-consuming according to organizational culture, give robust leadership, comprehensible expectations, and long-term objectives, and render training programs (Lockwood, 2004). Centennial workforce prefers to lead toward a technology-driven environment, and automatic processes, work freely & solitarily, and be self-reliant (Blazek, 2016).

7. FUTURE RESEARCH DIRECTIONS

This article focuses only on work values, communication style, and leadership style from the perspective of four generations. Now that there is evidence that generational differences exist in work values, communication style, and leadership style, further research should build on these findings, exploring the causes and consequences of these differences. Further research may also be conducted on other generational traits of distinct generations of employees to unearth the root causes of their differences in terms of social, economic, and cultural backgrounds. New studies may strive to probe generational differences in terms of work-life balance, work ethics, professional identity, and artificial intelligence of the employees of distinct generations. There are some other issues that need to be considered by future researchers such as Do racial and ethnic backgrounds of the employees of different generations and/or their color and creed affect generational difference? Do generational similarities or dissimilarities have any correspondence with the performance of the subjects? What kind of entrepreneurship development policies impact the younger generation of entrepreneurs? How do millennials prefer to be managed, and how do they manage their subordinates? What are the attitudes of millennials toward their subordinates, in particular toward Generation Z? Furthermore, various managerial issues faced by organizations must also be examined and reviewed with high-quality theoretical and empirical efforts to assist organizations in making the transition to the next generational cohort.

8. CONCLUSION

Employees nowadays are more diverse than ever before, and that diversity is manifested in these generational cohorts. The current context concerning generational differences at work is briefly outlined, followed by a description of the distinct characteristics underpinning the notion of generational cohorts. The introduction of the current study strives to render a brief background to the notion that there are generational differences at work. Generations are differentiated from cohorts, and the article discusses the relevance of the literature on cohort differences to an understanding of generational differences. This study has uncovered four generational cohorts and the differences and comparisons among them in work values, communication style, and leadership style. Comprehending differences among four distinct age groups at the workplace is a pivotal measure in meeting employees' desires and requirements. According to the above researchers, it is found out that there are significant differences among generations as well as they have different styles of communication, styles of leading their subordinates, and values of work. Table 3 has represented a comparison of distinct age groups (boomer, Gen X, Gen Y (millennials), and Gen Z (iGen or centennial) in work values, communication style, and leadership style at the workplace. According to the table above baby boomers have rich experience and a strong drive to deliver in organizations. Generation X is independent, self-assured, and balance oriented while Generation Y (millennials) focuses on nurturing itself and also looks at the bigger picture. According to Valickas and Jakstaite (2017), the baby boom generation at the workplace is faithful and devoted to the manager, Gen X shows devotion towards its occupation while employees of Generation Y are devoted to the occupation and to itself. Furthermore, generation Z is self-reliant, multitasking, efficient in technology utilization, and believes in face-to-face communication. At the workplace, there are discrete demands and inducing elements of centennials or iGen as compared to previous generations. Further, when they get a job in the organization, they try to find their unusual demands and needs to implement at work (Agarwal and Vaghela, 2018). Therefore, the present review or research is just a way of comprehending the comparisons or differentiation in work values, communication style, and leadership style between four distinct generational employees. This review has also the ability to aid organizations and supervisors to better explicate the differences between generations in work value, communication style, and leadership style within the workplace.

REFERENCES

Agarwal, H., & Vaghela, P. (2018). *Work values of Gen Z: Bridging the gap to the next generation*. In National Conference on Innovative Business Management Practices in 21st Century, Faculty of Management Studies, Parul University, Gujarat, India.

Ahmed, I., (2016). *Generational differences in workplace behaviour and their effective management with reference to professional education sector of Uttar Pradesh*. Research Gate.

Al-Asfour, A., & Lettau, L. (2014). Strategies for leadership styles for multi-generational workforce. *Journal of Leadership, Accountability and Ethics*, *11*(2), 52–69.

Alexander, C. (2018). Gen Z, The Future of Work, and HR Tech. *BizLibrary*. www.bizlibrary.com

Arora, N., & Dhole, V. (2019). Generation Y: Perspective, engagement, expectations, preferences and satisfactions from workplace; a study conducted in Indian context. *Benchmarking*, *26*(5), 1378–1404. doi:10.1108/BIJ-05-2018-0132

Aydemir, M., Dinc, M. S., & Caglar, M. (2016). How work-life balance and work values differ from generation to generation: An exploratory study. In *Proceedings of the 2nd Annual International Conference on Social Sciences (AICSS),* (pp. 77-89). Research Gate.

Berger, J., & Iyengar, R. (2013). 'Communication channels and word of mouth. How the medium shapes the message'. *The Journal of Consumer Research, 40*(3), 567–579. doi:10.1086/671345

Berkup, S. B. (2014). Working with generations X and Y in generation Z period: Management of different generations in business life. *Mediterranean Journal of Social Sciences, 5*(19), 218. doi:10.5901/mjss.2014.v5n19p218

Beutell, N. J., & Wittig-Berman, U. (2008). Work-family conflict and work-family synergy for generation X, baby boomers, and matures: Generational differences, predictors, and satisfaction outcomes. *Journal of Managerial Psychology, 23*(5), 507–523. doi:10.1108/02683940810884513

Blazek, K. (2016). *Leadership style of Generation Z.* TruScore. https://www.truscore.com/resources/Gen-z/

Burke, C. S., Sims, D. E., Lazzara, E. H., & Salas, E. (2007). 'Trust in leadership: A multi-level review and integration'. *The Leadership Quarterly, 18*(6), 606–632. doi:10.1016/j.leaqua.2007.09.006

Cennamo, L., & Gardner, D. (2008). Generational differences in work values, outcomes and person–organization values fit. *Journal of Managerial Psychology, 23*(8), 891–906. doi:10.1108/02683940810904385

Chu, K. H. A. (2007). A factorial validation of work value structure: Second-order confirmatory factor analysis and its implications. *Tourism Management, 29*(2), 320–330. doi:10.1016/j.tourman.2007.03.003

Coulter, J. S., & Faulkner, D. C. (2014). The multi-Generational workforce. *Professional Case Management, 19*(1), 46–51. doi:10.1097/NCM.0000000000000008 PMID:24300430

Crowder, B.R.R., (2017). *Work Motivation Theory: Identifying Multi-Generational Values in the Workplace*, 1-157. Walden University.

D'Amato, A., & Herzfeldt, R. (2008). 'Learning orientation, organizational commitment and talent retention across generations: A study of European managers'. *Journal of Managerial Psychology, 23*(8), 929–953. doi:10.1108/02683940810904402

Dimock, M. (2019). *Defining Generations: Where Millennials end and Generation Z begins*. Pew Research Center. https://pewrsr.ch/2szqtJz

Dolot, A. (2018). The characteristics of Generation Z. *E-mentor, 74*(2), 44-50.

Dose, J. J. (1997). Work values: An integrative framework and illustrative application to organizational socialization. *Journal of Occupational and Organizational Psychology*, *70*(3), 219–240. doi:10.1111/j.2044-8325.1997.tb00645.x

Eagly, A. H., & Johnson, B. T. (1990). 'Gender and leadership style: A meta-analysis'. *Psychological Bulletin*, *108*(2), 233–256. doi:10.1037/0033-2909.108.2.233

Fenzel, J. L. (2013). *Examining generational differences in the workplace: Work centrality, narcissism, and their relation to employee work engagement* [Doctoral dissertation, The University of Wisconsin-Milwaukee].

Ferri-Reed, J. (2014). Millennializing the workplace. *Journal for Quality and Participation*, *37*(1), 13.

French, A. M., & Shim, J. P. (2016). The digital revolution. Internet of things 5G, and beyond. *Communications of the Association for Information Systems*, *38*(1), 40. doi:10.17705/1CAIS.03840

Gallicano, T. D., Curtin, P., & Matthews, K. (2012). I love what I do, but… A relationship management survey of millennial generation public relations agency employees. *Journal of Public Relations Research*, *24*(3), 222–242. doi:10.1080/1062726X.2012.671986

Gibson, W. J., Greenwood, A. R., Edward, F., & Murphy, F. E. (2009). Generational differences In the workplace: Personal values, behaviors, and popular beliefs. *Journal of Diversity Management*, *4*(3), 1–8.

Goudreau, J. (2013). How to communicate in the new multi-generational office. *Forbes*. https://www.forbes.com/sites/jennagoudreau/2013/02/14/how-tocommunicate-in-the-new-multigenerational-office/#1652ee244a6b

Gursoy, D., Chi, C. G., & Karadag, E. (2013). Generational differences in work values and attitudes among front line and service contact employees. *International Journal of Hospitality Review*, *32*, 40–48.

Gursoy, D., Maier, A. T., & Chi, G. C. (2008). Generational differences: An examination of work values and Generational gaps in the hospitality workforce'. *International Journal of Hospitality Management*, *27*(3), 448–458. doi:10.1016/j.ijhm.2007.11.002

Hartman, J. L., & McCambridge, J. (2011). Optimizing millennials' communication styles. *Business Communication Quarterly, 74*(1), 22–44. doi:10.1177/1080569910395564

Hurrelmann, K., & Albrecht, E. (2014). *Die heimlichen Revolutionäre - Wie die Generation Y unsere Welt verändert.* Verlag Beltz.

Kicheva, T. (2017). 'Management of Employees from Different Generations - Challenge for Bulgarian Managers and HR Professionals'. *Economic Alternatives, 1*, 103–121.

Kovary, G. (2012). *'Leading A MultiGenerational Project Team'*. NGen Performance. https://www.nGenperformance.com

Lancaster & Stillman. (2002). *When the Generations collide: Traditionalist, baby boomers, Generation Xers and millennials: who they are, why they clash, how to solve Generational puzzle at work.* Harper collins.

Lester, S. W., Standifer, R. L., Schultz, N. J., & Windsor, J. M. (2012). Actual versus perceived Generational differences at work. *Journal of Leadership & Organizational Studies, 19*(3), 341–354. doi:10.1177/1548051812442747

Lockwood, N.R., (2004). Leadership Styles Series Part II: Leadership Styles: Generational Differences. SHRM Briefly Stated. *Society for Human Resource Management (SHRM), 2.*

Lockwood, N. R. (2009). The Multi-Generational Workforce: Opportunity for Competitive Success. *Research Quarterly*, 2.

Lyons, S., & Kuron, L. (2014). Generational differences in the workplace: A review of the evidence and directions for future research. *Journal of Organizational Behavior, 35*(S1), S139–S157. doi:10.1002/job.1913

Macky, K., Gardner, D., & Forsyth, S. (2008). Generational differences at work: Introduction and overview. *Journal of Managerial Psychology, 23*(8), 857–861. doi:10.1108/02683940810904358

McCrindle. (2020). *Leadership.* Generationz. https://Generationz.com.au/articles/leadership/#: ~:text=For%20Gen%20Z%2C%20a%20shift,and%20lead%20directionally%20and%20strategically.

Miller, K. (2012). *Organizational communication: Approaches and processes* (6th ed.). Cengage Learning.

Milligan, S.R., (2016). *Conflict and Diversity Associated with Four Generations in the Workforce*, 1-134. Walden University.

Northouse, P. G. (2004). *Leadership. Theory and practice* (3rd ed.). Sage Publications'.

Ozkana, M. & Solmaz, B., (2015). The Changing Face Of The Employees- Generation Z And Their Perceptions of Work. *Science Direct, 26*, 476 – 483.

Parker, C. C., (2007). *Generational differences in work life balance attitudes*, 1-41. SUNY.

Pasko, R., Maellaro, R., & Stodnick, M. (2020). A study of millennials' preferred work-related attributes and retention. *Employee Relations*, *43*(3), 774–787. doi:10.1108/ER-05-2020-0224

Perilus, B. (2020). *Engaging Four Generations in the Workplace: A Single Case Study* [Doctoral dissertation, University of Phoenix]

Price, A. (2000). *Principle of Human Resource Management: an active learning approach*. Blackwell business.

Rodriguez, R. O., Green, M. T., & Ree, M. J. (2003). Leading Generation X: Do the old rules apply? *Journal of Leadership & Organizational Studies*, *9*(4), 67–75. doi:10.1177/107179190300900406

Rohei. (2019). *'The MultiGenerational Workforce: From Challenges to Opportunities'*. Rohei. https://www.rohei.com/ resources/the-multiGenerational-workforce-from-challenges-to-opportunities

Russette, J., Scully, R., & Preziosi, R. (2008). Leadership across cultures: A comparative study. *Academy of Strategic Management Journal*, *7*(1), 47–61.

Salahuddin, M. M. (2010). Generational differences impact on leadership style and organizational success'. *Journal of Diversity Management*, *5*(2), 1–6. doi:10.19030/jdm.v5i2.805

Salahuddin, M.M., (2014). The Impact of Generational Differences on Organizational Relationships: A Communication Perspective, 1-130. Department of Education.

Schawbel, D. (2014). Gen Z Employees: The 5 Attributes You Need to Know. *Entrepreneur.* http://www. entrepreneur.com/article/236560

Sessa, V. I., Kabacoff, R. I., Deal, J., & Brown, H. (2007). Generational differences in leader values and leadership behaviors. *The Psychologist Manager Journal*, *10*(1), 47–74. doi:10.1080/10887150709336612

Shrivastava, A. (2019). Using collaborative project for learning effective ways of working harmoniously with people from different cultures'. *International Journal Marketing Business Communication*, *8*(1), 47–54.

Sirias, D., Karp, H., & Brotherton, T. (2007). Comparing the levels of individualism collectivism between baby boomers and Generation X: Implications for teamwork. *Management Research News*, *30*(10), 749–761. doi:10.1108/01409170710823467

Strauss, W., & Howe, N. (1991). *Generations: The history of America's future*. William Morrow.

Twenge, J. M., Campbell, S. M., Hoffman, B. J., & Lance, C. E. (2010). Generational differences in work values: Leisure and extrinsic values increasing, social and intrinsic values decreasing. *Journal of Management*, *36*(5), 1117–1142. doi:10.1177/0149206309352246

Valickas, A., & Jakstaite, K. (2017). Different Generations' attitude towards work and management in the business organizations. *Human Resources Management & Ergonomics*, *XI*, 108–119.

Wey Smola, K., & Sutton, C. D. (2002). Generational differences: Revisiting Generational work values for the new millennium. *Journal of Organizational Behavior*, *23*(4), 363–382. doi:10.1002/job.147

Yu, H. C., & Miller, P. (2005). Leadership style: The X Generation and Baby Boomers compared in different cultural contexts. *Leadership and Organization Development Journal*, *26*(1), 35–50. doi:10.1108/01437730510575570

Zemke, R., Raines, C., & Filipczak, B. (2000). *Generations at Work: Managing the Clash of Veterans, Boomers, Xers, and Nexters in Your Workplace*. American Management Association.

ADDITIONAL READING

Cox, A., Hannif, Z., & Rowley, C. (2014). Leadership styles and generational effects: Examples of US companies in Vietnam. *International Journal of Human Resource Management*, *25*(1), 1–22. doi:10.1080/09585192.2013.778311

Flores, S. (2023). *Boost the Surprising Benefits of Generational Differences in Today's Workplace.* https://www.espresa.com/blog/generational-differences/

Just, R. A. (2011). *The differences in leadership styles among generation cohorts of small business leaders and their relationship to organizational outcomes* [Doctoral dissertation, Capella University].

Notre Dame of Maryland University. (2019). *The Evolution of communication across generations.* Notre Dame of Maryland University. https://online.ndm.edu/news/ communication/evolution- of-communication/

Parry, E., & Urwin, P. (2011). Generational differences in work values: A review of theory and evidence. *International Journal of Management Reviews, 13*(1), 79–96. doi:10.1111/j.1468-2370.2010.00285.x

Receno, J. P. (2021). Generational Differences in Work Values, Employee Engagement, and Organizational Culture: Inputs for Human Resource Development Plan. *Asia Pacific Journal of Academic Research in Business Administration, 7*(1), 48–56.

Stiglbauer, B., Penz, M., & Batinic, B. (2022). Work values across generations: Development of the New Work Values Scale (NWVS) and examination of generational differences. *Frontiers in Psychology, 13*, 1028072. doi:10.3389/fpsyg.2022.1028072 PMID:36420391

Uzialko, A. (2023). Bridge the Gap: Communicating With a Multigenerational Workforce. *Business News Daily.* https://www.businessnewsdaily.com/9708-multigenerational-workforce-communication.html

Vdovin, A. (2020). *Managing Communication Differences Between Generations In The Workplace.* Software Alert. https://www.alert-software.com/blog/corporate-communications-strategies-for-a-cross-generational-workforce

KEY TERMS AND DEFINITIONS

Communication style: The process of conveying and taking in ideas and opinions in distinct ways.

Generational difference: refers to the difference of opinion about beliefs, thoughts, actions, policies, or values between one generation and another. In other words, it means the chasm that separates the beliefs and behaviors of the employees of two distinct generations.

Generations: The current living generations at the workplace are the baby boomers (1946-1964), Generation X (1965 - 1980), millennials (1981 - 1996), and Generation Z (1997 - 2012).

Leadership style: The behavioral approach employed by leaders to influence, motivate, and direct their followers. A leadership style evaluates how leaders implement plans and strategies to accomplish given objectives while accounting for colleague expectations, and the well-being and soundness of their team.

Work values: refers to an accumulation of qualities, principles, ideals, and beliefs that relate to the workplace. They underpin the motivation, attitude, and behavior that influence the employees' working style and the decisions that they make at work and throughout their careers.

Chapter 11
The Potential of Ethically Responsible and Persistent Leadership Theory

Ansar Abbas
https://orcid.org/0000-0003-4521-1920
Universitas Airlangga, Indonesia & MY Business School, Muslim Youth University, Islamabad, Pakistan

ABSTRACT

The central focus of leadership theories in social psychology and organizational studies is on inclusive leadership. Persistent, naturally inclusive leaders seek diverse viewpoints and evaluate their journey. They build strategic intent and cooperate more successfully with others. Inclusive leaders have original social and ethical values, innate personal systems, and moral responsibility. They shape followers' behaviors through consciousness, open-mindedness, fearlessness, humility, and tolerance, fostering an environment where employees from diverse backgrounds feel respected and valued.

INTRODUCTION

Stogdill, in Handbook of Leadership, posited many diverse definitions of leadership as some people have tried to define the term (Stogdill, 1974). In today's world, there are many various styles of leadership. However, there is no universally accepted definition of what it means to be a leader. When contemplating past and present great leaders, it is natural to wonder what it took for them to achieve such stratospheric stature, e.g. (Avolio, 2005). Where they get their leadership skills is a

DOI: 10.4018/978-1-6684-6602-5.ch011

million-dollar question that arises in the mind of leadership studies. According to Max De Pree, these are crucial tools for developing into a creative leader who can guide their team and business to new heights (DePree, 1993). According to Max De Pree, Leadership is an Art. It is well-established that the more research on a subject, the more complicated and unclear it becomes. The public debate on the issue has been hampered by destructive and unethical leadership behaviors, which has increased the demand and relevance of ethically and morally persistent leadership applications. Particularly in the business management field because it explains how top-level managers and executives may improve their leadership abilities to create a more productive and profitable company(DePree, 2011).

Thomas Carlyle's Great Man Theory, which gained traction in the 1840s, postulated that innate leadership abilities allow for the emergence of exceptional leaders when given the right circumstances (Thomas, 1888). These people excel in leadership because they have attributes like moral clarity, empathy, and selflessness. Leaders in the Great Man supposition are portrayed as all-knowing brainiacs. Persons can anticipate and prepare for any possibility with their plans and individuals who can coordinate massively complex group efforts (Mouton, 2019). Many leadership theories and concepts are related to the idea that leaders are not born as great men but instead develop abilities and learn leadership. Position, Permission, Production, People Development, and Pinnacle are the five tiers of leadership described in John Maxwell's "5 Levels of Leadership." Researchers may benefit from exploring these tiers better to comprehend their development as leaders in the workplace and beyond. The notion of persistent leadership is guiding this trip. No person possesses all the necessary leadership skills, and performance improves when everyone on the team is treated as equals (French, 2017). This concept passes with Inclusive leaders who are aware of their prejudices and actively seek other perspectives to influence decision-making and improve collaboration (Van Knippenberg & van Ginkel, 2022). This chapter uses a wide range of sources to make a case for how inclusive the potential of persistent leadership theory is. It would connect the idea of persistent leadership to the paradigm of social change or a leader's responsible and ethical development.

PURPOSE OF THE STUDY

Academic literature highly values debates and discussions on various leadership philosophies. For this and other reasons, much literature is dedicated to leadership. Because of this constant interest, academics in fields as diverse as business and education have reaped many benefits from studying leadership. This chapter contributes to the clarion appeal for more attention to robust leadership theories in the face of social change.

JUSTIFICATION OF THE STUDY

A debate is a method of comparing and contrasting ideas in which the value of persistent leadership is emphasized to arrive at a decision that is both theoretically relevant and true. Claims, supporting evidence, and consequences are the three pillars upon which resolves a dispute rests. The assertion states the point of view the arguer hopes to impress onto the viewers. Some say great leaders are born, while others argue they must be developed. The assertion is supported by proof or third-party verification provided by the consent. This chapter gathers literature and builds an argument to support the leadership persistence theory.

SIGNIFICANCE OF THE STUDY

Theories of influence and leadership provide context for the assertion and indicate why the readership should care about development. The leadership debate is organized as a point-by-point discussion of each side's evidence and counterargument, beginning with a review of the theoretical justification. All modern theories are represented in literature by the same patterns. Some scholars have advocated one argument, while others have opposed responses, and the debate continues without resolution. In a standard theory, proponents of different views regarding whether leaders are "born" or "made" can pose meaningful questions about why the former concept is better for study.

RESEARCH QUESTIONS

The question of whether competencies are innate or acquired remains open. All leadership theories, however, are consistent with keeping their argument and ideology intact. This argument provides insights into the value of persistent leadership in concluding the dispute.

LITERATURE REVIEW

Considering the critical stances of the postmodernist account of social transformation is essential since businesses and economies are expanding (Ahmad et al., 2016; Tyree, 1998). The current characteristics of the space of social positions and the patterns of change that led up to the current situation primarily rely on social justice throughout the social change (Abbas, Ekowati, & Suhariadi, 2022; Ahmad et al., 2016;

Barnes et al., 2020; Crosby, 2020; Tyree, 1998). This allows us to apply complete analysis to lifestyles, contemporary characteristics, and change patterns connected to them (Benabou & Tirole, 2011; Blau, 2017; Elder Jr, 1994). Therefore, leadership and social change are the two topics that will be analyzed together (French, 2017; Hollander, 1980; Keller & Dansereau, 1995). It will examine how the patterns of homology between the two spaces have shifted dramatically throughout the period during which social change is being occurred.

Management for social equality is a system constantly rebuilt to meet the demands of the cultural context (Brooks et al., 2007). Developing research on social equity management serves a variety of purposes, employs a wide range of approaches and conceptual frames, and, not surprisingly, uncovers nuanced aspects of social justice leadership. For this reason, as McKenzie points out, it is unreasonable to expect that studies will lead to a universal theory or an "essentialized" prescription for diversity and inclusion leadership (McKenzie et al., 2008). Nevertheless, when viewed as a whole, the theoretical, prescriptive, and related research on social justice leadership reveals a set of persistent patterns and common themes. There are three broad types of writings here: Leadership for social justice, according to these ideas, ought to be action-oriented and transformative; dedicated and persistent; inclusive and democratic; relational and caring; reflective; oriented toward a pedagogy that is fair to all (Furman, 2012). All of these ideas are related to one another. Some authors also discuss the challenges that leaders who engage in this activity encounter and give the beginnings of a "toolbox" for this leadership practice (Lester et al., 2020). Being able to function as transformative, activist change agents in challenging settings requires a deep commitment to a social justice agenda and a "stubborn persistence" in one's efforts on behalf of that agenda on the part of organizational leaders (Scheurich & Skrla, 2003). Research articles repeatedly emphasize the importance of dedication and persistence in social justice activists' work. The "inexcusable courage" of leaders who lead for social justice in South Africa's challenging circumstances is highlighted by Jansen (2006), for example. Perseverance, commitment, and courage are indispensable in addressing unavoidable challenges and resistance to social justice work and cooperation (French, 2017).

The idea put forth by Bourdieu is that there are two different versions of social reality (Bourdieu, 1984). All of us have a position within an invisible hierarchy of social hierarchies. At the same time, we actively produce our social realities through our behaviors. Bourdieu developed the ideas of the shared sphere and the realm of lifestyles to understand these two social universes (Rosenlund, 2019). He also suggested establishing social and lifestyle spaces, using representations as examples (Bourdieu, 2010). According to Bourdieu, society is best understood as a hierarchical model. It has a significant relationship with the social environment, where social agents occupy different levels of power and privilege depending on the capital they control (Bennett & Savage, 2004). The idea of Bourdieu's capitalist mode of production serves as the basis for this classification scheme.

The structuring principles of this social space tend to be reproduced in stable sets of social practices and distinctive and unique ways of being in the world. This phenomenon occurs because of the habitus of the agents, which mediates a process of structural causality (Swartz, 1977). This method can tailor an individual's subjective experiences to the world's objective experiences. From a scholarly perspective, Bourdieu recommends using multiple correspondence analysis (MCA). This is because MCA is well suited for the "spatial vision" of his structural theory and because MCA places a higher value on extracted structures than on a priori preconceptions (Frie & Janssen, 2009; Grenfell & Lebaron, 2014). Pierre Bourdieu assumed a close relationship between business and culture, or structural factors in cultural ideals and practices, while postmodernists, too, confirm these and assert a growing divide. This phenomenon is called "social duality." Bourdieu concluded that the individuals who make up a society are placed inside an objective social structure in positions of dominance and subordination (Sewell, 2004). The reality of the moment of creation is displayed throughout; Bourdieu gave modern management human agency and social and cultural context (Tatli et al., 2015).

PERSISTENCE AND CHANGE MANAGEMENT

Through the years, management literature has classified various approaches to leadership into distinct subfields. However, the Great Men Theory, e.g. (Spector, 2016), the Trait Theory, e.g. (Fleenor, 2006), the Behavioral Theory, e.g. (Conger & Kanungo, 1987), the Contingency Theory, e.g. (Abbas, Ekowati, et al., 2021b) and the Theory of Leadership as a Method, e.g. (Stogdill & Shartle, 1948) are the most commonly cited overarching models. Multiple concepts and conceptual frameworks, each contributing uniquely to the overarching theories, have been produced and are now undergoing further development (Abbas, 2022). Understanding the theories and models and their underlying assumptions is crucial to comprehend the research questions that leadership literature has asked over the years (Abbas, Ekowati, et al., 2021a). It is reasonable to assume that the concerns voiced by leadership experts and academics will track with the developing of various leadership paradigms (Bass, 1997; Judge et al., 2009; Kennedy et al., 2013; Sims & Lorenzi, 1992). The voyage of leadership theories has been surrounded by societies, people, organizational, spatial, and global vision development. The researcher called for tracking how we engage with, challenge, and defy intricate and coercive managerial discourses of leadership (Sinclair, 2004). The framework for understanding the various material and spiritual approaches to human growth that are at work in the world today can be understood as a consultation with material and spiritual elements, e.g., (Noy, 2009).

Persistence is an ingrained habit provided by nature and is groomed by nurture (Buller, 2006). Regardless of the fundamental impacts that nature decides to exert on humans, this tendency is innate. The survival of humans can be attributed to a wide variety of factors. It could be to accomplish something other people think is impossible or to demonstrate something to ourselves and others. The study of processes needs to take the factor of time more seriously.

Similarly, studies on leadership processes must investigate how effects develop over time. Conceptual and empirical research on leadership has known for decades that time is essential, and many calls have been made to include it (Fischer et al., 2017). As a more theoretical and intellectual idea, the shape of persistence in leadership is still up for debate (Kirkpatrick & Locke, 1991). Although the topic of discussion is management, the focus is on political figures rather than corporate leaders, e.g. (Bittner, 2018). It has happened due to the personal influence of a leader over social change (Kelly et al., 2018; Singer & Gershman, 2018). Leaders have a greater capacity for overcoming challenges than followers. They can work while keeping more distant items in view and exhibit a "certain morality and degree of power of will or endurance" (Bennis, 2002). Leaders must maintain grit and determination in all their endeavors and see their plans through to completion (Stoltz, 2015). Most organizational transformation programs require a few months to get off the ground. It may be several years before the advantages become apparent. The leaders of an organization need to be determined to continue with these programs, and they need to be persistent to make sure that the changes they implement become institutionalized (Burke & Noumair, 2015). Grit is the engine that has propelled human progress forward. It is a trait shared by all role models, and studies have shown that leaders value it above all others in the people they rely on (Stoltz, 2015). Those who follow a leader see grit in them, and those who lead see grit in individuals who serve their teams (Caza & Posner, 2018).

SOCIAL AWARENESS AND INCLUSION

According to studies, inclusive leadership requires specific strengths, such as personal risk-taking, humility, and empowerment. These are all essential components. On the other hand, its framework expands on these principles by situating them within the broader context of diversity regarding economies, ideologies, businesses, and competence (Randel et al., 2018). Inclusive leadership is differentiated by its unwavering commitment to diversity and inclusion (Van Knippenberg et al., 2022). A key component supported by the ideals of equal opportunity and equitable treatment can be achieved by incorporating varied elements (Abbas, Ekowati, et al., 2021b). individuals who, in addition to particular uniqueness being recognized and respected, also feel a feeling of social connectedness (via the creation of a social fabric) and group membership as a result of their use of social cognition building (Abbas, Ekowati, & Suhariadi, 2022; Abbas, Saud, et al., 2021). The commitment shown by those in equitable and sustainable leadership roles is a core component. A commitment that lasts and is defined by sharing the same ideals as the people around (Abbas, Saud, et al., 2022).

To uphold social justice, team leaders must ensure that all members are treated equally and respectfully (Tyler & Smith, 1995). Each team member should be valued for their unique skills and perspectives. If leaders commit to something that requires value, they must do so ethically and responsibly (Friedman, 2007; Stewart, 1985). Proactive leaders adapt their work habits, especially social interaction, to meet the needs of their followers by exchanging positivity (Blau, 1964; Hollander, 1980; Keller et al., 1995). Leaders in an organization's Beliefs in a business case are restricted to what is known in the workplace. Most company heads concentrate on the conventional benefit of diversity and inclusion regarding talent, creativity, clients, and new market expansion (Conger et al., 1987). They prioritize diversity and inclusion as an organizational value for this group. People would eventually be able to accept individual responsibility for the results of efforts to promote diversity and inclusion (Cottrill et al., 2014). For this, it is necessary to express the importance of diversity and inclusion clearly and sincerely. To accomplish these ends, they commit resources to fostering an environment that values and encourages a diversity and inclusion culture for all employees (McAndrew et al., 2020; Rattrie et al., 2020). Leaders aware of situations must constantly have a strategic intent (Colin & Grasser, 2018; Fenitra et al., 2022). They must consider statutory procedures for managing formal diversity and inclusion and the resulting workplace culture and environmental building (Martins & Terblanche, 2003). This intent is to strategize how to encourage employees to interact with one another through initiatives such as workplace innovation culture (Altındağ & Kösedağı, 2015). They argue this to counterbalance the strategic myopia of top executives who fail to maintain a firm grip on their organizations' cultural norms (Siebelink et al., 2021).

MANAGING LEADERSHIP JOURNEY

It is encouraging that the education sector has made the question of the value of producing so many strong leaders at all levels a topic of study. Fortunately, the shadow aspect of leadership has been exposed, e.g. (Harris & Jones, 2018). Researchers can ensure that they know that there are leaders different from what is generally expected.

These are soulless, cruel, fragmented, dictatorial, and authoritarian individuals who are the exception based on their journey or innate individual nature. Since many companies are headed by people better described as micromanagers, the opportunity to uncover their shadow sides is ideal, e.g. (Mackey et al., 2021). More research is needed to understand better organizations' contexts, cultures, and other factors that allow for and even support ineffective leadership and management practices. There is a need for more research. Hence these studies need to be done. As such, "dark-side" leadership behaviors are strenuously linked to a high risk of work stress, e.g. (Furnham, 2017). Significant consequences include a dramatic drop in productivity and enthusiasm for one's work.

Moreover, the current research results significantly reduced levels of personal well-being (Boddy, 2006; Ferguson et al., 2014; Lu et al., 2017; Volmer et al., 2016; Zhang et al., 2020). Researchers can address the negative aspects of leadership if they can generate more leaders who genuinely care about the people they are entrusted to manage. The most challenging aspect of visualization is planning the leadership journey (Blain et al., 2017). Recognizing one's own biases and levels of power is necessary to develop strategic intent into essential adjustments (Abbas, Ekowati, & Anwar, 2023; Blain et al., 2017; Greenleaf et al., 2002; Marvin, 2021; Rebelo et al., 2020). However, leaders often fail to do so due to the dark aspects, e.g., (George & McLean, 2018). However, this is not a situation where a single effort will suffice. Many leaders spend their entire careers on a leadership journey that requires constant evaluation and reassessment of their vision, e.g. (Greenleaf, 1977).

When leaders concentrate on the satisfaction they receive from others rather than the motivation they receive from inside, they risk losing their footing (Conger, 1990). They frequently dismiss the sincere opponent who confronts authority with the facts. Instead, they surround themselves with dimwits who will give them the answers they want. They become incapable of honest conversation, and those around them learn not to challenge them with the truth (George et al., 2018).

The path to leadership would be challenging, but those who persist with it will eventually emerge as competent leaders (Fischer et al., 2017; Vroom & Jago, 1974). Many leaders rise to power by intimidating and eliminating everyone (Judge et al., 2009). However, suppose they take responsibility for their actions and grow from their experiences. In that case, they may eventually develop a more optimistic outlook. If they stay the same after reaching the pinnacle, they may become paranoid that everyone is out to bring them down. Occasionally, they will feel like an intruder due to their underlying fears of being exposed as fraud (Clements & Washbush, 1999). The morality and ethics of the individual who sets out to lead somebody on this path are crucially important (Nevarez & Wood, 2014).

THE THEORY

A study discussed its conjectures regarding the kind of poor leadership that recognizes relevant information. It proposed to conquer marauding or myopia with the societal and organizational needs that an extreme bias for deeds in management may cause (Paukku & Välikangas, 2021). The study realizes the need for discussing persistent leadership suppositions under ethically responsible behavior to consistently eliminate any bad image of leadership that highlights the details. Thus, this chapter proposes that Persistent leadership overcomes strategic myopia in societies and organizations.

The immediate and persistent demands placed on leaders tend to exceed their capacity for reflection (also known as "bounded rationality" and their ability to pay attention, e.g. (Simon, 1991). This argument is one of the primary reasons to understand why so many leaders are poor (strategically) (Ocasio, 1997). This myth is encapsulated in the groundbreaking behavioral theory of the societies (modern organizations), e.g., (March, 1963). This theory laid the groundwork for the attention-based perspective of the firm (Ocasio, 2011). According to the behavioral theory of the firm, Levinthal and March (1993) reasoned that organizations tend to be myopic in their actions. They saw limiting the leadership options and defining where their attention was theoretically focused. It also renders leadership ineffective or incompetent in nonroutine circumstances that call for more radical responses regarding the action scope and timing. When the leadership team is swamped with the usual workload of managing organizations, it is hard for leaders to deal with out-of-the-ordinary situations. It can be hard to take a step back and assess the situation (Alvesson & Spicer, 2012a, 2012b). In everyday circumstances, however, a leadership style that is narrow-minded and conditioned by the organization could be completely acceptable.

Businesses and societies now allow leaders to develop routine-driven leadership styles that are limited to remaining unchanged. It could cause strategic myopia since, whether or not people realize it; biases are formed by a mind bug in society and themselves (Banaji & Greenwald, 2013). Three beliefs or forces continue to entwine themselves with leaders, society, and organizations. Certain social aspects of consciousness strengthen language and its spiritual dimensions. Life comprises three components: the process, the material, and the formation of consciousness in the social world (Capra, 2004). Meaning is added by humans, who use social theory to develop their psychology and culture. Social theory and structural analysis equip people with how to effect change and exercise autonomy (Abbas, Ekowati, Shuairidi, et al., 2022). Humans have intrinsic leadership abilities shaped by their social networks, independence, and purpose. Cultures and religions provide the initial impetus for shaping people's worldviews and influencing their development into fully realized individuals (Abbas, Ekowati, Suhairidi, & Anwar, 2022; Beattie

& Smith, 2010). Their biological, social, cultural, and technical systems evolve with social changes.

Nevertheless, the world's fundamental complexity and flux have forced them to find common ground through metaphor (Mio et al., 2005). Using a metaphor, such as calling a given country leader "Hitler," can convey emotional meaning and evoke strong feelings from the listener or reader (Allison & Goethals, 2016). Management's theoretical and practical underpinnings are based on a single, overarching concept: steering an organization toward achieving its goals. In this category, organizational financial objectives based on a broader vision stand out. Management theorist Peter Block argues that managers primarily care about articulating the organization's mission, exercising discretionary authority, and allocating resources. Organizational objectives sometimes incorporate attaining corporate goals as a metaphor for rising to the top (McKenna, 1999). According to this line of thinking, metaphors are a powerful motivator for leaders at all levels of government and business, e.g. (Mio et al., 2005).

It is worth noting that Maxwell incorporated a five-step leadership escalator into his thesis. A position they take at the outset and a crucial one to ensure that a positional leader's sway is limited to that inherent in their role (Maxwell, 2014). It is the bases for people to follow the leader; therefore, the authority of a Positional leader stems from the privileges that come with the position of authority and see nothing wrong with preaching morality. Achieving influence by position alone is not pointless. However, it is immoral to use one's status to push people into following is often useless.

Second, developing their position is utterly reliant upon the ties they maintain. They follow others because they want to do it of their free will, and as a result, people like and respect those who have value for them. This occurs on the permission level. Once a leader has obtained this authorization, they can establish influence with the people they lead by using their personality or chrisms to earn their trust. The atmosphere becomes significantly more pleasant whether at home, on the job, at play, or participating in volunteerism.

Some people may stop there after overcoming the public's resistance to embracing them as a leader. However, strong leaders cannot concentrate on their laurels because they have created a comfortable atmosphere for their followers. They do this as a means of determining what they are capable of accomplishing and forecasting their followers' potential. This is why a leader could ascend to the next level even if they remain unable to create outcomes at that level if they are morally persistent. At the production level, leaders develop influence and credibility, and others begin to follow them because of what they have done for the organization. This aligns them with the leader's vision and allows them to climb up in the organization. The growth of leadership, individuals, and groups is an essential activity. A leader can only achieve excellence with a strong group of followers. Because of this, they cannot rely entirely on their inherent or social authority. Because of this, leaders should select members of their team who share their vision and can be empowered by them. On Particular stage 4, leaders utilize their power, networks, and competence to reinvest in their followers and grow them to the point where those followers can become leaders in the future. This leads to reproduction, e.g., succession planning and future leadership development. Straight now, leaders can make a positive difference in the lives of the individuals they are responsible for (achieved at this level). Because of what their leaders have done for them personally, socially, and morally, their people follow them with fully developed or intense loyalties. It is essential to highlight that those captivated by the financial developments of any of their peers would not consider their loyalties to be lasting. If moral growth is ignored, followers may see their leaders as a means to an end rather than a source of inspiration. That is why people tend to hold political leaders in higher esteem for more prolonged periods than business executives, whose influence often fades quickly. As a result, these relationships are frequently maintained throughout an individual's lifetime.

The pinnacle, the highest and most challenging leadership level, is the optimum stage for leaving an eternal impact on history. It is only reached by leaders who make history. According to Maxwell, the path that leads an individual to become a leader typically ends between Levels 1 and 3. Some people make it to Level 4, but Level 5 necessitates work, skill, and intention and a high level of talent, perseverance, and adherence to ethics and morality. Since the perseverance required to attain this level is not trivial, it is difficult to understand whether they are born or made. Those naturally endowed as leaders are the only ones who ever make it to the top level and remain there. Getting organizational leaders to a stage where they are willing and able to develop other leaders is frequently cited as the most challenging leadership assignment. However, now we come to the benefits. Those with exceptional leadership persistence can imagine ways to generate possibilities that other leaders cannot. Leaders can leave a lasting legacy in whatever they accomplish if they are persistent, promote good morality, and take responsibility for their actions.

People have a low tolerance for those who lead empty lives since they do not desire to emulate them. The leaders at the pinnacle level are the only ones who know how to communicate hidden secrets so that they can use them as a metaphor. People adhere to them because of whom they are associated with concerning these metaphors and what they stand for. Individuals frequently do not speak about the social exchange they receive from leaders because everyone has several layers that disguise their fundamental goals and requirements. This is because everyone has a complex social life. Put another way, their leadership is gaining an excellent reputation, and they remain persistent with ethical responsibility. At the same time, society's hidden secrets are being revealed. As a direct consequence of this, leaders at Level 5 frequently transcend their positions within societies and on a worldwide scale.

The assertion that has been put out is supported by substantial evidence. Many ineffective leaders leap to conclusions too quickly, especially in a crisis, thinking that this demonstrates good leadership or determination, e.g. (Hurst, 2008; Robinson, 2017). They appear, and most of the time, they successfully reach some stage and gain people's attention. However, ultimately lose their moral position of leading others due to their incorrect manners. A bias is defined as something that is discovered later and can be caused by hurrying. Observing the bias for action in the concealed biases of decent individuals is possible.

In literature, there has been lauded in renowned managerially focused works like "In Search of Excellence." Literature compiles management advice from some of the most successful businesses in the United States (Dahlgaard-Park & Dahlgaard, 2006; Solomons, 1983; Waterman & Peters, 1982). It is also well known in previous literature that perseverance in leadership and moral conduct have been favored throughout their trip (Bruch & Ghoshal, 2004). The self-efficacy determination notions developed are congruent with this idea (Deci & Ryan, 2012; Niemiec & Ryan, 2009; Ryan & Deci, 2000; Ryan et al., 2008; Ryan & Ryan, 2019). Self-determination and free will subject has been detailed and discussed in natural philosophy under human psychology and their application to pro and anti-social behavior (Abbas, Ekowati, Suhairidi, & Hamid, 2022). Self-efficacy was first identified in the field of psychology by Bandura (Bandura, 1977). Self-dissemination is either a natural talent or a learned ideology that falls within a leader's strategic goal (Biddle et al., 1999). It is a notion that encompasses much ground.

Another problem is that hidden or visible bias tends to be difficult to grasp without a theory of persistent behavior that is revealed with time (Banaji et al., 2013; Bruch et al., 2004; Paukku et al., 2021). It is also interpreted as a sign of leadership in a path where the implications of their metaphor use and subsequent actions or policies are not quickly challenged. This topic focuses on compelling people to use their less visible qualities to influence others, e.g. (Neffinger & Kohut, 2014). This argument is also valid since interpreting metaphor is a methodological approach that cannot be addressed instantly. Morality and ethics are necessities in today's world. By using these principles, we contrast impulsive leadership with more deliberate approaches like intent and persistence to show that there are better ways to take charge. We do this to demonstrate that historically, practical leadership theory is evaluated on taking the proper position and performing according to what is socially and globally accepted.

These are the lessons as power players let people believe what they do after acquiring power (Sivanathan et al., 2008). Studying political leaders is the only option left because most firms do not use a democratic procedure for selecting their top executives. Moreover, the policies of the dictators game led people to believe that gaining power would not hurt promises made properly (Born et al., 2018). This world is replete with examples of such leadership tactics, in which numerous leaders have attained confident leaders solely for the benefits that they provide to themselves. Those who gain influence due to external factors, such as needs and wants or societal expectations, could be included here. Positive and negative behavior theory provides insight into a historical leader suited to control the globe based on their performance in their previous responsibilities. It is important to study topics like military history, business, and social change movements to determine the innate leadership talents of people at the pinnacle of leadership positions that have significant impacts worldwide.

METHOD

Synthesizing can help make writing more interesting and engaging, allowing readers to connect and gain a deeper understanding of the ideas presented. Synthesizing can also help identify knowledge gaps and allow for further exploration and research. By combining different sources and ideas into a single piece, synthesizing allows writers to create a more comprehensive and nuanced argument. It also allows them to explore a variety of perspectives and draw on a range of evidence to support their argument. This can make a piece of writing more persuasive and thought-provoking, enabling readers to understand better the ideas presented. (Harvey, 2014). The conceptual strength method can generate compelling arguments while reviewing an endless body of text (Machi & McEvoy, 2021; Xiao & Watson, 2019). If an understandable synthesis offers a peek and structure, drawing substance from what has been stated previously, then possibly a research study is sufficient. A researcher's job is to organize and critically evaluate existing literature to contribute to the ongoing discourse. Many published works in domains such as literature require historical arguments.

The synthesis process can prove advantageous for researchers, enabling them to amalgamate paraphrased information from various sources. This is particularly in cases where the concepts are progressive. The synthesis process indicates scholarly work, showcasing the writer's comprehension of literature and data. It also showcases their capacity to establish links between concepts and construct a coherent argument. Researchers can demonstrate their academic proficiency by synthesizing concepts and creating a robust dialogue. A synthesis is an important tool in the research process, helping researchers to evaluate existing research, evaluate data, and draw meaningful conclusions as an essential skill for any researcher, see further (Snyder, 2019; Torraco, 2016).

FINDINGS

This body of literature used an ongoing appeal for the efficacy of leadership that has been sparked in more recent times. This appeal has been largely in response to the uncertainty of the modern world and its effects on organizations. As a result, many organizations have begun to focus on developing leadership within their ranks. Leadership has become essential for organizations to remain competitive and successful. It is one of the most successful theories expanding their horizons in all fields. It has become a solution for effective management. Transformational leadership is one of the most effective theories. Transformational leadership focuses on motivating and inspiring individuals to strive for excellence and to be leaders in their own right. It emphasizes the importance of creating a positive and stimulating environment for employees to reach their highest potential. It also encourages collaboration and encourages employees to think outside the box to develop innovative solutions (Ahmad et al., 2023). It is now more important than ever for leaders to have the experience and insight to accurately assess their surroundings and act accordingly, see further (Abbas, Ekowati, Suhariadi, et al., 2023). This calls for leaders to adopt a more responsible perspective while formulating strategies. This highlights the need for scholars to delve deeper into the potential of ethically responsible and persistent leadership theory.

CONCLUSION, RECOMMENDATION, AND FUTURE DIRECTIONS

Numerous peaks and troughs in literary history indicate the development of a conflicted conception of leadership in the current day. Leadership and management theory have seen flaws, and opinions on both sides have become increasingly strident. For their small gain, leaders who err on the side of their dark traits can have far-reaching, systemic consequences. Therefore, it is increasingly difficult for positive, strategic, and transformative leadership to continue producing outcomes. Leadership and Management must be persistent, and further effort may increase the breadth of the problem.

The importance of dependable leadership in fostering introspective and administrative processes is highlighted. Although preventing persistence in the leadership journey is crucial, there is a surprising lack of conceptual and empirical development in the research. To have a broader perspective on how effective leadership in business and society may promote mutual benefit through fostering a welcoming environment for all group members. Insights from three overlapping but distinct areas—leadership for diversity attitudes, the persistence of character, and leadership's journey toward becoming inclusive—are woven together in this chapter. Research into the effects of team diversity can drive additive performance outcomes through information integration processes, which is why inclusive leadership is sought for tackling this issue. Persistent leadership can open the door to interpersonal approaches to studying the leadership development process. More teams may benefit from leadership development if tensions within the group can be reduced so that information can be integrated more smoothly. Persistence in leadership can spark theoretical breakthroughs because no leadership theory can ignore a leader's ethical and responsible responsibilities. As long as the argument persists that leaders are formed of stuff, the propositions can be tailored to it (Avolio, 2005; Boerma et al., 2017).

a) Considering that there are five tiers of leadership, e.g. (Maxwell, 2014), the three are relatively simple for best fits to attain (Scouller, 2011). However, there is a demand for additional research in the future to amplify what can be captured qualitatively.
b) Social change is typically slow, except for organization, due to the inevitability of change (Abbas, Ekowati, Shuairidi, et al., 2022). Quite frequently, management will provide organizational leaders with mandates well before their due dates, making it simple to evaluate changes in organizational procedure. Therefore, situational leadership is a practical choice for managing organizational change because it divides time frames and yields quantifiable results.
c) Leaders with a penchant for strategy may get to the top of their fields over time. Likewise, many potential leaders' paths are cut short by the length and complexity of this method before they have a permanent impact. This argument is especially valid if they cannot stay in contact and are ethically connected with individuals who share their allegiances. Hence, the ability to persist in one's actions necessitates consistent morals, intrinsic skills, and responsible behavior. Leaders cannot escape this principle since their followers will always hold them accountable for being socially responsible and ethically consistent. Leadership qualities such as perseverance and moral alignment with followers could be evaluated in such an application. Motivation factors that can be interpreted contextually include satisfaction, commitment, productivity, retention, and leadership growth.
d) In literature, themes of diversity and inclusion grounded in social fairness, cultural virtue, and the duty to support the development of positive change are persistently achieved. Such principles can be incorporated into any theory to ensure compatibility with the views of individuals who are not deviating from their original point. Compared to other leadership theories, the self-vision

and personal imaginations of the authentic, servant, or spiritual leaders are particularly noteworthy.

Whether leaders learn or are born with their skills will keep theorists engaged for a long time. However, testing a leader's natural qualities over time is "their persistence," which cannot be obscured from the equation.

REFERENCE

Abbas, A. (2022). *Individual psychological distance: A leadership task to assess and cope with invisible change.* [PhD Dissertation, Airlangga University]

Abbas, A., Ekowati, D., & Anwar, A. (2023). Authentic Leadership Journey: An empirical Discussion from Pakistani higher education employing the Lay theory of Psychology. *International Journal of Public Leadership*. doi:10.1108/IJPL-04-2022-0020

Abbas, A., Ekowati, D., Shuairidi, F., Fenitra, R. M., & Fahlevi, M. (2022). Integrating Cycle of Prochaska and DiClemente with Ethically Responsible behavior theory for Social Change Management: Post Covid-19 Social Cognitive Perspective for Change. In A. Pego (Ed.), *Challenges and Emerging Strategies for Global Networking Post COVID-19* (pp. 130–155). IGI Global. doi:10.4018/978-1-7998-8856-7.ch007

Abbas, A., Ekowati, D., Suhairidi, F., & Anwar, A. (2022). Human Capital Creation: A Collective Psychological, Social, Organizational and Religious Perspective. *Journal of Religion and Health*. doi:10.100710943-022-01665-8 PMID:36109469

Abbas, A., Ekowati, D., Suhairidi, F., & Hamid, A. R. (2022). Negative Vs Positive Psychology: A Review of Science of Well-being. *Integrative Psychological & Behavioral Science*. doi:10.100712124-022-09708-1 PMID:35759165

Abbas, A., Ekowati, D., & Suhariadi, F. (2021a). Individual psychological distance: A leadership task to assess and cope with invisible change. *Journal of Management Development*, *40*(3), 168–189. doi:10.1108/JMD-09-2020-0304

Abbas, A., Ekowati, D., & Suhariadi, F. (2021b). Managing Individuals, Organizations Through Leadership: Diversity Consciousness Roadmap. In B. Christiansen & H. Chandan (Eds.), *Handbook of Research on Applied Social Psychology in Multiculturalism* (Vol. 1, pp. 47–71). IGI Global. doi:10.4018/978-1-7998-6960-3.ch003

Abbas, A., Ekowati, D., & Suhariadi, F. (2022). Social Perspective: Leadership in Changing Society. In M. I. Hassan, S. Sen Roy, U. Chatterjee, S. Chakraborty, & U. Singh (Eds.), *Social Morphology, Human Welfare, and Sustainability* (pp. 89–107). Springer International Publishing. doi:10.1007/978-3-030-96760-4_4

Abbas, A., Ekowati, D., Suhariadi, F., Anwar, A., & Fenitra, R. M. (2023). Technology acceptance and COVID-19: A perspective for emerging opportunities from crisis. *Technology Analysis and Strategic Management*, 1–13. doi:10.1080/09537325.2023.2214642

Abbas, A., Saud, M., Ekowati, D., & Suhariadi, F. (2021). Social Psychology and Fabrication: A Synthesis of Individuals, Society, and Organization. In B. Christiansen & H. Chandan (Eds.), *Handbook of Research on Applied Social Psychology in Multiculturalism* (Vol. 1, pp. 89–109). IGI Global. doi:10.4018/978-1-7998-6960-3.ch005

Abbas, A., Saud, M., Suhariadi, F., Usman, I., & Ekowati, D. (2022). Positive leadership psychology: Authentic and servant leadership in higher education in Pakistan. *Current Psychology (New Brunswick, N.J.)*, *41*(10), 5859–5871. doi:10.100712144-020-01051-1

Ahmad, S., Rofie, M. K. H., & Salim, S. (2016). Rewards and commitment in social development: Equiping modern muslim communities with knowledge on Islamic work ethics towards better living conditions. *Mediterranean Journal of Social Sciences, 7*(1 S1), 395-400. doi:10.5901/mjss.2016.v7n1s1p395

Ahmad, T., Hamid, A., Abbas, A., Anwar, A., Ekowati, D., Fenitra, R., & Suhariadi, F. (2023). Empowering leadership: Role of Organizational Culture of Self-Esteem, and Emotional Intelligence on Creativity. *Journal of Management Development*, *42*(3), 201–214. doi:10.1108/JMD-10-2021-0288

Allison, S. T., & Goethals, G. R. (2016). Hero worship: The elevation of the human spirit. *Journal for the Theory of Social Behaviour*, *46*(2), 187–210. doi:10.1111/jtsb.12094

Altındağ, E., & Kösedağı, Y. (2015). The relationship between emotional intelligence of managers, innovative corporate culture and employee performance. *Procedia: Social and Behavioral Sciences*, *210*, 270–282. doi:10.1016/j.sbspro.2015.11.367

Alvesson, M., & Spicer, A. (2012a). Critical leadership studies: The case for critical performativity. *Human Relations*, *65*(3), 367–390. doi:10.1177/0018726711430555

Alvesson, M., & Spicer, A. (2012b). A Stupidity-Based theory of organizations. *Journal of Management Studies*, *49*(7), 1194–1220. doi:10.1111/j.1467-6486.2012.01072.x

Avolio, B. J. (2005). *Leadership development in balance: Made/born* (1st ed.). Psychology Press. doi:10.4324/9781410611819

Banaji, M. R., & Greenwald, A. G. (2013). *Blindspot: Hidden biases of good people*. Random House Publishing.

Bandura, A. (1977). Self-efficacy: Toward a Unifying Theory of Behavioral Change. *Psychological Review*, *84*(2), 191–215. doi:10.1037/0033-295X.84.2.191 PMID:847061

Barnes, M. L., Wang, P., Cinner, J. E., Graham, N. A., Guerrero, A. M., Jasny, L., Lau, J., Sutcliffe, S. R., & Zamborain-Mason, J. (2020). Social determinants of adaptive and transformative responses to climate change. *Nature Climate Change*, *10*(9), 823–828. doi:10.103841558-020-0871-4

Bass, B. M. (1997). Does the transactional–transformational leadership paradigm transcend organizational and national boundaries? *The American Psychologist*, *52*(2), 130–139. doi:10.1037/0003-066X.52.2.130

Beattie, V., & Smith, S. J. (2010). Human capital, value creation and disclosure. *Journal of Human Resource Costing & Accounting*, *14*(4), 262–285. doi:10.1108/14013381011105957

Benabou, R., & Tirole, J. (2011). Laws and Norms. *National Bureau of Economic Research Working Paper Series, 17579*. doi:10.3386/w17579

Bennett, T., & Savage, M. (2004). Introduction: Cultural capital and cultural policy. *Cultural Trends*, *13*(2), 7–14. doi:10.1080/0954896042000267116

Bennis, W. (2002). *Moral leadership: The theory and practice of power, judgment and policy*. John Wiley & Sons.

Biddle, S., Soos, I., & Chatzisarantis, N. (1999). Predicting physical activity intentions using goal perspectives and self-determination theory approaches. *European Psychologist*, *4*(2), 83–89. doi:10.1027//1016-9040.4.4.83

Bittner, A. (2018). Leaders always mattered: The persistence of personality in Canadian elections. *Electoral Studies*, *54*, 297–302. doi:10.1016/j.electstud.2018.04.013

Blain, M.-J., Fortin, S., & Alvarez, F. (2017). Professional journeys of international medical graduates in Quebec: Recognition, uphill battles, or career change. *Journal of International Migration and Integration*, *18*(1), 223–247. doi:10.100712134-016-0475-z

Blau, P. (1964). Social exchange theory. *CORE, 3*, 62.

Blau, P. (2017). *Exchange and power in social life*. Routledge. doi:10.4324/9780203792643

Boddy, C. R. (2006). The dark side of management decisions: Organisational psychopaths. *Management Decision*, *44*(10), 1461–1475. doi:10.1108/00251740610715759

Boerma, M., Coyle, E. A., Dietrich, M. A., Dintzner, M. R., Drayton, S. J., Early, J. L., & Lin, A. Y. F. (2017). Point/counterpoint: Are outstanding leaders born or made? *American Journal of Pharmaceutical Education*, *81*(3), 1–5. doi:10.5688/ajpe81358 PMID:28496278

Born, A., van Eck, P., & Johannesson, M. (2018). An experimental investigation of election promises. *Political Psychology*, *39*(3), 685–705. doi:10.1111/pops.12429

Bourdieu, P. (1984). Distinction a social critique of the judgement of taste. In *Inequality Classic Readings in Race, Class, and Gender* (1st ed., pp. 287–318). Routledge.

Bourdieu, P. (2010). The forms of capital (1986). In I. Szeman & T. Kaposy (Eds.), *Cultural theory: An anthology* (Vol. 1, pp. 81–93). John Wiley & Sons.

Brooks, J. S., Jean-Marie, G., Normore, A. H., & Hodgins, D. W. (2007). Distributed leadership for social justice: Exploring how influence and equity are stretched over an urban high school. *Journal of School Leadership*, *17*(4), 378–408. doi:10.1177/105268460701700402

Bruch, H., & Ghoshal, S. (2004). *A bias for action: How effective managers harness their willpower, achieve results, and stop wasting time*. Harvard Business Press.

Buller, D. J. (2006). *Adapting minds: Evolutionary psychology and the persistent quest for human nature*. MIT press.

Burke, W. W., & Noumair, D. A. (2015). *Organization development: A process of learning and changing* (3rd ed.). FT Press.

Capra, F. (2004). *The hidden connections: A science for sustainable living*. Random House, Inc.

Caza, A., & Posner, B. Z. (2018). How and when does grit influence leaders' behavior? *Leadership and Organization Development Journal*, *40*(1), 124–134. doi:10.1108/LODJ-06-2018-0209

Clements, C., & Washbush, J. B. (1999). The two faces of leadership: Considering the dark side of leader-follower dynamics. *Journal of Workplace Learning*, *11*(5), 170–176. doi:10.1108/13665629910279509

Colin, T., & Grasser, B. ı. (2018). How Competency Management Tools Can Influence Routines in Workshops Depending on New Strategic Intent. *Book of Abstracts ARTEM OCC 2020 Edition*, 330

Conger, J. A. (1990). The dark side of leadership. *Organizational Dynamics*, *19*(2), 44–55. doi:10.1016/0090-2616(90)90070-6

Conger, J. A., & Kanungo, R. N. (1987). Toward a behavioral theory of charismatic leadership in organizational settings. *Academy of Management Review*, *12*(4), 637–647. doi:10.2307/258069

Cottrill, K., Denise, L., & Patricia, C., & Hoffman, C. (2014). How authentic leadership and inclusion benefit organizations. *Equality, Diversity and Inclusion*, *33*(3), 275–292. doi:10.1108/EDI-05-2012-0041

Crosby, G. (2020). *Planned change: Why Kurt Lewin's social science is still best practice for business results, change management, and human progress*. Productivity Press. doi:10.4324/9781003082491

Dahlgaard-Park, S. M., & Dahlgaard, J. J. (2006). In search of excellence–past, present and future. *Kreativ und konsequent*, *2*(3), 57-84

Deci, E. L., & Ryan, R. M. (2012). Self-determination theory. In A. W. K. In P. A. M. Van Lange, & E. T. Higgins (Eds.), (Ed.), Handbook of theories of social psychology (Vol. 1, pp. 416–436). Sage Publications Ltd. doi:10.4135/9781446249215.n21

DePree, M. (1993). The leadership quest: Three things necessary. *Business Strategy Review*, *4*(1), 69–74. doi:10.1111/j.1467-8616.1993.tb00045.x

DePree, M. (2011). *Leadership is an art*. Currency Doubleday Publisher.

Elder, G. H. Jr. (1994). Time, human agency, and social change: Perspectives on the life course. *Social Psychology Quarterly*, *57*(1), 4–15. doi:10.2307/2786971

Fenitra, R. M., Abbas, A., Ekowati, D., & Suhairidi, F. (2022). Strategic Intent and Strategic Leadership: A Review Perspective for Post-covid Tourism and Hospitality Industry Recovery. In P. Mohanty, A. Sharma, J. Kennell, & A. Hassan (Eds.), *The Emerald Handbook of Destination Recovery in Tourism and Hospitality* (pp. 23–44). Emerald Group Publishing. doi:10.1108/978-1-80262-073-320221003

Ferguson, E., Semper, H., Yates, J., Fitzgerald, J. E., Skatova, A., & James, D. (2014). The 'dark side'and 'bright side'of personality: When too much conscientiousness and too little anxiety are detrimental with respect to the acquisition of medical knowledge and skill. *PLoS One*, *9*(2), 1–11. doi:10.1371/journal.pone.0088606 PMID:24586353

Fischer, T., Dietz, J., & Antonakis, J. (2017). Leadership process models: A review and synthesis. *Journal of Management*, *43*(6), 1726–1753. doi:10.1177/0149206316682830

Fleenor, J. W. (2006). Trait approach to leadership. *Psychology*, *37*(1), 651–665.

French, A. (2017). Toward a New Conceptual Model: Integrating the Social Change Model of Leadership Development and Tinto's Model of Student Persistence. *Journal of Leadership Education*, *16*(3), 97–117. doi:10.12806/V16/I3/T4

Frie, K. G., & Janssen, C. (2009). Social inequality, lifestyles and health–a non-linear canonical correlation analysis based on the approach of Pierre Bourdieu. *International Journal of Public Health*, *54*(4), 213–221. doi:10.100700038-009-8017-5 PMID:19418020

Friedman, M. (2007). The social responsibility of business is to increase its profits. In W. C. Zimmerli, M. Holzinger, & K. Richter (Eds.), *Corporate ethics and corporate governance* (pp. 173–178). Springer. doi:10.1007/978-3-540-70818-6_14

Furman, G. (2012). Social justice leadership as praxis: Developing capacities through preparation programs. *Educational Administration Quarterly*, *48*(2), 191–229. doi:10.1177/0013161X11427394

Furnham, A. (2017). Dark side correlates of job reliability and stress tolerance in two large samples. *Personality and Individual Differences*, *117*, 255–259. doi:10.1016/j.paid.2017.06.020

George, B., & McLean, A. (2018). Why leaders lose their way. In *Contemporary Issues in Leadership* (pp. 175–185). Routledge. doi:10.4324/9780429494000-20

Greenleaf, R. K. (1977). *Servant leadership: A journey into the nature of legitimate power and greatness*. Paulist Press.

Greenleaf, R. K., Spears, L. C., & Covey, S. R. (2002). *Servant Leadership: A Journey Into the Nature of Legitimate Power and Greatness*. Paulist Press.

Grenfell, M., & Lebaron, F. (2014). *Bourdieu and data analysis: Methodological principles and practice*. Peter Lang AG. doi:10.3726/978-3-0353-0571-5

Harris, A., & Jones, M. (2018). The dark side of leadership and management. *School Leadership & Management*, *38*(5), 475–477. doi:10.1080/13632434.2018.1509276

Harvey, S. (2014). Creative synthesis: Exploring the process of extraordinary group creativity. *Academy of Management Review*, *39*(3), 324–343. doi:10.5465/amr.2012.0224

Hollander, E. P. (1980). Leadership and social exchange processes. In *Social exchange* (pp. 103–118). Springer. doi:10.1007/978-1-4613-3087-5_5

Hurst, R. (2008). *Leadership when the sky falls: leadership lessons from the shuttle Columbia disaster*. AuthorHouse Publishing Inc.

Jansen, J. D. (2006). Leading against the grain: The politics and emotions of leading for social justice in South Africa. *Leadership and Policy in Schools*, *5*(1), 37–51. doi:10.1080/15700760500484027

Judge, T. A., Piccolo, R. F., & Kosalka, T. (2009). The bright and dark sides of leader traits: A review and theoretical extension of the leader trait paradigm. *The Leadership Quarterly*, *20*(6), 855–875. doi:10.1016/j.leaqua.2009.09.004

Keller, T., & Dansereau, F. (1995). Leadership and empowerment: A social exchange perspective. *Human Relations*, *48*(2), 127–146. doi:10.1177/001872679504800202

Kelly, J. T., Brown, E. R., Diekman, A. B., & Schneider, M. C. (2018). The change we believe in: The role of socioeconomic conditions in evaluations of black political candidates. *Electoral Studies*, *54*, 254–260. doi:10.1016/j.electstud.2018.04.008

Kennedy, F., Carroll, B., & Francoeur, J. (2013). Mindset not skill set: Evaluating in new paradigms of leadership development. *Advances in Developing Human Resources*, *15*(1), 10–26. doi:10.1177/1523422312466835

Kirkpatrick, S. A., & Locke, E. A. (1991). Leadership: Do traits matter? *The Academy of Management Perspectives*, *5*(2), 48–60. doi:10.5465/ame.1991.4274679

Lester, W. S., Strunk, K. K., & Hoover, P. D. (2020). Persistent myths about the psychology of education: Implications for social justice and equity. In L. Parson. & C. Ozaki (Eds.), Teaching and learning for social justice and equity in higher education (pp. 53-71). Cham: Palgrave Macmillan.

Levinthal, D. A., & March, J. G. (1993). The myopia of learning. *Strategic Management Journal*, *14*(S2), 95–112. doi:10.1002mj.4250141009

Lu, J. G., Brockner, J., Vardi, Y., & Weitz, E. (2017). The dark side of experiencing job autonomy: Unethical behavior. *Journal of Experimental Social Psychology*, *73*, 222–234. doi:10.1016/j.jesp.2017.05.007

Machi, L. A., & McEvoy, B. T. (2021). The literature review: Six steps to success (3rd ed.). Thousand Oaks, California, USA: Corwin, SAGE Publications Ltd.

Mackey, J. D., Ellen, B. P. III, McAllister, C. P., & Alexander, K. C. (2021). The dark side of leadership: A systematic literature review and meta-analysis of destructive leadership research. *Journal of Business Research*, *132*, 705–718. doi:10.1016/j.jbusres.2020.10.037

March, J. G. (1963). *A behavioral theory of the firm*. Prentice-Hall.

Martins, E.-C., & Terblanche, F. (2003). Building organisational culture that stimulates creativity and innovation. *European Journal of Innovation Management*, *6*(1), 64–74. doi:10.1108/14601060310456337

Marvin, S. (2021). A Journey to Fulfillment. *Journal of Ayn Rand Studies*, *21*(1), 114–117. doi:10.5325/jaynrandstud.21.1.0114

Maxwell, J. C. (2014). *The 5 Levels of Leadership: Proven Steps to Maximize Your Potential*. Center Street.

McAndrew, S., O'Brien, D., & Taylor, M. (2020). The values of culture? Social closure in the political identities, policy preferences, and social attitudes of cultural and creative workers. *The Sociological Review*, *68*(1), 33–54. doi:10.1177/0038026119871401

McKenna, S. (1999). Learning through complexity. *Management Learning*, *30*(3), 301–320. doi:10.1177/1350507699303003

McKenzie, K. B., Christman, D. E., Hernandez, F., Fierro, E., Capper, C. A., Dantley, M., González, M. L., Cambron-McCabe, N., & Scheurich, J. J. (2008). From the field: A proposal for educating leaders for social justice. *Educational Administration Quarterly*, *44*(1), 111–138. doi:10.1177/0013161X07309470

Mio, J. S., Riggio, R. E., Levin, S., & Reese, R. (2005). Presidential leadership and charisma: The effects of metaphor. *The Leadership Quarterly*, *16*(2), 287–294. doi:10.1016/j.leaqua.2005.01.005

Mouton, N. (2019). A literary perspective on the limits of leadership: Tolstoy's critique of the great man theory. *Leadership*, *15*(1), 81–102. doi:10.1177/1742715017738823

Neffinger, J., & Kohut, M. (2014). Compelling people: the hidden qualities that make us influential. Victoria Embankment London: Penguin.

Nevarez, C., & Wood, J. L. (2014). *Ethical leadership and the community college: Paradigms, decision-making, and praxis*. Charlotte, North Carolina: Information age publishing inc, IAP.

Niemiec, C. P., & Ryan, R. M. (2009). Autonomy, competence, and relatedness in the classroom: Applying self-determination theory to educational practice. *Theory and Research in Education*, *7*(2), 133–144. doi:10.1177/1477878509104318

Noy, D. (2009). Material and spiritual conceptions of development: A framework of ideal types. *Journal of Developing Societies*, *25*(3), 275–307. doi:10.1177/0169796X0902500301

Ocasio, W. (1997). Towards an attention-based view of the firm. *Strategic Management Journal*, *18*(S1), 187–206. doi:10.1002/(SICI)1097-0266(199707)18:1+<187::AID-SMJ936>3.0.CO;2-K

Ocasio, W. (2011). Attention to attention. *Organization Science*, *22*(5), 1286–1296. doi:10.1287/orsc.1100.0602

Paukku, M., & Välikangas, L. (2021). Harried or Myopic Leadership: An Undue Bias for Action. In A. Örtenblad (Ed.), *Debating Bad Leadership: Reasons and Remedies* (pp. 239–255). Springer International Publishing. doi:10.1007/978-3-030-65025-4_13

Randel, A. E., Galvin, B. M., Shore, L. M., Ehrhart, K. H., Chung, B. G., Dean, M. A., & Kedharnath, U. (2018). Inclusive leadership: Realizing positive outcomes through belongingness and being valued for uniqueness. *Human Resource Management Review*, *28*(2), 190–203. doi:10.1016/j.hrmr.2017.07.002

Rattrie, L. T., Kittler, M. G., & Paul, K. I. (2020). Culture, burnout, and engagement: A meta-analysis on national cultural values as moderators in JD-R theory. *Applied Psychology*, *69*(1), 176–220. doi:10.1111/apps.12209

Rebelo, T., Lourenço, P. R., & Dimas, I. D. (2020). The journey of team learning since "The Fifth Discipline". *The Learning Organization*, *27*(1), 42–53. doi:10.1108/TLO-10-2019-0144

Robinson, M. (2017). Why Hast The Mighty Fallen?: An Intrinsic and Extrinsic Examination of the Lack of Counsel among Fallen Leaders. Park Ave, Meadville: Christian Faith Publishing, Inc.

Rosenlund, L. (2019). The persistence of inequalities in an era of rapid social change. Comparisons in time of social spaces in Norway. *Poetics*, *74*, 101323. doi:10.1016/j.poetic.2018.09.004

Ryan, R. M., & Deci, E. L. (2000). Self-determination theory and the facilitation of intrinsic motivation, social development, and well-being. *The American Psychologist*, *55*(1), 68–78. doi:10.1037/0003-066X.55.1.68 PMID:11392867

Ryan, R. M., Huta, V., & Deci, E. L. (2008). Living well: A self-determination theory perspective on eudaimonia. *Journal of Happiness Studies*, *9*(1), 139–170. doi:10.100710902-006-9023-4

Ryan, W. S., & Ryan, R. M. (2019). Toward a social psychology of authenticity: Exploring within-person variation in autonomy, congruence, and genuineness using self-determination theory. *Review of General Psychology*, *23*(1), 99–112. doi:10.1037/gpr0000162

Scheurich, J. J., & Skrla, L. (2003). *Leadership for equity and excellence: Creating high-achievement classrooms, schools, and districts*. Corwin Press.

Scouller, J. (2011). *The three levels of leadership: How to develop your leadership presence, knowhow, and skill*. Cirencester, Gloucestershire, United Kingdom: Management Books 2000.

Sewell, W. H. (2004). A theory of structure: duality, agency and transformation. In *Practicing history* (pp. 157–179). Routledge.

Siebelink, R., Hofman, E., Halman, J. I. M., & Nee, I. (2021). Roadmapping:(Missed) opportunities to overcome strategic challenges. *Business Horizons*, *64*(4), 501–512. doi:10.1016/j.bushor.2021.02.014

Simon, H. A. (1991). Bounded rationality and organizational learning. *Organization Science*, *2*(1), 125–134. doi:10.1287/orsc.2.1.125

Sims, J. H. P., & Lorenzi, P. (1992). *The new leadership paradigm: Social learning and cognition in organizations*. Sage Publications, Inc.

Sinclair, A. (2004). Journey around leadership. *Discourse (Abingdon)*, *25*(1), 7–19. doi:10.1080/0159630042000178455

Singer, M., & Gershman, Z. (2018). Do changes in district magnitude affect electoral fragmentation? Evidence over time at the district level. *Electoral Studies*, *54*, 172–181. doi:10.1016/j.electstud.2018.06.003

Sivanathan, N., Pillutla, M. M., & Murnighan, J. K. (2008). Power gained, power lost. *Organizational Behavior and Human Decision Processes*, *105*(2), 135–146. doi:10.1016/j.obhdp.2007.10.003

Snyder, H. (2019). Literature review as a research methodology: An overview and guidelines. *Journal of Business Research*, *104*, 333–339. doi:10.1016/j.jbusres.2019.07.039

Solomons, D. (1983). In search of excellence: lessons from america's best-run companies. *Journal of Accountancy (pre-1986), 156*(6), 150-175

Spector, B. A. (2016). Carlyle, Freud, and the great man theory more fully considered. *Leadership, 12*(2), 250–260. doi:10.1177/1742715015571392

Stewart, D. (1985). Ethics and the profession of public administration: The moral responsibility of individuals in public sector organizations. *Public Administration Quarterly, 8*(48), 487–495.

Stogdill, R. M. (1974). *Handbook of leadership: A survey of theory and research.* Free Press.

Stogdill, R. M., & Shartle, C. L. (1948). Methods for determining patterns of leadership behavior in relation to organization structure and objectives. *The Journal of Applied Psychology, 32*(3), 286–291. doi:10.1037/h0057264 PMID:18867065

Stoltz, P. G. (2015). Leadership GRIT™: What new research reveals. *Leader to Leader, 2015*(78), 49–55. doi:10.1002/ltl.20205

Swartz, D. (1977). Pierre Bourdieu: The cultural transmission of social inequality. *Harvard Educational Review, 47*(4), 545–555. doi:10.17763/haer.47.4.q1475v2qg2661v58

Tatli, A., Özbilgin, M., & Karatas-Özkan, M. (2015). Introduction: Management and Organisation Studies Meet Pierre Bourdieu. In *Pierre Bourdieu, Organisation, and Management* (pp. 1–16). Routledge. doi:10.4324/9781315818146

Thomas, C. (1888). the Great Man Theory, On Heroes, Hero-Worship and the Heroic in History. New York: Fredrick A. Stokes & Brother.

Torraco, R. J. (2016). Writing integrative reviews of the literature: Methods and purposes. *International Journal of Adult Vocational Education and Technology, 7*(3), 62–70. doi:10.4018/IJAVET.2016070106

Tyler, T. R., & Smith, H. J. (1995). Social justice and social movements. In Handbook of social psychology. McGraw-Hill.

Tyree, T. M. (1998). Designing an instrument to measure socially responsible leadership using the Social Change Model of Leadership Development. *Dissertation Abstracts International, 59*(06), 1945 (AAT 9836493)

Van Knippenberg, D., & van Ginkel, W. P. (2022). A diversity mindset perspective on inclusive leadership. *Group & Organization Management, 47*(4), 779–797. doi:10.1177/1059601121997229

Volmer, J., Koch, I. K., & Göritz, A. S. (2016). The bright and dark sides of leaders' dark triad traits: Effects on subordinates' career success and well-being. *Personality and Individual Differences*, *101*, 413–418. doi:10.1016/j.paid.2016.06.046

Vroom, V. H., & Jago, A. G. (1974). Decision-Making as a Social Process: Normative and Descriptive Models of Leader Behavior (AD0779334). New Haven, United States.

Waterman, R. H., & Peters, T. J. (1982). *In search of excellence: Lessons from America's best-run companies*. Harper & Row.

Xiao, Y., & Watson, M. (2019). Guidance on conducting a systematic literature review. *Journal of Planning Education and Research*, *39*(1), 93–112. doi:10.1177/0739456X17723971

Zhang, X., Tian, G., Ma, C., Tian, Y., Li, Z., & Liang, L. (2020). "Too much of a good thing?": Exploring the dark side of empowering leadership by linking it with unethical pro-organizational behavior. *Leadership and Organization Development Journal*, *42*(1), 32–46. doi:10.1108/LODJ-02-2020-0033

ADDITIONAL READING

Abbasi, A., Sattar, Rehman, K. U., & Bibi, A. (2010). Islamic leadership model an accountability perspective. *World Applied Sciences Journal*, *9*(3), 230–238.

Bhatti, M. H., Akram, U., Bhatti, M. H., Rasool, H., & Su, X. (2020). Unraveling the effects of ethical leadership on knowledge sharing: The mediating roles of subjective well-being and social media in the hotel industry. *Sustainability (Basel)*, *12*(20), 8333. doi:10.3390u12208333

Hersey, P., Blanchard, K. H., & Natemeyer, W. E. (1979). Situational leadership, perception, and the impact of power. *Group & Organization Studies*, *4*(4), 418–428. doi:10.1177/105960117900400404

McCleskey, J. A. (2014). Situational, transformational, and transactional leadership and leadership development. *Journal of business studies quarterly*, *5*(4), 117-130.

Mujtaba, B. G., & Sungkhawan, J. (2009). Situational leadership and diversity management coaching skills. *Journal of Diversity Management*, *4*(1), 1–12. doi:10.19030/jdm.v4i1.4947

Petrick, J. A., & Quinn, J. F. (2001). The challenge of leadership accountability for integrity capacity as a strategic asset. *Journal of Business Ethics*, *34*(3), 331–343. doi:10.1023/A:1012597201948

Shen, W. (2019). Personal and Situational Antecedents of Workers' Implicit Leadership Theories: A Within-Person, Between-Jobs Design. *Journal of Leadership & Organizational Studies*, *26*(2), 204–216. doi:10.1177/1548051818784001

Zaccaro, S. J., Green, J. P., Dubrow, S., & Kolze, M. (2018). Leader individual differences, situational parameters, and leadership outcomes: A comprehensive review and integration. *The Leadership Quarterly*, *29*(1), 2–43. doi:10.1016/j.leaqua.2017.10.003

KEY TERMS AND DEFINITIONS

Persistence: Continues or attempts to perform something with determination but often invisibility (inner motivation).

Ethical Responsibility: The ability to perceive, comprehend, and act on different principles and values according to field/context standards (of organization or society).

Social Change: Interpersonal relationships that change cultural and societal organizations.

Great Man: According to the leadership philosophy, certain people are born with the traits that make them leaders.

Leadership: A key individual who is capable of leading a group or organization.

Chapter 12
Impact of Workplace Incivility on Employees' Attitudinal and Behavioral Outcomes at the Workplace:
Through the Lens of Bibliometric Analysis

Ishpreet Kaur Saini
Jagran Lakecity University, Bhopal, India

Anuja Akhouri
Indian Institute of Management, Jammu, India

ABSTRACT

The impact of workplace incivility cannot be exaggerated, nor it can be ignored. Academic researchers have demonstrated in their study that 71% of the employees had faced incivility in past five years wherein the fellow court personnel were the instigators and workplace incivility is a source of job stress. Studies have reported that 78% of respondents had experienced supervisor incivility and 8% had gone through co-worker incivility. The stress released from incivility is not only within the workplace, but it is also taken home by the employees to their family domain which causes family antipathy. Haun suggested that incivility has negative impact over work and family domains as well. Employees who experience incivility hide their knowledge, and also retaliate the treatment they are given in workplace. On the days when employees are treated with uncivil behaviour, they tend to have a higher level of stress.

DOI: 10.4018/978-1-6684-6602-5.ch012

INTRODUCTION

Incivility is observed in the workplaces at a greater extend which could affect the working of the employees in the organisation. Incivility does matter. Bibliometric basically helps in evaluating the growth, the prominent authors, trends and the relevant conceptual maps. The aim of the chapter is to carry out a bibliometric analysis of Workplace Incivility in academic research. The current chapter implies bibliometrics review analysis for the literature on workplace incivility and for the same it uses the bibliometrix package of R studio as well as biblioshiny application for the analysis. The data collected and analysed from the Scopus Database. The results revealed that the publications of the research work on the area of workplace incivility are going at a great pace with USA, Canada and Australia as the leading most productive nations. The three most relevant affiliations were from the Bowling Green State University, University of Michigan and National University of Singapore. The Journal of Occupational Health Psychology followed by Journal of Applied Psychology and Journal of Nursing Management are the most prominent sources of publications shifting their focus on nursing while ignoring the review analysis in a general domain. The chapter would help the researchers to understand the concept of workplace incivility and its various dimensions in the academic as well as corporate sector. The Chapter is one of the comprehensive chapters that exclusively analyse the articles published between the year 1999 to 2021 on workplace incivility.

Workplace Incivility refers to Low intensity deviant acts, such as rude and discourteous verbal and nonverbal behaviours enacted towards another organisational member with ambiguous intent to harm (Andersson & Pearson, 1999).The words rude, intimidating, disruptive and undesirable behaviour towards the other person is regarded as workplace incivility (Clark & Ahten, 2011). Some of the examples of workplace incivility are not listening to others, gossiping with other, degrading others (Schilpzand, De Pater, & Erez, 2016). Predominantly Incivility and minor negative behaviours are being ignored and the initial stages and are not being observed and then gradually thy add up and become a great deal to be tackled with. Furthermore, if the organisation does not deal with it at the right time, it might affect the people of the organisation as well as the organisation as a whole(Andersson & Pearson, 1999). Workplace Incivility is been focused way more as prior to the last two decades. It is of great contribution towards the development of the aspects of the organisational behaviour. Studies contributed towards its negative effect on organisation and individuals and also help helped in understanding its factors (Schilpzand, De Pater, & Erez, 2016).

According to Pearson, C.M., Porath, & C.L (2004) Organisational Misconduct and Incivility have few similarities like bullying and distrust but still they are different in ways like: -

Firstly, Incivility is unsuitable behaviour not towards the organisation but only towards the individuals, Secondly, it only involves minor acts like disrespecting or ignoring the other persons in the workplace, Thirdly, the intention behind the uncivil behaviour is not to harm the other person.

The Key elements that separate Incivility and interpersonal maltreatment is the notion of enigmatic aim. The interpersonal maltreatment is with a specific purpose or aim and the intention of the person leading to mistreatment is very clear whereas in the case of incivility it is hard to deal with the intention of the person showing incivil behaviour (Sliter, 2013).

The incivil behaviours are palpable in the following significant manners: -

Firstly, Incivility is interpersonal wherein it is observed that one person shows incivil behaviour to other irrespective of the intention. Secondly, Incivility is also evident as cyber incivility wherein uncivil behaviours are being observed via the technology that is it is mediated via computers, laptops or even cell phones. Thirdly, Also, incivility can be presented even without the presence of any victim. In such a case there is no prompt effect of uncivil behaviour on the other person (Sliter, 2013).

Incivility is observed in the workplaces at a greater extend which could affect the working of the employees in the organisation. Incivility does matter (Pearson, C.M., Porath, & C.L, 2004). Incivility in workplace can spoil the social relations within a workgroup which may lead to the fall in the commitment of the employees with their companies (Cortina, L.M, 2008).

Porath, Gerbasi, & Schorch (2015) suggests that workplace incivility has realized increase in cost for both individuals as well as organisations. It cannot be always stated that the relationships between the humans will always be about happiness, calmness, love and all positive emotions. There are times and situations wherein a human may depict negative emotions might it be unintentionally or intentionally. When such behaviour wherein the intentions of the persons are clouded and it hurts or harms the dignity of other person it becomes an uncivil behaviour. Workplace incivility acts as an unfavourable ingredient in the life of the target person may it be with their fellow members, their family, friends and even with the organisation itself (Pearson, Andersson, & Porath, 2000). Workplace Incivility will gradually lead to fall in job satisfaction, causes job stress and also psychological distress (Cortina, Magley, Williams, & Langhout, 2001)(Caza & Cortina, 2007). The workplace incivility is not that severe and it is modest as it has inambiguous intentions therefore, the executives might not pay attention to this, leading to having no interventions and making it all pervasive (Cortina, L.M, 2008). Workplace incivility may seem to be a minor hurdle but it will gradually lead to big problems in long term and can negatively affect the employees and the organisation.

Bibiliometric analysis is that aspect of the research domain that helps in the analysis of a particular trendy topic with its evolution, background and scrutinizing it for providing motivation and grounds for the its future researches. It provides a proper framework and structure build on that particular topic. Bibliometrics is one of the trendiest way of analysis in the field of management studies which as a basics have three vital indicators namely Quantity Indicator (which depicts about the production of researches in that particular area), Quality Indicator (which depicts the quality of researches produced in that area which relevance to its citation analysis) and Structural Indicator (which depicts the connection between various researches in that field from the aspect of authors, countries, topics beneath it and publications as well) (L. Radha & J. Arumugam, 2021).

One of the applications for quantitative analysis and statistics is bibliometrics. Bibliometrics involves the evaluation of the publications and citations of the data in quantitative terms for all scientific fields. It basically helps in evaluating the growth, the prominent authors, trends and the relevant conceptual maps. Research Implies Bibliometrics for performance evaluation by universities, researchers, government and policymakers.

REVIEW OF LITERATURE

The impact of workplace incivility cannot be exaggerated nor it can be Ignored. Cortina, Magley, Williams, & Langhout (2001) in the study found that 71% of the employees had faced incivility in past 5 years wherein the fellow court personnel were the instigators. Penney & Spector (2005) found out that workplace incivility is a source of job stress. Blau & Andersson (2011) grounded that instigated and experienced workplace incivility are two different shades. Reio & Reio (2011) study resulted that 78% of respondents had experienced supervisor incivility and 8% had gone through co-worker incivility in the past one year of their study. The stress released from incivility is not only within workplace but it is also taken home by the employees to their family domain which causes family to work antipathy (Ferguson, 2011). Naimon, Mullins, & Osatuke (2013) findings revealed that person involved in workplace spirituality will feel the less percentage of incivility at work. Trent & Allen (2019) study revealed that the volunteers were the major targets of incivility and they faced an increased level of burnout as well. Taylor, Bedeian, Cole, & Zhang (2017)findings suggest that a change in incivility will lead to significant difference. Park & Haun (2018) Suggest that email incivility has negative impact over work and family domains as well. Abubakar, A.M, Megeirhi, H.A, & Shneikat (2018) reveals that workplace incivility can have sabotage intention and can be twice the workplace ostracism. Arshad & Ismail (2018) found that employees who experience incivility, hide their knowledge and also retaliate the treatment they are given in workplace. On the days when employees are treated with an uncivil behaviour, they tend to have higher level of stress on those days (Beattie & Griffin, 2014). The literature suggests that the intention to harm separates incivility from the other forms of misconduct in the organisation may it be bullying(Felblinger, 2008). However, there is no guarantee that the other person will not be harmed or hurt as there is absence of the intention to harm or hurt(Estes & Wang, 2008).If the person gets harm due to the uncivil behaviour experienced by him in that case that harm could last for a long period of time and so the mental and physical damage faced by the victim cannot be redeemed in the short span of time(Pearson, Andersson, & Porath, 2005). The mental damage of the individuals due to incivility can include depression, stress, worry anxiety and so on. The physical damage may include high blood pressure, migraine, headaches and so on (Kirk, Schutte, & Hine, 2011).The researches on Workplace incivility had major focused on the factors, antecedents and unfavourable repercussions incivility has on the employees as well as on the organisations. The few pivotal elements connected to the incivility at workplace are age, generation, gender, race, styles of conflict management and the confusions in role of the individuals of the organisation (Schilpzand, De Pater, & Erez, 2016).

Leea & Kim (2021) in their study adopted the theories already formulated relating to customer incivility. It followed the existing literature to discuss the role of various mediators and moderators that makes the Customer incivility concept complex and dynamic. The study mainly focused on the frontline employees. A structural review was performed that state the direct impact of customer incivility on the various factor like behavioural changes, emotional stress, job performance and work attitudes. L. Radha & J. Arumugam (2021) paper studied quantity, quality and structural indicators of bibliometrics. The database opted for the study was of category of library and the publications relating to information science in web of science. The target time period of the study was from 2014-2018. The use of Vos viewer and Biblioshiny as bibliometric tool was being used in the study and it analysed the recent research trends, coupling, top 20 institutions as well as collaborations on the area of library and Information Science. Altaf & Masrek (2021) study used the database of web of science on the literature present on the work engagement for a bibliometric analysis. It acquired the literature present since 1980 to 2020. Analysis was done using Biblioshiny Application involving the top author, countries and institutions followed by collaborations, citations, keywords frequency as well as scientific productivity. The study resulted in Netherland being the most productive country and Erasmus University being the most productive institution in the field of work engagement.

Taşkaya and Aksoy's (2020) study uses the bibiometric indicators in order to present abridgement on the literature present on workplace incivility in nursing. For the same it analysed 269 abstracts gathered from the database of web of science. Excel and Vos viewer were used to present and perform calculations on the data.

The study resulted in USA being the top most contributor towards publication in this area. Marin, Merigo, & Popa (2018) The study analysed the publications of the journal of knowledge management in 2017 as it celebrated its 20th Anniversary. The publications were analysed through bibliometric analysis for the data present from 1997 to 2016. It opted for science mapping as well as performance analysis. USA and UK are the leading in the line for the number of publications as a result of the study. Cui, Liu, & Mou (2018) study uses the database of web of science and 1479 publications from 2005-2016 were analysed using citespace software in order to visually analyse the organisational culture. The study shows that USA is the leading country in the publication and the main focus were on knowledge management, performance and innovation. Khan, Wood, Kim, andMahmood (2016) study examines 1406 articles relating to the work engagement published between 1990 and 2015. Vos Viewer application was used to study the keyword occurrence in title as well as in abstract. A power law distribution was being observed in keywords as a result of the study. Deng, Liang, Li, & Wang (2020) study performed Bibliometric analysis involving science mapping in order to display rational communities and structure as well as trends in the field of female entrepreneurship from 1975 to 2018. Vos Viewer application was used for the same. The study shows that the leading nation in the field of female entrepreneurship is USA.

OBJECTIVES

The following are the goals for performing the current bibliometric analysis chapter on the workplace incivility domain:

1. To analyse the growth of the studies pertaining to Workplace Incivility.
2. To identify the most Productive Countries in this area.
3. To identify the most Productive Institutions in this area.
4. To Recognize the Most Relevant Sources for publication in the area of Workplace Incivility.
5. To Pinpoint the Most Cited Articles Relating to this Field.
6. To ascertain the position of India in the contribution relating to workplace incivility.
7. To ascertain the World Collaborations Pertaining to the Area of Workplace Incivility.

METHODOLOGY

For the current study, the data primarily collected is from the Scopus database. Strategy used for the retrieval was- the Title - "workplace" OR "work-place" OR "work place" AND "incivility" for a time span of 1999 to 2022 retrieve on May 4 2022. Researcher did not include the data pertaining to the year 2022 as it is not significant to cover only the data available for few Months and not for complete year. Further, only the reference type "Article was used for the study. The further analysis was performed on 816 records. The Bibliographic data gained from Scopus was in the form of ".csv" file format. The Bibliometrix R Package version 3.2.1 was being installed through the R studio. Further the "Biblioshiny()" command was being followed on R console for getting the biblioshiny application started.

Bibliometrics assist research scholars in three vital aspects:

Firstly, for importing of data and its conversion to the format of R. Secondly, Use of publication dataset for Bibliometric analysis. Thirdly, Using Input data (Matrices) for the network analysis, correspondence analysis and data reduction techniques (Aria & Cuccurullo, 2017).

The parameter used in the chapter for analysis are being adapted from Oliveira, Silva, Juliani, Barbosa, & Nunhes (2019) and are shown in figure 1. Also, Figure 2 shows the description of the procedure followed for this bibliometric study Wherein it begins with defining the field of the study (Workplace Incivility) followed by the search platform for the database (Scopus), further the search criteria is defined and data results were exported and then the data was imported to biblioshiny application and then the analysis was performed based on certain parameters namely Most Cited

Figure 1. Parameters (Oliveira, Silva, Juliani, Barbosa, & Nunhes, 2019)

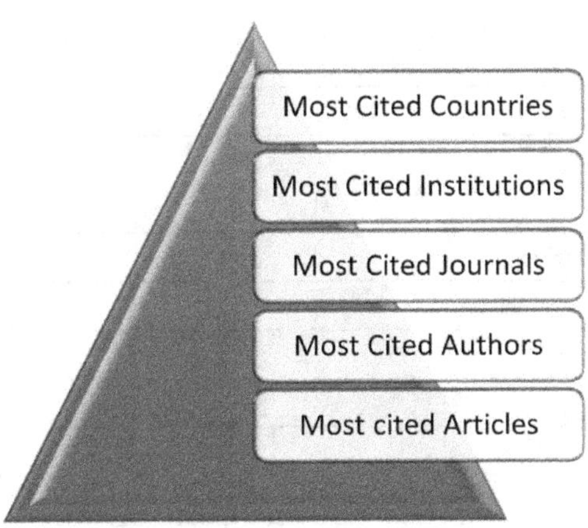

Figure 2. Procedure of the study

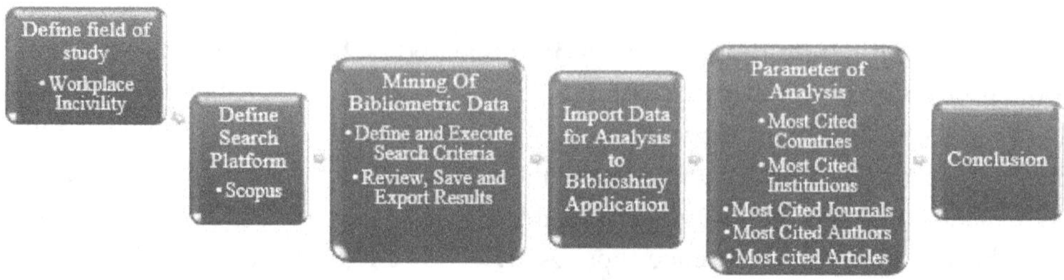

Countries, Most Cited Institutions, Most Cited Journals, Most Cited Authors, Most cited Articles and then lastly the conclusions were made.

Data Main Information

The Analysis with the help of Biblioshiny performed on 816 documents relating to workplace

Incivility disclosed that these documents were published in 429 Journals for the Time period from 1999 to 2021 that is for 22 Years. These documents were furnished by 1814 Authors and 2397 Author Appearances. It was revealed that the authors writing on Workplace incivility had a collaboration index of 2.53 and 2.94

Table 1. Data main information

Description	Result
Time Span	1999:2021
Sources (Journals)	429
Documents	816
References	36952
Authors	1814
Author's Keywords	1552
Author Appearances	2397
Authors of Single Author Documents	139
Authors of Multi Authored Documents	1675
Single Author Documents	152
Co-Authors Per Document	2.94
Documents Per Author	0.45
Collaboration Index	2.53

co-authors per document with 152 single authored documents and 0.45 Documents per author. Table 1 Provides these details.

Analysis of Annual Scientific Production

The Figure 3 and Table 2 shows the growth of the publication in the field of workplace incivility. It can be seen that the research in this specific field started with only 2 publications in the year 1999. This Number gradually grew to 11 articles in 2010.

Table 2. Annual scientific production

Year	Articles	Year	Articles
1999	2	2011	38
2001	4	2012	28
2002	1	2013	29
2003	1	2014	35
2004	2	2015	47
2005	8	2016	48
2006	5	2017	62
2007	5	2018	98
2008	5	2019	105
2009	18	2020	114
2010	11	2021	136

Figure 3. Annual scientific production

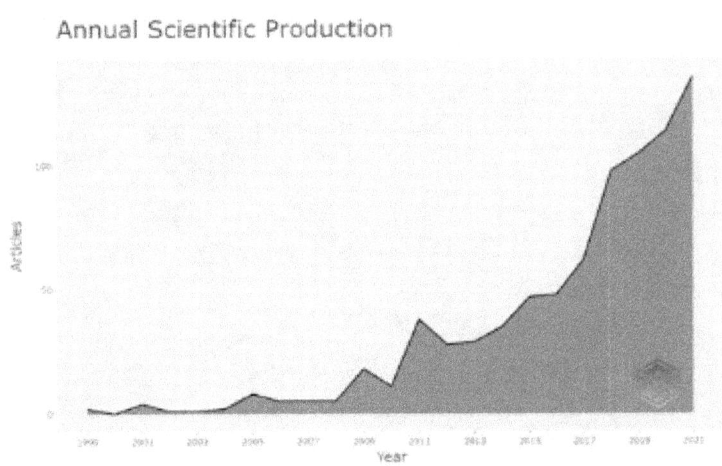

In the past 10 years that is from 2011-2021 the production has grown from 38 to 136 Respectively. As it can be seen in Figure 3 the publication trend in this field tends to grow at a great pace with an annual growth of 22.25% and there is a lot of scope for further researches and publications.

Figure 4. Most productive countries

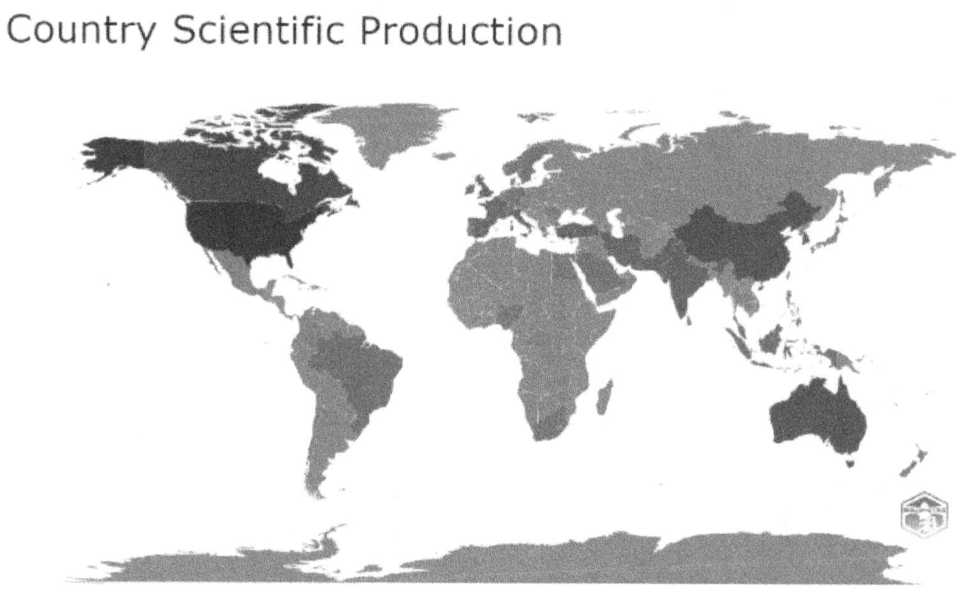

Figure 5. Most productive institutions

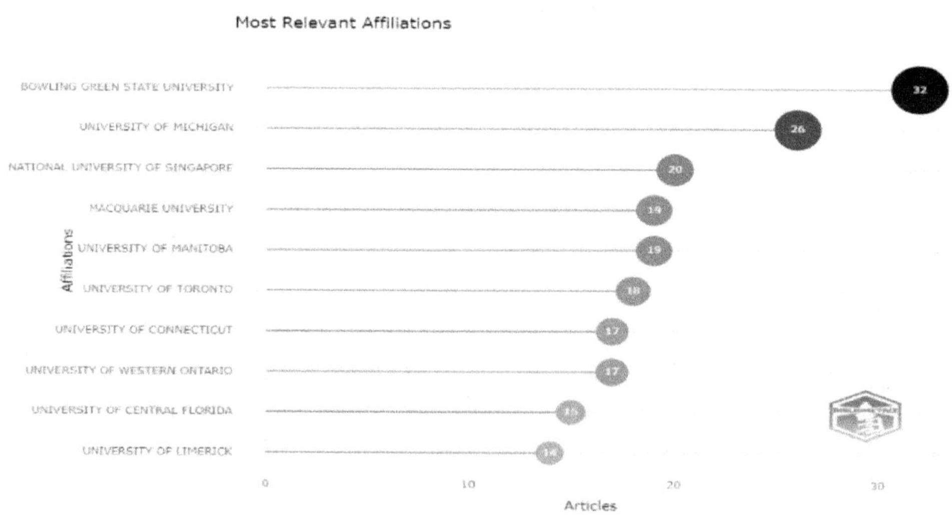

Analysis of Distribution of Countries and Institutions

The most prominent countries and institutions affiliated to the production of research work on workplace incivility are being plotted from biblioshiny(Figure 4 and 5). This will help the Researchers in identifying their collaboration they might have from various countries and institutions.

Most Productive Countries

The analytical results shown in table 3 represents that the overall 816 documents were distributed in 49 countries. The most effective scientific production was being observed by USA,Canada and Australia with a frequency of 1020,237 and 148 respectively. This reveals that USA, Canada and Australia are way ahead than other nations and they have major research power in the area of Workplace Incivility. India being on 8th Rank in the top 10 productive nations with a frequency of 44.

Table 3. Most productive countries and institutions

Country Production		Relevant Institutions	
Country	**Frequency**	**Affiliations**	**Articles**
USA	1020	BOWLING GREEN STATE UNIVERSITY	32
CANADA	237	UNIVERSITY OF MICHIGAN	26
AUSTRALIA	148	NATIONAL UNIVERSITY OF SINGAPORE	20
CHINA	144	MACQUARIE UNIVERSITY	19
UK	71	UNIVERSITY OF MANITOBA	19
SOUTH KOREA	59	UNIVERSITY OF TORONTO	18
PAKISTAN	56	UNIVERSITY OF CONNECTICUT	17
INDIA	44	UNIVERSITY OF WESTERN ONTARIO	17
TURKEY	42	UNIVERSITY OF CENTRAL FLORIDA	15
FRANCE	36	UNIVERSITY OF LIMERICK	14

Most Productive Institutions

The analytical results shown in table 3 represents the institutions affiliated are 794 in number where the top three institutions are Bowling Green State University,University of Michigan and National University of Singaporewith 32,26 and 20 affiliations respectively. The Interantional Collaborations and Cordinations would help in the more prominent researches in the coming future.

Most Relevant Sources

The current chapter discovered that the research on Workplace Incivility was published in the most prominent quality journals. Maximum Articles that are 33 in number were published in the Journal of Occupational Health Psychology followed by Journal of Applied Psychology with 20 articles and Journal of Nursing Management with 17 articles. The Impact Factor for these Journals are shown in the table 4. The Journal of Occupational Health Psychology has the highest h index of 26, g index of 32 and m index of 1.18. The data also disclosed that the publication in the journals relating to the area of workplace incivility started since 1999.

Table 4. Most relevant sources

Element	h_index	g_index	m_index	TC	NP	PY_start
JOURNAL OF OCCUPATIONAL HEALTH PSYCHOLOGY	26	32	1.181818182	3427	32	2001
JOURNAL OF APPLIED PSYCHOLOGY	13	17	0.722222222	1919	17	2005
JOURNAL OF NURSING MANAGEMENT	12	18	0.857142857	893	18	2009
JOURNAL OF ORGANIZATIONAL BEHAVIOR	12	15	0.666666667	1954	15	2005
JOURNAL OF NURSING ADMINISTRATION	9	12	0.529411765	607	12	2006
WORK AND STRESS	8	10	0.571428571	984	10	2009
ADVANCES IN DEVELOPING HUMAN RESOURCES	7	8	0.583333333	193	8	2011
JOURNAL OF BUSINESS AND PSYCHOLOGY	7	8	0.636363636	256	8	2012
INTERNATIONAL JOURNAL OF WORKPLACE HEALTH MANAGEMENT	6	8	0.6	155	8	2013
JOURNAL OF BUSINESS ETHICS	6	7	0.666666667	105	7	2014

Most Relevant Authors

The performance of the 10 most productive authors based on their publications and citations are shown in table 5. The number of publications by these authors ranged between 6 to 17. The topmost researcher CORTINA LM have 17 publications with 2743 citations, 12 h index and 0.545 m index. LEITER MP have 17 articles with 9 h index and 0.692 m index with 771 citations. Further, HERSHCOVIS MShas 12 articles with 9 h index, 0.692 m index and 991 citations.

Table 5. Most relevant authors

Element	h_index	g_index	m_index	TC	NP	PY_start
CORTINA LM	12	17	0.545	2743	17	2001
HERSHCOVIS MS	9	11	0.692	991	11	2010
LEITER MP	9	14	0.692	771	14	2010
MAGLEY VJ	9	10	0.409	2325	10	2001
CLARK CM	7	9	0.7	160	9	2013
LASCHINGER HKS	7	7	0.583	666	7	2011
LIM S	7	8	0.389	1164	8	2005
SPENCE LASCHINGER HK	7	7	0.5	861	7	2009
ABUBAKAR AM	6	6	1	213	6	2017
DAY A	6	6	0.429	917	6	2009

Most Global Cited References

Table 6 abridges the 10 most cited references globally with the Author, year, journal, DOI and number of citations. The ANDERSSON LM, 1999 tops the list with 1628 citations with 67.83 citations per year. Second is CORTINA LM, 2001 with 1003 citations and 45.59 citations per year. Third to the list is EINARSEN S, 2009 with 704 citations. And SPENCE LASCHINGER HK, 2009 is at the end of the top 10 list with 355 citations.

Table 6. Most global cited references

Paper	DOI	Total Citations	TC per Year	Normalized TC
ANDERSSON LM, 1999, ACAD MANAGE REV	10.5465/ AMR.1999.2202131	1628	67.8333	1.99877
CORTINA LM, 2001, J OCCUP HEALTH PSYCHOL	10.1037/1076-8998.6.1.64	1003	45.5909	2.84741
EINARSEN S, 2009, WORK STRESS	10.1080/02678370902815673	704	50.2857	5.05666
HERSHCOVIS MS, 2011, J ORGAN BEHAV	10.1002/job.689	481	40.0833	9.89069
PENNEY LM, 2005, J ORGAN BEHAV	10.1002/job.336	476	26.4444	2.12263
LIM S, 2008, J APPL PSYCHOL	10.1037/0021-9010.93.1.95	453	30.2	2.90757
AQUINO K, 2009, ANNU REV PSYCHOL	10.1146/annurev. psych.60.110707.163703	419	29.9286	3.00958
LIM S, 2005, J APPL PSYCHOL	10.1037/0021-9010.90.3.483	360	20	1.60535
PEARSON CM, 2005, ACAD MANAGE EXEC	10.5465/ ame.2005.15841946	360	20	1.60535
SPENCE LASCHINGER HK, 2009, J NURS MANAGE	10.1111/j.1365-2834.2009.00999.x	355	25.3571	2.54988

Analysis of Keyword Co-Occurrence

An analysis of the most frequent keywords in the studies of workplace incivility will help in identifying the skyline of the area. A keyword co-occurrence map (figure 6) and word cloud (figure 7) were created with the help of biblioshiny. Wherein few most frequent words are being displayed and if we compare the two figures (Fig 6 and 7) it is observed that workplace was at the top with 493 co-occurrences followed by human (371), female (363) and incivility (356) co-occurrences.

Bradford's Law

Table 7 makes it visible with the help of Bradford's law extracted from the Biblioshiny tool that JOURNAL OF OCCUPATIONAL HEALTH PSYCHOLOGY is the leading choice for publication by the researchers with a frequency of 33 followed by JOURNAL OF NURSING MANAGEMENT and JOURNAL OF APPLIED PSYCHOLOGY with a frequency of 20 and 17 respectively. The last rank in the top 10 list is of the NURSING FORUM with a frequency of 10.

Figure 6. Keyword co-occurrence map

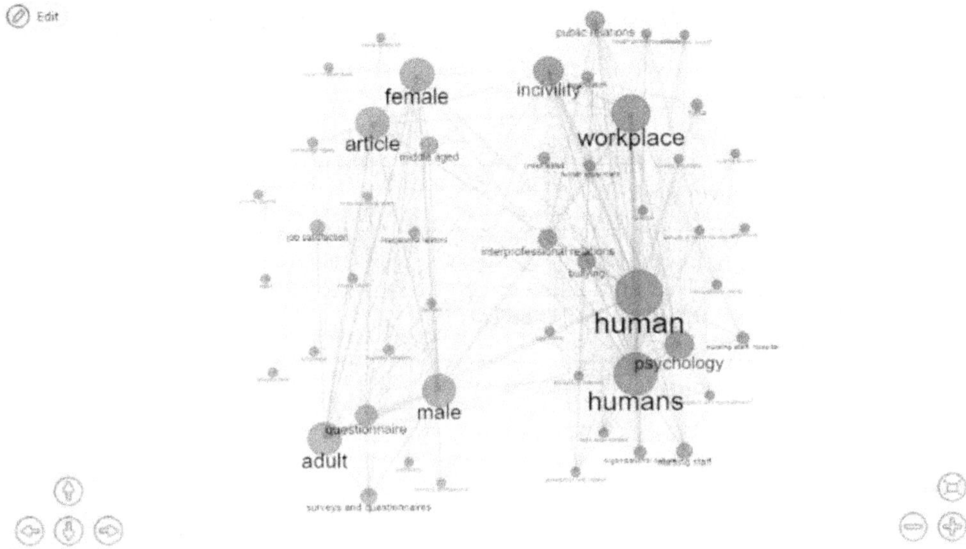

Figure 7. Word cloud

Table 7. Bradford's law

SOURCE	Rank	Freq	cumFreq	Zone
JOURNAL OF OCCUPATIONAL HEALTH PSYCHOLOGY	1	33	33	Zone 1
JOURNAL OF NURSING MANAGEMENT	2	20	53	Zone 1
JOURNAL OF APPLIED PSYCHOLOGY	3	17	70	Zone 1
JOURNAL OF ORGANIZATIONAL BEHAVIOR	4	15	85	Zone 1
INTERNATIONAL JOURNAL OF ENVIRONMENTAL RESEARCH AND PUBLIC HEALTH	5	13	98	Zone 1
JOURNAL OF NURSING ADMINISTRATION	6	12	110	Zone 1
FRONTIERS IN PSYCHOLOGY	7	11	121	Zone 1
WORK AND STRESS	8	11	132	Zone 1
INTERNATIONAL JOURNAL OF WORKPLACE HEALTH MANAGEMENT	9	10	142	Zone 1
NURSING FORUM	10	10	152	Zone 1

Trend Analysis

The Study is carried for the years 1999 to 2021. For the purpose of analysis of the topics in trend these years were divided into two phases. Phase 1 from 1999 to 2010 and phase 2 from 2011 to 2021.

The Figure 8 depicts the trendy topic from the phase 1(1999:2010) wherein it is observed that the trendiest topics for these years was the occupational health nursing. As we move forward towards the phase 2(2011:2021) it is observed that researchers were more focused on the workplace, human, adult, male and female aspects as shown in Figure 9.

World Collaboration Map

The articles relating to the workplace incivility of individual or multiple publications in each country can be visualized with the help of the world collaboration map. The top 10 International collaborations in the area of workplace incivility are shown in table 8 and figure 10 presenting the overall collaborations in the respective field. The

Figure 8. Phase 1 (1999:2010)

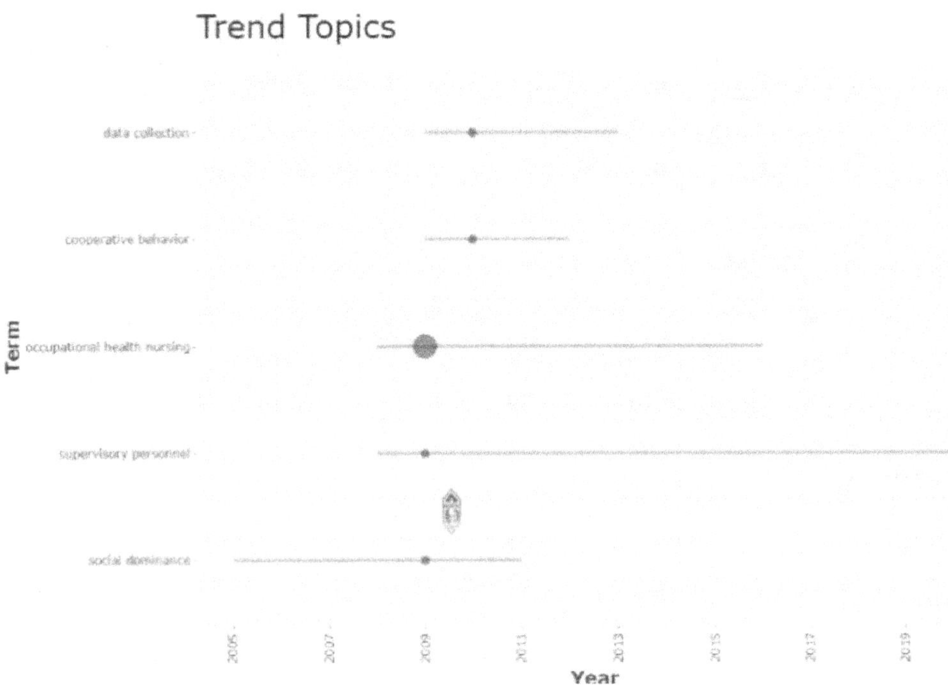

Figure 9. Phase 2 (2011:2021)

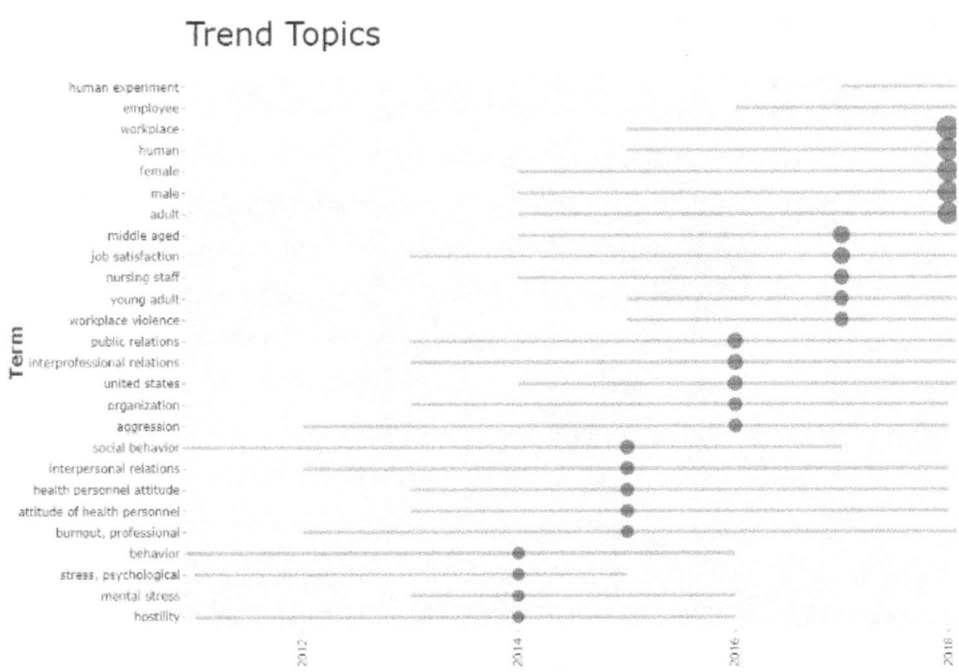

blue color in the map represents the articles published by the nation's collaborations and the degree of collaboration is represented by the borders in pink.

It can be observed from the table 8 and figure 10 that the frequency of collaborations from USA to Canada is highest that is 21 followed by Canada to UK with 11 frequencies. In the top 10 collaborations the countries which have collaborated the last but not the least is from the Pakistan to Malaysia with 4 frequencies.

Table 8. World collaborations

From	To	Frequency
USA	CANADA	21
CANADA	UNITED KINGDOM	11
USA	CHINA	10
CANADA	AUSTRALIA	7
USA	AUSTRALIA	7
USA	SINGAPORE	7
USA	KOREA	6
CHINA	PAKISTAN	5
USA	PAKISTAN	5
PAKISTAN	MALAYSIA	4

Figure 10. World collaboration map

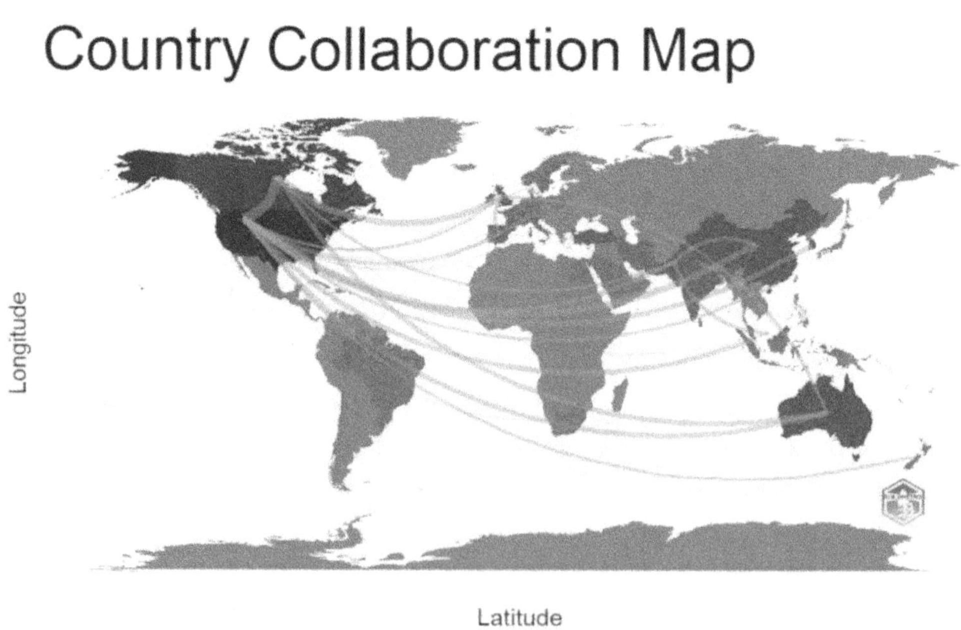

CONCLUSION

To Recapitulate, the research articles obtained from the database of Scopus were used for analysis via the biblioshiny application for a period of 1999-2021. Various tables and visual maps were drafted after analysis and the following treasurable closures are obtained from the chapter: -

1. The publications of the research work on the area of workplace incivility are going at a great pace.
2. USA, Canada and Australia are the leading most productive nations in the field of Workplace Incivility.
3. The three most relevant affiliations were from the Bowling Green State University, University of Michigan and National University of Singapore.
4. The Journal of Occupational Health Psychology followed by Journal of Applied Psychology and Journal of Nursing Management are the most prominent sources of publications.
5. Cortina Lm, Hershcovis MS and Leiter MP are the most relevant authors in the area of workplace incivility.
6. Citations Analysis revealed that the most cited reference is ANDERSSON LM (1999) in this field.
7. Workplace, Human, Female, Incivility are the most frequent keywords analysed through the keyword co-occurrence.
8. The world collaboration map disclosed the most remarkable collaborations were between USA, Canada and UK.

It is hard to be engaged in the workplace with the incivility involved in the communications happening in the organizations. From the knowledge gained form this chapter on Workplace incivility a better work environment can be created with the injections of respect and communication in the workplace. The first step towards stopping the incivility is to learn about incivility. Moreover, the analysis will further help the researchers to find the comprehension and references relating to the literature on Workplace Incivility.

The organisations must discourse their work culture and take the appropriate actions in order to abide by the norms of mutual respect and also for retaining their employees by avoiding the incivility at workplace.

The organisation can avoid the uncivil behaviour among their employees by following the standards of mutual respect and civil behaviour at the level of leaders itself this will have a positive impact on the employees of the organisation.

Further, an organisation must allow its employees to be open about their dignity that is whenever an employee feels disrespected, he/she can share the same and the problem can be resolved and the chances of evolution of the problem can be reduced.

The organisations are required to amend, improve and work upon their policies relating to the respectful culture an organisation must follow for the well-beingof the employees as well as for the effective working of the organisation(Monych, 2018). Organisation can also add civility training to the employee development programme in order to enhance the civil environment of the organisation.

Experimental studies will be helpful for the human resource department to spread awareness and create intervention on the workplace incivility.

The training related to the assorted group of people working together can be provided to the employees of the organisation which will help them in understanding the different nature and behaviour that might lead to a better communication which might gradually eliminate the uncivil behaviours.

FUTURE RESEARCH DIRECTIONS

As the data was considered only from Scopus, hence more analysis can be performed in future by researchers with the help of other indexing databases with some more specific area beneath workplace incivility and also with different data types as well.

REFERENCES

Abubakar, A. M., Megeirhi, H. A., & Shneikat, B. (2018). Tolerance for workplace incivility, employee cynicism and job search behavior. *Service Industries Journal, 38*(9/10), 629–643. doi:10.1080/02642069.2017.1420171

Alfonso, V., Boar, C., Frost, J., Gambacorta, L., & Liu, J. (n.d.). *E-commerce in the pandemic and beyond:online appendix*. BIS Bulletin.

Altaf, A., & Masrek, M. N. (2021). Visualizing the knowledge domain of Work Engagement through Bibliometric Analysis. *Library Philosophy and Practice (e-journal)*. https://digitalcommons.unl.edu/libphilprac/5300?utm_source=digitalcommons.unl.edu%2Flibphilprac%2F5300&utm_medium=PDF&utm_campaign=PDFCoverPages

Andersson, & Pearson. (1999). Tit for tat? The spiraling effect of incivility in the workplace. *Academy of Management Review, 24*(3), 452-471.

Aria, M., & Cuccurullo, C. (2017). A brief introduction to bibliometrix. *Journal of Informetrics, 11*(4), 959-975. doi:10.1016/j.joi.2017.08.007

Arshad, & Ismail. (2018). Workplace incivility and knowledge hiding behavior: does personality matter. *Journal of Organizational Effectiveness: People and Performance, 5*(3), 278-288.

Beattie, L., & Griffin, B. (2014). Day-level fluctuations in stress and engagement in response to workplace incivility: A diary study. *Work and Stress*, *28*(2), 124–142. doi:10.1080/02678373.2014.898712

Blau, G., & Andersson, L. (2011). Testing a measure of instigated workplace incivility. *Journal of occupational and oganizational psychology* . doi:10.1348/096317905X26822

Cao, W., Fang, Z., Hou, G., Han, M., Xu, X., Dong, J., & Zheng, J. (2020). *The psychological impact of the COVID-19 epidemic on college students in*. Elsevier. doi:10.1016/j.psychres.2020.112934

Carmeli, & Gefen. (2005). The relationship between work commitment models and employee withdrawal intentions. *Journal of Managerial Psychology, 20*(2), 63-86.

Carter, W. R, Nesbit, P. L., & Badham, R. J, & Parke. (2016). The effects of employee engagement and self-efficacy on job performance: A longitudinal field study. *International Journal of Human Resource Management*, *21*(17), 1–20.

Carton, W., Lund, J. F., & Dooley, K. (2021, April). Undoing Equivalence: Rethinking Carbon Accounting for just carbon removal. *Frontiers in Climate*, *3*, 1–7. doi:10.3389/fclim.2021.664130

Caza, B. B., & Cortina, L. M. (2007). 11 5). From Insult to Injury: Explaining the Impact of Incivility. *Basic and Applied Social Psychology*, *29*(4), 335–350. doi:10.1080/01973530701665108

Chawla, N., & Kumar, B. (2021). 07 09). E-Commerce and Consumer Protection in India: The Emerging Trend. *Journal of Business Ethics*, 1–24. doi:10.100710551-021-04884-3 PMID:34257470

Chugh, S., Vibhu, G., Kanijia, S., Kumar, V., & Pal, S. K. (2020). *To study the impact of advancement of e-payment technology used in India* . Sage.

Clark, C. M., & Ahten, S. (2011). 1 2). Beginning the Conversation: The Nurse Educator's Role in Preventing Incivility in the Workplace. *RN Idaho*, *33*(4), 9–10.

Cortina, L. M. (2008). Unseen injustice: Incivility as modern discrimination in organizations. *Academy of Management Review*, *33*(1), 55–75. doi:10.5465/amr.2008.27745097

Cortina, L. M., Magley, V. J., Williams, J. H., & Langhout, R. D. (2001). 1). Incivility in the workplace: Incidence and impact. *Journal of Occupational Health Psychology*, *6*(1), 64–80. doi:10.1037/1076-8998.6.1.64 PMID:11199258

Cui, Y., Liu, Y., & Mou, J. (2018). Bibliometric analysis of organisational culture using CiteSpace. *Suid-Afrikaanse Tydskrif vir Ekonomiese en Bestuurswetenskappe*, *21*(1). doi:10.4102ajems.v21i1.2030

Deng, W., Liang, Q., Li, J., & Wang, W. (2020). Science mapping: A bibliometric analysis of female entrepreneurship studies. *Gender in Management*. doi:10.1108/GM-12-2019-0240

Diamantopoulos, A. (2008, December). Formative indicators: Introduction to the special issue. *Journal of Business Research*, *61*(12), 1201–1302. doi:10.1016/j.jbusres.2008.01.008

Duraku, Z. H., & Hoxha, L. (2020). The impact of COVID-19 on education and on the well-being of teachers, parents, and students: Challenges related to remote (online) learning and opportunities for advancing the quality of education.

Estes, B. C., & Wang, J. (2008). Integrative Literature Review: Workplace Incivility: Impacts on Individual and Organizational Performance. *Human Resource Development Review*, *7*(2), 218–240. doi:10.1177/1534484308315565

Fan, L., Zhang, X., Rai, L., & Du, Y. (2021, May). Mobile Payment: The Next frontier of payment systems?-An emperical study based on Push Pull Mooring Framework. *Journal of Theoretical and Applied Electronic Commerce Research*, *16*(2), 155–169. doi:10.4067/S0718-18762021000200112

Felblinger, D. M. (2008). 3 11). Incivility and Bullying in the Workplace and Nurses' Shame Responses. *Journal of Obstetric, Gynecologic, and Neonatal Nursing*, *37*(2), 234–242. doi:10.1111/j.1552-6909.2008.00227.x PMID:18336449

Ferguson, M. (2011). 8 10). You cannot leave it at the office: Spillover and crossover of coworker incivility. *Journal of Organizational Behavior*, *33*(4), 571–588. doi:10.1002/job.774

GuptaA.GoplaniM. M. (2020, May). IMPACT OF COVID-19 ON EDUCATIONAL INSTITUTIONS IN INDIA. *Purakala, 31*(21), 661-671. doi:10.13140/RG.2.2.32141.36321

GuptaA.GoplaniM. M. (2020, May). IMPACT OF COVID-19 ON EDUCATIONAL INSTITUTIONS IN INDIA. *Purakala, 31*(21), 661-671. doi:10.13140/RG.2.2.32141.36321

He, R., Luo, L., Shamsuddin, A., & Tang, Q. (2021). Corporate Carbon Accounting: A literature Review of Carbon Accounting Research From the Koyoto Protocol to the Paris agreement. *Accounting and Finance Assosiation of Australia and New-Zealand*, 1-38. doi:10.1111/acfi.12789

Jena, P. K. (2020). Impact of Covid-19 on higher education in India. *International Journal of Advanced Education and Research*, *5*(3), 77–81.

Jena, P. K. (2020, June). Impact of Covid-19 on higher education in India. *International Journal of Advanced Education and Research*, *5*(3), 77–81.

Jena, P. K. (2020, July). Impact of Pandemic COVID-19 on Education in India. *International Journal of Current Research*, *12*(7), 12582–12586. doi:10.24941/ijcr.39209.07.2020

Jena, P. K. (2020, July). Impact of Pandemic COVID-19 on Education in India. *International Journal of Current Research*, *21*(07), 12582–12586. doi:10.24941/ijcr.39209.07.2020

Jha, C. (2020). *The Great Disruptive Transformation*. Wiley.

Joyce, D., & White, N. M. (2020). Colleges need a makeover: Adapting to change one class at a time. *Journal of Higher Education Theory and Practice*, *20*(5), 11–15.

Joyce, D., & White, N. M. (2020). Colleges Need a Makeover: Adapting to Change One Class at a Time. *Journal of Higher Education Theory and Practice*, *20*(5), 11–15.

Khan, G. F., Wood, J., Kim, W., & Mahmood, M. T. (2016). Work Engagement Research Domain: Keywords Analysis Using Social Network Analysis and Burst Detection Approach. *International Journal of Computers, 1*.

Kirk, B. A., Schutte, N. S., & Hine, D. W. (2011). The Effect of an Expressive-Writing Intervention for Employees on Emotional Self-Efficacy, Emotional Intelligence, Affect, and Workplace Incivility. *Journal of Applied Social Psychology*, *41*(1), 179–195. doi:10.1111/j.1559-1816.2010.00708.x

Kuckertz, A. (2020). Startups in times of crisis – A rapid response to the. *Journal of Business Venturing Insights*.

Kumar Mukul, G. K. (2021). Talent acquisition in startups in India: the role of social capital. *Journal of Entrepreneurship in Emerging Economies*.

Leea, K. J., & Kim, S. G. (2021). Structural Review of Customer Incivility and Social. *Journal of Quality Assurance in Hospitality & Tourism*. doi:10.1080/1528008X.2020.1864564

Ma, S., & Trigo, V. (2008). Winning the War for Managerial Talent in China:An EmpiricalStudy. *Chinese Economy, 41*(3), 34–57. doi:10.2753/CES1097-1475410303

Mahajan, D. Y. (2020). Study of impact of coronavirus pandemic on small and medium enterprises (SME's). *GIS SCIENCE JOURNAL, 7*(9), 1–6.

Marin, M. G., Merigo, J. M., & Popa, S. (2018). Twenty years of the Journal of Knowledge Management: A bibliometric analysis. *Journal of Knowledge Management, 22*(8), 1655–1687. doi:10.1108/JKM-10-2017-0497

Monych, B. (2018). *6 ways to combat workplace incivility*. Insperity. https://www.insperity.com/blog/workplace-incivility/

Nag, A. K. (2005). Covid paper. (bjhc, Ed.) Commerce, 8(2), 1*10.

Naimon, E. C., Mullins, M. E., & Osatuke, K. (2013). 1 10). The effects of personality and spirituality on workplace incivility perceptions. *Journal of Management, Spirituality & Religion, 10*(1), 91–110. doi:10.1080/14766086.2012.758049

Oliveira, O. J., Silva, F. F., Juliani, F., Barbosa, L. F., & Nunhes, T. V. (2019). *Bibliometric Method for Mapping the State-of-the-Art and Identifying Research Gaps and Trends in Literature: An Essential Instrument to Support the Development of Scientific Projects*. Scientometrics Recent Advances. doi:10.5772/intechopen.85856

Park, Y., & Haun, V. C. (2018). 12). The long arm of email incivility: Transmitted stress to the partner and partner work withdrawal. *Journal of Organizational Behavior, 39*(10), 1268–1282. doi:10.1002/job.2289

Pearson, C., Andersson, L., & Porath, C. (2005). Workplace incivility. In S. Fox & P. E. Spector (Eds.), Counterproductive work behavior: Investigations of actors and targets. *American Psychological Association.*, 177-200. https://psycnet.apa.org/doi/10.1037/10893-008

Pearson, C.M., & Porath, C.L. (2004). *On incivility, its impact, and directions for future research*, 403-425. Research Gate.

Pearson, C. M., Andersson, L. M., & Porath, C. L. (2000). 11 1). Assessing and attacking workplace incivility. *Organizational Dynamics, 29*(2), 123–137. doi:10.1016/S0090-2616(00)00019-X

Penney, L. M., & Spector, P. E. (2005). 11). Job Stress, Incivility, and Counterproductive Work Behavior (CWB): The Moderating Role of Negative Affectivity. *Journal of Organizational Behavior, 26*(7), 777–796. doi:10.1002/job.336

Porath, C. L., Gerbasi, A., & Schorch, S. L. (2015). The Effects of Civility on Advice, Leadership, and Performance. *The Journal of Applied Psychology*, *100*(5), 1527–1541. doi:10.1037/apl0000016 PMID:25798552

Radha, L., & Arumugam, J. (2021, October). The Research Output of Bibliometrics using Bibliometrix R Package and VOS Viewer. *International Journal of Arts. Science and Humanities*, *9*(2), 44–49. 10.34293

Reio, T. G., & Reio, J. S. (2011). 12 6). Thinking About Workplace Engagement: Does Supervisor and Coworker Incivility Really Matter? *Advances in Developing Human Resources*, *13*(4), 462–478. doi:10.1177/1523422311430784

Saxena, D., & Tripathi, D. N. (2021, February). Exploring The security risks and safety measures of mobile payments in Fintech Environment in India. *International Journal of Management*, *12*(2), 408–417. doi:10.34218/IJM.12.2.2021.041

Schaufeli, W. B., & Bakker, A. B. (2004). Job demands, job resources, and their relationship with burnout and engagement: A multi-sample study. *Journal of Organizational Behavior*, *25*(3), 293–315. doi:10.1002/job.248

Schilpzand, P., De Pater, I. E., & Erez, A. (2016). 2). Workplace incivility: A review of the literature and agenda for future research. *Journal of Organizational Behavior*, *37*(S1), S57–S88. doi:10.1002/job.1976

Sliter, M. (2013). *What is workplace incivility, why should we care, and what should we do?* HRZONE. https://www.hrzone.com/perform/people/what-is-workplace-incivility-why-should-we-care-and-what-should-we-do

Sundari, D. K., & Sowmiya, B. (2020). TIRUPUR TEXTILE START-UPS IN COVID 19 PANDEMIC. *SELP Journal of Social Science - A Blind Review & Refereed Quarterly Journal, XI*(46), 35-41.

Taşkaya, S., & Aksoy, A.TAŞKAYA. (2021, April). S., & AKSOY, A. (2020). A Bibliometric Analysis of Workplace Incivility in Nursing. *Journal of Nursing Management*, *29*(3), 518–525. doi:10.1111/jonm.13161

Taylor, S. G., Bedeian, A. G., Cole, M. S., & Zhang, Z. (2017). Developing and Testing a Dynamic Model of Workplace Incivility Change. *Journal of Management*, *43*(3), 645–670. doi:10.1177/0149206314535432

Toquero, C. M. (2020). Challenges and Opportunities for Higher Education amid the COVID19 Pandemic: The Philippine Context. *Pedagogical Research*, *5*(4), 1–5. doi:10.29333/pr/7947

Tran, L. T. (2020). Managing the effectiveness of e-commerce platforms in a pandemic. *Journal of Retailing and Consumer Services*, 1–9.

Trent, S. B., & Allen, J. A. (2019). 4 3). Resilience Only Gets You So Far: Volunteer Incivility and Burnout. *Organizational Management Journal*, *16*(2), 69–80. doi:10.1080/15416518.2019.1604199

Tsagkias, M., King, T. H., Kallumadi, S., Murdock, V., & Rijke, M. d. (2020). Challenges and Research Opportunites in e-commerce search and Recommendations. *ACM SIGIR Forum, 54*(1), 1-23.

Tysinger, J., Tysinger, D., Mcbrayer, J. S., & Daimanduros, T. (2020). Perspectives, Training and preparedness of frequently and infrequently Addressed Crisis events in online learning environment. *Journal of Higher Education Theory and Practice*, *20*(5), 61–69.

Yang, M., Mamun, A. A., Mohiuddin, M., Nawi, N., & Zainol, N. R. (2021). Cashless Transactions: A study on Intention and Adoption of e-wallets. *Sustainability (Basel)*, *13*(2), 1–18. doi:10.3390u13020831

ADDITIONAL READING

Agarwal, S., Pandey, R., Kumar, S., Lim, W. M., Agarwal, P. K., & Malik, A. (2023). Workplace incivility: A retrospective review and future research agenda. *Safety Science*, *158*, 105990. doi:10.1016/j.ssci.2022.105990

Al-Asfour, A. (2023). Workplace Incivility of Faculty Members in Higher Education Settings: A Bibliometric Analysis. *Journal of Faculty Development*, *37*(2), 5–16.

KEY TERMS AND DEFINITIONS

Bibliometrics: Bibliometrics is a quantitative analysis of the researches performed relating to a specific data theme involving the citation and content analysis.

Biblioshiny: Biblioshiny is an application which gets started through "Biblioshiny()" command on R console in the R studio application.

Scopus: Scopus is a multidisciplinary database for quality researches.

Workplace Incivility: Workplace Incivility refers to the rude, disrespectful and discourteous behaviour at the workplace.

Chapter 13
Opportunities and Barriers for Entrepreneurship in the Metaverse Age

Ömer Karademir
https://orcid.org/0000-0003-1109-4797
Kastamonu University, Turkey

ABSTRACT

The metaverse is a 3D (three-dimensional) virtual world synchronized with the real world, where users interact with a digital avatar using augmented reality technologies. The transformative impact of this virtual world is making itself felt in many areas, as are the opportunities and challenges it creates. Entrepreneurs' capacity to foresee these risks and assess opportunities may be crucial to the survival of their businesses in the future. This study aims to examine potential business opportunities, obstacles, and risks for entrepreneurs in the metaverse universe. To this end, studies in the metaverse literature were examined, and as a result of these studies, an attempt was made to determine the potential business opportunities that the metaverse universe could create. As a result, it was found that the metaverse offers very different business opportunities for entrepreneurs in different fields. This study considers it essential for entrepreneurs to invest in the metaverse to evaluate these business opportunities.

DOI: 10.4018/978-1-6684-6602-5.ch013

INTRODUCTION

In traditional times, who combined the factors of production to create goods and services that satiated consumer demands while also pursuing profit and taking on risk. Today, a new business ecosystem and a new parallel business universe emerge with the traditional world, called the "metaverse." New business opportunities and threats are revealed, a new form of entrepreneurship that will create added value that will create benefits. This situation necessitates new business opportunities and a new kind of entrepreneurial activity appropriate for the Metaverse's functioning universe. In the Metaverse universe, entrepreneurship must replace traditional times' local, regional, or national entrepreneurship. In this metaverse entrepreneurship, unlike industrial entrepreneurship, unlike creating a new product by processing raw materials, changing their shape, assembling and assembling, things are not done in the actual world, but a metaverse, world parallel to this one. This is a new example of creative entrepreneurship based on "web 3" technology. In innovative/creative entrepreneurship, work is done in a virtual environment and with virtual-world resources rather than in the real environment and with real-world resources. All of the work is done in the virtual environment and with the raw materials of the virtual environment. In contemporary society, rapidly increasing new technological developments create new opportunities for entrepreneurs. As a result of the development of information and communication technology and related innovations, a new economy known as the "digital economy" has been produced. The digital economy provides tremendous opportunities for numerous entrepreneurs to launch new businesses in a variety of industries (Hafezieh et al., 2011). The steady growth of digital technology, in particular since the mid-1990s, has created digital ventures whose business models are built on generating value through electronic information via data networks (Kollmann, 2006).

In a broad sense, digital entrepreneurship within the digital ecosystem refers to the creation of new ventures and the transformation of current businesses through the development of new digital technologies or applications (Shen et al., 2018; Ferreira et al., 2019). High-intensity digital technologies are a defining characteristic of digital entrepreneurs, who use them to enhance the operations of businesses and produce novel products and services, as well as new business models, while also interacting with stakeholders and customers. Digital entrepreneurs operate in a metaverse universe, taking advantage of different opportunities provided by the Internet, the World Wide Web, mobile technologies, the use of digital media, and other technological advances in communication and information (Beliaeva et al., 2020). With the development of the new generation of Internet (Web 3.0) infrastructure, the acceleration of digital transformation brings new business opportunities and entrepreneurship forms to the agenda. Digital transformation brings about current concepts and practices by creating changes in many areas (Lee et al., 2021). Digitization is becoming a new source of innovation in all sectors by forcing and restructuring business models. In this process, entrepreneurs are not only the driving forces of digitalization but also the affected actors. In addition to having numerous layers of connectivity and output forms as a stand-alone process of managing digital business platforms, the digital entrepreneurship area is becoming a significant driver of contemporary innovation structures and ecosystem models (Satalkina & Steiner 2020).

Whether its name is metaverse or virtual universe, the heart of the digital world beats in this "fictional universe." Almost everyone is trying to be included in this universe, attracting attention from 7 to 70. Some of them play games with the avatar they have created or participate in events such as concerts, while others are already looking for investments with tools such as fields. At the last point reached, many sectors from real estate to textile, from technology to tourism, are adapting their business models to the metaverse. In recent years, the development of digital technology has created new business models as a complex combination of interconnected augmented reality technologies. Virtual reality connected to augmented reality creates new business opportunities with digital transformations. In this virtual world, all the content is created by the users, and each user can have the experience they want in this world. The term "metaverse" refers to this digital transformation (Lee et al., 2021). Metaverse virtual environments are based on technologies that enable multi-sensory interactions with digital objects (Mystakidis, 2022). It refers to an immersive virtual world called the metaverse that serves as a place for business, education, and entertainment experiences. Caulfield's metaverse becomes a tethered platform for any application, becoming a virtual world of digital goods and identities (Caulfield, 2021). An immersive picture of the Internet as a single, shared space that is permanent and shared is at the core of the metaverse. Although the metaverse may appear futuristic, driven by emerging technologies like as 5G Artificial Intelligence, and Augmented Reality, it continues as augmented reality in cyberspace today (Lee et al., 2021). The metaverse depicted in books, movies, and games can potentially complement actual-world experiences and replace them largely (Allal-Chérif, 2022; Kim, 2021).

Firms aware of this potential show a broad interest in the metaverse. Microsoft's corporate metadata, Facebook Horizon, and Nvidia Omniverse lead this trend. On metaverse marketplaces such as Decentraland, consumer brands such as Gucci and Coca-Cola sell non-fungible tokens (Kim, 2021). It has been announced that the global bank giant HSBC will purchase a plot that it will develop in the metaverse to interact with sports, esports, and gaming fans. The Walking Dead, Snoop Dogg, Warner Music Group (WMG), and Adidas are among the global businesses investing in the metaverse world (Gkritsi, 2022). The world's third-largest sneaker brand headquartered in California, Skechers announced that it would open a store in the

Fashion District of Decentraland, its popular metaverse project (Ravi, 2020). We observe the emergence of this metaverse ecosystem, where several actors of all sizes are working together to build an alternate reality that mirrors the real one.

What opportunities and threats the rapidly developing metaverse ecosystem will bring to entrepreneurs is an issue that needs to be emphasized. By analyzing the metaverse ecosystem, which gained momentum with Web 3.0 internet technology, for entrepreneurs, the opportunities and threats that the technological transformation in the metaverse universe will create for both individual investors and companies will be examined. First of all, digital entrepreneurship and its historical background will be examined. Then, metaverse technology and the metaverse ecosystem will be examined. Then, we will focus on the opportunities and threats that this new technology will create for entrepreneurs and the opportunities and threats of entrepreneurship in the metaverse universe.

BACKGROUND

Metaverse

The incredibly rapid advances in information technology have changed the way we communicate with our fellow human beings, making interaction between the actual and virtual worlds possible. These innovations—which we can refer to as "information technology"—have played a crucial role in accelerating the metaverse's development. Information technologies have undergone great changes in every era. Today, we can say that the last point these developments have reached is the metaverse.

The term "metaverse" combines the words "universe," which refers to a virtual or parallel environment associated with the actual world, and the prefix "meta," which conveys transcendence (Dwivedi et al., 2022). Although it is still a relatively new concept in academia, the term first appeared in the early 1990s as research into virtual humans, real-time autonomous agents, and interactive worlds advanced. It was first used in Neal Stephenson's novel "Snow Crash" in 1992. People in this story attempt to escape the misery of the actual world by exploring a digital world with the aid of numerous digital avatars (Stephenson, 1992). The metaverse is referred to in the book as the realm of virtual reality and the Internet where software agents and avatars utilize augmented reality. The definition and boundaries of this term are still unclear, despite its growing popularity.

Meta-universes are described by Davis et al. (2009; 90) as immersive three-dimensional virtual environments where users can communicate using avatars created by software agents. When describing the metaverse as "an extensive 3D networked virtual world capable of supporting a large number of people simultaneously for social interaction," Wright et al., (2008) place special emphasis on the social aspects of metaverse. Collins (2021), on the other hand, portrays the metaverse as a large virtual world in which millions of individuals would engage in real time with their avatars. According to Gürcü (2022), the blockchain network is the "foundation" of the metaverse, "communication" takes place over the blockchain Internet, and "building material" is the metaverse, a three-dimensional (3D) virtual global network created by Web 3.0. These definitions all have the term "virtual world" in common. The phrase "virtual world" refers, according to Nevelsteen (2018), to a shared, persistent simulation environment in which numerous software agents or humans can interact virtually and react in real time to outside events. According to Srushti IMX (2021), the idea of the metaverse is more specifically described as the virtual shared space that generates a universe in which users select their avatars to construct homes and businesses, conduct meetings, go to classes, find partners, raid three-dimensional villages, conquer planets, and perform a variety of other possible and impractical real-life tasks via a computer. However, defining the metaverse solely in terms of virtual worlds would result in an inadequate definition. There is another approach that sees the metaverse as a way to connect the actual and virtual worlds. Smart et al., (2007) see the metaverse as a node or connecting point between the physical and virtual worlds. The reason for this is that virtual experiences in the metaverse can have direct reflections on the actual world. Contrarily, Go et al., (2021) emphasize the economic and cultural aspects of the metaverse, defining it as a 3D virtual reality in which avatars that are representations of reality carry out daily tasks and conduct economic life. In a similar way, Lee and Han (2021) define the metaverse as a universe in which virtual and actual worlds interact and co-evolve, and where economic, social, and cultural activities are carried out to produce value. Here, the metaverse is an interaction between the actual world and virtual reality rather than a simple combination of the two. This interaction takes place with avatars. The avatar in the metaverse is defined by the person's true self (Kye et al., 2021). Users participate in social, economic, and cultural activities in the metaverse with their avatars and reflect this in the actual world.

A universe in which both normal life and business transactions occur simultaneously is called a metaverse. The actual-world blends with virtual space, and reality expands into virtual space in everyday activities and business (Kye et al., 2021). A simulated digital environment known as the "metaverse" combines the principles of social media, augmented reality, and virtual reality to create dynamic interaction spaces for users that resemble the actual world (Laeeq, 2022). In this digital environment, the virtual and physical worlds are not simply combined. Instead, the physical world is given continuity in the virtual world to create an ecosystem that connects the two worlds (Tlili et al., 2022).

Table 1. Evolution of the metaverse concept over time

Illustrative Study	Scope	Definition of the "Metaverse"
Perlin& Goldberg (1996)	Single Virtual World (Narrow + Purely virtual)	"A future version of the Internet which appears to its participants as a quasi – physical world. Participants are represented by fully articulate human figures, or avatars. Body movements of avatars are computed automatically by the system"
Allbeck& Badler (1998)	Single Virtual World (Narrow + Purely virtual)	"A virtual reality world envisioned as a large cyber-planet. It contains homes, corporate headquarters, nightclubs, and virtually every other type of building found in reality and some that are not. Individuals from around the world materialize on this cyber-planet, and are represented there by avatars"
Wright et al. (2008)	Single Virtual World converging the physical and virtual realities (Narrow + Blended reality)	"An extensive 3D networked virtual world capable of supporting a large number of people simultaneously for social interaction" "implies the interaction of real people with the virtual environments and agents including avatars with increasing levels of immersion and presence" "the word metaverse (Meta-Universe) suggests the emergence of a new class of augmented social interaction which we term 'augmented duality'"
Frey et al. (2008)	Interoperable virtual worlds (Broad + Purely virtual)	"A system of numerous, interconnected virtual and typically user-generated worlds (or Meta-worlds) all accessible through a single-user interface"
Davis et al. (2009)	Single Virtual Worlds (Narrow + Purely Virtual)	"Immersive three-dimensional virtual worlds in which people interact as avatars with each other and with software agents, using the metaphor of the real world but without its physical limitations"
Dionisio et al. (2013)	Interoperable virtual worlds (Broad + Purely virtual)	"An integrated network of 3D virtual worlds"
Duan et al. (2021)	Interoperable convergence of the physical and virtual worlds (Broad + Blended reality)	"An evolving virtual world with unlimited scalability and interoperability" "real-time 3D rendering-related technologies like VR/AR are regarded as the main interaction interface."
Lee et al. (2021)	Interoperable convergence of the physical and virtual worlds (Broad + Blended reality)	"A virtual environment blending physical and digital, facilitated by the convergence between the Internet and Web technologies, and Extended Reality (XR)… all individual users own their respective avatars, in analogy to the user's physical self, to experience an alternate life in a virtuality that is a metaphor of the user's real worlds"

References: (Barrera & Shah 2023:3).

In summary, these definitions include the common characteristics of the metaverse: augmented reality, virtual world, continuity of people and objects, use of blockchain, shared environment, use of avatars, three-dimensionality, simultaneous interaction of real and virtual, sharing of social, cultural, and economic activities. Despite these commonalities, because the metaverse is still evolving as a concept and is new in terms of practice, it also contains some points of disagreement. However, taking all these characteristics together, the metaverse can be defined as a constantly evolving and growing three-dimensional virtual world ecosystem that is synchronized with the actual world and in which people participate socially, culturally, and economically through their avatars. As the metadata store is created and used more, this definition might be expanded upon and changed. The development of the term "metaverse" in recent literature is outlined in Table 1.

There are numerous areas of disagreement regarding the metaverse despite the fact that it has been described using numerous definitions, as was mentioned above. This may be due to two reasons. First, the metaverse is a new phenomenon that has entered our lives, and it is not yet fully understood what it is. The second reason is that the evolutionary emergence process of the metaverse is still in its infancy and is still ongoing. Technology that enables multisensory interaction between people, digital objects, and virtual environments is the foundation of the Metaverse (Mystakidis, 2022). Therefore, it would be wiser to concentrate on the underlying technology in order to comprehend the metaverse better.

Metaverse Technology

Web 3.0

When the revolutionary www was uncovered in 1991, the first website in the Web 1.0 version was combined with an IP address using html codes that were made up of distinct numbers and made available for use on all computers via a protocol. The initial stage of the Internet was referred to as Web 1.0. Web 1.0 was considerably simpler because the Internet's content was developed by a small group of people (Bansgopaul, 2021). There were few content creators, and the majority of Internet users were consumers.

In 1999, the term "Web 2.0" was used for the first time. Web 2.0 stands for the Internet that we all use today. Web 2.0 encourages users to become content creators when compared to Web 1.0. Instead of just passively using the Internet by viewing it, Web 2.0 provides an environment where more people can participate actively (Bansgopaul, 2021). Web 2.0 is characterized by the emergence of apps, self-publishing platforms like WordPress and Squarespace, and social media websites like Facebook, Instagram, LinkedIn, and YouTube.

The Internet is at the beginning of a new transformation process. This new phase of the Internet, called Web 3.0, is expected to bring new benefits to content creators and users. Therefore, Web 3.0 is commonly referred to as the Internet that belongs to its creators, users, and originators (Rai, 2022). Another feature that makes Web 3.0 very important is that it is a "semantic" Web. The semantic web is the synchronization of meaningful signs. Since it is not possible for the website itself to be semantic and synchronized, "network" structures can emerge that show that the elements (with virtual meaning) on our website are "synonymous" with those on other websites (Gürcü, 2022). Artificial intelligence and machine learning technologies will also enable users to interact with data. The semantic web and artificial intelligence will ultimately be combined in Web 3.0 (Bansgopaul, 2021). In this new system, websites will create a web of meaning that is open to surprise (Gürcü, 2022). Decentralized protocols will make Web 3.0 possible. Smart contracts are expected to be used in the future to automate and connect the Internet, blockchain technology, and cryptocurrencies (Bansgopaul, 2021). Web 3.0 further blurs the distinction between the digital and physical worlds by placing more emphasis on user identity persistence across different domains and websites. It also integrates augmented reality and virtual reality technologies. Thus, augmented reality and virtual reality are becoming more prevalent with Web 3.0, bringing more realistic graphics to applications and games. Considering all these reasons, it can be said that the metaverse Web 3.0 will emerge in the world of virtual existence with software technologies. It appears inevitable that Web 3.0 and the Metaverse will gain popularity and adoption over time (Entrepreneur, 2023).

Blockchain

The foundation of Metaverse started with blockchain software, and that software continues to grow as new rings are added to its continuous chain (Gürcü, 2022). Blockchain technology is not a new concept, but has been developed recently with its own unique advantages in ensuring transaction security. This concept was initially introduced in Satoshi Nakamoto's article "Bitcoin: A Peer-to-Peer Electronic Cash System," published in 2008. It explores how cryptography and an open distributed ledger can be merged in a digital currency application (Nakamoto, 2008). Blockchain is a detailed set of rules implemented via an encryption protocol or software to securely monitor and transmit data on the Internet (Gümüş & Erkuş, 2019). The blockchain consists of distributed ledgers in which all copies of a transaction or other process performed for the purpose of data verification are maintained by all participants (Türkmen & Durbilmez, 2019).

Blockchain advantages include distributed ledger, decentralization, information transparency, anti-theft, and openness. Distributed ledgers, commonly referred to as blockchains, are shared and managed by numerous parties and are comprised of identical copies of sequential lists of transactions. The real data is held by consensus among several parties and is not claimed to come from a single source. For this reason, "*blockchains are referred to as decentralized*" (Engelhardt, 2017). This arrangement shields the data not only from the blockchain's individual participants but also from damaging outside interference.

Blockchain is another piece of technology that can be used to realize the idea of smart contracts. According to Reyna et al. (2018), a smart contract is a general term for computer protocols or programs that enable a contract to be automatically executed and fulfilled under a predetermined set of conditions. Shrewd contracts offer features and conditions that go beyond cryptocurrency exchanges, such as validating assets within a certain range of transactions with non-monetary elements. This provides an excellent opportunity to extend blockchain technology into other areas. According to Engelhardt (2017) and Xu et al. (2019), blockchain technology has indeed broadened beyond digital currency into other industries such as finance, healthcare, supply chain management, smart energy, and copyright protection.

The foundation of the metaverse is smart contracts with blockchains (Jeon et al., 2021). For example, cryptocurrencies connected by blockchain act as an economic bridge between the virtual and real worlds, giving people deeper social meaning. On the other hand, blockchain also provides a solution to the problem of how to protect users' digital content and data in the metadata warehouse (Huynh-The et al. 2023b). For all these reasons, blockchain, with its various characteristics such as decentralization, immutability, and transparency, offers promising solutions for the metaverse world.

Extended Reality

Extended reality refers to immersive technologies in all interactive media that provide real and virtual continuity, such as virtual reality (VR), augmented reality (AR), and mixed reality (MR) (Huynh-The et al., 2023a). Augmented reality as a metaverse technology is a kind of magnification of the outside world. It exemplifies a type of technology that extends the real physical world beyond the individual, employing a location-based system and an interface with networked information that overlays our daily perception of the world. Virtual reality, on the other hand, is a kind of metaverse that simulates the inner world. On the other hand, virtual reality is a type of metaverse that simulates the inner world. Advanced 3D graphics, avatars, and rapid communication tools are all part of virtual reality technology. Users can completely submerge themselves in this virtual reality world (Kye et al., 2021). Augmented reality provides graphics, streaming, and hologram experiences in the physical world, while virtual reality provides a fully immersive viewing experience in the digital world. Mixed reality, on the other hand, provides a transitional experience between augmented reality and virtual reality (Huynh-The et al., 2023a). Virtual reality, for example, allows users to enter the virtual environment as avatars. Augmented reality is a technology that uses computer-generated virtual content to augment the physical world's environment. The use of mixed reality enables real-world objects to carry out virtual world functions. On the other hand, the role of extended reality in creating the metaverse environment is significant (Barrera & Shah, 2023). Through the creation of immersive user experiences between augmented reality and virtual reality, extended reality uses the capabilities of artificial intelligence (AI) to improve realism.

Artificial Intelligence

According to De Bruyn et al. (2020), artificial intelligence refers to technologies that allow machines to think, learn, and behave like people. Along with technologies such as virtual reality, augmented reality, blockchain, and, artificial intelligence plays a silent but important role in establishing and developing the metaverse (Huynh-The et al., 2023a). Artificial intelligence contributes to the creation of digital twins by automatically replicating virtual world actions in the metaverse's physical world (Barrera & Shah, 2023). In the background, artificial intelligence plays a crucial role in creating the imaginative and beautiful world of the metaverse and offering users a seamless virtual reality experience. Using artificial intelligence (AI), players can recognize computer characters that are not under their control as autonomous avatars and learn to adapt their behavior based on their interactions with users (Lee et al., 2021). Users' physical movements are reflected in the virtual worlds, giving them complete control over their avatars and the convenience of interacting with other things in the metaverse. AI can build safe, scalable, and realistic virtual worlds on an always-open platform in the metaverse by fusing augmented reality and virtual reality with other technologies like blockchain and networking (Huynh-The et al., 2023a).

Interface Devices

Interacting with other metaverse objects and having an identity are both made possible by interface devices. Head-mounted displays (HMD), wearable devices like virtual reality headsets and augmented reality glasses, and fixed (desktop computers) interface devices are currently the most widely used to give users a comparable experience in the metaverse (Barrera & Shah, 2023). Recent advances in extended reality interfaces include applications for tactile cues that transfer users' sense of touch, smell, and motor movements to avatars in the virtual environment, which can be transmitted in real time. For example, the emotional glove is a human-machine interface-based glove for augmented and virtual reality applications that can recognize gestures and provide users with haptic feedback about events in the virtual world (Njoku, 2023). Head-mounted displays (HMD), on the other hand, provide direction to movements in the virtual world through head movements. Full-spectrum mixed reality headsets, tactile gloves, and sensory clothing add depth to the metaverse by allowing users to interact with others while seeing the scene, hearing the sound, and feeling the touch (Buhalis et al., 2023). Therefore, these devices can allow users to develop a unique virtual environment. Users' physical movements are reflected in virtual environments, giving them complete control over their avatars and the convenience of interacting with other items in the metaverse (Huynh-The et al., 2023a). Interface tools can help users feel more present and embodied in the metaverse, which can help users' imaginations grow (Buhalis et al., 2023a). Therefore, it is important to create a human interface for the metaverse that is equipped with various interface technologies such as tactile gloves, sensory suits, virtual reality headsets and augmented reality goggles, and other technologies.

Digital Technology and Entrepreneurship

Entrepreneurship is frequently linked to the capacity to coordinate many production factors to produce economic goods and services by taking risks and innovating to seize new opportunities arising from environmental factors (Zahra, 2005). The most important driving force of innovation and seizing new opportunities in entrepreneurship is breakthroughs in technological development. Such breakthroughs not only lead to the emergence of new entrepreneurial activities, but also change the way existing startups operate and foster the emergence of new organizational structures which are better equipped for taking advantage of the opportunities created by technological advances (Autio et al., 2018). The mutually nourishing relationship between entrepreneurship and technology dates back to ancient times. Since the late 1700s, a series of interconnected technological breakthroughs have occurred roughly every half century, radically transforming entrepreneurial activity (Autio et al., 2018). Today, the final link in this breakthrough is digital technology.

Digital technology has a wide-ranging impact on entrepreneurship. A new generation of digital conveniences is provided by digital technologies, which may also lead to new business opportunities. In this way, the activities of entrepreneurs are facilitated, and entrepreneurs can connect with their customers, integrate with market offerings, or become an integral part of their business model (Steininger, 2019). As a result, the environments in which entrepreneurial activities occur are evolving and becoming more multidimensional at the same time as digital technological advancements (Nambisan, 2017). More specifically, the emergence of new economic activities and the creation of new opportunities that have an impact on businesses are made possible by rapid advancement of digital technologies and entrepreneurship infrastructures. According to Autio et al. (2018), three fundamental opportunities supported by digitization determine both the location of entrepreneurial opportunities in the economy and the most effective methods for seizing those opportunities. First, digitization promotes the separation of form and function and, as a result, changes and possibly diminishes the determinants of asset specificity in regulating power and dependency dynamics within manufacturing value chains. Second, digitization promotes disintermediation. It increases the freedom with which product and service providers can design their operating systems by reducing the impact of intermediaries in value chains. Finally, digitalization increases productivity by coordinating geographically dispersed target groups and creating new opportunities to develop and use the platform momentum thus created. Entrepreneurial processes are thus less constrained by digitization, especially in terms of their temporal and spatial structures.

Digital technologies manifest in entrepreneurship as three separate but interconnected elements. These elements are: digital works digital infrastructure, and digital platforms (Nambisan, 2017). A "digital artifact," as defined by Kallinikos et al. (2013), is a digital element, application, or piece of media that is a component of a brand-new good or service and offers the end user a particular functionality or benefit. Digital artifacts can either be individual pieces of software or hardware running on a physical device, or they can be a part of a larger ecosystem on a digital platform. According to Nambisan (2017), digital artifacts are present in a variety of products besides smartphones and other personal electronics, such as toys, clothing, shoes, and automobiles. A digital platform, according to Parker et al. (2016), is defined as a shared group of buildings and services that are used to house complementary goods, such as digital artifacts. Platforms such as Google's Android and Apple's iOS can be cited as examples. Digital platforms have given entrepreneurs many opportunities to produce complementary goods and services (Nambisan, 2017). The last point is that, in contrast to digital platforms, digital infrastructure offers computing, communication, and collaboration capabilities to support innovation and entrepreneurship. Examples include social media, online communities, 3D printing, cloud computing, data analytics, digital production spaces, and more. Such digital infrastructures help to democratize entrepreneurship by enabling participation of a wider and broader spectrum of people at all phases of the entrepreneurial process (Nambisan, 2017). The emergence of new digital infrastructure supports overall business operations. As a result, both in terms of the final product and the actual process, digital technologies are increasingly becoming a part of entrepreneurial opportunities.

How the new digital technologies support entrepreneurship is a topic that researchers are becoming more and more interested in (Nambisan, 2017; Steininger, 2019). In recent years, the metaverse has come to the forefront in the digital world with the possibilities and opportunities it offers users and businesses in both the virtual and physical worlds. Although metaverse entrepreneurship and digital entrepreneurship have many similarities, there are some differences that call for extra consideration, such as the blending of the virtual and physical worlds (Weking et al., 2023).

Metaverse and Entrepreneurship

Traditional models and approaches to entrepreneurship assume that there are relatively stable and fixed boundaries around entrepreneurial opportunities. (Nambisan, 2017). The seamless transition between the virtual and actual worlds in the unbounded space of the metaverse can change this assumption (Gursoy et al., 2022). The metaverse can almost realistically represent a physical world in a virtual world, but at the same time it seamlessly integrates the virtual world with the physical world. With this feature, the metaverse provides an immersive and permanent digital infrastructure that hosts more than a virtual world and supports entrepreneurs with technologies that enable the creation, sharing, and consumption of all types of digital works consisting of products, services, or experiences (Weking et al., 2023). By establishing a fully immersive, profoundly transformative online environment, metaverse enhances interaction between the virtual and physical worlds. This is not only the interaction of people and avatars, but also enabling new business models to emerge in terms of reconnecting real-world businesses (Shen et al., 2021). As the boundaries between the physical and digital worlds become increasingly blurred, the potential impact of the metaverse on the way we do business, interact with others and institutions, and create shared experiences could be profound (Dwivedi et al. 2022). This transformative impact will be evident across multiple dimensions of the business and offer entrepreneurs a wide range of entrepreneurial opportunities.

Many research and industry reports address expectations for the metaverse and attempt to demonstrate its business potential. In a study of senior executives by consulting firm PwC (PricewaterhouseCoopers), 46% of respondents said the metaverse is very important to their innovation strategy. The study estimates that by 2030, consultants and corporate industry observers expect the market for the metaverse to grow from hundreds of billions to trillions of dollars (Pratt, 2022). One of the many anticipated benefits is this tremendous economic potential. The CEO of Nvidia, Jensen Huang, predicted that the metaverse economy would surpass the size of the "real" economy (Worsley, 2021). All things considered; it is obvious that the metaverse will offer business owners a variety of new ventures.

Numerous multinational corporations have already taken notice of the Metaverse's business potential and are making investments there. Republic Realm, a New York-based company, invested a record-breaking $4.3 million in Metaverse real estate through The Sandbox in December 2021. Just before setting this record, the Canadian business Tokens.com spent $2.4 million on digital real estate on the Decentraland Metaverse platform (Seow, 2021). In parallel, it is evident from various digital news sources that many companies and entrepreneurs have started running their businesses in the metaverse. Samsung, Disney, McDonald's, Nike, Wir Asia, Rans Entertainment, PT Bank Rakyat Indonesia (Persero), and PT Bank Negara Indonesia (Persero) are some of the national and international companies operating in the metaverse (Samad & Hasan 2022).

Not just small, medium, or large businesses, but possibly everyone, could be impacted by the metaverse (Seow, 2021). According to Dwivedi et al. (2022), scalable and simultaneous experiences will inspire users of the metaverse to enrich their thoughts and fantasies by combining their fantasies and knowledge from different sources.

The most striking thing about the metaverse is its emphasis on ownership. Users can share in almost everything. They can vote on decisions about the communities they belong to and the applications they use. They can monetize, sell, rent, and even lend their digital assets. According to this viewpoint, user ownership represents a real revolution because it develops a new economy (Stackpole, 2022). But so far, it is unclear how the metaverse will work and what it will look like. In other words, it is difficult to say exactly what entrepreneurial opportunities will emerge because there are so many unknowns (Worsley, 2021). However, some predictions can be made by looking at the current trend. These potential business opportunities that the metaverse will create for entrepreneurs are discussed below.

New Business Opportunities in Metaverse

By providing more opportunities and diverse experiences than the real world, the metaverse can inspire the next generation of entrepreneurs (Weking et al., 2023). Several researchers have investigated the potential of the metaverse (Buhalis et al., 2023; Chengoden et al., 2023; Dwivedi et al., 2022; Enache, 2022). These studies have discussed the potential transformative and ameliorative impacts of the metaverse on collaborative work, education, tourism, marketing, and health services. Researches show that consumer uses of the metaverse are expanding in retail, entertainment, sports, health, tourism, and education experiences. Expectations for the metaverse are very high. These expectations are largely due to the ability to conduct business operations presently carried out in dissimilar and scattered domains in a single common domain as well as the viability of many business opportunities in the Metaverse (Enache, 2022). Potential business activities in the metaverse universe can be described as follows (Enache, 2022; Weston, 2022):

- Shopping in virtual retail stores and malls,
- Purchasing clothing, accessories, and other items for digital avatars,
- Purchasing digital art, assets, and collectibles as non-fungible tokens (NFTs),

- Interacting with users as digital avatars for customer service, employee retention, sales, service, and many other business communications,
- Creating and participating in virtual social experiences
- Developing digital real estate products such as virtual real estate purchases and virtual homes
- Creating or participating in virtual classrooms to create a unique learning experience

These features can all assist business owners in identifying and expanding metaverse business opportunities. The metaverse can promise more thanks to its high-tech features and large audience.

***Digital Product Design*:** The metaverse is a complex virtual and augmented reality experience where users can connect, play, and exchange transactions. With this aspect, it is an opportunity for entrepreneurs to reach a larger audience, identify their digital footprint, and leverage the earning potential (Mileva, 2022). A new platform called Metaverse may be essential for deciphering consumer culture and user behavior using novel techniques and metrics. Instead of being merely auxiliary players in a centralized platform ecosystem, entrepreneurs in the metaverse can actively shape their surroundings and monetize their own content (Weking et al., 2023). Entrepreneurs will have new opportunities to connect with their existing and potential customers thanks to the metaverse. With its different tools and functions, the metadata repository supports entrepreneurs create proposals that seem impossible in the actual world. Since the laws of nature do not apply in the virtual world, entrepreneurs can be extremely inventive and creative when designing unique products that go beyond the boundaries of the real world (Dwivedi, 2022a). Entrepreneurs can create value for their users with unique experiences. This includes creating virtual stores for extravagant or exclusive fashion and designing accessories for virtual events, art, and avatars (Weking et al., 2023). Many well-known brands (such as Gucci, Nike, Forever 21, etc.) have already entered the metaverse market by creating digital versions of their products. An analysis of marketing prospects in the Metaverse published recently highlights that sales of virtual goods through direct transactions with avatars will reach a $54 billion market by 2022 (Hazan et al., 2012). Recently, Samsung has opened its first Metaverse store, where the company showcases its digital products. Since its opening, Samsung's digital store has welcomed more than 120,000 customers (Mileva, 2022).

***Create a Unique Shopping Experience*:** The metaverse encompasses the entire social and economic structures of the real and virtual worlds (Petrigna & Musumeci, 2022). The metaverse provides users with not only the ability to interact with others but also an immersive three-dimensional experience of products and services. There are countless ways to display goods in the metaverse, including showing how tools or machines function, how clothing fits and appears on people, and how to interact with museums and other attractions (Seow, 2021). E-commerce companies can take advantage of the opportunity the metaverse provides to create captivating shopping experiences for their users as well as collect data on shopper behavior (Enache, 2022). One of the main factors limiting online shopping today is the customer's inability to try the product before purchasing it (Barta et al., 2023). Metaverse can provide a radical solution to this problem. In parallel with the deveoping interface technologies that underpin the metaverse universe, companies may be able to place kiosks in shopping malls, transportation hubs, and other high-traffic areas that provide highly accurate professional 3D scans to create metaverse avatars of customers' bodies (Seow, 2021). This allows customers to have an outfit they like tailored with an avatar that fits their body perfectly and see how they will look in the outfit.

***Designing Virtual Experiences*:** Businesses connect and interact with their customers in fresh and novel ways by using experiences that resemble metaverses (Pratt, 2022). The metaverse provides significant marketing and customer relationship opportunities for companies while saving customers time and money. At the 2022 World Economic Forum (WEF), it was emphasized that one of the most significant sectors that could gain from the metaverse is tourism. The possibilities for transforming traditional lodging and tourism offerings into virtual experiences are virtually unlimited in the Metaverse universe (Gursoy et al., 2022). The metaverse can allow tourists to experience the service environments of hotels and restaurants before purchasing them (Buhalis et al., 2023). Individuals can experience visiting a volcano, a landmark, or a museum at one end of the world or attending a concert or art event without being physically present (Gursoy et al., 2022). A recent study showed that more than 84% of consumers in different parts of the world are interested in using augmented reality or virtual reality for their travel experience, and 42% think it will shape tourism in the future (Buhalis & Karatay, 2022). Entrepreneurs have recognized this and begun to direct their investments into this area. For example, hotel groups such as Hotel Corporation have begun to develop virtual hotels to interact with different-minded hotel customers (Buhalis et al., 2023).

The phrase "metaverse" describes a virtual reality that exists outside of reality. The virtual experiences that people can have in this virtual reality universe are unlimited. In the metaverse, millions of people can come together to plan a festival, go to a concert by a favorite artist, or engage in any other kind of virtual activity (Kye et al., 2021). Moreover, before making a purchase, people can visit and view a real-time property in real time, so they can be sure of various criteria. In this way, real estate agents and buyers can save time and money (Howell, 2022).

***Designing a Unique Learning Environment*:** The application of metaverse technology in the field of education has gained significant momentum recently among promising metaverse business ideas. The metaverse could revolutionize education and skill development and dramatically reduce the time required to develop and acquire new skills (Purdy, 2022). The metaverse technology can be applied in a variety of fields, including higher education, the military, and medical education, to provide more immersive learning experiences (Weston, 2022). Students can benefit from an immersive learning environment where they can interact at a high level and engage in collaborative learning through the use of the metaverse. The metaverse can assist students in learning more effectively by allowing them to analyze how to use information in different scenarios and it can assist educators in creating metaverse teaching procedures (Tlili et al., 2022).

Disadvantages and Risks of Metaverse

Along with so many new opportunities for entrepreneurs in the metaverse, there are also risks and challenges. In addition to all these tremendous benefits, the metaverse also poses some significant risks. The challenges that entrepreneurs may face can be divided into economic, technological, consumer, legal, and ethical challenges (Buhalis et al., 2023). It remains unclear whether the metadata repository will be centralized or distributed. Because there are so many metaverse platforms, entrepreneurs may potentially encounter strategic difficulties, such choosing which metaverse to join (Dwivedi et al., 2022b). Technological challenges may arise because the metaverse is still largely conceptual and not practical. Metadata repositories are slowly evolving, and some businesses are taking small steps to explore their virtual assets (Buhalis et al., 2023). Because metadata repositories are still in the making, there are no recipes for solving potential problems. Therefore, solutions to potential problems can be risky and expensive.

Another important limitation is economic and based on user experience. The fact that metaverse technology is not at a level that is reasonably accessible to everyone in the world is a significant problem (Buhalis et al., 2023; WEF, 2022). Numerous businesses across the globe lack the financial resources to invest in metaverse technologies. Similarly, most individuals and organizations will lack the interface technologies needed to access the metaverse universe. It will take time for these technologies to become cheaper. The high purchase cost of the equipment may exclude many organizations and potential users from the system. As a result, individuals, as well as businesses, will need to budget for initial investments in order to participate in the metaverse universe (Buhalis et al., 2023). However, it should not be forgotten that it is always highly beneficial for individuals and institutions to be pioneers in digital transformation. On the other hand, overdependence on users and overuse of the meta-universe can lead to significant social impacts (WEF, 2022). Individuals may take shelter in the metaverse universe to escape the difficulties of real life. when people attempt to utilize the metaverse as an escape from their real-life suffering, it can lead to more addictive behaviors. Excessive playing virtual games and participation in digital activities can increase abuse and addiction (Buhalis et al., 2023).

One of the issues entrepreneurs should consider when entering the metaverse universe is its legal and ethical challenges. Legal challenges in the metaverse may include crimes such as fraud, money laundering, terrorist financing, drugs, illegal gambling, cybercrime, prostitution, and child abuse (Qin et al., 2022). Another important problem is ensuring the confidentiality of data. The metaverse is closely connected to the actual world and corresponds to a real identity. Confidentiality and security of user data are the most important problems in the real world (Yemenici, 2022). The potential for data collection in the metaverse repository is significantly greater than that of the current Internet (WEF, 2022). In order to ensure the privacy and security of customer data, businesses may need to make sizable investments (Yemenici, 2022). Companies are likely to collaborate in the future to create one or more metaverses.

Impact of Metaverse on Employee Equality and Diversity

The metaverse is expected to change not only the demand for digital products and services, but also the way we live and work (Momtaz, 2022). Communication and collaboration are fundamental metaverse virtues. For example, users can collaborate and share their experiences through their avatars (Dwivedi et al., 2022a). The metaverse's ability to provide collaborative and socially satisfying experiences, as well as face-to-face interactions, will enable companies to create a diverse and dispersed workforce around the world (Lawton, 2022). This demonstrates that employees from different parts of the world with different cultures can work together on the same project. Through such collaboration and sharing, new value is created. Through this collaboration, people are able to transcend time and space, which is unlike in the real world. It also gives employees a common goal and allows them to work as a team in the metaverse. Thus, the metaverse's remote work options could help integrate global labor markets and lower barriers to working in high-wage countries (Dwivedi et al., 2022b). UK-based PixelMax, for example, is a platform designed to improve team cohesion, employee wellbeing, and collaboration and to help companies create immersive work environments. Andy Sands, co-founder of the company, says its main vision is to connect different virtual workplaces. For a group of 40 top interior manufacturers in Manchester, England, the business is currently constructing a virtual workplace (Purdy, 2022). This can enrich employee diversity by allowing employees with different skills and cultures to work in different locations within the same environment. Employees will be able to collaborate as though they were all in the same room thanks to the metaverse's promise to replicate social interactions in the real world and represent physical objects in three dimensions (Momtaz, 2022). New metaverse experiences can make collaboration even better than in the real world (Lawton, 2022). Companies may push the limits on employee diversity as employee work practices like collaboration and interaction become more prevalent in the metaverse universe (WEF, 2022). The leading companies that are aware of this are already taking initiatives. The immersive avatar-based virtual reality platform NextMeet is based in India and specializes in interactive working, collaboration, and learning solutions. Its goal is to stop the isolation and labor shortages that can come from employees working remotely or in a hybrid environment. Using their avatars, staff members can give live presentations from booths, visit a virtual help desk, and enter and exit virtual offices and meeting rooms on this platform (Purdy, 2022).

Another impact of the metaverse on companies is their decision-making behavior. The metaverse can significantly improve the decision-making and operational efficiency of companies. It is difficult to develop sufficiently accurate mathematical models to analyze real-world, enterprise, or human behavior (Wang et al., 2022). It is therefore very challenging to predict the behavior of consumers, employees, or competing companies, to control their development, and to study them empirically. Therefore, when analyzing complex systems such as societies and people, the traditional "one-world view" no longer works and the "multi-world view" must be adopted (Wang et al., 2022).

Companies can make more accurate decisions by designing experiments with different alternatives, creating simulations of the decision situation before making a decision. This can help companies continuously optimize their decisions and more accurately determine future development directions. It can also create a more participative management style by incorporating more employees into decision-making. The Metaverse can be quite significant in ensuring employee equality, especially in companies that have employees who prefer to work in fulfilling jobs rather than financially rewarding ones, such as Generation Z.

FUTURE RESEARCH DIRECTIONS

The Metaverse is a future world whose foundations are being laid today. It is difficult to predict the direction in which this ecosystem, still in its formative stages, will evolve. However, it seems to be an undeniable fact for mankind that this new change will be experienced as in previous technological revolutions. This new world will bring opportunities and threats that will radically change the way we currently work and do business. Advances in artificial intelligence and virtual reality technologies are accelerating this change. For the metaverse ecosystem to function properly, its potential opportunities must be made clear to all, and its threats must be mitigated.

This study has focused specifically on the potential opportunities that the Metaverse can create for entrepreneurs and managers. Future research could focus on the threats that this new world may pose to individuals, consumers, and businesses. In this way, the potential threats that the metaverse may bring can be reduced and a more livable and healthier ecosystem for individuals, organizations, and societies can be created.

CONCLUSION

Entrepreneurship is one of the areas that are most rapidly affected by technological developments. The essence of entrepreneurship is seizing opportunities. The age of digital transformation we live in is called the metaverse. It is very important to anticipate the opportunities that the metaverse can create and seize new business opportunities. This study attempted to analyze the literature on the advantages and challenges that entrepreneurs may face in the Metaverse universe.

The term "metaverse" refers to virtual worlds that function synchronously with the actual world. This new world order holds many opportunities. The metaverse has the potential to have an impact on many industries, including marketing, healthcare, and education. Numerous innovations are brought about by metaverse, including the ability to design digital goods, launch online shops, and set up virtual organizations. With the opportunities it creates, it is attracting the attention of new entrepreneurs. While many entrepreneurs have started to invest in the Metaverse universe, many more are trying to do so.

Although not as many as the opportunities it offers for entrepreneurs, the metaverse universe does present some challenges and risks. Some of these difficulties stem from technological problems; others arise from user experiences and ethical and legal violations. Despite all these obstacles, the metaverse universe continues to create new opportunities for entrepreneurs. Entrepreneurs who are interested in taking advantage of these opportunities can gain an edge over rivals by taking the lead.

REFERENCES

Allal-Chérif, O. (2022). Intelligent cathedrals: Using augmented reality, virtual reality, and artificial intelligence to provide an intense cultural, historical, and religious visitor experience. *Technological Forecasting and Social Change*, *178*, 121604. doi:10.1016/j.techfore.2022.121604

Allbeck, J. M., & Badler, N. I. (1998). Avatars agrave/ la snow crash. *Proceedings Computer Animation* '98 (Cat. No.98EX169), 19-24. doi:10.1109/CA.1998.681903

Autio, E., Nambisan, S., Thomas, L. D., & Wright, M. (2018). Digital affordances, spatial affordances, and the genesis of entrepreneurial ecosystems. *Strategic Entrepreneurship Journal, 12*(1), 72–95. doi:10.1002ej.1266

Bansgopaul, N. (2021). What is Web 3.0 and why should you care?: If you understand the benefits of decentralization, it's time to recognize the importance of Web 3.0. *Newsweek*, https://www.newsweek.com/what-web-30-why-should-youcare-1627 250

Barrera, K. G., & Shah, D. (2023). Marketing in the metaverse: Conceptual understanding, framework, and research agenda. *Journal of Business Research, 155*, 113420. doi:10.1016/j.jbusres.2022.113420

Barta, S., Gurrea, R., & Flavián, C. (2023). How augmented reality increases engagement through its impact on risk and the decision process. *Cyberpsychology, Behavior, and Social Networking*, *26*(3), 177–187. doi:10.1089/cyber.2022.0087 PMID:36706429

Beliaeva, T., Ferasso, M., Kraus, S., & Damke, E. J. (2020). Dynamics of digital entrepreneurship and the innovation ecosystem: A multilevel perspective. *International Journal of Entrepreneurial Behaviour & Research*, *26*(2), 266–284. doi:10.1108/IJEBR-06-2019-0397

Buhalis, D., & Karatay, N. (2022). Mixed reality (mr) for generation z in cultural heritage tourism towards metaverse. Stienmetz, J.L., Ferrer-Rosell, B., Massimo, D. (eds) Information and Communication Technologies in Tourism 2022. ENTER 2022. Springer. doi:10.1007/978-3-030-94751-4_2

Buhalis, D., Leung, D., & Lin, M. (2023). Metaverse as a disruptive technology revolutionising tourism management and marketing. *Tourism Management*, *97*, 104724. doi:10.1016/j.tourman.2023.104724

Caulfield, B. (2021). What is the metaverse? *The official nvidia blog* https://blogs.nvidia.com/blog/2021/08/10/what-is-the-metaver se/

Chengoden, R., Victor, N., Huynh-The, T., Yenduri, G., Jhaveri, R. H., Alazab, M., Bhattacharya, S., Hegde, P., Maddikunta, P. R. K., & Gadekallu, T. R. (2023). Metaverse for healthcare: A survey on potential applications, challenges and future directions. IEEE Access, 4. IEEE. https://doi.org/ doi:10.48550/arXiv.2209.04160

Collins, B. (2021). The Metaverse: How to Build a Massive Virtual World. *Forbes*. https://www.forbes.com/sites/barrycollins/2021/09/25/the-met averse-how-to-build-a-massive-virtual-world/?sh=60735bad6d1c

Davis, A., Murphy, J., Owens, D., Khazanchi, D., & Zigurs, I. (2009). Avatars, people, and virtual worlds: Foundations for research in metaverses. *Journal of the Association for Information Systems, 10*(2), 1. https://aisel.aisnet.org/jais/vol10/iss2/1. doi:10.17705/1jais.00183

De Bruyn, A., Viswanathan, V., Beh, Y. S., Brock, J. K. U., & Von Wangenheim, F. (2020). Artificial intelligence and marketing: Pitfalls and opportunities. *Journal of Interactive Marketing*, *51*(1), 91–105. doi:10.1016/j.intmar.2020.04.007

Dionisio, J. D. N., Borns, W. G. III, & Gilbert, R. (2013). 3D virtual worlds and the metaverse: Current status and future possibilities. [CSUR]. *ACM Computing Surveys*, *45*(3), 1–38. doi:10.1145/2480741.2480751

Duan, H., Li, J., Fan, S., Lin, Z., Wu, X., & Cai, W. (2021). Metaverse for social good: A university campus prototype. *In Proceedings of the 29th ACM international conference on multimedia* (pp. 153-161). ACM. 10.1145/3474085.3479238

Dwivedi, Y. K., Hughes, L., Baabdullah, A. M., Ribeiro-Navarrete, S., Giannakis, M., Al-Debei, M. M., Dennehy, D., Metri, B., Buhalis, D., Cheung, C. M. K., Conboy, K., Doyle, R., Dubey, R., Dutot, V., Felix, R., Goyal, D. P., Gustafsson, A., Hinsch, C., Jebabli, I., & Wamba, S. F. (2022b). Metaverse beyond the hype: Multidisciplinary perspectives on emerging challenges, opportunities, and agenda for research, practice and policy. *International Journal of Information Management*, *66*, 102542. doi:10.1016/j.ijinfomgt.2022.102542

Dwivedi, Y. K., Hughes, L., Wang, Y., Alalwan, A. A., Ahn, S. J., Balakrishnan, J., Barta, S., Belk, R., Buhalis, D., Dutot, V., Felix, R., Filieri, R., Flavián, C., Gustafsson, A., Hinsch, C., Hollensen, S., Jain, V., Kim, J., Krishen, A. S., & Wirtz, J. (2022a). Metaverse marketing: How the metaverse will shape the future of consumer research and practice. *Psychology and Marketing*. doi:10.1002/mar.21767

Enache, M. C. (2022). Metaverse Opportunities for Businesses. *Annals of the University Dunarea de Jos of Galati: Fascicle: I. Economics & Applied Informatics*, *28*(1), 67–71. doi:10.35219/eai15840409246

Engelhardt, M. A. (2017). Hitching healthcare to the chain: An Introduction to blockchain technology in the healthcare sector. *Technology Innovation Management Review*, *7*(10), 22–34. doi:10.22215/timreview/1111

Entrepreneur. (2023) *What is the metaverse and why is it important to entrepreneurs?* Entrepreneur. https://www.entrepreneur.com/science-technology/what-is-the-metaverse-and-why-is-it-important-to/442015

Ferreira, J. J. M., Fernandes, C. I., & Ferreira, F. A. F. (2019). To be or not to be digital that is the question: Firm innovation and performance. *Journal of Business Research, 101*, 583–590. doi:10.1016/j.jbusres.2018.11.013

Frey, D., Royan, J., Piegay, R., Kermarrec, A. M., Anceaume, E., & Le Fessant, F. (2008). *Solipsis: A decentralized architecture for virtual environments.* [Paper presentation] 1st International Workshop on Massively Multiuser Virtual Environments. Reno, NV, United States.

Gkritsi, E. (2022). HSBC enters the metaverse through partnership with the sandbox. *Coindesk.* https://www.coindesk.com/business/2022/03/16/hsbc-enters-the-metaverse-through-partnership-with-the-sandbox/

Go, S. Y., Jeong, H. G., Kim, J. I., & Sin, Y. T. (2021). Concept and developmental direction of metaverse. *Korea Inf Process Soc Rev*, *28*, 7–16.

Gümüş, A., & Erkuş, H. (2019). Blockchain ve kripto paraların kullanımı üzerine bir değerlendirme [An assessment on the use of blockchain and cryptocurrencies]. *Anemon Muş Alparslan Üniversitesi Sosyal Bilimler Dergisi*, *7*(2), 41–49. doi:10.18506/anemon.427976

Gürcü, A. (2022). *Metavers nedir ne değildir*?[What is metaverse and what is it not?]. Insaniyet. https://www.insaniyet.net/metavers-nedir-ne-degildir

Gursoy, D., Malodia, S., & Dhir, A. (2022). The metaverse in the hospitality and tourism industry: An overview of current trends and future research directions. *Journal of Hospitality Marketing & Management*, *31*(5), 527–534. doi:10.1080/19368623.2022.2072504

Hafezieh, N., Akhavan, P., & Eshraghian, F. (2011). Exploration of Process and Competitive Factors of Entrepreneurship in Digital Space: A Multiple Case Study in Iran. *Education, Business and Society*, *4*(4), 267–279. doi:10.1108/17537981111190051

Hazan, E., Kelly, G., Khan, H., Spillecke, D., & Yee, L. (2022). *Marketing in the metaverse: An opportunity for innovation and experimentation.* McKinsey. https://www.mckinsey.com/capabilities/growth-marketing-and-sales/our-insights/marketing-in-the-metaverse-an-opportunity-for-innovation-and-experimentation

Howell, J. (2022). *Top 5 Metaverse Applications.* 101 Bloackchains. https://101blockchains.com/top-metaverse-applications/

Huynh-The, T., Gadekallu, T. R., Wang, W., Yenduri, G., Ranaweera, P., Pham, Q. V., Costa, D. B., & Liyanage, M. (2023b). Blockchain for the metaverse: A Review. *Future Generation Computer Systems, 143*, 401–419. doi:10.1016/j.future.2023.02.008

Huynh-The, T., Pham, Q. V., Pham, X. Q., Nguyen, T. T., Han, Z., & Kim, D. S. (2023a). Artificial intelligence for the metaverse: A survey. *Engineering Applications of Artificial Intelligence, 117*, 105581. doi:10.1016/j.engappai.2022.105581

Jeon, H. J., Youn, H. C., Ko, S. M., & Kim, T. H. (2022). Blockchain and AI Meet in the Metaverse. *Advances in the Convergence of Blockchain and Artificial Intelligence, 73*(10.5772). https://www.intechopen.com/chapters/77823

Kallinikos, J., Aaltonen, A., & Marton, A. (2013). The ambivalent ontology of digital artifacts. *Management Information Systems Quarterly, 37*(2), 357–370. https://www.jstor.org/stable/43825913. doi:10.25300/MISQ/2013/37.2.02

Kim, J. (2021). Advertising in the Metaverse: Research Agenda. *Journal of Interactive Advertising, 21*(3), 141–144. doi:10.1080/15252019.2021.2001273

Kollmann, T. (2006). What is e-entrepreneurship? Fundamentals of company founding in the net economy. *International Journal of Technology Management, 33*(4), 322–340. doi:10.1504/IJTM.2006.009247

Kye, B., Han, N., Kim, E., Park, Y., & Jo, S. (2021). Educational applications of metaverse: Possibilities and limitations. *Journal of Educational Evaluation for Health Professions, 18*, 1149230. doi:10.3352/jeehp.2021.18.32 PMID:34897242

Laeeq, K. (2022). *Metaverse: Why, how and what.* Research Gate. https://www.researchgate.net/profile/Kashif-Laeeq/publication/358505001_Metaverse_Why_How_and_What/links/62053bb0afa8884cabd70210/Metaverse-Why-How-and-What.pdf

Lawton, G. (2022). *How will the metaverse affect the future of work?* Tech Target. https://www.techtarget.com/searchcio/tip/How-will-the-metaverse-affect-the-future-of-work

Lee, L. H., Braud, T., Zhou, P., Wang, L., Xu, D., Lin, Z., Kumar, A., Bermejo, C., & Hui, P. (2021). All one needs to know about metaverse: A complete survey on technological singularity, virtual ecosystem, and research agenda. https://doi.org/doi:10.48550/arXiv.2110.05352

Lee, S., & Han, S. H. (2021). *Metaverse begins: Five issues and perspectives.* SPRI. https://spri.kr/posts/view/23197?code=issue_reports

Mileva, G. (2022). *20 Brands Leaping into the Metaverse.* Influencer Market Hub. https://influencermarketinghub.com/metaverse-brands/

Momtaz, P. P. (2022). Some very simple economics of web3 and the metaverse. *FinTech, 1*(3), 225–234. doi:10.3390/fintech1030018

Mystakidis, S. (2022). Metaverse. *Encyclopedia*, *2*(1), 486–497. doi:10.3390/encyclopedia2010031

Nakamoto, S. (2008). Bitcoin: A peer-to-peer electronic cash system. *SSRN*, *21260*. doi:10.2139srn.3440802

Nambisan, S. (2017). Digital Entrepreneurship: Toward a Digital Technology Perspective of Entrepreneurship. *Entrepreneurship Theory and Practice*, *41*(6), 1029 1055. doi:10.1111/etap.12254

Nevelsteen, K. J. (2018). Virtual world, defined from a technological perspective and applied to video games, mixed reality, and the metaverse. *Computer Animation and Virtual Worlds*, *29*(1), e1752. doi:10.1002/cav.1752

Njoku, J. N., Nwakanma, C. I., Amaizu, G. C., & Kim, D. S. (2023). Prospects and challenges of Metaverse application in data-driven intelligent transportation systems. *IET Intelligent Transport Systems*, *17*(1), 1–21. doi:10.1049/itr2.12252

Parker, G., Van Alstyne, M., & Choudary, S. P. (2016). *Platform revolution: How networked markets are transforming the economy–and how to make them work for you*. Norton & Company.

Perlin, K., & Goldberg, A. (1996). Improv: A system for scripting interactive actors in virtual worlds. In *Proceedings of the 23rd annual conference on Computer graphics and interactive techniques* (pp. 205-216). Association for Computing Machinery. 10.1145/237170.237258

Petrigna, L., & Musumeci, G. (2022). The metaverse: A new challenge for the healthcare system: A scoping review. *Journal of Functional Morphology and Kinesiology*, *7*(3), 63. doi:10.3390/jfmk7030063 PMID:36135421

Pratt, M. K. (2022). *Metaverse pros and cons: Top benefits and challenges*. Tech Target. https://www.techtarget.com/searchcio/tip/Metaverse-pros-and-cons-Top-benefits-and-challenges

Purdy, M. (2022). *How the metaverse could change work*. HBR. https://hbr.org/2022/04/how-the-metaverse-could-change-work

Qin, H. X., Wang, Y., & Hui, P. (2022). *Identity, crimes, and law enforcement in the metaverse*. https://doi.org//arXiv.2210.06134 doi:10.48550

Rai, R. (2022). An overview of Web3 venture capital activity in 2021. *Forbes*. https://www.forbes.com/sites/rahulrai/2022/01/02/an-overview-of-web3-venture-capital-activity-in-2021/?sh=631611601f16

Ravi, R. (2022) *Skechers joins the metaverse, planning to open a store in decentraland*. NFT Evening. https://nftevening.com/skechers-joins-the-metaverse-planning-to-open-a-store-in-decentraland/

Reyna, A., Martín, C., Chen, J., Soler, E., & Díaz, M. (2018). On blockchain and its integration with IoT. Challenges and opportunities. *Future Generation Computer Systems*, *88*, 173–190. doi:10.1016/j.future.2018.05.046

Samad, T. F. D., & Hasan, N. (2022). Women entrepreneurs in the era of metaverse: An Islamic economic perspective. *Review of Islamic Social Finance and Entrepreneurship*, 131-140. https:// doi:10.20885/RISFE.vol1.iss2.art5

Satalkina, L., & Steiner, G. (2020). Digital entrepreneurship and its role in innovation systems: A systematic literature review as a basis for future research avenues for sustainable transitions. *Sustainability (Basel)*, *12*(7), 2764. doi:10.3390u12072764

Seow, J. H. I. (2021). Metaverse: A Game-changing innovation for entrepreneurs, entrepreneur, 2021. *Entrepreenuer.* https://www.entrepreneur.com/en-in/technology/metaverse-a-game-changing-innovation-for-entrepreneurs/403080

Shen, K. N., Lindsay, V., & Xu, Y. (2018). Digital entrepreneurship. *Information Systems Journal*, *28*(6), 1125–1128. doi:10.1111/isj.12219

Smart, J., Cascio, J., Paffendorf, J., Bridges, C., Hummel, J., Hursthouse, J., & Moss, R. (2007). *Metaverse Roadmap Overview.* W3. https://www.w3.org/2008/WebVideo/Annotations/wiki/images/1/19/MetaverseRoadmapOverview.pdf

Stackpole, T. (2022). Exploring the metaverse. *Harvard Business Review*. https://hbr.org/2022/07/exploring-the-metaverse

Steininger, D. M. (2019). Linking information systems and entrepreneurship: A review and agenda for IT-associated and digital entrepreneurship research. *Information Systems Journal*, *29*(2), 363–407. doi:10.1111/isj.12206

Stephenson, N. (1992). *Snow crash: A novel*. Spectra.

Tlili, A., Huang, R., Shehata, B., Liu, D., Zhao, J., Metwally, A. H. S., Wang, H., Denden, M., Bozkurt, A., Lee, L. H., Beyoglu, D., Altinay, F., Sharma, R. C., Altinay, Z., Li, Z., Liu, J., Ahmad, F., Hu, Y., Salha, S., & Burgos, D. (2022). Is Metaverse in education a blessing or a curse: A combined content and bibliometric analysis. *Smart Learning Environments*, *9*(1), 1–31. doi:10.118640561-022-00205-x

Türkmen, S. Y., & Durbilmez, S. E. (2019). Blockchain teknolojisi ve Türkiye finans sektöründeki durumu. [Blockchain technology and its situation in the Turkish financial sector]. *Finans Ekonomi ve Sosyal Araştırmalar Dergisi*, *4*(1), 30–45. doi:10.29106/fesa.509254

Wang, F. Y., Qin, R., Wang, X., & Hu, B. (2022). Metasocieties in metaverse: Metaeconomics and metamanagement for metaenterprises and metacities. *IEEE Transactions on Computational Social Systems*, *9*(1), 2–7. doi:10.1109/TCSS.2022.3145165

Weking, J., Desouza, K. C., Fielt, E., & Kowalkiewicz, M. (2023). Metaverse-enabled entrepreneurship. *Journal of Business Venturing Insights*, *19*, e00375. doi:10.1016/j.jbvi.2023.e00375

Weston, G. (2022). *5 Profitable business opportunities in metaverse.* 101 Blockchains. https://101blockchains.com/business-opportunities-in-metaverse/

World Economic Forum. (2022). *How the metaverse can be a force for good in an uncertain world.* WEF. https://www.weforum.org/agenda/2022/05/how-metaverse-can-be-a-force-for-good-in-an-uncertain-world/

Worsley, B. (2021) For entrepreneurs, the metaverse is already here. *Medium.* https://medium.com/masterplans/for-entrepreneurs-the-metaverse-is-already-here-78909ffb405e

Wright, M., Ekeus, H., Coyne, R., Stewart, J., Travlou, P., & Williams, R. (2008). Augmented duality: overlapping a metaverse with the real world. *In Proceedings of the 2008 International Conference on Advances in Computer Entertainment Technology*, (pp. 263–266). ACM. 10.1145/1501750.1501812

Xu, M., Chen, X., & Kou, G. (2019). A systematic review of blockchain. *Financial Innovation*, *5*(1), 1–14. doi:10.118640854-019-0147-z

Yemenici, A. D. (2022). Entrepreneurship in the world of Metaverse: Virtual or real? *Journal of Metaverse*, *2*(2), 71–82. doi:10.57019/jmv.1126135

Zahra, S. A. (2005). Entrepreneurial risk taking in family firms. *Family Business Review*, *18*(1), 23–40. doi:10.1111/j.1741-6248.2005.00028.x

ADDITIONAL READING

Caboni, F., & Pizzichini, L. (2023). Smart Extended Reality in the Metaverse-Tailing: The Rise of New Retail Landscape. In *Augmented Reality and Artificial Intelligence: The Fusion of Advanced Technologies* (pp. 307–321). Springer Nature Switzerland. doi:10.1007/978-3-031-27166-3_17

Mohamed, E. S., Naqishbandi, T. A., & Veronese, G. (2023). Metaverse!: Possible Potential Opportunities and Trends in E-Healthcare and Education. [IJEA]. *International Journal of E-Adoption*, *15*(2), 1–21. doi:10.4018/IJEA.316537

Schöbel, S. M., & Leimeister, J. M. (2023). Metaverse platform ecosystems. *Electronic Markets*, *33*(1), 12. doi:10.100712525-023-00623-w

Sebastian, G. (2022). A Study on Metaverse Awareness, Cyber Risks, and Steps for Increased Adoption. [IJSPPC]. *International Journal of Security and Privacy in Pervasive Computing*, *14*(1), 1–11. doi:10.4018/IJSPPC.308785

Singla, A., Gupta, N., Aeron, P., Jain, A., Garg, R., Sharma, D., Gupta, B. B., & Arya, V. (2022). Building the Metaverse: Design Considerations, Socio-Technical Elements, and Future Research Directions of Metaverse. [JGIM]. *Journal of Global Information Management*, *31*(2), 1–28. doi:10.4018/JGIM.315283

Valle-Cruz, D., Muñoz-Chávez, J. P., & García-Contreras, R. G. (2023). Towards the Understanding of Consumer Behavior in the Metaverse: A Systematic Literature Review Using the PRISMA Methodology. *Handbook of Research on Consumer Behavioral Analytics in Metaverse and the Adoption of a Virtual World*, (pp 1-21). IGI Global. https://www.igi-global.com/chapter/virtual-world-and-the-teaching-of-literature-studies-in-ir-40-era/321608

KEY TERMS AND DEFINITIONS

Blockchain: Interconnected ledgers where data and transactions are stored.

Business Opportunity: It is an opportunity seized or created to invest and make money.

Digital Technology: The use of information technologies such as computers, software, and microchips to process data and information.

Entrepreneurship: The process of transforming business opportunities into investments.

Extended Reality: It is an umbrella term for all immersive technologies, including augmented reality, virtual reality, and mixed reality.

Interface Technologies: Software and hardware technologies that provide a link between two different systems.

Metaverse: Synchronized virtual copy of the real world.

Compilation of References

Abbas, A. (2022). *Individual psychological distance: A leadership task to assess and cope with invisible change.* [PhD Dissertation, Airlangga University]

Abbas, A., Ekowati, D., & Anwar, A. (2023). Authentic Leadership Journey: An empirical Discussion from Pakistani higher education employing the Lay theory of Psychology. *International Journal of Public Leadership*. doi:10.1108/IJPL-04-2022-0020

Abbas, A., Ekowati, D., Shuairidi, F., Fenitra, R. M., & Fahlevi, M. (2022). Integrating Cycle of Prochaska and DiClemente with Ethically Responsible behavior theory for Social Change Management: Post Covid-19 Social Cognitive Perspective for Change. In A. Pego (Ed.), *Challenges and Emerging Strategies for Global Networking Post COVID-19* (pp. 130–155). IGI Global. doi:10.4018/978-1-7998-8856-7.ch007

Abbas, A., Ekowati, D., Suhairidi, F., & Anwar, A. (2022). Human Capital Creation: A Collective Psychological, Social, Organizational and Religious Perspective. *Journal of Religion and Health*. doi:10.100710943-022-01665-8 PMID:36109469

Abbas, A., Ekowati, D., Suhairidi, F., & Hamid, A. R. (2022). Negative Vs Positive Psychology: A Review of Science of Well-being. *Integrative Psychological & Behavioral Science*. doi:10.100712124-022-09708-1 PMID:35759165

Abbas, A., Ekowati, D., & Suhariadi, F. (2021a). Individual psychological distance: A leadership task to assess and cope with invisible change. *Journal of Management Development*, *40*(3), 168–189. doi:10.1108/JMD-09-2020-0304

Abbas, A., Ekowati, D., & Suhariadi, F. (2021b). Managing Individuals, Organizations Through Leadership: Diversity Consciousness Roadmap. In B. Christiansen & H. Chandan (Eds.), *Handbook of Research on Applied Social Psychology in Multiculturalism* (Vol. 1, pp. 47–71). IGI Global. doi:10.4018/978-1-7998-6960-3.ch003

Abbas, A., Ekowati, D., & Suhariadi, F. (2022). Social Perspective: Leadership in Changing Society. In M. I. Hassan, S. Sen Roy, U. Chatterjee, S. Chakraborty, & U. Singh (Eds.), *Social Morphology, Human Welfare, and Sustainability* (pp. 89–107). Springer International Publishing. doi:10.1007/978-3-030-96760-4_4

Abbas, A., Ekowati, D., Suhariadi, F., Anwar, A., & Fenitra, R. M. (2023). Technology acceptance and COVID-19: A perspective for emerging opportunities from crisis. *Technology Analysis and Strategic Management*, 1–13. doi:10.1080/09537325.2023.2214642

Abbas, A., Saud, M., Ekowati, D., & Suhariadi, F. (2021). Social Psychology and Fabrication: A Synthesis of Individuals, Society, and Organization. In B. Christiansen & H. Chandan (Eds.), *Handbook of Research on Applied Social Psychology in Multiculturalism* (Vol. 1, pp. 89–109). IGI Global. doi:10.4018/978-1-7998-6960-3.ch005

Abbas, A., Saud, M., Suhariadi, F., Usman, I., & Ekowati, D. (2022). Positive leadership psychology: Authentic and servant leadership in higher education in Pakistan. *Current Psychology (New Brunswick, N.J.)*, *41*(10), 5859–5871. doi:10.100712144-020-01051-1

Aboramadan, M., Dahleez, K. A., & Farao, C. (2022). Inclusive leadership and extra-role behaviors in higher education: Does organizational learning mediate the relationship? *International Journal of Educational Management*, *36*(4), 397–418.

Abraham, R. (2000). Organizational cynicism: Bases and consequences. *Genetic, Social, and General Psychology Monographs*, *126*(3), 269–292. PMID:10950198

Abubakar, A. M., & Arasli, H. (2016). Dear top management please don't make me cynic: Intention to sabotage. *Journal of Management Development*, *35*(10), 1266–1286. doi:10.1108/JMD-11-2015-0164

Abubakar, A. M., Megeirhi, H. A., & Shneikat, B. (2018). Tolerance for workplace incivility, employee cynicism and job search behavior. *Service Industries Journal*, *38*(9/10), 629–643. doi:10.1080/02642069.2017.1420171

Acker, J. (2006). Inequality regimes: Gender, class, and race in organizations. *Gender & Society*, *20*(4), 441–464. doi:10.1177/0891243206289499

Adams, B. G., Meyers, M. C., & Sekaja, L. (2020). Positive leadership: Relationships with employee inclusion, discrimination, and well-being. *Applied Psychology*, *69*(4), 1145–1173. doi:10.1111/apps.12230

Adapa, S., & Sheridan, A. (Eds.). (2018). *Inclusive Leadership*. Springer International Publishing. doi:10.1007/978-3-319-60666-8

Agarwal, H., & Vaghela, P. (2018). *Work values of Gen Z: Bridging the gap to the next generation*. In National Conference on Innovative Business Management Practices in 21st Century, Faculty of Management Studies, Parul University, Gujarat, India.

Agarwal, U. A., Stokes, P., & Smith, S. (2016). Examining perceived organizational politics among Indian managers: Engagement as mediator and locus of control as moderator. *The International Journal of Organizational Analysis*, *24*(3), 415–437. doi:10.1108/IJOA-07-2014-0786

Aggarwal, I., Woolley, A. W., Chabris, C. F., & Malone, T. W. (2019). The impact of cognitive style diversity on implicit learning in teams. *Frontiers in Psychology*, *10*, 112. doi:10.3389/fpsyg.2019.00112 PMID:30792672

Aguinis, H. (2013). *Performance management* (3rd ed.). Pearson/Prentice-Hall.

Agustiningsih, H. N., Armanu, T., Djumilah, H., & Noermijati, N. (2016). The effect of remuneration, job satisfaction and OCB on the employee performance. *Science Journal of Business and Management*, *4*(6), 212–222. doi:10.11648/j.sjbm.20160406.16

Ahearne, M., Mathieu, J., & Rapp, A. (2005). To empower or not to empower your sales force? An empirical examination of the influence of leadership empowerment behavior on customer satisfaction and performance. *The Journal of Applied Psychology*, *90*(5), 945–955. doi:10.1037/0021-9010.90.5.945 PMID:16162066

Ahmad, S., Rofie, M. K. H., & Salim, S. (2016). Rewards and commitment in social development: Equiping modern muslim communities with knowledge on Islamic work ethics towards better living conditions. *Mediterranean Journal of Social Sciences, 7*(1 S1), 395-400. doi:10.5901/mjss.2016.v7n1s1p395

Ahmad, T., Hamid, A., Abbas, A., Anwar, A., Ekowati, D., Fenitra, R., & Suhariadi, F. (2023). Empowering leadership: Role of Organizational Culture of Self-Esteem, and Emotional Intelligence on Creativity. *Journal of Management Development*, *42*(3), 201–214. doi:10.1108/JMD-10-2021-0288

Ahmed, I., (2016). *Generational differences in workplace behaviour and their effective management with reference to professional education sector of Uttar Pradesh.* Research Gate.

Ahmed, F., Zhao, F., & Faraz, N. A. (2020). How and when does inclusive leadership curb psychological distress during a crisis? Evidence from the COVID-19 outbreak. *Frontiers in Psychology*, *11*, 1898. doi:10.3389/fpsyg.2020.01898 PMID:32849111

Ahmed, F., Zhao, F., Faraz, N. A., & Qin, Y. J. (2021). How inclusive leadership paves way for psychological well-being of employees during trauma and crisis: A three-wave longitudinal mediation study. *Journal of Advanced Nursing*, *77*(2), 819–831. doi:10.1111/jan.14637 PMID:33231300

Ainscow, M., & Sandill, A. (2010). Developing inclusive education systems: The role of organisational cultures and leadership. *International Journal of Inclusive Education*, *14*(4), 401–416. doi:10.1080/13603110802504903

Al-Ababneh, M. M. (2015). Employees' service innovation behavior and new service development in four- and five-star hotels. *International Journal of Tourism & Hospitality Reviews*, *1*(1), 13–22. doi:10.18510/ijthr.2014.113

Alam, J., Mendelson, M., Boamah, M. I., & Gauthier, M. (2022). Exploring the antecedents of employee engagement. *International Journal of Organizational Analysis*.

Al-Asfour, A., & Lettau, L. (2014). Strategies for leadership styles for multi-generational workforce. *Journal of Leadership, Accountability and Ethics*, *11*(2), 52–69.

Albrecht, S. L. (2015). Meaningful work: Some key questions for research and practice. In R. J. Burke, K. M. Page, & C. L. Cooper (Eds.), *Flourishing in life, work, and careers: Individual wellbeing and career experiences* (pp. 210–234). Edward Elgar. doi:10.4337/9781783474103.00021

Alexander, C. (2018). Gen Z, The Future of Work, and HR Tech. *BizLibrary*. www.bizlibrary.com

Alfes, K., Truss, C., Soane, E., Rees, C., & Gatenby, M. (2010). *Creating an engaged workforce: findings from the Kingston employee engagement consortium project*. Chartered Institute of Personnel and Development.

Alfonso, V., Boar, C., Frost, J., Gambacorta, L., & Liu, J. (n.d.). *E-commerce in the pandemic and beyond:online appendix*. BIS Bulletin.

Allal-Chérif, O. (2022). Intelligent cathedrals: Using augmented reality, virtual reality, and artificial intelligence to provide an intense cultural, historical, and religious visitor experience. *Technological Forecasting and Social Change*, *178*, 121604. doi:10.1016/j.techfore.2022.121604

Allbeck, J. M., & Badler, N. I. (1998). Avatars agrave/ la snow crash. *Proceedings Computer Animation* '98 (Cat. No.98EX169), 19-24. doi:10.1109/CA.1998.681903

Allinson, C. W., & Hayes, J. (1996). The cognitive style index: A measure of intuition-analysis for organizational research. *Journal of Management Studies*, *33*(1), 119–135. doi:10.1111/j.1467-6486.1996.tb00801.x

Allison, S. T., & Goethals, G. R. (2016). Hero worship: The elevation of the human spirit. *Journal for the Theory of Social Behaviour*, *46*(2), 187–210. doi:10.1111/jtsb.12094

Altaf, A., & Masrek, M. N. (2021). Visualizing the knowledge domain of Work Engagement through Bibliometric Analysis. *Library Philosophy and Practice (e-journal)*. https://digitalcommons.unl.edu/libphilprac/5300?utm_source=digitalcommons.unl.edu%2Flibphilprac%2F5300&utm_medium=PDF&utm_campaign=PDFCoverPages

Altındağ, E., & Kösedağı, Y. (2015). The relationship between emotional intelligence of managers, innovative corporate culture and employee performance. *Procedia: Social and Behavioral Sciences*, *210*, 270–282. doi:10.1016/j.sbspro.2015.11.367

Aluwi, A. R., & Saihani, M. S. (2013). Managing diversity at the workplace: A case study in a Malaysian government agency. *Journal of Management and Sustainability*, *3*(4), 155–167.

Alvesson, M., & Spicer, A. (2012a). Critical leadership studies: The case for critical performativity. *Human Relations*, *65*(3), 367–390. doi:10.1177/0018726711430555

Alvesson, M., & Spicer, A. (2012b). A Stupidity-Based theory of organizations. *Journal of Management Studies*, *49*(7), 1194–1220. doi:10.1111/j.1467-6486.2012.01072.x

Alvesson, M., & Sveningsson, S. (2015). *Changing Organizational Culture: Cultural change work in progress* (2nd ed.). Routledge., doi:10.4324/9781315688404

American Psychological Association. (2021). *COVID-19 one year later: Workplace mental health matters more than ever*. APA.

Amin, M., Till, A., & McKimm, J. (2018). Inclusive and person-centred leadership: Creating a culture that involves everyone. *British Journal of Hospital Medicine*, *79*(7), 402–407. doi:10.12968/hmed.2018.79.7.402 PMID:29995546

Anand, R. (2022). *Leading global diversity, equity, and inclusion: A guide for systemic change in multinational organizations* (1st ed.). Berrett-Koehler.

Anderson, AH, McEwan, R, Bal, J & Carletta, J. (2007). Virtual team meetings: An analysis of communication and context. *Computers in Human Behavior*, *23*(5), 2558- 2580.

Andersson, & Pearson. (1999). Tit for tat? The spiraling effect of incivility in the workplace. *Academy of Management Review, 24*(3), 452-471.

Ang'ana, G. A., & Chiroma, J. A. (2021). Collaborative Leadership and its Influence in Building and Sustaining Successful Cross-Functional Relationships in Organizations in Kenya. *Journal of Business and Management*, *23*(8), 18–26.

Ang, S., & Van Dyne, L. (2008). Conceptualization of cultural intelligence: Definition, distinctiveness, and nomological network. In S. Ang & L. Van Dyne (Eds.), *Handbook of Cultural Intelligence: Theory, Measurement, and Applications* (pp. 3–15). M. E. Sharpe.

Aria, M., & Cuccurullo, C. (2017). A brief introduction to bibliometrix. *Journal of Informetrics, 11*(4), 959-975. doi:10.1016/j.joi.2017.08.007

Ariani, D. W. (2014). Relationship leadership, employee engagement, and organizational citizenship behavior. *International Journal of business and social research, 4*(8), 74-90.

Arnold, J. A., Arad, S., Rhoades, J. A., & Drasgow, F. (2000). The empowering leadership questionnaire: The construction and validation of a new scale for measuring leader behaviors. *Journal of Organizational Behavior*, *21*(3), 249–269. doi:10.1002/(SICI)1099-1379(200005)21:3<249::AID-JOB10>3.0.CO;2-#

Arora, N., & Dhole, V. (2019). Generation Y: Perspective, engagement, expectations, preferences and satisfactions from workplace; a study conducted in Indian context. *Benchmarking*, *26*(5), 1378–1404. doi:10.1108/BIJ-05-2018-0132

Arshad, & Ismail. (2018). Workplace incivility and knowledge hiding behavior: does personality matter. *Journal of Organizational Effectiveness: People and Performance, 5*(3), 278-288.

Arslan, M., & Roudaki, J. (2019). Examining the role of employee engagement in the relationship between organisational cynicism and employee performance. *The International Journal of Sociology and Social Policy*, *39*(1/2), 118–137. doi:10.1108/IJSSP-06-2018-0087

Arun, K., & Kahraman Gedik, N. (2022). Impact of Asian cultural values upon leadership roles and styles. *International Review of Administrative Sciences*, *88*(2), 428–448. doi:10.1177/0020852320935982

Aryee, S., Budhwar, P. S., & Chen, Z. X. (2002). Trust as a mediator of the relationship between organizational justice and work outcomes: Test of a social exchange model. *Journal of Organizational Behavior*, *23*(3), 267–285. doi:10.1002/job.138

Ashikali, T., & Groeneveld, S. (2015). Diversity management in public organizations and its effect on employees' affective commitment: The role of transformational leadership and the inclusiveness of the organizational culture. *Review of Public Personnel Administration*, *35*(2), 146–168. doi:10.1177/0734371X13511088

ASIS. (2009). *Organizational Resilience: Security, Preparedness, and Continuity Management Systems - Requirements with Guidance for Use ASIS SPC 1-2009*. ASIS.

Audia, G., Locke, E. A., & Smith, K. G. (2000). The paradox of success: An archival and laboratory study of strategic persistence following a radical environmental change. *Academy of Management Journal*, *43*(5), 837–853. doi:10.2307/1556413

Ausburn, L. J., & Ausburn, F. B. (1978). Cognitive styles: Some information and implications for instructional design. *Educational Communication and Technology*, *26*(4), 337–354. doi:10.1007/BF02766370

Autio, E., Nambisan, S., Thomas, L. D., & Wright, M. (2018). Digital affordances, spatial affordances, and the genesis of entrepreneurial ecosystems. *Strategic Entrepreneurship Journal*, *12*(1), 72–95. doi:10.1002ej.1266

Avolio, B. J. (2005). *Leadership development in balance: Made/born* (1st ed.). Psychology Press. doi:10.4324/9781410611819

Avolio, B., & Kahai, S. (2003). Adding the 'E' to E-leadership: How it may impact your leadership. *Organizational Dynamics*, *31*(4), 325–338. doi:10.1016/S0090-2616(02)00133-X

Aydemir, M., Dinc, M. S., & Caglar, M. (2016). How work-life balance and work values differ from generation to generation: An exploratory study. In *Proceedings of the 2nd Annual International Conference on Social Sciences (AICSS),* (pp. 77-89). Research Gate.

Bailey, C., Madden, A., Alfes, K., & Fletcher, L. (2017). The meaning, antecedents and outcomes of employee engagement: A narrative synthesis. *International Journal of Management Reviews*, *19*(1), 31–53. doi:10.1111/ijmr.12077

Banaji, M. R., & Greenwald, A. G. (2013). *Blindspot: Hidden biases of good people*. Random House Publishing.

Bandura, A. (1977). Self-efficacy: Toward a unifying theory of behavioral change. *Psychological Review*, *84*(2), 191–215. doi:10.1037/0033-295X.84.2.191 PMID:847061

Bandura, A. (1986). *Social foundation of thought and action: A social cognitive theory*. Prentice-Hall.

Bandura, A. (1997). *Self-efficacy: The exercise of control*. Freeman.

Bandura, A. (2002). Social cognitive theory in cultural context. *Applied Psychology, 51*(2), 269–290. doi:10.1111/1464-0597.00092

Bang, H., & Reio, T. G. Jr. (2017). Examining the role of cynicism in the relationships between burnout and employee behavior. *Journal of Work and Organizational Psychology, 33*(3), 217–227. doi:10.1016/j.rpto.2017.07.002

Bannay, D. F., Hadi, M. J., & Amanah, A. A. (2020). The impact of inclusive leadership behaviors on innovative workplace behavior with an emphasis on the mediating role of work engagement. *Problems and Perspectives in Management, 18*(3), 479.5e5

Bansgopaul, N. (2021). What is Web 3.0 and why should you care?: If you understand the benefits of decentralization, it's time to recognize the importance of Web 3.0. *Newsweek*, https://www.newsweek.com/what-web-30-why-should-youcare-1627250

Bardin, L. (1977). *Análise de conteúdo*. Edições 70.

Barnes, M. L., Wang, P., Cinner, J. E., Graham, N. A., Guerrero, A. M., Jasny, L., Lau, J., Sutcliffe, S. R., & Zamborain-Mason, J. (2020). Social determinants of adaptive and transformative responses to climate change. *Nature Climate Change, 10*(9), 823–828. doi:10.103841558-020-0871-4

Baron, A., & Armstrong, M. (2007). *Human capital management: achieving added value through people*. Kogan Page. https://www.123library.org/book_details/?id=98763

Barrera, K. G., & Shah, D. (2023). Marketing in the metaverse: Conceptual understanding, framework, and research agenda. *Journal of Business Research, 155*, 113420. doi:10.1016/j.jbusres.2022.113420

Barringer, B. R., Jones, F. F., & Neubaum, D. O. (2005). A quantitative content analysis of the characteristics of rapid-growth firms and their founders. *Journal of Business Venturing, 20*(5), 663–687. doi:10.1016/j.jbusvent.2004.03.004

Barta, S., Gurrea, R., & Flavián, C. (2023). How augmented reality increases engagement through its impact on risk and the decision process. *Cyberpsychology, Behavior, and Social Networking, 26*(3), 177–187. doi:10.1089/cyber.2022.0087 PMID:36706429

Basadur, M. S., & Head, M. M. (2001). Team performance and satisfaction: A link to cognitive style within a process framework. *The Journal of Creative Behavior, 35*(3), 1–22. doi:10.1002/j.2162-6057.2001.tb01048.x

Bass, B. M. (1997). Does the transactional–transformational leadership paradigm transcend organizational and national boundaries? *The American Psychologist, 52*(2), 130–139. doi:10.1037/0003-066X.52.2.130

Bass, B. M., & Riggio, R. E. (2006). *Transformational leadership* (2nd ed.). Lawrence Erlbaum Associates. doi:10.4324/9781410617095

Bassett-Jones, N. (2005). The paradox of diversity management, creativity and innovation. *Creativity and Innovation Management, 14*(2), 169–175. doi:10.1111/j.1467-8691.00337.x

Bateman, T. S., & Crant, J. M. (1993). The proactive component of organizational behavior: Ameasure and correlates. *Journal of Organizational Behavior, 14*(2), 103–118. doi:10.1002/job.4030140202

Baumeister, R. F. (2012). Need-to-belong theory. In P. A. M. van Lange, A. W. Kruglanski, & E. T. Higgins (Eds.), Handbook of theories of social psychology (pp. 121–140). Thousand Oaks, CA: Sage. doi:10.4135/9781446249222.n32

Beattie, L., & Griffin, B. (2014). Day-level fluctuations in stress and engagement in response to workplace incivility: A diary study. *Work and Stress, 28*(2), 124–142. doi:10.1080/02678373.2014.898712

Beattie, V., & Smith, S. J. (2010). Human capital, value creation and disclosure. *Journal of Human Resource Costing & Accounting, 14*(4), 262–285. doi:10.1108/14013381011105957

Becker, B. E., & Huselid, M. A. (1998). Human resources strategies, complementarities, and firm performance. *SUNY Buffalo: Unpublished manuscript.*

Beck, J. W., Beatty, A. S., & Sackett, P. R. (2014). On the distribution of job performance: The role of measurement characteristics in observed departures from normality. *Personnel Psychology, 67*, 531–566.

Belanger, F., & Watson-Manheim, M. B. (2006). Virtual teams and multiple media: Structuring media use to attain strategic goals. *Group Decision and Negotiation, 15*(4), 299–321. doi:10.100710726-006-9044-8

Beliaeva, T., Ferasso, M., Kraus, S., & Damke, E. J. (2020). Dynamics of digital entrepreneurship and the innovation ecosystem: A multilevel perspective. *International Journal of Entrepreneurial Behaviour & Research, 26*(2), 266–284. doi:10.1108/IJEBR-06-2019-0397

Benabou, R., & Tirole, J. (2011). Laws and Norms. *National Bureau of Economic Research Working Paper Series, 17579.* doi:10.3386/w17579

Bennett, T., & Savage, M. (2004). Introduction: Cultural capital and cultural policy. *Cultural Trends, 13*(2), 7–14. doi:10.1080/0954896042000267116

Bennis, W. (2002). *Moral leadership: The theory and practice of power, judgment and policy.* John Wiley & Sons.

Berger, J., & Iyengar, R. (2013). 'Communication channels and word of mouth. How the medium shapes the message'. *The Journal of Consumer Research, 40*(3), 567–579. doi:10.1086/671345

Berkup, S. B. (2014). Working with generations X and Y in generation Z period: Management of different generations in business life. *Mediterranean Journal of Social Sciences, 5*(19), 218. doi:10.5901/mjss.2014.v5n19p218

Berson, Y., Waldman, D. A., & Pearce, C. L. (2016). Enhancing our understanding of vision in organizations: Toward an integration of leader and follower processes. *Organizational Psychology Review*, *6*(2), 171–191. doi:10.1177/2041386615583736

Beutell, N. J., & Wittig-Berman, U. (2008). Work-family conflict and work-family synergy for generation X, baby boomers, and matures: Generational differences, predictors, and satisfaction outcomes. *Journal of Managerial Psychology*, *23*(5), 507–523. doi:10.1108/02683940810884513

Bhattacharya, M., Gibson, D. E., & Doty, D. H. (2005). The effects of flexibility in employee skills, employee behaviors, and human resource practices on firm performance. *Journal of Management*, *31*(4), 622–640. doi:10.1177/0149206304272347

Biddle, S., Soos, I., & Chatzisarantis, N. (1999). Predicting physical activity intentions using goal perspectives and self-determination theory approaches. *European Psychologist*, *4*(2), 83–89. doi:10.1027//1016-9040.4.4.83

Bindl, U. K., & Parker, S. K. (2011). Proactive work behavior: Forward-thinking and change-oriented action in organizations. In S. Zedeck (Ed.), APA handbook of industrial and organizational psychology, Vol. 2. Selecting and developing members for the organization (pp. 567–598). American Psychological Association. doi:10.1037/12170-019

Bittner, A. (2018). Leaders always mattered: The persistence of personality in Canadian elections. *Electoral Studies*, *54*, 297–302. doi:10.1016/j.electstud.2018.04.013

Blackburn, D., & Smallbone, D. (2015). *Sustaining self-employment for disadvantaged entrepreneurs: A background paper for the OECD Centre for Entrepreneurship, SMEs and Local Development*. OECD and LEED.

Black, C., Akintoye, A., & Fitzgerald, E. (2000). An analysis of success factors and benefits of partnering in construction. *International Journal of Project Management*, *18*(6), 423–434. doi:10.1016/S0263-7863(99)00046-0

Blain, M.-J., Fortin, S., & Alvarez, F. (2017). Professional journeys of international medical graduates in Quebec: Recognition, uphill battles, or career change. *Journal of International Migration and Integration*, *18*(1), 223–247. doi:10.100712134-016-0475-z

Blau, G., & Andersson, L. (2011). Testing a measure of instigated workplace incivility. *Journal of occupational and oganizational psychology* . doi:10.1348/096317905X26822

Blau, P. (1964). Social exchange theory. *CORE, 3*, 62.

Blau, P. M. (1964). *Exchange and Power in Social Life*. John Wiley and Sons.

Blau, P. M. (1964). *Exchange and power in social life*. Wiley.

Blau, P. M. (1964). Justice in social exchange. *Sociological Inquiry*, *34*(2), 193–206. doi:10.1111/j.1475-682X.1964.tb00583.x

Blazek, K. (2016). *Leadership style of Generation Z*. TruScore. https://www.truscore.com/resources/Gen-z/

Bligh, M. C., Kohles, J. C., & Meindl, J. R. (2004). Charisma under crisis: Presidential leadership, rhetoric, and media responses before and after the September 11th terrorist attacks. *The Leadership Quarterly*, *15*(2), 211–239. doi:10.1016/j.leaqua.2004.02.005

Bligh, M. C., Pearce, C. L., & Kohles, J. C. (2006). The importance of self-and shared leadership in team based knowledge work: A meso-level model of leadership dynamics. *Journal of Managerial Psychology*, *21*(4), 296–318. doi:10.1108/02683940610663105

Bloom, N., Sadun, R., & Van Reenen, J. (2012). Does management really work? *Harvard Business Review*, *90*(11), 76–82. PMID:23155999

Blouch, R., & Azeem, M. F. (2019). Effects of perceived diversity on perceived organizational performance: Mediating role of perceived organizational justice. *Employee Relations*, *41*(5), 1079–1097. doi:10.1108/ER-05-2018-0150

Boddy, C. R. (2006). The dark side of management decisions: Organisational psychopaths. *Management Decision*, *44*(10), 1461–1475. doi:10.1108/00251740610715759

Boekhorst, J. A. (2015). The role of authentic leadership in fostering workplace inclusion: A social information processing perspective. *Human Resource Management*, *54*(2), 241–264. doi:10.1002/hrm.21669

Boerma, M., Coyle, E. A., Dietrich, M. A., Dintzner, M. R., Drayton, S. J., Early, J. L., & Lin, A. Y. F. (2017). Point/counterpoint: Are outstanding leaders born or made? *American Journal of Pharmaceutical Education*, *81*(3), 1–5. doi:10.5688/ajpe81358 PMID:28496278

Borekci, D., Rofcanin, Y., & Sahin, M. (2014). Effects of organizational culture and organizational resilience over subcontractor riskiness: A multi-method study in longitudinal time setting. *European Business Review*, *26*(1), 2–22. doi:10.1108/EBR-07-2013-0099

Born, A., van Eck, P., & Johannesson, M. (2018). An experimental investigation of election promises. *Political Psychology*, *39*(3), 685–705. doi:10.1111/pops.12429

Bortini, P., Paci, A., Rise, A., & Rojnik, I. (2018). *Inclusive leadership: Theoretical framework*. Inclusive Leadership. http://inclusiveleadership. eu/il_theoreticalframework_en. p df.

Boschma, R. (2005). Proximity and innovation: A critical assessment. *Regional Studies*, *39*(1), 61–74. doi:10.1080/0034340052000320887

Bourdieu, P. (1984). Distinction a social critique of the judgement of taste. In *Inequality Classic Readings in Race, Class, and Gender* (1st ed., pp. 287–318). Routledge.

Bourdieu, P. (2010). The forms of capital (1986). In I. Szeman & T. Kaposy (Eds.), *Cultural theory: An anthology* (Vol. 1, pp. 81–93). John Wiley & Sons.

Bourke, J. (2018). The diversity and inclusion revolution: Eight powerful truths. *Deloitte Review* (22). https://www2.deloitte.com/us/en/insights/deloitte-review/issue-22/diversity-and-inclusion-at-work-eight-powerful-truths.html.

Bourke, J. (2016). *Which Two Heads Are Better Than One?: How Diverse Teams Create Breakthrough Ideas and Make Smarter Decisions*. Australian Institute of Company Directors.

Bourke, J., & Dillon, B. (2018). The diversity and inclusion revolution: Eight powerful truths. *Deloitte Review*, *22*, 82–95.

Bourke, J., & Espedido, A. (2019). Why inclusive leaders are good for organizations, and how to become one. *Harvard Business Review*, *96*, 3–8.

Bourke, J., & Titus, A. (2020). The key to inclusive leadership. *Harvard Business Review*, *97*, 2–5.

Bowen, D. E., & Ostroff, C. (2004). Understanding HRM–firm performance linkages: The role of the "strength" of the HRM system. *Academy of Management Review*, *29*(2), 203–221.

Boxall, P., & Macky, K. (2009). Research and theory on high-performance work systems: Progressing the high-involvement stream. *Human Resource Management Journal*, *19*(1), 3–23. doi:10.1111/j.1748-8583.2008.00082.x

Bradley, E. H. (2020). Diversity, inclusive leadership, and health outcomes. *International Journal of Health Policy and Management*, *9*(7), 266–268. doi:10.15171/ijhpm.2020.12 PMID:32613797

Brady, L. M., Kaiser, C. R., Major, B., & Kirby, T. A. (2015). It's fair for us: Diversity structures cause women to legitimize discrimination. *Journal of Experimental Social Psychology*, *57*, 100–110. doi:10.1016/j.jesp.2014.11.010

Brannen, M. Y., & Thomas, D. C. (2010). Bicultural individuals in organizations: Implications and opportunity. *International Journal of Cross Cultural Management*, *10*(1), 5–16. doi:10.1177/1470595809359580

Braun, V., & Clarke, V. (2006). Using thematic analysis in psychology. *Qualitative Research in Psychology*, *3*(2), 77–101. doi:10.1191/1478088706qp063oa

Brewer, M. B. (1991). The social self: On being the same and different at the same time. *Personality and Social Psychology Bulletin*, *17*(5), 475–482. doi:10.1177/0146167291175001

Brooks, J. S., Jean-Marie, G., Normore, A. H., & Hodgins, D. W. (2007). Distributed leadership for social justice: Exploring how influence and equity are stretched over an urban high school. *Journal of School Leadership*, *17*(4), 378–408. doi:10.1177/105268460701700402

Brown, J. (2019). *How to be an inclusive leader: Your role in creating cultures of belonging where everyone can thrive*. Berrett-Koehler Publishers.

Bruch, H., & Ghoshal, S. (2004). *A bias for action: How effective managers harness their willpower, achieve results, and stop wasting time*. Harvard Business Press.

Buengeler, C., Leroy, H., & De Stobbeleir, K. (2018). How leaders shape the impact of HR's diversity practices on employee inclusion. *Human Resource Management Review*, *28*(3), 289–303. doi:10.1016/j.hrmr.2018.02.005

Buhalis, D., & Karatay, N. (2022). Mixed reality (mr) for generation z in cultural heritage tourism towards metaverse. Stienmetz, J.L., Ferrer-Rosell, B., Massimo, D. (eds) Information and Communication Technologies in Tourism 2022. ENTER 2022. Springer. doi:10.1007/978-3-030-94751-4_2

Buhalis, D., Leung, D., & Lin, M. (2023). Metaverse as a disruptive technology revolutionising tourism management and marketing. *Tourism Management*, *97*, 104724. doi:10.1016/j.tourman.2023.104724

Buller, D. J. (2006). *Adapting minds: Evolutionary psychology and the persistent quest for human nature*. MIT press.

Bundy, J., & Pfarrer, M. D. (2015). A burden of responsibility: The role of social approval at the onset of a crisis. *Academy of Management Review*, *40*(3), 345–369. doi:10.5465/amr.2013.0027

Bundy, J., Pfarrer, M. D., Short, C. E., & Coombs, W. T. (2017). Crises and crisis management: Integration, interpretation, and research development. *Journal of Management*, *43*(6), 1661–1692. doi:10.1177/0149206316680030

Bureau of Labor Statistics. (2021). *White-collar workers: An overview*. Bureau of Labor Statistics.

Burgess, Z., & Tharenou, P. (2002). Women board directors: Characteristics of the few. *Journal of Business Ethics*, *37*(1), 39–49. doi:10.1023/A:1014726001155

Burke, C. S., Fiore, S. M., & Salas, E. (2003). The role of shared cognition in enabling shared leadership and team adaptability. In C. L. Pearce & J. A. Conger (Eds.), *Shared Leadership: Reframing the Hows and Whys of Leadership* (pp. 103–122). Sage Publications. doi:10.4135/9781452229539.n5

Burke, C. S., Sims, D. E., Lazzara, E. H., & Salas, E. (2007). 'Trust in leadership: A multi-level review and integration'. *The Leadership Quarterly*, *18*(6), 606–632. doi:10.1016/j.leaqua.2007.09.006

Burke, C. S., Stagl, K. C., Salas, E., Pierce, L., & Kendall, D. (2006). Understanding team adoption: A conceptual analysis and model. *The Journal of Applied Psychology*, *91*(6), 1189–1207. doi:10.1037/0021-9010.91.6.1189 PMID:17100478

Burke, P. J. (1991). Identity processes and social stress. *American Sociological Review*, *56*(6), 836–849. doi:10.2307/2096259

Burke, W. W., & Noumair, D. A. (2015). *Organization development: A process of learning and changing* (3rd ed.). FT Press.

Bushee, B. J. (1998). The influence of institutional investors on myopic R&D investment behavior. *The Accounting Review*, *73*, 305–333.

Busse, R., & Regenberg, S. (2019). Revisiting the "authoritarian versus participative" leadership style legacy: A new model of the impact of leadership inclusiveness on employee engagement. *Journal of Leadership & Organizational Studies*, *26*(4), 510–525. doi:10.1177/1548051818810135

Cadinu, M., & Galdi, S. (2012). Gender differences in implicit gender self-categorization lead to stronger gender self-stereotyping by women than by men [Article]. *European Journal of Social Psychology*, *42*(5), 546–551. doi:10.1002/ejsp.1881

Cao, W., Fang, Z., Hou, G., Han, M., Xu, X., Dong, J., & Zheng, J. (2020). *The psychological impact of the COVID-19 epidemic on college students in*. Elsevier. doi:10.1016/j.psychres.2020.112934

Capra, F. (2004). *The hidden connections: A science for sustainable living*. Random House, Inc.

Carli, L. L. (1999). Gender, interpersonal power, and social influence. *The Journal of Social Issues*, *55*(1), 81–99. doi:10.1111/0022-4537.00106

Carmeli, & Gefen. (2005). The relationship between work commitment models and employee withdrawal intentions. *Journal of Managerial Psychology, 20*(2), 63-86.

Carmeli, A., Reiter-Palmon, R., & Ziv, E. (2010). Inclusive leadership and employee involvement in creative tasks in the workplace: The mediating role of psychological safety. *Creativity Research Journal*, *22*(3), 250–260. doi:10.1080/10400419.2010.504654

Caron, J., Asselin, H., Beaudoin, J. M., & Muresanu, D. (2019). Promoting perceived insider status of indigenous employees. *Cross Cultural & Strategic Management*, *26*(4), 609–638. doi:10.1108/CCSM-02-2019-0031

Carson, J. B., Tesluk, P. E., & Marrone, J. A. (2007). Shared leadership in teams: An investigation of antecedent conditions and performance. *Academy of Management Journal*, *50*, 1217–1234.

Carter, R. T., & Brown, S. A. (2020). Racialized trauma and the use of employee resource groups for support and advocacy. *The American Psychologist*, *75*(5), 661–670.

Carter, W. R, Nesbit, P. L., & Badham, R. J, & Parke. (2016). The effects of employee engagement and self-efficacy on job performance: A longitudinal field study. *International Journal of Human Resource Management*, *21*(17), 1–20.

Carton, W., Lund, J. F., & Dooley, K. (2021, April). Undoing Equivalence: Rethinking Carbon Accounting for just carbon removal. *Frontiers in Climate*, *3*, 1–7. doi:10.3389/fclim.2021.664130

Cascio, W. F., & Shurygailo, S. (2003). E-Leadership and Virtual Teams. *Organizational Dynamics*, *31*(4), 362–376. doi:10.1016/S0090-2616(02)00130-4

Catalyst. (2018). *The business case for employee resource groups*. Catalyst. https://www.catalyst.org/research/business-case-employee-resource-groups/

Catalyst. (2020). *Intersectionality: A critical lens for gender equality*. Ccatalyst.

Caulfield, B. (2021). What is the metaverse? *The official nvidia blog* https://blogs.nvidia.com/blog/2021/08/10/what-is-the-metaverse/

Caza, A., & Posner, B. Z. (2018). How and when does grit influence leaders' behavior? *Leadership and Organization Development Journal*, *40*(1), 124–134. doi:10.1108/LODJ-06-2018-0209

Caza, B. B., & Cortina, L. M. (2007). 11 5). From Insult to Injury: Explaining the Impact of Incivility. *Basic and Applied Social Psychology*, *29*(4), 335–350. doi:10.1080/01973530701665108

Cenkci, A. T., Bircan, T., & Zimmerman, J. (2020). Inclusive leadership and work engagement: The mediating role of procedural justice. *Management Research Review*, *44*(1), 158–180. doi:10.1108/MRR-03-2020-0146

Cennamo, L., & Gardner, D. (2008). Generational differences in work values, outcomes and person–organization values fit. *Journal of Managerial Psychology*, *23*(8), 891–906. doi:10.1108/02683940810904385

Center for Talent Innovation. (2018). *Sponsorship and the high-potential employee: A guide to understanding and overcoming the barriers*. Center for Talent Innovation.

Chak, C. M., Carminati, L., & Wilderom, C. P. (2022). Hope, goal-commitment and-stress mediating between collaborative leadership, financial resources, and performance. *International Journal of Productivity and Performance Management*.

Champion, D. (1999). The price of under management. *Harvard Business Review*, *77*(2), 14–15.

Chawla, N., & Kumar, B. (2021). 07 09). E-Commerce and Consumer Protection in India: The Emerging Trend. *Journal of Business Ethics*, 1–24. doi:10.100710551-021-04884-3 PMID:34257470

Cheng, X., Liu, W., & Li, Y. (2022). Is online collaboration process suitable for digital youth organization? A design approach. *Journal of Electronic Business & Digital Economics*.

Chengoden, R., Victor, N., Huynh-The, T., Yenduri, G., Jhaveri, R. H., Alazab, M., Bhattacharya, S., Hegde, P., Maddikunta, P. R. K., & Gadekallu, T. R. (2023). Metaverse for healthcare: A survey on potential applications, challenges and future directions. IEEE Access, 4. IEEE. https://doi.org/ doi:10.48550/arXiv.2209.04160

Chen, L., Luo, F., Zhu, X., Huang, X., & Liu, Y. (2020). Inclusive leadership promotes challenge-oriented organizational citizenship behavior through the mediation of work engagement and moderation of organizational innovative atmosphere. *Frontiers in Psychology*, *11*, 560594. doi:10.3389/fpsyg.2020.560594 PMID:33329187

Chen, Y., Wang, L., Liu, X., Chen, H., Hu, Y., & Yang, H. (2019). The trickle-down effect of leaders' pro-social rule breaking: Joint moderating role of empowering leadership and courage. *Frontiers in Psychology*, *9*, 2647. doi:10.3389/fpsyg.2018.02647 PMID:30666224

Chiaburu, D. S., Diaz, I., & Pitts, V. E. (2011). Social and economic exchanges with the organization: Do leader behaviors matter? *Leadership and Organization Development Journal*, *32*(5), 442–461. doi:10.1108/01437731111146569

Chiaburu, D. S., & Harrison, D. A. (2008). Do peers make the place? Conceptual synthesis and meta-analysis of coworker effects on perceptions, attitudes, OCBs, and performance. *The Journal of Applied Psychology*, *93*(5), 1082–1103. doi:10.1037/0021-9010.93.5.1082 PMID:18808227

Choi, S. B., Tran, T. B. H., & Kang, S. W. (2017). Inclusive leadership and employee well-being: The mediating role of person-job fit. *Journal of Happiness Studies*, *18*(6), 1877–1901. doi:10.100710902-016-9801-6

Choi, S. B., Tran, T. B. H., & Park, B. I. (2015). Inclusive leadership and work engagement: Mediating roles of affective organizational commitment and creativity. *Social Behavior and Personality*, *43*(6), 931–943. doi:10.2224bp.2015.43.6.931

Chow, I. H. S. (2018). Cognitive diversity and creativity in teams: The mediating roles of team learning and inclusion. *Chinese Management Studies*, *12*(2), 369–383. doi:10.1108/CMS-09-2017-0262

Choy, W. K. (2007). Globalisation and workforce diversity: HRM implications for multinational corporations in Singapore. *Singapore Management Review*, *29*(2), 1–20.

Chrobot-Mason, D., Ruderman, M., & Nishii, L. (2013). Leadership in a diverse workplace. In Q. Roberson (Ed.), *The Oxford handbook of diversity and work* (pp. 315–340). University Press. doi:10.1093/oxfordhb/9780199736355.013.0018

Chugh, S., Vibhu, G., Kanijia, S., Kumar, V., & Pal, S. K. (2020). *To study the impact of advancement of e-payment technology used in India* . Sage.

Chu, K. H. A. (2007). A factorial validation of work value structure: Second-order confirmatory factor analysis and its implications. *Tourism Management*, *29*(2), 320–330. doi:10.1016/j.tourman.2007.03.003

Cioffi, D. (1991). Beyond attentional strategies: A cognitive-perceptual model of somatic interpretation. *Psychological Bulletin*, *109*(1), 25–41. doi:10.1037/0033-2909.109.1.25 PMID:2006227

Clark, C. M., & Ahten, S. (2011). 1 2). Beginning the Conversation: The Nurse Educator's Role in Preventing Incivility in the Workplace. *RN Idaho*, *33*(4), 9–10.

Clements, C., & Washbush, J. B. (1999). The two faces of leadership: Considering the dark side of leader-follower dynamics. *Journal of Workplace Learning*, *11*(5), 170–176. doi:10.1108/13665629910279509

Cletus, U., Isah, M. A., & Kifordu, A. A. (2018). Diversity management and performance of selected Nigerian firms. [CompTIA.]. *African Journal of Economic and Management Studies*, *9*(1), 71–84.

Cloudman, R., & Hallahan, K. (2006). Crisis communication preparedness among U.S. organizations: Activities and assessments by public relations practitioners. *Public Relations Review, 32*(4), 367–376. doi:10.1016/j.pubrev.2006.09.005

Cohen, J. (1988). *Statistical power analysis for the behavioural sciences*. Lawrence Erlbaum Associates.

Colin, T., & Grasser, B. ı. (2018). How Competency Management Tools Can Influence Routines in Workshops Depending on New Strategic Intent. *Book of Abstracts ARTEM OCC 2020 Edition*, 330

Collins, B. (2021). The Metaverse: How to Build a Massive Virtual World. *Forbes*. https://www.forbes.com/sites/barrycollins/2021/09/25/the-metaverse-how-to-build-a-massive-virtual-world/?sh=60735bad6d1c

Colquitt, J. A., & Rodell, J. B. (2011). Justice, trust, and trustworthiness: A longitudinal analysis integrating three theoretical perspectives. *Academy of Management Journal, 54*(6), 1183–1206. doi:10.5465/amj.2007.0572

Conger, J. A. (1990). The dark side of leadership. *Organizational Dynamics, 19*(2), 44–55. doi:10.1016/0090-2616(90)90070-6

Conger, J. A., & Kanungo, R. N. (1987). Toward a behavioral theory of charismatic leadership in organizational settings. *Academy of Management Review, 12*(4), 637–647. doi:10.2307/258069

Conger, J. A., & Kanungo, R. N. (1988). The empowerment process: Integrating theory and practice. *Academy of Management Review, 13*(3), 471–482. doi:10.2307/258093

Connolly, W. E. (1995). *The ethos of pluralization*. University of Minnesota Press.

Cook, K. S., Cheshire, C., Rice, E. R., & Nakagawa, S. (2013). Social exchange theory. In *Handbook of social psychology* (pp. 61–88). Springer. doi:10.1007/978-94-007-6772-0_3

Cools, E., & Van den Broeck, H. (2007). Development and validation of the Cognitive Style Indicator. *The Journal of Psychology, 141*(4), 359–387. doi:10.3200/JRLP.141.4.359-388 PMID:17725071

Coombs, W. (2007). *Ongoing Crisis Communication: Planning, Managing and Responding* (2nd ed.). Sage.

Coombs, W. T., & Holladay, S. J. (2002). Helping crisis managers protect reputational assets. *Management Communication Quarterly, 16*(2), 165–186. doi:10.1177/089331802237233

Cooper-Cunningham, D. (2020). Drawing Fear of Difference: Race, Gender, and National Identity in *Ms. Marvel* Comics. *Millennium, 48*(2), 165–197. doi:10.1177/0305829819889133

Cortina, L. M. (2008). Unseen injustice: Incivility as modern discrimination in organizations. *Academy of Management Review, 33*(1), 55–75. doi:10.5465/amr.2008.27745097

Cortina, L. M., Magley, V. J., Williams, J. H., & Langhout, R. D. (2001). 1). Incivility in the workplace: Incidence and impact. *Journal of Occupational Health Psychology*, *6*(1), 64–80. doi:10.1037/1076-8998.6.1.64 PMID:11199258

Costello, M. L., Brunner, P. W., & Hasty, K. (2002). Preparing students for the empowered workplace: The risks and rewards in a management classroom. *Active Learning in Higher Education*, *3*(2), 117–127. doi:10.1177/1469787402003002002

Cottrill, K., Denise, L., & Patricia, C., & Hoffman, C. (2014). How authentic leadership and inclusion benefit organizations. *Equality, Diversity and Inclusion*, *33*(3), 275–292. doi:10.1108/EDI-05-2012-0041

Coulter, J. S., & Faulkner, D. C. (2014). The multi-Generational workforce. *Professional Case Management*, *19*(1), 46–51. doi:10.1097/NCM.0000000000000008 PMID:24300430

Coutu, D. L. (2002). How resilience works. *Harvard Business Review*, *80*(5), 46–56. PMID:12024758

Cox, C. B., & Blake, A. (2021). Diversity and organizational resilience: Insights for leaders navigating COVID-19. *Journal of Leadership Studies*, *15*(1), 81–88. doi:10.1002/jls.21686

Crant, J. M., & Bateman, T. S. (2000). Charismatic leadership viewed from above: The impact of proactive personality. *Journal of Organizational Behavior*, *21*(1), 63–75. doi:10.1002/(SICI)1099-1379(200002)21:1<63::AID-JOB8>3.0.CO;2-J

Cronin, M. A., & Weingart, L. R. (2007). Representational gaps, information processing, and conflict in functionally diverse teams. *Academy of Management Review*, *32*(3), 761–773. doi:10.5465/amr.2007.25275511

Cropanzano, R., Anthony, E. L., Daniels, S. R., & Hall, A. V. (2017). Social exchange theory: A critical review with theoretical remedies. *The Academy of Management Annals*, *11*(1), 479–516. doi:10.5465/annals.2015.0099

Cropanzano, R., & Mitchell, M. S. (2005). Social exchange theory: An interdisciplinary review. *Journal of Management*, *31*(6), 874–900. doi:10.1177/0149206305279602

Crosby, G. (2020). *Planned change: Why Kurt Lewin's social science is still best practice for business results, change management, and human progress*. Productivity Press. doi:10.4324/9781003082491

Crowder, B.R.R., (2017). *Work Motivation Theory: Identifying Multi-Generational Values in the Workplace*, 1-157. Walden University.

Cui, Y., Liu, Y., & Mou, J. (2018). Bibliometric analysis of organisational culture using CiteSpace. *Suid-Afrikaanse Tydskrif vir Ekonomiese en Bestuurswetenskappe*, *21*(1). doi:10.4102ajems.v21i1.2030

Cullen, K. L., Fan, J., & Liu, C. (2014). Employee popularity mediates the relationship between political skill and workplace interpersonal mistreatment. *Journal of Management*, *40*(6), 1760–1778. doi:10.1177/0149206311435104

Cunningham, G. B., & Sagas, M. (2004). Group diversity, occupational commitment, and occupational turnover intentions among NCAA Division IA football coaching staffs. *Journal of Sport Management, 18*(3), 236–254. doi:10.1123/jsm.18.3.236

Cunningham, J., O'Reilly, P., Dolan, B., O'Kane, C., & Mangematin, V. (2017). Gender differences and academic entrepreneurship: A study of scientists in the principal investigator role. In A. Link (Ed.), *Gender and entrepreneurial activity* (pp. 221–251). Edward Elgar. doi:10.4337/9781785364747.00013

D'Amato, A., & Herzfeldt, R. (2008). 'Learning orientation, organizational commitment and talent retention across generations: A study of European managers'. *Journal of Managerial Psychology, 23*(8), 929–953. doi:10.1108/02683940810904402

D'Innocenzo, L., Mathieu, J. E., & Kukenberger, M. R. (2014). A Meta-Analysis of Different Forms of Shared Leadership–Team Performance Relations. *Journal of Management, 20*(10), 1–28.

Daft, R. L. (2001). *Organization theory and design.* Australia, South-western Thomson learning.

Dahlgaard-Park, S. M., & Dahlgaard, J. J. (2006). In search of excellence–past, present and future. *Kreativ und konsequent, 2*(3), 57-84

Dallalfar, A. (2011). *Transforming classroom culture inclusive pedagogical practices.* Palgrave Macmillan. doi:10.1057/9780230370319

Danneels, E. (2002). The dynamics of product innovation and firm competences. *Strategic Management Journal, 23*(12), 1095–1121. doi:10.1002mj.275

Daspit, J., Tillman, C., Boyd, N., & Mckee, V. (2013). Cross-functional team effectiveness: An examination of internal team environment, shared leadership, and cohesion influences. *Team Performance Management, 19*(1/2), 19. doi:10.1108/13527591311312088

Davis, A., Murphy, J., Owens, D., Khazanchi, D., & Zigurs, I. (2009). Avatars, people, and virtual worlds: Foundations for research in metaverses. *Journal of the Association for Information Systems, 10*(2), 1. https://aisel.aisnet.org/jais/vol10/iss2/1. doi:10.17705/1jais.00183

De Bruyn, A., Viswanathan, V., Beh, Y. S., Brock, J. K. U., & Von Wangenheim, F. (2020). Artificial intelligence and marketing: Pitfalls and opportunities. *Journal of Interactive Marketing, 51*(1), 91–105. doi:10.1016/j.intmar.2020.04.007

De Jong, J. P., & Den Hartog, D. N. (2007). How leaders influence employees' innovative behaviour. *European Journal of Innovation Management, 10*(1), 41–64. doi:10.1108/14601060710720546

De Jong, J., & Den Hartog, D. (2010). Measuring innovative work behaviour. *Creativity and Innovation Management, 19*(1), 23–36. doi:10.1111/j.1467-8691.2010.00547.x

Dean, J. W. Jr, Brandes, P., & Dharwadkar, R. (1998). Organizational cynicism. *Academy of Management Review, 23*(2), 341–352. doi:10.2307/259378

Deci, E. L., & Ryan, R. M. (2012). Self-determination theory. In A. W. K. In P. A. M. Van Lange, & E. T. Higgins (Eds.), (Ed.), Handbook of theories of social psychology (Vol. 1, pp. 416–436). Sage Publications Ltd. doi:10.4135/9781446249215.n21

Decuypere, A., & Schaufeli, W. (2020). Leadership and work engagement: Exploring explanatory mechanisms. *German Journal of Human Resource Management*, *34*(1), 69–95. doi:10.1177/2397002219892197

Delanty, G., & O'Mahony, P. (2002). Nationalism and social theory: Modernity and the recalcitrance of the nation. *Sage (Atlanta, Ga.)*.

Deloitte. (2018). *The Diversity and Inclusion Revolution: Eight Powerful Truths*. Deloitte.

Deloitte. (2019). *Leading the social enterprise: Reinvent with a human focus*. Deloitte.

Deng, W., Liang, Q., Li, J., & Wang, W. (2020). Science mapping: A bibliometric analysis of female entrepreneurship studies. *Gender in Management*. doi:10.1108/GM-12-2019-0240

DeNisi, A. S., & Murphy, K. R. (2017). Performance appraisal and performance management: 100 years of progress? *The Journal of Applied Psychology*, *102*(3), 421–433. doi:10.1037/apl0000085 PMID:28125265

DeNisi, A., Wilson, M., & Biteman, J. (2014). Research and practice in hrm: A historical perspective. *Human Resource Management Review*, *14*(3), 219–231. doi:10.1016/j.hrmr.2014.03.004

Denning, S. (2012). Why is diversity vital for innovation. *Forbes*. https://www.forbes.com/sites/stevedenning/2012/01/16/why-is-diversity-vital-for-innovation/?sh=6c63f62c13e2. *Retrieved on December*, 20, 2022.

Dennissen, M., Benschop, Y., & van den Brink, M. (2020). Rethinking diversity management: An intersectional analysis of diversity networks. *Organization Studies*, *41*(2), 219–240. doi:10.1177/0170840618800103

DePree, M. (1993). The leadership quest: Three things necessary. *Business Strategy Review*, *4*(1), 69–74. doi:10.1111/j.1467-8616.1993.tb00045.x

DePree, M. (2011). *Leadership is an art*. Currency Doubleday Publisher.

Derks, B., Van Laar, C., & Ellemers, N. (2016). The queen bee phenomenon: Why women leaders distance themselves from junior women. *The Leadership Quarterly*, *27*(3), 456–469. doi:10.1016/j.leaqua.2015.12.007

Derven, M. (2016). Four drivers to enhance global virtual teams. *Industrial and Commercial Training*, *48*(1), 1–8. doi:10.1108/ICT-08-2015-0056

Devine, D. J., & Philips, J. L. (2001). Do smarter teams do better: A meta-analysis of cognitive ability and team performance. *Small Group Research*, *32*(5), 507–532. doi:10.1177/104649640103200501

Devloo, T., Anseel, F., De Beuckelaer, A., & Feys, M. (2016). When the fire dies: Perceived success and support for innovation shape the motivating potential of innovative work behaviour. *European Journal of Work and Organizational Psychology*, *25*(4), 512–524. doi:10.1080/1359432X.2016.1182157

Di Stefano, G., Gambardella, A., & Verona, G. (2021). Cognitive diversity, team performance, and firm growth: Evidence from a large panel of firms. *Strategic Management Journal*, *42*(2), 301–329. doi:10.1002mj.3218

Diamantopoulos, A. (2008, December). Formative indicators: Introduction to the special issue. *Journal of Business Research*, *61*(12), 1201–1302. doi:10.1016/j.jbusres.2008.01.008

Dias, J. H., & Paraíso, I. (2011). O sistema de gestão e avaliação do desempenho na Administração Pública Portuguesa: Efeitos da sua prática no contrato psicológico dos colaboradores. *Interações*, *20*, 101–132. https://www.interacoes-ismt.com/index.php/revista/article/viewFile/276/282

Dickersin, K. (1997). How important is publication bias? A synthesis of available data. *AIDS Education and Prevention*, *9*, 15–21. PMID:9083596

Diehl, M., & Stroebe, W. (1991). Productivity loss in idea-generating groups: Tracking down the blocking effect. *Journal of Personality and Social Psychology*, *61*(3), 392–403. doi:10.1037/0022-3514.61.3.392

Dillon, B., & Bourke, J. (2016). *The six signature traits of inclusive leadership: Thriving in a diverse new world.* Deloitte University Press. https://www2.deloitte.com/content/dam/Deloitte/au/Documents/human-capital/ deloitte-au-hc-six-signature-traits-inclusive-leadership020516.pdf

Dimock, M. (2019). *Defining Generations: Where Millennials end and Generation Z begins.* Pew Research Center. https://pewrsr.ch/2szqtJz

Dionisio, J. D. N., Borns, W. G. III, & Gilbert, R. (2013). 3D virtual worlds and the metaverse: Current status and future possibilities. [CSUR]. *ACM Computing Surveys*, *45*(3), 1–38. doi:10.1145/2480741.2480751

Dionne, S. D., Gupta, A., Sotak, K. L., Shirreffs, K., Serban, A., Hao, C., & Yammarino, F. J. (2014). A 25-year perspective on levels of analysis in leadership research. *The Leadership Quarterly*, *25*(1), 6–35. doi:10.1016/j.leaqua.2013.11.002

Dolot, A. (2018). The characteristics of Generation Z. *E-mentor, 74*(2), 44-50.

Dongrey, R., & Rokade, V. (2022). A Framework to Assess the Impact of Employee Perceived Equality on Contextual Performance and Mediating Role of Affective Commitment to Enhance and Sustain Positive Work Behavior. *Discrete Dynamics in Nature and Society*, *2022*, 1–14. doi:10.1155/2022/5407947

Dorsey, S., & Villwock, J. (2020). Employee resource groups: Best practices for organizational success. *Journal of Business Diversity*, *20*(2), 1–16.

Dose, J. J. (1997). Work values: An integrative framework and illustrative application to organizational socialization. *Journal of Occupational and Organizational Psychology*, *70*(3), 219–240. doi:10.1111/j.2044-8325.1997.tb00645.x

Downey, S. N., van der Werff, L., Thomas, K. M., & Plaut, V. C. (2015). The role of diversity practices and inclusion in promoting trust and employee engagement. *Journal of Applied Social Psychology*, *45*(1), 35–44. doi:10.1111/jasp.12273

Duan, H., Li, J., Fan, S., Lin, Z., Wu, X., & Cai, W. (2021). Metaverse for social good: A university campus prototype. *In Proceedings of the 29th ACM international conference on multimedia* (pp. 153-161). ACM. 10.1145/3474085.3479238

Dubovitskaya, T., Maznichenko, M., Romanova, G., & Yakubova, F. (2022). *The Teacher's Inclusive Culture: Assessing, Adjusting and Nurturing*. 351–369. doi:10.3897/ap.5.e0351

Duffy, M. K., Scott, K. L., Shaw, J. D., Tepper, B. J., & Aquino, K. (2012). A social context model of envy and social undermining. *Academy of Management Journal*, *55*(3), 643–666. doi:10.5465/amj.2009.0804

Du, J., Ma, E., & Lin, X. (2021). Can proactivity translate to creativity? Examinations at individual and team levels. *International Journal of Hospitality Management*, *98*, 103034. doi:10.1016/j.ijhm.2021.103034

Duraku, Z. H., & Hoxha, L. (2020). The impact of COVID-19 on education and on the well-being of teachers, parents, and students: Challenges related to remote (online) learning and opportunities for advancing the quality of education.

Dwertmann, D. J., Nishii, L. H., & Van Knippenberg, D. (2016). Disentangling the fairness & discrimination and synergy perspectives on diversity climate: Moving the field forward. *Journal of Management*, *42*(5), 1136–1168. doi:10.1177/0149206316630380

Dwivedi, Y. K., Hughes, L., Baabdullah, A. M., Ribeiro-Navarrete, S., Giannakis, M., Al-Debei, M. M., Dennehy, D., Metri, B., Buhalis, D., Cheung, C. M. K., Conboy, K., Doyle, R., Dubey, R., Dutot, V., Felix, R., Goyal, D. P., Gustafsson, A., Hinsch, C., Jebabli, I., & Wamba, S. F. (2022b). Metaverse beyond the hype: Multidisciplinary perspectives on emerging challenges, opportunities, and agenda for research, practice and policy. *International Journal of Information Management*, *66*, 102542. doi:10.1016/j.ijinfomgt.2022.102542

Dwivedi, Y. K., Hughes, L., Wang, Y., Alalwan, A. A., Ahn, S. J., Balakrishnan, J., Barta, S., Belk, R., Buhalis, D., Dutot, V., Felix, R., Filieri, R., Flavián, C., Gustafsson, A., Hinsch, C., Hollensen, S., Jain, V., Kim, J., Krishen, A. S., & Wirtz, J. (2022a). Metaverse marketing: How the metaverse will shape the future of consumer research and practice. *Psychology and Marketing*. doi:10.1002/mar.21767

Eagly, A. H., & Johnson, B. T. (1990). 'Gender and leadership style: A meta-analysis'. *Psychological Bulletin*, *108*(2), 233–256. doi:10.1037/0033-2909.108.2.233

Earley, P. C., & Mosakowski, E. (2004). Cultural intelligence. *Harvard Business Review*, *82*(10), 139–146. PMID:15559582

Eaton, J. A. (2000). *A social motivation approach to organizational cynicism*. York University.

Edelman. (2019). 2019 Edelman trust barometer. *The Importance of Employee Engagement in the Modern Workplace*. Entrepreneur.

Edmondson, A. C., Kramer, R. M., & Cook, K. S. (2004). Psychological safety, trust, and learning in organizations: A group-level lens. *Trust and distrust in organizations: Dilemmas and approaches, 12*, 239-272.

Ehsan, S. M. A. (2021). Managing Workforce Diversity Through Human Resource Management. A. Farazmand (ed.), Global Encyclopedia of Public Administration, Public Policy, and Governance, 1-9. Cornell University.

Eid, R., & Agag, G. (2020). Determinants of innovative behaviour in the hotel industry: A cross-cultural study. *International Journal of Hospitality Management*, *91*, 102642. doi:10.1016/j.ijhm.2020.102642

Ekíci, S., & Tuncel, G. (2015). Göç ve İnsan. *Birey ve Toplum Sosyal Bilimler Dergisi*, *5*(1), 9. doi:10.20493/bt.71783

Elder, G. H. Jr. (1994). Time, human agency, and social change: Perspectives on the life course. *Social Psychology Quarterly*, *57*(1), 4–15. doi:10.2307/2786971

Elsaied, M. M. (2020). A moderated mediation model for the relationship between inclusive leadership and job embeddedness. *American Journal of Business*, *35*(3/4), 191–210. doi:10.1108/AJB-06-2019-0035

Elsbach, K. D., & van Knippenberg, D. (2020). Creating high-impact literature reviews: An argument for 'integrative reviews'. *Journal of Management Studies*, *57*(6), 1277–1289. doi:10.1111/joms.12581

eMarketer. (2021). *Global e-commerce update 2021: Amid a pandemic shockwave*. eMarketer.

Enache, M. C. (2022). Metaverse Opportunities for Businesses. *Annals of the University Dunarea de Jos of Galati: Fascicle: I. Economics & Applied Informatics*, *28*(1), 67–71. doi:10.35219/eai15840409246

Engelhardt, M. A. (2017). Hitching healthcare to the chain: An Introduction to blockchain technology in the healthcare sector. *Technology Innovation Management Review*, *7*(10), 22–34. doi:10.22215/timreview/1111

Entrepreneur. (2023) *What is the metaverse and why is it important to entrepreneurs?* Entrepreneur. https://www.entrepreneur.com/science-technology/what-is-the-metaverse-and-why-is-it-important-to/442015

Erkutlu, H. (2012). The impact of organizational culture on the relationship between shared leadership and team proactivity. *Team Performance Management*, *18*(1/2), 102–119. doi:10.1108/13527591211207734

Erkutlu, H., & Chafra, J. (2012). The impact of team empowerment on proactivity: The moderating roles of leader's emotional intelligence and proactive personality. *Journal of Health Organization and Management*, *26*(5), 560–577. doi:10.1108/14777261211256918 PMID:23115905

Esmaeilikia, M., & Groth, M. (2022). A motivational approach to emotional labor: Examining the link between goal orientation and emotional labor strategies. *Journal of Management & Organization*, *28*(6), 1280–1300. doi:10.1017/jmo.2019.63

Espinoza, O. (2007). Solving the equity–equality conceptual dilemma: A new model for analysis of the educational process. *Educational Research*, *49*(4), 343–363. doi:10.1080/00131880701717198

Estes, B. C., & Wang, J. (2008). Integrative Literature Review: Workplace Incivility: Impacts on Individual and Organizational Performance. *Human Resource Development Review*, *7*(2), 218–240. doi:10.1177/1534484308315565

Eva, N., Robin, M., Sendjaya, S., van Dierendonck, D., & Liden, R. C. (2019). Servant leadership: A systematic review and call for future research. *The Leadership Quarterly*, *30*(1), 111–132. doi:10.1016/j.leaqua.2018.07.004

Fang, Y. C., Chen, J. Y., Wang, M. J., & Chen, C. Y. (2019). The impact of inclusive leadership on employees' innovative behaviors: The mediation of psychological capital. *Frontiers in Psychology*, *10*, 1803. doi:10.3389/fpsyg.2019.01803 PMID:31447740

Fang, Y., Dai, X., & Zhang, X. (2021). An empirical study of the relationship between inclusive leadership and business model innovation. *Leadership and Organization Development Journal*, *42*(3), 480–494. doi:10.1108/LODJ-11-2019-0484

Faniko, K., Ellemers, N., Derks, B., & Lorenzi-Cioldi, F. (2017). Nothing Changes, Really: Why Women Who Break Through the Glass Ceiling End Up Reinforcing It. *Personality and Social Psychology Bulletin*, *43*(5), 638–651. doi:10.1177/0146167217695551 PMID:28903635

Fan, L., Zhang, X., Rai, L., & Du, Y. (2021, May). Mobile Payment: The Next frontier of payment systems?-An emperical study based on Push Pull Mooring Framework. *Journal of Theoretical and Applied Electronic Commerce Research*, *16*(2), 155–169. doi:10.4067/S0718-18762021000200112

Fatima, T., Majeed, M., & Zulfiqar Ali Shah, S. (2021). A moderating mediation model of the antecedents of being driven to work: The role of inclusive leaders as change agents. *Canadian Journal of Administrative Sciences/Revue Canadienne des Sciences de l'Administration*, 1–21. doi:10.1002/cjas.1605

Faulkner, B. (2001). Towards a framework for tourism disaster management. *Tourism Management*, *22*(2), 135–147. doi:10.1016/S0261-5177(00)00048-0

Felblinger, D. M. (2008). 3 11). Incivility and Bullying in the Workplace and Nurses' Shame Responses. *Journal of Obstetric, Gynecologic, and Neonatal Nursing*, *37*(2), 234–242. doi:10.1111/j.1552-6909.2008.00227.x PMID:18336449

Fenitra, R. M., Abbas, A., Ekowati, D., & Suhairidi, F. (2022). Strategic Intent and Strategic Leadership: A Review Perspective for Post-covid Tourism and Hospitality Industry Recovery. In P. Mohanty, A. Sharma, J. Kennell, & A. Hassan (Eds.), *The Emerald Handbook of Destination Recovery in Tourism and Hospitality* (pp. 23–44). Emerald Group Publishing. doi:10.1108/978-1-80262-073-320221003

Fenzel, J. L. (2013). *Examining generational differences in the workplace: Work centrality, narcissism, and their relation to employee work engagement* [Doctoral dissertation, The University of Wisconsin-Milwaukee].

Ferdman, B. M., Prime, J., & Riggio, R. E. (2020). *Inclusive Leadership: Transforming Diverse Lives, Workplaces, and Societies* (B. M. Ferdman, J. Prime, & R. E. Riggio, Eds.; 1st ed.). Routledge. doi:10.4324/9780429449673

Ferguson, E., Semper, H., Yates, J., Fitzgerald, J. E., Skatova, A., & James, D. (2014). The 'dark side'and 'bright side'of personality: When too much conscientiousness and too little anxiety are detrimental with respect to the acquisition of medical knowledge and skill. *PLoS One*, *9*(2), 1–11. doi:10.1371/journal.pone.0088606 PMID:24586353

Ferguson, M. (2011). 8 10). You cannot leave it at the office: Spillover and crossover of coworker incivility. *Journal of Organizational Behavior*, *33*(4), 571–588. doi:10.1002/job.774

Fernandes, C., de Carvalho, G. B., & de Oliveira Cruz, G. (2018). The relationship between cognitive diversity and team creativity. *Journal of Business Research*, *86*, 78–86. doi:10.1016/j.jbusres.2018.01.040

Ferreira, J. J. M., Fernandes, C. I., & Ferreira, F. A. F. (2019). To be or not to be digital that is the question: Firm innovation and performance. *Journal of Business Research*, *101*, 583–590. doi:10.1016/j.jbusres.2018.11.013

Ferri-Reed, J. (2014). Millennializing the workplace. *Journal for Quality and Participation*, *37*(1), 13.

Filion, L. J. (2021). Defining the entrepreneur. In L. P. Dana (Ed.), *World encyclopedia of entrepreneurship* (2nd ed., pp. 72–83). Edward Elgar Publishing. doi:10.4337/9781839104145.00015

Filstad, C., Traavik, L. E., & Gorli, M. (2019). Belonging at work: The experiences, representations, and meanings of belonging. *Journal of Workplace Learning*, *31*(2), 116–142. doi:10.1108/JWL-06-2018-0081

Findler, L., Wind, L. H., & Barak, M. E. M. (2007). The Challenge of Workforce Management in a Global Society: Modeling the Relationship Between Diversity, Inclusion, Organizational Culture, and Employee Well-Being, Job Satisfaction and Organizational Commitment. *Administration in Social Work*, *31*(3), 63–94. doi:10.1300/J147v31n03_05

Fine, C., Sojo, V., & Lawford-Smith, H. (2020). Why does workplace gender diversity matter? Justice, organizational benefits, and policy. *Social Issues and Policy Review*, *14*(1), 36–72. doi:10.1111ipr.12064

Fischer, T., Dietz, J., & Antonakis, J. (2017). Leadership process models: A review and synthesis. *Journal of Management*, *43*(6), 1726–1753. doi:10.1177/0149206316682830

Fitzgerald, T. H. (1988). Can change in organizational culture really be managed? *Organizational Dynamics*, *17*(2), 5–15. doi:10.1016/0090-2616(88)90015-0

Fleenor, J. W. (2006). Trait approach to leadership. *Psychology*, *37*(1), 651–665.

Flexera. (2020). *2020 State of the cloud report*. Flexera.

Folger, R., Sheppard, B. H., & Buttram, R. T. (1995). Equity, equality, and need: Three faces of social justice. In B. B. Bunker & J. Z. Rubin (Eds.), *Conflict, cooperation, and justice: Essays inspired by the work of Morton Deutsch* (pp. 261–289). Jossey-Bass/Wiley.

Forbes. (2019). Why the Human Workforce Is Still the Future of Work. *Forbes*.

Fowler, K. L., Kling, N. D., & Larson, M. D. (2007). Organizational preparedness for coping with a major crisis or disaster. *Business & Society*, *46*(1), 88–103. doi:10.1177/0007650306293390

Franco, A., Malhotra, N., & Simonovits, G. (2014). Publication bias in the social sciences: Unlocking the file drawer. *Science*, *345*(6203), 1502–1505. doi:10.1126cience.1255484 PMID:25170047

French, A. (2017). Toward a New Conceptual Model: Integrating the Social Change Model of Leadership Development and Tinto's Model of Student Persistence. *Journal of Leadership Education*, *16*(3), 97–117. doi:10.12806/V16/I3/T4

French, A. M., & Shim, J. P. (2016). The digital revolution. Internet of things 5G, and beyond. *Communications of the Association for Information Systems*, *38*(1), 40. doi:10.17705/1CAIS.03840

Frese, M., & Fay, D. (2001). Personal initiative: An active performance concept for the 21st century. In B. M. Staw & R. I. Sutton (Eds.), *Research in Organizational Behavior,23, 133–187*. JAI Press. doi:10.1016/S0191-3085(01)23005-6

Frese, M., Fay, D., Hilburger, T., Leng, K., & Tag, A. (1997). The concept of personal initiative: Operationalization, reliability and validity in two German samples. *Journal of Occupational and Organizational Psychology*, *70*(2), 139–161. doi:10.1111/j.2044-8325.1997.tb00639.x

Frey, D., Royan, J., Piegay, R., Kermarrec, A. M., Anceaume, E., & Le Fessant, F. (2008). *Solipsis: A decentralized architecture for virtual environments*. [Paper presentation] 1st International Workshop on Massively Multiuser Virtual Environments. Reno, NV, United States.

Friedman, M. (2007). The social responsibility of business is to increase its profits. In W. C. Zimmerli, M. Holzinger, & K. Richter (Eds.), *Corporate ethics and corporate governance* (pp. 173–178). Springer. doi:10.1007/978-3-540-70818-6_14

Frie, K. G., & Janssen, C. (2009). Social inequality, lifestyles and health–a non-linear canonical correlation analysis based on the approach of Pierre Bourdieu. *International Journal of Public Health, 54*(4), 213–221. doi:10.100700038-009-8017-5 PMID:19418020

Fujimoto, Y., & Härtel, C. E. J. (2017). Organizational diversity learning framework: Going beyond diversity training programs. *Personnel Review, 46*(6), 1120–1141. doi:10.1108/PR-09-2015-0254

Furman, G. (2012). Social justice leadership as praxis: Developing capacities through preparation programs. *Educational Administration Quarterly, 48*(2), 191–229. doi:10.1177/0013161X11427394

Furnham, A. (2017). Dark side correlates of job reliability and stress tolerance in two large samples. *Personality and Individual Differences, 117*, 255–259. doi:10.1016/j.paid.2017.06.020

Fu, S., Cheng, X., Su, L., Bilgihan, A., & Okumus, F. (2020). Designing collaboration process facilitation in hotel management teams to improve collaboration performance. *International Journal of Hospitality Management, 88*, 102527. doi:10.1016/j.ijhm.2020.102527

Galinsky, A. D., Maddux, W. W., White, J. B., & Dubois, D. (2018). Cultural borders and mental barriers: The relationship between living abroad and creativity. *Journal of Personality and Social Psychology, 114*(2), 168–184. doi:10.1037/pspp0000138

Gallicano, T. D., Curtin, P., & Matthews, K. (2012). I love what I do, but… A relationship management survey of millennial generation public relations agency employees. *Journal of Public Relations Research, 24*(3), 222–242. doi:10.1080/1062726X.2012.671986

Gallicano, T. D., Martin, L. M., & Wingreen, S. C. (2021). A multilevel examination of cultural diversity, diversity climate, and innovation in US organizations. *Journal of Business Research, 131*, 731–743. doi:10.1016/j.jbusres.2021.03.038

Gallup. (2019). *State of the American workplace*. Gallup.

Gardenswartz, L., & Rowe, A. (1994). Diversity management: Practical application in a health care organization. *Frontiers of Health Services Management, 11*(2), 36–40. doi:10.1097/01974520-199410000-00004 PMID:10139136

Gardner, P., Moynihan, T., & Wright, L. (2007). The influence of human resource practices on the performance of business units. *Human Resource Management Journal, 13*, 21–36.

Gardner, T. M., Wright, P. M., & Moynihan, L. M. (2011). The impact of motivation, empowerment, and skill-enhancing practices on aggregate voluntary turnover: The mediating effect of collective affective commitment. *Personnel Psychology, 64*(2), 315–350. doi:10.1111/j.1744-6570.2011.01212.x

George, B., & McLean, A. (2018). Why leaders lose their way. In *Contemporary Issues in Leadership* (pp. 175–185). Routledge. doi:10.4324/9780429494000-20

Gerhart, B., & Fang, M. (2015). Pay, intrinsic motivation, extrinsic motivation, performance, and creativity in the workplace: Revisiting long-held beliefs. *Annual Review of Organizational Psychology and Organizational Behavior*, *2*(1), 489–521. doi:10.1146/annurev-orgpsych-032414-111418

Ge, T., Abbas, J., Ullah, R., Abbas, A., Sadiq, I., & Zhang, R. (2022). Women's entrepreneurial contribution to family income: Innovative technologies promote females' entrepreneurship amid COVID-19 crisis. *Frontiers in Psychology*, *13*, 1–10. doi:10.3389/fpsyg.2022.828040 PMID:35422737

Ghafoor, A., & Haar, J. (2020). A climate and personality approach towards creativity behaviours: A moderated mediation study. *International Journal of Innovation Management*, *24*(06), 2050080. doi:10.1142/S1363919620500802

Gibbons, J. M. (2006). *Employee engagement: A review of current research and its implications*. Conference Board.

Gibson, W. J., Greenwood, A. R., Edward, F., & Murphy, F. E. (2009). Generational differences In the workplace: Personal values, behaviors, and popular beliefs. *Journal of Diversity Management*, *4*(3), 1–8.

Gillespie, N., & Dietz, C. (2009). Trust Repair after an Organization-Level Failure. *Academy of Management Review*, *34*(1), 127–145. doi:10.5465/amr.2009.35713319

Gioia, D. A., Corley, K. G., & Hamilton, A. L. (2013). Seeking qualitative rigor in inductive research: Notes on the Gioia methodology. *Organizational Research Methods*, *16*(1), 15–31. doi:10.1177/1094428112452151

Gkritsi, E. (2022). HSBC enters the metaverse through partnership with the sandbox. *Coindesk*. https://www.coindesk.com/business/2022/03/16/hsbc-enters-the-metaverse-through-partnership-with-the-sandbox/

Godkin, L., Parayitam, S., & Natarajan, L. (2010). An empirical study of attitudes toward recognition among civilian municipal employees in a U.S. City. Journal of Organizational Culture. *Communication and Conflict*, *14*(2), 51–61.

Goldberg, K., & Kumar, V. (2018). Cognitive Diversity: AI & The Future of Work. Tata Communications. https://www.tatacommunications.com/wp-content/uploads/2018/09/Report_Cognitive-Diversity_AI-and-The-Future-of-Work.pdf

Gong, Z., Yang, J., Gilal, F. G., Van Swol, L. M., & Yin, K. (2020). Repairing police psychological safety: The role of career adaptability, feedback environment, and goal-self concordance based on the conservation of resources theory. *SAGE Open*, *10*(2), 2158244020919510. doi:10.1177/2158244020919510

Go, S. Y., Jeong, H. G., Kim, J. I., & Sin, Y. T. (2021). Concept and developmental direction of metaverse. *Korea Inf Process Soc Rev*, *28*, 7–16.

Goswami, S., & Kishor, B. (2018). Exploring the relationship between workforce diversity, inclusion and employee engagement. *Drishtikon: A Management Journal, 9*(1), 65-89.

Gotsis, G., & Grimani, K. (2016a). The role of servant leadership in fostering inclusive organizations. *Journal of Management Development*, *35*(8), 985–1010. doi:10.1108/JMD-07-2015-0095

Gotsis, G., & Grimani, K. (2016b). Diversity as an aspect of effective leadership: Integrating and moving forward. *Leadership and Organization Development Journal*, *2*(37), 241–264. doi:10.1108/LODJ-06-2014-0107

Gotsis, G., & Grimani, K. (2017). The role of spiritual leadership in fostering inclusive workplaces. *Personnel Review*, *46*(5), 908–935. doi:10.1108/PR-11-2015-0286

Goudreau, J. (2013). How to communicate in the new multi-generational office. *Forbes*. https://www.forbes.com/sites/jennagoudreau/2013/02/14/how-to communicate-in-the-new-multigenerational-office/#1652ee244a6
b

Gouldner, A. W. (1960). The norm of reciprocity: A preliminary statement. *American Sociological Review*, *25*(2), 161–178. doi:10.2307/2092623

Goulet, L., Krentz, C., & Christiansen, H. (2003). Collaboration in education: The phenomenon and process of working together. *The Alberta Journal of Educational Research*, *49*(4), 325–340.

Granovetter, M. (1985). Economic action and social structure: The problem of embeddedness. *American Journal of Sociology*, *91*(3), 481–510. doi:10.1086/228311

Grant, A. M., & Ashford, S. J. (2008). The dynamics of proactivity at work. *Research in Organizational Behavior*, *28*, 3–34. doi:10.1016/j.riob.2008.04.002

Grant, A. M., Gino, F., & Hofmann, D. A. (2011). Reversing the extraverted leadership advantage: The role of employee proactivity. *Academy of Management Journal*, *54*(3), 528–550. doi:10.5465/amj.2011.61968043

Greenleaf, R. K. (1977). *Servant leadership: A journey into the nature of legitimate power and greatness*. Paulist Press.

Greenleaf, R. K., Spears, L. C., & Covey, S. R. (2002). *Servant Leadership: A Journey Into the Nature of Legitimate Power and Greatness*. Paulist Press.

Grenfell, M., & Lebaron, F. (2014). *Bourdieu and data analysis: Methodological principles and practice*. Peter Lang AG. doi:10.3726/978-3-0353-0571-5

Grichnik, D., Brinckmann, J., Singh, L., & Manigart, S. (2014). Beyond environmental scarcity: Human and social capital as driving forces of bootstrapping activities. *Journal of Business Venturing*, *29*(2), 310–326. doi:10.1016/j.jbusvent.2013.02.006

Grossnickle, E. M. (2016). Disentangling curiosity: Dimensionality, definitions, and distinctions from interest in educational contexts. *Educational Psychology Review, 28*(1), 23–60. doi:10.100710648-014-9294-y

Guillaume, Y. R., Dawson, J. F., Woods, S. A., Sacramento, C. A., & West, M. A. (2013). Getting diversity at work to work: What we know and what we still don't know. *Journal of Occupational and Organizational Psychology, 86*(2), 123–141. doi:10.1111/joop.12009

Guinalíu, M., & Jordán, P. (2016). Building trust in the leader of virtual work teams. *Spanish Journal of Marketing-ESIC, 20*(1), 58–70. doi:10.1016/j.reimke.2016.01.003

Gümüş, A., & Erkuş, H. (2019). Blockchain ve kripto paraların kullanımı üzerine bir değerlendirme [An assessment on the use of blockchain and cryptocurrencies]. *Anemon Muş Alparslan Üniversitesi Sosyal Bilimler Dergisi, 7*(2), 41–49. doi:10.18506/anemon.427976

Guo, Y., Zhu, Y., & Zhang, L. (2020). Inclusive leadership, leader identification and employee voice behavior: The moderating role of power distance. *Current Psychology (New Brunswick, N.J.)*, 1–10. doi:10.100712144-020-00647-x

GuptaA.GoplaniM. M. (2020, May). IMPACT OF COVID-19 ON EDUCATIONAL INSTITUTIONS IN INDIA. *Purakala, 31*(21), 661-671. doi:10.13140/RG.2.2.32141.36321

Gu, R., & Nie, F. Y. (2021). Does empowering women benefit poverty reduction? Evidence from a multi-component program in the Inner Mongolia Autonomous Region of China. *Journal of Integrative Agriculture, 20*(4), 1092–1106. doi:10.1016/S2095-3119(20)63436-0

Gürcü, A. (2022). *Metavers nedir ne değildir*?[What is metaverse and what is it not?]. Insaniyet. https://www.insaniyet.net/metavers-nedir-ne-degildir

Gursoy, D., Chi, C. G., & Karadag, E. (2013). Generational differences in work values and attitudes among front line and service contact employees. *International Journal of Hospitality Review, 32*, 40–48.

Gursoy, D., Maier, A. T., & Chi, G. C. (2008). Generational differences: An examination of work values and Generational gaps in the hospitality workforce'. *International Journal of Hospitality Management, 27*(3), 448–458. doi:10.1016/j.ijhm.2007.11.002

Gursoy, D., Malodia, S., & Dhir, A. (2022). The metaverse in the hospitality and tourism industry: An overview of current trends and future research directions. *Journal of Hospitality Marketing & Management, 31*(5), 527–534. doi:10.1080/19368623.2022.2072504

Hackman, J., & Wageman, R. (2005). A Theory of Team Coaching. *Academy of Management Review, 302*(2), 269–287. doi:10.5465/amr.2005.16387885

Hafezieh, N., Akhavan, P., & Eshraghian, F. (2011). Exploration of Process and Competitive Factors of Entrepreneurship in Digital Space: A Multiple Case Study in Iran. *Education, Business and Society, 4*(4), 267–279. doi:10.1108/17537981111190051

Hamel, G., & Valikangas, L. (2004). The quest for resilience. *Icade. Revista de la Facultad de Derecho (Montevideo)*, *62*, 355–358.

Hammond, M., Cross, C., Farrell, C., & Eubanks, D. (2019). Burnout and innovative work behaviours for survivors of downsizing: An investigation of boundary conditions. *Creativity and Innovation Management*, *28*(3), 306–317. doi:10.1111/caim.12327

Hanh Tran, T. B., & Choi, S. B. (2019). Effects of inclusive leadership on organizational citizenship behavior: The mediating roles of organizational justice and learning culture. *Journal of Pacific Rim Psychology*, *13*(17), e17. doi:10.1017/prp.2019.10

Han, S. J., & Hazard, N. (2022). Shared Leadership in Virtual Teams at Work: Practical Strategies and Research Suggestions for Human Resource Development. *Human Resource Development Review*, *21*(3), 300–323. doi:10.1177/15344843221093376

Harrell-Cook, G., Ferris, G. R., & Dulebohn, J. H. (1999). Political behaviors as moderators of the perceptions of organizational politics—Work outcomes relationships. *Journal of Organizational Behavior*, *20*(7), 1093–1105. doi:10.1002/(SICI)1099-1379(199912)20:7<1093::AID-JOB945>3.0.CO;2-#

Harris, A., & Jones, M. (2018). The dark side of leadership and management. *School Leadership & Management*, *38*(5), 475–477. doi:10.1080/13632434.2018.1509276

Harrison, D. A., & Klein, K. J. (2007). What's the difference? Diversity constructs as separation, variety, or disparity in organizations. *Academy of Management Review*, *32*(4), 1199–1228. doi:10.5465/amr.2007.26586096

Harrison, D. A., Price, K. H., & Bell, M. P. (1998). Beyond relational demography: Time and the effects of surface- and deep-level diversity on work group cohesion. *Academy of Management Journal*, *41*(1), 96–107. doi:10.2307/256901

Harrison, J. K., & Brower, H. H. (2011). The impact of cultural intelligence and psychological hardiness on homesickness among study abroad students. *Frontiers: The Interdisciplinary Journal of Study Abroad*, *21*(1), 41–62. doi:10.36366/frontiers.v21i1.303

Harter, J. K., Schmidt, F. L., & Hayes, T. L. (2002). Business-unit-level relationship between employee satisfaction, employee engagement, and business outcomes: A meta-analysis. *The Journal of Applied Psychology*, *87*(2), 268–279. doi:10.1037/0021-9010.87.2.268 PMID:12002955

Hartman, J. L., & McCambridge, J. (2011). Optimizing millennials' communication styles. *Business Communication Quarterly*, *74*(1), 22–44. doi:10.1177/1080569910395564

Harvard Business Review. (2019). The Business Case for Diversity in the Workforce. *Harvard Business Review*.

Harvard Business Review. (2019). The Importance of a Skilled Workforce in the Digital Age. *Harvard Business Review*.

Harvey, S. (2014). Creative synthesis: Exploring the process of extraordinary group creativity. *Academy of Management Review*, *39*(3), 324–343. doi:10.5465/amr.2012.0224

Haslam, S. A. (2004). *Psychology in Organizations: The Social Identity Approach* (2nd ed.). SAGE Publications.

Hassanein, E. E. A. (2015). *Inclusion, Disability and Culture*. SensePublishers. doi:10.1007/978-94-6209-923-4

Hassan, S., & Jiang, Z. (2021). Facilitating learning to improve performance of law enforcement workgroups: The role of inclusive leadership behavior. *International Public Management Journal*, *24*(1), 106–130. doi:10.1080/10967494.2019.1680465

Hazan, E., Kelly, G., Khan, H., Spillecke, D., & Yee, L. (2022). *Marketing in the metaverse: An opportunity for innovation and experimentation.* McKinsey. https://www.mckinsey.com/capabilities/growth-marketing-and-sales/our-insights/marketing-in-the-metaverse-an-opportunity-for-innovation-and-experimentation

He, R., Luo, L., Shamsuddin, A., & Tang, Q. (2021). Corporate Carbon Accounting: A literature Review of Carbon Accounting Research From the Koyoto Protocol to the Paris agreement. *Accounting and Finance Assosiation of Australia and New-Zealand*, 1-38. doi:10.1111/acfi.12789

He, L., Zhou, W., He, M., Nie, X., & He, J. (2021). Openness and COVID-19 induced xenophobia: The roles of trade and migration in sustainable development. *PLoS One*, *16*(4), e0249579. doi:10.1371/journal.pone.0249579 PMID:33831012

Henseler, J., Ringle, C. M., & Sarstedt, M. (2015). A new criterion for assessing discriminant validity in variance-based structural equation modeling. *Journal of the Academy of Marketing Science*, *43*(1), 115–135. doi:10.100711747-014-0403-8

Herring, C. (2019). Does diversity pay? Race, gender, and the business case for diversity. *American Sociological Review*, *84*(2), 208–235. doi:10.1177/000312240907400203

Herring, C., Woolley, A. W., & Xin, K. R. (2019). Demographic diversity and creativity in small groups: A review and integration of the literature. *Small Group Research*, *50*(6), 715–770. doi:10.1177/1046496419883426

Hertel, G. T., Geister, S., & Konradt, U. (2005). Managing virtual teams: A review of current empirical research. *Human Resource Management Review*, *15*(1), 69–95. doi:10.1016/j.hrmr.2005.01.002

Hesselbein, F. (1999). The key to cultural transformation: THE KEY TO CULTURAL TRANSFORMATION. *Leader to Leader*, *1999*(12), 1–7. doi:10.1002/ltl.40619991201

Heuven, E., Bakker, A. B., Schaufeli, W. B., & Huisman, N. (2006). The role of self-efficacy in performing emotion work. *Journal of Vocational Behavior*, *69*(2), 222–235. doi:10.1016/j.jvb.2006.03.002

Hilal, O. A. (2021). The moderating role of self-efficacy in the relationship between workplace envy and social undermining. *Global Business and Organizational Excellence*, *40*(6), 28–40. doi:10.1002/joe.22091

Hinds, P. J., & Mortensen, M. (2021). The key to managing remote work: Functional diversity. *Harvard Business Review*, *99*(1), 124–133.

Hirak, R., Peng, A. C., Carmeli, A., & Schaubroeck, J. M. (2012). Linking leader inclusiveness to work unit performance: The importance of psychological safety and learning from failures. *The Leadership Quarterly*, *23*(1), 107–117. doi:10.1016/j.leaqua.2011.11.009

Hoch, J. E. (2013). Shared leadership and innovation: The role of vertical leadership and employee integrity. *Journal of Business and Psychology*, *28*(2), 159–174. doi:10.100710869-012-9273-6

Hofstede, G. (2023). Hofstede insights: Country comparison tool. *Hofstede-Insights (E-Article),* Https://Www. Hofstede-Insights. Com/.

Hollander, E. P. (1980). Leadership and social exchange processes. In *Social exchange* (pp. 103–118). Springer. doi:10.1007/978-1-4613-3087-5_5

Hollander, E. P. (2009). *Inclusive leadership: The essential leader-follower relationship.* Routledge.

Holvino, E., Ferdman, B. M., & Merrill-Sands, D. (2004). *Creating and sustaining diversity and inclusion in organizations: Strategies and approaches.*

Homan, A. C., Buengeler, C., Eckhoff, R. A., Ginkel, W. P. V., & Voelpel, S. C. (2019). The interplay of diversity training and diversity beliefs on team creativity in nationality diverse teams. *Journal of Organizational Behavior*, *40*(7), 812–832. doi:10.1002/job.2381

Home, J. F. III, & Orr, J. E. (1997). Assessing behaviors that create resilient organizations. *Employment Relations Today*, *24*(4), 29–39. doi:10.1002/ert.3910240405

Hope Pelled, L., Ledford, G. E. Jr, & Albers Mohrman, S. (1999). Demographic dissimilarity and workplace inclusion. *Journal of Management Studies*, *36*(7), 1013–1031. doi:10.1111/1467-6486.00168

Horwitz, S. K., & Horwitz, I. B. (2007). The effects of team diversity on team outcomes: A meta-analytic review of team demography. *Journal of Management*, *33*(6), 987–1015. doi:10.1177/0149206307308587

Houghton, J., Neck, C. P., & Manz, C. C. (2003). Self-leadership and Super Leadership: the heart and the art of creating shared leadership in teams. In C. L. Pearce & J. A. Conger (Eds.), *Shared Leadership: Reframing the Hows and Whys of Leadership* (pp. 123–140). Sage Publications. doi:10.4135/9781452229539.n6

House, R. J., & Global Leadership and Organizational Behavior Effectiveness Research Program (Eds.). (2004). *Culture, leadership, and organizations: The GLOBE study of 62 societies*. Sage Publications.

Howell, J. (2022). *Top 5 Metaverse Applications*. 101 Bloackchains. https://101blockchains.com/top-metaverse-applications/

Hsiao, A., Auld, C., & Ma, E. (2015). Perceived organizational diversity and employee behavior. *International Journal of Hospitality Management*, *48*, 102–112. doi:10.1016/j.ijhm.2015.04.009

Huang, X., Wang, J., & Zhang, Y. (2021). Exploring the relationship between functional diversity and team innovation in the manufacturing industry: The role of organizational learning capability. *Sustainability*, *13*(3), 1102. doi:10.3390u13031102

Hüffmeier, J., Krumm, S., Kanthak, J., & Hertel, G. (2012). "Don't let the group down": Facets of instrumentality moderate the motivating effects of groups in a field experiment. *European Journal of Social Psychology*, *42*(5), 533–538. doi:10.1002/ejsp.1875

Hughes, M., Rigtering, J. C., Covin, J. G., Bouncken, R. B., & Kraus, S. (2018). Innovative behaviour, trust and perceived workplace performance. *British Journal of Management*, *29*(4), 750–768. doi:10.1111/1467-8551.12305

Human Rights Campaign Foundation. (2019). *LGBTQ diversity and inclusion in ERGs*. HRCF.

Hu, N., Wu, J., & Gu, J. (2019). Cultural intelligence and employees' creative performance: The moderating role of team conflict in interorganizational teams. *Journal of Management & Organization*, *25*(1), 96–116. doi:10.1017/jmo.2016.64

Hunter, S. T., Ouimet, G., Thompson, L. F., & Lee, M. K. (2020). Diversity, faultlines, and team effectiveness in health care organizations. *Journal of Health Organization and Management*, *34*(2), 236–249.

Hunt, V., & Ajao, B. (2021). How to promote diversity and inclusion during a crisis. *Harvard Business Review*.

Hunt, V., Layton, D., & Prince, S. (2019). *Diversity wins: How inclusion matters*. McKinsey & Company.

Hurrelmann, K., & Albrecht, E. (2014). *Die heimlichen Revolutionäre - Wie die Generation Y unsere Welt verändert*. Verlag Beltz.

Hurst, R. (2008). *Leadership when the sky falls: leadership lessons from the shuttle Columbia disaster*. AuthorHouse Publishing Inc.

Huynh-The, T., Gadekallu, T. R., Wang, W., Yenduri, G., Ranaweera, P., Pham, Q. V., Costa, D. B., & Liyanage, M. (2023b). Blockchain for the metaverse: A Review. *Future Generation Computer Systems*, *143*, 401–419. doi:10.1016/j.future.2023.02.008

Huynh-The, T., Pham, Q. V., Pham, X. Q., Nguyen, T. T., Han, Z., & Kim, D. S. (2023a). Artificial intelligence for the metaverse: A survey. *Engineering Applications of Artificial Intelligence*, *117*, 105581. doi:10.1016/j.engappai.2022.105581

Hyatt, D. E., & Ruddy, T. M. (1997). An examination of the relationship between work group characteristics and performance: Once more into the breech. *Personnel Psychology*, *50*(3), 553–585. doi:10.1111/j.1744-6570.1997.tb00703.x

IES. (2004). *Employee Studies*. The Institute for Employment Studies. http://www.employmentstudies. co.uk/system/files/resources/files/408.pdf

Ince, F. (2022). Transformational Leadership in a Diverse and Inclusive Organizational Culture. In R. I. Perez-Uribe, D. Ocampo-Guzman, & N. Moreno-Monsalve (Eds.), (pp. 188–201). Advances in Human Resources Management and Organizational Development. IGI Global., doi:10.4018/978-1-6684-5216-5.ch010

Isidro, H., & Sobral, M. (2015). The effects of women on corporate boards on firm value, financial performance, and ethical and social compliance. *Journal of Business Ethics*, *132*(1), 1–19. doi:10.100710551-014-2302-9

ISO. (2011). *ISO 28002:2011(en), Security management systems for the supply chain—Development of resilience in the supply chain—Requirements with guidance for use*. ISO. https://www.iso.org/obp/ui/fr/#iso:std:iso:28002:ed-1:v1:en

Itam, U., & Bagali, M. M. (2019). Diversity and inclusion management: a focus on employee engagement. In Gender and Diversity: Concepts, Methodologies, Tools, and Applications (pp. 1771-1788). IGI Global.. doi:10.4018/978-1-5225-6912-1.ch093

Iyer, A., & Ryan, M. K. (2009). Why Do Men and Women Challenge Gender Discrimination in the Workplace? The Role of Group Status and In-group Identification in Predicting Pathways to Collective Action. *The Journal of Social Issues*, *65*(4), 791–814. doi:10.1111/j.1540-4560.2009.01625.x

Iyer, D. N., & Miller, K. D. (2008). Performance feedback, slack, and the timing of acquisitions. *Academy of Management Journal*, *51*(4), 808–822.

Jackson, S. E., Li, Y., Zhao, Y., & Liu, J. (2020). The effects of cognitive diversity on team effectiveness in professional service organizations. *Journal of Organizational Behavior*, *41*(8), 801–818. doi:10.1002/job.2391

Jackson, S. E., Ruderman, M. N., & DeFillippi, R. J. (2019). Diversity, creativity, and innovation: A meta-analytic review of the relationship. *Journal of Business and Psychology*, *34*(1), 3–26.

James, J. B., McKechnie, S., Swanberg, J., & Besen, E. (2013). Exploring the workplace impact of intentional/unintentional age discrimination. *Journal of Managerial Psychology*, *28*(7/8), 907–927. doi:10.1108/JMP-06-2013-0179

Janis, I. L. (1972). *Victims of Groupthink: A Psychological Study of Foreign-Policy Decisions and Fiascoes*. Houghton Mifflin.

Jansen, J. D. (2006). Leading against the grain: The politics and emotions of leading for social justice in South Africa. *Leadership and Policy in Schools*, *5*(1), 37–51. doi:10.1080/15700760500484027

Jans, L., Postmes, T., & Van der Zee, K. I. (2012). Sharing differences: The inductive route to social identity formation. *Journal of Experimental Social Psychology*, *48*(5), 1145–1149. doi:10.1016/j.jesp.2012.04.013

Janssen, O. (2004). How fairness perceptions make innovative behavior more or less stressful. *Journal of Organizational Behavior*, *25*(2), 201–215. doi:10.1002/job.238

Janssen, O., & Van Yperen, N. W. (2004). Employees' goal orientations, the quality of leader-member exchange, and the outcomes of job performance and job satisfaction. *Academy of Management Journal*, *47*(3), 368–384. doi:10.2307/20159587

Jaques, T. (2007). Issue management and crisis management: An integrated, non-linear, relational construct. *Public Relations Review*, *33*(2), 147–157. doi:10.1016/j.pubrev.2007.02.001

Jarvenpaa, S. L., Shaw, T. R., & Staples, D. S. (2004). Toward contextualized theories of trust: The role of trust in global virtual teams. *Information Systems Research*, *15*(3), 250–267. doi:10.1287/isre.1040.0028

Jarvenpaa, S. L., & Tanriverdi, H. (2002). Leading virtual knowledge networks. *Organizational Dynamics*, *31*(4), 403–412. doi:10.1016/S0090-2616(02)00127-4

Javed, B., Khan, A. K., & Quratulain, S. (2018). Inclusive leadership and innovative work behavior: Examination of LMX perspective in small capitalized textile firms. *The Journal of Psychology*, *152*(8), 594–612. doi:10.1080/00223980.2018.1489767 PMID:30260768

Javed, B., Naqvi, S. M. M. R., Khan, A. K., Arjoon, S., & Tayyeb, H. H. (2017). Impact of inclusive leadership on innovative work behavior: The role of psychological safety. *Journal of Management & Organization*, *25*(1), 117–136. doi:10.1017/jmo.2017.3

Jehn, K. A., Northcraft, G. B., & Neale, M. A. (1999). Why differences make a difference: A field study of diversity, conflict and performance in workgroups. *Administrative Science Quarterly*, *44*(4), 741–763. doi:10.2307/2667054

Jena, P. K. (2020). Impact of Covid-19 on higher education in India. *International Journal of Advanced Education and Research*, *5*(3), 77–81.

Jena, P. K. (2020, July). Impact of Pandemic COVID-19 on Education in India. *International Journal of Current Research*, *12*(7), 12582–12586. doi:10.24941/ijcr.39209.07.2020

Jeon, H. J., Youn, H. C., Ko, S. M., & Kim, T. H. (2022). Blockchain and AI Meet in the Metaverse. *Advances in the Convergence of Blockchain and Artificial Intelligence*, *73*(10.5772). https://www.intechopen.com/chapters/77823

Jha, C. (2020). *The Great Disruptive Transformation*. Wiley.

Jiang, H., & Zhang, Q. P. (2014). Development and validation of team creativity measures: A complex systems perspective. *Creativity and Innovation Management*, *23*(3), 264–275. doi:10.1111/caim.12078

Jiang, Z., Hu, X., Wang, Z., & Jiang, X. (2019). Knowledge hiding as a barrier to thriving: The mediating role of psychological safety and moderating role of organizational cynicism. *Journal of Organizational Behavior*, *40*(7), 800–818. doi:10.1002/job.2358

Jneid, C. (2022). How Social Self-Efficacy and Emotional Self-Efficacy moderate the relationship between Occupational stress and knowledge hiding in Brazilian software industry. Evidence-based HRM: a global forum for empirical scholarship. doi:10.1108/EBHRM-03-2021-0040

Johnson, S. K. (2020). *Inclusify: The power of uniqueness and belonging to build innovative teams*. Harper Business, an imprint of HarperCollins Publishers.

Johnson, J. L., & O'Leary-Kelly, A. M. (2003). The effects of psychological contract breach and organizational cynicism: Not all social exchange violations are created equal. *Journal of Organizational Behavior: The International Journal of Industrial. Journal of Organizational Behavior*, *24*(5), 627–647. doi:10.1002/job.207

Johnson, R. E., & Johnson, D. W. (2019). Functional diversity and innovation in interdisciplinary teams. *The Journal of Creative Behavior*, *53*(4), 501–515. doi:10.1002/jocb.398

Johnson, S. K., & Hekman, D. R. (2021). Intersectionality as a necessary framework for diverse and inclusive organizations. *Academy of Management Review*, *46*(2), 221–231. doi:10.5465/amr.2019.0464

Jolly, P. M., & Lee, L. (2021). Silence is not golden: Motivating employee voice through inclusive leadership. *Journal of Hospitality & Tourism Research (Washington, D.C.)*, *45*(6), 1092–1113. doi:10.1177/1096348020963699

Jones, J. R., & Harter, J. K. (2005). Race effects on the employee engagement turnover intention relationship. *Journal of Leadership & Organizational Studies*, *11*(2), 78–88. doi:10.1177/107179190501100208

Jones, P., & Danforth, S. (Eds.). (2015). *Foundations of inclusive education research* (1st ed.). Emerald. doi:10.1108/S1479-363620156

Joyce, D., & White, N. M. (2020). Colleges need a makeover: Adapting to change one class at a time. *Journal of Higher Education Theory and Practice*, *20*(5), 11–15.

Joyce, D., & White, N. M. (2020). Colleges Need a Makeover: Adapting to Change One Class at a Time. *Journal of Higher Education Theory and Practice*, *20*(5), 11–15.

Judge, T. A., & Bono, J. E. (2001). Relationship of core self-evaluations trait self-esteem, generalized self-efficacy. Locus of control, and emotional stability – with job satisfaction and job performance: A meta-analysis. *The Journal of Applied Psychology*, *86*(1), 80–92. doi:10.1037/0021-9010.86.1.80 PMID:11302235

Judge, T. A., Piccolo, R. F., & Kosalka, T. (2009). The bright and dark sides of leader traits: A review and theoretical extension of the leader trait paradigm. *The Leadership Quarterly*, *20*(6), 855–875. doi:10.1016/j.leaqua.2009.09.004

Kahn, W. A. (1990). Psychological conditions of personal engagement and disengagement at work. *Academy of Management Journal, 33*(4), 692–724. doi:10.2307/256287

Kahn, W. A., Barton, M. A., & Fellows, S. (2013). Organizational crises and the disturbance of relational systems. *Academy of Management Review, 38*(3), 377–396. doi:10.5465/amr.2011.0363

Kalinoski, Z. T., Steele-Johnson, D., Peyton, E. J., Leas, K. A., Steinke, J., & Bowling, N. A. (2013). A meta-analytic evaluation of diversity training outcomes. *Journal of Organizational Behavior, 34*(8), 1076–1104. doi:10.1002/job.1839

Kallinikos, J., Aaltonen, A., & Marton, A. (2013). The ambivalent ontology of digital artifacts. *Management Information Systems Quarterly, 37*(2), 357–370. https://www.jstor.org/stable/43825913. doi:10.25300/MISQ/2013/37.2.02

Kaminski, M., Kaufman, J. S., Graubarth, R., & Robins, T. G. (2000). How do people become empowered? A case study of union activists. *Human Relations, 53*(10), 1357–1383. doi:10.1177/a014108

Kanter, R. M. (2018). The diversity and inclusion revolution: Eight powerful truths. *Harvard Business Review, 96*(1), 54–61.

Karau, S. J., & Williams, K. D. (1993). Social loafing: A meta-analytic review and theoretical integration. *Journal of Personality and Social Psychology, 65*(4), 681–706. doi:10.1037/0022-3514.65.4.681

Kelan, E. K. (2020). The inclusive leader, the smart strategist and the forced altruist: Subject positions for men as gender equality partners. *European Management Review, 17*(3), 603–613. doi:10.1111/emre.12372

Keller, T., & Dansereau, F. (1995). Leadership and empowerment: A social exchange perspective. *Human Relations, 48*(2), 127–146. doi:10.1177/001872679504800202

Kelly, C., & Breinlinger, S. (1995). Identity and injustice: Exploring women's participation in collective action. *Journal of Community & Applied Social Psychology, 5*(1), 41–57. doi:10.1002/casp.2450050104

Kelly, J. T., Brown, E. R., Diekman, A. B., & Schneider, M. C. (2018). The change we believe in: The role of socioeconomic conditions in evaluations of black political candidates. *Electoral Studies, 54*, 254–260. doi:10.1016/j.electstud.2018.04.008

Kennedy, F., Carroll, B., & Francoeur, J. (2013). Mindset not skill set: Evaluating in new paradigms of leadership development. *Advances in Developing Human Resources, 15*(1), 10–26. doi:10.1177/1523422312466835

Kenski, K. (2021). *The impact of COVID-19 on the IT workforce: A year of disruption.*

Kerr, N. L. (1983). Motivation losses in task-performing groups: A social dilemma analysis. *Journal of Personality and Social Psychology, 45*(4), 819–828. doi:10.1037/0022-3514.45.4.819

Kerr, N. L., & Tindale, R. S. (2004). Group performance and decision making. *Annual Review of Psychology, 55*(1), 623–655. doi:10.1146/annurev.psych.55.090902.142009 PMID:14744229

Khalili, A. (2016). Linking transformational leadership, creativity, innovation, and innovation-supportive climate. *Management Decision, 54*(9), 2277–2293. doi:10.1108/MD-03-2016-0196

Khan, G. F., Wood, J., Kim, W., & Mahmood, M. T. (2016). Work Engagement Research Domain: Keywords Analysis Using Social Network Analysis and Burst Detection Approach. *International Journal of Computers, 1.*

Khan, J., Jaafar, M., Javed, B., Mubarak, N., & Saudagar, T. (2020). Does inclusive leadership affect project success? The mediating role of perceived psychological empowerment and psychological safety. *International Journal of Managing Projects in Business, 13*(5), 1077–1096. doi:10.1108/IJMPB-10-2019-0267

Khan, M. W., & Altaf, M. (2015). Important dimensions influencing employee engagement in organizations of Pakistan. *Journal of Business and Management Research, 9*(1), 270–275.

Khattak, S. R., Zada, M., Nouman, M., Rahman, S. U., Fayaz, M., Ullah, R., Salazar-Sepúlveda, G., Vega-Muñoz, A., & Contreras-Barraza, N. (2022). Investigating Inclusive Leadership and Pro-Social Rule Breaking in Hospitality Industry: Important Role of Psychological Safety and Leadership Identification. *International Journal of Environmental Research and Public Health, 19*(14), 8291. doi:10.3390/ijerph19148291 PMID:35886142

Kicheva, T. (2017). 'Management of Employees from Different Generations - Challenge for Bulgarian Managers and HR Professionals'. *Economic Alternatives, 1*, 103–121.

Kim, E., & Glomb, T. M. (2014). Victimization of high performers: The roles of envy and work group identification. *The Journal of Applied Psychology, 99*(4), 619–634. doi:10.1037/a0035789 PMID:24490964

Kimhi, A. (2010). Entrepreneurship and income inequality in southern Ethiopia. *Small Business Economics, 34*(1), 81–91. doi:10.100711187-009-9196-4

Kim, J. (2021). Advertising in the Metaverse: Research Agenda. *Journal of Interactive Advertising, 21*(3), 141–144. doi:10.1080/15252019.2021.2001273

Kim, J., Kim, J. N., & Park, H. J. (2020). The relationship between functional diversity and firm performance in the technology industry: The moderating role of environmental dynamism. *Asia Pacific Journal of Management, 37*(1), 81–107. doi:10.100710490-019-09657-9

King, G. III. (2002). Crisis management and team effectiveness: A closer examination. *Journal of Business Ethics, 41*(3), 235–249. doi:10.1023/A:1021200514323

Kirk, B. A., Schutte, N. S., & Hine, D. W. (2011). The Effect of an Expressive-Writing Intervention for Employees on Emotional Self-Efficacy, Emotional Intelligence, Affect, and Workplace Incivility. *Journal of Applied Social Psychology, 41*(1), 179–195. doi:10.1111/j.1559-1816.2010.00708.x

Kirkman, B. L., Chen, G., Farh, J. L., Chen, Z. X., & Lowe, K. B. (2009). Individual power distance orientation and follower reactions to transformational leaders: A cross-level, cross-cultural examination. *Academy of Management Journal*, *52*(4), 744–764. doi:10.5465/amj.2009.43669971

Kirkman, B. L., & Rosen, B. (1999). Beyond self-management: Antecedents and consequences of team empowerment. *Academy of Management Journal*, *42*(1), 58–74. doi:10.2307/256874

Kirkpatrick, S. A., & Locke, E. A. (1991). Leadership: Do traits matter? *The Academy of Management Perspectives*, *5*(2), 48–60. doi:10.5465/ame.1991.4274679

Kirton, G., & Greene, A. M. (2015). *The Dynamics of Managing Diversity: A Critical Approach*. Routledge. doi:10.4324/9781315767147

Kirton, M. (1976). Adaptors and innovators: A description and measure. *The Journal of Applied Psychology*, *61*(5), 622–629. doi:10.1037/0021-9010.61.5.622

Ko, C. H. (2015). Exploring the Motivators Stimulating Hotel Employees' Innovation. *Journal of Human Resource and Sustainability Studies*, *3*(03), 156–161. doi:10.4236/jhrss.2015.33021

Kollmann, T. (2006). What is e-entrepreneurship? Fundamentals of company founding in the net economy. *International Journal of Technology Management*, *33*(4), 322–340. doi:10.1504/IJTM.2006.009247

Komives, S. R., Lucas, N., & McMahon, T. R. (2013). *Exploring leadership: For college students who want to make a difference* (3rd ed.). Jossey-Bass.

Koopman, J., Lanaj, K., & Scott, B. A. (2016). Integrating the bright and dark sides of OCB: A daily investigation of the benefits and costs of helping others. *Academy of Management Journal*, *59*(2), 414–435. doi:10.5465/amj.2014.0262

Korkmaz, A. V., van Engen, M. L., Knappert, L., & Schalk, R. (2022). About and beyond leading uniqueness and belongingness: A systematic review of inclusive leadership research. *Human Resource Management Review*, *32*(4), 100894. doi:10.1016/j.hrmr.2022.100894

Kostopoulos, K. C., & Bozionelos, N. (2011). Team exploratory and exploitative learning: Psychological safety, task conflict, and team performance. *Group & Organization Management*, *36*(3), 385–415. doi:10.1177/1059601111405985

Kouzes, J. M., & Posner, B. Z. (2023). *The leadership challenge: How to make extraordinary things happen in organizations*. John Wiley & Sons.

Kovary, G. (2012). *'Leading A MultiGenerational Project Team'*. NGen Performance. https://www.nGenperformance.com

Kozhevnikov, M. (2007). Cognitive styles in the context of modern psychology: Toward an integrated framework of cognitive style. *Psychological Bulletin*, *133*(3), 464–481. doi:10.1037/0033-2909.133.3.464 PMID:17469987

Kozlowski, S. W. J., & Klein, K. J. (2000). A Multilevel Approach to Theory and Research in Organizations: Contextual, Temporal, and Emergent Processes. In K. J. Klein & S. W. J. Kozlowski (Eds.), *Multilevel Theory, Research, and Methods in Organizations: Foundations, Extensions, and New Directions* (pp. 3–90). Jossey-Bass.

Krebs, V. (2007). Managing the 21st century organization. *ihrim Journal, 11*(4), 2-8.

Kremer, M. (1993). The O-ring theory of economic development. *The Quarterly Journal of Economics, 108*(3), 551–575. doi:10.2307/2118400

Kress, G., Steinert, M., & Price, T. (2012). Cognition as a measure of team diversity. In *2012 2nd interdisciplinary engineering design education conference (IEDEC)* (pp. 67-72). 10.1109/IEDEC.2012.6186925

Kuckertz, A. (2020). Startups in times of crisis – A rapid response to the. *Journal of Business Venturing Insights.*

Kuknor, S. C., & Bhattacharya, S. (2020a). Inclusive leadership: New age leadership to foster organizational inclusion. *European Journal of Training and Development.* doi:10.1108/EJTD-07-2019-0132

Kuknor, S., & Bhattacharya, S. (2020b). Exploring organizational inclusion and inclusive leadership in Indian companies. *European Business Review, 33*(3), 450–464. doi:10.1108/EBR-04-2020-0089

Kular, S., Gatenby, M., Rees, C., Soane, E., and Truss, K. (2008). *Employee Engagement: A literature review.* Kingston University.

Kumar Mukul, G. K. (2021). Talent acquisition in startups in India: the role of social capital. *Journal of Entrepreneurship in Emerging Economies.*

Kumar, V., & Pansari, A. (2016). Competitive advantage through engagement. *JMR, Journal of Marketing Research, 53*(4), 497–514. doi:10.1509/jmr.15.0044

Kundu, S. C., & Mor, A. (2017). Workforce diversity and organizational performance: A study of IT industry in India. *Employee Relations, 39*(2), 160–183. doi:10.1108/ER-06-2015-0114

Kurthen, H., Bergmann, W., & Erb, R. (Eds.). (1997). *Antisemitism and xenophobia in Germany after unification.* Oxford University Press.

Kurtzberg, T. R. (2005). Feeling creative, being creative: An empirical study of diversity and creativity in teams. *Creativity Research Journal, 17*(1), 51–65. doi:10.120715326934crj1701_5

Kuusela, P., Keil, T., & Maula, M. (2017). Driven by aspirations, but in what direction? Performance shortfalls, slack resources, and resource-consuming vs. resource-freeing organizational change. *Strategic Management Journal, 38*(5), 1101–1120. doi:10.1002mj.2544

Kye, B., Han, N., Kim, E., Park, Y., & Jo, S. (2021). Educational applications of metaverse: Possibilities and limitations. *Journal of Educational Evaluation for Health Professions, 18,* 1149230. doi:10.3352/jeehp.2021.18.32 PMID:34897242

Lacerenza, C. N., Reyes, D. L., Marlow, S. L., Joseph, D. L., & Salas, E. (2017). Leadership training design, delivery, and implementation: A meta-analysis. *The Journal of Applied Psychology, 102*(12), 1686–1718. doi:10.1037/apl0000241 PMID:28749153

Laeeq, K. (2022). *Metaverse: Why, how and what.* Research Gate. https://www.researchgate.net/profile/Kashif-Laeeq/publication/358505001_Metaverse_Why_How_and_What/links/62053bb0afa8884cabd70210/Metaverse-Why-How-and-What.pdf

Lall-Trail, S. F., Salter, N. P., & Xu, X. (2021). How Personality Relates to Attitudes Toward Diversity and Workplace Diversity Initiatives. *Personality and Social Psychology Bulletin*, 01461672211057755. PMID:34930046

Lampel, J., Shamsie, J., & Shapira, Z. (2009). Experiencing the improbable: Rare events and organizational learning. *Organization Science, 20*(5), 835–845. doi:10.1287/orsc.1090.0479

Lancaster & Stillman. (2002). *When the Generations collide: Traditionalist, baby boomers, Generation Xers and millennials: who they are, why they clash, how to solve Generational puzzle at work.* Harper collins.

Landells, E. M., & Albrecht, S. L. (2019). Perceived organizational politics, engagement, and stress: The mediating influence of meaningful work. *Frontiers in Psychology, 10*, 1612. doi:10.3389/fpsyg.2019.01612 PMID:31354596

Lawler, E. E. III. (1994). Performance management: The next generation. *Compensation and Benefits Review, 26*(3), 16–19. doi:10.1177/088636879402600303

Lawrence-Brown, D., Sapon-Shevin, M., & Erevelles, N. (2014). *Condition critical: Key principles for equitable and inclusive education.* Teachers College Press.

Lawton, G. (2022). *How will the metaverse affect the future of work?* Tech Target. https://www.techtarget.com/searchcio/tip/How-will-the-metaverse-affect-the-future-of-work

Lazarus, R. S. (1991). *Emotion and adaptation.* Oxford university press.

Lazear, E. P., & Gibbs, M. (2014). *Personnel economics in practice.* John Wiley & Sons.

Lee, E. (2021). America for Americans: A history of xenophobia in the United States. Basic Books.

Lee, L. H., Braud, T., Zhou, P., Wang, L., Xu, D., Lin, Z., Kumar, A., Bermejo, C., & Hui, P. (2021). All one needs to know about metaverse: A complete survey on technological singularity, virtual ecosystem, and research agenda. https://doi.org/ doi:10.48550/arXiv.2110.05352

Lee, S., & Han, S. H. (2021). *Metaverse begins: Five issues and perspectives.* SPRI. https://spri.kr/posts/view/23197?code=issue_reports

Leea, K. J., & Kim, S. G. (2021). Structural Review of Customer Incivility and Social. *Journal of Quality Assurance in Hospitality & Tourism.* doi:10.1080/1528008X.2020.1864564

Lee, C., & Wong, C. S. (2019). The effect of team emotional intelligence on team process and effectiveness. *Journal of Management & Organization, 25*(6), 844–859. doi:10.1017/jmo.2017.43

Lee, J. Y., Swink, M., & Pandejpong, T. (2011). The roles of worker expertise, information sharing quality, and psychological safety in manufacturing process innovation: An intellectual capital perspective. *Production and Operations Management*, *20*(4), 556–570. doi:10.1111/j.1937-5956.2010.01172.x

Lee, K., Duffy, M. K., Scott, K. L., & Schippers, M. C. (2018). The experience of being envied at work: How being envied shapes employee feelings and motivation. *Personnel Psychology*, *71*(2), 181–200. doi:10.1111/peps.12251

Leenders, R. T. A. J., Engelen, J. M. L. V., & Kratzer, J. (2003). Virtuality, communication, and new product team creativity: A social network perspective. *Journal of Engineering and Technology Management*, *2003*(20), 69–92. doi:10.1016/S0923-4748(03)00005-5

LePine, J. A., Colquitt, J. A., & Erez, A. (2000). Adaptability to changing task contexts: Effects of general cognitive ability, conscientiousness, and openness to experience. *Personnel Psychology*, *53*(3), 563–593. doi:10.1111/j.1744-6570.2000.tb00214.x

Lester, W. S., Strunk, K. K., & Hoover, P. D. (2020). Persistent myths about the psychology of education: Implications for social justice and equity. In L. Parson. & C. Ozaki (Eds.), Teaching and learning for social justice and equity in higher education (pp. 53-71). Cham: Palgrave Macmillan.

Lester, S. W., Standifer, R. L., Schultz, N. J., & Windsor, J. M. (2012). Actual versus perceived Generational differences at work. *Journal of Leadership & Organizational Studies*, *19*(3), 341–354. doi:10.1177/1548051812442747

Leung, A., Der Foo, M., & Chaturvedi, S. (2013). Imprinting effects of founding core teams on HR values in new ventures. *Entrepreneurship Theory and Practice*, *37*(1), 87–106. doi:10.1111/j.1540-6520.2012.00532.x

Levinthal, D. A., & March, J. G. (1993). The myopia of learning. *Strategic Management Journal*, *14*(S2), 95–112. doi:10.1002mj.4250141009

Liao, Y., & Thomas, D. C. (2020). Conceptualizing cultural intelligence. In *Cultural intelligence in the world of work* (pp. 17–30). Springer. doi:10.1007/978-3-030-18171-0_2

Liao, Z., & Long, S. (2016). Cognitive diversity, alertness, and team performance. *Social Behavior and Personality*, *44*(2), 209–220. doi:10.2224bp.2016.44.2.209

Li, H., Feng, Z., Liu, C., & Cheng, D. (2014). The impact of relative leader-member exchange on employees' work behaviors as mediated by psychological contract fulfillment. *Social Behavior and Personality*, *42*(1), 79–88. doi:10.2224bp.2014.42.1.79

Li, M., & Hsu, C. H. (2016). Linking customer-employee exchange and employee innovative behavior. *International Journal of Hospitality Management*, *56*, 87–97. doi:10.1016/j.ijhm.2016.04.015

Lin, C., Standing, C., & Liu, Y. C. (2008). A model to develop effective virtual teams. *Decision Support Systems*, *45*(4), 1031–1045. doi:10.1016/j.dss.2008.04.002

LinkedIn. (2020). *The most in-demand hard and soft skills of 2020*. LinkedIn.

Lisdiono, P., Said, J., Yusoff, H., & Hermawan, A., A. (2022). Risk management practice, alliance management capability, and enterprise resilience: Findings from Indonesian state-owned enterprises. *Problems and Perspectives in Management*, *20*(1), 190–202. doi:10.21511/ppm.20(1).2022.17

Liu, X. R., Yu, J. J., Guo, Q., & Li, J. J. (2022). Employee engagement, its antecedents and effects on business performance in hospitality industry: a multilevel analysis. *International Journal of Contemporary Hospitality Management*.

Liu, Y., Dai, X., & Zhu, W. (2020). The impact of demographic diversity on team performance in the financial services industry. *International Journal of Human Resource Management*, *31*(8), 1082–1107. doi:10.1080/09585192.2017.1418659

Lockwood, N.R., (2004). Leadership Styles Series Part II: Leadership Styles: Generational Differences. SHRM Briefly Stated. *Society for Human Resource Management (SHRM)*, *2*.

Lockwood, N. R. (2009). The Multi-Generational Workforce: Opportunity for Competitive Success. *Research Quarterly*, 2.

Lu, J. G., Brockner, J., Vardi, Y., & Weitz, E. (2017). The dark side of experiencing job autonomy: Unethical behavior. *Journal of Experimental Social Psychology*, *73*, 222–234. doi:10.1016/j.jesp.2017.05.007

Luke, B., Verreynne, M. L., & Kearins, K. (2007). Measuring the benefits of entrepreneurship at different levels of analysis. *Journal of Management & Organization*, *13*(4), 312–330. doi:10.5172/jmo.2007.13.4.312

Luo, Y., Permzadian, V., Fan, J., & Meng, H. (2019). Employees' social self-efficacy and work outcomes: Testing the mediating role of social status. *Journal of Career Assessment*, *27*(4), 661–674. doi:10.1177/1069072718795401

Lüscher, L. S., Scholz, R. W., Berlowitz, I., & Schwaninger, M. (2021). Diversity, culture and innovation in health care: Insights from a Swiss case study. *European Journal of Innovation Management*, *24*(1), 149–172. doi:10.1108/EJIM-03-2019-0080

Luthans, F., Avolio, B. J., Avey, J. B., & Norman, S. M. (2007). Positive psychological capital: Measurement and relationship with performance and satisfaction. *Personnel Psychology*, *60*(3), 541–572. doi:10.1111/j.1744-6570.2007.00083.x

Luu, T. T. (2021). A tale of two countries: How do employees with disabilities respond to disability inclusive HR practices in tourism and hospitality industry? *Journal of Sustainable Tourism*, 1–31. doi:10.1080/09669582.2021.1876073

Luu, T. T., Rowley, C., & Vo, T. T. (2019). Addressing employee diversity to foster their work engagement. *Journal of Business Research*, *95*, 303–315. doi:10.1016/j.jbusres.2018.08.017

Lyons, S., & Kuron, L. (2014). Generational differences in the workplace: A review of the evidence and directions for future research. *Journal of Organizational Behavior*, *35*(S1), S139–S157. doi:10.1002/job.1913

Lyons, W. E., Thompson, S. A., & Timmons, V. (2016). 'We are inclusive. We are a team. Let's just do it': Commitment, collective efficacy, and agency in four inclusive schools. *International Journal of Inclusive Education*, *20*(8), 889–907. doi:10.1080/13603116.2015.1122841

Maalouf, G. Y. (2019). Effects of collaborative leadership on organizational performance. *International Journal of Multidisciplinary Research and Development*, *6*(1), 138–144. doi:10.22271/ijmrd.2019.v6.i1.25

Machi, L. A., & McEvoy, B. T. (2021). The literature review: Six steps to success (3rd ed.). Thousand Oaks, California, USA: Corwin, SAGE Publications Ltd.

MacKenzie, S. B., Podsakoff, P. M., & Podsakoff, N. P. (2011). Construct measurement and validation procedures in MIS and behavioral research: Integrating new and existing techniques. *Management Information Systems Quarterly*, *35*(2), 293–334. doi:10.2307/23044045

Mackey, J. D., Ellen, B. P. III, McAllister, C. P., & Alexander, K. C. (2021). The dark side of leadership: A systematic literature review and meta-analysis of destructive leadership research. *Journal of Business Research*, *132*, 705–718. doi:10.1016/j.jbusres.2020.10.037

Macky, K., Gardner, D., & Forsyth, S. (2008). Generational differences at work: Introduction and overview. *Journal of Managerial Psychology*, *23*(8), 857–861. doi:10.1108/02683940810904358

MacLeod, D., & Clarke, N. (2011). *Engaging for success: enhancing performance through employee engagement, a report to Government.* IoE.

Madera, J. M., Dawson, M., & Neal, J. A. (2013). Hotel managers' perceived diversity climate and job satisfaction: The mediating effects of role ambiguity and conflict. *International Journal of Hospitality Management*, *35*, 28–34. doi:10.1016/j.ijhm.2013.05.001

Madi Odeh, R. B. S., Obeidat, B. Y., Jaradat, M. O., Masa'deh, R., & Alshurideh, M. T. (2021). The transformational leadership role in achieving organizational resilience through adaptive cultures: The case of Dubai service sector. *International Journal of Productivity and Performance Management*. Advance online publication. doi:10.1108/IJPPM-02-2021-0093

Maeda, J. (2019). *Design in Tech Report.* Design InTech. https://designintech.report/wp-content/uploads/2019/03/dit2019_v00.pdf

Mahajan, D. Y. (2020). Study of impact of coronavirus pandemic on small and medium enterprises (SME's). *GIS SCIENCE JOURNAL*, *7*(9), 1–6.

Mahmood, M., Uddin, M. A., & Fan, L. (2018). The influence of transformational leadership on employees' creative process engagement: A multi-level analysis. *Management Decision*, *57*(3), 741–764. doi:10.1108/MD-07-2017-0707

Malik, M. S., Suleman, F., Ali, N., & Arshad, F. (2017). An Empirical Analysis of Impact of Inclusive Leadership on Employee Engagement in International Non-Government Organizations (INGO's) of Punjab (Pakistan). *International Journal of Economics and Management Science*, *6*, 2–6.

Mallak, L. (1998). Putting organizational resilience to work. *Industrial Management-Chicago Then Atlanta*, 8–13.

Mallak, L. A. (1998). Measuring resilience in health care provider organizations. *Health Manpower Management*, *24*(4), 148–152. doi:10.1108/09552069810215755 PMID:10346317

Mandal, S. (2017). The influence of organizational culture on healthcare supply chain resilience: Moderating role of technology orientation. *Journal of Business and Industrial Marketing*, *32*(8), 1021–1037. doi:10.1108/JBIM-08-2016-0187

Manoharan, A., Madera, J. M., & Singal, M. (2021). Walking the talk in diversity management: Exploring links between strategic statements, management practices, and external recognition. *International Journal of Hospitality Management*, *94*, 102864. doi:10.1016/j.ijhm.2021.102864

Mansoor, A., Farrukh, M., Wu, Y., & Abdul Wahab, S. (2021). Does inclusive leadership incite innovative work behavior? *Human Systems Management*, *40*(1), 93–102. doi:10.3233/HSM-200972

Mansoor, A., Wahab, S. A., & Jahan, S. (2021). Stimulation of innovative behavior through the inclusive leaders and engaged workers. *Business: Theory and Practice*, *22*(2), 249–255. doi:10.3846/btp.2021.13363

Mao, Y., He, J., & Yang, D. (2021). The dark sides of engaging in creative processes: Coworker envy, workplace ostracism, and incivility. *Asia Pacific Journal of Management*, *38*(4), 1261–1281. doi:10.100710490-020-09707-z

March, J. G. (1963). *A behavioral theory of the firm*. Prentice-Hall.

Marin, M. G., Merigo, J. M., & Popa, S. (2018). Twenty years of the Journal of Knowledge Management: A bibliometric analysis. *Journal of Knowledge Management*, *22*(8), 1655–1687. doi:10.1108/JKM-10-2017-0497

Marks, M. A., Mathieu, J. E., & Zaccaro, S. J. (2001). A temporally based framework and taxonomy of team processes. *Academy of Management Review*, *26*(3), 356–376. doi:10.2307/259182

Martins, E.-C., & Terblanche, F. (2003). Building organisational culture that stimulates creativity and innovation. *European Journal of Innovation Management*, *6*(1), 64–74. doi:10.1108/14601060310456337

Martins, L. L., Schilpzand, M. C., Kirkman, B. L., Ivanaj, S., & Ivanaj, V. (2013). A contingency view of the effects of cognitive diversity on team performance: The moderating roles of team psychological safety and relationship conflict. *Small Group Research*, *44*(2), 96–126. doi:10.1177/1046496412466921

Marvin, S. (2021). A Journey to Fulfillment. *Journal of Ayn Rand Studies*, *21*(1), 114–117. doi:10.5325/jaynrandstud.21.1.0114

Ma, S., & Trigo, V. (2008). Winning the War for Managerial Talent in China:An Empirical Study. *Chinese Economy*, *41*(3), 34–57. doi:10.2753/CES1097-1475410303

Maslach, C., Schaufeli, W. B., & Leiter, M. P. (2001). Job burnout. *Annual Review of Psychology*, *52*(1), 397–422. doi:10.1146/annurev.psych.52.1.397 PMID:11148311

Mathis, R. L., & Jackson, J. H. (2010). *Human resource management.* South-Western College.

Maxwell, J. C. (2014). *The 5 Levels of Leadership: Proven Steps to Maximize Your Potential.* Center Street.

Mayan, M., Lo, S., Oleschuk, M., Paucholo, A., & Laing, D. (2016). Leadership in community-based participatory research: Individual to collective. *Engaged Scholar Journal: Community-Engaged Research, Teaching, and Learning*, *2*(2), 11–24.

May, D. R., Gilson, R. L., & Harter, L. M. (2004). The psychological conditions of meaningfulness, safety and availability and the engagement of the human spirit at work. *Journal of Occupational and Organizational Psychology*, *77*(1), 11–37. doi:10.1348/096317904322915892

McAndrew, S., O'Brien, D., & Taylor, M. (2020). The values of culture? Social closure in the political identities, policy preferences, and social attitudes of cultural and creative workers. *The Sociological Review*, *68*(1), 33–54. doi:10.1177/0038026119871401

McCrindle. (2020). *Leadership.* Generationz. https://Generationz.com.au/articles/leadership/#:~:text=For%20Gen%20Z%2C%20a%20shift,and%20lead%20directionally%20and%20 strategically.

McKenna, S. (1999). Learning through complexity. *Management Learning*, *30*(3), 301–320. doi:10.1177/1350507699303003

McKenzie, K. B., Christman, D. E., Hernandez, F., Fierro, E., Capper, C. A., Dantley, M., González, M. L., Cambron-McCabe, N., & Scheurich, J. J. (2008). From the field: A proposal for educating leaders for social justice. *Educational Administration Quarterly*, *44*(1), 111–138. doi:10.1177/0013161X07309470

McKinsey & Company. (2020). *COVID-19 and jobs: Monitoring the real-time effects on the labor market.* McKinsey.

McKinsey & Company. (2020). *Diversity Wins: How Inclusion Matters.* McKinsey.

Mealor, A. D., Simner, J., Rothen, N., Carmichael, D. A., & Ward, J. (2016). Different dimensions of cognitive style in typical and atypical cognition: New evidence and a new measurement tool. *PLoS One*, *11*(5), e0155483. doi:10.1371/journal.pone.0155483 PMID:27191169

Meeuwissen, S. N. E., Gijselaers, W. H., van Oorschot, T. D., Wolfhagen, I. H. A. P., & Oude Egbrink, M. G. A. (2021). Enhancing team learning through leader inclusiveness: A one-year ethnographic case study of an interdisciplinary teacher team. *Teaching and Learning in Medicine*, *33*(5), 498–508. doi:10.1080/10401334.2021.1887738 PMID:33632034

Mello, A. L., & Delise, L. A. (2015). Cognitive diversity to team outcomes: The roles of cohesion and conflict management. *Small Group Research*, *46*(2), 204–226. doi:10.1177/1046496415570916

Mello, A. L., & Rentsch, J. R. (2015). Cognitive diversity in teams: A multidisciplinary review. *Small Group Research*, *46*(6), 623–658. doi:10.1177/1046496415602558

Mello, A., & Rentsch, J. (2014). Cognitive style diversity in decision making teams: A conceptual framework. *International Journal of Business and Social Research*, *4*(4), 123–135.

Meraku, A. (2017). Role of leadership in organizational effectiveness. *Journal of Economics. Business and Management*, *5*(11), 336–340.

Messick, S. (1976). Personality consistencies in cognition and creativity. In S. Messick & ... (Eds.), *Individuality in Learning* (pp. 4–22). Jossey-Bass.

Messick, S. (1984). The nature of cognitive styles: Problems and promise in educational practice. *Educational Psychologist*, *19*(2), 59–74. doi:10.1080/00461528409529283

Metcalfe, B. D. (2011). Women, work organization, and social change: Human resource development in Arab Gulf States. *Human Resource Development International*, *14*(2), 123–129. doi:10.1080/13678868.2011.558309

Metzger, M., Dowling, T., Guinn, J., & Wilson, D. T. (2020). Inclusivity in Baccalaureate Nursing Education: A Scoping Study. *Journal of Professional Nursing*, *36*(1), 5–14. doi:10.1016/j.profnurs.2019.06.002 PMID:32044053

Meyer, J. P., Becker, T. E., & Vandenberghe, C. (2004). Employee commitment and motivation: A conceptual analysis and integrative model. *The Journal of Applied Psychology*, *89*(6), 991–1007. doi:10.1037/0021-9010.89.6.991 PMID:15584837

Mikolajczak, M., Menil, C., & Luminet, O. (2007). Explaining the protective effect of trait emotional intelligence regarding occupational stress: Exploration of emotional labor processes. *Journal of Research in Personality*, *41*(5), 1107–1117. doi:10.1016/j.jrp.2007.01.003

Mikyoung, K., & Moon, J. (2019). Inclusive leadership and creative performance: The role of psychological safety, feedback-seeking behavior and power-distance. *Korean Journal of Human Resources Development*, *22*(4), 181–205. doi:10.24991/KJHRD.2019.12.22.4.181

Mileva, G. (2022). *20 Brands Leaping into the Metaverse*. Influencer Market Hub. https://influencermarketinghub.com/metaverse-brands/

Miller, C. C. (2019). The power of cognitive diversity. *Harvard Business Review*, *97*(3), 96–103.

Miller, C. C., Burke, L. M., & Glick, W. H. (1998). Cognitive diversity among upper-echelon executives: Implications for strategic decision processes. *Strategic Management Journal*, *19*(1), 39–58. doi:10.1002/(SICI)1097-0266(199801)19:1<39::AID-SMJ932>3.0.CO;2-A

Miller, K. (2012). *Organizational communication: Approaches and processes* (6th ed.). Cengage Learning.

Miller, K. D., & Chen, W. R. (2004). Variable organizational risk preferences: Tests of the march-Shapira model. *Academy of Management Journal*, *47*(1), 105–115. doi:10.2307/20159563

Milligan, S.R., (2016). *Conflict and Diversity Associated with Four Generations in the Workforce*, 1-134. Walden University.

Minehart, R. D., Foldy, E. G., Long, J. A., & Weller, J. M. (2020). Challenging gender stereotypes and advancing inclusive leadership in the operating theatre. *British Journal of Anaesthesia*, *124*(3), e148–e154. doi:10.1016/j.bja.2019.12.015 PMID:32000976

Mio, J. S., Riggio, R. E., Levin, S., & Reese, R. (2005). Presidential leadership and charisma: The effects of metaphor. *The Leadership Quarterly*, *16*(2), 287–294. doi:10.1016/j.leaqua.2005.01.005

Mir, A., Rafique, M., & Mubarak, N. (2021). Impact of inclusive leadership on project success: Testing of a model in information technology projects. *International Journal of Information Technology Project Management*, *12*(1), 63–79. doi:10.4018/IJITPM.2021010103

Mitroff, I. I., & Alpaslan, M. C. (2003). Preparing for Evil. *Harvard Business Review*, *81*(4), 109–115. PMID:12687925

Mohammed, A. A., & Hadi, A. A. (2022). The impact of empowering and transformational leadership on organizational performance and innovation: the mediating role of shared leadership and moderating role of organizational culture in the Iraqi healthcare sector. *International Journal of Organizational Analysis*.

Mohanty, A., Pradhan, R. K., & Jena, L. K. (2015). Curiosity and Meaning of life leading towards Personal Growth: The role of Emotional Intelligence. *Journal of the Indian Academy of Applied Psychology*, *41*(2), 1–35.

Mohr, D. M. (2008). *Embracing the other: Addressing xenophobia in the new literatures in English*. Rodopi. doi:10.1163/9789401205672

Moliner, O., Sales, A., Ferrández, R., & Traver, J. (2011a). Inclusive cultures, policies and practices in Spanish compulsory secondary education schools: Teachers' perceptions in ordinary and specific teaching contexts. *International Journal of Inclusive Education*, *15*(5), 557–572. doi:10.1080/13603110903165158

Momtaz, P. P. (2022). Some very simple economics of web3 and the metaverse. *FinTech*, *1*(3), 225–234. doi:10.3390/fintech1030018

Mone, E., Eisinger, C., Guggenheim, K., Price, B., & Stine, C. (2011). Performance management at the wheel: Driving employee engagement in organizations. *Journal of Business and Psychology, 26*(2), 205–212. doi:10.100710869-011-9222-9

Montani, F., Odoardi, C., & Battistelli, A. (2015). Envisioning, planning and innovating: A closer investigation of proactive goal generation, innovative work behaviour and boundary conditions. *Journal of Business and Psychology, 30*(3), 415–433. doi:10.100710869-014-9371-8

Monych, B. (2018). *6 ways to combat workplace incivility*. Insperity. https://www.insperity.com/blog/workplace-incivility/

Mor Barak, M. E. (2011). *Managing diversity: Toward a globally inclusive workplace*. Sage.

Mor Barak, M. E., Lizano, E. L., Kim, A., Duan, L., Rhee, M. K., Hsiao, H. Y., & Brimhall, K. C. (2016). The promise of diversity management for climate of inclusion: A state-of-the-art review and meta-analysis. *Human Service Organizations, Management, Leadership & Governance, 40*(4), 305–333. doi:10.1080/23303131.2016.1138915

Mor Barak, M. E., Luria, G., & Brimhall, K. C. (2021). What leaders say versus what they do: Inclusive leadership, policy-practice decoupling, and the anomaly of climate for inclusion. *Group & Organization Management*. doi:10.1177/2F10596011211005916

Morales, S. N., Martínez, L. R., Gómez, J. A. H., López, R. R., & Torres-Argüelles, V. (2019). Predictors of organizational resilience by factorial analysis. *International Journal of Engineering Business Management, 11*, 184797901983704. doi:10.1177/1847979019837046

Morgeson, F. P., & Hofmann, D. A. (1999). The structure and function of collective constructs: Implications for multilevel research and theory development. *Academy of Management Review, 24*(2), 249–265. doi:10.2307/259081

Morrow, P. C., & Crum, M. R. (1998). The effects of perceived and objective safety risk on employee outcomes. *Journal of Vocational Behavior, 53*(2), 300–313. doi:10.1006/jvbe.1997.1620

Mouton, N. (2019). A literary perspective on the limits of leadership: Tolstoy's critique of the great man theory. *Leadership, 15*(1), 81–102. doi:10.1177/1742715017738823

Mujtaba, B. G. (2013). Ethnic diversity, distrust and corruption in Afghanistan: Reflections on the creation of an inclusive culture. *Equality, Diversity and Inclusion, 32*(3), 245–261. doi:10.1108/EDI-12-2012-0113

Mukherjee, D., Lahiri, S., & Billing, T. K. (2012). Leading virtual teams: How do social, cognitive, and behavioral capabilities matter? *Management Decision, 50*(2), 273–290. doi:10.1108/00251741211203560

Mulvaney, M. A., McKinney, W. R., & Grodsky, R. (2012). The development of a pay-for-performance appraisal system for municipal agencies: A case study. *Public Personnel Management, 41*(3), 505–533. doi:10.1177/009102601204100307

Murphy, K. R., Cleveland, J. N., & Hanscom, M. (2018). Performance appraisal and management: Why does it fail and how can it be fixed? *Sage (Atlanta, Ga.)*.

Murphy, P. (2006). Chaos Theory As A Model For Managing Issues And Crises. *Public Relations Review*, *22*(2), 95–113. doi:10.1016/S0363-8111(96)90001-6

Mystakidis, S. (2022). Metaverse. *Encyclopedia*, *2*(1), 486–497. doi:10.3390/encyclopedia2010031

Nae, E. Y., Moon, H. K., & Choi, B. K. (2015). Seeking feedback but unable to improve work performance? Qualified feedback from trusted supervisors matters. *Career Development International*, *20*(1), 81–100. doi:10.1108/CDI-08-2014-0107

Nafei, W. (2015). The effects of job embeddedness on organizational cynicism and employee performance: A study on Sadat City University. *International Journal of Business Administration*, *6*(1), 8.

Nag, A. K. (2005). Covid paper. (bjhc, Ed.) Commerce, 8(2), 1*10.

Naidoo, V. (2010). Firm survival through a crisis: The influence of market orientation, marketing innovation and business strategy. *Industrial Marketing Management*, *39*(8), 1311–1320. doi:10.1016/j.indmarman.2010.02.005

Naimon, E. C., Mullins, M. E., & Osatuke, K. (2013). 1 10). The effects of personality and spirituality on workplace incivility perceptions. *Journal of Management, Spirituality & Religion*, *10*(1), 91–110. doi:10.1080/14766086.2012.758049

Nakamoto, S. (2008). Bitcoin: A peer-to-peer electronic cash system. *SSRN, 21260*. doi:10.2139srn.3440802

Nambisan, S. (2017). Digital Entrepreneurship: Toward a Digital Technology Perspective of Entrepreneurship. *Entrepreneurship Theory and Practice*, *41*(6), 1029 1055. doi:10.1111/etap.12254

Naqshbandi, M. M., Tabche, I., & Choudhary, N. (2018). Managing open innovation: The roles of empowering leadership and employee involvement climate. *Management Decision*, *57*(3), 703–723. doi:10.1108/MD-07-2017-0660

National Center for Women & Information Technology. (2019). *By the numbers*. NCWIT. https://www.ncwit.org/bythenumbers

Neal, D. (1995). Industry-specific human capital: Evidence from displaced workers. *Journal of Labor Economics*, *13*(4), 653–677. doi:10.1086/298388

Neeley, T. B. (2020). The challenge of leading diverse teams. *Harvard Business Review*, *98*(6), 62–71.

Neffinger, J., & Kohut, M. (2014). Compelling people: the hidden qualities that make us influential. Victoria Embankment London: Penguin.

Nembhard, I. M., & Edmondson, A. C. (2006). Making it safe: The effects of leader inclusiveness and professional status on psychological safety and improvement efforts in health care teams. *Journal of Organizational Behavior*, *27*(7), 941–966. doi:10.1002/job.413

Nevarez, C., & Wood, J. L. (2014). *Ethical leadership and the community college: Paradigms, decision-making, and praxis*. Charlotte, North Carolina: Information age publishing inc, IAP.

Nevelsteen, K. J. (2018). Virtual world, defined from a technological perspective and applied to video games, mixed reality, and the metaverse. *Computer Animation and Virtual Worlds*, *29*(1), e1752. doi:10.1002/cav.1752

Neves, P. (2012). Organizational cynicism: Spillover effects on supervisor–subordinate relationships and performance. *The Leadership Quarterly*, *23*(5), 965–976. doi:10.1016/j.leaqua.2012.06.006

Niemiec, C. P., & Ryan, R. M. (2009). Autonomy, competence, and relatedness in the classroom: Applying self-determination theory to educational practice. *Theory and Research in Education*, *7*(2), 133–144. doi:10.1177/1477878509104318

Nishii, L. H. (2013). The benefits of climate for inclusion for gender-diverse groups. *Academy of Management Journal*, *56*(6), 1754–1774. doi:10.5465/amj.2009.0823

Nishii, L. H., Khattab, J., Shemla, M., & Paluch, R. M. (2018). A multi-level process model for understanding diversity practice effectiveness. *The Academy of Management Annals*, *12*(1), 37–82. doi:10.5465/annals.2016.0044

Nishii, L. H., & Mayer, D. M. (2009). Do inclusive leaders help to reduce turnover in diverse groups? The moderating role of leader–member exchange in the diversity to turnover relationship. *The Journal of Applied Psychology*, *94*(6), 1412–1426. doi:10.1037/a0017190 PMID:19916652

Nishii, L. H., & Ozbilgin, ¨. M. F. (2007). Global diversity management: Towards a conceptual framework. *International Journal of Human Resource Management*, *18*(11), 1883–1894. doi:10.1080/09585190701638077

Nishii, L. H., & Paluch, R. M. (2018). Leaders as HR sensegivers: Four HR implementation behaviors that create strong HR systems. *Human Resource Management Review*, *28*(3), 319–323. doi:10.1016/j.hrmr.2018.02.007

Njoku, J. N., Nwakanma, C. I., Amaizu, G. C., & Kim, D. S. (2023). Prospects and challenges of Metaverse application in data-driven intelligent transportation systems. *IET Intelligent Transport Systems*, *17*(1), 1–21. doi:10.1049/itr2.12252

Noland, C. M., Steffens, N. K., & Haslam, S. A. (2019). When empowerment limits diversity: A study of employee resource groups in the technology sector. *Frontiers in Psychology*, *10*, 2149. 10

Nooteboom, B. (2000). *Learning and innovation in organizations and economies*. OUP Oxford.

Norman, L., Rankin-Wright, A. J., & Allison, W. (2018). "It'sa concrete ceiling; it's not even glass": Understanding tenets of organizational culture that supports the progression of women as coaches and coach developers. *Journal of Sport and Social Issues*, *42*(5), 393–414. doi:10.1177/0193723518790086

Northouse, P. G. (2004). *Leadership. Theory and practice* (3rd ed.). Sage Publications'.

Noy, D. (2009). Material and spiritual conceptions of development: A framework of ideal types. *Journal of Developing Societies*, *25*(3), 275–307. doi:10.1177/0169796X0902500301

Nunnally, J. C. (1978). *Psychometric Theory* (2nd ed.). McGraw-Hill.

Obuobisa-Darko, T., & Domfeh, K. A. (2019). Leader behaviour to achieve employee engagement in Ghana: A qualitative study. *International Journal of Public Leadership*, *15*(1), 19–37. doi:10.1108/IJPL-04-2018-0018

Ocasio, W. (1997). Towards an attention-based view of the firm. *Strategic Management Journal*, *18*(S1), 187–206. doi:10.1002/(SICI)1097-0266(199707)18:1+<187::AID-SMJ936>3.0.CO;2-K

Ocasio, W. (2011). Attention to attention. *Organization Science*, *22*(5), 1286–1296. doi:10.1287/orsc.1100.0602

OECD. (2011). *OECD Reviews of Risk Management Policies, Future Global Shocks, Improving Risk Governance*. OECD Publishing.

Okun, O., Şen,Cem, & Arun, K. (2020). How Do Paternalistic Leader Behaviors Shape Xenophobia in Business Life? *International Journal of Organizational Leadership*. doi:10.33844/ijol.2020.60487

Okun, O., Arun, K., & Kılınç, S. (2021). Organizational Xenophobia: Effects of Leadership with Moderation of Satisfaction with Life: A field study in the Sample of Dense Migrated Province. *Journal for East European Management Studies*, *26*(4), 665–687. doi:10.5771/0949-6181-2021-4-665

Oliveira, O. J., Silva, F. F., Juliani, F., Barbosa, L. F., & Nunhes, T. V. (2019). *Bibliometric Method for Mapping the State-of-the-Art and Identifying Research Gaps and Trends in Literature: An Essential Instrument to Support the Development of Scientific Projects*. Scientometrics Recent Advances. doi:10.5772/intechopen.85856

Olson, B. J., Parayitam, S., & Bao, Y. (2007). Strategic decision making: The effects of cognitive diversity, conflict, and trust on decision outcomes. *Journal of Management*, *33*(2), 196–222. doi:10.1177/0149206306298657

Ongori, H., & Agolla, J. E. (2007). Critical review of literature on workforce diversity. *African journal of business management, 1*(4). 072-076

Overstreet, R. E., Hazen, B. T., Skipper, J. B., & Hanna, J. B. (2014). Bridging the gap between strategy and performance: Using leadership style to enable structural elements. *Journal of Business Logistics*, *35*(2), 136–149. doi:10.1111/jbl.12043

Ozkana, M. & Solmaz, B., (2015). The Changing Face Of The Employees- Generation Z And Their Perceptions of Work. *Science Direct, 26*, 476 – 483.

Page, S. (2017). The diversity bonus. In *The Diversity Bonus*. Princeton University Press. doi:10.2307/j.ctvc77c0h

Page, S. E. (2007). Making the difference: Applying a logic of diversity. *The Academy of Management Perspectives*, *21*(4), 6–20. doi:10.5465/amp.2007.27895335

Pande, R. & Ford, D. (2012). Gender Quotas And Female Leadership: A Review. *Background Paper For The World Development Report On Gender.*

Pandolfo, A. M. (2017). What is the "cognitive" in cognitive diversity? *Investigating the convergent validity of cognitive diversity measures.* UWO. https://ir.lib.uwo.ca/cgi/viewcontent.cgi?article=1034&context=psychd_uht.

Panicker, A., Agrawal, R. K., & Khandelwal, U. (2018). Inclusive workplace and organizational citizenship behavior. *Equality, Diversity and Inclusion*, *37*(6), 530–550. doi:10.1108/EDI-03-2017-0054

Paraskevas, A. (2006). Crisis Management or Crisis Response System? A Complexity Science Approach to Organizational Crises. *Management Decision*, *44*(7), 892–907. doi:10.1108/00251740610680587

Parker, C. C., (2007). *Generational differences in work life balance attitudes*, 1-41. SUNY.

Parker, G., Van Alstyne, M., & Choudary, S. P. (2016). *Platform revolution: How networked markets are transforming the economy–and how to make them work for you*. Norton & Company.

Parker, S. K., Williams, H., & Turner, N. (2006). Modeling the antecedents of proactive behavior at work. *The Journal of Applied Psychology*, *91*(3), 636–652. doi:10.1037/0021-9010.91.3.636 PMID:16737360

Park, Y., & Haun, V. C. (2018). 12). The long arm of email incivility: Transmitted stress to the partner and partner work withdrawal. *Journal of Organizational Behavior*, *39*(10), 1268–1282. doi:10.1002/job.2289

Parris, D. L., & Peachey, J. W. (2013). A systematic literature review of servant leadership theory in organizational contexts. *Journal of Business Ethics*, *113*(3), 377–393. doi:10.100710551-012-1322-6

Parrott, W. G., & Smith, R. H. (1993). Distinguishing the experiences of envy and jealousy. *Journal of Personality and Social Psychology*, *64*(6), 906–920. doi:10.1037/0022-3514.64.6.906 PMID:8326472

Pasko, R., Maellaro, R., & Stodnick, M. (2020). A study of millennials' preferred work-related attributes and retention. *Employee Relations*, *43*(3), 774–787. doi:10.1108/ER-05-2020-0224

Paukku, M., & Välikangas, L. (2021). Harried or Myopic Leadership: An Undue Bias for Action. In A. Örtenblad (Ed.), *Debating Bad Leadership: Reasons and Remedies* (pp. 239–255). Springer International Publishing. doi:10.1007/978-3-030-65025-4_13

Payne, R., Kruwinnus, J., & Grant-Smith, D. (2023). Handbook of Research on Promoting an Inclusive Organizational Culture for Entrepreneurial Sustainability, p. 86-109. IGI Global.

Pearce, C. L. (2007). The future of leadership development: The importance of identity, multilevel approaches, self-leadership, physical fitness, shared leadership, networking, creativity, emotions, spirituality and on-boarding processes. *Human Resource Management Review*, *17*(4), 355–359. doi:10.1016/j.hrmr.2007.08.006

Pearce, C. L., & Conger, J. A. (2003). *Shared leadership: Reframing the hows and whys of leadership*. Sage. doi:10.4135/9781452229539

Pearce, C. L., & Manz, C. C. (2005). The new silver bullets of leadership: The importance of self and shared leadership in knowledge work. *Organizational Dynamics*, *34*(2), 130–140. doi:10.1016/j.orgdyn.2005.03.003

Pearson, C., Andersson, L., & Porath, C. (2005). Workplace incivility. In S. Fox & P. E. Spector (Eds.), Counterproductive work behavior: Investigations of actors and targets. *American Psychological Association.*, 177-200. https://psycnet.apa.org/doi/10.1037/10893-008

Pearson, C.M., & Porath, C.L. (2004). *On incivility, its impact, and directions for future research*, 403-425. Research Gate.

Pearson, C. M., Andersson, L. M., & Porath, C. L. (2000). 11 1). Assessing and attacking workplace incivility. *Organizational Dynamics*, *29*(2), 123–137. doi:10.1016/S0090-2616(00)00019-X

Penney, L. M., & Spector, P. E. (2005). 11). Job Stress, Incivility, and Counterproductive Work Behavior (CWB): The Moderating Role of Negative Affectivity. *Journal of Organizational Behavior*, *26*(7), 777–796. doi:10.1002/job.336

Perilus, B. (2020). *Engaging Four Generations in the Workplace: A Single Case Study* [Doctoral dissertation, University of Phoenix]

Perlin, K., & Goldberg, A. (1996). Improv: A system for scripting interactive actors in virtual worlds. In *Proceedings of the 23rd annual conference on Computer graphics and interactive techniques* (pp. 205-216). Association for Computing Machinery. 10.1145/237170.237258

Perrin, T. (2003). Working today: Understanding what drives employee engagement. *The 2003 Towers Perrin talent report*. Perrin Talent. http://www.keepem.com/doc_files/Towers_Perrin_Talent_2003%28 TheFinal%29.pdf

Perry, E. L., Block, C. J., & Noumair, D. A. (2020). Leading in: Inclusive leadership, inclusive climates and sexual harassment. *Equality, Diversity and Inclusion*, *40*(4), 430–447. doi:10.1108/EDI-04-2019-0120

Petrie, E. J., Nieto, A. G., & Andrews, K. (2021). Racial Differences in Perceptions of Shared Leadership Among IT Managers. In *Effective Strategies for Communicating Insights in Business* (pp. 101–128). IGI Global. doi:10.4018/978-1-7998-3964-4.ch007

Petrigna, L., & Musumeci, G. (2022). The metaverse: A new challenge for the healthcare system: A scoping review. *Journal of Functional Morphology and Kinesiology*, *7*(3), 63. doi:10.3390/jfmk7030063 PMID:36135421

Pfarrer, M. D., DeCelles, K. A., Smith, K. G., & Taylor, M. S. (2008). After the fall: Reintegrating the corrupt organization. *Academy of Management Review*, *33*(3), 730–749. doi:10.5465/amr.2008.32465757

Pfeffer, J. (2007). Human resources from an organizational behavior perspective: Some paradoxes explained. *The Journal of Economic Perspectives*, *21*(4), 115–134. doi:10.1257/jep.21.4.115

Pfister, I. B., Jacobshagen, N., Kalin, W., & Semmer, N. K. (2020). How does appreciation lead to higher job satisfaction? *Journal of Managerial Psychology*, *35*(6), 465–479. doi:10.1108/JMP-12-2018-0555

Pless, N., & Maak, T. (2004). Building an inclusive diversity culture: Principles, processes and practice. *Journal of Business Ethics*, *54*(2), 129–147. doi:10.100710551-004-9465-8

Podsakoff, N. P., LePine, J. A., & LePine, M. A. (2007). Differential challenge stressor-hindrance stressor relationships with job attitudes, turnover intentions, turnover, and withdrawal behavior: A meta-analysis. *The Journal of Applied Psychology*, *92*(2), 438–454. doi:10.1037/0021-9010.92.2.438 PMID:17371090

Porath, C. L., Gerbasi, A., & Schorch, S. L. (2015). The Effects of Civility on Advice, Leadership, and Performance. *The Journal of Applied Psychology*, *100*(5), 1527–1541. doi:10.1037/apl0000016 PMID:25798552

Prajogo, W., Kusumawati, H., & Wijaya, N. H. S. (2020). Organizational culture as determinant of employee-based antecedents to organizational cynicism. *Humanities & Social Sciences Reviews*, *8*(1), 881–886. doi:10.18510/hssr.2020.81105

Pratt, M. K. (2022). *Metaverse pros and cons: Top benefits and challenges*. Tech Target. https://www.techtarget.com/searchcio/tip/Metaverse-pros-and-cons-Top-benefits-and-challenges

Pratto, F., & Stewart, A. L. (2012). Group Dominance and the Half-Blindness of Privilege [Article]. *The Journal of Social Issues*, *68*(1), 28–45. doi:10.1111/j.1540-4560.2011.01734.x

Price, A. (2000). *Principle of Human Resource Management: an active learning approach*. Blackwell business.

PricewaterhouseCoopers International. (2019). *Unraveling the fabric ceiling*. PricewaterhouseCoopers. https://www.pwc.com/us/en/industries/consumer-markets/assets/pwc-unraveling-the-fabric-ceiling.pdf

Prime, J., & Salib, E. R. (2014). *Inclusive leadership: The view from six countries.* Catalyst. https://www.catalyst.org/research/inclusive-leadership-the-view-from-six-countries/

Priola, V., Smith, J. L., & Armstrong, S. J. (2004). Group work and cognitive style: A discursive investigation. *Small Group Research, 35*(5), 565–595. doi:10.1177/1046496404265143

Pulakos, E. D., & O'Leary, R. S. (2011). Why is performance management so broken? *Industrial and Organizational Psychology: Perspectives on Science and Practice*, *4*(2), 146–164. doi:10.1111/j.1754-9434.2011.01315.x

Purdy, M. (2022). *How the metaverse could change work.* HBR. https://hbr.org/2022/04/how-the-metaverse-could-change-work

PwC. (2019). *Global Culture Survey 2018: Building a culture of innovation and purpose.* PwC.

Qi, L., Liu, B., Wei, X., & Hu, Y. (2019). Impact of inclusive leadership on employee innovative behavior: Perceived organizational support as a mediator. *PLoS One*, *14*(2), e0212091. doi:10.1371/journal.pone.0212091 PMID:30817753

Qin, H. X., Wang, Y., & Hui, P. (2022). *Identity, crimes, and law enforcement in the metaverse.* https://doi.org//arXiv.2210.06134 doi:10.48550

Quantum Workplace. (2020). Future of work: 17 performance review templates to motivate employees. *Quantum Workplace.* https://www.quantumworkplace.com/future-of-work/17-performance-review-templates-to-motivate-employees.

Radha, L., & Arumugam, J. (2021, October). The Research Output of Bibliometrics using Bibliometrix R Package and VOS Viewer. *International Journal of Arts. Science and Humanities*, *9*(2), 44–49. 10.34293

Ragins, B. R., & Gonzalez, J. A. (2003). Understanding diversity in organizations: getting a grip on a slippery construct. In J. Greenberg (Ed.), *Organizational Behavior: The State of the Science* (2nd ed., pp. 125–163). Lawrence Erlbaum Associates.

Rai, R. (2022). An overview of Web3 venture capital activity in 2021. *Forbes.* https://www.forbes.com/sites/rahulrai/2022/01/02/an-overview-of-web3-venture-capital-activity-in-2021/?sh=631611601f16

Ramarajan, L., & Reid, E. (2013). Shattering the myth of separate worlds: Negotiating non work identities at work. *Academy of Management Review*, *38*(4), 621–644. doi:10.5465/amr.2011.0314

Randel, A. E., Dean, M. A., Ehrhart, K. H., Chung, B., & Shore, L. (2016). Leader inclusiveness, psychological diversity climate, and helping behaviors. *Journal of Managerial Psychology*, *31*(1), 216–234. doi:10.1108/JMP-04-2013-0123

Randel, A. E., Galvin, B. M., Shore, L. M., Ehrhart, K. H., Chung, B. G., Dean, M. A., & Kedharnath, U. (2018). Inclusive leadership: Realizing positive outcomes through belongingness and being valued for uniqueness. *Human Resource Management Review*, *28*(2), 190–203. doi:10.1016/j.hrmr.2017.07.002

Rattrie, L. T., Kittler, M. G., & Paul, K. I. (2020). Culture, burnout, and engagement: A meta-analysis on national cultural values as moderators in JD-R theory. *Applied Psychology*, *69*(1), 176–220. doi:10.1111/apps.12209

Raub, S., & Robert, C. (2013). Empowerment, organizational commitment, and voice behavior in the hospitality industry: Evidence from a multinational sample. *Cornell Hospitality Quarterly*, *54*(2), 136–148. doi:10.1177/1938965512457240

Ravi, R. (2022) *Skechers joins the metaverse, planning to open a store in decentraland.* NFT Evening. https://nftevening.com/skechers-joins-the-metaverse-planning-to-open-a-store-in-decentraland/

Rawls, J. (1971). *A theory of justice*. Belknap Press. doi:10.4159/9780674042605

Rayisi, A., & Nastiezaie, N. (2019). The Relationship between organizational cynicism and organizational anti-citizenship behavior with the mediating role of organizational envy. *Career and Organizational Counseling*, *11*(38), 117–136. doi:10.29252/jcoc.11.1.117

Rayner, S. (2009). Educational diversity and learning leadership: A proposition, some principles and a model of inclusive leadership? *Educational Review*, *61*(4), 433–447. doi:10.1080/00131910903404004

Rayner, S., & Riding, R. (1997). Towards a categorisation of cognitive styles and learning styles. *Educational Psychology*, *17*(1-2), 5–27. doi:10.1080/0144341970170101

Rebelo, T., Lourenço, P. R., & Dimas, I. D. (2020). The journey of team learning since "The Fifth Discipline". *The Learning Organization*, *27*(1), 42–53. doi:10.1108/TLO-10-2019-0144

Reichers, A. E., Wanous, J. P., & Austin, J. T. (1997). Understanding and managing cynicism about organizational change. *The Academy of Management Perspectives*, *11*(1), 48–59. doi:10.5465/ame.1997.9707100659

Reio, T. G., & Reio, J. S. (2011). 12 6). Thinking About Workplace Engagement: Does Supervisor and Coworker Incivility Really Matter? *Advances in Developing Human Resources*, *13*(4), 462–478. doi:10.1177/1523422311430784

Rese, M., & Fay, D. (2001). *Personal initiative: An active performance conceptforthe 21st century.*

Reuters. (2021). *Google to train 100,000 African coders in digital skills program*. Reuters.

Reyna, A., Martín, C., Chen, J., Soler, E., & Díaz, M. (2018). On blockchain and its integration with IoT. Challenges and opportunities. *Future Generation Computer Systems*, *88*, 173–190. doi:10.1016/j.future.2018.05.046

Reynolds, A., & Lewis, D. (2017). Teams solve problems faster when they're more cognitively diverse. *Harvard Business Review*, *30*, 1–8.

Rezvani, A., Chang, A., Wiewiora, A., Ashkanasy, N. M., Jordan, P. J., & Zolin, R. (2016). Manager emotional intelligence and project success: The mediating role of job satisfaction and trust. *International Journal of Project Management*, *34*(7), 1112–1122. doi:10.1016/j.ijproman.2016.05.012

Rich, B. L., Lepine, J. A., & Crawford, E. R. (2010). Job engagement: Antecedents and effects on job performance. *Academy of Management Journal*, *53*(3), 617–635. doi:10.5465/amj.2010.51468988

Riffkin, R., & Harter, J. (2016). *Using Employee Engagement to Build a Diverse Workforce*. Gallup Inc.

Rijamampianina, R., & Carmichael, T. (2005). A pragmatic and holistic approach to managing diversity. *Problems and Perspectives in Management*, (1), 109–117.

Robbins, S. P., & Judge, T. (2017). *Organizational behavior*. Pearson Boston.

Roberge, M. É., & Van Dick, R. (2010). Recognizing the benefits of diversity: When and how does diversity increase group performance? *Human Resource Management Review*, *20*(4), 295–308. doi:10.1016/j.hrmr.2009.09.002

Roberson, Q. M. (2006). Disentangling the meanings of diversity and inclusion in organizations. *Group & Organization Management*, *31*(2), 212–236. doi:10.1177/1059601104273064

Roberson, Q. M. (2019). Diversity, equity, and inclusion at work: A review and research agenda. *Journal of Organizational Behavior*, *40*(4), 387–400. doi:10.1002/job.2353

Roberson, Q. M., Kulik, C. T., & Pepper, M. B. (2019). The threat of increasing diversity: Why organizations need psychological safety for diversity initiatives. *Organizational Dynamics*, *48*(1), 36–44. doi:10.1016/j.orgdyn.2018.10.004

Roberson, Q., & Perry, J. L. (2022). Inclusive leadership in thought and action: A thematic analysis. *Group & Organization Management*, *47*(4), 755–778. doi:10.1177/10596011211013161

Robinson, M. (2017). Why Hast The Mighty Fallen?: An Intrinsic and Extrinsic Examination of the Lack of Counsel among Fallen Leaders. Park Ave, Meadville: Christian Faith Publishing, Inc.

Rock, D., & Grant, H. (2020). Leading through cognitive diversity. *Harvard Business Review*, *98*(4), 76–84.

Rodriguez, R. O., Green, M. T., & Ree, M. J. (2003). Leading Generation X: Do the old rules apply? *Journal of Leadership & Organizational Studies*, *9*(4), 67–75. doi:10.1177/107179190300900406

Rogov, M. A. (2006). Global Risk Factors. *Journal of Business Economics and Management*, *7*(1), 25–28. doi:10.3846/16111699.2006.9636119

Rohei. (2019). *'The MultiGenerational Workforce: From Challenges to Opportunities*'. Rohei. https://www.rohei.com/ resources/the-multiGenerational-workforce-from-challenges-to-opportunities

Rosenlund, L. (2019). The persistence of inequalities in an era of rapid social change. Comparisons in time of social spaces in Norway. *Poetics*, *74*, 101323. doi:10.1016/j.poetic.2018.09.004

Rudman, L. A., & Fairchild, K. (2004). Reactions to Counterstereotypic Behavior: The Role of Backlash in Cultural Stereotype Maintenance. *Journal of Personality and Social Psychology*, *87*(2), 157–176. doi:10.1037/0022-3514.87.2.157 PMID:15301625

Rupp, G. (2015). *Beyond individualism: The challenge of inclusive communities*. Columbia University Press. doi:10.7312/columbia/9780231174282.001.0001

Russette, J., Scully, R., & Preziosi, R. (2008). Leadership across cultures: A comparative study. *Academy of Strategic Management Journal*, *7*(1), 47–61.

Ryan, R. M., & Deci, E. L. (2000). Self-determination theory and the facilitation of intrinsic motivation, social development, and well-being. *The American Psychologist*, *55*(1), 68–78. doi:10.1037/0003-066X.55.1.68 PMID:11392867

Ryan, R. M., Huta, V., & Deci, E. L. (2008). Living well: A self-determination theory perspective on eudaimonia. *Journal of Happiness Studies*, *9*(1), 139–170. doi:10.100710902-006-9023-4

Ryan, S. M. (2014). An inclusive rural post secondary education program for students with intellectual disabilities. *Rural Special Education Quarterly*, *33*(2), 18–28. doi:10.1177/875687051403300204

Ryan, W. S., & Ryan, R. M. (2019). Toward a social psychology of authenticity: Exploring within-person variation in autonomy, congruence, and genuineness using self-determination theory. *Review of General Psychology*, *23*(1), 99–112. doi:10.1037/gpr0000162

Ryssen, S. V., & Godar, S. H. (2000). Going international without going international: Multinational virtual teams. *Journal of International Management*, *6*(1), 49–60. doi:10.1016/S1075-4253(00)00019-3

Sajjad, M., Kaleem, N., Chani, M. I., & Ahmed, M. (2020). Worldwide role of women entrepreneurs in economic development. *Asia Pacific Journal of Innovation & Entrepreneurship*, *14*(2), 151–160. doi:10.1108/APJIE-06-2019-0041

Saks, A. M. (2006). Antecedents and consequences of employee engagement. *Journal of Managerial Psychology*, *21*(7), 600–619. doi:10.1108/02683940610690169

Saks, A. M., & Gruman, J. A. (2014). What do we really know about employee engagement? *Human Resource Development Quarterly*, *25*(2), 155–182. doi:10.1002/hrdq.21187

Salahuddin, M.M., (2014). The Impact of Generational Differences on Organizational Relationships: A Communication Perspective, 1-130. Department of Education.

Salahuddin, M. M. (2010). Generational differences impact on leadership style and organizational success'. *Journal of Diversity Management, 5*(2), 1–6. doi:10.19030/jdm.v5i2.805

Samad, T. F. D., & Hasan, N. (2022). Women entrepreneurs in the era of metaverse: An Islamic economic perspective. *Review of Islamic Social Finance and Entrepreneurship*, 131-140. https:// doi:10.20885/RISFE.vol1.iss2.art5

Sapriel, C. (2003). Effective crisis management: Tools and best practice for the new millennium. *Journal of Communication Management (London), 7*(4), 348–355. doi:10.1108/13632540310807485

Sarason, I. G., Sarason, B. R., Brock, D. M., & Pierce, G. R. (1996). Social support: Current status, current issues. Stress and Emotion. *Anxiety, Anger, and Curiosity, 16*, 3–27.

Satalkina, L., & Steiner, G. (2020). Digital entrepreneurship and its role in innovation systems: A systematic literature review as a basis for future research avenues for sustainable transitions. *Sustainability (Basel), 12*(7), 2764. doi:10.3390u12072764

Sauer, J., Felsing, T., Franke, H., & Rüttinger, B. (2006). Cognitive diversity and team performance in a complex multiple task environment. *Ergonomics, 49*(10), 934–954. doi:10.1080/00140130600577502 PMID:16803725

Saxena, A. (2014). Workforce diversity: A key to improve productivity. *Procedia Economics and Finance, 11*, 76–85. doi:10.1016/S2212-5671(14)00178-6

Saxena, A., Meschino, D., Hazelton, L., Chan, M., Benrimoh, D., Matlow, A., Dath, D., & Busari, J. (2019). Power and physician leadership. *BMJ Leader, 3*(3), 92–98. doi:10.1136/leader-2019-000139

Saxena, D., & Tripathi, D. N. (2021, February). Exploring The security risks and safety measures of mobile payments in Fintech Environment in India. *International Journal of Management, 12*(2), 408–417. doi:10.34218/IJM.12.2.2021.041

Schaufeli, W. B., & Bakker, A. B. (2004). Job demands, job resources, and their relationship with burnout and engagement: A multi-sample study. *Journal of Organizational Behavior, 25*(3), 293–315. doi:10.1002/job.248

Schaufeli, W. B., Salanova, M., González-Romá, V., & Bakker, A. B. (2002). The measurement of engagement and burnout: A two sample confirmatory factor analytic approach. *Journal of Happiness Studies, 3*(1), 71–92. doi:10.1023/A:1015630930326

Schawbel, D. (2014). Gen Z Employees: The 5 Attributes You Need to Know. *Entrepreneur.* http://www. entrepreneur.com/article/236560

Schein, E. H., & Bennis, W. G. (1965). *Personal and organizational change through group methods: The laboratory approach.* Wiley.

Scheurich, J. J., & Skrla, L. (2003). *Leadership for equity and excellence: Creating high-achievement classrooms, schools, and districts.* Corwin Press.

Schilpzand, P., De Pater, I. E., & Erez, A. (2016). 2). Workplace incivility: A review of the literature and agenda for future research. *Journal of Organizational Behavior, 37*(S1), S57–S88. doi:10.1002/job.1976

Schwarz, A., Seeger, M. W., & Auer, C. (Eds.). (2016). *The handbook of international crisis communication research.* John Wiley & Sons. doi:10.1002/9781118516812

Schwarzwald, J., Koslowsky, M., & Allouf, M. (2005). Group Membership, Status, and Social Power Preference. *Journal of Applied Social Psychology, 35*(3), 644–665. doi:10.1111/j.1559-1816.2005.tb02139.x

Scott, B. A. (2013). A conceptual framework for the study of popularity in the workplace. *Organizational Psychology Review, 3*(2), 161–186. doi:10.1177/2041386612464092

Scott, K. L., Tams, S., Schippers, M. C., & Lee, K. (2015). Opening the black box: Why and when workplace exclusion affects social reconnection behaviour, health, and attitudes. *European Journal of Work and Organizational Psychology, 24*(2), 239–255. doi:10.1080/1359432X.2014.894978

Scott, S. G., & Bruce, R. A. (1994). Determinants of innovative behavior: A path model of individual innovation in the workplace. *Academy of Management Journal, 37*(3), 580–607. doi:10.2307/256701

Scouller, J. (2011). *The three levels of leadership: How to develop your leadership presence, knowhow, and skill.* Cirencester, Gloucestershire, United Kingdom: Management Books 2000.

Seers, A., Keller, T., & Wilkerson, J. M. (2003). Can team members share leadership? Foundations in research and theory. In C. L. Pearce & J. A. Conger (Eds.), *Shared Leadership: Reframing the Hows and Whys of Leadership* (pp. 77–102). Sage Publications. doi:10.4135/9781452229539.n4

Seow, J. H. I. (2021). Metaverse: A Game-changing innovation for entrepreneurs, entrepreneur, 2021. *Entrepreenuer.* https://www.entrepreneur.com/en-in/technology/metaverse-a-game-changing-innovation-for-entrepreneurs/403080

Sessa, V. I., Kabacoff, R. I., Deal, J., & Brown, H. (2007). Generational differences in leader values and leadership behaviors. *The Psychologist Manager Journal, 10*(1), 47–74. doi:10.1080/10887150709336612

Sewell, W. H. (2004). A theory of structure: duality, agency and transformation. In *Practicing history* (pp. 157–179). Routledge.

Shah, A. K. (2022). *Inclusive and Sustainable Finance: Leadership, Ethics and Culture* (1st ed.). Routledge., doi:10.4324/9781003164746

Shakil, R. M., Memon, M. A., & Ting, H. (2021). Inclusive leadership and innovative work behaviour: The mediating role of job autonomy. *Quality & Quantity*, 1–15. doi:10.100711135-021-01102-0

Shamir, B., & Howell, J. M. (1999). Organizational and contextual influences on the emergence and effectiveness of charismatic leadership. *The Leadership Quarterly*, *10*(2), 257–283. doi:10.1016/S1048-9843(99)00014-4

Shankar, S., & Tewari, V. (2021). Impact of Collective Intelligence and Collective Emotional Intelligence on the Psychological Safety of the Organizations. *Vision (Basel)*, 9722629211012256.

Sharma, N. E., Chaudhary, N. E., & Singh, V. K. E. (2019). *Management techniques for employee engagement in contemporary organizations*. Business Science Reference/IGI Global. doi:10.4018/978-1-5225-7799-7

Shen, H., & Jiang, H. (2019). Engaged at work? An employee engagement model in public relations. *Journal of Public Relations Research*, *31*(1-2), 32–49. doi:10.1080/1062726X.2019.1585855

Shen, J., Chanda, A., D'netto, B., & Monga, M. (2009). Managing diversity through human resource management: An international perspective and conceptual framework. *International Journal of Human Resource Management*, *20*(2), 235–251. doi:10.1080/09585190802670516

Shen, K. N., Lindsay, V., & Xu, Y. (2018). Digital entrepreneurship. *Information Systems Journal*, *28*(6), 1125–1128. doi:10.1111/isj.12219

Shenoy, V., & Kumar, M. (2021). Common biases found in the workplace: Visible and invisible inequalities. *Strategic HR Review*, *20*(5), 183–185. doi:10.1108/SHR-10-2021-188

Shimizu, K. (2007). Prospect theory, behavioral theory, and the threat-rigidity thesis: Combinative effects on organizational decisions to divest formerly acquired units. *Academy of Management Journal, 50*(6), 1495-1514.

Shin, S. J., Kim, T. Y., Lee, J. Y., & Bian, L. (2012). Cognitive team diversity and individual team member creativity: A cross-level interaction. *Academy of Management Journal*, *55*(1), 197–212. doi:10.5465/amj.2010.0270

Shore, L. M., & Chung, B. G. (2022). Inclusive leadership: How leaders sustain or discourage work group inclusion. *Group & Organization Management*, *47*(4), 723–754. doi:10.1177/1059601121999580

Shore, L. M., Chung-Herrera, B. G., Dean, M. A., Ehrhart, K. H., Jung, D. I., Randel, A. E., & Singh, G. (2009). Diversity in organizations: Where are we now and where are we going? *Human Resource Management Review*, *19*(2), 117–133. doi:10.1016/j.hrmr.2008.10.004

Shore, L. M., Cleveland, J. N., & Sanchez, D. (2018). Inclusive workplaces: A review and model. *Human Resource Management Review*, *28*(2), 176–189. doi:10.1016/j.hrmr.2017.07.003

Shore, L., Randel, A., Chung, B., Dean, M., Ehrhart, K., & Singh, G. (2011). Inclusion and diversity in work groups: A review and model for future research. *Journal of Management*, *37*(4), 1262–1289. doi:10.1177/0149206310385943

Shrivastava, A. (2019). Using collaborative project for learning effective ways of working harmoniously with people from different cultures'. *International Journal Marketing Business Communication, 8*(1), 47–54.

Shu, C. Y., & Lazatkhan, J. (2017). Effect of leader-member exchange on employee envy and work behavior moderated by self-esteem and neuroticism. *Journal of Work and Organizational Psychology, 33*(1), 69–81. doi:10.1016/j.rpto.2016.12.002

Shuck, B. (2011). Four Emerging Perspectives of Employee Engagement: An integrative literature review. *Human Resource Development Review, 10*(3), 304–328. doi:10.1177/1534484311410840

Shuck, B., Osam, K., Zigarmi, D., & Nimon, K. (2017). Definitional and conceptual muddling: Identifying the positionality of employee engagement and defining the construct. *Human Resource Development Review, 16*(3), 263–293. doi:10.1177/1534484317720622

Shuck, B., & Wollard, K. (2010). Employee engagement and HRD: A seminal review of the foundations. *Human Resource Development Review, 9*(1), 89–110. doi:10.1177/1534484309353560

Shu, Q., & Wang, Y. (2021). Collaborative leadership, collective action, and community governance against public health crises under uncertainty: A case study of the quanjingwan community in China. *International Journal of Environmental Research and Public Health, 18*(2), 598. doi:10.3390/ijerph18020598 PMID:33445697

Siebelink, R., Hofman, E., Halman, J. I. M., & Nee, I. (2021). Roadmapping:(Missed) opportunities to overcome strategic challenges. *Business Horizons, 64*(4), 501–512. doi:10.1016/j.bushor.2021.02.014

Siegrist, J. (2005). Social reciprocity and health: New scientific evidence and policy implications. *Psychoneuroendocrinology, 30*(10), 1033–1038. doi:10.1016/j.psyneuen.2005.03.017 PMID:15951124

Simha, A., Elloy, D. F., & Huang, H. C. (2014). The moderated relationship between job burnout and organizational cynicism. *Management Decision, 52*(3), 482–504. doi:10.1108/MD-08-2013-0422

Simon, H. A. (1991). Bounded rationality and organizational learning. *Organization Science, 2*(1), 125–134. doi:10.1287/orsc.2.1.125

Simpson, B., & Macy, M. W. (2004). Power, Identity, and Collective Action in Social Exchange. *Social Forces, 82*(4), 1373–1409. doi:10.1353of.2004.0096

Sims, J. H. P., & Lorenzi, P. (1992). *The new leadership paradigm: Social learning and cognition in organizations.* Sage Publications, Inc.

Sinclair, A. (2004). Journey around leadership. *Discourse (Abingdon), 25*(1), 7–19. doi:10.1080/0159630042000178455

Singer, M., & Gershman, Z. (2018). Do changes in district magnitude affect electoral fragmentation? Evidence over time at the district level. *Electoral Studies, 54*, 172–181. doi:10.1016/j.electstud.2018.06.003

Sirias, D., Karp, H., & Brotherton, T. (2007). Comparing the levels of individualism collectivism between baby boomers and Generation X: Implications for teamwork. *Management Research News*, *30*(10), 749–761. doi:10.1108/01409170710823467

Sivanathan, N., Pillutla, M. M., & Murnighan, J. K. (2008). Power gained, power lost. *Organizational Behavior and Human Decision Processes*, *105*(2), 135–146. doi:10.1016/j.obhdp.2007.10.003

Siyal, S., Xin, C., Umrani, W. A., Fatima, S., & Pal, D. (2021). How do leaders influence innovation and creativity in employees? The mediating role of intrinsic motivation. *Administration & Society*, *53*(9), 1337–1361. doi:10.1177/0095399721997427

Sliter, M. (2013). *What is workplace incivility, why should we care, and what should we do?* HRZONE. https://www.hrzone.com/perform/people/what-is-workplace-incivility-why-should-we-care-and-what-should-we-do

Small, E. E., & Rentsch, J. R. (2010). Shared leadership in teams: A matter of distribution. *Journal of Personnel Psychology*, *9*(4), 203–211. doi:10.1027/1866-5888/a000017

Smart, J., Cascio, J., Paffendorf, J., Bridges, C., Hummel, J., Hursthouse, J., & Moss, R. (2007). *Metaverse Roadmap Overview.* W3. https://www.w3.org/2008/WebVideo/Annotations/wiki/images/1/19/MetaverseRoadmapOverview.pdf

Smith-Tran, A. (2020). Exploring the benefits and drawbacks of age disclosure among women faculty of color. *Teaching Sociology*, *48*(1), 3–12. doi:10.1177/0092055X19869983

Snellman, K., & Solal, I. (2022). Does investor gender matter for the success of female entrepreneurs? Gender homophily and the stigma of incompetence in entrepreneurial finance. *Organization Science*.

Snyder, H. (2019). Literature review as a research methodology: An overview and guidelines. *Journal of Business Research*, *104*, 333–339. doi:10.1016/j.jbusres.2019.07.039

Society for Human Resource Management. (2020). *How to support employee resource groups.* SHRM.

Solomons, D. (1983). In search of excellence: lessons from america's best-run companies. *Journal of Accountancy (pre-1986), 156*(6), 150-175

Sommer, S. A., Howell, J. M., & Hadley, C. N. (2016). Keeping Positive and Building Strength: The Role of Affect and Team Leadership in Developing Resilience During an Organizational Crisis. *Group & Organization Management*, *41*(2), 172–202. doi:10.1177/1059601115578027

Spector, B. A. (2016). Carlyle, Freud, and the great man theory more fully considered. *Leadership*, *12*(2), 250–260. doi:10.1177/1742715015571392

Spreitzer, G. M. (1995). Psychological empowerment in the workplace: Dimensions, measurement, and validation. *Academy of Management Journal*, *38*(5), 1442–1465. doi:10.2307/256865

Srivastava, A., Bartol, K. M., & Locke, E. A. (2006). Empowering leadership in management teams: Effects on knowledge sharing, efficacy, and performance. *Academy of Management Journal*, *49*(6), 1239–1251. doi:10.5465/amj.2006.23478718

Stackpole, T. (2022). Exploring the metaverse. *Harvard Business Review*. https://hbr.org/2022/07/exploring-the-metaverse

Stajkovic, A. D., & Luthans, F. (1998). Self-efficacy and work-related per-formance: A meta-analysis. *Psychological Bulletin*, *124*(2), 240–261. doi:10.1037/0033-2909.124.2.240

Starr, R., Newfrock, J., & Delurey, M. (2003). Enterprise resilience: Managing risk in the networked economy. *Strategy & Business*, *30*, 70–79.

Staw, I. B. M., & Sutton, R. I. (Eds.), *Research in Organizational Behavior* (Vol. 23, pp. 133–187). JAIPress.

Steininger, D. M. (2019). Linking information systems and entrepreneurship: A review and agenda for IT-associated and digital entrepreneurship research. *Information Systems Journal*, *29*(2), 363–407. doi:10.1111/isj.12206

Stephenson, N. (1992). *Snow crash: A novel*. Spectra.

Sterling, A., & Srivastava, S. B. (2018). *The inclusion dividend: Why investing in diversity & inclusion pays off*. Center for Talent Innovation.

Sternberg, R. J., Siriner, I., Oh, J., & Wong, C. H. (2022). Cultural Intelligence: What Is It and How Can It Effectively Be Measured? *Journal of Intelligence*, *10*(3), 54. doi:10.3390/jintelligence10030054 PMID:35997410

Sternberg, R. J., Wong, C. H., & Kreisel, A. P. (2021). Understanding and assessing cultural intelligence: Maximum-performance and typical-performance approaches. *Journal of Intelligence*, *9*(3), 45. doi:10.3390/jintelligence9030045 PMID:34564293

Stewart, D. (1985). Ethics and the profession of public administration: The moral responsibility of individuals in public sector organizations. *Public Administration Quarterly*, *8*(48), 487–495.

Steyaert, C., & Katz, J. (2004). Reclaiming the space of entrepreneurship in society: Geographical, discursive and social dimensions. *Entrepreneurship and Regional Development*, *16*(3), 179–196. doi:10.1080/0898562042000197135

Stocker, D., Keller, A. C., Meier, L. L., Elfering, A., Pfister, I. B., Jacobshagen, N., & Semmer, N. K. (2019). Appreciation by supervisors buffers the impact of work interruptions on well-being longitudinally. *International Journal of Stress Management*, *26*(4), 331–343. doi:10.1037tr0000111

Stogdill, R. M. (1974). *Handbook of leadership: A survey of theory and research*. Free Press.

Stogdill, R. M., & Shartle, C. L. (1948). Methods for determining patterns of leadership behavior in relation to organization structure and objectives. *The Journal of Applied Psychology*, *32*(3), 286–291. doi:10.1037/h0057264 PMID:18867065

Stoltz, P. G. (2015). Leadership GRIT™: What new research reveals. *Leader to Leader, 2015*(78), 49–55. doi:10.1002/ltl.20205

Strauss, K., Griffin, M. A., & Rafferty, A. E. (2009). Proactivity directed toward the team and organization: The role of leadership, commitment and role-breadth self-efficacy. *British Journal of Management, 20*(3), 279–291. doi:10.1111/j.1467-8551.2008.00590.x

Strauss, W., & Howe, N. (1991). *Generations: The history of America's future*. William Morrow.

Subašić, E., Hardacre, S., Elton, B., Branscombe, N. R., Ryan, M. K., & Reynolds, K. J. (2018). "We for She": Mobilizing men and women to act in solidarity for gender equality. *Group Processes & Intergroup Relations, 21*(5), 707–724. doi:10.1177/1368430218763272

Sugiyama, K., Cavanagh, K. V., van Esch, C., Bilimoria, D., & Brown, C. (2016). Inclusive leadership development: Drawing from pedagogies of women's and general leadership development programs. *Journal of Management Education, 40*(3), 253–292. doi:10.1177/1052562916632553

Sundari, D. K., & Sowmiya, B. (2020). TIRUPUR TEXTILE START-UPS IN COVID 19 PANDEMIC. *SELP Journal of Social Science - A Blind Review & Refereed Quarterly Journal, XI*(46), 35-41.

Sundstrom, E., De Meuse, K. P., & Futrell, D. (1990). Work Teams: Applications and Effectiveness. *The American Psychologist, 45*(2), 120–133. doi:10.1037/0003-066X.45.2.120

Sun, L. Y., Aryee, S., & Law, K. S. (2007). High performance human resources practices, citizenship behavior, and organizational performance: A relational perspective. *Academy of Management Journal, 50*(3), 558–577. doi:10.5465/amj.2007.25525821

Su, S., Baird, K., & Munir, R. (2022). Organisational resilience: The role of organisational culture from an organisational life cycle perspective. *International Journal of Manpower*. doi:10.1108/IJM-11-2021-0631

Suzue, K. (2020). *The Cognitive Diversity-creative Performance Relationship and the Mediating Effect of Power-distance Orientation: A Study of Japan-based Organizations in the US* [Doctoral dissertation, The Chicago School of Professional Psychology].

Swartz, D. (1977). Pierre Bourdieu: The cultural transmission of social inequality. *Harvard Educational Review, 47*(4), 545–555. doi:10.17763/haer.47.4.q1475v2qg2661v58

Tabatabaei, S. A. N., & Bigdelli, E. (2015). The mediating role of employee cynicism in the relationship between perceived organizational justice and employee silence. *Journal UMP Social Sciences and Technology Management, 3*(3), 121–127.

Tarmo, C. G., & Issa, F. H. (2022). An analysis of groupthink and decision making in a collectivism culture: The case of a public organization in Tanzania. *International Journal of Public Leadership, 18*(1), 15–29. doi:10.1108/IJPL-08-2020-0072

Tasa, K., Taggar, S., & Seijts, G. H. (2007). The development of collective efficacy in teams: A multilevel and longitudinal perspective. *The Journal of Applied Psychology*, *92*(1), 17–27. doi:10.1037/0021-9010.92.1.17 PMID:17227148

Taşkaya, S., & Aksoy, A.TAŞKAYA. (2021, April). S., & AKSOY, A. (2020). A Bibliometric Analysis of Workplace Incivility in Nursing. *Journal of Nursing Management*, *29*(3), 518–525. doi:10.1111/jonm.13161

Tatli, A., Özbilgin, M., & Karatas-Özkan, M. (2015). Introduction: Management and Organisation Studies Meet Pierre Bourdieu. In *Pierre Bourdieu, Organisation, and Management* (pp. 1–16). Routledge. doi:10.4324/9781315818146

Taylor, S. G., Bedeian, A. G., Cole, M. S., & Zhang, Z. (2017). Developing and Testing a Dynamic Model of Workplace Incivility Change. *Journal of Management*, *43*(3), 645–670. doi:10.1177/0149206314535432

Tesluk, P. E., & Mathieu, J. E. (1999). Overcoming roadblocks to effectiveness: Incorporating management of performance barriers into models of work group effectiveness. *The Journal of Applied Psychology*, *84*(2), 200–217. doi:10.1037/0021-9010.84.2.200

Theurer, C. P., Tumasjan, A., & Welpe, I. M. (2018). Contextual work design and employee innovative work behavior: When does autonomy matter? *PLoS One*, *13*(10), e0204089. doi:10.1371/journal.pone.0204089 PMID:30286104

Thomas, C. (1888). the Great Man Theory, On Heroes, Hero-Worship and the Heroic in History. New York: Fredrick A. Stokes & Brother.

Thomas, D. A., & Ely, R. J. (2019). Making work more meaningful for everyone. *Harvard Business Review*, *97*(5), 118–127.

Thomas, D. C., Liao, Y., Aycan, Z., Cerdin, J. L., Pekerti, A. A., Ravlin, E. C., Stahl, G. K., Lazarova, M. B., Fock, H., Arli, D., Moeller, M., Okimoto, T. G., & Van De Vijver, F. (2015). Cultural intelligence: A theory-based, short form measure. *Journal of International Business Studies*, *46*(9), 1099–1118. doi:10.1057/jibs.2014.67

Tlili, A., Huang, R., Shehata, B., Liu, D., Zhao, J., Metwally, A. H. S., Wang, H., Denden, M., Bozkurt, A., Lee, L. H., Beyoglu, D., Altinay, F., Sharma, R. C., Altinay, Z., Li, Z., Liu, J., Ahmad, F., Hu, Y., Salha, S., & Burgos, D. (2022). Is Metaverse in education a blessing or a curse: A combined content and bibliometric analysis. *Smart Learning Environments*, *9*(1), 1–31. doi:10.118640561-022-00205-x

Topcic, M., Baum, M., & Kabst, R. (2016). Are high-performance work practices related to individually perceived stress? A job demands-resources perspective. *International Journal of Human Resource Management*, *27*(1), 45–66. doi:10.1080/09585192.2015.1043136

Toquero, C. M. (2020). Challenges and Opportunities for Higher Education amid the COVID19 Pandemic: The Philippine Context. *Pedagogical Research*, *5*(4), 1–5. doi:10.29333/pr/7947

Torraco, R. J. (2005). Writing integrative literature reviews: Guidelines and examples. *Human Resource Development Review*, *4*(3), 356–367. doi:10.1177/1534484305278283

Torraco, R. J. (2016). Writing integrative reviews of the literature: Methods and purposes. *International Journal of Adult Vocational Education and Technology*, *7*(3), 62–70. doi:10.4018/IJAVET.2016070106

Tran, L. T. (2020). Managing the effectiveness of e-commerce platforms in a pandemic. *Journal of Retailing and Consumer Services*, 1–9.

Tran, T. B. H., & Choi, S. B. (2019). Effects of inclusive leadership on organizational citizenship behaviour: The mediating roles of organizational justice and learning culture. *Journal of Pacific Rim Psychology*, *13*, 1–11.

Trehan, K. (2018, October 18). Why the world needs more women CEOs. *The Conversation*. https://theconversation.com/why-the-world-needs-more-women-ceos-104876

Trent, S. B., & Allen, J. A. (2019). 4 3). Resilience Only Gets You So Far: Volunteer Incivility and Burnout. *Organizational Management Journal*, *16*(2), 69–80. doi:10.1080/15416518.2019.1604199

Triandis, H. C., Kurowski, L. L., & Gelfand, M. J. (1994). Workplace diversity. In H. Triandis, M. Dunnette, & L. Hough (Eds.), *Handbook of industrial and organizational psychology* (pp. 769–827). Consulting Psychologists Press.

Triguero-Sánchez, R., Peña-Vinces, J., & Guillen, J. (2018). How to improve firm performance through employee diversity and organisational culture. *Revista Brasileira de Gestão de Negócios*, *20*(3), 378–400. doi:10.7819/rbgn.v20i3.3303

Tsagkias, M., King, T. H., Kallumadi, S., Murdock, V., & Rijke, M. d. (2020). Challenges and Research Opportunites in e-commerce search and Recommendations. *ACM SIGIR Forum, 54*(1), 1-23.

Turkmen, A. A. (2013). *Cognitive diversity and innovation: Does cognitive diversity in multinational corporations influence workgroup innovation?* [Doctoral dissertation, Fielding Graduate University].

Türkmen, S. Y., & Durbilmez, S. E. (2019). Blockchain teknolojisi ve Türkiye finans sektöründeki durumu. [Blockchain technology and its situation in the Turkish financial sector]. *Finans Ekonomi ve Sosyal Araştırmalar Dergisi*, *4*(1), 30–45. doi:10.29106/fesa.509254

Twenge, J. M., Campbell, S. M., Hoffman, B. J., & Lance, C. E. (2010). Generational differences in work values: Leisure and extrinsic values increasing, social and intrinsic values decreasing. *Journal of Management*, *36*(5), 1117–1142. doi:10.1177/0149206309352246

Tyler, T. R., & Smith, H. J. (1995). Social justice and social movements. In Handbook of social psychology. McGraw-Hill.

Tyree, T. M. (1998). Designing an instrument to measure socially responsible leadership using the Social Change Model of Leadership Development. *Dissertation Abstracts International, 59*(06), 1945 (AAT 9836493)

Tysinger, J., Tysinger, D., Mcbrayer, J. S., & Daimanduros, T. (2020). Perspectives, Training and preparedness of frequently and infrequently Addressed Crisis events in online learning environment. *Journal of Higher Education Theory and Practice*, *20*(5), 61–69.

Tzafrir, S. S., Dolan, S. L., & Yakhnich, L. (2018). Functional diversity and team performance in health care organizations: The role of transformational leadership. *Journal of Health Organization and Management*, *32*(2), 254–270. doi:10.1108/JHOM-05-2017-0117

Ucal, M., Ozcan, K. M., Bilgin, M. H., & Mungo, J. (2010). Relationship Between Financial Crisis And Foreign Direct Investment in Developing Countries Using Semiparametric Regression Approach. *Journal of Business Economics and Management*, *11*(1), 20–33. doi:10.3846/jbem.2010.02

Uhl-Bien, M. (2006). Relational leadership theory: Exploring the social processes of leadership and organizing. *The Leadership Quarterly*, *17*(6), 654–676. doi:10.1016/j.leaqua.2006.10.007

Ullrich, A., Lambert, R. G., & McCarthy, C. J. (2012). Relationship of German elementary teachers' occupational experience, stress, and coping resources to burnout symptoms. *International Journal of Stress Management*, *19*(4), 333–342. doi:10.1037/a0030121

Vakira, E., Shereni, N. C., Ncube, C. M., & Ndlovu, N. (2022). The effect of inclusive leadership on employee engagement, mediated by psychological safety in the hospitality industry. *Journal of Hospitality and Tourism Insights*.

Valickas, A., & Jakstaite, K. (2017). Different Generations' attitude towards work and management in the business organizations. *Human Resources Management & Ergonomics*, *XI*, 108–119.

Valle-Flórez, R.-E., de Caso Fuertes, A. M., Baelo, R., & Marcos-Santiago, R. (2022). Inclusive Culture in Compulsory Education Centers: Values, Participation and Teachers' Perceptions. *Children (Basel, Switzerland)*, *9*(6), 813. doi:10.3390/children9060813 PMID:35740750

Valliere, D., & Peterson, R. (2009). Entrepreneurship and economic growth: Evidence from emerging and developed countries. *Entrepreneurship and Regional Development*, *21*(5-6), 459–480. doi:10.1080/08985620802332723

van Baalen, S., Alessandri, G., Perugini, M., & Borgogni, L. (2021). The relationship between team diversity and team innovation: A meta-analysis. *European Journal of Work and Organizational Psychology*, *30*(1), 87–111. doi:10.1080/1359432X.2020.1840199

van Breda, A. D. (2016). Building Resilient Human Service Organizations. *Human Service Organizations, Management, Leadership & Governance*, *40*(1), 62–73. doi:10.1080/23303131.2015.1093571 van der Berg, P. (2010). Stimulating Knowledge Sharing by Error Management and Leader-Member Exchange: Psychological Safety as a Mediator. *Psihologia Resurselor Umane*, *8*(2), 42–52. doi:10.24837/pru.v8i2.417

van der Klift, E., & Kunc, N. (2019). *Being realistic isn't realistic: Collected essays on disability, identity, inclusion and innovation*. Tellwell Talent.

Van der Vegt, G. S., & Janssen, O. (2003). Joint impact of interdependence and group diversity on innovation. *Journal of Management*, *29*(5), 729–751. doi:10.1016/S0149-2063_03_00033-3

Van Dierendonck, D. (2011). Servant leadership: A review and synthesis. *Journal of Management*, *37*(4), 1228–1261. doi:10.1177/0149206310380462

Van Dyne, L., Ang, S., Ng, K. Y., Rockstuhl, T., Tan, M. L., & Koh, C. (2012). Sub-dimensions of the four factor model of cultural intelligence: Expanding the conceptualization and measurement of cultural intelligence. *Social and Personality Psychology Compass*, *6*(4), 295–313. doi:10.1111/j.1751-9004.2012.00429.x

Van Gulick, R. (2000). Inward and upward: Reflection, introspection, and self-awareness. *Philosophical Topics*, *28*(2), 275–305. doi:10.5840/philtopics200028222

Van Knippenberg, D., De Dreu, C. K., & Homan, A. C. (2004). Work group diversity and group performance: An integrative model and research agenda. *The Journal of Applied Psychology*, *89*(6), 1008–1022. doi:10.1037/0021-9010.89.6.1008 PMID:15584838

Van Knippenberg, D., & Schippers, M. C. (2007). Work group diversity. *Annual Review of Psychology*, *58*(1), 515–541. doi:10.1146/annurev.psych.58.110405.085546 PMID:16903805

Van Knippenberg, D., & Sitkin, S. B. (2013). A critical assessment of charismatic—transformational leadership research: Back to the drawing board? *The Academy of Management Annals*, *7*(1), 1–60. doi:10.5465/19416520.2013.759433

Van Knippenberg, D., & van Ginkel, W. P. (2022). A diversity mindset perspective on inclusive leadership. *Group & Organization Management*, *47*(4), 779–797. doi:10.1177/1059601121997229

Van Laar, C., Meeussen, L., Veldman, J., Van Grootel, S., Sterk, N., & Jacobs, C. (2019). Coping with stigma in the workplace: Understanding the role of threat regulation, supportive factors, and potential hidden costs. *Frontiers in Psychology*, *10*, 1879. doi:10.3389/fpsyg.2019.01879 PMID:31507478

Vancouver, J. B., & Kendall, L. N. (2006). When self-efficacy negatively relates to motivation and performance in a learning context. *The Journal of Applied Psychology*, *91*(5), 1146–1153. doi:10.1037/0021-9010.91.5.1146 PMID:16953775

Varshney, R.(2020). AI and machine learning trends in 2020. *Forbes*.

Vecchio, R. (2005). Explorations in employee envy: Feeling envious and feeling envied. *Cognition and Emotion*, *19*(1), 69–81. doi:10.1080/02699930441000148

Vecchio, R. P. (1995). It's not easy being green: Jealousy and envy in the workplace. In G. R. Ferris (Ed.), *Research in personnel and human resources management* (Vol. 13, pp. 201–244). JAI Press.

Veldman, J., Van Laar, C., Meeussen, L., & Lo Bue, S. (2021). Daily coping with social identity threat in outgroup-dominated contexts: Self-group distancing among female soldiers. *Personality and Social Psychology Bulletin*, *47*(1), 118–130. doi:10.1177/0146167220921054 PMID:32431224

Vescio, T., Gervais, S. J., Snyder, M., & Hoover, A. "Power and the Creation of patronizing Environments: The Stereotype-Based Behaviors of the Powerful and Their Effects on Female Performance in Masculine Domains" (2005). Faculty Publications, Department of Psychology. 341.

Volmer, J., Koch, I. K., & Göritz, A. S. (2016). The bright and dark sides of leaders' dark triad traits: Effects on subordinates' career success and well-being. *Personality and Individual Differences*, *101*, 413–418. doi:10.1016/j.paid.2016.06.046

Vorina, A., Simonič, M., & Vlasova, M. (2017). An analysis of the relationship between job satisfaction and employee engagement. *Economic themes, 55*(2), 243-262

Vroom, V. H., & Jago, A. G. (1974). Decision-Making as a Social Process: Normative and Descriptive Models of Leader Behavior (AD0779334). New Haven, United States.

Wagstaff, G. F. (1994). Equity, equality, and need: Three principles of justice or one? An analysis of 'equity as desert'. *Current Psychological Research & Reviews*, *13*(2), 138–152. doi:10.1007/BF02686797

Walumbwa, F. O., Wu, C., & Orwa, B. (2008). Contingent reward transactional leadership, work attitudes, and organizational citizenship behavior: The role of procedural justice climate perceptions and strength. *The Leadership Quarterly*, *19*(3), 251–265. doi:10.1016/j.leaqua.2008.03.004

Walvoord, A. A. G., Redden, E. R., Elliot, L. R., & Coovert, M. D. (2008). Empowering followers in virtual teams: Guiding principles from theory and practice. *Computers in Human Behavior*, *24*(5), 1884–1906. doi:10.1016/j.chb.2008.02.006

Wang, D., Waldman, D. A., & Zhang, Z. (2014). A meta-analysis of shared leadership and team effectiveness. *The Journal of Applied Psychology*, *99*(2), 181–198. doi:10.1037/a0034531 PMID:24188392

Wang, F. Y., Qin, R., Wang, X., & Hu, B. (2022). Metasocieties in metaverse: Metaeconomics and metamanagement for metaenterprises and metacities. *IEEE Transactions on Computational Social Systems*, *9*(1), 2–7. doi:10.1109/TCSS.2022.3145165

Wang, F., & Shi, W. (2021). Inclusive leadership and pro-social rule breaking: The role of psychological safety, leadership identification and leader-member exchange. *Psychological Reports*, *124*(5), 2155–2179. doi:10.1177/0033294120953558 PMID:32878545

Wang, H., Chen, M., & Li, X. (2021). Moderating multiple mediation model of the impact of inclusive leadership on employee innovative behavior. *Frontiers in Psychology*, *12*, 666477. doi:10.3389/fpsyg.2021.666477 PMID:34456787

Wang, M., Hu, Q., & He, W. (2020). The relationship between workforce diversity and turnover: A meta-analysis. *Journal of Management*, *46*(7), 1097–1125.

Wang, Q., Wang, J., Zhou, X., Li, F., & Wang, M. (2020). How inclusive leadership enhances follower taking charge: The mediating role of affective commitment and the moderating role of traditionality. *Psychology Research and Behavior Management*, *13*, 1103–1114. doi:10.2147/PRBM.S280911 PMID:33299363

Wang, Y. X., Yang, Y. J., Wang, Y., Su, D., Li, S. W., Zhang, T., & Li, H. P. (2019). The mediating role of inclusive leadership: Work engagement and innovative behaviour among Chinese head nurses. *Journal of Nursing Management*, *27*(4), 688–696. doi:10.1111/jonm.12754 PMID:30702790

Wang, Z., Xu, S., Sun, Y., & Liu, Y. (2019). Transformational leadership and employee voice: An affective perspective. *Frontiers of Business Research in China*, *13*(1), 2. doi:10.118611782-019-0049-y

Waterman, R. H., & Peters, T. J. (1982). *In search of excellence: Lessons from America's best-run companies*. Harper & Row.

Wei, L. Q., & Wu, L. (2013). What a diverse top management team means: Testing an integrated model. *Journal of Management Studies*, *50*(3), 389–412. doi:10.1111/joms.12013

Weintraub, P., & McKee, M. (2019). Leadership for innovation in healthcare: An exploration. *International Journal of Health Policy and Management*, *8*(3), 138–144. doi:10.15171/ijhpm.2018.122 PMID:30980629

Weiss, M., Kolbe, M., Grote, G., Spahn, D. R., & Grande, B. (2018). We can do it! Inclusive leader language promotes voice behavior in multi-professional teams. *The Leadership Quarterly*, *29*(3), 389–402. doi:10.1016/j.leaqua.2017.09.002

Weking, J., Desouza, K. C., Fielt, E., & Kowalkiewicz, M. (2023). Metaverse-enabled entrepreneurship. *Journal of Business Venturing Insights*, *19*, e00375. doi:10.1016/j.jbvi.2023.e00375

Weston, G. (2022). *5 Profitable business opportunities in metaverse*. 101 Blockchains. https://101blockchains.com/business-opportunities-in-metaverse/

Wey Smola, K., & Sutton, C. D. (2002). Generational differences: Revisiting Generational work values for the new millennium. *Journal of Organizational Behavior*, *23*(4), 363–382. doi:10.1002/job.147

Williams, H. M., Parker, S. K., & Turner, N. (2010). Proactively performing teams: The role of work design, transformational leadership, and team composition. *Journal of Occupational and Organizational Psychology*, *83*(2), 301–324. doi:10.1348/096317910X502494

Wise, C. R. (2006). Organizing for homeland security after Katrina: Is adaptive management what's missing? *Public Administration Review*, *66*(3), 302–318. doi:10.1111/j.1540-6210.2006.00587.x

Wishart, M. (2018). *Under represented entrepreneurs: A literature review.* Enterprise Research Centre. https://www.enterpriseresearch.ac.uk/wp-content/uploads/2018/07/Under-represented-entrepreneurs-Revised-10.18.pdf

Witkowski, E. (2021). Ally networks: The future of employee resource groups. *Harvard Business Review.*

Witte, L. (2012). Creating and Leading in an Environment of Collaboration. *SPNHA Review*, *8*(1), 7.

Woll, E. S. M. (2021). *Inclusive Leadership: 6 Behaviors to Embody.* Betterup. https://www.betterup.com/blog/what-makes-an-inclusive-leader-and-6-ways-to-up-your-game

Woodard, C. R., & Pury, C. L. (2007). The construct of courage: Categorization and measurement. *Consulting Psychology Journal*, *59*(2), 135–147. doi:10.1037/1065-9293.59.2.135

Woodrow, C., & Guest, D. E. (2014). When good HR gets bad results: Exploring the challenge of HR implementation in the case of workplace bullying. *Human Resource Management Journal*, *24*(1), 38–56. doi:10.1111/1748-8583.12021

Woodside, A. G. (2013). Moving beyond multiple regression analysis to algorithms: Calling for adoption of a paradigm shift from symmetric to asymmetric thinking in data analysis and crafting theory. *Journal of Business Research*, *66*(4), 463–472. doi:10.1016/j.jbusres.2012.12.021

World Economic Forum. (2022). *How the metaverse can be a force for good in an uncertain world.* WEF. https://www.weforum.org/agenda/2022/05/how-metaverse-can-be-a-force-for-good-in-an-uncertain-world/

Worsley, B. (2021) For entrepreneurs, the metaverse is already here. *Medium.* https://medium.com/masterplans/for-entrepreneurs-the-metaverse-is-already-here-78909ffb405e

Wright, M. P., Gardner, M. T., & Moynihan, M. L. (2003). The impact of HR practices on the performance of business units. *Human Resource Management Journal*, *13*(3), 21–36. doi:10.1111/j.1748-8583.2003.tb00096.x

Wright, M., Ekeus, H., Coyne, R., Stewart, J., Travlou, P., & Williams, R. (2008). Augmented duality: overlapping a metaverse with the real world. *In Proceedings of the 2008 International Conference on Advances in Computer Entertainment Technology*, (pp. 263–266). ACM. 10.1145/1501750.1501812

Wright, P. M., Dunford, B. B., & Snell, S. A. (2001). Human resources and the resource based view of the firm. *Journal of Management*, *27*(6), 701–721. doi:10.1177/014920630102700607

Xanthopoulou, D., Bakker, A. B., Demerouti, E., & Schaufeli, W. B. (2009). Reciprocal relationships between job resources, personal resources, and work engagement. *Journal of Vocational Behavior*, *74*(3), 235–244. doi:10.1016/j.jvb.2008.11.003

Xiaotao, Z., Yang, X., Diaz, I., & Yu, M. (2018). Is too much inclusive leadership a good thing? An examination of curvilinear relationship between inclusive leadership and employees' task performance. *International Journal of Manpower*, *39*(7), 882–895. doi:10.1108/IJM-01-2017-0011

Xiao, Y., & Watson, M. (2019). Guidance on conducting a systematic literature review. *Journal of Planning Education and Research*, *39*(1), 93–112. doi:10.1177/0739456X17723971

Xu, C., & Zhao, L. (2022). Collective achievement, cohesive support, complementary expertise: 3Cs emergent model for shared leadership. *Human Resource Development International*, 1–26.

Xu, M., Chen, X., & Kou, G. (2019). A systematic review of blockchain. *Financial Innovation*, *5*(1), 1–14. doi:10.118640854-019-0147-z

Xu, X., Jiang, L., & Wang, H. J. (2019). How to build your team for innovation? A cross-level mediation model of team personality, team climate for innovation, creativity, and job crafting. *Journal of Occupational and Organizational Psychology*, *92*(4), 848–872. doi:10.1111/joop.12277

Yammarino, F. J., & Dansereau, F. (2008). Multi-level nature of and multi-level approaches to leadership. *The Leadership Quarterly*, *19*(2), 135–141. doi:10.1016/j.leaqua.2008.01.001

Yang, M., Mamun, A. A., Mohiuddin, M., Nawi, N., & Zainol, N. R. (2021). Cashless Transactions: A study on Intention and Adoption of e-wallets. *Sustainability (Basel)*, *13*(2), 1–18. doi:10.3390u13020831

Yemenici, A. D. (2022). Entrepreneurship in the world of Metaverse: Virtual or real? *Journal of Metaverse*, *2*(2), 71–82. doi:10.57019/jmv.1126135

Ye, Q., Wang, D., & Guo, W. (2019). Inclusive leadership and team innovation: The role of team voice and performance pressure. *European Management Journal*, *37*(4), 468–480. doi:10.1016/j.emj.2019.01.006

Ye, Q., Wang, D., & Li, X. (2018). Promoting employees' learning from errors by inclusive leadership: Do positive mood and gender matter? *Baltic Journal of Management*, *13*(1), 125–142. doi:10.1108/BJM-05-2017-0160

Ye, Q., Wang, D., & Li, X. (2019). Inclusive leadership and employees' learning from errors: A moderated mediation model. *Australian Journal of Management*, *44*(3), 462–481. doi:10.1177/0312896218805796

Ye, Y., Lyu, Y., Kwan, H. K., Chen, X., & Cheng, X. M. (2021). The antecedents and consequences of being envied by coworkers: An investigation from the victim perspective. *International Journal of Hospitality Management*, *94*, 102751. doi:10.1016/j.ijhm.2020.102751

Yu, L., & Duffy, M. K. (2016). A moral licensing perspective of abusive supervision and career consequences. In Academy of Management Proceedings (pp. 15269). Academy of Management. doi:10.5465/ambpp.2016.15269abstract

Yuan, F., & Zhou, J. (2015). Effects of cultural power distance on group creativity and individual group member creativity. *Journal of Organizational Behavior*, *36*(7), 990–1007. doi:10.1002/job.2022

Yu, H. C., & Miller, P. (2005). Leadership style: The X Generation and Baby Boomers compared in different cultural contexts. *Leadership and Organization Development Journal*, *26*(1), 35–50. doi:10.1108/01437730510575570

Zahra, S. A. (2005). Entrepreneurial risk taking in family firms. *Family Business Review*, *18*(1), 23–40. doi:10.1111/j.1741-6248.2005.00028.x

Zaitouni, M., Harraf, A., & Kisswani, A. M. (2020). Resources for development: The relationship of HRM practices and continuous learning culture with training success. *International Journal of Human Resources Development and Management*, *20*(1), 75–92. doi:10.1504/IJHRDM.2020.105099

Zanoni, P., & Janssens, M. (2007). Minority employees engaging with (diversity) management: An analysis of control, agency, and micro-emancipation. *Journal of Management Studies*, *44*(8), 1371–1397. doi:10.1111/j.1467-6486.2007.00700.x

Zemke, R., Raines, C., & Filipczak, B. (2000). *Generations at Work: Managing the Clash of Veterans, Boomers, Xers, and Nexters in Your Workplace*. American Management Association.

Zeng, H., Zhao, L., & Zhao, Y. (2020). Inclusive leadership and taking-charge behavior: Roles of psychological safety and thriving at work. *Frontiers in Psychology*, *11*, 62. doi:10.3389/fpsyg.2020.00062 PMID:32153448

Zhang, X., Tian, G., Ma, C., Tian, Y., Li, Z., & Liang, L. (2020). "Too much of a good thing?": Exploring the dark side of empowering leadership by linking it with unethical pro-organizational behavior. *Leadership and Organization Development Journal*, *42*(1), 32–46. doi:10.1108/LODJ-02-2020-0033

Zhao, F., Ahmed, F., & Faraz, N. A. (2020). Caring for the caregiver during COVID-19 outbreak: Does inclusive leadership improve psychological safety and curb psychological distress? A cross-sectional study. *International Journal of Nursing Studies*, *110*, 103725. doi:10.1016/j.ijnurstu.2020.103725 PMID:32810720

Zhu, J., Xu, S., & Zhang, B. (2020). The paradoxical effect of inclusive leadership on subordinates' creativity. *Frontiers in Psychology*, *10*, 2960. doi:10.3389/fpsyg.2019.02960 PMID:32038369

About the Contributors

Çağlar Doğru, (Ph.D.) is an associate professor of Management and Strategy and serves as the head of the management and organization department at Ufuk University, Ankara, Turkey. He completed his bachelor's degree at Hacettepe University, department of business administration. He received a master's degree in human resources management and a doctoral degree in business administration from Gazi University, Ankara, Turkey. His research interests are concentrated on management, leadership, organization, organizational behavior, human resources management, and strategic management. He has given lessons in his research areas, both at bachelor's and master's degrees. He has supervised many master's theses on management and organization as well. Additionally, he has numerous research articles in both national and international journals. Moreover, he has many book chapters in the international publishing houses and he presented numerous studies at many national and international conferences and published at proceedings. He serves as an editor for both international books and national/international prestigious journals. Having conducted national and international projects so far, he serves as a management consultant to the biggest trade companies in Turkey besides holding several leadership roles at the University.

* * *

Ansar Abbas received from the The Airlangga Development Scholarship the financial support he needed to earn his Ph.D. at the University of Airlangga in Surabaya, Indonesia. He is an associate professor at MYU Business School in Islamabad, Pakistan. He published various qualitative and quantitative journal articles and book chapters throughout his academic career. He researched and wrote about leadership theory, leadership psychology, modern slavery, human capital value creation, positive and negative elements of psychology, spirituality, spiritual intelligence, research modeling, framework design, well-being, and positive psychology. In addition to reading widely, he is also contributing to the advancement of knowledge by examining submissions, assisting in the editing process, and acting as an editor for several national and international periodicals. He has 15 years of experience in management, administration, higher education, and the research and development sectors.

Richard Afedzie is a senior lecturer at Pentecost University. He is the Dean of Evening & Weekend school. His research interests are in the areas of Business Ethics, Sustainability, Leadership, Change Management and Organisational Development. He finished his PhD at the University of Texas at Tyler in the USA. He teaches at both the undergraduate and graduate levels in management courses, entrepreneurship and leadership

Diksha Dhar is a Ph.D research scholar in the Department of Business Administration, Assam University Silchar. She has completed her M.Phil (Gold Medalist) from Babasaheb Bhimrao Ambedkar University, Lucknow and has one year of teaching experience. Her research interests are focused on leadership and organizational behaviour.

Ömer Karademir graduated from Gazi University, Faculty of Commerce and Tourism Education, in 2009, and from Anadolu University, Faculty of Economic and Administrative Sciences, Department of Business Administration, in 2014. In the same year, he graduated from Gazi University, Graduate School of Educational Sciences, and in 2020 from Sakarya University, Faculty of Business Administration, Department of Business Administration, Management, and Organization. He worked in the Turkish Grain Board from 2009 to 2011. Since 2011, he has been teaching as an academic at the Kastamonu University at the undergraduate and associate levels. He studies the fields of management, organizational behaviour, strategic management, entrepreneurship, and human resources and has published several studies in these fields.

Praveen Kumar is an Assistant Professor at the University School of Business at Chandigarh University, with 5.5 years of experience in teaching and Research. He has cleared the Junior Research Fellowship (UGC-JRF) which is conducted by University Grant Commission (UGC). He has awarded his Ph.D. in Management with the research topic "Consumers Perception and Purchase Intention towards Organic Food Products". He has attended many international and national conferences, workshops, seminars, and faculty development programs. He has published many Scopus-indexed research papers and book chapters in reputed Journals in the field of Marketing, Finance, and Human Resource Management. He has also written many book chapters in different areas of Management and published national and International Patents in various fields. He has practical experience and knowledge of

Statistical software viz. SPSS, AMOS- SEM, PLS. He has been invited as a keynote speaker in various workshops, and seminars related to Research methodology at different colleges and Universities.

Inês Maximino completed her Masters in Management at ISAG - European Business School and is a researcher at Research Center in Business Sciences and Tourism (CICET-FCVC), Porto, Portugal.

Theresa Obuobisa-Darko holds a PhD in Public Administration and Policy Management and an MBA in Human Resource Management both from University of Ghana and an MA in Organisational Development from University of Cape Coast. Theresa is a Professor in Human Resource Management in the Department of Human Resource Management in her University. She has experience in teaching and research. Her research interest includes Leadership in Organisation, Performance Management, Conflict Management, Employee Health and Safety, and Employee Engagement. Theresa has published in peer reviewed journals and presented papers at both international and national conferences.

Olcay Okun graduated from the National Defense University. He received his PhD in Business Administration. Since 1998, he has held various positions in the Ministry of National Defense and NATO staff. He is currently a lecturer at the National Defense University. He adopted positive social psychology and positive organizational behavior phenomena as communication and management style in his duties and worked in this direction. In his academic studies, he tries to produce results by trying to carry the phenomena of management and organization to daily life. Publications and Book Chapters are available in Social Science Scitation Index (SSCI), Sciences Citation Index (SCI), Sci-Expanded, Scopus Scanned Journals.

Ana Pinto Borges has a PhD in Economics, Faculty of Economics, University of Porto, in 2009. Since 2010 is Coordinating Professor at ISAG - European Business School. Scientific Coordinator of Research Center in Business Sciences and Tourism (CICET – FCVC) since 2021 and coordinated the ISAG Research Center between 2015 and 2021. Author of several publications of papers and book chapters indexed to the main bibliographic databases (WoS - Clarivate Analytics and Scopus). She also publishes books of international distribution, namely "New Techniques for Brand Management in the Healthcare Sector", "Building Consumer-Brand Relationship in Luxury Brand Management" and "Gastronomy, Hospitality, and the Future of the Restaurant Industry". Participation in presentations in various national and international congresses and member of the scientific committees in academic events. Editor and one of the founding members of the European Journal of Applied Business and Management (EJABM). She supervised several final master's and doctoral works. Former Accenture consultant in the financial area. Economist at the Health Regulatory Entity since 2010 with the main function of carrying out sectoral studies and issuing opinions in the scope of access, quality and competition in the health sector.

Henrique Pires is a specialist and master in Human Resources Management and has a degree in Psychology from the University of Coimbra. Professor and sub-director of ISAG - European Business School and researcher at the Research Center in Business Sciences and Tourism (CICET-FCVC), Porto, Portugal

Soni Rathi is a research scholar at the University School of Business at Chandigarh University, Punjab. Her current research interests include work-life balance, job stress, work-life conflict, job satisfaction, employees' creativity, human resource management, and generational differences. She has attended many international and national conferences, workshops, and faculty development programs. She has practical experience and knowledge of Statistical software viz. Smart PLS 3 & 4, SPSS v.25, Vos viewer.

Ishpreet Kaur Saini is a research scholar in the field of HR & OB. She has qualified UGC NET. Her area of research is workplace incivility

Lata Bajpai Singh (PhD) is currently working as Assistant Professor OB/HR in the Department of Management Studies, Babasaheb Bhimrao Ambedkar University, Lucknow, U.P. India. Her research work has published in Personnel Review, Journal of Hospitality & Tourism Management, International Journal of Conflict Management, Employee Relations, Journal of Management Development, Journal of International Education in Business, The International Journal of Management Education, and Journal of Enterprising Communities: People and Places in the Global Economy.

Evans Sokro holds a PhD from Federation University Australia, MPhil Human Resource Management and BA Psychology and Sociology all from the University of Ghana, Legon. He is a senior lecturer and Head, Department of Human Resource Management at the Central Business School, where he teaches courses in HRM at the MBA and undergraduate levels. He is also an associate member of Chartered Institute of Human Resource Management, Ghana. He has considerable research, teaching and consulting experience in the application of management principles and theory to everyday management and human resource challenges in organisations. Evans has a couple of publications in internationally peer-reviewed academic journals and presented conference papers at international conferences. His research interests include Expatriation in sub-Saharan Africa, Organisational culture and values, Leadership effectiveness and HRIS. He was a recipient of Federation University Australia postgraduate research scholarship and a special overseas student scholarship award in 2014.

Sachitaa Srivastava is a Ph.D. Scholar from Babasaheb Bhimrao Ambedkar University, Lucknow. Her research interests revolve around various aspects of Organizational Behavior/Human Resources, aiming to contribute valuable insights to enhance workplace dynamics and organizational practices. Her scholarly work published in the International Journal of Conflict Management (IJCMA) and the IUP Journal of Organizational Behavior (IUP JOB).

Sukhada Tambe is an Associate Professor at IES's Management College and Research Centre. Her areas of interest are Organizational Behaviour, Communication Skills, Quality Management and Human Resource Management. She holds Ph.D in Management Studies and is a double postgraduate with Masters in Labour Studies and Masters in Economics. She is also UGC-NET qualified. She has published numerous articles and research papers and has presented several papers in national and international conferences. She has also edited books in the area of General Management. She is a reviewer for reputed international journals.

Mary Rani Thomas is currently working as an Assistant professor in CHRIST (Deemed to be University), Bengaluru, India from 2010. Has completed MPhil and her PhD from CHRIST (Deemed to be University), Bengaluru. Areas of specialisation and subjects handled are Marketing, Management, Human Resource Management and Organisation Behaviour. Research interests and publications are in the fields of consumer behaviour and Organisation behaviour Also published in reputed UGC-listed and Scopus journals.

Bruno Miguel Vieira is an Adjunct Professor at the ISAG – European Business School since 2013. He is doing his PhD in Informatics MAP-i at a joint program between the Universities of Minho, Aveiro and Porto, with international partnerships (e.g. University of Texas in Austin and with Carnegie Mellon University). He develops business consulting activity in the field of management information systems, keeping a close connection to the businesses. Currently, he is the coordinator of the scientific area of Computer Science at ISAG and coordinates the Higher Professional Technical Course in Digital Marketing Management and the Post-graduation program in Digital Marketing Strategy.

Elvira Vieira holds a PhD in Applied Economics from the University of Santiago de Compostela (Spain) is currently the Dean of ISAG-EBS (Porto, Portugal), where is also a Coordinating Professor and Researcher. President of the Board of Directors of the Consuelo Vieira da Costa Foundation (FCVC), Scientific Coordinator and Researcher in its Research Centre in Business Sciences and Tourism (CICET-FCVC). Adjunct Professor at the Polytechnic Institute of Viana do Castelo (IPVC) and Researcher at UNIAG – Applied Management Research Unit. She is the author of several indexed articles, papers, book chapters and 2 books, in the areas of Economics and Management, Business Sciences, and Tourism.

Index

L

M

O

P

S

www.ingramcontent.com/pod-product-compliance
Lightning Source LLC
LaVergne TN
LVHW080345011026
849161LV00009B/2191
* 9 7 8 1 6 6 8 4 6 6 0 2 5 *